The Physical World

The Political World

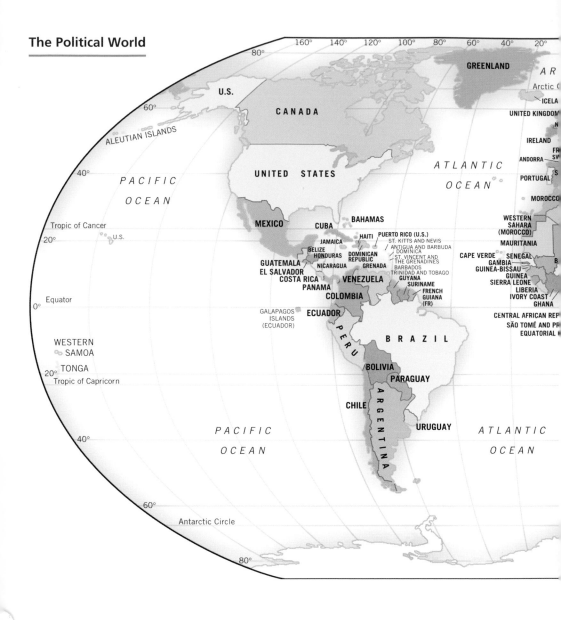

160°   140°   120°   100°   80°   60°   40°   20°

80°

GREENLAND

AR

Arctic C

ICELA

UNITED KINGDOM

N

IRELAND

FR

ANDORRA   SW

PORTUGAL

MOROCCO

WESTERN
SAHARA
(MOROCCO)

MAURITANIA

CAPE VERDE   SENEGAL
GAMBIA
GUINEA-BISSAU
GUINEA
SIERRA LEONE
LIBERIA
IVORY COAST
GHANA

CENTRAL AFRICAN REP
SÃO TOMÉ AND PR
EQUATORIAL

U.S.

CANADA

60°

ALEUTIAN ISLANDS

40°

PACIFIC

OCEAN

UNITED STATES

ATLANTIC

OCEAN

BAHAMAS

Tropic of Cancer

20°

U.S.

MEXICO

CUBA

PUERTO RICO (U.S.)
HAITI
ST. KITTS AND NEVIS
JAMAICA   ANTIGUA AND BARBUDA
DOMINICA
BELIZE
HONDURAS   DOMINICAN
REPUBLIC   ST. VINCENT AND
THE GRENADINES
GUATEMALA   NICARAGUA   GRENADA   BARBADOS
EL SALVADOR   TRINIDAD AND TOBAGO
COSTA RICA   VENEZUELA   GUYANA
PANAMA   SURINAME
FRENCH
COLOMBIA   GUIANA
(FR)

0°

Equator

GALAPAGOS
ISLANDS
(ECUADOR)

ECUADOR

PERU

BRAZIL

WESTERN
SAMOA

TONGA

20°

Tropic of Capricorn

BOLIVIA

PARAGUAY

CHILE

ARGENTINA

URUGUAY

40°

PACIFIC

OCEAN

ATLANTIC

OCEAN

60°

Antarctic Circle

80°

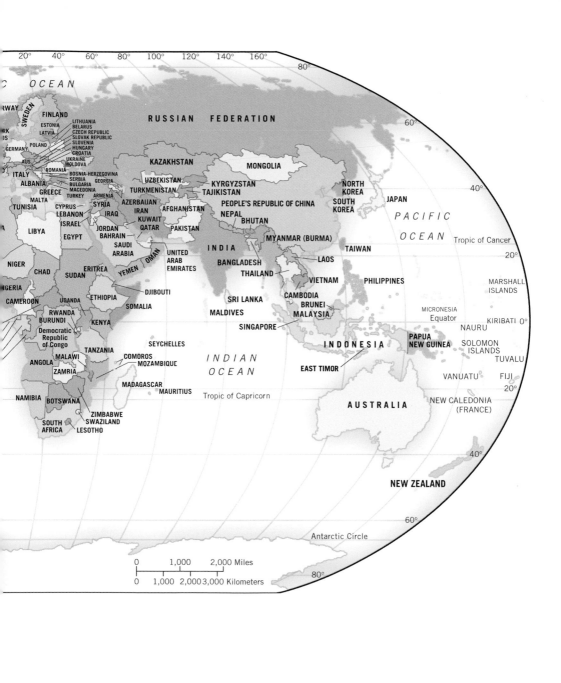

A comprehensive way to present the history of the world without falling into the trap of great men, battles, and politics. . . . Excellent use of the story lines to provide a more humanistic approach to world history.

Craig Pascoe
Georgia College and State University

It is one of the best, if not the best, textbook in the field.

John Weakland
Ball State University

An excellent synthesis of world civilizations. The narrative and overview are brilliant. This is an exceptional intellectual effort that everyone teaching world civilizations should be familiar with.

Timothy Pytell
California University, San Bernardino

Quite refreshing and ambitious, pushing the boundaries of world history teaching. . . . A must read for those eager to explore more fully the question of human interaction with the environment.

Wing Chung Ng
University of Texas at San Antonio

One of the most impressive . . . world history textbooks on the market. The lively authorial voice and global approach provoke students to engage with novel perspectives on history.

William Womack
Samford University

A brilliant work of historical analysis. It is perhaps the best world history survey book I have had the pleasure of perusing.

Wesley Underhill
Arkansas State University

Scholarly, comprehensive, critical and penetrating. The best text I've seen to date. . . . The main strength is the way [the author] makes interconnections between events and patterns, thereby creating deeper meaning.

David Underwood
University of South Florida

PENGUIN ACADEMICS

THE WORLD
A HISTORY

Volume 1: To 1500

FELIPE FERNÁNDEZ-ARMESTO
University of Notre Dame

Prentice Hall

Boston   Columbus   Indianapolis   New York   San Francisco   Upper Saddle River
Amsterdam   Cape Town   Dubai   London   Madrid   Milan   Munich   Paris   Montréal   Toronto
Delhi   Mexico City   São Paulo   Sydney   Hong Kong   Seoul   Singapore   Taipei   Tokyo

Editorial Director: Craig Campanella
Executive Editor: Jeff Lasser
Editorial Project Manager:
   Rob DeGeorge
Director of Marketing:
   Brandy Dawson
Senior Marketing Manager:
   Maureen E. Prado Roberts
Senior Managing Editor:
   Ann Marie McCarthy
Project Manager: Debra A. Wechsler
Operations Specialist:
   Christina Amato
Cover Designer: Bruce Kenselaar
Manager, Visual Research:
   Beth Brenzel

Photo Researcher: Tim Herzog
Manager, Cover Visual Research & Permissions:
   Rita Wenning
Cover Art: "Three scribes at work, painted limestone
   decoration from the mastaba tomb (no. 60)
   of the official Ty from Saqqara, 5th Dynasty
   2450–2325 B.C." The Art Archive / Dagli Orti,
   Picture Desk, Inc. / Kobal Collection.
Media Director: Brian Hyland
Lead Media Project Manager: Alison Lorber
Full-Service Project Management:
   Roxanne Klaas, S4Carlisle Publishing Services
Composition: S4Carlisle Publishing Services
Printer/Binder: R. R. Donnelley/Crawfordsville
Cover Printer: Lehigh-Phoenix Color/Hagerstown
Text Font: Glypha, 9.75/13

Credits and acknowledgments borrowed from other sources and reproduced, with permission, in this textbook appear on appropriate page within text.

Library of Congress Cataloging-in-Publication Data
Fernández-Armesto, Felipe.
   The world : a history / Felipe Fernández-Armesto.
      p. cm.—(Penguin academics)
   Includes bibliographical references and index.
   ISBN 978-0-205-75930-9 (combined : alk. paper)—ISBN 978-0-205-77615-3 (exam copy: alk. paper)—ISBN 978-0-205-75931-6 (volume 1 : alk. paper)—ISBN 978-0-205-75932-3 (volume 2 : alk. paper)   1. World history—Textbooks.   I. Title.
   D21.F46 2011
   909—dc22

                                                                2010029067

10 9 8 7 6 5 4 3 2 1

                                                 Combined Volume
                                      ISBN 10:   0-205-75930-0
                                      ISBN 13: 978-0-205-75930-9
                                                 Examination Copy
                                      ISBN 10:   0-205-77615-9
                                      ISBN 13: 978-0-205-77615-3
                                                       Volume 1
                                      ISBN 10:   0-205-75931-9
                                      ISBN 13: 978-0-205-75931-6
                                                       Volume 2
                                      ISBN 10:   0-205-75932-7
                                      ISBN 13: 978-0-205-75932-3

Prentice Hall
is an imprint of

www.pearsonhighered.com

brief contents

contents

maps

about felipe fernández-armesto

FELIPE FERNÁNDEZ-ARMESTO holds the William P. Reynolds Chair of History at the University of Notre Dame. He has master's and doctoral degrees from the University of Oxford, where he spent most of his teaching career, before taking up the Chair of Global Environmental History at Queen Mary College, University of London, in 2000, and the Prince of Asturias Chair at Tufts University (2005–2009). He is on the editorial boards of the History of Cartography for the University of Chicago Press, Studies in Overseas History (Leiden University), *Comparative Studies in Society and History, Journeys,* and *Journal of Global History.* Recent awards include the World History Association Book Prize (2007), Spain's Premio Nacional de Gastronomía (2005, for his work on the history of food), and the Premio Nacional de Investigación (Sociedad Geográfica Española, 2004). He has had many distinguished visiting appointments, including a Fellowship of the Netherlands Institute of Advanced Study in the Humanities and Social Sciences and a Union Pacific Visiting Professorship at the University of Minnesota. He won the Caird Medal of the National Maritime Museum in 1995 and the John Carter Brown Medal in 1999 and has honorary doctorates from La Trobe University and the Universidad de los Andes. He has served on the Council of the Hakluyt Society, on the Committee of English PEN, and as Chairman of the PEN Literary Foundation. His work in journalism includes regular columns in the British and Spanish press, and, among his many contributions to broadcasting, he is the longest-serving presenter of BBC radio's flagship current affairs program, *Analysis.* He has been short-listed for the most valuable literary prize in the United Kingdom.

Fernández-Armesto is the author, coauthor, or editor of 30 books and numerous papers and scholarly articles. His work has been translated into 25 languages. His books include *Before Columbus; The Times Illustrated*

History of Europe; Columbus; Millennium: A History of the Last Thousand Years (the subject of a ten-part series on CNN); *Civilizations: Culture, Ambition, and the Transformation of Nature; Near a Thousand Tables; The Americas; Humankind: A Brief History; Ideas That Changed the World; The Times Atlas of World Exploration; The Times Guide to the Peoples of Europe; Amerigo: The Man Who Gave His Name to America;* and *Pathfinders: A Global History of Exploration.*

Dear Reader,

History is stories. There are hundreds of tales in this book about real, flesh-and-blood people—commoners and kings, sons and mothers, heroes and villains, the famous and the failed. I try to combine them in two narratives that crisscross throughout the book. One is the story of how people connect and separate, as cultures take shape and influence and change one another. Alongside this story, there is another one of how humans interact with the rest of nature—other species, the unstable natural environment, the dynamic planet.

History is global. The whole world stays in view in almost every chapter. Readers can compare and connect what was happening in every region and every continent in every period—like observers from another galaxy, gazing at the world from outer space and seeing it whole.

History is universal. This book tries to say something about every sphere of life—including science and art, suffering and pleasure, thought and imagination.

History is a problem-posing discipline. This book is full of provocations, contested claims, debated speculations, open horizons, and questions too complex and too interesting to answer easily. I employ facts not just for their own sake but also to make my readers—and myself—think.

History is evidence. Readers of this book confront the sources on every page—the words, images, and objects people really used in the past—to reveal vivid pictures of what history looked like and what it felt like to live in the past.

History enhances life. I believe that a textbook can be entertaining, even amusing, as well as instructive and accessible; challenging without being hostile; friendly without being cloying.

History isn't over. This book is about how the world got to be the way it is, confronting present problems and perspectives for the future—which is, after all, only the past that hasn't yet happened.

By the standards of astronauts, say, or science fiction writers, historians seem timid, unadventurous creatures who are only interested in one puny species—our species, the human species—on one tiny planet—our planet, Earth. But Earth is special. So far, we know of nowhere else in the cosmos where so much has happened and is happening today. By galactic standards, global history is a small story—but it's a good one.

Humans, moreover, compared with other animals, seem outward looking. Our concerns range over the universe, and beyond it, to unseen worlds, vividly imagined or mysteriously revealed. Not just everything we do but also everything that occurs to our minds is part of our history and, therefore, is part of this book, including science and art, fun and philosophy, speculations and dreams. We continually generate stories—new stories—at an amazing rate.

But the present passes instantly into the past. The present is always over, transformed into history. And the past is always with us, tugging at our memories, shaping our thoughts, launching and limiting our lives. Human history may seem narrowly self-interested, but it focuses on an undeniably riveting subject that is also our favorite subject—ourselves.

The Way of Humankind

Although the story of this book is a human story, it can never be merely human because, in isolation humankind does not make perfect sense. Humans are animals, and to understand ourselves thoroughly and to know what, if anything, makes us unique, we have to compare ourselves with other animals. As with other animals, we are best studied in our habitats. We cannot begin to comprehend our own history except in context. Our story is inseparable from the climates where it takes place and the other life forms that we depend on or compete with. We lord it over other species, but we remain linked to them by the food chain. We transform our environment, but we can never escape from it. We differentiate ourselves from nature—we speak loosely, for instance, of nature as if we were not natural creatures ourselves. We distance ourselves from our fellow animals by adopting what we think are unnatural behaviors—wearing clothes, for instance, cooking food, replacing nature with culture. In short, we do what is natural to us, and all the elaborate culture we produce generates new, intimate relationships with the environment we refashion and the life forms we exploit.

We are exceptionally ambitious compared to other animals, consciously remodeling environments to suit our own purposes. We carve out fields, turn prairies into wheat lands, deserts into gardens, and gardens into deserts. We fell forests where we find them and plant them where none exist; we dam rivers, wall seas, cultivate plants, breed creatures, extinguish some species, and call others into being by selection and hybridization. Sometimes we smother terrain with environments we build for ourselves. Yet none of these practices liberates us from nature. As we shall see, one of the paradoxes of the human story is that the more we change the environment, the more vulnerable we become to ecological lurches and unpredictable disasters. Failure to establish the right balance between exploitation and conservation has often left civilizations in ruins. History becomes a path picked across the wreckage. This does not mean that the environment determines our behavior or our lives, but it does set the framework in which we act.

We are an exceptionally successful species in terms of our ability to survive in a wide range of diverse climates and landscapes—more so than just about any other creature, except for the microbes we carry around with us. But we are still explorers of our planet, engaged in an ongoing effort to change it. Indeed, we have barely begun to change planet Earth, though, as we shall see, some human societies have devoted the last ten thousand years to trying to do it. We call ourselves lords, or, more modestly, stewards of creation, but about 90 percent of the biosphere is too far underwater or too deep below the Earth for us to inhabit with the technology we have at present: These are environments that humans have only recently begun to invade and that we still do not dominate.

If we humans are peculiarly ambitious creatures, who are always intruding in the life of the planet, we are also odd compared to other animals in the way we generate change among ourselves. We are an unpredictable, unstable species. Lots of other animals live social lives and construct societies. But those societies are remarkably stable compared to ours. As far as we know, ants and elephants have the same lifeways and the same kinds of relationships that they have had since their species first appeared. That is not to say animals never change their cultures. One of the fascinating discoveries in primatology is that apes and monkeys develop cultural differences from one another, even between groups living in similar and sometimes adjacent environments. In one forest region of East Africa, chimpanzees have developed a termite-catching technology. They "fish" with stripped branches that they plunge into termite nests but do not use tools to break open nuts. Chimps in a neighboring region ignore the termites but are experts in nut cracking, using rocks like hammers and anvils. In Sumatra in Indonesia, orangutans play a game—jumping from falling trees—that is unknown to their cousins in nearby Borneo. In Ethiopia in East Africa, males in some baboon groups control harems while others nearby have one mate after another. In some chimpanzee societies, hunting and meat eating seem to have increased dramatically in recent times.

These are amazing facts, but the societies of nonhuman animals still change little compared with ours. So, alongside the theme of human interaction with the rest of nature is another great theme of our history: the ways our societies have changed, grown apart from one another, reestablished contact, and influenced one another in their turn.

The Way of This Book

This book, then, interweaves two stories—stories of our interactions with nature and stories of our interactions with each other. The environment-centered story is about humans distancing themselves from the rest of nature and searching for a relationship that strikes a balance between constructive and destructive exploitation. The culture-centered story is of how human cultures have become mutually influential and yet mutually differentiating. Both stories have been going on for thousands of years. We do not know whether they will end in triumph or disaster.

There is no prospect of covering all of world history in one book. Rather, the fabric of this book is woven from selected strands. Readers will see these at every turn, twisted together into yarn, stretched into stories. Human-focused historical ecology—the environmental theme—will drive readers back, again and again, to the same concepts: sustenance, shelter, disease, energy, technology, art. (The last is a vital category for historians, not only because it is part of our interface with the rest of the world, but also because it forms a record of how we see reality and of how the way we see it changes.) In the global story of human interactions, which is the cultural theme, we return constantly to the ways people make contact with each another—migration, trade, war, imperialism, pilgrimage, gift exchange, diplomacy, travel—and to their social frameworks: the economic and political arenas, the human groups and groupings, the states and civilizations, the sexes and generations, the classes and clusters of identity.

The stories that stretch before us are full of human experience. "The stork feeds on snakes," said the ancient Greek sage, Agathon, "the pig on acorns, and history on human lives." The only way to build up our picture of human societies and ecosystems of the past is to start with the evidence people have left. Then we reassemble it bit by bit, with the help of imagination disciplined by the sources. Anyone reading a history book needs to bear in mind that interpreting evidence is a challenge—half burden and half opportunity. The subject matter of history is not the past directly because the past is never available to our senses. We only have evidence about it. This makes history an art, not a science, an art disciplined by respect for the sources, just as patterns impose discipline on poets or as the limitations of stagecraft discipline a play.

For a book like this, the sources set the limits of my imagination. Sometimes these are concrete clues to what people really did—footprints of their wanderings, debris of their meals, fragments of their technologies, wreckage of their homes, traces of diseases in their bones. Usually, however, the sources do not reflect the way things were but the way people wished to represent them in their arts and crafts and writings. In short, most sources are evidence of what happened only in the minds of those who made them. This means, in turn, that our picture of what went on in the world beyond human minds is always tentative and open to reinterpretation. The historian's job is not—cannot be—to say what the past was like, but rather, what it felt like to live in it because that is what the evidence tends to reveal.

One of the most admirable historians of the twentieth century, R. G. Collingwood, who was also a professor of philosophy at Oxford, said that "all history is intellectual history." He was right. History—even the environmental and cultural history that is the subject of this book—is largely about what people perceived rather than what they really saw, what they thought or felt rather than what happened outwardly, what they represented rather than what was real. The nineteenth-century philosopher Arthur Schopenhauer, one of the most pessimistic thinkers ever, who drew on Hindu and Buddhist writings for his inspiration, said that history's only subject was "humankind's oppressive, muddlesome dream." He thought that made history pointless. I think the dream makes it intriguing.

Because the evidence is always incomplete, history is not so much a matter of describing or narrating or question-answering as it is a matter of problem-posing. No one reading this book should expect to be instructed in straightforward facts or to acquire proven knowledge. The thrill of history is asking the right question, not getting the right answer. Most of the time, the most we can hope for is to identify interesting problems that stimulate debate. And we have to accept that the debate is worthwhile for its own sake, even if we have insufficient knowledge to reach conclusions.

There is no agreement among historians even about what are the right sorts of questions to ask. Some—including me—are interested in huge philosophical questions: How does history happen? What makes change? Is it random or is it subject to scientific laws? Do impersonal forces beyond human control—environmental factors or economics or some world force called fate or evolution or God or progress—determine it? Or is change the externalization of ideas, which arise in minds and are projected onto the world through human action? And if it's a mixture, what's the balance?

At a slightly lower level of analysis, some historians ask questions about how human societies function: How and why do societies grow and fragment and take different forms? How do some people get power over others? How and why do revolutions happen and states and civilizations rise and fall?

Other historians like to pose problems about the present: How did we get into the mess we're in? Can we trace the causes of present dilemmas back into the past and, if so, how far? Why do we have a globally connected world without global governance? Why is peace always precarious? Why does ecological overkill menace our global environment? Having accounted—or failed to account—for the present, some historians like to focus on the future. They demand lessons from history about how to change our behavior or cope with recurrences of past difficulties. Others, again, search to make sense of the past, to find an overall way of characterizing it or narrating it that makes us feel we understand it.

Yet others—the majority, in the current state of historical fashion, and again including me—like to study the past for its own sake and try to identify the questions that mattered to people at the time they first asked them. This does not mean that the sort of history found in this book is useless (although I do not necessarily think it would be a bad thing if it were). For to penetrate the minds of people of the past—especially the remote past of cultures other than your own—you have to make a supreme effort of understanding. The effort has dividends for the person who practices it. It enhances life by sharpening responses to the streetscapes and landscapes, art and artifacts, laws and letters we have inherited from the past. And understanding is what we need most today in our multicultural societies and multicivilizational world.

How This Book Is Arranged

After finding the time, accumulating the knowledge, posing the questions, stiffening the sinews, and summoning the blood, the big problem for the writer of a global history textbook is organizing the material. The big problem for the reader is navigating it. It is tempting to divide the world up into regions or cultures or even—as I did in a previous book—into biomes and devote successive chapters to each. You could call that "world history," if you genuinely managed to cover the world. But "global history" is different: an attempt to see the planet whole—as if from an immense, astral height—and discern themes that truly transcend geographical and cultural boundaries. In this book, therefore, I try to look at every continent in just about every chapter (there are a couple of chapters that, for reasons described in their place, focus only on part of the world). Each chapter concentrates on themes from the two great global stories: how human societies diverge and converge and how they interact with the rest of nature.

Because history is a story in which the order of events matters, the chapters are grouped into 10 parts, arranged chronologically. There are 30 chapters—one for each week in a typical U.S. academic year (though of course, every reader or group of readers will go at their own pace). I hope there is plenty to surprise readers without making the parts perversely defiant of the "periods" historians conventionally speak of. Part I runs from roughly 150,000 to roughly 20,000 years ago, and, on the whole, the periods covered get shorter as sources accumulate, cultures diverge, data multiply, and readers' interests quicken. Of course, no one should be misled into thinking the parts are more than devices of convenience. Events that happened in, say, 1850, are in a different part of this book from those that happened in, say, 1750. But the story is continuous, and the parts could equally well be recrafted to start and end at different moments.

At every stage, some parts of the world are more prominent than others because they are more influential, more populous, more world-shaping. For great stretches of the book, China occupies relatively more space; this is not for reasons of political correctness, but because China has, for much of the past, been immensely rich in globally influential initiatives. In the coverage of the last couple of hundred years, Europe and the United States get a lot of attention: this is not "Eurocentrism" or "Westocentrism" (if there is such a word), but an honest reflection of how history happened. But I have tried not to neglect the peoples and parts of the world that historians usually undervalue: Poor and peripheral communities sometimes have a stunning impact on the world. The margins and frontiers of the world are often where world-changing events happen—the fault lines of civilizations, which radiate seismic effects.

A Wealth of Powerful Teaching and Learning Tools

The pedagogical features found in the Penguin Academics edition of *The World* have been carefully devised to complement the narrative, reinforce important concepts, and prompt students to ask questions and formulate arguments.

Chapter-Opening Vignettes use dramatic and unusual stories to put the main themes of each chapter in relief.

Focus Questions open each chapter and encourage students to think critically about the key questions raised in the chapter.

Making Connections tables throughout the text help students see the global linkages behind important historical developments. Praised by users of *The World,* every chapter in the Penguin Academics edition of *The World* now includes a Making Connections table.

Maps The maps in the Penguin Academics edition of *The World* employ innovative perspectives to help the reader see world history in a fresh and dynamic way. A range of different maps connect with the discussion on a variety of different levels. See page xii for a listing of the maps in the book.

Visual Sources Users of *The World* consistently rank its photo program as the best found in any textbook available today. Intimately connected to the narrative, each photo provides a compelling visual record. Detailed captions, crafted by the author, explicate the meaning behind each visual source.

In Perspective sections conclude each chapter and do much more than summarize the preceding discussion. They put the developments covered in the chapter into historical perspective, and they make explicit for the student the process by which historians interpret the past.

Chronologies at the end of each chapter arrange key historical developments in the order in which they occurred.

Key Terms are defined in the Glossary and are set in boldface type in the text.

Problems and Parallels At the end of each chapter, a series of questions helps students focus on the important issues discussed within the chapter. These questions can also be used to facilitate classroom discussion and as short essay topics.

Changes to the Penguin Academics Edition of *The World*

The many helpful readers' reports and reviews of the First Edition by both users and nonusers formed the basis for preparing the Second Edition, upon which the Penguin Academics edition is based. Every chapter was either updated with new and accepted scholarship or reorganized to clarify its presentation. In many chapters, more substantive changes were made in response to feedback and advice from teachers.

Chapters 1–15

Chapter 1 now begins with a discussion of Imo, the famous Japanese macaque. Chapter 2 examines the archaeological remains of an ancient feast to highlight the main problems of the chapter. In Chapter 5, coverage of Babylon has been expanded. Chapter 6 now includes a new section on the Israelites and more discussion of Buddhism. Discussion of Rome has been increased in Chapter 7. Chapter 8 includes fuller treatment of Tang China. Both the Crusades and Ghana are examined in more depth in Chapter 12. The Renaissance receives more discussion in Chapter 15.

For Students

- **World History Study Site** (www.pearsonhighered.com) This course-based, open-access online companion provides a wealth of resources for both students and professors, including test questions, flash cards, links for further research, and Web-based assignments.
- **CourseSmart Textbooks Online** is an exciting new choice for students looking to save money. As an alternative to purchasing the print textbook, students can subscribe to the same content online and save up to 50 percent off the suggested list price of the print text. With a CourseSmart eTextbook, students can search the text, make notes online, print out reading assignments that incorporate lecture notes,

and bookmark important passages for later review. For more information, or to subscribe to the CourseSmart eTextbook, visit www.coursesmart.com.

Acknowledgments

Without being intrusive, I have tried not to suppress my presence—my voice, my views—in the text because no book is objective, other than by pretense, and the reader is entitled to get to know the writer's foibles and failures. In overcoming mine, I have had a lot of help (though there are sure still to be errors and shortcomings through my fault alone). Textbooks are teamwork, and I have learned an immense amount from my friends and helpers at Pearson Prentice Hall, especially my editors, Jeff Lasser and Gerald Lombardi, whose indefatigability and forbearance made the book better at every turn. I thank Maureen Prado Roberts, senior marketing manager, for her creativity. I also thank the members of the production and cartographic sections of the team who performed Herculean labors: Ann Marie McCarthy, senior managing editor; Debra Wechsler, production project manager; Mirella Signoretto, map project manager; and Peter Bull, cartographer.

I also owe a debt of gratitude to the senior management team at Pearson Prentice Hall who supported this endeavor every step of the way: Bill Barke, CEO, Pearson Arts & Sciences; Yolanda de Rooy, president of the Humanities and Social Sciences division; Craig Campanella, editorial director; Rochelle Diogenes, editor-in-chief for development; Brandy Dawson, director of marketing; Maureen E. Prado Roberts, senior marketing manager.

I could not have gotten through the work without the help and support of my wonderful colleagues at Queen Mary, University of London; the Institute of Historical Research, University of London; and the History Departments of Tufts University and the University of Notre Dame. I owe special thanks to the many scholars who shared and still share their knowledge of global history at the Pearson Prentice Hall Seminar Series in Global History, and through the World History Association, the *Journal of Global History*, the *Journal of World History,* and H-NET. David Ringrose of University of California, San Diego, was a constant guide, whose interest never flagged and whose wisdom never failed. Many colleagues and counterparts advised me on their fields of expertise or performed heroic self-sacrifice in putting all of the many pieces of the book together: Natia Chakvetadze, Shannon Corliss, Maria Guarascio, Anita Castro, Conchita Ordonez, Sandra Garcia, Maria Garcia, Hector Grillone, the late Jack Betterley, Jeremy Greene, Jai Kharbanda, Ernest Tucker (United States Naval Academy), Steve Ortega (Simmons College), David Way (British Library), Antony Eastmond (Courtland Institute), Morris Rossabi (Columbia University), David Atwill and Jade Atwill (Pennsylvania State University), Stephen Morillo (Wabash College), Peter Carey (Oxford University), Jim Mallory (Queens University, Belfast), Matthew Restall (Pennsylvania State University), Roderick Whitfield (School of Oriental and African Studies, University of London), Barry Powell (University of Wisconsin), Leonard Blussé (Harvard University), Guolong Lai (University of Florida), Frank Karpiel (The Citadel), George Kosar (Tufts University), David Kalivas and Eric Martin of H-NET and the many subscribers to their service who commented on the book or posted or e-mailed queries and suggestions, and the faculty, staff, and students of the many colleges where I got the chance to discuss the book (Boston College, Colorado State University, Essex Community College, Georgetown University, Jackson State University, Northern Kentucky University, Ohio State University, Penn State University, St John's University [New York], Salem State University, San José State University, Simmons College, U.S. Air Force Academy, U.S. Naval Academy, University at Buffalo, University of California [San Diego], San Diego State University, University of Arkansas [Little Rock], and University of Memphis), as well as the many good people whose assistance I may have failed to acknowledge.

FELIPE FERNÁNDEZ-ARMESTO
Notre Dame, Indiana

developing *the world*

Developing a project like *The World* required the input and counsel of hundreds of individuals. David Ringrose, from the University of California at San Diego, served as *The World*'s editorial consultant, closely reading and commenting on every draft of the book. His experience and understanding of classroom issues were invaluable to the development of *The World*. Nearly 100 reviewers critiqued portions of the manuscript from the first to the final draft. In addition, the manuscript was class-tested with more than 1,000 students across the country who provided invaluable feedback and advice. Additionally, 15 focus groups were held with teachers of world history to gather feedback and test ideas. An additional 75 reviewers critiqued portions of *The World* to help prepare the Second Edition. We thank all those who shared their time and effort to make *The World* a better book.

Reviewers of the First Edition

Donald R. Abbott, *San Diego Mesa College*
Wayne Ackerson, *Salisbury University*
Roger Adelson, *Arizona State University*
Alfred J. Andrea, *University of Vermont (Emeritus)*
David G. Atwill, *Pennsylvania State University*
Leonard Blussé, *Harvard University*
Mauricio Borrero, *St. John's University*
John Brackett, *University of Cincinnati*
Gayle K. Brunelle, *California State University—Fullerton*
Fred Burkhard, *Maryland University College*
Antoinette Burton, *University of Illinois*
Jorge Cañizares-Esguerra, *University of Texas—Austin*
Elaine Carey, *St. John's University*
Tim Carmichael, *College of Charleston*
Douglas Chambers, *University of Southern Mississippi*
Nupur Chaudhuri, *Texas Southern University*
David Christian, *San Diego State University*
Duane Corpis, *Georgia State University*

Dale Crandall-Bear, *Solano Community College*
Touraj Daryaee, *University of California, Irvine*
Jeffrey M. Diamond, *College of Charleston*
Brian Fagan, *University of California—Santa Barbara*
Nancy Fitch, *California State University—Fullerton*
Alison Fletcher, *Kent State University*
Patricia Gajda, *The University of Texas at Tyler*
Richard Golden, *University of North Texas*
Stephen S. Gosch, *University of Wisconsin—Eau Claire*
Jonathan Grant, *Florida State University*
Mary Halavais, *Sonoma State University*
Shah M. Hanifi, *James Madison University*
Russell A. Hart, *Hawaii Pacific University*
Phyllis G. Jestice, *University of Southern Mississippi*
Amy J. Johnson, *Berry College*
Deborah Smith Johnston, *Lexington High School*
Eric A. Jones, *Northern Illinois University*
Ravi Kalia, *City College of New York*
David M. Kalivas, *Middlesex Community College*
Frank Karpiel, *College of Charleston*
David Kenley, *Marshall University*
Andrew J. Kirkendall, *Texas A&M University*
Dennis Laumann, *The University of Memphis*
Donald Leech, *University of Minnesota*
Jennifer M. Lloyd, *SUNY—Brockport*
Aran MacKinnon, *University of West Georgia*
Moria Maguire, *University of Arkansas—Little Rock*
Susan Maneck, *Jackson State University*
Anthony Martin, *Wellesley College*
Dorothea Martin, *Appalachian State University*
Adam McKeown, *Columbia University*
Ian McNeely, *University of Oregon*
Margaret E. Menninger, *Texas State University—San Marcos*
Stephen Morillo, *Wabash College*
William Morison, *Grand Valley State University*
Laura Neitzel, *Brookdale Community College*
Kenneth J. Orosz, *University of Maine—Farmington*
Michael Pavkovic, *Hawaii Pacific University*
Phyllis E. Pobst, *Arkansas State University*
Kenneth Pomeranz, *University of California—Irvine*
Sara B. Pritchard, *Montana State University*
Norman Raiford, *Greenville Technical College*
Stephen Rapp, *Georgia State University*

Vera Blinn Reber, *Shippensburg University*
Matthew Redinger, *Montana State University—Billings*
Matthew Restall, *Pennsylvania State University*
Jonathan Reynolds, *Arkansas State University*
Richard Rice, *University of Tennessee—Chattanooga*
Peter Rietbergen, *Catholic University (Nijmegen)*
David Ringrose, *University of California—San Diego*
Patricia Romero, *Towson University*
Morris Rossabi, *Queens College*
David G. Rowley, *University of Wisconsin—Platteville*
Sharlene Sayegh, *California State University—Long Beach*
William Schell, *Murray State University*
Linda Bregstein Scherr, *Mercer County Community College*
Patricia Seed, *University of California, Irvine*
Lawrence Sondhaus, *University of Indianapolis*
Richard Steigmann-Gall, *Kent State University*
John Thornton, *Boston University*
Ann Tschetter, *University of Nebraska—Lincoln*
Deborah Vess, *Georgia College & State University*
Stephen Vinson, *SUNY—New Paltz*
Joanna Waley-Cohen, *New York University*
Anne M. Will, *Skagit Valley College*
John Wills, *University of Southern California*
Theodore Jun Yoo, *University of Hawaii—Manoa*

Reviewers of the Second Edition

Jeffrey Alexander, *Douglas College/The University of British Columbia*
Emma Alexander-Mudaliar, *University of Winnipeg*
Gerald D. Anderson, *North Dakota State University*
Ellen Arnold, *Macalester College*
Daniel Ayana, *Youngstown State University*
Lt. David Bachler, *United States Air Force Academy*
Alan Baumler, *Indiana University of Pennsylvania*
Cynthia Bisson, *Belmont University*
Robert Blackey, *California State University—San Bernardino*
Robert Bond, *Youngstown State University*
Connie Brand, *Meridian Community College*
Tanya Brown, *Pittsburgh State University*
Byron Canner, *University of Utah*
Robert Carriedo, *United States Air Force Academy*
Carole R. Carter, *University of Central Arkansas*

Martin Scott Catino, *University of South Carolina—Aiken*
Yuan-ling Chao, *Middle Tennessee State University*
Gregory Crider, *Wingate University*
Eric Cunningham, *Gonzaga University*
Shawn Dry, *Oakland Community College*
Jeffrey Dym, *California State University—Sacramento*
Lisa Edwards, *University of Massachusetts—Lowell*
Jari Eloranta, *Appalachian State University*
Ken Faunce, *Washington State University*
Jeffrey Gaab, *SUNY College at Farmingdale*
Trevor Getz, *San Francisco State University*
Peter H. Griffin, *Lindenwood University*
William W. Haddad, *California State University—Fullerton*
Laura J. Hilton, *Muskingum College*
Matt Hopper, *California Polytechnic State University*
Ahmed H. Ibrahim, *Missouri State University*
Robert Irwin, *Grant MacEwan College*
Eric Johnson, *Pennsylvania State University*
Lisa Kazmier, *Drexel University*
Keith P. Knuuti, *University of Hawaii—Windward Community College*
Stephen Laffer, *Florida State University*
Eugene Larson, *Los Angeles Pierce College*
Paul Lococo Jr., *Leeward Community College*
David Longfellow, *Baylor University*
M. Lois Lucas, *West Virginia State University*
David McCarter, *Indiana State University*
Tom McCarthy, *United States Naval Academy*
Emerson Thomas McMullen, *Georgia Southern University*
Gerald Mills, *University of Oklahoma*
Ruma Niyogi, *Saint Xavier University*
Bradley Parker, *University of Utah*
Charles Parker, *St. Louis University*
Robert W. Patch, *University of California—Riverside*
Alice K. Pate, *Columbus State University*
Patrick Patterson, *Honolulu Community College*
Patricia M. Pelley, *Texas Tech University*
Wendy Pojmann, *Sienna College*
Timothy Pytell, *California State University—San Bernardino*
Scott S. Reese, *Northern Arizona University*
Jeremy Rich, *Middle Tennessee State University*
Paul Richgruber, *Minneapolis Community and Tech College;*
Inver Hills Community College
William S. Rodner, *Tidewater Community College*

Anthony R. Santoro, *Christopher Newport University*
Adam R. Seipp, *Texas A & M University*
Elizabeth Sharpe, *Jackson State University*
Jeffrey M. Shumway, *Brigham Young University*
James J. Simon, *Genesee Community College*
Phillip Luke Sinitiere, *University of Houston*
Timothy G. Sistrunk, *California State University—Chico*
Rachel Stocking, *Southern Illinois University—Carbondale*
Jacky Swansinger, *SUNY at Fredonia*
Michael Tarver, *Arkansas Tech University*
Patricia L. Thompson, *University of Texas at San Antonio*
Kate Transchel, *California State University*
Mary A. Valante, *Appalachian State University*
Gilmar Visoni, *Queensborough Community College*
Paul Voisey, *University of Alberta*
Rick Warner, *Wabash College*
Joshua Weiner, *American River College*
Claude Welch, *University at Buffalo, State University of New York*
Scott N. West, *University of Dayton*
Kristina Wilson, *Morehead State University*

Reviewers of the Penguin Academics Edition

Daniel Albert, *Salem State College*
James De Lorenzi, *John Jay College—CUNY*
David Dorrell, *Nicholls State University*
Mary Ann Mahony, *Central Connecticut State University*
Richard Warner, *Wabash College*

a note on dates and spellings

In keeping with common practice among historians of global history, we have used B.C.E. (before the common era) and C.E. (common era) to date events. For developments deep in the past, we have employed the phrase "years ago" to convey to the reader a clear sense of time. Specific dates are only given when necessary and when doing so improves the context of the narrative.

Recognizing that almost every non-English word can be transliterated in any number of ways, we have adopted the most widely used and simplest systems for spelling names and terms. The *pinyin* system of Chinese spelling is used for all Chinese words with the exception of such words as *Yangtze*, which are still widely referred to in its Wade-Giles form. Following common usage, we have avoided using apostrophes in the spelling of Arabic and Persian words, as well as words from other languages—thus, *Quran* and *Kaaba* instead of *Qu'ran* and *Ka'ba*, and *Tbilisi* instead of *T'bilisi*. Diacritical marks, accents, and other specialized symbols are used only if the most common variant of a name or term employs such devices (such as *Çatalhüyük*), if they are part of a personal noun (such as *Nicolás*), or if the inclusion of such markings in the spelling of a word makes pronouncing it easier (*Teotihuacán*).

Throughout the text, the first appearance of important non-English words whose pronunciation may be unclear for the reader are followed by phonetic spellings in parentheses, with the syllable that is stressed spelled in capital letters. So, for example *Ugarit* is spelled phonetically as "OO-gah-riht." Chinese words are not stressed, so each syllable is spelled in lowercase letters. Thus, the city of Hangzhou in China is rendered phonetically as "hahngjoh." For monosyllabic words, the phonetic spelling is in lowercase letters. So *Rus* is spelled as "roos." The following table provides a guide for how the vowel sounds in *The World* are represented phonetically.

a	as in *cat, bat*	ih	as in *if, sniff*
ah	as in *car, father*	o	as in *more, door*
aw	as in *law, paw*	oh	as in *row, slow*
ay	as in *fate, same*	oo	as in *loop, moo*
eh	as in *bet, met*	ow	as in *cow, mouse*
ee	as in *beet, ease*	uh	as in *but, rul*
eye	as in *dine, mine*		

Out of the Ice: Peopling the Earth

focus questions

1. Where in the evolutionary record do humans begin?
2. Why did the population of *Homo sapiens* grow so rapidly?
3. Why was the Ice Age a time of abundance?
4. What does its art tell us about Ice Age society?
5. When did *Homo sapiens* migrate to the Americas?
6. How did human life change when the Ice Age ended?

Imo was less than two years old. But she displayed precocious talents as an innovator and teacher. Her tribe loved to eat freshly cleaned sweet potatoes, scraping the dirt off with their hands. But Imo figured out how to wash the vegetables and passed the knowledge on, first to her mother and then to other relatives who in turn taught others, until the tribe had mastered the idea. Imo later found a new way to separate wheat grains from the sand that clung to them: she dropped them in water. The sand, heavier than the cereal, sank while Imo scooped up the wheat. Again, she taught the practice to the tribe.

The most surprising thing about Imo's achievement, when scientists in Japan observed it in 1953, was that she was a monkey. She excited the scientific world because she helped prove that humans are not the only species with culture—behaviors transmitted by learning, which become routines or rites, practiced not necessarily because they are useful but because they are traditional or conventional. To this day, the monkeys of Imo's tribe wash their sweet potatoes before eating them and teach their youngsters to do the same, even if you give them ready-washed food from a supermarket shelf.

Meanwhile, examples of culture in nonhuman species have multiplied. Human culture is still special in curious ways: it changes faster than that of other species, and it diverges more widely, but we are beginning to realize that to understand human peculiarities we must take other cultural animals into account. Some of the most challenging recent discoveries have brought animal politics to light. Even baboons can change their political systems. In Kenya in 1986, the aggressive elite that ruled a group of about ninety baboons all died suddenly after raiding a contaminated garbage dump for food. After that, the group adopted a much looser power structure and taught male "immigrants" from other tribes to adopt collaborative approaches to power. Mutual grooming replaced force as the main way to gain authority and attract mates. New research is focusing on even more surprising examples of what looks like cultural behavior in dolphins, elephants, and rats. The assumption that humans are easily separable from the rest of creation now looks shaky.

So You Think You're Human

Species are just convenient categories for grouping together closely related forms of life. The boundaries between species are fuzzy. There is no standard of how closely related you have to be to a fellow creature to be classed in the same species. DNA evidence reveals that all the people we now recognize as human had a common ancestor in Africa, probably more than 150,000 years ago. Five to 7 million years back, we share ancestors with chimpanzees. Double the length of time, and fossils reveal ancestors we share with other great apes. Further back, the differences between our ancestors and other creatures are only matters of degree. If we accept the theory of **evolution**—and, in outline, it does present a true account of how life forms change—we cannot find any transforming moment when humankind began.

Even today, there are nonhuman species—especially among apes—who seem morally indistinguishable from humans and should, according to some biologists and philosophers, be included in the same genus and even the same moral community as ourselves, with similar rights. In terms of their cultures, emotions, societies, and behaviors, chimpanzees share many characteristics with the fellow apes we call humans. To a lesser extent, gorillas and orangutans are also like us. All of us apes use tools, learn from each other, practice altruism and deceit, like to play, detest boredom, and seem self-aware. Our bodies and our behaviors are so like those of chimpanzees that the physiologist and historian Jared Diamond has suggested we reclassify our species as a kind of chimp. The first big question for this chapter, then, is where in the evolutionary record does it make sense to talk about humans? When does the story of humankind begin?

Human Evolution

A creature known as **Homo habilis** ("handy"), about 2.5 million years ago, chipped hand axes from stones. In calling this species the first humans, scholars defined humans as toolmakers—a now discredited concept. At one time, anthropologists backed a slightly later species, **Homo erectus** ("standing upright"), of about 1.5 million years ago, as the first human, largely because they admired the symmetrical flints for tools and weapons that *erectus* carved. From finds over 800,000 years ago, variant (or, perhaps, different) species called **Homo ergaster** ("workman") and *antecessor* ("predecessor") appeared, who later—at one site at least—stacked the bones of the dead. But reverence for the dead is not a uniquely human trait either. All these creatures, and others like them, have had champions who have claimed them as the first humans. Clearly, these instances of backing one set of ancestors over another reflect subjective criteria: supposed resemblances to ourselves. We are like the bereaved of some horrible disaster, scanning the remains of the dead for signs that we can recognize.

Species that occurred earlier than those classed under the heading "Homo," or who resembled us less, have tended to get labeled with less human-sounding names. Anthropologists used to call them *pithecanthropoi*—literally, ape-men. Current terminology favors **australopithecines** ("southern apelike creatures"), or *paranthropoi* ("next to humans"), as if they were identifiably nonhuman or prehuman. In 1974, the archaeologist Dan Johansen made a discovery that blew away all notion of a clear dividing line. He spotted the bones of an australopithecine sticking out of the mud in Hadar in Ethiopia in East Africa. He dug her up and called her "Lucy" after the title of a song on a Beatles record he played that night in camp. Lucy

Lucy. The bones shown here aren't connected to each other, but modern imaginations have reconstructed the 3-million-year-old skeleton known as "Lucy," as human or nearly so. Lucy walked on two legs and was closer to humans, in evolutionary terms, than any nonhuman creature that exists today.
© *The Natural History Museum, London*

had died more than 3 million years ago. She was only about three feet tall, but she and her kind walked on two legs and lived in family groups—characteristics that were thought to belong exclusively to later species of *Homo*. Then Johansen discovered tools 2.5 million years old near the site the following year, and in 1977, he found footprints, dating back 3.7 million years, of creatures who stood and walked on two legs. Finds with similar characteristics may date as far back as 6 million years ago.

It is tempting to try to settle the issue of who's human by reserving the term *human* for ourselves—members of the species we call **Homo sapiens**. Literally, the term *sapiens* means "wise," a grandiose name that betrays the foolishness of self-ascribed wisdom. For other species also have strong claims. One example is *Homo neanderthalensis*, who vanished only 30,000 years ago. The name means "of the Neander Valley"—the spot in northern Germany where remains of this species were found in 1856. We can be fairly certain that no one living today has a **Neanderthal** ancestor because there are no known cases of interbreeding between Neanderthals and our own ancestors. But *Homo neanderthalensis* and *Homo sapiens* coexisted for something like 100,000 years. Neanderthals had distinctive vocal tracts, so it is unlikely that they and our ancestors could speak each others' languages. They could have used nonverbal communication, however, just as we do today to talk with apes and even with humans whose spoken language we do not understand.

In most other respects, the two species of *Homo* were alike. Neanderthals were as big as *sapiens* and had a similar appearance. The brains were also similar, but, on average, the Neanderthal brain was slightly larger. They followed the same hunting, foraging ways of life in overlapping habitats. They made the same kinds of tools our ancestors made, lived in the same types of society, ate the same foods, and had many of the same customs and rites. They cared for their old and sick, and buried their dead with signs that suggest a sense of religion. Yet some paleoanthropologists seem determined to deny Neanderthals the name of humans—using arguments startlingly reminiscent of those of nineteenth-century scientific racism. Meanwhile, the evidence of Neanderthals' accomplishments is explained away. The ritual objects found at their graves, detractors say, must be "tricks of evidence," deposited accidentally by streams, winds, or animals.

Paleoanthropologists continue to dig up specimens that challenge believers in human uniqueness. In October 2004, excavators published news of a stunning find in Southeast Asia on the island of Flores in Indonesia, which included the remains of a female whose teeth, when they found her, were mashed to pulp, her bones rotted and soggy. She died 18,000 years ago. She was dwarfishly tiny. Her brain was barely as big as a chimpanzee's. But she had the power to subvert anthropological orthodoxy. *Homo floresiensis*, as her finders called her and her relatives whose bones lay alongside hers, proved that big brains do not make their possessors superior to other creatures. To judge from adjoining finds, these "hobbits," as the press dubbed them, had tools typical of early *Homo sapiens*, despite chimp-sized brains in imp-sized bodies. *Floresiensis* almost certainly made those tools. In known cases where nonhuman creatures lie alongside *sapiens*-made tools, *sapiens* ate them. But the remains of *floresiensis* showed no signs of having been butchered.

Out of Africa

Since no clear line separates human from nonhuman species, we might rationally start our story with our last common ancestor, roughly 150,000 years ago. All of us—as far as we can tell without actually testing everyone alive today—have a chemical component in our cells that a mother in East Africa passed on to her daughters at about that time. We nickname her Eve after the first woman in the Book of Genesis, but of course she was not our first ancestor nor was she the only woman of her day. By the best available estimates, perhaps 20,000 individuals of the species *Homo sapiens* lived in the same region at that time. In 2003, archaeological evidence of Eve's world turned up in Herto, in Ethiopia, near the remains of a butchered hippopotamus. Three skulls—a child's and two adults'—dated to about 154,000 to 160,000 years ago, resemble those of humans today, except that they are larger than what is now average. They had been stripped of flesh and polished after death, which suggests that the culture they belonged to practiced some death-linked ritual. We can begin to picture not only the appearance of the African Eve—we can do that by looking in a mirror—but also something of her way of life or, at least, life at a time close to her own.

Eve's homeland of mixed grassland and woodland was no Eden, but it was suitable for the creatures into which our ancestor and her off-spring had evolved. In this environment they could make up for their deficiency as climbers by standing erect to look out around them. They could exploit their modest physical advantages over competitor species. Humans are poorly equipped physically, with inferior senses of sight, smell, hearing, and unthreatening teeth and nails. But we can sweat pro-fusely over our hairless skins to keep cool during long chases, and we can ward off rival predators with our relatively accurate throwing-arms and well-coordinated eye–arm movements. In short, like most creatures, we are physically well equipped for a particular kind of habitat.

Peopling the Old World

From their beginnings in East Africa, Eve's descendants spread over the world (see Map 1.1). The first great problems these migrants pose for us are why they wanted to move, and what made them so adaptable to dif-ferent environments. Most species stay in the environments where they are best adapted. Even when human migrants move, they try to re-create the feel of home in their adopted country, carrying with them the bag-gage of their **culture**. They transport and transplant familiar animals and crops, which usually means finding a new area similar to the one they left. English settlers in America called the place they chose New England and tried to re-create the ways of life of the land they had left.

Yet when groups of *Homo sapiens* left Africa to people the world, about 100,000 years ago, they often relocated in challengingly different environments. These new habitats bred unfamiliar diseases. Yet people kept on moving through them and into them. We are still struggling to understand how it happened.

Such migration had happened before—or something like it had. Between about 1.75 and 1.25 million years ago, before *Homo sapiens* set out, *Homo erectus* migrated from a similar region in East Africa and spread over most of what is now Africa and Eurasia. This was a slower and more selective peopling of the Earth, and its circumstances are too obscure to cast much light on how and why *sapiens* became so widely dispersed. We can, however, look at other species that have crossed environments slowly and selectively. For example, the mountain gorillas of Rwanda in Central Africa moved into their present high, relatively cold habitat to escape the competitive environment of the tropical forest lowlands. Now, probably because food sources are relatively scarce in their new homeland, these exclusively vegetarian creatures are smaller and weaker than other goril-las. Nonetheless, they have forged a viable way of life.

Though the archaeological evidence is patchy, we can reconstruct where and when *Homo sapiens* traveled while peopling the Earth. One way is to measure differences in blood type, genetic makeup, and language among populations in different parts of the world. The greater the differences, the longer the ancestors of the people concerned are likely to have been out of touch with the rest of humankind. This is inexact science, because people are rarely isolated for long. Over most of Eurasia and Africa, populations have moved about tremendously in recorded history. Groups of people have frequently been mixed and restirred. There are, moreover, no agreed ways to measure the differences among languages. Still, for what it is worth, the best-informed research puts *Homo sapiens* in the Middle East by about 100,000 years ago. The colony failed, but new migrants reestablished it about 60,000 years ago. Settlement then proceeded along the coasts of Africa and Asia, probably by sea. The earliest agreed-upon archaeological evidence of *Homo sapiens* in China is about 67,000 years old (although some sites have yielded puzzlingly earlier dates for remains that seem like those of *Homo sapiens*).

Humans developed nautical technology surprisingly early. They crossed seas in boats to colonize what is now Australia 50,000 years ago. *Homo sapiens* reached Europe only a little later. Northern Asia and America—isolated by impenetrable screens of cold climate—were probably colonized much later. The most generally accepted archaeological evidence indicates the New World was settled no earlier than about 15,000 years ago.

If these dates are correct, the expansion of *Homo sapiens* implies an astonishing rate of population growth. Though we have no idea—beyond guesswork—of the actual numbers that migrated, we can estimate a figure in millions by the end of the process. A handful of Eve's children had multiplied to the point where they could colonize most of the habitable Old World in less than 100,000 years. But was the increase in population cause or effect of the migrations? And how did it relate to the other changes migration brought? Migrating groups were doubly dynamic: not just mobile, but also subject to huge social changes—divisive and violent, but with constructive ways of organizing their lives.

Migration, Population, and Social Change

Migration changed people's relationships with each other, the size and organization of their groups, the way they saw the world, and the way they interacted with other species—including those they competed with, preyed on, and outlasted. As far as we know, everyone at the time lived by foraging and moved on foot. Because mothers cannot easily carry more than one or two infants, large numbers of children are unsuited to foraging life. Consequently, foragers usually limit their families, either by strictly regulating who can mate with whom (to reduce the numbers of breeding couples) or by practicing other forms of population control. Their main contraceptive method is a long period of lactation.

Map 1.1 Early Human Migration, 150,000–40,000 Years Ago

8

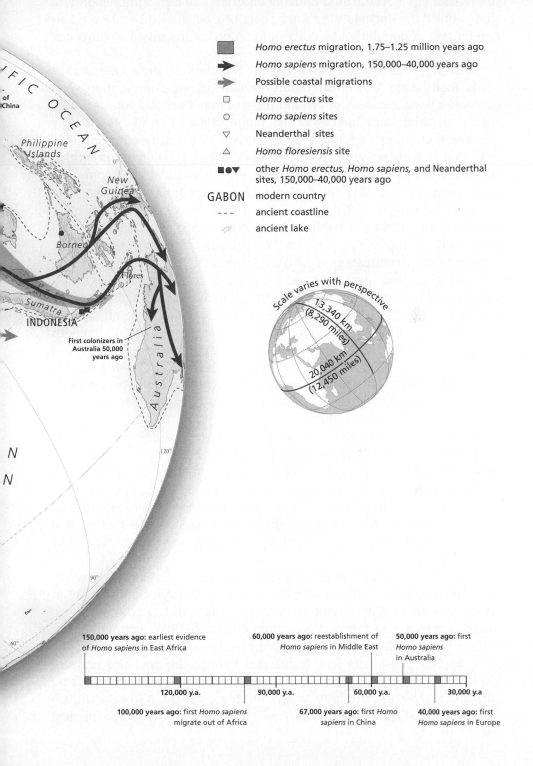

Homo erectus migration, 1.75–1.25 million years ago

➤ Homo sapiens migration, 150,000–40,000 years ago

➤ Possible coastal migrations

☐ Homo erectus site

○ Homo sapiens sites

▽ Neanderthal sites

△ Homo floresiensis site

■●▼ other Homo erectus, Homo sapiens, and Neanderthal sites, 150,000–40,000 years ago

GABON modern country

- - - ancient coastline

ancient lake

IFIC OCEAN

of China

Philippine Islands

New Guinea

Borneo

Flores

Sumatra

INDONESIA

First colonizers in Australia 50,000 years ago

Australia

Scale varies with perspective
13,340 km (8,290 miles)
20,040 km (12,450 miles)

150,000 years ago: earliest evidence of *Homo sapiens* in East Africa

60,000 years ago: reestablishment of *Homo sapiens* in Middle East

50,000 years ago: first *Homo sapiens* in Australia

120,000 y.a.   90,000 y.a.   60,000 y.a.   30,000 y.a

100,000 years ago: first *Homo sapiens* migrate out of Africa

67,000 years ago: first *Homo sapiens* in China

40,000 years ago: first *Homo sapiens* in Europe

Breast-feeding mothers are relatively infertile. The demographic growth that peopled the Earth is surprising, therefore, because it breaks the normal pattern of population stability in foraging communities. So how can we explain it?

Cooking with fire probably helped populations grow, because it made food easier to digest. Creatures like us, who have short guts and weak jaws, can only chew and digest limited energy sources. As a result, anything that increased the range of foods available to early humans was a major evolutionary advantage. The earliest indisputable evidence of cooking with fire dates back about 150,000 years, which coincides neatly with the beginning of the population boom. But we cannot be sure that fire-fueled cooking first happened then. The paleoanthropologist R. Wrangham has argued for a starting date more than 2 million years ago, based on the evolving shape of hominid guts and teeth, which, apparently, got smaller and blunter at that time, in response to the modification of food by flames. There is, however, no direct evidence that fire was used for cooking at that time. Fires that burned in caves between 500,000 and 1.5 million years ago appear to have been deliberately kindled, perhaps with cooking in mind. We are similarly uncertain about when other technologies started that might have improved diet by improving hunting, such as making driving lanes and corrals to herd animals for killing, but, though much earlier dates have been proposed, the earliest known examples of fire-hardened spears are only 150,000 years or so old—again taking us back to a date near the start of the migrations.

Whether or not new technologies empowered humans to migrate, new stresses or opportunities drove or drew them on. Food shortages or ecological disasters might explain the necessity to move, but no evidence supports this or fits with the evidence of rising population. In every other case we know of, in all species, population declines when food sources shrink. Another possible source of stress is warfare. Plague, famine, and natural disaster tend to inhibit human action, whereas war spurs us to new responses.

One of the most fascinating problems of history is how and when war started. Some anthropologists argue that evolution implanted aggressive and violent instincts in humans as it did in other animals. When people asked Bernard Montgomery (1887–1976), commander of British forces in World War II, how he justified war, he would refer them to *The Life of the Ant*. Romantics defend the opposite point of view. Human nature, they say, is essentially peaceful until competition corrupts it. War, according to Margaret Mead, the great liberal anthropologist of the 1920s and 1930s, was an invention, not a biological necessity.

At first, the evidence seemed divided. The earliest archaeological proof we have of large-scale warfare is a battle fought at Jebel Sahaba, near the modern border of Egypt and Sudan, about 11,000 years ago. The victims included women and children, savaged by multiple wounds. One female was stabbed twenty-two times. At the time, agriculture was in its infancy, encouraging speculation that warfare began—or, at least, entered a new, more systematic phase—when settled communities started to fight one another to control land and resources.

In the 1970s, the primatologist Jane Goodall observed something like what we would now call gang warfare among chimpanzee communities in West Africa. When chimpanzee splinter groups secede from their societies, their former fellows try to kill them. Similar conflicts may have made early human splinter groups migrate to safety. It is an intriguing speculation, but it poses other problems. What stresses could have caused people to divide and fight each other 100,000 years ago? Rising population again? Or are we driven back to more speculation about increasing competition for supposedly diminishing food stocks, or even to assertions about innate animal aggression?

In societies of increasing violence, men have enhanced roles. This is because, among all primates, including humans, greater competitiveness in mating makes males, on average, bigger and stronger than females. Yet women are more valuable in most societies than men. A society can dispense with most of its men and still reproduce itself. That is why societies more commonly risk men in war than women. Women, moreover, are more easily mistaken as sacred because of the obvious correspondences between the cycles of their bodies and the rhythms of the heavens. Menstruation and the cycle of female fertility match the phases of the moon.

So how did male domination come to be normal in human societies? One theory ascribes it to a deliberate, collective power-seeking strategy

Making Connections | THE FIRST POPULATION BOOM: REASONS FOR POPULATION GROWTH

Fire-managed grazing of animals; driving lanes; corrals	Control over food supply	More food available for consumption
Throwing-arms; fire-hardened spears	Improved hunting	Improved diet
Cooking with fire	Improved taste and digestibility	Increase in range of available food
Sexual economic specialization	Hunting and gathering	Women liberated for childbearing

by males, inspired by dislike of women or resentment or envy or a desire to get control of the most elementary of resources—the means of reproducing the species. By analogy with chimpanzees, a rival theory suggests that male dominance is a consequence of hunting, which, in the few chimpanzee groups known to practice it, is an almost exclusively male activity. Hunting increases male dominance in chimpanzee society because the hunters distribute the meat, in almost ritual fashion. Females line up and, in effect, beg for morsels. Female chimps often exchange sex for food, especially meat. By contrast, among bonobos, who are like chimps but are strictly plant-eating, both sexes share foraging, and females tend to be socially equal or even dominant. Hunting, however, seems to be a recent development in chimpanzee society and to have followed and strengthened male dominance—not caused it.

Without evidence to the contrary, it is unwise to assume that early in the migration period either sex monopolized political power. Still, migrating groups must have developed ways to liberate more women for childbirth or increase the fertile period of women's lives. Given the practical limitations on the number of children a woman can carry around with her, population can only have increased that way. Improved nutrition helped. Was there also some redistribution of economic activities, with men taking on more food-supplying roles?

As far as we know, in the earliest kind of economic specialization by sex, men did most of the hunting, while women did most of the gathering. Women's work seems to have been more productive in terms of calorific value per unit of energy expended. But we do not know when this specialization started or how rigid or widespread it was. In any case, the balance between hunted and gathered foods in the diets of the migrants varied according to the environment. In known cases, hunters supplied about a third of the nutrition. The migrations, and the accompanying demographic changes, would not have been possible without both hunting and gathering.

The Last Great Ice Age

Whatever caused it, the peopling of the world spanned the most convulsive period of climatic change that *Homo sapiens* experienced before our own times. The cooling and warming phases of the planet are regular occurrences, and one or the other is always going on. Every 100,000 years or so, a distortion in the Earth's orbit tugs the Northern Hemisphere away from the sun. On more frequent cycles, the Earth tilts and wobbles on its axis. When these phenomena coincide, temperatures change dramatically and ice ages set in. A great cooling began about 150,000 years ago. The great migrations roughly coincided with the Ice Age, as if humans did not just welcome the cold, but actively sought it. We think of global warming as a current phenomenon, and indeed it is. The world only began to emerge from the last Ice Age about 15,000 to 20,000 years ago. The intensive global warming we experience today is the most dramatic phase of that trend.

This is how the world we inhabit today came about. As the Earth tilted and the sun blazed, the ice cap began to shrink. At its most extensive, about 20,000 years ago, it had reached the present lower courses of the Missouri and Ohio rivers in North America and deep into what are now the British Isles. It covered what is today Scandinavia. Most of the rest of Europe was **tundra**, a treeless region with permanently frozen subsoil, or coniferous forest, with trees such as spruce, fir, and pine. In central Eurasia, tundra reached almost to the present latitudes of the Black Sea. **Steppe**—dry plain covered with scrub grass—licked the shores of the Mediterranean. In North America, tundra and coniferous forest extended to where Virginia is today.

Warming started about 18,000 years ago. Not long after, between about 16,000 and 8,000 years ago, the geological record shows enormous regional fluctuations in temperature. Melting ice meant cooling seas and temporary reversals of warming in affected latitudes. As the fluctuations subsided, temperatures leaped. Glaciers retreated worldwide. Seas flooded and spilled over land, until—broadly speaking—the world map as we know it today took shape.

Ice Age Hunters

The severity of the Ice Age is unimaginable, but it was not an entirely hostile world. For the hunters who inhabited the vast tundra that covered much of Eurasia, the edge of the ice was the best place to be. Over thousands of years of cold, a lot of mammals had adapted by efficiently storing their own body fat—and that was the hunters' target. Fat has a bad reputation today, but for most of history, most people have eagerly sought it. Relatively speaking, animal fat is the world's most energy-abundant source of food.

Hunters favored species they could kill in large numbers by driving them over cliffs or into bogs or lakes. The bones of Ice Age horses are often found near the bottom of precipitous cliffs, and remains of 100 mammoths have turned up in pits at a site in the Czech Republic in Central Europe. About 20,000 years ago, the invention of the bow and arrow revolutionized hunting. For some hunted species, the new weapon hastened extinction, though climate change had perhaps already condemned them. But for the killers, the result was a fat bonanza, achieved with relatively modest effort.

Venus of Laussel. An image of a woman carved in relief on a cave wall in central France more than 20,000 years ago reveals much about Ice Age life: esteem for big hips and body fat; the love of revelry suggested by the uplifted drinking-horn; the involvement of women in presumably sacred activity; and the existence of accomplished, specialized artists.
© *Charles & Josette Lenars/CORBIS*
All Rights Reserved

For Ice Age artists, fat was beautiful. One of the oldest artworks in the world is the Venus of Willendorf—a plump little carving of a fat female, 30,000 years old and named for the place in Germany where she was found. Critics have interpreted her as a goddess, a ruler, or, since she could be pregnant, a means of conjuring fertility. However, her slightly more recent look-alike, the Venus of Laussel, carved on a cave wall in France, evidently got fat the way most of us do: by enjoyment and indulgence. She raises a horn, surely containing food or drink.

The remains of Ice Age people reveal that, on average, they were better nourished than later populations. Only modern industrialized societies surpass their intake of 3,000 calories a day. In some Ice Age communities, people ate about five pounds of food a day. The nature of the plant foods they gathered—few starchy grains, relatively large amounts of fruit and plants that grow underground—and the high vitamin C content of animal organ meats provided five times the average intake of vitamin C of an American today. Abundant game guaranteed **Ice Age affluence**. High levels of nutrition and long days of leisure, unequaled in most later societies, meant people had time to observe nature and think about what they saw. The art of the era shows the sublime results.

Ice Age Art

In the depths of the Ice Age, a stunningly resourceful way of life took shape. We know most about the period in Europe, where extensive art has survived because it was made in deep caves evidently chosen because they were inaccessible. Most prehistoric art has been found in northern Spain and southwest France. Examples of sculptures, carvings, and other art objects are also scattered across Europe, from Britain and the Atlantic to the Ural Mountains in Russia.

This art told stories and had magical, ritual uses. Some animal images are slashed or punctured many times over, as if in symbolic sacrifice. A good case has been made for seeing the cave paintings as aids to track prey. The shapes of hooves, the tracks, dung, seasonal habits, and favorite foods of the beasts are among the artists' standard images. By analogy with the rock paintings of hunter–gatherers of later periods, Ice Age art depicts an imagined world, full of the spirits of the animals people needed and admired: a magical world, accessed in mystical trances.

Outside Europe, what little we know of the peoples of the time suggests that they created equally skillful work. Four painted rock slabs from Namibia in southwest Africa are about 26,000 years old—almost as old as any art in Europe—and bear similar animal images. A clue to the very idea of representing life in art fades today from a rock face in Kenniff, Australia, where stencils of human hands and tools were made 20,000 years ago.

Lions from Chauvet Cave, France. In 1994, three cave explorers spent the Christmas holiday in the gorges of the Ardéche region in southeastern France. In the area, explorers had already discovered numerous caves that Ice Age people had decorated between about 14,000 and 21,000 years ago. But nothing already known about the region prepared the team for the breathtaking find that awaited them. It soon became apparent that the Chauvet cave was one of the most extensive collections of Ice Age art in the world. Furthermore, carbon dating from many of the images led to an inescapable conclusion. These were the world's oldest known paintings, yielding three dates of more than 30,000 years, and none less than 23,000. The paintings also subverted everything previously thought about Ice Age art. Scholarship had assumed that Ice Age art had evolved in style from "primitive" sketches by the earliest artists to the sublime images painted toward the end of the era in the caves of Altamira in Spain and Lascaux in France. In technique and skill, the Chauvet paintings are equal to paintings done in similar environments 10,000 or 15,000 years later. The Chauvet painters' favorite subjects were rhinoceroses and lions often shown stalking like the group above.
French Ministry of Culture and Communication, Regional Direction for Cultural Affairs—Rhone-Alps, Regional Department of Archaeology

Ice Age Culture and Society

The Ice Age was the last great era of what we would now call a kind of **globalization**. That is, key elements of culture were similar all over the inhabited world. Although languages and the structures of political and social life were probably already highly various, people practiced hunter–gatherer economies with similar kinds of technology, ate similar foods, and—as far as we can tell—had similar religious practices. Social change and intellectual shifts were challenging for people who experienced them, but they happened slowly by comparison with later periods. The earliest of the art-filled caves of southern France, at Chauvet, is 30,000 years old. That at Lascaux dates from 10,000 years later. Yet the subjects the artists painted, and the techniques and styles they used, hardly changed at all.

Mammoth Hut. Between 40,000 and 16,000 years ago, on what are now the Russian and Ukranian steppe, people built dwellings made out of the bones of woolly mammoths and other creatures. The biggest surviving dwelling at Mezhirich (Ukraine) has 385 bones from about 100 different beasts that, when alive, weighed more than 46,000 pounds in all. *CM Dixon/Ancient Art and Architecture Collection*

The **material culture** that many archaeological digs yield provides clues to what goes on in the mind. For instance, the people who hunted mammoths to extinction 20,000 years ago on the Ice Age steppes of what is now southern Russia built dome-shaped dwellings of mammoth bones on a circular plan twelve or fifteen feet in diameter that seem sublime triumphs of the imagination. They are reconstructions of mammoth nature, humanly reimagined, perhaps to acquire the beast's strength or magically to assume power over the species. Ordinary, everyday activities went on inside these extraordinary dwellings—sleeping, eating, and all the routines of family life—in communities, on average, of fewer than 100 people. But no dwelling is purely practical. Your house reflects your ideas about your place in the world.

Thanks to the clues material culture yields, we can make some confident assertions about other aspects of Ice Age people's lives: their symbolic systems, their magic, and the kind of social and political units in which they lived. Although Ice Age people had nothing we recognize as writing, they did have highly expressive symbols, which we struggle to translate. Realistic drawings made 20,000 to 30,000 years ago show recurring gestures and postures. Moreover, they often include what seem to be numbers, signified by dots and notches. One widely occurring mark that looks like a "P" may be a symbol for female because it resembles the curves of a woman's body. What looks like a calendar was made 30,000 years ago in the Dordogne region in France. It is a flat bone inscribed with crescents and circles that may record phases of the moon.

Clues to the spiritual life of the time appear in traces of red ocher, the earliest substance that seems to have had a role in ritual. The oldest known ocher mine in the world, about 42,000 years old, is at Lion Cave in what is now Lesotho in southern Africa. The vivid, lurid color was applied in burials—perhaps as a precious offering, perhaps to imitate blood and reinvest the dead with life.

Ice Age people also used symbols and pigments in magic. Those who controlled them wielded power. In paintings and carvings, we can glimpse the Ice Age elite, people considered special and set apart from the group. In figures wearing animal masks—antlered or lionlike—the wearer is transformed. From anthropological studies of the recent past, we know such disguises are normally efforts to communicate with the dead or with the gods. Bringing messages from other worlds is the role of a **shaman**, who acts as an intermediary between humans and spirits or gods. The shaman may seek a state of ecstasy induced by drugs or dancing or drumming, to communicate with normally inaccessible realms. Among the Chukchi hunters of northern Siberia, whose way of life and environment are similar to those of Ice Age peoples, the shaman's experience is represented as a journey to consult the spirits in a realm that only the dead can normally enter. The shaman may adopt an animal disguise to acquire the animal's speed or strength or identify with an animal ancestor. The shaman's role can be an awesome source of authority. Shamans can challenge alpha males. Like other religions, shamanism involves spiritual insight that people of both sexes, various levels of intellect, and all kinds of physical makeup can acquire. By choosing elites who had the gift of communicating with spirits, Ice Age societies could escape the oppression of the physically powerful or those privileged by birth.

Although we cannot be sure about the nature of the Ice Age power class, we know it existed because of the inequalities of Ice Age graves. In a cemetery at Sunghir, near Moscow, dated about 24,000 years ago, the highest-status person seems, at first glance, to have been an elderly man. His burial goods include a cap sewn with fox's teeth and about twenty ivory bracelets. Nearby, however, two boys about eight or ten years of age have even more spectacular ornaments. In addition to ivory bracelets and necklaces and fox-tooth buttons, the boys have animal carvings and beautifully wrought weapons, including spears of mammoth ivory, each more than six feet long. About 3,500 finely worked ivory beads had been drizzled over the head, torso, and limbs of each boy. Here was a society that marked leaders for greatness from boyhood and perhaps from birth.

In our attempt to understand where power lay in Ice Age societies, the final bits of evidence are crumbs from rich tables. Archaeologists have found ashes from large-scale cooking and the calcified debris of food that indicate feasting at sites in northern Spain, perhaps from as long as 23,000 years ago. By analogy with modern hunting peoples, the most likely reason for the feasts was to forge alliances between communities. From the moment of its emergence, the idea of the feast had practical consequences: to build and strengthen societies and enhance the power of those who organized the feasts and controlled the food.

Peopling the New World

The New World was one of the last parts of the planet *Homo sapiens* peopled. According to the formerly dominant theory, a gap opened between glaciers toward the end of the Ice Age. A race of hunters crossed the land link between North America and Asia, where the Bering Strait now flows, to enter a paradise where no human hunter had ever trod before. The abundance was so great and the animals were so unwary that the invaders ate enormously and multiplied greatly. They spread rapidly over the hemisphere, hunting the great game to extinction as they went. The story appealed to an unsophisticated form of U.S. patriotism. The Clovis people, as these hunters were dubbed after an early archaeological site in New Mexico, seemed to resemble modern American pioneers. They exhibited quick-fire locomotion, hustle and bustle, technical prowess, big appetites, irrepressible strength, enormous cultural reach, and a talent for reforging the environment.

But the truth about the peopling of the hemisphere is disappointingly undramatic. These first great American superheroes—like most of their successors—did not really exist. Although archaeologists have excavated too few sites for a complete and reliable picture to emerge, a new theory now dominates. We have evidence of early human settlement scattered from the northernmost to the southernmost limits of the Americas. This evidence is so widespread, spanning so long a period, embedded in so many different geological layers, and exhibiting such a vast range of cultural diversity that one conclusion is inescapable—colonists came at different times, bringing different cultures with them.

No admissible evidence dates any inhabited sites in the American hemisphere earlier than about 13,000 B.C.E. The first arrivals came while glaciers covered much of North America. They stuck close to the cold, where the game was fattest. They followed corridors between walls of ice or along narrow shores away from glaciers. Around 10,000 years ago, a cluster of extinctions wiped out the mammoth, mastodon, horse, giant sloth, saber-toothed tiger, and at least thirty-five other large species in the Americas. New hunting techniques and new hunters were partly responsible. But we can only explain the events in the context of vast climatic changes that affected habitats and the whole ecology on which these animals depended.

Many supposedly early sites of human habitation have proved to be delusions of overenthusiastic archaeologists. A few sites, however, offer strong evidence of the antiquity and range of settlement. Most are in the eastern United States—a long way from the vicinity of the modern Bering Strait. In the mid-1970s, 15,000-year-old basketwork and tools made with fine flints emerged from deep under the discarded beer cans that topped a dig at Meadowcroft, on the Ohio River, near the border of Pennsylvania and

West Virginia. Later in the 1970s, excavations at Monte Verde in southern Chile revealed a twenty-foot long, wooden, hide-covered dwelling preserved in a peat bog for about 12,500 years. Nearby were a big mastodon-butchery and a space devoted to making tools. The inhabitants brought salt and seaweed from the coast, forty miles away, and medicinal herbs from mountains equally far in the opposite direction. If Meadowcroft is a long way from the colonizers' entry point near the Bering Strait, southern Chile is a world away again—almost as far as you can get in the Western Hemisphere. How long would it have taken the settlers of Monte Verde to cross the hemisphere, over vast distances and through many different kinds of environments, each demanding new forms of adaptation? Most specialists think it must have taken thousands of years. The question of the date of the first peopling of the New World therefore remains open.

Survival of the Foragers

As the ice cap retreated and the great herds shifted with it, many human communities opted to follow them. Archaeology has unearthed traces of their routes. Along the way, in what is now Germany, about 12,000 years ago, people sacrificed reindeer by sewing stones into their stomachs and drowning them in a lake. About 1,000 years later, hunters as far north as Yorkshire in England found an environment as abundant as the cave artists' had been. Not only was it filled with tundra-loving species such as red deer, elk, and aurochs—huge, shaggy wild cattle—but also with wild boar in surroundings that were becoming patchily wooded.

At Skateholm in Sweden, about 8,000 years ago, hunters founded the largest known settlement of the era. It was a winter camp in an area, abundant with animals the inhabitants ate. In summer, the people must have moved farther north. They lie today in graves decorated with beads and ocher and filled with the spoils of their careers, including antlers and boar's tusks. Their dogs are buried nearby. These burly, wolflike companions are sometimes interred with more signs of honor than humans were given. Dogs were full members of societies where hunting prowess and skill in war determined status.

The most persistently faithful followers of the ice were the Inuit of North America. About 4,000 years ago, they invented the blubber-filled soapstone lamp, enabling them to follow big game beyond the tundra and into the darkness of an arctic winter. They could track the caribou on its winter migrations, when its fur is thickest and its fat most plentiful. This way of life persisted until the late twentieth century, although its first practitioners have disappeared. Migrants from the Arctic Ocean replaced them 1,000 years ago.

Climate change trapped other foraging peoples in environments where they had to develop new ways of life. Some of these environments offered new kinds of abundance. Here were broad-leaved forests and lakes and rivers full of aquatic life. New World prairies held apparently inexhaustible stocks of bison (though the largest bison species was rapidly hunted to extinction). Between the unstable periods of climate change around 12,000 years ago, foragers even colonized dense, tropical forests at Pedra Pintada in Brazil, where the Amazon River now flows. Today, foragers in this region have to struggle to find foods they can digest, but it seems to have been more environmentally diverse toward the end of the Ice Age.

Some societies perpetuated their foraging life in hot, arid deserts, as different from the best hunting grounds of the Ice Age as it is possible to imagine. This required two forms of adaptation. First, the thinly dispersed populations had to create collaborative networks. Second, poor environments demanded that inhabitants develop what we might call orally transmitted science. For only with accurate and extensive knowledge of their habitat can people survive in harsh environments.

The San or Bushmen of southern Africa's Kalahari Desert illustrate the difficulties and solutions. Their domain has shrunk in recent centuries, as Bantu farmers, Khoi herdsmen, and white invaders have overrun much of their former territory. But their heartland was already dry at the time of the San's first occupancy, about 14,000 years ago. There are underground rivers but few permanent water holes. The people watch for rare signs of rain and hurry to gather the vegetation that accompanies it. The scrubland plant foods, including water-bearing tubers and a kind of cactus, supply 30 percent of their sustenance. The rest comes from game, which grazes on desert shrubs that humans cannot digest.

In one sense, the world's food supply still depends on foraging. The amount of food from hunting actually increased in the twentieth century, which may go down in history not only as the last age of hunting but as the greatest. Throughout the world today, we practice a highly specialized, mechanized, and unusual form of hunting—deep-sea trawling. Fish farming is likely to replace it in the future, but deep-sea fishing is a historical throwback.

IN PERSPECTIVE
After the Ice

In the post–Ice Age world, little by little, over thousands of years, most societies abandoned foraging and adopted farming or herding as the way to get their food. Among peoples who still live close to the ice cap, the

CHRONOLOGY	
Over 3 million years ago	Lucy
1 million years ago	*Homo erectus* migrates from East Africa to Africa and Eurasia
100,000 years ago	*Homo sapiens* migrates out of Africa
67,000 years ago	*Homo sapiens* in Asia
50,000 years ago	*Homo sapiens* colonizes Australia and New Guinea; *Homo sapiens* reaches Europe
30,000 years ago	Last Neanderthals vanish
20,000–15,000 B.C.E.	World emerges from the Ice Age
20,000 B.C.E.	Invention of the bow and arrow
13,000 B.C.E.	*Homo sapiens* in the Americas
(All dates are approximate)	

Inuit remain faithful to their hunting tradition in North America. Most of their Old World counterparts, however, have long abandoned it. In Eurasia, though some hunting cultures still cling to the old ways at the eastern end of Siberia, the peoples on the western Arctic rim adopted reindeer herding over 1,000 years ago. The Ice Age way of life, if not over, is drawing to a close. Hunting is now thought of as a primitive way to get food, long abandoned except as an aristocratic indulgence in some countries or as a supposedly manly sport in others.

The disappearance of foraging lifeways seems a remarkable turn-around for a predator species such as *Homo sapiens*. There was a time, before hunting, when our ancestors were scavengers; for hundreds of thousands, perhaps millions, of years, however, foraging was reliable and rewarding. It fed people through every change of climate. Its human practitioners spread over the world and adapted to every kind of habitat. They dominated every ecosystem they became part of and competed successfully with most other species. They achieved startling increases in their numbers, which we struggle to explain. They founded more var-ied societies than any other species (though the differences among these societies were slight compared to later periods). They had art-rich cul-tures with traditions of learning and symbolic systems to record informa-tion. They had their own social elites, political customs, ambitious magic, and practical methods to exploit their environment.

Our next task is to ask why, after the achievements recounted in this chapter, people abandoned the foraging life? Renouncing the hunt and pursuing new ways of life after the Ice Age are among the most far-reaching and mysterious transformations of the human past. If the puzzle of why *Homo sapiens* spread over the Earth is the first great question in our history, the problem of why foragers became farmers is the second.

PROBLEMS AND PARALLELS

1. Is it possible to define what it means to be human?
2. Why did *Homo sapiens* migrate out of Africa, and why did the population of *Homo sapiens* increase so rapidly?
3. What theories attempt to explain how and why war started?
4. How did male domination come to be normal in human societies?
5. Why was the Ice Age a time of affluence?
6. Why has the foraging way of life persisted today?

CHAPTER 2

Out of the Mud: Farming and Herding after the Ice Age

focus questions

1. Why are foragers often better off than farmers?
2. What kinds of environments are suited to herding?
3. Where did farming begin, and what were the first crops farmers grew?
4. Why did people in most areas of the world switch from foraging to farming?

Early in the third millennium B.C.E., on a hilltop at Hambledon in southwest England, in the midst of a complex of ceremonial enclosures and defensive earthworks, people gathered for purposes we can no longer identify, but one thing is obvious from the archaeological record. They were there to eat and drink. They brought a mixture of food with them—some, such as venison, was from hunting; other edibles, especially the large quantities of hazlenuts, were from gathering. But there were also foods the people produced for themselves by herding and farming: cattle, pigs, sheep, and wheat and barley that had already been cleaned of chaff. They intended to eat the food, not store it, because the site is strewn with the fragments of broken plates and cups. Some of the animals they reared were enormous, yielding 600 pounds of meat, organ meats, and fat; on some of the days of feasting at the site, two or three such creatures were butchered at one time. So these were gatherings of hundreds or thousands of people, who knew how to breed livestock for size. The people who lived in the area at the time exhibited strikingly varied food habits, which implies that there were different ranks or orders of society, marked by differences of diet. Most people lived mainly on meat and milk, but some ate only vegetable foods. They probably washed their feast down with wine, because archaeologists have found the remains of grapes and grape vines at the site.

The feasting at Hambledon Hill perhaps sprang from a hunter–gatherer way of life, which people in the region had not yet altogether abandoned in favor of farming. Once hunters kill a large animal, such as a deer or even a wild ox, they have to eat the meat quickly in communal meals before it rots. Yet the eaters who gathered at Hambledon were engaged in a huge transformation of their way of life—from foraging for food to growing and breeding it—that had already been going on for centuries in their part of the world and, in some places, for thousands of years. The transition has been gathering pace ever since and now includes most of the Earth's inhabitants.

To most people, in most societies, for most of the time, food is and always has been the most important thing in the world. Nothing can happen without it. Changes in how we get food and whether we get it are among history's biggest changes. During the global warming that followed the Ice Age, **husbandry**—breeding animals and cultivating crops—began to replace hunting and gathering and introduced the biggest change of all. The menu at the Hambledon feast—the mix of wild and cultivated plants, and hunted and domesticated meat—raises one of the most perplexing sets of problems in history: When, where, how, and why did people abandon the life of foragers and take up farming? Why did food procurers become food producers?

The Problem of Agriculture

Husbandry happened in two distinct ways, involving different types of environments and different levels of environmental intervention. In some environments, people could exploit creatures that had a herd instinct by managing the herds, rather than by hunting them. Breeding enhanced qualities that evolution did not necessarily favor, such as docility; size; and yield of meat, milk, eggs, and fat. On the negative side, close contact between humans and animals often allowed disease-bearing organisms to thrive, threatening human lives and health and sometimes unleashing plagues. Otherwise, however, animal husbandry barely affected the environment. Herds, on the whole, kept to their traditional patterns of migration, and people continued to accompany them—driving the beasts rather than following them. Domesticated animals remained recognizably the heirs of their wild ancestors, and the landscapes through which they traveled did not change much, except that the herds' feeding and manure probably encouraged the grasses they ate to flourish at the expense of other plant species.

In other environments, however, plant husbandry involved massive human intervention. In the long run, tillage of the soil changed the world more than any previous innovation by *Homo sapiens*. From postglacial mud, people coaxed what we now call "civilization"—a way of life based on radically modifying the environment. Instead of merely trying to manage the landscape nature provided, farmers recarved it with fields and boundaries, ditches and irrigation canals. They stamped the land with a new look, a geometrical order. Agriculture enabled humans to see the world in a new way—to imagine that magic and science had the power to change nature. Such power, in turn, changed people's sense of where they fit into the panorama of life on Earth. Now they could become masters or, in more modest moments or cultures, stewards of creation.

Together, farming and herding revolutionized humans' place in their ecosystems. Instead of merely depending on other life forms to sustain us, we forged a new relationship of interdependence with those species we eat. We rely on them for food; they rely on us for their reproduction. Domesticated animals would not exist without humans. Husbandry was the first human challenge to evolution. Instead of evolving species through **natural selection**, farming and herding proceed by what might be called unnatural selection—sorting and selecting by human hands, for human needs, according to human agenda.

Herding and tilling also changed human societies. By feeding people on a greater scale, agriculture allowed societies to grow bigger than ever before. Larger populations demanded new forms of labor control and food distribution, which nurtured strong states and powerful elites.

In almost every case, for reasons we still do not understand, when people begin to practice agriculture, the pace of change quickens immeasurably. States and civilizations do not seem to last long. Societies that we think of as being the most highly evolved turn out to be least fitted for survival. Compared with the relative stability of forager communities, societies that depend on agriculture are prone to lurch and collapse.

In other words, farming is a disastrous, self-destructive option for many of the societies that adopt it: As we shall see in this chapter, it commonly brings devastating new diseases, oppressive political systems, and recurrent famines to many of the societies that choose it as their means of life. This implies that cultures do not necessarily change like living organisms, according to the rules of evolution. Typically, living creatures evolve because successful adaptations, which help the species survive, become generalized. Cultures, however, often respond to changes in their environments by adopting dysfunctional new features.

A Case in Point: Aboriginal Australians

In August 1770, Captain James Cook reached the north coast of Australia, on the first of his spectacular voyages of exploration that charted the lands and limits of the Pacific Ocean. Near Cape York, he paused at an island he named Possession. Though his stated purpose was scientific, he was also an officer of the Royal Navy with orders to extend the British Empire. To Cook's mind, the island, though inhabited, was waiting to be grabbed. The natives could not be said to possess it because they had left no marks of possession on its soil. A wealth of plants that they could have domesticated was growing wild. Yet, Cook wrote, the people "know nothing of cultivation. . . . It seems strange."

Cook and his contemporaries saw only two reasons why foragers would reject agriculture: They were either stupid or subhuman. Early European painters in Australia depicted **aborigines** as apelike creatures, grimacing oddly and crawling in trees. The colonists ignored the natives, or, when they got in the way, hunted them down—as they would beasts. Not only did the native Australians reject agriculture, in some areas, they appeared to shun every technical convenience. In Arnhem Land, in the extreme north, they used boomerangs to make music but no longer as weapons for the hunt. Progress, which the European discoverers of Australia believed in fervently, seemed to have gone into reverse.

But the aborigines did not lack the knowledge necessary to switch from foraging to farming if they had wanted to do so. When they gathered wild yams or the root known as nardoo, they ensured that enough of the plant remained in the ground so that it would grow back. In many regions, too, they used fire to control the grazing grounds of kangaroos and concentrate them for hunting. Along the Murray and Darling rivers, aborigines watered and weeded wild crops and policed their boundaries against human and animal predators.

In the far north of Australia, aboriginal communities traded with the farming cultures of New Guinea. So, even if they hadn't developed agriculture on their own, they could have learned it from outsiders. If the aborigines did not farm, it is because they were doing well without it. Similar cases all over the world support this conclusion. Where wild foods are abundant, there is no incentive to domesticate them. Of course, people often adopt practices that do them no good. We can concede this general principle, but, case by case, we still want to know why.

Preagricultural Settlements

Archaeological evidence in the Middle East shows that people can settle in one place without the trouble of farming. After the Ice Age ended, by about 15,000 B.C.E., a frontier zone between forest and grassland stretched across the eastern shore of the Mediterranean and what are now Iran, eastern Turkey, and Iraq (see Map 2.1). The forests were full of acorns, pistachios, and almonds, which gatherers ground into flour and paste. The grasslands bred vast quantities of wild grass with edible seeds. These foods could all be warehoused between harvests and had the additional advantage of ripening at different times. Dense herds of gazelle in the grasslands provided more nutrition for hunters to bring home. Food was so plentiful that foragers did not have to move around much to find it.

	forest	●	preagricultural settlement
	grassland	○	other preagricultural settlements
TURKEY	modern-day country	-------	ancient coastlines

Map 2.1 Preagricultural Settlements in the Middle East

Jomon Pottery. Ten thousand years ago, the Jomon potters of Japan produced the world's earliest known earthenware vessels. Other pottery-making peoples also practiced farming, but the Jomon people were sedentary foragers—living in permanent or long-term settlements, but managing the environment in minimal ways and relying on abundant wild foods, including nuts, seeds, acorns, some seventy marine animal species, and land mammals—eating not just boar, deer, and hare, but also wolves, wildcats, flying squirrels, and monkeys. © Sakamoto Photo Research Laboratory/CORBIS All Rights Reserved

By about 14,000 to 15,000 years ago, permanent settlements arose throughout the region: clusters of dwellings with stone walls, or those made of wood on stone foundations, or cut from soft stone and roofed with reeds. The foragers who lived in these sedentary communities apparently kept to themselves. Villages had distinctive habits, which almost amounted to badges of identity. To judge from the evidence of inherited physical characteristics, they married within their own communities. Some settlers cut what look like plans of their fields on limestone slabs, which suggests that they were territorial—that they had a sense of possession that Captain Cook would have recognized.

But the settled foragers were better off than farmers. Their remains, on the whole, show better health and nutrition than the farming peoples who followed later in the same region. A diet rich in seeds and nuts had ground down their teeth, but—unlike the farmers—they have none of the streaked tooth enamel common among people who suffer from food shortages.

Similar evidence of preagricultural settlements exists in other places. The Jomon people of central Honshu Island in Japan lived in permanent villages 13,000 years ago, feeding themselves by fishing and gathering acorns and chestnuts. Underwater archaeology has recently discovered what seem to be the remains of substantial stone buildings of the Jomon period submerged offshore as the result of an ancient landslide. At Göbekli Tepe, a hilltop site in southeast Turkey, contemporaries who lived mainly by gathering wild wheat hewed seven-ton pillars from limestone. They erected them in a sunken chamber in their village and decorated them with carvings of snakes, boar, gazelles, cranes, and symbols that look suspiciously like writing.

What was life like in these earliest settlements? Small, permanent houses suggest that nuclear families—parents and children—predominated, though some sites clearly have communal work areas for grinding seeds and nuts. As for who did the work, the most stunning finding of recent archaeology in the Middle East suggests that work was probably shared between the sexes. After a long period during which they had evolved to look different, male and female bodies began to converge. As food production replaced hunting and gathering, war and child-rearing became the main sex-specific jobs in society.

The Disadvantages of Farming

Preagricultural communities do not simply progress to farming. If foraging produces abundance and security, it does not necessarily follow that farming can deliver more of the same. The consequences of adopting agriculture are by no means all positive. In the early stages of moving from foraging to farming, people depend on a relatively small range of farmed foods. As a result, a community becomes vulnerable to ecological disasters. Famine becomes more likely as diet narrows. Moreover, when people have to plant and grow food as well as gather it, they have to use up more energy to get the same amount of nourishment (although domesticated foods, once harvested, tend to be easier to process for eating). The need to organize labor encourages inequalities and exploitation. Concentrations of domesticated animals spread disease.

So the problem is really the opposite of what Cook supposed: It is farmers' behavior, not foragers' behavior, that is strange. Husbandry is not a step along a march of improvement because, in some ways, it makes life worse. Questions must be raised: Why farm? Why work harder for less nutritious food and a more capricious supply? Why invite famine, plague, pestilence, and crowded living conditions?

Husbandry in Different Environments

Scholars used to suppose that agriculture was so extraordinary it must have begun in some particular spot and that **diffusion** spread it from there—carried by migrants or conquerors, or transmitted by trade, or imitated. The past forty years of research have shown, on the contrary, that the transition to food production happened over and over again, in a range of regions and a variety of environments, with different foodstuffs and different techniques. The most obvious contrast in environments is between **herders** and **tillers**. Herding develops where plants are too sparse or indigestible to sustain human life, but animals can convert these plants into meat—an energy source that people can access by eating the animals. Tilling develops where the soil is suitable or enough

FORAGERS		FARMERS
Food procurers		**Food producers**
• Hunt and gather		• Husbandry (breed animals, cultivate crops)
Fit into nature		**Change nature**
• Little environmental impact		• Herders: some environmental impact tillers: massive environmental impact
Manage the landscape		**Nature remade and reimagined**
Dependence on wild animals and plants		**Interdependence among humans, plants, and animals**
		• Animals and plants exploited and domesticated
Stable food supply		**Unstable food supply**
• Nomadic foragers move in response to environmental change; sedentary foragers vulnerable to changes of climate		• Small range of farmed foods increases vulnerability to ecological disasters
Stable population		**Expanding population**
• Relatively little labor needed		• Breeding livestock and cultivating plants leads to increased food supply and increased population
• Population control available, mainly by managed lactation		• Concentrations of domesticated animals spread disease
Stable society		**Radically changed, unstable society**
• Kinship and age fix individual's place in society		• Need to control labor and food distribution leads to social inequalities
• Sexes usually share labor by specializing in different economic tasks		• Work shared between the sexes, increased reliance on female labor
		• Strong states develop with powerful elites, complex technologies

ecological diversity exists to sustain plant husbandry or mixed farming of plants and animals.

Herders' Environments

In three types of environment tundra, the evergreen forests of northern Eurasia, and great grasslands—it is impossible to grow enough humanly digestible plant foods to keep large numbers of people alive. These environments offer only two options. People can remain foragers—and primarily hunters, seeking the fat-rich species typical of such zones. The Inuit in the North American Arctic, for example, hunt seal and walrus. Or people can become herders, like the Sami and Samoyeds of northern Europe and northwest Asia, who live off reindeer.

Similarly, the soils of the world's vast grasslands—known as prairie in North America, pampa in South America, steppe in Eurasia, and the **Sahel** in Africa—have, for most of history, been unfavorable for tillage. Except for patches of exceptionally favorable soil, herding has been the only possible form of husbandry in these areas. The peoples of the Eurasian and African grasslands were probably herding by about 5000 B.C.E. In contrast, native American grassland dwellers of the New World retained a foraging way of life because available species—bison, various types of antelope—were, for the most part, more abundant for the hunt and less suitable for herding.

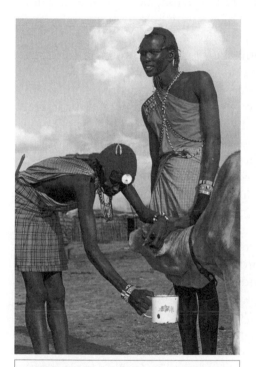

Masai. Humans need vitamin C, but the meat and dairy products from herds do not supply much of it. So people in herding cultures eat half-digested plants from animals' stomachs and organ meats, such as the liver, in which vitamin C tends to get concentrated. Fresh blood—drawn here from the veins of a calf by Masai women in Kenya—is also a useful source of the vitamin. Drinking blood confers an added advantage: nomads can draw it from their animals "on the hoof," without slaughtering them or halting the migrations of their flocks.

Herding has three special consequences. First, it imposes a mobile way of life. The proportion of the population who follow the herds—and, in some cases, it is the entire population—cannot settle into permanent villages. Herder peoples are not unwilling or unable to build permanently or on a large scale. The Scythians, for instance, people of the western Asian steppe who first domesticated the horse and invented the wheel and axle about 6,000 to 7,000 years ago, built impressive stone structures. But these were underground tombs, dwellings for the dead, while the living inhabited temporary camps. Some herding societies in Asia and Africa have become rich enough to found cities for elites or specialists working outside of food production. In the thirteenth century c.e., a city of this type, Karakorum in Mongolia, was one of the most admired cities in the world. On the whole, however, herding does not favor the development of cities or the kind of culture that cities nourish, such as monumental buildings, large-scale institutions for education and the arts, and industrial technology.

Second, because herders breed from animals that naturally share their grassland habitats, their herds consist of milk-yielding stock. To get the full benefit from their animals, herding peoples have to eat dairy products. To modern, milk-fed Americans, this may sound perfectly normal. But it required a modification of human evolution. Most people, in most parts of the world, do not naturally produce lactase, the substance that enables them to digest milk, after infancy. They respond to dairy products with distaste or even intolerance. Whereas the Masai of Kenya in East Africa get 80 percent of their energy intake from milk, their Kikuyu neighbors, who are tillers, detest the stuff. People from the steppes of Eurasia invented an amazing variety of products, including butter, yogurt, and cheese to make milk digestible.

Third, herders' diets, relying heavily on meat, milk, and blood, lack variety compared to those of people in more ecologically diverse environments. This does not mean that the herders' diet is nutritionally deficient. If you eat organ meats (especially liver, kidneys, heart, lungs, and glands), drink animal blood, and prepare dairy products in a variety of ways to harness beneficial bacteria, you can get everything the human body needs, including adequate vitamin C. But, herders still highly prize farmers' cultivated plants and import them at great cost or take them as tribute or booty. The same goes for the products of the sedentary industries that only farming folk have land or leisure for, or that are possible only in tree-rich environments, such as wood products, silk, linen, and cotton.

Violence between herders and farmers was common until about 300 years ago, when the war technology of sedentary societies left herding societies unable to compete. Conflict arose from herders' desire to share the benefits of farming culture. On the other hand, farmers have not normally had to depend on herding cultures for meat or dairy products. Typically, they can farm their own animals, feeding them on the waste or surplus of their crops or by grazing them between their tillage. Or they can graze sheep or goats upland, at higher altitudes above their fields. Therefore, in herder–settler warfare, the herders have typically been aggressive and the settlers defensive.

Tillers' Environments

In the tundra, northern Eurasian evergreen forests, and great grasslands, tilling isn't an option. Husbandry is restricted to herding. But numerous other environments are suited to farming. The first essential prerequisite for farming was soil loose enough for a dibble—a pointed stick for poking holes in the ground—to work. At first, this was the only technology available. Where the sod had to be cut or turned—where, for instance, the soil was heavy clay or a dense or sticky mixture—agriculture had to wait for the slightly more advanced technology of the spade and the plow.

Equally necessary prerequisites were sufficient water, by rain or flood or irrigation, to grow the crop; enough sun to ripen it; and some way to nourish the soil. This last was generally the hardest to ensure, because farming can exhaust even the richest soils fairly rapidly. Flooding and layering with silt or dredging and dressing new topsoil is needed to replace nutrients. Alternatively, farmers can add fertilizer: ash from burned wood, leaf mold from forest clearings, guano from bird colonies if there are any nearby, mined potassium, manure from domesticated animals, or night soil—if all else fails, for human excretion is poor fertilizer.

We can divide environments suited to early agriculture into three broad types: swampy wetlands, uplands, and alluvial plains, where flooding rivers or lakes renew the topsoil. Each of the three types developed with peculiar characteristics and specialized crops. It is worth looking at each in turn.

Swampland Swamp is no longer much in demand for farming. Nowadays, in the Western world, if we want to turn bog into farmland we drain it. But it had advantages early on. Swamp soil is rich, moist, and easy to work with simple technology. At least one staple grows well in waterlogged land—*rice*. We still do not know where or when rice was first cultivated, or even whether any of these wetland varieties preceded the dryland rice that has gradually become more popular around the world. Most evidence, however, suggests that people were producing rice at sites on the lower Ganges River in India and in parts of Southeast Asia some 8,000 years ago, and in paddies in the Yangtze River valley in China not long afterward.

Where rice is unavailable, swampland cultivators can adapt the land for other crops by dredging earth—which they can do by hand in suitable conditions—and by building up mounds. Not only can they plant the mounds, but they can also farm water-dwelling creatures and plants in the ditches between mounds. In the western highlands of New Guinea, the first agriculture we know of started fully 9,000 years ago in the boggy valley bottoms. Drains, ditches, and mounds still exist in the Kuk swamp there. More extensive earthworks were in place by 6000 B.C.E. The crops have vanished—biodegraded into nothingness—but the first farmers probably planted *taro*, the most easily cultivated, indigenous native root. Modern varieties of taro exhibit signs of long domestication. A diverse group of plants—native bananas, yams and other tubers, the sago palm, and nuts from the palmlike *pandanus* tree—was probably added early. At some point, pigs arrived on the island.

Having a variety of crops made New Guinea's agriculture exceptionally sustainable. Variety may also help explain why farming has remained a small-scale enterprise there that numerous, politically independent villages, and not a large, centralized state, conduct. New Guinea never generated the big states and cities that grew up where the range of available crops was narrower and agriculture more fragile. Empire-building was unknown on the island until European colonizers got there in the late nineteenth century.

We know of no other swamps that people adapted so early, but many later civilizations arose from similar sorts of ooze. We do not know much about the origins of **Bantu** agriculture in West Africa, but it is more likely to have begun in the swamp than in the forest. Swampland is suited to the native *yams* on which Bantu farming first relied. Waterlogged land is also the favorite habitat of the other mainstay of Bantu tradition, the *oil palm*. The earliest archaeological evidence of farming based on yams and oil palms dates from about 5,000 years ago in swampy valley bottoms of Cameroon, above the forest level.

Swampland also contributed to the agriculture that began along the Amazon River in South America 4,000 or 5,000 years ago. At first, the crops were probably richly diverse, supplemented by farming turtles and snails or similar mollusks. Later, however, from about 500 C.E., farmers increasingly focused on *bitter manioc*, also known as cassava or yucca, which has the great advantage of being poisonous to predators. Human consumers can process the poison out. Olmec civilization, which was enormously influential in the history of **Mesoamerica**, was founded in swamps thick with mangrove trees about 3,000 years ago.

Uplands Like swamplands, regions of high altitude are not places that people today consider good for farming. Farmers have usually left these regions to the herdsmen and native upland creatures, such as sheep, goats, yaks, and llamas. There are three reasons for doing so: First, as altitude increases, cold and the scorching effects of solar radiation in the thin atmosphere diminish the variety of viable plants. Second, slopes are subject to erosion (although this has a secondary benefit because relatively rich soils collect in valley bottoms). Finally, slopes in general are hard to work once you have come to rely on plows, but this does not stop people who do not use plows from farming them.

The Andes Highlands usually contain many different microclimates at various altitudes and in valleys where sun and rain can vary tremendously

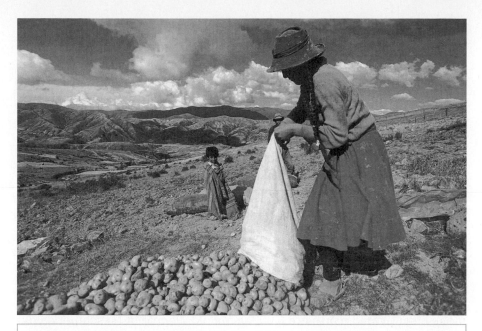

The Valley of Cuzco, Peru, the Homeland of the Inca. Potatoes—which were first cultivated in the Andes at least 7,000 years ago and spread from there to the rest of the world—remain a staple in this region. They are the only food that—if eaten in sufficient quantities—contains all the nutrients necessary to sustain life. Suitable varieties of potatoes flourish at more than 13,000 feet above sea level. In mountain climates, they can be freeze-dried for year-round nutrition.
Jon Spaull/Panos Pictures

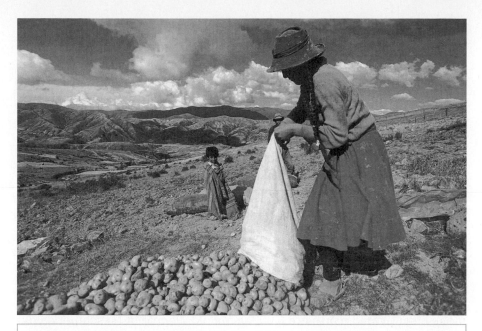

within a short space. Some of the world's earliest farming, therefore, happened at surprisingly high altitudes. Evidence of mixed farming survives from between about 12,000 and 7,000 years ago near Lake Titicaca, elevation 13,000 feet, in the Andes of South America. Nearby in the cave of Pachamachay, bones of domesticated llamas cover those of hunted camelios—the llamalike but smaller *vicuña* and *guanaco*. The domesticated animals fed on *quinoa*, an extremely hardy grainlike food that resembles some kinds of grass. It grows at high altitudes thanks to a bitter, soapy coating that cuts out solar radiation. The llamas ingested the leafy part and deposited the seeds in their manure. Their corrals therefore became nurseries for a food fit for humans to grow and eat.

The earliest known experiments in domesticating the *potato* probably occurred at about the same time in the same area. Potatoes were ideal for mountain agriculture. Not only were some naturally occurring varieties of potato hardy enough to grow at altitudes of up to 14,000 feet, but they also provided total nutrition. Eaten in sufficient quantities, potatoes provide everything the human body needs to survive. Moreover, the high-altitude varieties have a hidden advantage. Whereas wild kinds of lowland potatoes are poisonous and need careful processing to become edible, the concentration of poison in potatoes diminishes the higher you climb. There is an obvious evolutionary reason for this. The poison is there to deter predators, which are most numerous at low altitudes.

The potato gave Andean mountain dwellers the same capacity to support large populations as peoples of the valleys and plains, where a parallel story began in the central coastal region of what is now Peru. There, around 10,000 years ago, farmers grew *sweet potato* tubers similar to modern varieties. If agriculture did indeed produce sweet potatoes, they would have to be counted as the New World's earliest farmed crop. Once both regions had the capacity to feed dense populations, Andean history became a story of highland–lowland warfare, punctuated by the rise and fall of mountain-based empires.

Mesoamerica The Mesoamerican highlands, stretching from central Mexico to Central America, produced their own kind of highland-adapted food: a trinity of **maize**, *beans*, and *squash*. The earliest surviving specimens of cultivated maize are 6,000 years old. People in Mesoamerica developed maize from a wild grass known as teosinte, of which a type still grows in the state of Oaxaca in central Mexico, along with the wild ancestors of modern domesticated beans. By working out how long it would take wild species to mutate, botanists estimate that people domesticated beans about 9,000 years ago. The earliest domesticated squashes date from about the same period and are found at the same site as teosinte and wild beans, at Guilá Naquitz, in Oaxaca. The fact that their wild ancestors have disappeared suggests that farming here might have started with squashes when gatherers of wild beans and grains needed to provide food during droughts. Squash grows well during dry spells severe enough to wither teosinte and blight beans, so it would have provided a food reserve that people did not need to store.

The Old World The Old World had no potatoes, quinoa, or even maize for highland farmers to work with. The hardiest staples available in most of Eurasia and Africa were *rye* and *barley*. Surprisingly, however, people in lowlands first domesticated both of them in what are now Jordan and Syria, probably about 10,000 years ago. Rye germinates at just a couple of degrees above freezing, but its drawbacks made it more popular as a winter crop in wheat-growing lowlands than as a mountain staple. Its yield is lower than other grains, it is less nutritious, and it is also vulnerable to fungus infection. Barley did not fulfill its potential to be an Old World equivalent of quinoa or potatoes until the sixth century C.E., when it became the staple food of a farming society in Tibet (see Chapter 10).

Alluvial Plains Although swamps and rain-fed highlands have produced spectacularly successful agriculture, farmers get the best help from nature in **alluvial plains**, flatlands where mud carried by overflowing rivers or lakes renews the soil. If people can channel the floods to keep crops from being swept away on these plains, alluvium, made up of sediment and other organic matter, restores nutrients and compensates for lack of rain. As we shall see in the next chapter, alluvial soils in arid climates sustained some of the world's most productive economies until late in the second millennium B.C.E. *Wheat* and barley grew in the black earth that lines Egypt's Nile, the floodplains of the lower Tigris and Euphrates rivers in what is now Iraq, and the Indus River in what is now Pakistan. People first farmed millet on alluvial soils in a somewhat cooler, moister climate in China, in the crook of the Yellow River and the Guanzhong Basin around 7,000 years ago. And in the warm, moist climate of Indochina in what is now Cambodia, three crops of rice a year could grow on soil that the annual counter flow of the Mekong River created.

Smaller patches of alluvium, deposited by floods, nourished the world's earliest known fully farming economies. Among the first of these farming economies was Jericho on the river Jordan. Today, the Jordan valley looks inhospitable. Ten thousand years ago, however, Jericho overlooked an alluvial fan that trickling streams washed down from the Judaean hills, filling the river as it crept south from the Sea of Galilee. The Jordan was thick with silt. The banks it deposited formed the biblical "jungle of Jericho," from where lions padded to raid the sheepfolds.

Jericho Skull. No one knows why people in Jericho, in the eighth millennium B.C.E., kept skulls, painted them with plaster, and inserted cowrie shells into the eye sockets. But these decorated skulls have, in a sense, helped the dead to survive. Some of the skulls even show traces of painted hair and mustaches. *Ashmolean Museum, Oxford, England, U.K.*

In much the same period, between about 9,000 and 11,000 years ago, farming towns also appeared in Anatolia in Turkey. Çatalhüyük, the most spectacular of these towns, stood on an alluvial plain that the river Çarsamba flooded. Nourished by wheat and beans, the people filled an urban area of 32 acres. By exchanging craft products—weapons, metalwork, and pots—for primary materials such as cowrie shells from the Red Sea, timber from the Taurus Mountains in Anatolia, and copper from beyond the Tigris, the inhabitants of Çatalhüyük became rich by the standards of the time. Archaeologists have unearthed such treasures as fine blades and mirrors made from local obsidian and products of the copper-smelting technology that these people gradually developed.

Yet the inhabitants of Çatalhüyük never got safely beyond the mercy of nature. They worshiped images of its strength: bulls with monstrous horns and protruding tongues, crouching leopards that guard goddesses leaning on grain bins, fuming volcanoes, giant boars with laughing jaws and bristling backs. This is surely farmer's art, animated by fear of the wild and loathing of the savage. Most people died in their late twenties or early thirties. Their corpses were ritually fed to vultures and jackals—as surviving paintings show—before their bones were buried in communal graves.

Çatalhüyük lasted for nearly 2,000 years, remarkable longevity by the standards of later cities. It became doomed as the waters that supplied it dried up. Even during its greatest prosperity, its space was limited and its resource base restricted. But, along with Jericho and other settlements of the era, it pointed to the future, showing how farming, despite all its short-term disadvantages and the sacrifices it demanded, could sustain life through hard times.

The Spread of Agriculture

The development of food production in diverse environments with different foods and techniques points to an important conclusion: Farming was not a unique occurrence—a one-of-a-kind accident or a stroke of genius. Rather, it was an ordinary and fairly frequent process that could therefore be open to a variety of explanations.

Where we can be sure agriculture developed independently, we can see that early food producers focused on what they could grow or raise most easily in their particular environment. Nevertheless, connections between neighboring regions were unquestionably important in spreading husbandry. Some crops were undoubtedly transferred from the places they originated to other regions.

Europe

It seems likely that migrants from Asia colonized Europe. They brought their farming materials and knowledge with them, as well as their **Indo-European languages**, from which most of Europe's present languages descend. Colonization was a gradual process, beginning about

6,000 years ago. Early farmers may have cleared land, but probably did not undertake large-scale deforestation, which more likely occurred naturally, perhaps through tree diseases. Between 4,500 and 5,000 years ago, for instance, in northern Europe, the broad-leaved forest receded, creating areas that were well suited to farming. When the woodland grew back after a few hundred years, farmers unquestionably cut it away.

Asia

Similar migrations probably spread farming to parts of Central Asia south of the steppeland. The farming that developed in alluvial environments in Anatolia and the Jordan valley colonized or converted every viable part of the region by 8,000 or 9,000 years ago. At altitudes above 1,800 feet, inhabitants of sites east of the Zagros Mountains (in what is now Iran) replaced wild grains with cultivated varieties. Then, too, by about 6,000 years ago, comprehensive irrigation systems for farming crisscrossed the oases in southern Turkmenistan, which had a moister climate than it has now.

In the Indian subcontinent, the sudden emergence of well-built villages in the same period was probably the result of outside influence. No intermediate phase between foraging and farming occurred; there was no period when foragers led settled lives. We can trace the spread of farming from southwest Asia by way of Baluchistan (southern Pakistan). Here, remnants of domestic barley and wheat in mud bricks and the bones of domestic goats confirm the presence of agriculture about 9,000 years ago.

The Americas

In much of North America, the spread of maize northward from its birthplace in central Mexico marked the transmission of agriculture. This process took thousands of years and demanded the development of new varieties as the crop crossed climate zones on its northward route. The best estimate puts maize farming in the southwestern United States about 3,000 years ago. Meanwhile, some North American peoples began to farm sunflowers and sumpweed for their edible seeds and roots. In South America, the idea of agriculture spread from, or across, the high Andes, through the upper Amazon Basin.

Africa

How agriculture spread in Africa is less clear. People began to cultivate similar plant foods in the Egyptian Sahara and in the Nile valley about 9,000 years ago. It therefore appears that one region might have influenced the other. A little later, wheat cultivation along the Nile followed developments of a similar kind in the Jordan valley. Between 4,500 and

5,000 years ago, agriculture spread southward from West Africa along with Bantu languages. We can trace the path from what are now Cameroon and Nigeria in West Africa southward and then eastward across the expanding Sahara to the Nile valley, before turning south again.

The Pacific Islands

Scholars debate when agriculture originated in the Pacific Islands. In particular, we do not know how or when the sweet potato—which, together with the pig, is the basis of food production in most of the region—got there. The most widely respected theory sees agriculture as the result of diffusion from New Guinea. It was a slow process requiring many adaptations as it spread across the ocean with seaborne migrants.

So Why Did Farming Start?

Why, despite the short-term difficulties, did some peoples originate farming and others adopt it? Though scholars ferociously advocate rival explanations, we do not have to choose among them. Different explanations, or different combinations of the same explanations, may have applied in different places. Nor do we have to go through all the theories. We can group them under seven manageable headings.

Population Pressure

The first group of theories explains agriculture as a response to stress from population growth and overexploitation of wild foods. Examples include hunting game to extinction and overgathering plants, grubs, and mollusks. Logically, population should not grow if resources are getting scarce. But anthropological studies of contemporary cultures making the transition to agriculture in Botswana and Lesotho in southern Africa support the theory. Apparently, once farming starts, people cannot abandon it without catastrophe. A ratchet effect makes it impossible, while population rises, to go back to less intensive ways of getting food. As an explanation, however, for why agriculture arose in the first place, population pressure does not match the facts of chronology. Populations certainly grew in the most dedicated farming cultures, but, in most places, growth was probably more a consequence of agriculture than a cause.

The Outcome of Abundance

A group of theories has arisen in direct opposition to stress theory. These claim that husbandry was a result of abundance. Farming, therefore, was a by-product of the leisure of fishermen in Southeast Asia who devoted their spare time to experimenting with plants. Or it was invented by hill dwellers in northern Iraq, whose habitat was peculiarly rich in easily domesticated grasses and grazing herds. Or it was the natural result of concentrations of pockets of abundance in Central Asia in the post–Ice Age era of global warming. As temperatures rose, oases opened up where different species congregated peacefully. Humans discovered they could domesticate animals that would otherwise be rivals, enemies, or prey. Abundance theory is a convincing description for why agriculture developed in some key areas, but it does not explain why, in good times, people would want to change how they got their food and take on extra work.

The Power of Politics

Stress theory and abundance theory may apply to why agriculture arose in different areas, but they cannot be true simultaneously. Therefore, beyond the food supply, it is worth considering possible political, social, or religious influences on food strategies. After all, food is for more than nourishment. It also confers power and prestige, symbolizes identity, and generates rituals.

Societies bound by feasting, where leaders buy allegiance with food, will always favor intensive agriculture and massive storage. Even in societies with looser forms of leadership or with collective decision making, feasting can be a powerful incentive to boost food production and storage. Feasting can celebrate collective identity or cement relations with other communities.

Cult Agriculture

Religion may well have been the inspiration for farming. Planting may have originated as a fertility rite, or irrigation as libation, or enclosure as an act of reverence for a sacred plant. To plow or dibble and sow and irrigate can carry profound meaning. They can be understood as rites of birth and nurture of the god on whom you are going to feed. In exchange for labor—a kind of sacrifice—the god provides nourishment. Most cultures have considered the power to make food grow to be a divine gift or curse or a secret that a hero stole from the gods. People have domesticated animals for use in sacrifice and prophecy as well as for food. Many societies cultivate plants that play a part at the altar rather than at the table. Examples include incense, ecstatic or hallucinatory drugs, the sacrificial corn of some high Andean communities, and wheat, which, in orthodox Christian traditions, is the only grain permitted for the Eucharist. And if religion inspired agriculture, alcohol as a drink that can induce ecstasy might have had a special appeal. In short, where crops are gods, farming is worship.

Climatic Instability

Global warming presented foragers with thousands of years of abundance. But warming is unpredictable. Sometimes it intensifies, causing droughts; sometimes it goes into reverse, causing little ice ages. In the agrarian heartland of the Middle East, warming squeezed the environment of nut-bearing trees but favored some grasses. The forest receded dramatically as the climate got drier and hotter. Between about 13,000 and 11,000 years ago, a spell of cooling, when temperatures dropped a degree or so, seems to have affected much of the Northern Hemisphere. The new conditions encouraged people to rely more and more on grains for food and perhaps try to find ways to increase the amount of edible wheat. Gatherers who knew the habits of their plants tended them ever more carefully.

Agriculture by Accident

The nineteenth century's most popular theory of how farming started attributed it to accident. One can hardly open a nineteenth-century book on the subject without encountering the myth of the primitive forager, usually a woman, discovering agriculture by observing how seeds, dropped by accident, germinated on fertilized soil. But historians are never satisfied to fall back on what might have happened. We want to know what really did happen.

Production as an Outgrowth of Procurement

Still, the accident theory may be right in one respect. Early practitioners may not have consciously thought of food production as a different strategy from foraging. It makes sense, for instance, to see herding as a natural development of hunting techniques, such as improving a species by culling weak or old animals, managing grazing by setting fires, driving herds down lanes to a place of slaughter, or corralling them for the kill. Similarly, farming and gathering might have been parts of a single continuous attempt to manage food sources. It is hard to tell where one leaves off and the other begins. "Even the simplest hunter–gatherer society," as archaeologist Brian Fagan has said, "knows full well that seeds germinate when planted."

The archaeological evidence has begun to yield clues to how gatherer communities of southwest Asia transformed themselves into farming communities after the Ice Age. Grasses on the whole are naturally too indigestible to be human food. But the region produced wild barley and two kinds of wheat—einkorn and emmer. We know people ate them because archaeologists have found remains that grinders processed from

14,000 to 15,000 years ago. Kernels of these grains are hard to free from their covering, so people who ate large amounts of them may have had an incentive to try to breed varieties that were easier to process. At first, the gatherers beat sheaves of wheat with sticks where they grew and collected edible seeds in baskets as they fell. Increasingly, as time went on, they cut stalks with flint sickles, which meant that fewer seeds fell when the wheat was harvested. This new method suggests that people were selecting preferred seeds for replanting. Modern experiments show that this process could produce a self-propagating species within twenty years. Alternatively, the new method itself might have encouraged changes in the species because heavier, larger seeds would be more likely to fall to the ground at the point of harvesting. Eventually, new varieties would emerge, but the process would be much slower.

Even earlier, humans used a similar process with snails and other mollusks. Mollusks are an efficient food, self-packaged in a shell for carrying and cooking. Compared with the large four-legged beasts that are usually claimed as the first domesticated animal food sources, mollusks are readily managed. People can gather marine varieties, such as mussels and clams, in a natural rock pool. On land, a snail-rich spot can be enclosed with a ditch. Moreover, snails are grazers and do not need to be fed with foods that humans would otherwise eat themselves. They can be herded without equipment, danger, or the need to train animals. By culling small or undesirable types by hand, the early snail farmers enjoyed the benefits of selective breeding. Shell mounds from the late Ice Age or soon thereafter contain varieties of snails that are bigger on average than today's, so it looks as if the snail eaters were already selecting for size.

A Conservative Revolution?

The archaeologist Martin Jones has suggested a speculative but attractive way of making sense of competing theories about how agriculture started. In warming environments, where climate change threatened settled foragers' stands of crops, they would be bound to take increasing care of those crops to preserve their existing way of life. They would weed them, tend them, water them, winnow them, and even transplant them to more favorable spots. They would adopt similar practices to conserve the creatures they hunted, managing their grazing grounds ever more zealously, until eventually the humans and the species they ate became locked in mutual dependence—each unable to survive without the other. A conservative trait—a strategy of survival and resistance to change—ended by transforming the environment and committing people to a new way of life.

CHRONOLOGY	
15,000 B.C.E.	End of Ice Age
13,000–14,000 B.C.E.	First permanent settlements in Middle East
11,000 B.C.E.	Appearance of Jomon culture, Japan
10,000–5000 B.C.E.	Mixed farming and potato cultivation develop (South America)
9000–7000 B.C.E.	Farming towns appear in Anatolia and Egypt
8000 B.C.E.	Rye and barley cultivation in Jordan and Syria; farming spreads from Jordan and Anatolia to Central Asia
7000 B.C.E.	"Trinity" of maize, beans, and squash develops in Andes; farming spreads in Egyptian Sahara and Nile valley; evidence of agriculture in Indian subcontinent; earliest evidence of agriculture in New Guinea
6000 B.C.E.	Rice cultivation in India, Southeast Asia, and China
4000 B.C.E.	Scythians domesticate the horse and invent wheel and axle; Indo-European languages spread as migrants from Asia colonize Europe; millet farmed in Yellow River valley, China
5000–2000 B.C.E.	River valley civilizations flourish
3000 B.C.E.	Teff cultivated in Ethiopia; Bantu languages and agriculture begin to spread southward from West Africa; earliest specimens of cultivated maize (Mexico)
1000 B.C.E.	Maize cultivation moves northward from Mexico to southwestern United States
(All dates are approximate)	

IN PERSPECTIVE
Seeking Stability

So gathering, hunting, herding, and tillage, which conventional chronologies usually place one after the other, were complementary techniques to obtain food. They developed together, over thousands of years, in a period of relatively intense climatic change. The warming, drying effects of the post–Ice Age world multiplied the opportunities and incentives for people to experiment with food strategies in changing environments. Foragers turned to farming and herding by slow stages and one case at a time, as relationships between people and other species changed and accumulated little by little. Eventually, foodstuffs developed that needed human involvement to survive and reproduce. For instance, emerging kinds of edible grasses (maize, for example) would not survive because their seeds would not fall to the ground unless a person removed the seeds from their husks.

The continuities in the worlds of the food procurers and early food producers are, in many ways, more impressive than the differences. The settled way of life, the art, the religious cults, even the kinds of foods (though obtained by different means) are often of the same order. The similarities suggest a new way to look at the transition to agriculture. We can see it as an attempt to stabilize a world convulsed by climatic instability—a way to cope with environmental change that was happening too fast and to preserve ancient traditions. In other words, the peoples who switched to herding or farming and those who clung to hunting and gathering shared a common, conservative mentality. Both wanted to keep what they had.

Perhaps, then, we should stop thinking of the beginnings of food production as a revolution, the overthrow of an existing state of affairs and its replacement by an entirely different one. Rather, we should think of it as a **climacteric**—a long period of critical change in a world poised between different possible outcomes. Indeed, the concept of a climacteric can be a useful way to understand change. It is worth keeping it in mind throughout the rest of this book as we confront other so-called revolutions that were really uncertain, slow, and sometimes unconscious transitions. Yet if early farmers' motivations were indeed conservative, in most cases they failed to maintain the status quo. On the contrary, they inaugurated the spectacular changes and challenges that are the subject of the next chapter.

PROBLEMS AND PARALLELS

1. What are the disadvantages of farming compared to foraging?
2. Why were agricultural settlements less stable than foraging communities?
3. Why has violence between farmers and foragers been so common in history?
4. What theories attempt to explain the switch from foraging to farming among early peoples?
5. How did early farmers exploit different environments to grow crops? Why were alluvial plains the most hospitable environment for early agricultural societies?

The Great River Valleys: Accelerating Change and Developing States

focus questions

1. Why did intensified agriculture lead to cultural differences?
2. Where did the first great river valley civilizations develop?
3. How can we account for the differences and similarities in political institutions, social structure, and ways of life in the four great river valleys?
4. Is writing a defining characteristic of civilizations?

Witnesses in court swear to tell "the whole truth." This would be a risky oath for a historian to take because we see the past only in glimpses and patches. Sometimes-contrasting, sometimes-contradictory sources confuse or distract us. To get close to the whole picture, we have to shift perspective, dodging and slipping between rival viewpoints. With every shift, we get a bit more of the picture—like glimpsing a scene in a forest, between the leaves and the trees.

The boldest possible perspective shift is imaginary, to envision history from a viewpoint outside it—perhaps from an enormous distance of time and space, and ask how it might look to visitors from a remote future in another world. They would have an enviable advantage: objectivity, which we, who are entangled in our history, can never attain. Today, globalization is spreading uniform ways of life across the world, but galactic observers could see that, since agriculture started, the main theme of our past has been increasingly rapid cultural divergence. Compared with foragers, herders and tillers generated much more change of all kinds. More spectacular, however, were the differences that separated farming cultures from each other.

Some of them came to occupy vast zones, feed huge populations, and sustain spectacular material achievements—including cities, monumental arts, and world-changing technologies. Other farmers' societies remained relatively small and static. This does not mean they were backward or primitive. Their modest scale and relative isolation kept them stable. These were peoples who succeeded in adapting to climate change without subjecting their societies to social and political convulsions that were often part of the price other peoples paid for material achievements that seem impressive to us. The big problem we need to look at in this chapter, then, is what made the difference?

It is also worth asking whether within these diverse societies we can detect any common patterns. This is a long-standing quest for historians and, especially, for sociologists, who look for models that they can use to describe and predict how societies change. At a simple level, intensified agriculture clearly unlocks a potential pattern. More food makes it possible to sustain larger populations, to concentrate them in bigger settlements, and to divert more manpower into nonagricultural activities. But intensification also requires organization, and broadly speaking, the more intensive the farming, the more organized it has to be. It calls for someone—or some group—with power to divide land, marshal labor, and regulate the distribution of water and—if necessary—fertilizers. Surplus production needs storage under guard, in case crops fail or natural disasters strike. A legal elite is necessary to resolve the frequent disputes that arise in thickly settled communities where people have to compete for resources. So intensively farmed areas all tend to develop similar political institutions and personnel, including bureaucrats and enforcers.

These effects are the themes of this chapter, which focuses on the most conspicuous examples, in regions with common environmental features. The next chapter follows the crises, catastrophes, and transformations large-scale farming societies faced, up to the end of the second millennium B.C.E. Chapter 5 covers the recovery or renewal of ambitious states and cultural experiments after the crises had passed.

Growing Communities, Divergent Cultures

Most of the communities that early agriculture fed resembled the forager settlements that preceded them, though there is little evidence to inform our assumptions. With no reason to think otherwise, we imagine that early farming societies in New Guinea, in North America, along the Amazon River, and among the Bantu people in West Africa were like those in most of the rest of the world: extended family businesses where everyone in the community felt tied by kinship. Elsewhere, owing to greater resources or to the enlivening effects of cross-cultural contacts through migration or trade, different patterns prevailed. Communities became territorially defined. Economic obligations, not kinship, shaped allegiance. Chiefs or economic elites monopolized or largely controlled the distribution of food.

Scholars have tried to divide subsequent change in societies of this type into sequences or stages of growth—chiefdoms become states, towns become cities. But these are relative terms—no hard-and-fast lines divide them.

The difference between a small city and a big town or a small town and a big village is a matter of judgment. Some of the characteristics we traditionally associate with particular ways of life turn out, in the light of present knowledge, to provide little or no help for defining the societies in which they occur. Metallurgy, pottery, and weaving, for example, exist among herding and foraging peoples, as well as in settled communities. Where people settle together, however, predictable changes usually follow. As markets grow, settlements acquire more craftsmen, who engage in more specialized trades and organize into more and larger units. As they get bigger, settlements and politically linked or united groups of settlements also expand the number of government functions. Where once there were just a chief and his counselors, now there are aides, advisers, officials, and administrators.

As society gets bigger, people seek groups within it, of manageable size, with whom they can identify and to whom they can appeal for help in times of need. At the same time, rulers organize subjects into categories according to the needs of the state, which include collective labor, taxation, and war. The categories get more numerous and varied as opportunities for economic specialization multiply and as more districts or quarters appear in growing settlements. If we want to try to trace the early history of cultural divergence, we should look for certain sorts of changes: intensified settlement, population concentrated in relatively large settlements, multiplying social categories and functions of government, emergence of chiefs and fledgling states, and increasingly diversified and specialized economic activity. Between 5000 and 3000 B.C.E., we can detect these changes in widely separated places around the world. We can take a few examples in a selective tour through cultures launched into divergent futures.

Intensified Settlement and Its Effects

In the New World, Mesoamerica and Central America remained a region of small villages. We can document monumental cities and large states there only from about 2000 B.C.E. In North America, agriculture barely appeared. By contrast, at the base of the high Andes in South America, archaeology has unearthed early evidence of many different social rankings, economic specializations, and grossly unequal concentrations of wealth and power.

In about 3500 B.C.E., large farming settlements began to appear on alluvial plains in coastal Peru, especially in the Supe Valley, which has more than thirty archaeological sites. The most impressive was Aspero, where seventeen mounds supported half a dozen platforms and various terraces, with large, complex dwellings and storehouses. The platforms were built up with loads of rubble in uniform containers, which suggests that a system existed to measure the labor of different groups of workers. An infant's grave gives us a glimpse into the society and perhaps the politics of the time. Under a grinding stone, he lies painted with red ocher, wrapped in textiles, and scattered with hundreds of beads. This is evidence of inherited wealth and, perhaps, power in an economy dependent on grain, where a flour-making tool literally marked the difference between life and death.

Covering more than thirty-two acres, Aspero must have had a big population—uniquely big by the standards of the Americas at the time. There were, however, many settlements of between 2,000 and 3,000 people. They were trading centers where people exchanged the products of different ecosystems—marine shells, mountain foods, and featherwork made from the brightly colored birds that lived in the forests east of the Andes.

Comparable developments occurred across Eurasia. In parts of eastern Europe, for instance, innovations in technology and government emerged, without, as far as we know, any influence from outside the region. In the shadow of the Carpathian Mountains, in what is now Serbia, Europe's oldest copper mine at Rudna Glava made the region a center of early metallurgy. In Tisza in what is now Hungary, more than 7,000 years ago smelters worked copper into beads and small tools—magic that made smiths powerful figures of myth. To the people who left offerings, the mines were the dwellings of gods.

In Bulgaria during the same period, trenches and palisades sur-rounded settlements, with gateways exactly aligned at the points of the compass, as in later Roman army camps. Here, prospectors in metal-rich hills traded gold for the products of agriculture. No place in prehistoric Europe gleams more astonishingly than Varna on the Black Sea, where a chief was buried clutching a gold-handled axe, with his penis sheathed in gold, and with nearly 1,000 gold ornaments, including hundreds of discs that must have spangled a dazzling coat. This single grave contained more than three pounds of fine gold.

A little to the east, also around 5000 B.C.E., at Sredny Stog on the middle Dnieper River in what is now Ukraine, the earliest known domes-ticators of horses filled their garbage dumps with horse bones. In graves of about 3500 B.C.E., as if for use in an afterlife, lie covered wagons, arched with hoops and designed to be pulled by oxen, rumbling on vast wheels of solid wood: evidence that rich and powerful chiefdoms could carry out ambitious building projects despite a herding way of life that required constant mobility. Few other societies in the world were rich enough to bury objects of such size and value. Central Eurasia became a birthplace for early transportation technology. For instance, the earliest recognizable chariot dates from early in the third millennium B.C.E. in the southern Ural Mountains that divide Europe from Asia.

Meanwhile, monumental building projects, on a scale only agriculture could sustain and only a state could organize, were under way in the Mediterranean. The remains of the first large stone dwellings known anywhere in the world are on the island of Malta. Here, at least half a dozen temple complexes arose in the fourth and third millennia B.C.E. The biggest temple is almost seventy feet wide under a thirty-foot wall. Inside one building was a colossal, big-hipped goddess with small female mod-els scattered around her. There were altars and wall carvings—some in spirals, some with deer and bulls—and thousands of bodies piled in com-munal graves. We wonder how Malta's soil, so poor and dry, could sustain a population large and leisured enough to build so lavishly.

Even on Europe's Atlantic edge, in the fourth millennium B.C.E., luxury objects could find a market, and monumental buildings arose. Some of the earliest signs of the slow-grinding social changes lie among the bones of aristocrats in individual graves with the possessions that define their status and suggest their way of life—weapons of war and drinking cups that once held liquor or poured offerings to the gods. Then come the graves of chiefs, buried under enormous standing stones, near stone circles probably designed to resemble glades that preceded them as places of worship. In the Orkney Islands, for instance, off the north coast of Scotland, settled about 5,500 years ago, an elaborate tomb at Maes Howe lies close to a temple building, filled with light on midsummer's day. Nearby stone circles hint, on a smaller scale, at attempts to monitor the sun and, perhaps, control nature by magic. A stone-built village to the west has hearths and fitted furniture still in place. It is tempting to imagine this as a far-flung colonial station, preserving the styles and habits of a distant home in southwest Britain and northwest France, where the big tombs and stone circles are found.

The Ecology of Civilization

In this world of increasing diversification, four river valleys stand out in terms of scale: the middle and lower Nile in Egypt; the Indus (and the now dried-up Saraswati), mainly in what is now Pakistan; the Tigris and Euphrates in what is now Iraq; and the Yellow River in China. Between 5000 and 2000 B.C.E., people in these regions exploited more land and changed at a faster pace than other regions. Change was measured in terms of intensified agriculture, technological innovation, development of state power, and construction of cities.

In recent times, these valleys have occupied disproportionate space in our history books and a privileged place in our store of images and memories. Their ruins and relics still inspire movie makers, advertisers, artists, toy makers, and writers of computer games. They shape our ideas of what civilizations ought to be: We picture Egyptian pyramids, sphinxes, and mummies; Chinese bronzes, jades, and clays; Mesopotamian **ziggurats**—tall, tapering, steplike temples—and writing tablets smothered with ancient wedge-shaped letter forms. Or we conjure the windblown wrecks of almost-vanished cities in landscapes turning to desert. We even call these seminal—or nursery—civilizations, as if they were seed plots from which civilized achievements spread around the world. Or we call them great civilizations, and we begin our conventional histories of civilization by describing them.

For some scholars, civilization is now a discredited word. They argue that people have abused it as a name for societies they approve of, which usually means societies that resemble their own. Or writers have misapplied it as the name of a supposedly universal stage of social development, even though we have no evidence that societies follow any universal course of development. We can, however, understand a civilization as a society that, for good or ill, engages ambitiously with its environment, seeking to remodel the rest of nature to suit human purposes. In this sense of the word, the four river valleys housed societies more civilized than earlier cases we know of. They modified the landscape with fields and irrigation works or smothered it with monumental buildings on a scale that no people before attained or, perhaps, even conceived.

The Great Floodplains

The four valleys shared certain environmental features: a gradually warming climate, relatively dry soils, and a reliance on seasonally flooding rivers and therefore, on irrigation. If we consider them together, however, we can see how relentless divergence opened cultural chasms inside this common ecological framework.

The Ecology of Egypt

In the north, where the lower Nile empties into the Mediterranean, distinctive food sources and useful plants complemented what farmers could grow in the irrigated lands to the south. In the delta's teeming marshlands, birds, animals, fish, and plants clustered for the gatherer and hunter. A painter showed Nebamun—a scribe and counter of grain who lived probably about 3,500 years ago—hunting in a land "full of

Nebamun's Tomb from the fourteenth century B.C.E. shows the Egyptian vizier hunting in the lush Nile delta, abundant in fish below his reed-built boat, prolific in the bird and insect life flushed from the blue thickets at his approach. He grabs birds by the handful and wields a snake like a whip.
© Copyright The British Museum/Art Resource, NY

everything good—its ponds with fish and its lakes with birds. Its meadows are verdant; its banks bear dates; its melons are abundant."

Most of Egypt, however, lay above the delta. The Nile flows from south to north, from the highlands of Ethiopia in Central Africa to the Mediterranean, and where the ground breaks from higher altitudes or where the riverbed narrows, dangerous rapids hinder navigation. Soil samples reveal the history of climate change. By about 4,000 years ago, the valley was already a land of "black" earth between "red" earths. Floods fed the fertile, alluvial black strip along the Nile; slowly drying red desert lay on either side. Hunting scenes painted at Memphis, Egypt's first capital, in the Nile delta, showed game lands turning to scrub, sand, and bare rock. Rain became rare. Thirst was called "the taste of death." Other lands had rain, as an Egyptian priest told a Greek traveler, "Whereas in our country water never falls on fields from above, it all wells up from below."

The Nile turns green with algae in early summer, then red with tropical earth in August. In September and October, if all goes well, the river floods and spreads the dark, rich silt thinly over the earth. Between floods, the nitrogen content of the soil decreases by two-thirds in the top six inches. But the annually renewed topsoil grew some of the densest concentrations of wheat in the ancient world. If the flood is too high, the land drowns. If the level of the river falls below about eighteen feet, drought follows. In one of the oldest surviving documents of Egyptian history, probably of about 2500 B.C.E., a king reveals a dream. The river failed to flood because the people neglected the gods who ruled beyond the rapids, where the waters came from. Still, compared to the other river valleys of the period, the Nile flood waters were—and still are—exceptionally regular and, therefore, easy to exploit.

The economy guaranteed basic nutrition for a large population, not individual abundance. Most people lived on bread and grainy, nutritious beer, in amounts only modestly above subsistence level. Most of the courtly luxuries that today's Western museum goers see in exhibits on ancient Egypt came from raids, conquest, and trade driven by agricultural surplus. Gold and ivory came from Nubia, an African kingdom beyond the cataracts. Copper and turquoise came from Sinai, a region of desert uplands linking Egypt to the Middle East (see Map 3.1).

Shifting Rivers of the Indus Valley

In the Indus valley, the sparse remains of the society called Harappan lie frustratingly beyond historians' reach. The rising water table has drowned evidence of the earliest phases, and the literate period is obscure because scholars have been unable to decipher the writing system. Here, the Indus and Saraswati rivers were more powerful and capricious than the Nile,

Map 3.1 Ancient Egypt

changing course and cutting new channels that might deprive settlements of water supplies. Ultimately, perhaps, they were fatally unpredictable, for Egypt lasted thousands of years longer. When, the Indus altered course and the Saraswati dried up, Harappan cities dwindled to faint traces in the dust.

But 3,000 to 5,000 years ago, the Indus floodplain was broader than the Nile's. The Indus and Saraswati flooded twice a year—first with the spring snowmelt when the rivers rose and then in summer when warm air, rising in Central Asia, sucks moisture in from the sea. As a result, farmers here could grow two crops annually. The basic patterns were the same as in Egypt. Wheat and barley grew on rainless, irrigated soil, and cattle—mainly humped-back zebu—grazed on marginal grassland. No region was as rich as the Nile delta, but Harappa had a coastal outpost at the seaport of Lothal, on the Gulf of Cambay on the Indian Ocean (see Map 3.2).

200 km
200 miles

Aral Sea

Caspian Sea

CENTRAL ASIA

AFGHANISTAN

IRAN

Mundigak

Harappa

Himalayas

Saraswati

PAKISTAN

BALUCHISTAN

Indus

Mohenjodaro

INDIA

Tropic of Cancer

Lothal

INDIAN

OCEAN

Gulf of Cambay

extent of Harappan culture

⊙   other important Harappan site

INDIA   modern-day country

Map 3.2 Harappan Civilization

The Harappan heartland had few valuables of its own. As in Egypt, the basis of its wealth was the surplus of its agriculture. Around 2000 B.C.E., the Harappan-culture area was the biggest in the world, stretching over 500,000 square miles. Territorial expansion was the Harrapan solution to feeding its increasingly dense population in the heartland, but no society can keep expanding forever.

Most surviving Harappan art is engraved on seals used to mark trading goods. These little masterpieces capture how people of the time saw their world. Some show naturalistic representations of animals— especially bearded zebus, feasting tigers, and elegant, humpless bulls— but violations of realism are more characteristic and include comical elephants and rhinoceroses. Perplexing scenes, probably from Harappan mythology, include transformations of human into tiger, starfish into unicorn, horned serpent into flourishing tree. In one case, a human is transforming into a tree after sex with a rampant bull.

Fierce Nature in Early Mesopotamia

The waters of the Nile and the Indus spill and recede according to a reasonably predictable rhythm, but the Tigris and Euphrates flood at any time, washing away dikes and overflowing ditches. At other times, desert sandstorms choke the farmers and bury their crops. In the wind, according to the poets, earth shattered "like a pot." "Will new seed grow?" asked a proverb. "We do not know. Will old seed grow? We do not know."

In lower Mesopotamia, where the first big cities sprang up around 3000 B.C.E., the rivers fell through a parched landscape from a distant land of rain, like trickles across a windowpane (see Map 3.3). Summers were too dry to produce food, and the early cities had to rely on winter crops of wheat, barley, onions, chickpeas, and sesame. Rain fell more often than it does today, but it was largely confined to winter when ferocious storms made the sky flare with sheet lightning. "Ordered by the storm-god in hate," according to a poet, "it wears away the country." The floods that created the life-giving alluvial soils were also life-threateningly capricious. Unleashed in early summer by mountain rains, rivers could swell and sweep away crops.

The ferocity of the climate demanded hardy plants, so Mesopotamia produced much more barley than wheat. Exhaustive digging raised dwellings above the flood and diverted and conserved water. The people who lived along the lower stretches of the river depicted themselves in their art as dome-headed, potbellied lovers of music, feasts, and war. But they were necessarily resourceful people who made ships in a country with no timber, worked masterpieces in bronze in a part of the world where no metal could be found, built fabulous cities without stone by baking mud into bricks, and dammed rivers as the Marsh Arabs of southern Iraq do to this day—with brushwood, reeds, and earth.

Map 3.3 Early Mesopotamia

The Good Earth of Early China

Mesopotamia and Harappa traded with each other. Mesopotamia and
Egypt were close to each other and in constant touch. However, long distance and physical barriers surrounded China's Yellow River valley (see
Map 3.4). Nevertheless, perhaps in part because the environment was
similar, developments here unfolded in familiar ways.

Map 3.4 Early China

Legend:
- Yellow River valley
- distribution of Yellow River loess soils
- desert regions
- mountain regions
- area of early wet rice cultivation
- area of early millet cultivation
- city
- core area of Shang Empire

Mongolia

Yellow River

Huai River

Yangtze River

Panlongcheng

PACIFIC OCEAN

Scale varies with perspective

7,780 km (4,830 miles)

8,370 km (5,220 miles)

The Yellow River collects rain in the mountains of Shaanxi province, where rapid thaws bring torrents of water. Where it disgorges, the stream broadens suddenly and periodically overflows. Here, the climate has been getting steadily drier for thousands of years. The region today is torrid in summer; icy in winter; stung by chill, gritty winds; and rasped by rivers full of ice. The winds blow dust from the Mongolian desert over the land, creating the crumbly, yellow earth that gives the river its name. This soil is almost sterile if it is not watered, but the fierce, unpredictable flood coaxes it into amazing fertility. The river needs careful management, with dikes to stem the flood, ditches to channel it, and artificial basins to conserve water against drought. When farmers first began to till them, these lands were a sort of savanna, where grasslands mixed with woodland. 3,000 to 4,000 years ago, water buffalo were still plentiful, together with other creatures of marsh and forest.

During the Shang dynasty, between about 3000 and 1000 B.C.E., millet sustained what were perhaps already the densest populations in the world and kept armies of tens of thousands of warriors in the field. The earliest known cultivators cleared the ground with fire before dibbling and sowing. They harvested each cluster of ears by hand and threshed seeds by rubbing between hands and feet. Crop rotation secured the best yields. Eventually, soya beans provided the alternating crop, but it is not clear when soya cultivation began.

Even at its wettest, the Yellow River valley could not sustain a rice-eating civilization. Rice could only become a staple when people colonized new areas. Some later poets recalled expansion from the Yellow River southward as a process of conquest, grasping at the Yangtze River. But conquest makes more interesting myths than colonization does. Colonists and conquerors probably combined with other communities, where similar changes were already in progress, in a slow process of expansion on many levels, beginning more than 3,500 years ago.

Configurations of Society

All four valleys faced the same problems—population was growing denser and society was becoming more complex. Yet they adopted contrasting solutions.

Patterns of Settlement and Labor

We do not know how many people lived in the great river valley civilizations, but they surely numbered in the millions. In Egypt, the people were spread fairly uniformly throughout the narrow floodplain of the Nile. Cities strew the other three valleys.

The Ziggurat of Ur. Typically, farming in any climate demands large-scale, highly disciplined labor and generates seasonal manpower surpluses. Elites, therefore, have both the means and need to build on a monumental scale. This temple stairway at Ur in Mesopotamia is representative of the results: towering dimensions and precisely geometrical forms seem calculated to defy nature, symbolize order, and project triumphs of human imaginations. *George Gerster/Photo Researchers, Inc.*

In lower Mesopotamia, for instance, Ur (Abraham's home in the bible story), had royal tombs of staggering wealth and towering ziggurats, built more than 4,000 years ago—inspired, as recent archaeology shows—by even earlier structures in what is now Iran. By the beginning of the second millennium B.C.E., new frontier towns also marked the growth of China—modest places like Panlongcheng, or Curled Dragon Town, in the northern province of Hubei, where a colonnade of forty-three pillars surrounded the governor's house.

In Harappan cities, the streetscapes—the layouts of residential and administrative zones—were always roughly identical, as were the houses. Every brick was uniform—sometimes kiln baked, sometimes pan dried. Mohenjodaro was big enough to house perhaps 50,000 or 60,000 people and Harappa, more than 30,000. No other settlements were as big, but there were plenty of them—at least 1,500 are known to archaeologists.

Population density made specialization possible. People could devote themselves to particular crafts and trades. Each sex specialized in certain occupations. Outside the home, urban life created new opportunities for specialized female labor. Women and children, for instance, were the textile workers in Ashur, a large city in northern Mesopotamia, and probably

Dancing Girl. One of a collection of bronze figures known as "dancing girls" unearthed at Mohenjodaro. Their sinuous shapes, sensual appeal, and provocative poses suggest to some scholars that they may portray temple prostitutes. They are modeled with a freedom that contrasts with the formality and rigidity of the handful of representations of male figures that survive from the same civilization.
Dancing girl. Bronze statuette from Mohenjo Daro. Indus Valley Civilization. National Museum, New Delhi, India. Borromeo/Art Resource, NY

wove cotton in Harappan cities. Moreover, women were not necessarily excluded from power. These societies employed them as rulers, prophetesses, and priestesses and included them as subjects of art. Yet art also depicted women in servile roles. For instance, pouting, languid bronze dancing girls—or are they temple prostitutes?—figure among the few art works excavated from Harappan cities of the second millennium B.C.E. Mesopotamian law codes and Chinese texts show people increasingly inheriting status from their fathers rather than their mothers and depict women's talents increasingly focused on the family home and child-rearing. This is understandable because population increase created more domestic work, while increasingly ambitious agriculture and construction were more efficiently enthrusted to males. Concentrating on domestic life, however, gave women opportunities to exercise informal power. Surviving texts show some of the consequences. Women had the right to initiate divorce, to recover their property, and, sometimes, to win additional compensation on divorce. A wife, says the Egyptian *Book of Instructions*, "is a profitable field. Do not contend with her at law and keep her from gaining control."

Politics

All four river valley societies shared, in one respect, a type of environment suited to tyranny, or, at least, to strong states exercising minute control over subjects' lives. Even without agriculture, people could have no security of life without collective action to manage the floods. Even foragers would need ditches and dikes to protect wild foodstuffs and defend dwellings. The importance of collectively managing the floods helps account for the obvious resemblances between the political systems of all these regions. All practiced divine or sacred kingship; all had rigid social hierarchies; all placed the lives and labor of the inhabitants at the disposal of the state. The mace head of an Egyptian king of the fourth millenium B.C.E. shows him digging a canal. Proverbially, a just judge was "a dam for the sufferer, guarding lest he drown," a corrupt one "a flowing lake."

We can see how one irrigation system worked, in Larsa in Mesopotamia, from the archive of a contractor named Lu-igisa, which has survived from around 2000 B.C.E. His job was to survey land for canal building, organize the laborers and their pay and provisions, and supervise the digging and the dredging of accumulated silt. Procuring labor was the key task—5,400 workers to dig a canal and 1,800 on one occasion for emergency repairs. In return, he had the potentially profitable job of controlling the opening and closing of the locks that released or shut off the water supplies. Failure was fatal. "What is my sin," he complained when he was fired, "that the king took my canal from me?"

The Egyptian State

In Egypt—a scorching environment that floods periodically soak—defying nature meant more than refashioning the landscape. Above all, it meant stockpiling against disaster, to safeguard humans from the invisible forces that let loose the floods. A temple at Abu Simbel had storehouses big enough to feed 20,000 people for a year. The taxation yields proudly painted on the walls of a high official's tomb are an illustrated menu for feeding an empire: sacks of barley, piles of cakes and nuts, hundreds of head of livestock. The state as stockpiler existed, it seems, not to redistribute goods but for famine relief.

Methods of collecting and storing grain were as vital as the systems of flood control, precisely because the extent of the flood could vary from one year to the next. The biblical story of Joseph, an Israelite who became a pharaoh's chief official and saved Egypt from starvation, recalls "seven lean years" at one stretch. Such bad times were part of folk memories, as were spells when "every man ate his children." A tomb scene from the city of Amarna shows a storehouse with only six rows of stacked victuals, including grain sacks and heaps of dried fish, laid on shelves supported on brick pillars. A strong state was an inseparable part of this kind of farsightedness. Grain had to be taxed under compulsion, transported under guard, and kept under watch.

If pharaohs were highly glorified storekeepers, what did the Egyptians mean when they said their king was a god? Furthermore, how could pharaohs bear the names and exercise the functions of many gods, each with a separate identity? A possible aid to understanding is the Egyptian habit of making images. The image "was" the god only when the god inhabited the image. The pharaoh's person could provide a similar opportunity for a god to take up residence. In a letter of around 1500 B.C.E., pharaoh is "my sun-god" and the ruler of a city in Palestine, "thy servant and the dirt whereon thou dost tread." Some 400 years earlier, a father, Sehetep-ib-Re, wrote advice to his children—"a counsel of eternity and a manner of living aright." The king is the sun-god, but he is more. "He illumines Egypt more than the sun, he makes the land greener than does the Nile."

In Egypt, the law remained in the mouth of the divine pharaoh, and the need to put it in writing was never strong. Instead, religion defined a moral code that the state could not easily modify or subvert. The evidence comes from Egyptian tombs. Early grave goods include the cherished possessions and everyday belongings of this world, suggesting that the next world would reproduce the inequalities and lifestyles of this one. At an uncertain date, however, a new idea of the afterlife emerged. This world was called into existence to correct the imbalances of the one we know. It is particularly well documented in ancient Egyptian sources that most of the elite seem to have changed their attitude toward the afterlife around 2000 B.C.E. Earlier tombs are antechambers to a life for which the world was practical training. Tombs built later are places of interrogation after a moral preparation for the next life.

Wall paintings from the later tombs show the gods weighing the souls of the dead. Typically, the deceased's heart lies in one scale, and a feather symbolizing truth lies in the other. The jackal-headed god of the underworld, Anubis, supervises the scales. The examined soul renounces a long list of sins that concentrate on three areas: sacrilege, sexual perversion, and the abuse of power against the weak. Then the good deeds appear: obedience to human laws and divine will, acts of mercy, offerings to the gods and the spirits of ancestors, bread to the hungry, clothing to the naked, "and a ferry for him who was marooned." The reward of the good is a new life in the company of Osiris, the sometime ruler of the universe. For those who fail the test, the punishment is extinction.

Statecraft in Mesopotamia

Unlike Egypt, which was a single state under a single ruler, Mesopotamia was divided into many small rival kingdoms, each based on a single city. In Mesopotamia, kings were not gods, which is probably why the earliest known law codes come from there. The codes of Ur from the third millennium B.C.E. are fragmentary—essentially, lists of fines. But the code of King Lipit-Ishtar of Sumer and Akkad, around 2000 B.C.E., is clearly an attempt to regulate the entire society. It explains that the laws were divinely inspired. Their purpose was to make "children support the father and the father children, . . . abolish enmity and rebellion, cast out weeping and lamentation . . . bring righteousness and truth and give well-being."

Hammurabi, ruler of Babylon in the first half of the 1700s B.C.E., gets undue credit because his code happens to survive intact, having been carried off as a war trophy to Persia. It is engraved in stone and shows the king receiving the text from the hands of a god. It was clearly intended to substitute for the physical presence and words of the ruler. "Let any oppressed man who has a cause come into the presence of the statue of me, the king of justice, and then read carefully my inscribed stone, and give heed to my precious words. May my stone make his case clear to him." These were not laws as we know them, handed down by tradition or enacted to restrain the ruler's power. Rather, they were means to perpetuate royal commands. Obedience was severely enforced in Mesopotamia—to the vizier in the fields, the father in the household, the king in everything. "The king's word is right," says a representative text, "his word, like a god's, cannot be changed."

Even if we had no written evidence to confirm it, royal power would gleam from the luxurious artifacts that filled rulers' tombs, evidence of the realm's wealth: a gilded harp carved in the form of a ram, dice and gaming boards of inlaid shell and polished stone, lively animals sculpted in gold and silver, tapering vessels of gold, and golden cups modeled on ostrich eggs. The stunning collections of jewelry seem to have religious themes, as if each had a distinct ritual function.

In Mesopotamian carvings, the king is commonly the biggest figure in any scene that includes him. He drinks. He receives supplicants who petition his help and citizens and ambassadors who pay him tribute. He presides over armies and processions of chariots drawn by wild asses. He carries bricks to build cities and temples, purifying them with fire and consecrating them with oil. To form the first brick from the mud was the king's exclusive right, and bricks from the state kilns were stamped with royal names. Royal seals make plain why this was the case. They show gods building the world up out of mud. They mix it, carry it up ladders, and fling mud bricks up to the men who set them layer by layer. The transformation of mud into city was royal magic.

Oracles—means of supposed access to knowing the future—told kings what to do. Augurers were the hereditary interpreters of oracles. They read the will of the gods in the livers of sacrificed sheep, in the drift of incense, and above all, in the movements of heavenly bodies. Their predictions of royal victory, danger, anger, and recovery from sickness fill surviving records. Religion, however, did not necessarily limit royal power. Normally, kings controlled the oracles. Kings themselves sometimes slept in temples to induce prophetic dreams, especially during a crisis, such as the failure of the floods. Of course, the predictions they reported may have merely legitimated the policies they had already decided to follow.

Yet these rulers were there to serve the people: to mediate with the gods on behalf of the whole society, to organize the collective effort of tillage and irrigation, to warehouse food against hard times, and to redistribute it for the common good. A comic dialogue from Akkad illustrates the delicate politics and economics of control of the food supply in the second millennium B.C.E. "Servant, obey me," the master begins.

> I shall give food to our country.
> Give it, my lord, give it. The man who gives food to his country.
>> keeps his own barley and gets rich on the interest other people
>> pay him.
> No, my servant, I shall not give food to my country.
> Do not give, my lord, do not give. Giving is like loving . . . or like
>> having a son. . . . They will curse you. They will eat your barley
>> and destroy you.

The most famous relic of ancient Mesopotamian literature, the epic of *Gilgamesh*, sheds further light on the nature of leadership. There was a real Gilgamesh, or at least a king of that name who ruled the city of Uruk, probably around 2700 B.C.E. The poem quotes a proverbial saying about him: "Who has ever ruled with power like his?" In the surviving versions, written down, perhaps about 1800 B.C.E., the same natural forces that molded the Mesopotamian environment shaped the story. When Gilgamesh, the hero of the poem, confronts a monster who breathes fire and plague, the gods blind the creature with a scorching wind. When Gilgamesh explores the Ocean of Death to find the secret of immortality, he encounters the only family to have survived a primeval flood. The disaster, wrought by divine whim, had destroyed the rest of the human race and even left the gods themselves "cowering like dogs crouched against a wall."

The First Documented Chinese State

The earliest recorded kingship traditions of China resemble those of Egypt and Mesopotamia, with the same connection between royal status and the management of food and water. The legendary engineer— Emperor Yu the Great—was praised for having "mastered the waters and caused them to flow in great channels." Early folk poetry describes a period of city building after his time, so fast "that the drums could not keep pace." The legendary ruler Tan-fu supervised builders of houses and temples, as they "lashed the boards and erected the frames."

The earliest China we know of was a unitary state. The dynasty known as Shang dominated the Yellow River valley for most of the second millennium B.C.E. Diviners, whose job was to detect the gods' messages, heated animal bone to breaking point and read the gods' answers along the lines of the cracks. Scribes transcribed the answers onto the fragments, so the bones tell of the lives and duties of kings. The court treasury held millet, turtle shells, and oracle bones paid in tribute. The king was most often engaged in war and sometimes in diplomacy. Marriage was part of it; later emperors called it "extending my favor." To their soldiers, "our prince's own concerns" rolled them "from misery to misery" and gave them homes "like tigers and buffaloes . . . in desolate wilds." The court treasury held millet, turtle shells, and oracle bones in tribute and stored them.

Above all, the king was a mediator with the gods, performing sacrifices, preparing for and conducting oracle readings, breaking the soil, praying for rain, founding towns. He spent half his time hunting—presumably as a way to entertain counselors and ambassadors, train horsemen, and add meat to his diet. Scholars claim to detect an increasingly businesslike tone in the oracles. References to dreams and sickness diminish as time goes on, the style becomes terser, and the tone more optimistic. Sometimes the bones reveal revolutions in the conduct of rites from reign to reign, evidence that kings fought tradition and tried to give the world a stamp of their own. Tsu Jia, for instance, a king of the late second millennium B.C.E., discontinued sacrifices to mythical ancestors, mountains, and rivers and increased those to historical figures. Beyond reasonable doubt, he was modifying the practices of the longest-lived and most renowned of his dynasty, Wu Ding.

The chronology is uncertain, but Wu Ding must have ruled about 1400 B.C.E. He was remembered 1,000 years later as a conqueror who ruled his empire as easily "as rolling it on his palm." He was a glorious hunter, whose oracles predicted, on one occasion, a bag of "tigers, one; deer, forty; foxes, one hundred and sixty-four; hornless deer, one hundred and fifty-nine; and so forth." One of his sixty-four consorts was buried in the richest known tomb of the period, with her human servants, dogs, horses, hundreds of bronzes and jades, and thousands of cowrie shells, which were used as money. Although there is room for confusion because of the court habit of calling different people by the same name, court records probably identify her correctly. Wu Ding repeatedly consulted the oracles about her childbeds and sickbeds. She was one of his three principal wives and was not only a wife and mother, but an active participant in politics. She had a domain of her own, including a walled town, and could mobilize 3,000 warriors on command.

As mediator with the gods, the king was a substitute for the shaman, the middleman between humans and gods, eliciting the "sharp-eared, keen-eyed" wisdom of ghosts and spirits and restoring contact with heaven after disordered times. By taking over the divination of bones and turtle shells, the king transferred to the state the most important political functions of magic and religion—foretelling the future and interpreting the will of the spirits. The king became the guardian of a secular bureaucracy—a slowly developing corps of court historians, who could acquire experience on which predictions could be based more reliably than on the shamans' supposed insights.

At this stage, the Chinese viewed kingship in practical terms—how well the ruler looked after his subjects. Shang rulers claimed to have come to power as executors of divine justice against an earlier—doubtless mythical—dynasty, the Xia, whose last representative had forfeited his right to rule by "neglecting husbandry": failing, that is, in his duty to look after the realm as a farmer cares for his fields. The earliest scholars' texts that describe the emergence of China probably reflect traditional propaganda fairly accurately. They depict kind, generous rulers who fostered the arts of peace. The Yellow Emperor, a mythical figure, was credited with inventing the carriage, the boat, the bronze mirror, the cooking pot, the crossbow, "and a kind of football." Poems and popular legends, however, reveal more of the bloody business of kingship, which inherited ancient clan leaders' rights of life and death. An axe engraved with the emblems of the executioner—hungry smiles and devouring teeth—signified the original term for rulership. "Bring your tongues under the rule of law," says a late Shang ruler in an approving poet's lines, "lest punishment come upon you when repentance will be of no avail."

Wealth and warfare were inseparable essentials of kingship. The tombs of Shang rulers around 1500 B.C.E. display the nature of their power: thousands of strings of cowrie shells, bronze axes and chariots, lacquer ware, and hundreds of intricately carved treasures of jade and bone. The greatest treasures were bronzes of unparalleled quality, cast in ceramic molds. Bronze making was the supreme art of Shang China, and its products were a privilege of rank. Thousands of human sacrifices, buried with kings to serve them in the next world or to sanctify their tombs, were—to those who buried them—among the cheapest sacrifices.

Ruling the Harappan World

In the Harappan world, the extraordinary consistency in urban layout and building design did not necessarily arise from political unity. Hierarchically ordered dwelling spaces hint at a class or even a more rigid caste structure. In a class system, individuals can rise or fall through the ranks of society. In a caste system, they are stuck with the status with which they are born. In Harappan cities, the extensive communal quarters must have had something to do with the organization of

Harappan Elite. Society and politics of ancient Harappa remain mysterious because little art survives as a clue to what went on, and we do not know how to decipher Harappan writings. A few sculptures, like this one from Mohenjodaro, depict members of an elite. The embroidered robe, jeweled crown, combed beard, and grave face all imply power—but is it priestly power, political power, or both? *Andy Crawford © Dorling Kindersley, Courtesy of the National Museum, New Delhi*

manpower—soldiers, perhaps, or slaves, or scholars. Huge warehouses suggest a system to distribute food. The waste-disposal system looks like a masterpiece of urban planning, with clay pipes laid under the streets. The uniform bricks must have come from state kilns and pans. The imposing citadels or fortresses enclosed spaces that might have had an elite function, like the spacious bathing tank at Mohenjodaro. Harappan sites, however, have no rich graves, and the absence of kingly quarters or regal furnishings tempts us to imagine Harappan societies as republics or theocracies.

For a society like Harappa's, whose writings we cannot read, archaeological evidence normally tells us what little we know. We would hope to learn something from works of art, but no pictorial art has survived, and Harappan artists seem to have produced little sculpture, except on a small scale in clay and sometimes bronze. One extraordinary figure from Mohenjodaro—of great seriousness, with almond eyes and rigidly fluted beard—wears a headband with what looks like the setting for a gem. He has a rich garment slung over one shoulder and extends what is left of his arm in what must surely have been a symbolic or ritual gesture. He has been called a priest-king or a philosopher-king, but these romantic terms are valueless. With no context for interpreting him, we can only describe him.

The Politics of Expansion

Although just about everything in Harappan politics remains mysterious, the reach of the culture seems so vast it is hard to imagine how it can have spread so far, into a range of different environments, except by force of arms. A sense of what the Harappan frontier was like—expanding and violent—grips you when you see the garrisons that reached toward the interior of Asia, in unirrigatable deserts and siltless hills. In what is now northern Afghanistan, lapis lazuli and copper were traded at oasis settlements that reached westward toward the Caspian Sea. Mundigak, a fortified trading center, was equipped to house entire caravans. Today, behind formidable walls with square bastions, the wreck of a great citadel lunges over the landscape, baring rows of deep, round columns at its flank, like the ribs of a huge, squat beast crouched to guard the routes of commerce.

In Egypt, Mesopotamia, and China, the sources are ample enough to reveal how states grew by conquest. In Egypt, the Nile was the spine that supported a unitary state. More than the source of life-giving mud, the river was a highway through a long, thin land. Culture and trade could flow freely from the coast to the cataracts. When the owner of a fleet died, his ships were illustrated on the walls of his tomb, like that of a royal chancellor at Thebes, painted more than 3,000 years ago, with yachts, barges, and fishing boats. Models and paintings of river craft are among the most common decorations of tombs. At Thebes, you can still see painted scenes of grain-laden barges and others with oil jars and bundles of fodder, docking by the marketplace.

The river was politically unifying, too. Pharoahs took the river route for inspection tours of the kingdom, mooring at royal docks with brick shrines and exercise yards for chariots. Egypt was an empire shaped like the fans Egyptians used to rake and beat their wheat—the long staff of the Nile linked to the spread of the delta where the river meets the Mediterranean. Mythology preserved the memory of a prehistoric Egypt divided into two realms: an upriver South Kingdom, or Upper Egypt, and Lower Egypt, occupying the delta region. Pharaohs wore a double crown to recall this past. Egypt's traditional lists of dynasties began with Menes, the culture hero who supposedly conquered the delta from his own kingdom in the south around 3000 B.C.E. He united the kingdoms and founded Memphis, his capital, at the point on the Nile where Upper and Lower Egypt joined, a little to the south of modern Cairo.

Conveyance by river was one of the features this world had in common with heaven. To accompany the immortals as they were ferried across the sky, the pharaoh Cheops was provided with transport. In one pit adjoining his pyramid lies the barge that carried his body to the burial place. Egyptologists are currently excavating an adjoining pit, where his celestial boat is buried. In this sailing vessel, he would navigate the darkness, joining the fleet that bore the Sun back to life every night.

In retrospect, the unity of Egypt seems "natural"—river shaped. Mesopotamia was not so easy to unify. Competition was probably the driving force behind Mesopotamian city-states. Inscriptions addressed to their cities' patron gods are full of victories against rivals, each one's propaganda bewilderingly contradicting the others. Around 2000 B.C.E., the most boastful author of inscriptions, Lugal Zagesi, king of the city of Umma in Sumer, claimed more. The supreme god, Enlil, "put all the lands at his feet and from east to west made them subject to him" from the Persian Gulf to the Mediterranean.

This was almost certainly just a boast. Left to themselves, the warring Sumerian city-states could never have united for long. Around 2500 B.C.E., however, invaders from northern Mesopotamia forced political change. The conquering king, Sargon of Akkad, was one of the great empire builders of antiquity. His armies poured downriver and made him King of Sumer and Akkad. "Mighty mountains with axes of bronze I conquered," he declared in a surviving chronicle fragment and dared kings who came after him to do the same. His armies were said to have reached Syria and Iran.

Such a vast empire could not last. After a century or two, native Sumerian forces expelled Sargon's successors. Nevertheless, Sargon's achievement set a new pattern—an imperial direction—for the political history of the region. City-states sought to expand by conquering each other.

Making Connections | POLITICS AND STATE POWER IN GREAT RIVER VALLEY SOCIETIES

STATE	LEADER AND SYMBOLIC ROLE	METHOD OF UNIFICATION	RULER'S MEANS OF CONTROL
Egypt	Pharaoh (herdsman) sometimes functions as god	Organizing labor to manage floods; distributing food; use of Nile River as highway to unify, control	Pharaoh's commands, policies function as law, regarded as divine
Mesopotamia city-states	Kings/royals meditate, lead worship, receive oracles	Organizing labor; distributing food; competition with other city-states	Earliest law codes; rituals performed by oracles guide decision making
China	Emperor/ engineer, builder, hunter, takes on shamans' role in receiving prophecies	Organizing dike building, irrigation; use of Yellow River as highway to unify and control	Ritual divination using oracle bones— foretelling future, interpreting will of spirits
Harappa	Uncertain if singular ruler or priests dominated ruling class	Harnessing river, irrigation; distributing food; engineering and construction of complex urban systems	Unknown; widespread standardization of measurements and trade point to coordination/ leadership

For a time, Lagash, a northern neighbor of Ur, dominated Sumer. One of its kings was the subject of twenty-seven surviving images. We have no better index of any ruler's power. But around 2100 B.C.E., Ur displaced Lagash. The new capital began to acquire the look for which it is renowned, with showy ziggurats and daunting walls. Within a few years more, tribute, recorded on clay tablets, was reaching Ur from as far away as the Iranian highlands and the Lebanese coast. A 4,000-year-old box—the soundbox of a harp, perhaps—gorgeously depicts the cycle of royal life in imperial Ur: victory, tribute-gathering, and celebration. Thereafter, leadership in the region shifted among rival centers, but it always remained in the south.

In China, itineraries for royal travel dating around 1500 B.C.E. reveal a different political geography. Kings constantly rattled up and down the great vertical artery of the realm, the eastern arm of the Yellow River, and frenziedly did the round of towns and estates to the south, as far as the river Huai. Occasionally, they touched the northernmost reach of the Yangtze River. This was a telltale sign. Shang civilization was expanding south from its heartlands on the middle Yellow River, growing into a regionally dominant superstate. Gradually, the worlds of Chinese culture and politics absorbed the Yangtze valley. The result was a unique state containing complementary environments: the millet-growing lands of the Yellow River, the rice fields of the Yangtze. The new ecology of China helped protect it against ecological disaster in either zone. It also formed the basis of the astonishingly resilient and productive state seen in subsequent Chinese history. The consequences will be apparent throughout the remainder of this book. For most of the rest of our story, China wields disproportionate power and influence.

Moreover, the broadening of China's frontiers stimulated rulers' ambitions. They became boundless. Religion and philosophy conspired. The sky was a compelling deity: vast and pregnant with gifts—of light and warmth and rain—and bristling with threats of storm and fire and flood. A state that touched its limits would fulfill a kind of "manifest destiny"—a reflection of divine order. Comparing the state to the cosmos prompted rulers to seek a dominion as boundless as the sky's. The Chinese came to see imperial rule over the world as divinely ordained. Emperors treated the whole world as rightfully or potentially subject to them. By the time of the Zhou, the dynasty that succeeded the Shang, the phrase **mandate of heaven** came into use to express these doctrines.

The concept of the mandate of heaven spread to neighboring peoples. On the Eurasian steppes, the immense flatlands and vast skies encouraged similar thinking. We have no documentation for the ambitions of the steppe dynasties until much later. But, as we shall see, steppelanders with conquest in mind repeatedly challenged empires around the edges of Eurasia in the first millennium B.C.E. It is probably fair to say that for hundreds, perhaps thousands, of years, the concept of a right to rule the world drove imperialism in Eurasia.

Literate Culture

It used to be thought—some people still think—that one reason the early Egyptians, Mesopotamians, Chinese, and Harappans qualified as "civilized" was because they were the first to use symbolic methods to record information and pass it on to future generations.

Mesopotamians devised the wedge shapes of the writing known as **cuneiform** to be easily incised, or cut, in the clay tablets used to keep records. The hieroglyphs of the earliest Egyptian texts and the symbols carved on Chinese oracle bones were **logograms**, stylized pictures that provoked mental associations with ideas they were intended to represent or with the sounds of their spoken names. The surviving Harappan texts marked the cord or sacks of merchants' goods. Archaeologists have retrieved many of them from heaps of discarded produce.

So, all these civilizations developed useful and expressive writing systems. For three reasons, however, we can no longer claim that writing was a special and defining feature that made these the first civilizations. First, writing systems originated independently in widely separated parts of the world and were far more varied than traditional scholarship has supposed. Notched sticks and knotted strings can be forms of writing as much as letters on a page or in an inscription. Some writing systems were much older than the civilizations of the river valleys. The chronology and definition of writing are in turmoil.

Second, it is not clear why we should consider writing special compared to information-retrieval systems based on memory. The earliest writing systems were usually employed for trivia—merchants' price lists, tax collectors' memoranda, potters' marks, and similar jottings. Real art—the great creative poems and myths, like *Gilgamesh*—were too sacred for writing to taint and too memorable for such a crude method of transmission. Instead, for centuries, people memorized them and transmitted them orally from one generation to the next.

Finally, how much information does a system have to be able to convey before we can call it writing? Will knotted strings or notched sticks do? Surviving Shang oracle bones of the second millennium B.C.E. bear the ancestral language of modern Chinese. Yet a symbolic system of recording information appears on pottery more than 2,000 years older from Banpo in the Yellow River region. The symbols might be numerals and potters' marks. They do not seem to be connected sentences because the symbols are simple and used one at a time. So is this writing or something else unworthy of the name? Turtle shells recently discovered at Wuyang in China, which are even older, bear marks that we can only explain as part of a system of symbolic representation.

Instead of restricting our definition of writing, we ought to feel awe at the adventure of combining isolated symbols to tell stories and make arguments. But familiarity disperses awe. Some cultures may have taken thousands of years to make this leap, even while they used writing systems for other purposes, such as labels, oracles, bureaucracy, and magic charms.

CHRONOLOGY	
5000–2000 B.C.E.	Four great river valley civilizations develop: Middle and Lower Nile, Egypt; Indus and Saraswati rivers; Tigris and Euphrates rivers, Mesopotamia; Yellow River, China
4000 B.C.E.	*Shaduf* invented in Egypt
3000 B.C.E.	Menes unites Upper and Lower Egypt
2500 B.C.E.	Cities of Harappa and Mohenjodaro flourish; Sargon of Akkad conquers Sumer
2250–2000 B.C.E.	Ziggurat of Ur built
2000–1000 B.C.E.	Shang dynasty, China
1800 B.C.E.	*Epic of Gilgamesh* written down
1700 B.C.E.	Law code of Hammurabi
(All dates are approximate)	

IN PERSPECTIVE
What Made the Great River Valleys Different?

Still, thanks in part to writing, the civilizations of the four great river valleys—or, at least, the three whose writings we can decipher—are, to us, the best known of their time. For that reason, not because of their supposed influence on other peoples, they fairly occupy so much space in books like this one. Studying their written works helps us identify at least two reasons for the cultural divergence of the era, of which they are extreme examples. First, in part, divergence was environmentally conditioned. That is, the greater or more diverse the resource base, the bigger and more durable the society it feeds. The great river valleys were large, continuous areas of fertile, easily worked soil, and for farming societies, exploitable land is the most basic resource of all. Environmental diversity gave the river valley peoples extra resources, compared with civilizations in less privileged regions. Egypt had the Nile delta at hand. In the Yellow River and Yangtze valleys, China had two complementary ecological systems. Mesopotamia had a hinterland of pastures, and Mesopotamia and Harappa had access to each other by sea.

Second, interactions matter. Societies learn from each other, compete with each other, and exchange culture with each other. The more societies are in touch with other societies, the more these activities occur. By contrast, isolation retards. Egypt was in touch with Mesopotamia and Mesopotamia with Harappa. China's relative isolation perhaps helps explain its late start in some of the common processes of change that these societies all experienced. All these societies enclosed, within their own bounds, relatively large zones of exchange. But all were remarkably self-contained. As we shall see in the next chapter, however, travel and trade were increasingly important. These were the means of communicating the cultures from the great river valleys to other regions, some of which were less environmentally fortunate. Invasions and migrations, too, were—and still are—effective forms of interaction because they shift many people around, and people carry their culture with them.

The grandeur of the great river valley civilizations raises questions about their sustainability. Their wealth and productivity excited envy from outsiders and invited attack. Continued population growth demanded ever-more intensive exploitation of the environment. At the same time, climates and ecosystems continued to change. The vast collective efforts required for irrigation, storage, and monumental building left huge classes of people oppressed and resentful of elites. As a result of these and other stresses, beginning around 1500 B.C.E., transformation or collapse threatened all these societies. Meanwhile, peoples in less easily exploitable environments found the will and means to reproduce, challenge, or exceed the achievements of these four civilizations. The question of how well they succeeded is the focus of the next chapter.

Because they all made fairly extensive use of bronze, nineteenth-century archaeology—classifying societies according to their characteristic technology—called the era of the great river valley civilizations the Bronze Age. In the late second millennium B.C.E., the crises that afflicted them seemed to herald transition to an "Iron Age." Such labels no longer seem appropriate. Though there were bronze-using and iron-making societies, there was never an "age" of either. Some societies in Africa never used bronze. Many societies never adopted iron, and few used it to make tools and weapons until well into the first millennium B.C.E. Although bronze making came to have an important place in the economies and art of many Eurasian peoples during the second millennium B.C.E., other societies achieved similar standards of material culture and developed comparable states without it. In any case, there are aspects of civilization—ways of thinking and feeling and behaving—more deeply influential than technology, "more lasting"—as a Roman poet said of his poems—"than bronze," and therefore more worthy of attention.

PROBLEMS AND PARALLELS

1. Where did the four great river valley civilizations arise?
2. How did the different environments in which these civilizations arose affect their economic activity, religious beliefs, and political systems?
3. How did rulers in the four river valley civilizations seek to expand their states?
4. What was the connection between religion and Egypt, China, and Mesopotamia?

A Succession of Civilizations: Ambition and Instability

focus questions

1. Why were the Hittite, Cretan, and Mycenean states more fragile than the great river valley civilizations?

2. What fundamental problems to their survival did all large ancient civilizations face?

3. Why did Harappan civilization disappear?

4. What were the continuities between the Shang and the Zhou in China?

5. Where did the first states arise in the New World?

For a moment, the scribe thought the king was already dead. He ruled a line under his notes.

They formed a grim, faltering record of an old man's regrets: his hatred of his treacherous sister—"a serpent" who "bellows like an ox"; the faithlessness of his adopted heir—"an abomination . . . without compassion"; the disloyalty of relatives "heedless of the word of the king." The dying monarch railed against his daughter, too. "She incited the whole land to rebellion." Rebels taunted him, "There is no son for your father's throne. . . A servant will become king."

With his last bit of strength, Hattusili, the great king of the Hittites, ruler of the land of Hatti, south of the Black Sea, and of an empire that touched upper Mesopotamia and the Mediterranean, sought to keep a grasp on power beyond the grave. With no suitable adult to succeed him, he decided that his infant grandson must be the next king. The administrators of the kingdom must protect the child and prepare him for manhood, reading to him every month his grandfather's testament, with its warnings against disloyalty in the realm and its exhortations to mercy, piety, and forgiveness.

Around the deathbed in the city of Kussara, in a room gleaming with lapis lazuli and gold, the assembled warriors and officials contemplated an insecure future. But the king was not yet dead. He stirred, striving to speak. The scribe hastily picked up his stylus and, straining to catch the royal words, scratched hurried characters onto his clay tablet. A woman's name fell from the king's lips: Hastayar. Who was she? Wife or concubine, sorceress or daughter? No one now knows. But she was at the bedside, consulting with the old women who were the court's official prophetesses, even as the king's life ebbed. With Hattusili's last breath came these final words: "Is she even now interrogating the soothsayers? . . . Do not forsake me. Interrogate me! I will give you words as a sign. Wash me well. Hold me to your breast. Keep me from the earth."

Hattusili dictated this deathbed testament in about 1600 B.C.E. It is the most intimate and lively document to survive from its time, our only glimpse of a king with his guard down, disclosing his own personality.

It also reveals the nature and problems of a state at this time: the all-importance of the king, the sacred nature of his word, the ill-defined rules of succession, the power and jealousies of military and administrative elites, an intelligence system that relied on soothsayers, and an atmosphere of danger and insecurity. In short, it was a political environment made to be volatile.

In the Hittite kingdom, we see the great themes of the second millennium B.C.E. First, features that characterized the great river valley civilizations of the previous chapter began to emerge in other environments. These features included intensive agriculture, densely distributed populations, stratified societies, large cities, and states often seeking to build empires. Second, the number of complex states—those with large-scale systems to organize production, control distribution, and regulate life—rapidly increased. These new states also developed a great variety of political institutions and ways to structure society and organize economic activity. Finally, accelerating change claimed victims. By about 1000 B.C.E., war, natural disaster, environmental overexploitation, and social and political disintegration had strained or shattered most of the big states and civilizations that had emerged from the transition to agriculture.

Students of history often dislike this period, with its bewildering succession of empires and civilizations that rise and fall, sometimes with baffling speed. Textbook pages resemble a bad TV soap opera—crowded with action, empty of explanation, with too many characters and too few insights into their behavior. If we are to try to make sense of the millennium between 2000 and 1000 B.C.E., we need to understand the problems associated with accelerating change. This was an era of extended and critical change that extinguished some civilizations, changed others, and might have wiped all of them out. The question for this chapter, then, is why were some ambitions in the world of around 3,000 years ago realized and others were not? What made the difference between success and failure for states and civilizations?

The Case of the Hittite Kingdom

Anatolia, where Hattusili's kingdom took shape, seems an unlikely place to found a large state. Most of it suffers alternating seasonal extremes that scorch and freeze crops. Rainfall was, and still is, less than twenty inches a year. Desert stretched between cultivatable patches.

Yet from the central part of this region, between about 1800 and 1500 B.C.E., the people who called themselves children of Hatti—Hittites—drew thousands of such patches and millions of people into a single network of production and distribution, under a common allegiance. They went on to build a state we can call an empire. It had palace complexes, storehouses, towns, and armies. And all were comparable in scale with those of the river valley peoples of the last chapter. Egyptian pharaohs treated Hittite kings as equals. When one pharaoh died without heirs, his widow sent to the king of Hatti for "one of your sons to be my husband, for I will never take a servant of mine and make him my husband." We can picture the Hittites with the help of images they have left us of themselves: hook-nosed, short-headed, and—more often than not—arrayed for war. But how did their state and empire happen in such a hostile environment?

The Importance of Trade

Hatti became a regional power through enrichment by trade. In the second millennium B.C.E., new potential trading partners arose in nearby regions, as, for unknown reasons, the economic center of gravity in Mesopotamia gradually shifted upriver. Changes in the course of the Tigris and Euphrates rivers stranded formerly important cities. Accumulations of silt kept merchants offshore. Wars at the far end of the Persian Gulf and the disappearance of some of the great cities of the Indus valley probably disrupted commerce in the Arabian Sea and Persian Gulf. New opportunities, meanwhile, arose in the north as economic development created new markets, or expanded old ones, in Syria, the Iranian highlands, and Anatolia.

For instance, the archives of Ebla, an independent city-state in Syria, reveal exchanges with Mesopotamia. Ebla's commerce was a state monopoly. Its merchants were ambassadors. A dozen foreign cities delivered gold, silver, copper, and textiles to its markets and treasury. Its royal granary stored enough food for 18 million meals. The most complete surviving record of a tour of inspection of the state warehouses names twelve kinds of wheat, abundant wine and cooking oil, and more than

Ebla's Palace Walls in the mid-third millennium B.C.E. were forty or fifty feet high. The ceremonial court in the foreground was 165 feet long. The holes show where pillars supported the roof. Akkadian invaders destroyed the palace around 2300 B.C.E., but left intact the precious archives that recorded the range of trade with Mesopotamia, Anatolia, and Egypt.
The Art Archive/Dagli Orti

80,000 sheep. The city's ceramic seals, ivory figurines, and metalsmith work reached the courts of chiefs in central Anatolia.

With the shift of economic activity from Lower to Upper Mesopotamia and beyond, networks of traders spread, east and north, from growing upriver cities such as Ashur on the Tigris and Mari on the Euphrates. Thousands of documents—16,000 in Ebla, 17,000 in Mari—describe wealthy private merchants underwritten by the state and stateless middlemen who served as deal makers. Trade forges social obligations, establishes new relationships of power, and legitimates old ones. Merchant-diplomats carried gifts between palaces. The king of the city of Ugarit rewarded an official called Tamkaru for this kind of work with a grant of land in the mid-1200s B.C.E. Leaders who accumulated imported luxuries or who were tough enough to tax passing trade could reinvest in more goods or buy the allegiance of other chiefs. They might build palace centers like those of Mesopotamia and Egypt to redistribute goods.

Business had its human side. The royal family of Ashur had a farm at Sabi Abyad, a frontier trading post on the routes to Anatolia and the Mediterranean. More than 1,000 people lived there—migrants from Ashur, exiled foreigners, prisoners of war. The steward, permanently frustrated by impractical orders, frustrated the king in turn, who wrote: "What is this, that whatever I tell you, you fail to do as I say?" The supply of beer and tableware to entertain passing embassies provoked many quarrels. So did the problems of enforcing tolls on luxuries.

Anitta, king of Kanes, early in the second millennium had "a throne of iron and a sceptre of iron." Iron was new, originating in this region but still rare and soft, smelted at a temperature only slightly higher than that required for copper. The technique of combining it with carbon to make it hard was unreliable. Bronze remained the metal of choice for weapons and agricultural tools. One of the towns Anitta saw as a rival was Kussara, the hometown of the dynasty that later founded the kingdom of Hatti. According to one of his inscriptions, he demolished the place, sowed it with salt, and cursed it, so that it might never arise again. The curse failed. His example, however, inspired the Hittites and showed them how trade and conquest could build a state.

Hittite Society and Politics

The Hittite kingdom brought farmers and herders into a single state and economic system. This was how to make the most of the rugged Anatolian environment, with its small concentrations of cultivatable soil surrounded by marginal grazing land. Herders' wool combined with small farmers' food production. Such mixed farming by independent peasants—not bonded or enslaved workers or wage earners—was of the highest importance. Livestock produce fertilizer to help feed growing populations. Milk-rich diets can improve human fertility. The consequences are more opportunity for economic specialization, urbanization, and the mobilization of manpower for war.

The surviving inventory of the estate of a typical Hittite peasant, Tiwapatara, lists one house for his family of five; three dozen head of livestock; one acre of pasture; and three and a half acres of vineyard, with forty-two pomegranate and forty apple trees. Farmers like Tiwapatara were the manpower that, for a time, made Hatti invincible. Children such as his worked the farms during military campaigns, which usually coincided with sowing and harvest. He and his kind were willing, presumably, to support the state that in turn protected them, because Hittite law laid down harsh penalties for theft or trespassing on private property. We do not know the total productivity of the economy, but a single grain silo excavated in the major city, Hattusa, held enough grain for 32,000 people for a year.

Hatti's king was the sun god's earthly deputy. His responsibilities were war, justice, and relations with the gods. Hardly any case at law was too trivial to be referred to the king, although, in practice, professional clerks dealt with most of them on his behalf. It was a bureaucratic court, where writing perpetuated the king's commands and conveyed them to subordinates.

To judge from surviving law codes, Hittites observed many apparently arbitrary sexual taboos. Intercourse with pigs or sheep was punishable by death, but not cases involving horses or mules. Hittites evidently measured the civilization of other societies by the severity of their incest laws. Their own code forbade intercourse between siblings or cousins. Any sexual act, however, was polluting in some degree and had to be cleansed by bathing before prayer. If we knew more about Hittite religion, we might understand their morality better. Strong sexual taboos are usually found in "dualist" religions, alongside belief in the eternal struggle of forces of good and evil or spirit and matter. Hittite attitudes toward sex contrasted with those in Mesopotamia, where—in what seems to have been a more typical pattern—sex was in some sense sacred and temples employed prostitutes.

In some ways, Hatti was a man's world, with the masculine attitudes and values typical of a war state. The oath army officers took indicates this:

Do you see here a woman's garments? We have them for the oath. Whoever breaks these oaths and does the king harm, let the oaths change him from a man to a woman!

But women exercised power. Old women acted as diviners at court. Others, lower down the social scale, were curers, waving sacrificial piglets over the victims of curses, with the cry, "Just as this pig shall not see the sky . . . , so let the curse not see the sacrificers!"

Fragility and Fall: The End of Hatti

The Hittite state was formidable in war. It had to be. Its domestic economy was fragile and its homeland poor in key resources. It needed to grow. Conquests were, in extreme circumstances, the only way to guarantee supplies of food for an increasing population and of tin to make bronze weapons. But even successful conflicts can weaken a state by overextending its power and disrupting its trade. Growth butts against immovable limits. In Hatti's case, those limits were the frontiers of Egypt and Mesopotamia.

The Hittite kingdom suffered from other weaknesses. As with all communities that made the transition to agriculture, it was vulnerable to famine and disease. Around 1300 B.C.E., King Mursili II reproached the gods for a plague: "Now no one reaps or sows your fields, for all are dead!" A couple of generations later, there was reputedly "no grain in Hatti." For one of the last Hittite kings, Tudhaliya IV, an order not to detain a grain ship bound for his country was "a matter of life and death." Nomadic prowlers from the hinterlands were another common hazard. People the Hittites called *Kaska* invaded repeatedly to grab booty or extort protection. On at least one of their raids, they robbed the royal court.

In the last few decades of the 1300s B.C.E., the Hittite state was in obvious decline. Hatti lost southern provinces to an expanding kingdom in Upper Mesopotamia. The oaths the king demanded from his subordinates have an air of desperation: "if nobody is left to yoke the horses . . . , you must show even more support. . . . If . . . the chariot-driver jumps down from the chariot, and the valet flees the chamber, and not even a dog is left, . . . your support for your king must be all the greater." Among the last documents the court issued are complaints that formerly subject kings were neglecting tribute or diplomatic courtesies. After 1210 B.C.E., the Hittite kingdom simply disappeared from the record.

Instability and Collapse in the Aegean

The Hittite story is a case study of the problems of global history in the second millennium B.C.E. It demonstrates how agrarian communities became consolidated into states, elevated into empires, and how most of them failed to survive past 1000 B.C.E. Echoes, parallels, and connected cases occurred in many regions near the experiments in civilization building that we discussed in the previous chapter.

The civilization scholars call Minoan or Cretan, for instance, took shape in the second millennium on the large Mediterranean island of Crete, which lies between what are now Greece and Turkey (see Map 4.1). Nearby in the southern Peloponnese, the peninsula that forms the southern part of

Map 4.1 The Eastern Mediterranean, ca. 2000–1200 B.C.E.

Cretan palace complexes

Mycenean palace

important cities

Hittite empire at its greatest extent

Hyksos

trade route

2,000 B.C.E. First palace storehouses on Crete

1,750

1,500 B.C.E. Hyksos conquer Egypt and fortified cities appear on Peloponnese

1,400 B.C.E. Knossos rebuilt after earthquake

1,250

1,190 B.C.E. Ramses III of Egypt defeats Sea Peoples

1,180 B.C.E. Sea Peoples conquer Ugarit in Syria

1,100 B.C.E. Minoan and Mycenean cities abandoned

1,000 B.C.E.

MESOPOTAMIA

SYRIA

Carchemish

Ugarit

Anatolia
TURKEY

EGYPT

Nile

Black Sea

Zakros

Akrotiri

Thera

Knossos

Mallia

Crete

Phaistos

Aegean
Sea

GREECE

Thebes

Mycenae

Pylos

Peloponnese

Mediterranean Sea

Libyan Desert

Hyksos ca. 1500 B.C.E.

Carpathian Mts.

Scandinavia

Baltic Sea

Adriatic Sea

Rundholm

DENMARK

North
Sea

E U R O P E

A F R I C A

Atlas Mountains

ATLANTIC OCEAN

65°
60°
55°
50°
45°
40°
35°
30°

40°
45°
50°
55°
60°
65°

10°
15°
20°
25°
30°
35°

5°
10°
15°
20°
25°
30°
35°

0°

N

83

Greece, the civilization we call Mycenean emerged. Both have inspired Western imaginations. Europeans and Americans view Crete and Mycenae as part of their history, assuming that they can trace the civilization of classical Greece—and therefore of the Western world—to these glamorous, spendthrift cultures of three and a half thousand years ago, about 1500 B.C.E. That now seems a doubtful assumption. Crete and Mycenae were subjects of myth—civilizations almost as mysterious to the Greeks as they are to us, and almost as remote. Still, they are worth studying for their own sake and the light they cast on their own times.

Cretan Civilization

Crete is big enough to be self-sustaining, but mountains cover two-thirds of it, leaving little land to cultivate amid devastating droughts and earthquakes. But wall paintings from around 2000 B.C.E., when the first palace-storehouses arose there, show fields of grain, vines, and orchards of olives, almonds, and quince. Forests of honey and venison surround gardens of lilies and iris, gladioli and crocuses. The seas seem full of dolphin and octopus, under skies where partridge and brightly colored birds fly.

This lavish world was painfully carved from a tough environment, harsh soil, and dangerous seas. And it depended on two despotic methods to control an unpredictable food supply: organized agriculture, embracing, as in Hatti, both farming and herding, and state-regulated trade. The function of the palace as storehouse was a vital part of the system. The greatest palace complex on the island, Knossos, covers more than 40,000 square feet. When it lay in ruins, visitors from Greece who saw its galleries and corridors imagined an enormous maze, built to house a monster who fed on human sacrifices. In fact, the labyrinth was an immense storage area for clay jars, twelve feet high, filled with wool, wine, cooking oil, and grain, some still in place.

Stone chests, lined with lead to protect the foodstuffs they contained, were like strongboxes in a central bank waiting to be distributed or traded. Cretans were such skilled sailors that the Greeks said Cretan ships knew their own way through the water, bringing ivory tusks and ostrich eggs from Africa and blue baboons from Egypt. Craft workshops inside the palaces added value to imports by spinning and weaving fine garments, delicately painting stone jars, and hammering gold and bronze into jewels and chariots. Palace records suggest a staff of 4,300 people.

Yet Knossos and buildings like it were also dwellings of an elite who lived in luxury. Squat columns with tops like fat pumpkins supported majestic staircases. Pillars were lacquered red, and the wall paintings glowed with a wonderful sky blue—scenes of feasting, gossiping, playing, and bull leaping. At Zakros, a site that was never plundered, you can see marble-veined chalices, stone storage jars, and a box of cosmetic ointment with an elegant little handle in the form of a reclining greyhound.

Lesser dwellings, grouped in towns, were tiny imitations of the palace. Many had columns, balconies, and upper-storey galleries. In the houses of more prosperous inhabitants, colorful, delicate pottery, stone vases ground into seductively sinuous shapes, and elaborately painted baths survive in large numbers. Yet, at lower levels of society, there was little surplus for luxury or time for leisure. Few people lived beyond their early forties. If the purpose of the state was to recycle food, its efficiency was limited. Skeletons show that the common people lived near the margin of malnutrition.

The cities' environment was destructive. On the nearby island of Thera, which a volcanic eruption blew apart around 1500 B.C.E., ash and rock buried the lavish city of Akrotiri. Knossos and similar palaces along the coasts of Crete at Phaistos, Mallia, and Zakros were all rebuilt once or twice on an increasingly generous scale, after unknown causes (possibly earthquakes) destroyed them.

Fortifications—evidence of internal warfare—began to appear. At the time of the last rebuilding of Knossos, generally dated around 1400 B.C.E., a major change in culture occurred. The archives began to be written in an early form of Greek. By this time, the fate of Crete seems to have become closely entangled with another Aegean civilization—the Mycenean.

Mycenean Civilization

The fortified cities and gold-rich royal tombs of the Mycenean civilization began to appear early in the 1500s B.C.E. States in the region already had kings who made war, hunted lions, and inhabited palace-storehouses similar to those of Crete. At Pylos, one of the largest Mycenean palaces, clay tablets list the vital and tiresome routines of numerous palace officials: levying taxes, checking that the landowner class observed its social obligations, mobilizing resources for public works, and gathering raw materials for manufacture and trade. Workshops turned out bronzeware and perfumed oils for export to Egypt and the Hittite empire. Trade reached north as far as Scandinavia, for eastern Mediterranean elites craved Baltic amber for glowing jewels.

The essential duty of the palace bureaucrats was to equip their rulers for almost constant warfare. Palaces were heavily and cleverly fortified. As well as fighting each other, the kingdoms felt the threat of the barbarian hinterland, which may, in the end, have overwhelmed them. Paintings on the walls of Pylos show warriors, in the boar's-head helmets also worn on Crete and Thera, in battle with skin-clad savages.

Stunned by earthquakes, strained by wars, Mycenean cities followed those of Crete into abandonment by 1100 B.C.E. What is surprising is not, perhaps, that they should ultimately have perished, but that their fragile economies, sustained by elaborate and expensive methods of collecting, storing, and redistributing food, should have managed to feed the cities and support the elite culture for so long.

A General Crisis in the Eastern Mediterranean World?

Although we could explain the extinction of Crete, Mycenae, and Hatti in terms of local political failures or ecological disasters, it is tempting to try to relate them to a general crisis in the eastern Mediterranean. Not only was the grandeur of the Aegean civilizations blotted out and the Hittite empire of Anatolia overwhelmed, but nearby states also reported fatal or near-fatal convulsions. The Egyptians almost succumbed to unidentified **Sea Peoples**, who exterminated numerous states and cities in the region. Meanwhile, in Upper Mesopotamia, an anguished king of Ashur prayed to Assur, the city's god, "Darkness without sunshine awaits the evildoers who stretch out threatening hands to scatter the armies of Assur. Wickedly, they conspire against their benefactor."

The Egyptian Experience

Egypt had survived invasion before the Sea Peoples. Perhaps toward 1500 B.C.E., the Hyksos arrived, sweating from the Libyan desert, to overwhelm the land and commission carvings of a sphinx seizing an Egyptian by the ears. Like so many nomadic conquerors of sedentary cultures around the world, the Hyksos adopted Egyptian culture and became Egyptianized before they were expelled. For their part, Egyptians considered all foreigners barbarians and viewed them with contempt.

Sea Peoples. "Now the northern peoples in their isles were quivering in their bodies," says the inscription that accompanies a ship-borne battle-scene of the reign of Ramses III. "They penetrated the channels of the mouths of the Nile. . . . They are capsized and overwhelmed where they stand. . . . Their weapons are scattered on the sea." Pharaohs' propaganda tended to lie or exaggerate, but the "Sea Peoples" really existed, and Egypt really escaped conquest or colonization by them.
© Erich Lessing/Art Resource, NY

But the narrowness of the Black Land, as Egyptians called the fertile Nile valley, was a cause of unease, and Egyptians alternated between arrogance and insecurity. On the one hand, desert and sea constituted protection against barbarian attack. Egypt was flanked by almost uninhabitable spaces, difficult to cross, whereas civilizations, like those of Mesopotamia and Harappa, with more attractive environments at their frontiers, were under constant threat from marauders and invaders. On the other hand, sea and desert were the realm of Seth, the god of chaos who threatened to overwhelm the cosmic order of life along the Nile.

Exposure to invasion continued. The descent of the Sea Peoples—about 1190 B.C.E.—is well documented because the pharaoh who defeated them, Ramses III, devoted a long inscription to his achievement. It is glaring propaganda, a celebration of the pharaoh's power and preparation: "Barbarians," it says vaguely, "conspired in their islands . . . No land could withstand their arms." A list of victims follows, including Hatti and a string of cities in southern Anatolia and along the eastern Mediterranean. "They were heading for Egypt, while we prepared flame before them . . . They laid their hands on the land as far as the edges of the Earth, their hearts confident and trusting, 'We will succeed!' " The Nile delta, however, "made like a strong wall with warships . . . I was the valiant war-god, standing fast at their head. Those who came forward together on the sea, the full flame was in front of them at the river mouths, while a stockade of lances surrounded them on the shore. They were dragged in, enclosed, and prostrated on the beach, killed and made into heaps."

The Roots of Instability

Even after unpicking the propaganda, we can be confident that the pharaoh's boasts reflect real events. Other documents confirm the existence of the Sea Peoples. For example, when the city of Ugarit in Syria fell, probably early in the twelfth century B.C.E., never to be reoccupied, messages begging for seaborne reinforcements were left unfinished. The reply from the governor of Carchemish, an inland trading center on the way to Hatti and Mesopotamia, was typical—too little, too late: "You must remain firm. . . . Surround your towns with ramparts . . ., and await the enemy with great resolution."

The image of a general crisis brought about by barbarian invasions has appealed to Western historians influenced by a familiar episode of their own past: the decline and fall of the Roman Empire. A general crisis also fits with a popular conception of the past as a battlefield of barbarism versus civilization. However, such an idea is, at best, a gross oversimplification because both barbarism and civilization are relative, subjective terms.

We can best understand the intruders as a symptom of a broader phenomenon of the period: the widespread instability of populations driven by hunger and land shortages. Egyptian carvings show desperate migrants, with ox carts full of women and children. From Mesopotamia and Anatolia comes evidence of marauders in the late thirteenth century B.C.E. But migrants probably did not cause the decline of the states they ravaged. Rather, they were among its consequences. Environmental and economic historians have scoured the evidence unsuccessfully for some sign of a deeper trauma, such as earthquakes or droughts or commercial failures, that might explain grain shortages and disrupted trade.

The causes of the crisis lay in common structural problems of the states that faltered or failed, namely, their ecological fragility and unstable, competitive politics. In this respect, the crisis was even more general, not just confined to the civilizations around the eastern Mediterranean where the Sea People roamed. If we turn to trace the fate of communities elsewhere in Asia, and even to some examples in the New World, we can detect similar strains and comparable effects.

The Extinction of Harappan Civilization

In the Indus valley, city life and intensive agriculture were in danger of collapse even when they were at their most productive. Many sites were occupied only for a few centuries. Some sites were abandoned by about 1800 B.C.E., and by 1000 B.C.E., all had dwindled to ruins. Meanwhile, in Turkmenia, on the northern flank of the Iranian plateau, relatively young but flourishing fortified settlements on the Oxus River, such as Namazga and Altin, shrank to the dimensions of villages. Some scholars believe a sudden and violent invasion was responsible, while others think of a gradual ecological disaster.

The Evidence of the *Rig Veda*

A collection of hymns and poems called the **Rig Veda** inspired the invasion theory. The people who created this literature of destruction were sedentary speakers of an Indo-European language, living in what is now the Punjab, the area north of the Indus valley where northern India and Pakistan meet from about 1500 B.C.E. They were not newcomers or nomads, though strong in horses and chariots. When poets wrote down the *Rig Veda*, some time around 800 B.C.E., after centuries of oral transmission, it still had the power to carry hearers and readers back to a lost age of heroes.

The hymns tell of a people who wanted a world of fat and opulence, basted with butter, flowing with milk, dripping with honey. They valued boasting and drinking. Their rites of fire included burning down their enemies' dwellings. Their favorite god, Indra, was a "breaker of cities," but this was part of his generally destructive role, which included mountain smashing and serpent crushing.

Some of the cities seem already to have been in ruins when the *Rig Veda* poets beheld them. Excavators who claimed that they could read such traumatic events at Mohenjodaro, in the bones of massacre victims and scorch marks on the walls, seem to have been wrong. Few of the supposed massacre victims have any wounds. Instead of a single violent event, the more likely explanation speaks of a gradual decline—a climacteric, a point at which Harappan civilization collapsed, and its cities were abandoned.

The Environment of Stress

The climate was getting drier in the Indus valley. The Saraswati River, along which settlements were once densely clustered, disappeared into the advancing Thar Desert. Yet not even the loss of a river adequately explains the abandonment of the cities. The Indus River is still disgorging its wonderful silt, year by year, over vast, shining fields, which would have been sufficient to maintain the urban populations. Presumably, something happened to the food supply that was connected with the drying climate or human mismanagement of environmental resources—the cattle and hinterland products that supplemented the wheat and barley of the fields.

In addition—or instead—the inhabitants apparently fled from some plague more deadly than the malaria that anthropologists have detected in buried bones. In an environment where irrigation demands standing water, mosquitos can breed. Malaria is inevitable. The people left, "expelled by the fire-god," as the *Rig Veda* says, and "migrated to a new land." This is probably an exaggeration. People stayed on or squatted in the decaying cities, inhabiting the ruins for generations. But the fall of Harappan civilization remains the most dramatic case of large-scale failure in the second millennium B.C.E. In broad terms, Harappa suffered essentially the same fate as the Hittite and eastern Mediterranean civilizations: The food distribution system outran the resource base. And when networks of power began to break down, invaders broke in.

Conflict on the Yellow River

China's problems toward the end of the second millennium B.C.E. were part of what looks increasingly like a global pattern, yet different in some ways from those of Egypt or Harappan. China suffered no large-scale population loss, no wholesale abandonment of regions, no wreck of cities.

The basis of the Shang state had always been shaky. War, rituals, and oracles are all gamblers' means of power, vulnerable to the lurches of luck. Manipulating the weather, the rains, the harvests, for instance, was a big part of the king's job, but in reality, of course, it was not one he could accomplish. Failure was built into his job description. It was a common problem for monarchs of the time, exposing pharaohs to blame for natural disasters, driving Hittite kings to depend on soothsayers.

The late Shang state was shrinking. Beginning about 1100 B.C.E., the names of subject, tribute-paying, and allied states gradually vanished from the oracle bones. The king's hunting grounds grew smaller. The king became the sole diviner and commander as the numbers at his disposal fell. Former allies became enemies.

Bronze Drum. This intricate geometric design on the face of a Vietnamese drum shows a sunburst at the center. Rulers often displayed these impressive bronze drums as emblems of their royal status.
Lee Boltin/American Museum of Natural History

Meanwhile, just as Mesopotamian culture had been exported to Anatolia and Cretan ways of life to Mycenae, so Shang was exported beyond the Shang state. New chiefdoms were developing in less favorable environments under the influence of trade. As far away as northern Vietnam and Thailand, bronze-making techniques similar to those of China, appeared at the courts of chiefs who delighted in personal ornaments, spittoons, and, in Vietnam, heavily decorated drums. More ominously and closer to home, right on the Shang border, a state arose in imitation and, increasingly, in rivalry: Zhou.

The Rise of Zhou

The earliest Zhou sites—of the 1100s B.C.E.—are burials in the mountains above the Wei River in western China. This was probably not the Zhou heartland, but the area they had migrated to from grazing country farther to the north. Their own legends recalled time spent "living among the barbarians." The Zhou were highland herders, an upland, upriver menace to the Shang just as Akkad was to Sumer in Mesopotamia (see Map 4.2).

According to chronicle evidence, Shang-style turtle shell oracles had inspired the Zhou to conquest, and later Zhou rulers upheld that tradition. Chronicles composed in the third century B.C.E. tell the same story as texts hundreds of years older. If they can be believed, the Zhou "captured"—as they put it—the Shang state in a single battle in 1045 B.C.E. at Muye. They annexed it as a kind of colony and established garrisons all along the

Map legend:

✂ battle of Muye, 1045 B.C.E.   ▬ approximate extent of Zhou state

▬ approximate extent of Shang cultural area   - - - ancient coastline

Map 4.2 Zhou China

lower Yellow River to the coast. Archaeological evidence shows that they shifted the center of the empire north, to the hilly region west of where the Yellow River turns toward the sea.

The Zhou Political System

Inscriptions on bronze loving cups are the only contemporary written sources to survive from the period of Zhou supremacy, which lasted from about 1000 through the 700s B.C.E. Those who could afford them—and, of course, few could—recorded their inheritances, their legacies to their families, and, above all, the key moments in their family's relationships with the imperial house. Documenting the family's achievements was related to a belief in inherited virtue. Indeed, as Shao Gong, uncle and adviser to an early Zhou king, put it: "there is nothing—neither wisdom nor power—that is not present at a son's birth."

The inscriptions tend to combine self-praise and self-justification. Shortly before 1000 B.C.E., for instance, a king's nephew recorded how he had been made ruler of the colony of Xing. He tells us first of the royal decision to make the appointment. Then we get the circumstances: The nominee performs a rite of gratitude. He accompanies the king on a lake hunt in a ship with a red banner. The king bags a goose and gives the nominee a black axe. "In the evening, the lord was awarded many axe-men as vassals, two hundred families, and was offered the use of a chariot-team in which the king rode; bronze harness-trappings, an overcoat, a robe, cloth and slippers." The gifts apparently mattered a great deal because all such inscriptions mention them. The special clothes conferred status. The newly ennobled lord then commissioned a commemorative cup, which bore the inscription: "With sons and grandsons, may he use it for ever to confer virtue, invoke blessings, and recall the order to colonize Xing."

The Zhou did not continue all Shang traditions. Despite pious declarations, they gradually abandoned divination by bone oracles. Though they extended China's cultural frontiers before their own state dissolved in its turn in the eighth century B.C.E., their leaders were not universal emperors in the mold of the Shang, ruling all the world that mattered to them. Rival states multiplied around them, and their own power tended to erode and fragment. But they originated the ideology of the mandate of heaven, which "raised up our little land of Zhou." All subsequent Chinese states inherited the same notion that the emperor was divinely chosen. Furthermore, all subsequent changes in rule appealed to the same claim that heaven transferred power from a decayed dynasty to one of greater virtue. The Zhou created an effective myth of the unity and continuity that dominated the way the Chinese came to think of themselves. This myth is now the part of the standard Western view of China, too, as a monolithic state—massive, uniform, durable, and hungry for world dominance.

State-Building in the Americas

On a relatively smaller scale and over a longer time span, communities in parts of the New World experimented with some of the same processes of state-building and civilization that we have seen in the Old World. Some peoples of the Andean region and in Mesoamerica were particularly ambitious in modifying their environments.

Andean Examples

About 3,500 years ago, experiments in civilization spread from alluvial areas on the Peruvian coast to less obviously favorable environments (see Map 4.3). In Cerro Sechín, only about 300 feet higher than the Supe valley in north-central Peru (see Chapter 2), an astounding settlement existed in about 1500 B.C.E. on a site of about twelve acres. On a stone platform 170 feet square, hundreds of carved warrior images slash their victims in two, exposing their entrails, or slicing off their heads in a rite of victory. By about 1200 B.C.E., nearby Sechín Alto was one of the world's

inset map A

Gulf of Mexico

V E R A   C R U Z

Olmec

La Venta

San Lorenzo

TABASCO

M E X I C O

Coatzacoalcos

Usumacinta

50 km
50 miles

90°

Gulf of
Mexico

Tropic of Cancer

see inset map A

Mesoamerica

Caribbean Sea

CENTRAL
AMERICA

0°

Amazon

see inset map B

P E R U

S O U T H
A M E R I C A

PACIFIC
OCEAN

Peru (Humboldt) Current

El Niño Current

Tropic of Capricorn

90°

Tropic of Capricorn

30°

inset map B

Lambayeque

Cajamarca
Valley

Cupinisque
Gorge

Moche

Viru

Huaca de los Reyes

Nepeña

Sechin Alto

Cerro Sechin

Chavín de
Huantar

Huarmey

P E R U

Supe
Valley

PACIFIC
OCEAN

Huaura

Chillon

Huallaga Valley

Huallaga

Marañon

A n d e s

100 km
100 miles

10°

ATLANTIC
OCEAN

N

1,000 km
1,000 miles

60°

Olmec cultural area

Chavín cultural area

normal flow of Pacific Ocean current

El Niño current

Olmec sculptural site

PERU   modern-day country

TABASCO   state province

Map 4.3 State-Building in the Americas, ca. 1500–1200 B.C.E.

great ceremonial complexes, with gigantic mounds erected to perform rituals, and monumental buildings arrayed along two boulevard like spaces, each more than a mile long, at its heart. The biggest mound covers thirty square miles and is almost 140 feet tall.

These places, and others like them, suggest new experiments to manage the environment and coordinate food production in numerous small, hilly areas, each irrigated by a gravity canal and organized from a central seat of power. The violent carvings of Cerro Sechín show the price paid in blood to defend or enlarge them.

In the same period—in the last three centuries or so of the second millennium B.C.E.—farther up the coast, new settlements took shape around the Cupisnique gorge. Though the environment was similar, the physical remains suggest a different culture and different politics. Huaca de los Reyes, for instance, had dozens of stucco-fronted buildings and colonnades of fat pillars, each up to 6.5 feet thick, guarded by huge, saber-toothed heads in clay. At Pampa de Caña Cruz, a gigantic mosaic, 170 feet long, represented a similar head, embedded in the earth, so that a viewer could only appreciate its shape from a height humans could not reach—but their gods, perhaps, could. These regions traded with nearby highlands, where building on a monumental scale followed soon afterward at sites that exhibit extraordinary cultural diversity.

Most Andean experiments in civilization were short lived. With modest technologies, they struggled to survive in unstable environments. At irregular intervals, usually once or twice a decade, **El Niño**—the periodic reversal of the normal flow of Pacific currents—drenched the region in torrential rain and killed or diverted the ocean fish. Population levels outgrew food supplies, or overexploitation impoverished the soil, or envious neighbors unleashed wars.

The city of Chavín de Huantar began to emerge about 1000 B.C.E., more than 3,300 feet up in the Andes, on the Mosna River. Chavín demonstrates how people could achieve prosperity and magnificence at middling altitudes. Essential prerequisites were command of trade routes and the availability of diverse foodstuffs in the microclimates of mountain environments. Gold-working technology, already at least a thousand years old in the highlands, provided objects for luxury trade. Forest products from east of the mountains were also in demand in the lowland cities. Chavín was in the middle of these trades.

Even in the impressive world of early Andean civilizations, the sheer workmanship of Chavín stood out and attracted imitators in architecture, water management, engineering, metalwork, and ceramics. Today, the ceremonial spaces, storehouses, and barrack-like dwellings inspire speculation about how this society was organized and ruled. The best clues are probably in the sculptures of humans half-transformed into jaguars, often with traces of drug-induced ecstasy. Nausea and bulging eyes contort their faces; their nostrils stream with mucus. Here is the evidence of a society ruled by shamans—the go-betweens who rise above the level of their subjects by drug-induced ecstasies. Proof of their power lay in the messages they brought back from the gods and the spirit world.

Developments in Mesoamerica

States developed in the Andes the same way they developed in the Old World—as responses to the stimulation of trade. Both followed the model described in Chapter 3: beginning with intensified agriculture and leading to population density, economic specialization, growing markets, and trade. In the Andes, the model emerged from the soil of Aspero in the Supe valley and climaxed in Chavín. In Mesoamerica, however, stunning experiments in civilization began, as far as we know, without the benefit of trade.

Olmec Head. The Olmec carving known to archaeologists as Head No. 1, in San Lorenzo, Veracruz, in Mexico, where nine such sculptures, each more than six feet high, are concentrated. San Lorenzo is far from the source of the basalt from which the heads were carved. Their close-fitting helmets have inspired the fantasy that they were representations of space men. Their thick-lipped faces have induced almost equally incredible speculations about prehistoric arrivals from Africa. More probably—like later monumental portraits in Mesoamerica—they represent stylized images of rulers.
Nathaniel Tarn/Photo Researchers, Inc.

The culture we call Olmec arose in what is now Tabasco in southern Mexico in the second millennium B.C.E. (see Map 4.3). We can picture the Olmecs with help from portraits they left: heads, carved from stones and columns of basalt, each of up to forty tons, toted or dragged over distances of up to a hundred miles. Some have jaguarlike masks or almond eyes, parted lips, and sneers of cold command. Perhaps they, too, are shaman-rulers with the power of divine self-transformation, though they are never as thoroughly transformed as the coca-crazed shamans of Chavín.

The swamps of Tabasco had supported agriculture for at least a thousand years before the first monumental art and ceremonial centers in the Olmec tradition appeared. The Olmec chose settlement sites near mangrove swamps and rain forests, close to beaches and oceans, where they could exploit a variety of environments. Marshy lakes, full of aquatic prey, were alluring to settlers. They dredged mounds for farming from the swamp and, between the mounds, coaxed canals into a grid for raising fish, turtles, and perhaps caymans.

The agricultural mounds became the model for ceremonial platforms. The earliest known ceremonial center was built on a rise above the river Coatzalcos around 1200 B.C.E. Two large centers soon followed, at La Venta, deep among the mangrove swamps on the Tonalá River, and at nearby San Lorenzo. By about 1000 B.C.E., San Lorenzo had substantial reservoirs and drainage systems, integrated into a plan of causeways, plazas, platforms, and mounds. At La Venta, there are early examples of the ritual spaces that fitted into these gridworks. The center was built with stones toted and rolled from more than sixty miles away. The focus of La Venta is a mound over a hundred feet tall—evidently a setting for the most important rituals. One of the ceremonial courts has a mosaic pavement that resembles a jaguar mask that its creators appear to have deliberately buried. Similar buried offerings were placed under other buildings, perhaps the way some Christians bury relics from saints in the foundations and altars of churches. Although the stone buildings—those that survive—were designed for ritual life, these were cities: dense settlements clustered around the ceremonial centers.

Two unsolved problems exist in connection with the Olmecs: How and why did intensive food production begin? And how and why did ambitious attempts to modify the environment begin? Monumental building requires ample food supplies to support manpower and generate spare energy. Many scholars still believe that the Olmecs could have produced sufficient food by slashing forest clearings, setting fire to the stumps, and planting seeds directly in the ash. But this theory is unconvincing because, as far as we know, no society using such methods ever prospered the way the Olmecs did. It is more likely that the transition to city-building began when the Olmecs started farming high-yielding varieties of maize. With beans and squash, maize provided complete nourishment. The three plants together were so important to Olmec life that they depicted them on gods' and chieftains' headgear.

It is risky to make inferences on the basis of such scanty evidence, but it looks as if a determined, visionary leadership energized by shamanism drove Olmec civilization forward. An exquisite scene of what seems to be a ceremony in progress suggests the seemingly pivotal role of shamanism. Archaeologists found it buried in sand, perhaps as an offering. Carved figures with misshapen heads, suggesting that the skull was deliberately deformed, stand in a rough circle of upright stone slabs. They wear nothing but loincloths and ear ornaments. Their mouths are open, their postures relaxed. Similar figures include a *were-jaguar*—a small creature, half jaguar, half human. Others carry torches on phallic staffs. Or else they kneel or sit in a restless posture, as if ready to be transformed from shaman into jaguar, as other works depict. For the rites these figures suggest, the Olmecs built stepped platforms—forerunners, perhaps, or maybe just early examples of the angular mounds and pyramids typical of later New World civilizations.

Rulers were buried in the sort of disguises they wore for ritual performances. They became fantastic creatures with a cayman's body and nose, a jaguar's eyes and mouth, and feathered eyebrows that evoke raised hands. They lay in pillared chambers with bloodletting tools of jade or stingray spine beside them. We can still see their images carved on benchlike thrones of basalt, where they sat to shed blood—their own and their captives'. One of these carvings shows a throne with a submissive figure roped to a majestic character in an eagle headdress, who leans outward as if to address an audience.

Believers in the diffusionist theory of civilization have often hailed the Olmecs as the mother civilization of the Americas. Diffusionism states, in brief, that civilization is such an extraordinary achievement that we can credit only a few gifted peoples with creating it. It then diffused—or spread by example and instruction—to other less inventive peoples. This theory is almost certainly false. Rather, several civilizations probably emerged independently, in widely separated places.

Nevertheless, Olmec influence seems to have spread widely in Mesoamerica and perhaps beyond. Numerous aspects of Olmec life became characteristic of later New World civilizations: mound building; a tendency to seek balance and symmetry in art and architecture; ambitious urban planning around angular temples and plazas; specialized elites, including chieftains commemorated in monumental art; rites of rulership involving bloodletting and human sacrifice; a religion rooted in shamanism with bloody rites of sacrifice and ecstatic performances by kings and priests; and agriculture based on maize, beans, and squash.

Assessing the Damage

By 1000 B.C.E., failed states littered the landscape. Some of the world's spectacular empires broke up. Mysterious catastrophes cut short the histories of complex cultures. Food distribution centers controlled from palace labyrinths shut down. Trade was disrupted. Settlements and monuments were abandoned. Harappan civilization vanished, as did Crete's and Mycene's. Hatti was obliterated.

In Mesopotamia, Akkadian armies spread their language the length of the Tigris and Euphrates. Sumerian speech dwindled from everyday use to become—like Latin in the Western world today—a purely ceremonial language. Sumer's cities crumbled. Their memory was preserved chiefly in the titles that invaders from uplands and deserts used to dignify the rule of their own kings. Ur declined to a cult center and tourist resort.

Something similar occurred in China, which succumbed to conquerors from neighboring uplands. Aspects of the civilization survived, but its center of gravity was shunted upriver. As we shall see in a later chapter, when numerous competing kingdoms in turn succeeded Zhou in the 700s B.C.E., continuity was not broken. Society and everyday life remained essentially intact. This was a pattern often repeated in Chinese history. In the New World, meanwhile, Mesoamerica and the Andean region undertook environmentally ambitious initiatives, but none showed much staying power.

The Survival of Egypt

Though there were more losers than winners after the climacteric of the second millennium B.C.E., the outstanding case of endurance, as we saw in the last chapter, was Egypt. Invasions in the late second millennium failed, and the basic productivity of the agrarian system remained intact. But even Egypt was reined in.

Nubia—the region upriver of the cataracts, what is now Sudan—disappeared from Egyptian records by 1000 B.C.E. This was a major reversal because extending its empire along the Nile had been one of Egypt's most constant objectives. The abundant ivory, the mercenaries that Nubia supplied, and the river trade that made gold in Egypt "as plentiful as the sand of the sea" had long drawn Egypt southward. Egypt originally became interested in Central Africa when the explorer Harkhuf made three expeditions around 2500 B.C.E. He brought back "incense, ebony, scented oil, tusks, arms, and all fine produce." Harkhuf's captive pygmy, "who dances divine dances from the land of the spirits . . ." fascinated the boy pharaoh Pepi. Writing to the explorer, the pharaoh commanded the utmost care in guarding him: "inspect him ten times a night. For my Majesty wishes to see this pygmy more than all the products of Sinai and Punt."

Contact and commerce led to the formation of a Nubian state in imitation of Egypt. From about 2000 B.C.E. on, Egypt tried to influence or control this state, sometimes by erecting fortifications, sometimes by invasion, sometimes by pushing its own frontier southward to beyond the third cataract. Pharoahs' inscriptions piled curses on the Nubians as the latter became more powerful and more difficult to handle. Eventually, around 1500 B.C.E., Pharoah Tut-mose I launched a campaign beyond the fourth cataract, conquering the kingdom of Kush and making Nubia a colonial territory. Egypt studded Nubia with forts and temples. The last temple, to Pharoah Ramses II, at Abu Simbel, was the most crushingly monumental that Egyptians had built for 2,000 years. It has remained a symbol of power ever since. But during the reigns of his immediate

KINGDOM AND REGION	PRIMARY PROBLEMS	CONSEQUENCES
Egypt	Exposure to invasion; limited areas of soil fertility; occasional grain shortages	Famines, land shortages, and sizable migrations; invasion by Sea Peoples exploits instability
Northern Anatolia—Hatti	Growth overlaps with frontiers of Egypt, Mesopotamia; overextension of power; disruption of trade through warfare; vulnerability to famine and disease in early stages of agriculture	Nomadic prowlers attack during weak periods, conquered subjects revolt
Crete—Minoan Civilization	Uneven organization of labor; distribution of food; competition with other city-states; destruction of environment; little fertile soil; dangerous seas	Social inequality, internal warfare combine with nearby volcanic activity and earthquakes to force abandonment of cities, palaces
Greece— Mycenaean Civilization	Barbarian raiders from north attracted by wealth of palaces; earthquakes; social inequality; internal warfare	Social inequality, internal warfare combine with nearby volcanic activity and earthquakes to force abandonment of cities, palaces
Indus River— Harappa and Mohenjodaro	Gradually drying climate; evidence of earthquakes, shifting riverbeds, disease; overuse of environmental resources	Gradual collapse of food distribution system; political control; cities and towns abandoned
China—Shang and Zhou Dynasties	Overdependence of Shang leaders on rituals, oracles, war, conquest to manipulate harvest, weather	Collapse of Shang rule; rise of Zhou state; shifting center of empire; lessened dependence on divination by bone oracles
Andes—Supe Valley, Cajarmarca Valley, and Cupinisque Gorge	Vulnerability to climate change from El Niño; population levels dependent on sufficient food supplies	Overexploitation of soil leads to famines; envious neighbors unleash war; Chavín de Huantar emerges as dominant state
Mesoamerica— Olmec	Intensive food production unable to support large populations	Building on large scale declines by 300 B.C.E.

ASSESSING THE DAMAGE

99

CHRONOLOGY	
2500 B.C.E.	Egypt expands southward
2000–1000 B.C.E.	Climacteric: critical and accelerating change; state-building in Hatti, Crete, Egypt; Shang China, the Andes, and Mesoamerica
2000 B.C.E.	Nubian state formed, emulating Egypt; Cretan civilization emerges
1800–1500 B.C.E.	Hittite kingdom flourishes
1500 B.C.E.	Mycenae civilization appears; Cerro Sechín flourishes in Andes (Peru)
1210 B.C.E.	Last record of Hatti
1190 B.C.E.	Ramses III defeats Sea Peoples
1000 B.C.E.	Cretan and Mycenaean cities abandoned; Shang state in decline; Harappan cities in ruin; Chavín civilization emerges; Nubia disappears from Egyptian records
300 B.C.E.	Olmec civilization declines (Mesoamerica)
(All dates are approximate)	

successors, disastrously little flooding of the Nile, on which the success of Egyptian agriculture depended, was recorded. This was the era, toward the end of the thirteenth century B.C.E., when Egypt came closer to collapse than at any time since the invasion of the Hyksos. To abandon Nubia in the late second millennium B.C.E., after investing so much effort and emotion, shows how severe Egypt's need for retrenchment must have been.

IN PERSPECTIVE
The Fatal Flaws

Paradox racked the most ambitious states of the era. They were committed to population growth, which imposed unsustainable goals of expansion on overextended frontiers. They were founded on intensified methods of production, which drove them to overexploit the environment. They concentrated large populations in a limited area, making them more vulnerable to famine and disease. Enemies surrounded them, jealous of their wealth and resentful of their power. They created more enemies for themselves by inspiring rivals and imitators in their hinterlands. When their food-distribution programs failed, disruptive migrations resulted. Their rulers condemned themselves to failure and rebellion because they lived a lie, manipulating unreliable oracles, negotiating with heedless gods, and bargaining with hostile nature. If Harappan society was unsustainable in the silt-rich Indus valley, how realistic were the Hittite or Olmec or Cretan or Andean ambitions in much less favorable environments?

In some cases, the traditions that failed or faltered during the great climacteric simply got displaced, to reemerge elsewhere. In others, dark ages of varying duration—periods of diminished achievement, about which we have little evidence—followed the climacteric. Chavín survived for about 500 years, until around 500 B.C.E., but during the following centuries, people in the Andes attempted nothing on a comparable scale for centuries. After the Olmec stopped building on a large scale, probably in the 300s B.C.E., they had no successors for many centuries. Squatters occupied the cities of Harappa and Mycenae. The literacy of these civilizations was lost, their writing systems forgotten. When writing resumed in these regions hundreds of years later, the inhabitants had to invent new alphabets.

Our next problem is to penetrate that darkness and trace the displaced traditions from failed states. We want to examine the context that would produce a different world after the climacteric, post-1000 B.C.E. In the last millennium B.C.E.—thanks to an extraordinary blossoming of intellectual and spiritual life—the world was literally rethought.

PROBLEMS AND PARALLELS

1. Why did the number of complex states increase during the second millennium B.C.E.?
2. Why did the Hittite kingdom and the Cretan and Mycenaean civilizations collapse and disappear while Egypt survived?
3. What factors might explain the long-term survival of Chinese civilization and the disappearance of Harappan/Indus valley civilization?
4. Why is the period between 2000 and 1000 B.C.E. a climacteric in world history?

Rebuilding the World: Recoveries, New Initiatives, and Their Limits

focus questions

1. What were the political and economic foundations of the Assyrian Empire?
2. Why were colonization and trade so important for the Greeks and Phoenicians?
3. Why did the Zhou state decline in China?
4. How was civilization built anew in India and Sri Lanka?
5. How did geography influence the transmission of culture in the Americas and Africa?

The time was high summer, a little more than 3,000 years ago; the place, the eastern Mediterranean. Wenamun, an Egyptian ambassador, was on his way to the city-state of Byblos, in Phoenicia, on the shore of Lebanon. His mission: to procure timber for the Egyptian fleet from the mountain forests the king of Byblos controlled. Egypt had no timber of its own.

On arrival, he set up an altar to Egypt's chief god, Amun. King Zeker Baal kept Wenamun waiting for weeks before suddenly summoning the ambassador in the dead of night. Presumably, the summons was a negotiating ploy. But Wenamun reported it as a dramatic change of heart that Amun had brought about. The ambassador recorded his dialogue with the king—doctored, no doubt, but still revealing.

Wenamun began by reminding Zeker Baal that his father and grandfather had sent timber to Egypt, but the king resented the implication that timber was due as tribute.

"They did so by way of trade," he replied. "When you pay me I shall do it." The two men bickered over the price, and each threatened to call off the negotiations. "I call loudly to the Lebanon which makes the heavens open," claimed Zeker Baal, "and the wood is delivered to the sea."

"Wrong!" retorted Wenamun. "There is no ship which does not belong to Amun. His also is the sea. And his is the Lebanon of which you say, 'It is mine.' Do his bidding and you will have life and health."

It was an impressive speech, but in the end, the Egyptians had to pay Zeker Baal's price: four jars of gold and five of silver, unspecified amounts of linen, 500 ox hides, 500 ropes, twenty sacks of lentils, and twenty baskets of fish.

The Egyptian ambassador's document is vivid and dramatic, a true story better than fiction. But its value goes deeper. It opens a window into a world recovering from the crises of the late second millennium B.C.E. The confidence of a small city-state like Byblos in the face of demands from a giant like Egypt seems astounding. But new opportunities that were opening up, thanks to increasing trade and cultural exchange in Eurasia, justified it.

The question for this chapter, then, is what happened between 1000 and 500 B.C.E. that led some places to recover from the failures of the second millennium? Investigating the nature of those recoveries will equip us to approach a far bigger problem in the next part of this book: How do we explain the vitality and influence—the intellectual and spiritual achievements—of some groups and centers in Eurasia in the period that followed, beginning about 500 B.C.E.?

Equally important in its way is the problem of why new initiatives were so rare, late, and slow beyond Eurasia. In particular, why did the promising initiatives in parts of the Americas and sub-Saharan Africa wither instead of grow and thrive in this period? Why, for example, was Greece's dark age after the fall of Mycenae so much shorter than the dark ages of the Andes after Chavín or Mesoamerica after the Olmecs? Why did big states and monumental cities appear later in sub-Saharan Africa than in China, say, or India, or the Mediterranean? And why did so much historical initiative—the power of some human groups to influence others—become so concentrated in a few regions?

Trade and Recovery in the Middle East

Byblos was one of the largest city-states of Phoenicia, a maritime culture along the eastern coast of the Mediterranean. The name "Phoenicia" expresses the Phoenicians' chief interest—trade—because the word almost certainly means "suppliers of purple dye." Tyre, an even bigger port near Byblos, developed a deep, rich purple from the crushed shells of sea mollusks that became Western antiquity's favorite and most expensive color. (It took 12,000 shells to make the dye for just one cloak.) Beginning early in the first millennium B.C.E., Phoenician traders and colonists spread around the Mediterranean. Meanwhile new, land-based empires arose that grew rich as much by conquest as by trade, threatening Phoenicia and, eventually, engulfing it (see Map 5.1).

The Phoenician Experience

In front of them, Phoenicians had waters accessible through excellent harbors. Behind them, they had mountains with forests of cedar and fir for shipbuilding and timber exports. But they did not have much land to farm. They turned, therefore, to industry and trade. In legend, at least, Phoenician ships brought gold for the biblical King Solomon from distant Ophir, a mythical or lost kingdom. Timber from Tyre built the Temple of Solomon in Jerusalem, in exchange for food and oil.

This was a period when the only way to trade with a region that did not have its own merchant class or tradition of long-distance commerce was to colonize it. According to legend, the Phoenicians' earliest colonies were in what is now Tunisia in North Africa and at Cadiz in Spain. Phoenicians founded the Tunisian city of Carthage around 800 B.C.E. and colonized the Mediterranean islands of Malta and Sardinia by 700 B.C.E. From these bases, Phoenician navigators broke into the Atlantic and established a trading post as far away as Mogador on the northwest coast of Africa.

Where they built cities, the Phoenicians were agents of cultural exchange, borrowing from all over the eastern Mediterranean, while introducing clay-lined beehives, glass blowers' techniques, and their own vats for mixing Tyrian dye.

The colonies remained, even when the cities of Phoenicia fell to foreign raiders or rulers. Egyptian and Babylonian rulers—and by the early sixth century, conquerors from Persia—then preyed on the region in their turn. By 500 B.C.E., Carthage aspired to be an imperial capital of its own, fighting to control Mediterranean trade—first with Greek cities, then with Rome. It had a harbor just where it was needed—in the center of the Mediterranean—and a fertile hinterland of flocks, wheat fields, irrigated gardens, and vineyards. Its aspirations seemed justified. The city's worst enemy, the Roman statesman, Cato the Elder (234–149 B.C.E.), preached, to the Roman Senate, "Carthage must be destroyed." To show why, he displayed plump, fresh figs, a delicate fruit that spoils quickly, newly imported from there. With this single gesture, he conveyed that the land was fertile, the city was rich and strong—and Rome was within its easy reach.

A Roman poet later recalled Phoenicians as "a clever people who prospered in war and peace. They excelled in writing and literature and the other arts, as well as in seamanship, naval warfare, and ruling over an empire." Their records might illuminate for us the dark age of lack of sources after the fall of Mycenae, but the Romans, who defeated Carthage in three wars and destroyed the city in 146 B.C.E., were too thorough in victory. The Phoenician language gradually yielded in North Africa and in Phoenicia itself to Latin and Greek—the languages the Romans introduced for administrative and literary purposes—and almost the whole of Phoenician literature disappeared. Only fragments of stone inscriptions survive, along with the Phoenicians' unique gift to the world, the alphabet.

The Assyrian Empire

By 1000 B.C.E., Hatti's extinction was Assur's opportunity (see Chapter 4). Kings of Assur, who were already wide-scale raiders, forged a state along the Upper Tigris, in the hills where enough rain fell to make agriculture possible without irrigation. By about 750 B.C.E., Assyrian rulers considered themselves successful enough to contend for more than regional power. King Tiglath-Pilaser III adopted the title of King of the Four Quarters, or, as we would say, King of the World.

Close to home, within Upper Mesopotamia, the Assyrian kings appointed governors to run provinces, which were too small to mount successful rebellions. Beyond this core, Assyrian supremacy was looser, exercised by more varied means, adjusted according to local feeling and custom. In Babylon, for instance, the king of Assyria performed the annual rite of allegiance to the city god; in the city of Gaza, near the border

▨	Assyrian Empire at its greatest extent
▬	Babylonian Empire at its peak under Nebuchadnezzar II
▦	Phoenicia and Phoenician colonies
▦	Areas frequented or settled by Greeks
▤	Etruria
●	Greek colony
○	Phoenician colony

SLOVENIA	modern country
▨	copper
▨	gold
◆	tin
——	Greek trade route
——	Phoenician trade r[o]
- - -	ancient coastline

1,000 B.C.E.
Beginning
of Phoenician
colonization

750 B.C.E. Assyria contends
for power in Middle
East and Mediterranean

650 B.C.E. Reign
of Ashurbanipal

500 B.C.E. Greek colonies
spread; Carthage
aspires to dominate
Mediterranean

900   800   700   600

800 B.C.E. Carthage
founded by
Phoenician traders

689 B.C.E. Assyrian
King Sennacherib
destroys Babylon

605–562 B.C.E. Peak of
Babylonian Empire under
Nebuchadnezzar II

Map 5.1 The Middle East and the Mediterranean, ca. 1000–500 B.C.E.

Black Sea

Caspian Sea

Caucasus Mts

COLCHIS

P E R S I A

Anatolia

TURKEY

Nineveh
Nimrud

Tigris

Carchemish

M E S O P O T A M I A

Euphrates

Babylon

Persian Gulf

SYRIA

LEBANON

Byblos

PHOENICIA

Cyprus

Tyre

Crete

ISRAEL

Jerusalem

PALESTINE

Gaza

JUDAH

A R A B I A

Tropic of Cancer

rian Sea)

Naucratis

E G Y P T

Nile

S a h a r a

R e d   S e a

500 km
500 miles

107

between modern Israel and Egypt, he was enrolled among local divinities. Elsewhere, he destroyed temples and statues of gods to demonstrate his power and then restored them to show his generosity.

Inscriptions from the reign of King Ashurbanipal in the mid-seventh century B.C.E. best capture the character of the Assyrian state. He was probably the most self-celebrated monarch in the history of the Mesopotamian world. While never dethroning war as the Assyrians' priority, he made a cult of literacy, looting the learning of Babylon for his library at Nineveh. He was proud of the canals dug in his reign, the wine pressed, and the 120 layers of bricks in the foundations of his palace. A portrait survives of him picnicking with his wife under the dangling head of an enemy.

To celebrate a new palace and flaunt the wealth of his realm, Ashurbanipal held a banquet for 16,000 citizens, 5,000 visiting dignitaries, 1,500 palace officials, and 47,074 workmen. They consumed history's biggest meal: 10,000 jugs of beer; 10,000 skins of wine; 30,000 quarts each of figs, dates, and shelled pistachios; 1,000 each of lambs and fat oxen; 14,000 sheep; 20,000 pigeons; 10,000 eggs; 10,000 desert rats; and hundreds of deer. "For ten days I gave them food, I gave them drink, I had them bathed, I had them anointed. I honored them and sent them back to their lands in peace and joy." Like Egyptian and Chinese rulers, the Assyrian kings sought to enhance their power by claiming to communicate with forces in Nature—a doomed enterprise. When their supposed magic failed, they lost power, and competing factions arose. Some Assyrian monarchs asserted their legitimacy so vigorously as to make us doubt it. Ashurbanipal's father tried to secure the succession against rebellion with 150 lines of oaths and curses:

> May you, your women, your sons, your daughters, be bitter towards each other . . . May your waterskin break in a place of thirst and famine, so that you die of thirst.

In the background of internal conflicts was a harem of ambitious women with time to conspire in favor of their own sons. In the early eighth century B.C.E., Sammuramat was one such woman who effectively ruled the empire and accompanied her son on military campaigns. Naqia was another. She was virtual co-ruler with her husband, Sennacherib, the Assyrian monarch famed in the Bible for descending on Jerusalem "like a wolf on the fold." She did everything kings did, from dedicating inscriptions to building a palace and receiving important war dispatches.

The Babylonian Revival

As the old cities of Lower Mesopotamia declined and trade shifted upriver, the city of Babylon became the resting place of all the learning and much of the remaining wealth. To the Assyrians, Babylon was

Babylon. No king of Babylon built more grandly than Nebuchadnezzar II (r. 604–562 B.C.E.), who gave the city center a gate, shown here in reconstruction, dedicated to the goddess Ishtar. Precious lapis lazuli colored the tiles that smother the gate. Guardian bulls and dragons adorn it.
© Nik Wheeler/CORBIS

always the great prize, and it became part of their expanding empire. But Babylonians never forgot their independence and frequently tried to reclaim it. In 689 B.C.E., Sennacherib attempted a definitive solution. He massacred or dispersed the population, razed buildings to the ground, threw the debris into the river, and dug channels across the site of the city to turn it into a swamp. His son relented and set to rebuilding the city, but Ashurbanipal resumed the policy of vengeance in the next generation.

In 649 B.C.E., Ashurbanipal claimed to have deported 500,000 people to prevent anyone from stealing back to Babylon and to have sacrificed those still living. Yet the name of Babylon still retained mythic power as a rallying point for native resistance to Assyria, and a reversal of fortunes was at hand. Overextended along the Euphrates, Assyria succumbed to enemies on other fronts. In the late seventh century B.C.E., Nabopolassar—"the son of nobody," as his inscriptions admit—masterminded a Babylonian revival. He boasted that he "defeated Assyria, which, from olden days had made people of the land bear its heavy yoke."

Babylon's fame peaked during the long reign (605–562 B.C.E.) of Nebuchadnezzar II. He attacked the kingdom of Judah, destroyed King Solomon's temple at Jerusalem, and deported the Jews into exile. He fought off the Egyptians at Carchemish in Palestine. His building projects, however, made a more worthy monument. Ancient Greek guidebooks attributed two of the proverbial wonders of the world to him: the terraced "hanging" gardens of Babylon, supposedly built to please a concubine, and city walls broad enough to race four chariots abreast. Nebuchadnezzar was a master of theatrical gestures, a genius at attracting esteem. He cultivated an image of himself as the restorer of ancient glories by rebuilding ziggurats and city walls all over Mesopotamia.

Nebuchadnezzar's dynasty was Babylon's last era of greatness. In effect, Babylon and Egypt fought each other to exhaustion in their efforts to replace Assyria. From 539 B.C.E., Babylon was merely a provincial center under the rule of foreigners. Five centuries later, the Greek geographer Strabo reported that Babylon had been "turned to waste" by the blows of invaders and the indifference of rulers. "The great city has become a great desert."

Greece and Beyond

In the late second millennium B.C.E., when the Sea Peoples and other displaced communities disrupted the eastern Mediterranean and threatened Egypt (see Chapter 4), a similar upheaval took place on land. Migrants from the north swept into southern Greece, eradicating literate culture. Refugees streamed across the Aegean and Ionian Seas to Italy, Anatolia, and islands in the eastern and central Mediterranean.

The Greek Environment

By early in the first millennium B.C.E., the Mycenaean palace centers were in ruins. The only stone or rubble buildings from this period that we know of in Greece were in the city of Eretria, on the island of Euboea. Few iron tools were available for farming. Barley was the staple crop, laboriously cultivated. Most Greeks lived by goat farming and in thatched huts.

Industry and trade were ways to escape. In the tenth century B.C.E., Athens, Corinth, and a few other centers exported decorated pots and pressed olives—the only surplus farm product—for oil, which, unlike barley, was exportable and came from a crop with advantages. Harvesting olives was seasonal work and left plenty of time for seafaring. Olive trees would grow in ground that grains disdained at remarkably high altitudes. Olive oil added fat to poor diets, could be burned in lamps for lighting, and was used like soap for cleansing the body. Olive processors invested in promoting trade. Commercial enterprise soon lined the Aegean and Ionian seas with cities; then, from the mid-eighth century B.C.E. onward, spread all over the Mediterranean and the Black Sea.

The Greek poet Hesiod recorded a conversation that evokes the way Greece took to the sea. Perses, his younger brother, was lolling around their humble farm while Hesiod sweated at the plow. "How can I make money easily?" asked Perses. Hesiod recommended work on the land. But Perses was the type of person who asks for advice only because he wants to confirm his own opinion. He revealed what he really wanted: "to buy and sell in distant markets."

"Please don't be a fool," rejoined Hesiod. "Money may be all you want in life, but it is not worth the risk of drowning. . . . Be moderate, my brother. Moderation is best in everything."

All over Greece, however, men like Perses won the arguments. Greek writers included merchants and explorers among their heroes, something unthinkable, for example, in China of the time, which valued only farmers, warriors, and scholars. In the 500s B.C.E., trade was growing so rapidly that some Greek states introduced their own coinage and designed and built new, larger types of ships.

Greek Colonialism

By Hesiod's time, iron tools had improved agriculture and increased food production, which in turn led to an increase in population. But more people meant more demands on food and land. Now, not only were the Greeks a trading people, they also became colonizers.

They founded colonies on the advice of gods who spoke through oracles. At Delphi, where smoke rose from deep crevices in the earth, a priestess uttered divine pronouncements from a three-legged throne. One supplicant went to the shrine to find a remedy for childlessness and received orders to found the city of Croton in southern Italy. Others were told to colonize to escape famine. Founding colonies became so much a part of the Greek way of life that the comic playwright Aristophanes joked about founding one in the sky.

Most colonists were outcasts, exiles, and criminals—frontiersmen forging a new society. But wherever they went, they reproduced Greek ways of life. At Naucratis in the Nile delta, for example, colonists dedicated shrines to gods from their hometowns. In the sixth and fifth centuries B.C.E., offerings to Aphrodite, goddess of love, show a steady stream of Greek sex-tourists to Naucratis' brothels.

Meanwhile, growing contacts with Egypt and the Near East inspired Greek artists and thinkers at home. The sea washed new cultural influences back toward Greece. The most striking example is the creation of a writing system, loosely based on Phoenician models. Unlike so many of the earlier systems that were developed to catalog merchandise or record trade transactions, the Greek alphabet was rapidly used to record creative literature and preserve epic poems that bards recited at warriors' drinking parties. Poems attributed to Homer, for instance, were written down in their surviving versions probably toward the end of the second century B.C.E. They have been revered—and imitated—ever since in the West for the brilliance with which they evoke war and seafaring. The *Iliad* tells a story of the interplay of gods and mortals during a military expedition from Mycenae to the city of Troy in what is now

The Parthenon. The temple of the goddess Athene, dominates the acropolis of Athens, a huge, natural, flat-topped rock that rises above the city. Here, the civic life of the community centered in ancient times. Most of the surviving ruins are of buildings of the fifth century B.C.E., the product of a building program inaugurated by Pericles, who was a tireless advocate of democracy but who, in effect, used his popularity to seize power over the city and to be its ruler from about 461 to 429 B.C.E.
Copyright © Georg Gerster/Photo Researchers, Inc.

western Turkey. The *Odyssey* recounts the wanderings of one of the heroes of the same war on his way home. The *Iliad* bristles with ships' masts. The *Odyssey* is loud with waves. Greek literature rarely strayed far from the sea.

Early Greek Society

Greeks had a remarkably uniform set of ideas about themselves—"our community of blood and language and religion and ways of life." Some of their notions were mythical, and Western tradition has multiplied the myths. We have idealized the Greeks as originators of our civilization and embodiments of all our values. However, scholars have been revising almost everything that has traditionally been said about them. Their world—and the imagination of most Greeks who shared it—was run not by reason but by weird and bloody rites, goat dances, orgiastic worship, sacrifices, signs, and omens.

The Greeks formed two kinds of community, which they called *ethne* and *poleis*—'tribes' and 'cities'. *Demokrateia* meant a state where supreme power belonged to an assembly of all citizens. But most Greeks disapproved of such an arrangement. Women were excluded. So were slaves, who made up 40 percent of the population in fifth-century B.C.E. Athens. In some Greek states, citizens used bits of broken pottery as ballots on which to scrawl their votes to exile unpopular leaders. When we look at them now, we see fragments of an oppressive system that made slaves of captives, victims of women, battle fodder of men, and scapegoats of failures.

Families were the basis of society in Greek communities. When Aristotle speculated in the fourth century B.C.E about the origins of the state, he assumed that it arose from the voluntary alliance of families.

In Athens, some of the earliest group burials known to archaeologists are in family plots. Typically, girls were married at age fourteen or fifteen to men twice their age. So men dominated. "The Greeks," said a writer of the fourth century B.C.E., "expect their daughters to keep quiet and do wool-work." Myth eliminated women from Athenian origins: the founders of the community supposedly sprang from the soil. Wives and daughters did not normally inherit property. They rarely appeared in public, except as extravagant mourners or as priestesses in religious cults. In art of the first half of the millennium, men are shown more and more in the company only of other men, women only with other women. Women's function was to serve the community by bearing and raising children and thereby increasing manpower for production and war. In the city-state of Sparta—which Greeks always regarded as "utterly different" from other Greek states—all women had to train for motherhood, and women who died in childbirth were commemorated in the same way as heroic warriors killed in battle.

Scholars used to infer Greek values and morality from philosophical writings, but now we also look to popular plays and satires and find that the average Greek's social attitudes were different from the philosophers'. Athenian elites, for instance, tended to idealize homosexual relationships between older men and adolescents, but the playwrights' audiences despised them.

One of the discredited notions is of Greek "purity"—the idea that the Greeks were a self-made civilization, owing almost nothing to other cultures. This was one of their myths of themselves: a way of differentiating themselves from foreigners. Indeed, the Greeks went beyond mere imitation when they received influences, whether from abroad or from an antiquity that they saw as their own. But they were heavily indebted to what they called Asia, which to them included Egypt; and especially, to Lydia, Lycia, Phrygia in Anatolia; and to the Ionian islands in the Aegean. Greece was open to the eastern Mediterranean, and influences from around the sea's rim fashioned Greek culture.

The Spread of State-Building and City-Building

Phoenician and Greek colonization and trade made the Mediterranean a highway of cultural exchange. Around and across its peninsulas lay a crust of peoples who could build up a large surplus of resources, strong states, monumental cities, literate culture, and vibrant art. Most of them tend to get left out of books on global history because they are little known or underrated. But they help us to see the Phoenicians and Greeks in context and understand what made the Mediterranean a potential forge of empires and fount of influence for the future. A tour is in order.

The Thracians The lands of the Thracians lay along the Aegean Sea, north and east of Greece. Their written works have perished, and surviving inscriptions are indecipherable. But archaeology gives us inklings of their culture.

Because Thrace was close to the trading centers of the eastern Mediterranean, its chiefs made an early start accumulating wealth and state-building. They practiced rites of fire, commemorated in spiraling incisions that swirled on their hearths. A fine example imitates a shimmering sun. A horseback hero dominated their art. In surviving examples, he hunts with hounds, wrestles a three-headed monster, leads a bear in triumph, and does battle among severed heads.

Around 500 B.C.E., energetic rulers unified the Thracian city-states into a kingdom and sought to expand their domain. These were flesh-and-blood figures whom we know from Greek sources, not mythic heroes. In 429, the Thracian King Sitalkes invaded Macedonia in northern Greece with an army said to number 150,000. There he built a palace-city of 12.5 acres, mostly of mud bricks and painted stucco. His failure to build a permanent empire marks a new period, when Thracian states squirmed to survive alongside mightier neighbors.

The Illyrians and Garamantes To the Thracians' west, along the coast of the Adriatic Sea around 500 B.C.E., lay Illyria, whose rulers and elites were buried with hoards of gold and silver and sacrifices of oxen and wild boar. An urn found in present-day Slovenia depicts the luxurious life of an Illyrian court: Warriors parade. Hawkers and deer hunters stalk. Dignitaries display their authority with double-headed scepters or play on pipes. Voluptuous, long-haired women feed them.

Across the Mediterranean in North Africa, in the ferociously hot and dry region of Libya called the Fezzan, lived the Garamantes. They dug nearly 1,000 miles of irrigation tunnels under the Sahara, carving out the limestone that lies between the water table and the sand. On all sides, desert surrounded their cities, of which, according to Roman reports, there were fourteen. The Garamantes grew wheat where they could and barley elsewhere. No records of their own survive, but early Greek descriptions call them a slave-trading elite, driving four-horse chariots. Romans depicted their tattooed and ritually scarred faces under ostrich-plume helmets.

The Etruscans On the north shore of the Mediterranean, stretching across central Italy, was Etruria, the land of the Etruscans. Their "loamy, fat and stoneless" soil had to be plowed nine times to make a furrow, so they needed iron mines and powerful smelting technology. Much of the region, however, lay under malarial marshes that the Etruscans drained.

Their language, which their neighbors could not understand, became a soothsayers' tongue in Roman times and was then forgotten. We cannot decipher their inscriptions.

We can, however, glimpse Etruscan culture through their arts. Theater was their specialty. They gave the Romans their word for actor: *hister*. After acting, soothsaying was the skill they esteemed most, reading omens from sheep's livers and the flight of birds. These were borrowed techniques. Like the Phoenicians (and perhaps thanks to trade with them), Etruscan culture drew from all over the Mediterranean.

Etruscan cities were the earliest in Italy. The biggest, Caere, could have accommodated 20,000 inhabitants. The layout of their tombs imitated their houses, as if to prepare for an afterlife. At Caere, a warrior lies alongside two chariots, with shields and arrows nailed to the walls. It is tempting to identify him as a king of Caere whom Roman sources reviled for having "mocked the gods" with cruelty to his captives. But the tomb was not made for him. Its best chamber houses a heavily bejeweled woman. Strewn around her, objects of gold, silver, and ivory are marked with her name: Larthia.

Among the Etruscans, women had freedom Greeks and Romans of the time mistook for immodesty. They could go out of their homes, attend games, and dine with men. In Greek art, the only women who did such things were prostitutes, but Etruscan wives routinely dined with their husbands. In one tomb, a married couple was buried under a portrait showing them reclining as companions. With easy affection, he draws her close, as she offers him a garland of flowers. Because mirrors and combs often display inscriptions, we can assume upper-class Etruscan women were literate.

Spain In the mid-millennium, Greeks said, "The god of riches dwells in Spain." Treasures of Spain survive. From western Spain comes a belt decorated with a hero in combat with a lion and a huge funeral monument depicting a banquet of monsters—one with two heads, one with a forked tongue—feeding on wild boar. In another scene, a hero challenges a fire-breathing monster. The region evidently had an elite with the resources needed to build on a large scale and the power to inspire heroic and terrible images of authority.

From eastern Spain comes an imposing female sculpture—startling in its realism—called the Lady of Elche. Originally, she was probably enthroned in a tomb. A hollow space in her back may have held an offering to the gods or the ashes or bones of a human fellow occupant. Her luxurious dress, elaborate hairstyle, grand headdress, and enormous jewels—which bulge like Hollywood costume pieces—leave no doubt of her social status or the wealth of the society that produced her.

From the Mediterranean to the Atlantic From deep inside the steamship age, it is hard to imagine how inhibiting was the strength of the eight-knot current—the "rapacious wave," a Greek poet called it—that stoppered the Atlantic entrance to the Mediterranean. Here, according to myth, the divine hero Hercules erected his pillars as a warning against the monster-haunted "sea of darkness" beyond. But Greek and Phoenician traders braved them. Tartessos, their first destination, was the Eldorado of its day. At its heart lay the iron pyrites belt—an area in southern Portugal and Spain, rich in iron, copper, silver, gold. The banks of the Rio Tinto are blotched with the flow of copper-bearing ores. Miners dug deep underground galleries, drained with siphons.

Greek tales help us reconstruct Tartessos's history. Early stories are of a shepherd king, Geryon, followed by Theron, a conqueror so powerful it took the strength of Hercules to halt him. Then, in the mid-first millennium B.C.E., King Arganthonios was said to have subsidized the city walls that protected the marketplace of Phocaea at the other end of the Mediterranean. For a transition of this kind, from pastoralism to plutocracy, trading partners were essential. But Tartessos belongs to a long tradition of civilization-building in Spain, dimly detectable in even earlier treasure hordes. Native cultures, given the resources, were capable of spontaneous economic growth.

Empires and Recovery in China and South Asia

Summaries nearly always distort. But it is probably fair to say that the story of this chapter so far is one of formerly marginal regions becoming—at least for a while—rich and powerful like Phoenicia and Greece, Assyria and Babylon, and parts of the western and central Mediterranean, as if to replace the old centers of power and wealth in Lower Mesopotamia, Hatti, and Crete. This suggests problems to bear in mind when confronting what happened in China and South Asia in the same period: Were the traditions of the Shang and Zhou in China and of Harappa in India passed on to successors in new places? Or was the continuity of history ruptured, and a new beginning made in new locations? (See Map 5.2.)

The Zhou Decline

When the Zhou conquered the Shang, they explained their victory as a mandate from heaven—they were divinely chosen to rule the world because they were more virtuous than the Shang (see Chapter 4). This was all well and good, but as Zhou supremacy spread, the realm became increasingly decentralized. Moreover, the impossibility of using magic to manage the state undermined royal authority. Zhou rituals to appease the gods became ever more elaborate: The vessels got bigger, the ceremonies more elaborate, the hymns of praise to Zhou ancestors more extravagant. "Heaven's mandate is unending," intoned the court poets

Map 5.2 China and South Asia, ca. 750 B.C.E.

and congregations, with evident unease. A poet in the provinces disagreed: "Drought has become so severe, . . . glowing, burning. . . . The great mandate is about to end."

King Li (LEE) ascended the throne in 857 B.C.E. Chroniclers portrayed him as a failure—self-indulgent and heedless of advice. After all, if he had been virtuous, he would not have lost the mandate of heaven. A bronze inscription preserves Li's own version: "Although I am but a young boy, I have no leisure day or night," sacrificing to ancestors, elevating "eminent warriors" and well-recommended sages. But there was more urgent business than these ceremonial acts. In 842 B.C.E., rebels drove him from his capital, eventually installing the young heir, Xuan (shoo-ehn). For a reign of forty-six years, Xuan held off the main external threat, the western barbarians, while trying to confront natural disasters with magic.

When Xuan died in 782 B.C.E.—reputedly murdered by the ghost of a subordinate he had unjustly executed—an earthquake hit. "The hundred rivers bubble and jump, the mountains and mounds crumble and fall." Following tradition, the poet blamed the disaster on the government's shortcomings. But the problems went much deeper. As wealth from Zhou trickled outward from trade, outlying states grew more powerful and insubordinate. In 771 B.C.E., people whom the Zhou called "Dog barbarians" drove them from their ancestral lands forever.

The Zhou moved east, to a region much changed since its glorious era under the Shang. Zhou garrisons had colonized it and divided it among 148 *fiefs* that Zhou relatives or nominees ruled. Consolidation and reconfiguration gradually reduced the number, and by the sixth century B.C.E., the former empire had been transformed into jostling states. Leadership among them was usually determined by war—and, within states, by assassination and massacre. In 541 B.C.E., at one of the periodic summits of rulers, Zhao Yang (jaow yahng), the leading minister of the largest state north of the Yellow River, summed up what Chinese historians came to call the "Warring States Period":

> *Ever since the time when there has not been a true king, rulers of states have competed to preside at the inter-state conferences, which therefore rotate among the rulers. Is there a constant leader? . . . Which presiding state can pass judgment?*

The kind of instability that Yang described seems bound to inhibit cultural and economic development and unleash violence. Yet the consequences were, in some respects, the opposite. As we will see in the next chapter, the vibrant era of thinking and learning from the sixth century B.C.E. onward mainly coincided with the failures or absence of imperial initiatives. Politically, fragmentation encouraged intellectual creativity. Indeed, well before the turn of the mid-millennium, this fact was evident in the new initiatives and new thinking in South Asia.

South Asia: Relocated Centers of Culture

After the erosion and disappearance of the Harappan cities, Indian history differed in an important respect from other regions of large-scale state-building and city-building. In Europe, Mesopotamia, Phoenicia, and China, as we have seen, people tried to cope with the instabilities of the late second millennium in various ways. All depended on the survival or revival of previous traditions or on stimulation by outside influences. But India provides clear proof that such conditions were not necessary.

Historical orthodoxy has long insisted that something of the Harappan past—some migrants, some aspects of culture—must have survived. Indian civilization seems to deserve a pedigree as old as the Indus cities, and those cities, in turn, deserve to have left lasting traditions. But written and archaeological sources are few, and we have no evidence of real continuities or unmistakable transmissions of culture across the dark, undocumented centuries of Indian history. When civilization did reemerge in South Asia in the first millennium B.C.E., it was in two areas. One was the Ganges valley and the other was the island of Sri Lanka, which was once known as Ceylon.

The Ganges Valley

After a lapse of centuries, iron axes cleared the way for farming in the Ganges valley, a different environment from the hot, dry floodplains of the Indus valley. It was a region of abundant rain and rich forests. We have no knowledge that the Ganges received colonists from Harappa at the time. The only artifacts from the region during this period are fine copperware, which no one has found in the art of the Indus people, although some decorative designs may be similar.

Later Indian cultural history does not exhibit strong evidence that Harappan culture was transplanted to the Ganges either. Only pottery fragments exist, with glazes similar to Harappan wares. Moreover, the first urban sites and fortifications in the Ganges valley have none of the tell-tale signs of Harappan order: no seals, no weights and measures, no uniform bricks. This makes it hard to believe that the Ganges civilization could be the Harappan civilization transplanted. On the contrary, the lack of material evidence makes early Indian civilization seem even more distant from the Harappan than Greek civilization was from the Cretan and Mycenaean. In only one respect does the world of the Ganges clearly resemble that of Harappa—we know all but nothing about its political and social life.

The literature of its sages, however, survives in abundance. It is impossible to find evidence for traditional claims that the earliest texts originate from orally transmitted traditions from deep in the previous millennium. But surviving versions could have begun to be written down early in the first millennium B.C.E. The theoretical sections of these texts, the **Upanishads** (oo-PAH-nee-shahdz), show the recollection of a time when teaching passed from one generation to another by word of mouth. The very name "Upanishad" means something like "the seat close to the master."

One of the earliest Upanishads tells how the powers of nature rebelled against nature itself—how the lesser gods challenged the supreme god **Brahman** and failed. "But the fire could not burn straw without Brahman. The wind could not blow the straw away without Brahman." On its own, the story might suggest no more than divine omnipotence, similar to the doctrines Jews, Christians, and Muslims hold. But in the context of the other Upanishads, it seems part of a more general, mystical belief in the oneness of the universe, infinite and eternal. Such a "theory of everything" does not appear in the thought of earlier civilizations.

Sages of the time proclaimed two, more stunning, new ideas. The first was that matter is an illusion. The world is Brahman's dream; the creation of the world was like falling asleep. Sense organs can tell us nothing that is true. Speech is illusory since it relies on lips and tongues. Thought is illusory, since it happens in—or at least passes through—the body. Most feelings are illusory because our nerves and guts register them. We can glimpse truth only in purely spiritual visions or certain kinds of feeling, like selfless love and unspecific sadness, which do not arise from particular physical stimuli. Second, the Upanishads describe a cycle of reincarnation or rebirth. Through a series of lives virtuously lived, the soul can advance toward perfection, at which time its identity is submerged in the divine "soul of the world" known as Brahman.

These profound ideas are so startling and innovative that we want to know how they occurred. And who were the patrons and pupils of the sages who uttered them? Why did society value such sublimely unworldly—such apparently useless—speculations? We have no evidence on which to base answers to these questions. But these ideas are glimmerings of a new era of unprecedented and intense intellectual activity. Ideas from this period—from about the sixth century B.C.E. to about the first century C.E.—are antiquity's most influential legacy to us and are the subject of our next chapter. They still inform the questions that confront our religions and philosophies and still mold the way we think about them.

Building Anew in Sri Lanka

South Asia's other nursery of large-scale cities and states was in Sri Lanka, off the southern tip of India, in the Indian Ocean. Here, the *Mahavamsa*, chronicles of the long-lived "Lion Kingdom," are deceptive documents. In surviving versions, they were written down in what Westerners think of as the sixth century C.E. to serve a partisan political purpose: to justify the ruling *Sinhalese* people, sanctify their ground, and legitimize their conquests. Their account of the early history of the kingdom features a prince born of a lion who battles with amorous female demons. The founders of the realm are characters in a familiar moral fable of the sea: storm-driven exiles, redeemed from sins that are bemoaned but never described. The chronicles begin the history of the kingdom with a credible event: colonization by seafarers from the Indian Ocean Gulf of Cambay, on the edge of the Harappan culture area. But the *Sinhalese* had no known connection with the Harappans. They became large-scale builders and irrigators but produced nothing to rival the logic, creative literature, mathematics, and speculative science written down along the Ganges about 2,500 years ago.

The heartland of the early kingdom was in the relatively dry northern plateau, where annual rainfall is heavy—about sixty inches a year—but painfully long dry spells are common. In summer, droughts crack the earth, shrivel the scrub, and scatter dust everywhere. Nowadays in the dry zone, rice cultivation relies on village reservoir tanks dug out of seasonal streams, dammed with earth. There is not always enough water for annual crops of rice. Even if we allow for changes in the climate, the *Sinhalese* colonists could not have built great cities without considerable feats of hydraulic ingenuity. At Maduru Oya, for instance, watertight valves dammed the flow of water from artificial lakes six miles long. Even before the adoption of Buddhism, which tradition dates to the third century B.C.E., Anuradhapura (an-uh-rad-PO-ra) was a large and splendid capital, with the largest artificial reservoir in the world.

The new initiatives in the Ganges valley and in Sri Lanka exhibit so little connection to earlier civilizations or to others of this era that we have to acknowledge that civilizations can arise without the help either of recovered traditions or stimulation from outside influences. Yet the question remains, Why didn't what happened in India occur in most of the rest of the world? If people in the Ganges valley and Sri Lanka could build states and cities without traditions from the past or influences from outside, why did something similar not occur in the Americas and most of Africa? Why were these vast regions relatively dormant for so long, despite the promising starts described in earlier chapters?

The Frustrations of Isolation

In discussing developments in the Americas and Africa, we have to allow for a trick of the evidence. The cultures of Eurasia churned out huge amounts of documents and literature, much of which we can read today. This alone accounts for their dominant place in historical tradition, compared with cultures that employed other, less accessible ways to record events and ideas. In the West, prejudice also favors Eurasian cultures over others. That is, we pay more attention to history that seems to anticipate the way we live now. Sometimes we read into that history the origins of our own societies. Conversely, we overlook or fail to recognize history that appears too different from our own.

Compared to Eurasia, the geography of the Americas and sub-Saharan Africa discourages communication and cultural exchange. Much of Africa and Central and South America lies in the tropics, where dense rain forests make it difficult and unhealthy for outsiders attempting to cross them. Africa has relatively few rivers, and for the most part, they do not allow long-range navigation. In Eurasia, cultural exchange was rapid. It happened across zones of similar climate, with no need for either the people or the food plants and livestock they brought with them to adapt. Cultural transmission in Africa and the Americas, on the other hand, had to cross vast chasms of climate from north to south and south to north, calling for different survival strategies along the way.

Monsoonal wind systems in much of maritime Asia and relatively stable weather in the Mediterranean favor navigation. By contrast, lee shores and hostile winds enclose and hem in much of sub-Saharan Africa. Except in the Caribbean, the Americas have none of the narrow seas with which parts of Europe and Asia are relatively well endowed that encourage communication. Even the civilizations of the Ganges and Sri Lanka, though they originated independently, could take advantage of the communications systems of maritime Asia and trans-Eurasian trade routes early in their histories, linking up with China and southwest Asia by land and sea.

Developments in North America

In any case, there were plenty of developments in the world beyond Eurasia between 1000 and 500 B.C.E., but they tend to get left out of the global story, overshadowed by more spectacular changes in Eurasia. In the American far north, for instance, the Dorset culture transformed life. People there began to build semisubterranean longhouses and stone alleys for driving caribou into lakes. Their art realistically depicted all the species that shared their environment.

The critical new technology was the blubber-fueled soapstone lamp, which enabled the Dorset people to colonize deserts of ice. Now hunters could go far from home in the Arctic darkness, tracking the musk ox to graveyards on the shore of the Arctic, devouring its entrails, boiled and dressed with seal oil. They could pursue the caribou to remote salt licks: The caribou cannot be hunted at the hunters' pleasure; they have to wait until the beginning of winter, when its hair is thick enough to make the warmest clothing. No longer limited to the forest, the users of oil lamps could hunt on the ice, where abundant fat game waited without competitors and where the climate preserved carcasses. People of the Dorset culture speared seals and harpooned walruses from kayaks on the open sea. Now that their prey was too fat to be felled by arrows, they abandoned the bow for the barbed harpoon. Ingenious notched blades stayed in the victim's flesh, until the animal was so tired that it could be hauled in, butchered, and sped home on hand-drawn sleds with runners of walrus ivory.

Equally dramatic new ways of life developed in the same period—between the late-second and mid-first millennia B.C.E.—on the lower Mississippi River and the coast of the Gulf of Mexico. The culture—inappropriately called Poverty Point after the location of its biggest site in Louisiana—worked in copper and manufactured fine tools and jewelry of colorful stones. Trade goods arrived along the Mississippi, Red, and Tennessee rivers. More than one hundred sites, grouped around ten major centers, appear to be forager settlements comparable to settlements in the Middle East (see Chapter 2). The biggest covers a square mile and is divided by a series of semicircular earthen ridges. Alongside is a mound almost seventy feet high, which appears oriented to the spring and autumn equinox. The mound is a ceremonial center utterly unlike anything seen earlier in Mesoamerica and therefore likely to have grown up independently.

Meanwhile, burial mounds in the Ohio River valley provide evidence of new social patterns and perhaps chiefdoms. Here, settled foragers planted grains and sunflowers to supplement the food they gathered and hunted, painted their dead in lively colors, and buried them with ornaments of copper and shell.

In the same period, contact with Mesoamerica brought about changes in parts of the North American Southwest. In the San Juan and Tucson basins in Arizona, people developed a new variety of maize that matured in 120 days. They could now cultivate maize in drier areas where squash also grew. From around 500 B.C.E., the number of sites with traces of beans greatly increased. Farmers in the region were working their way toward the same complete system of nutrition—maize, squash, beans—that the Olmecs had developed in Mexico (see Chapter 4).

New Initiatives in Africa

As in North America, change in Africa between 1000 and 500 B.C.E. was slow and localized compared to the most dynamic parts of Eurasia. Nonetheless, events set a direction for the future. Four developments in particular are worth mentioning (see Map 5.3). First, around 750 B.C.E., Egypt weakened, and a Nubian state reemerged on the Upper Nile (see Chapter 4), with its chief cities at Napata and Meroe. Ever since Egypt had first colonized Nubia, Egyptian culture had heavily influenced it. Late in the millennium, however, the language of the Nubian royal court

■   hard-iron technology, ca. 500 B.C.E

➤   expansion of Bantu languages

—   trade route

⌀   aromatics

Map 5.3 Africa, ca. 1000–500 B.C.E.

changed from Egyptian to an indigenous Nubian tongue. Scholars today have difficulty reading the distinctive script in which this language was written. This change shows that Nubia was becoming less Egyptian and more Sudanic, or, as some scholars like to say, more African.

Second, Africans developed hard-iron technology. This was almost certainly an independent discovery. African smiths had smelted soft iron and copper for centuries. The first iron foundries emerged along the Niger River in West Africa around 500 B.C.E., and again, perhaps independently, in Central Africa's Great Lakes region soon after. Natural drafts fanned the furnaces that melted the iron ore through long clay tubes. The people who made the tubes also left clay heads—wide-eyed, open-mouthed, partly shaved, with decoratively scarred foreheads. The use of fired clay suggests how Africans may have made the breakthrough in iron forging. These were people who knew the seemingly magical uses of fire—how fire turns hard what is soft and helps make art out of mud. Forging iron was a further stage in the process of exploring the potential of fire.

Third, Bantu languages continued their slow spread south (see Chapter 1), reaching the Great Lakes of Central Africa by about 1000 B.C.E. In this region, farmers could grow grains as well as yams, a major improvement in nutrition. Surplus production of food made trade with Nubia possible. Trade was part of a broader shift to new ways of life. At about this time, too, round dwellings with conical roofs replaced rectangular ones with ridged roofs. By the end of the first millennium B.C.E., thanks, perhaps, to improved tools made of iron, Bantu farmers reached what are now Kenya in East Africa and South Africa.

Finally, the growth of trade was pregnant with consequences for the future. The slaving activities of the Garamantes from what is today Libya

Heads Sculpted from coarse-grained clay, in what is now central Nigeria, in the second half of the first millennium B.C.E., are not just fine works of art—as this example of the first century B.C.E. shows. They are also evidence of the technical accomplishments of the craftsmen who made clay tubing for the forges in which iron tools were made.
Nigeria, Nok head, 900 BC–200 AD, Rafin Kura, Nok. Prehistoric West African sculpture from the Nok culture. Terracotta, 36 cms high. © Werner Forman/Art Resource, NY

REGION	MEANS OF CULTURAL, ECONOMIC, POLITICAL DEVELOPMENT	DISTINCTIVE ACHIEVEMENTS
Greece	Seaborne trade; colonization of Mediterranean basin; extensive cultural exchange	New forms of government *(demokrateia)* and communities *(poleis, ethne)*; colonial autonomy; highly developed written literature
Zhou Dynasty/ Warring States Period (China)	Centralized rule; elaborate court rituals; ancestor worship; trade and taxation; constant threat from barbarians	Political instability fosters intellectual endeavors
Ganges Valley	Highly developed spiritual literature (Vedas, Upanishads); agriculture with iron tools; little understanding of political, economic policies	First philosophies focused on doctrine of reincarnation, *maya* (matter as illusion), large-scale urban settlements, fortifications
Sri Lanka	Sophisticated water-management systems combined with urbanization	Large-scale cities, early adoption of Buddhism from neighboring India
North America	In the far north: decentralized communities, simple technologies, group hunting techniques; South/Midwest: widespread trade networks connecting to Mesoamerica, settlements	Northern regions: long-term adaptation to hostile environments, gradual depletion of wildlife; South/Midwest: forager settlements, mound building, mixed agriculture/ hunting–gathering culture
Sub-Saharan Africa/ Southwest Arabia	Widespread trade, cultural exchange with hard-iron technology accelerating tool and weapon making, spread of Bantu language	Growth of Nubian state south of Egypt; sophisticated art, industry in Niger region; building and farming techniques spread with Bantu speakers; trade and state-building in southwest Arabia (Saba)

suggest that one of the major routes to tropical Africa was already developing across the Sahara from the Mediterranean. The other great potential link was across the Indian Ocean from Asia to the Horn of Africa in what is today Somalia and Ethiopia. This link was at least as important for the history of civilization in East Africa as the link to the Mediterranean was to Europe. We do not know when this route opened, but developments in southern Arabia provide clues about how it may have begun. Southern and southeast Arabia have fertile valleys, where seasonal streams flow from the mountains before they soak into the desert and evaporate into the air. Here, the areas that are now Oman and Bahrain forged copper goods, and Yemen produced frankincense and myrrh, aromatic resins from trees that are used in perfumes and, as biblical accounts show, were in demand for religious rituals. Some of these goods reached Mesopotamia and Harappan cities. But when those civilizations collapsed in the second millennium B.C.E., so did most economic development in this region.

Only Saba, a state in the southwest corner of Arabia, closest to Africa, continued to grow. This was where the Queen of Sheba supposedly came from to King Solomon in Jerusalem in the tenth century B.C.E., if we can trust traditional biblical chronology. Numerous inscriptions survive from soon after that time. A temple outside Marib, the Sabaeans' chief city, bears bronze plaques commemorating victories—grisly scenes of warriors in triumph, brandishing the severed hands of their victims. This same temple houses bronze sculptures—tribute from

CHRONOLOGY	
1000–500 B.C.E.	Traditions and states of the late second millennium recover; Dorset culture in American far north thrives; peoples of lower Mississippi and Gulf of Mexico develop new ways of life
1000 B.C.E.	Civilization reemerges in Ganges valley; Bantu languages continue slow spread southward
800 B.C.E.	Phoenicians colonize the Mediterranean
771 B.C.E.	Zhou driven eastward from their ancestral lands
750–500 B.C.E.	Rapid expansion of Greek trading and colonization
750 B.C.E.	Egypt declines and Nubian state reemerges
605–562 B.C.E.	Peak of Babylonian empire
500 B.C.E.	Carthage seeks control of Mediterranean trade until defeated by Romans in 146 B.C.E.; West Africans develop and spread hard-iron technology southward
100s B.C.E.	Bantu languages reach present-day South Africa

(All dates are approximate)

kings and landowners, some, evidently, personal likenesses. Piecing together the inscriptions, we see how the Sabaean state expanded at its neighbors' expense. Understanding what happened in Saba is the best way to study one of the most intriguing problems in the next part of this book—the growth of great states, great buildings, and great ambitions in East Africa.

IN PERSPECTIVE
The Framework of Recovery

The climacteric of the late second millennium B.C.E. damaged and changed the frameworks of civilization but, in most cases, did not break them. Recovery was possible because traditions survived—or could be revived—or because there were stimulating outside influences. In Greece and India, people forgot the art of writing, and they had to reinvent it from scratch after hundreds of years. Recovery sometimes happened in new places and among new peoples. After the extinction of the Harappan world, civilization gradually emerged in India, far from the Indus. In Sri Lanka, monumental irrigation works and buildings arose. In Mesopotamia and China, the centers of activity and initiative were relocated, but, again, the continuities of tradition, which are the foundations of progress, were never entirely lost. Traditions spread through neighboring regions. Greek civilization crystallized on the edges of the Greek world, in islands and small colonies around the Ionian and Aegean seas. Fertilized by Phoenicia and Greece, a ring of ambitious cities and states formed around the Mediterranean and Black seas.

Gradually, fitfully, and despite reversals, people continued to make ambitious attempts to modify the environment, transforming new areas. In some parts of Eurasia, the pace of state-building and economic expansion not only resumed, but quickened. The imperial experiments between 1000 and 500 B.C.E. failed to take hold, but efforts to expand borders and dominate other states became a typical feature of regions where change was accelerating. Political instability among competing states may seem unfavorable, but it stimulated technological change: hotter furnaces, more iron. It also, perhaps, multiplies the opportunities of patronage for artists and intellectuals. An "age of sages" was detectable in India and would soon be apparent in other parts of Eurasia.

In the Mediterranean and what we think of as the Middle East, between 1000 and 500 B.C.E., state-building and growing trade led to imperial ambitions that eventually failed. Elsewhere, imperial projects ran out of steam or into trouble—as in China—or simply did not happen.

Was this because the contenders were too well matched? Or was it because the economic environment was too undeveloped or the ecological environment too fragile? Or was it because no conqueror had found an enduring formula or a means to solidify states that were prone to failure? Whatever the problems that frustrated imperial ambitions in the first half of the millennium, states soon found ways to overcome them. The second half of the millennium was remarkable not only as an age of sages in Eurasia, but also as an age of robust empires. A zone of connected, communicating cultures began to take shape across Eurasia and the Mediterranean, from the Pacific to the Atlantic. They nourished each other. Faint links were beginning to put parts of this central zone in touch with northern Europe and parts of Africa. In the rest of the world, isolated cultures, still organized in kinship groups or chiefdoms or small states, were able, at best, to develop regional networks on a relatively small scale.

As a result, the focus of the next part of this book is on Eurasia and, in particular, the regions where sages founded well-rooted intellectual traditions that have continued, ever since, to shape the way we think: in China, India, southwest Asia, and Greece. These were homelands of huge ambitions to understand the world, change it, or—in some cases—conquer it. Their stories occupy the next chapters.

PROBLEMS AND PARALLELS

1. Why was the ruler of a city-state like Byblos able to stand up to a giant nation-state like Egypt?
2. Why were trade and colonization so important to the Phoenicians and the Greeks?
3. What roles did war, conquest, and terror play in the Assyrian Empire? Why was the city of Babylon so important to the peoples and rulers of the Middle East?
4. How did Greek culture spread around the Mediterranean world? How did the interplay of cultures in the Mediterranean and Indian Ocean basins affect the development of civilization in those areas?
5. How did the isolation of cultures in the Americas affect the development of civilization there?
6. What important cultural and technological developments occurred in Africa between 1000 and 500 B.C.E.?

The Great Schools

focus questions

1. What do historians mean by the term *axial age*?
2. Where were the main centers of axial age thinking in Eurasia?
3. Why are the religious, political, and scientific ideas of the axial age so important?
4. What similarities developed among Indian, Greek, and Chinese science and medicine during the axial age?
5. How did political optimists differ from pessimists in their thinking about human nature and the role of government?
6. Why was the axial age confined to such a limited area of the world?

Just over halfway through the first millennium B.C.E., a frustrated police administrator set out from the small Chinese state of Lu, south of the Yellow River, in search of a worthy master. Conflicting traditions claim him as the descendant of kings and the child of a humble home. By what is said to be his own account, he was a studious child, who worked his way through his education learning menial jobs, including grain-counting and book-keeping. He could never get ahead in the bureaucracy of Lu, perhaps because he was openly disgusted with the immorality of its politics. A book later published under his name recounts the history of his times, listing the violence and injustice of the kings and aristocrats, in deadpan fashion, heightening the reader's revulsion.

Far as the exile wandered, he never found the ideal ruler he sought. Instead, he lived by attracting pupils and left a body of thought that still influences ideas on the conduct of politics and the duties and opportunities of daily life. For him—and for most other thinkers in an era disfigured by the disintegration of China—loyalty was the key virtue: loyalty to God, to the state, to one's family, and to the true meanings of the words one uses. Most of the world knows him today by a name that is a corruption of his honorific title: "Master Kong"—Kong Fuzi (koong foo-tzeh) in Chinese, "Confucius" in the West.

The importance of Confucius is a reminder of how much the world of our own day owes to the world of his—how thinkers of the time anticipated and influenced the way we think now. Heroic teachers gathered disciples and handed down traditions. Typically, followers treated the founders with awestruck reverence, recast them as supermen or even gods, and clouded our knowledge of them with legends and lore. We can unpick enough evidence, however, to get tentative pictures of some and impressions of what they taught.

Between them, these sages came up with ideas so influential that they justify a term that has become popular with scholars: the **axial age**. Different writers assign different meanings to this term. In this book, it designates the 500 years or so leading roughly up to the beginning of the Christian era. The image of an axis suits the period, for three reasons. First, as a glance at the map shows, the areas in which the thought of the sages and their schools unfolded stretched, axislike, across Eurasia, in regions that more or less bordered on and influenced each other (see Map 6.1). Second, the thought of the period has remained central to, and supporting of, so much later thought. The religious leaders of the time founded traditions of such power that they have huge followings. The secular thinkers spun out grooves of logic and science in which people still think. They raised problems of human nature—and of how to devise appropriate social and political solutions—that still preoccupy us. And because disciples wrote down much of their teaching, a body of texts has survived to become reference points for later study.

THE GREAT SCHOOLS

132

territory ruled by David and Solomon, ca. 1000–900 B.C.E.   Kingdom of Judah, 9th–8th c. B.C.E.

Kingdom of Israel, 9th–8th c. B.C.E.

Map 6.1 Ancient Israel

No one should try to study this material expecting it to be easy. Part of the fun, part of the excitement, is engaging with minds active long ago, but still—with a bit of effort—intelligible to us today. We could dodge the difficulties by talking about the personalities instead of the problems of the axial age. But this chapter is designed to concentrate on what the axial age sages thought and why they thought it—not on their own lives and characters. So, after first outlining who the sages were and where they operated, we shall turn to the common content of their minds: the religious, political, and scientific ideas that characterized the age and made it "axial"—the shared features, which for students of global history, are the most interesting.

Finally, the big problem arises: Why was there an axial age at all? Why did so much thinking—so much enduring thinking, so much thinking that has shaped the world ever since—happen in such a relatively concentrated period? We will explore this question toward the end of the chapter by investigating the networks to which the sages and their disciples belonged. The next chapter describes the political and economic context that surrounded, nourished, and transmitted axial age ideas.

The Thinkers of the Axial Age

As we saw in the last chapter, the work of thinkers of great depth and complexity was recorded earlier in India. Gradually, however, as disciples began to confide sages' secrets to writing, evidence emerged that issues similar to those already familiar, in Indian sources, were also attracting attention in other parts of Asia.

In what we now call Iran, the sage usually known as Zoroaster is insecurely dated to the late seventh and early sixth centuries B.C.E. Texts ascribed to him are so partial, corrupt, and obscure that we cannot confidently reconstruct them. As practiced by his followers, however, and twisted by tradition, **Zoroastrianism** assumed that conflicting forces of good and evil shaped the world. The single good deity, **Ahura Mazda**, was present in fire and light; the rites of his worshippers were connected with dawn and fire-kindling, while night and darkness were the province of **Ahriman**, the god of evil. By influence or coincidence, similar ideas, which dominated mainstream thinking in Iran for 1,000 years, have appeared in other Eurasian religions (see the discussion of Manichaenism in Chapter 9). Zoroastrian communities are still scattered around the world, but Zoroaster had no comparable successor in his homeland.

In India, meanwhile, around the middle of the millennium, texts of the Veda multiplied. In particular, teachings about Brahman, handed down in the early Upanishads and described in Chapter 5, were studied and written down. Alongside this *defining*—as we might call it—of Brahmanism in written texts, new thinking explored the moral implications of religious life, in a world of competing states comparable to that of China during its Warring States period. Vardhamana Jnatrputra, for instance, whose life is traditionally assigned to the sixth or early fifth century B.C.E., is universally known as "Mahavira" —"the great hero." He founded **Jainism**, a way of life designed to free the soul from evil by ascetic practices: chastity, detachment, truth, and charity so complete that a religious Jain should accept only what is freely given, preferring starvation to ungenerous life. Jainism, though it attracted lay followers, is so demanding that it could only be practiced with full rigor in monasteries and religious communities. It never drew a following outside India.

Gautama Siddharta, however, who probably lived between the mid-sixth and early fourth centuries B.C.E., founded in India a religion of potentially universal appeal. Or perhaps the tradition he launched is better described as a code of life than as a religion, because Gautama himself seems never to have made any assertions about God. Rather, he prescribed practices that would liberate devotees from the troubles of this world. Gautama, whose followers called him "the Buddha" or "the Enlightened One," taught that a combination of meditation, prayer, and unselfish behavior could achieve happiness. The object was to escape desire—the cause of unhappiness. For the most privileged practitioners of what came to be called *Buddhism*, the aim was the ultimate extinction of all sense of self in a mystical state: **nirvana**, or "extinction of the flame." Devotees gathered in monasteries to help guide each other toward this end—but individuals in worldly settings could also achieve it. Many early Buddhist stories of the attainment of enlightenment concern people in everyday occupations, including merchants and rulers. This helped create powerful constituencies for the religion.

Buddhists now avoid the word "soul" because the Buddha decried the notion that there is anything essential or immutable about an individual. But most early Buddhist texts clung to the notion that the self survives the death of the body—perhaps many such deaths in the course of a long cycle of death and rebirth. To liberate the self from the world, either by individual self-refinement or by losing oneself in selflessness, was likely to be a long job. Most religions of Indian origin agreed about that and expected reincarnation to recycle the soul. The distinctive element in the Buddhist view of this process was that it was ethical. A principle of justice—or at least retribution—would govern the fate of the soul, which would be assigned a "higher" or "lower" body in each successive life depending on its virtuousness in its previous incarnation. In a famous text, recorded in eighth-century China, the Buddha promises that a righteous person can be born as an emperor for hundreds or thousands of eons while remembering what happened in his previous life.

Critics sometimes claim that these new religions were really forms of old magic: that the desire to "escape the world" or "extinguish the self" or achieve "union with Brahman" was, in effect, a bid for immortality and that mystical practice was a kind of alternative medicine designed to prolong or enhance life. Or else such practices as prayer and self-denial could be seen as a bid for the charismatic power of self-transformation of the shaman (see Chapter 1), obtained without using mind-bending drugs. These analyses may have some validity. The Buddha called himself healer as well as teacher. Many legends of the era associate miracles

Nature Worship. This rare Daoist scroll from about 1150 C.E.—only a portion of which is reproduced here—depicts some of the feats of the "Eight Immortals," the most famous characters in Daoist folklore. The serene landscape is typical of Daoist painting.
Courtesy of the Library of Congress

of therapy with founders of religions. The identification of detachment from the world with the pursuit of immortality is explicit, for instance, in writings attributed to Laozi, who probably lived in the fourth century B.C.E. and founded **Daoism** in China. Amid the insecurities of life among the warring states described in the last chapter, he recommended disengagement to give the Daoist power over suffering—power like that of water, which erodes even when it seems to yield: "There is nothing more soft and weak; for attacking the hard and strong there is nothing better."

Yet, however much the new religions owed to traditional magic, they were genuinely new. They upheld the effectiveness of moral practice, alongside formal rituals, as ways to adjust humans' relationship with nature or with whatever was divine: not just sacrificing prescribed offerings fittingly to God or gods, but modifying the way people behaved toward each other. They attracted followers with programs of individual moral progress, rather than with rites to appease nature. In other words, they were emerging as religions of salvation, not just of survival. They promised the perfection of the human capacity for goodness, or "deliverance from evil"—attainable in this world or, if not, by transfer to another world after death, or by a total transformation of this world at the end of time.

The Jews

Traditions developed during the axial age among the people later known as Jews also showed a drift in this direction. This relatively small and politically insignificant people of southwest Asia's Mediterranean coastal region (see Map 6.1) demands attention because of the enormous long-term influence of some Jewish thinking and the contribution Jews and their descendants made to almost every aspect of the life of Western societies. We cannot satisfactorily reconstruct the Jews' early history, though they were self-consciously a people of pastoral origins, as the biblical story of Cain and Abel shows. The blood sacrifice of Abel, the herdsman, was more "acceptable" to God than were the crops of his brother Cain, the "tiller of the soil."

Traditionally, in the attempt to retrieve the facts of early Jewish history, scholars have relied on supposedly historical narratives in the Bible, the sacred writings of the Jews. But archaeological investigation has made this history increasingly difficult to confirm. Thus, any account has to be tentative.

Like most people, the Jews seem to have started with a religion tailored to worldly ends, worshipping a tribal deity who promised material success, prosperity, and victory. Their sacred writings tell a story of disillusionment: of defeats and dispossessions by their enemies. From the eighth century B.C.E., Egyptian, Assyrian, and Babylonian inscriptions confirm that Jews inhabited two kingdoms they called Israel and Judah, which fought each other and fell victim to the wars of neighboring empires. Large-scale deportations—including a massive forced migration to Babylon after the fall of the Jews' holy city of Jerusalem in the 580s (see Chapter 5)—incited a "diaspora mentality": exiles' sense of loss, resignation, nostalgia, defeat, and hope. "By the waters of Babylon," as the writer of the psalm put it, "we lay down and wept. . . . If I ever forget Jerusalem, let my tongue cleave to my mouth."

Instead of turning the Jews against their deity, their disasters inspired them to reevaluate their relationship with him and to see him not just as superior to the gods of other peoples, but as the only true God, beside whom all other gods were false. Sufferings were trials of faith and punishments for sin—especially for failures to acknowledge God's uniqueness. God promised deliverance, if not in this life, then in the afterlife; or at the end of history; or, at best, in a remote future, as a reward for present fidelity to prescribed rituals and rules of life, known as "the Law." Jews differed among themselves about what deliverance would mean. For some, it would be individual immortality; for some, relief from a sense of sinfulness; for some, the elimination of evil from the world; for some, national independence; for some, an empire over their enemies.

The last great teacher of the age—the greatest, in terms of his influence—was the Jew we usually call Jesus, who died in or about 33 C.E. Scholars have questioned traditions concerning his life, on the grounds that his own followers were virtually the only ones who collected and wrote down the sources and that we have almost no independent confirmation that he even existed. Actually, however, we are much better informed about him than we are about most other figures of his time or type. Collections of stories and sayings were written down within thirty or forty years of his death. The brevity of this interval makes them unusually reliable by the standards of most such sources for ancient history.

To the secular historian, Jesus is best understood as an independent-minded Jewish rabbi, with a radical message. Indeed, some of his followers saw him as the culmination of Jewish tradition—embodying, renewing, and even replacing it. The name *Christ*, which his followers gave him, is a corruption of a Greek attempt to translate the Hebrew term *ha-mashiad*, or **Messiah**, meaning "the anointed," which Jews used to designate the king they hoped for at the end of history to bring heaven to earth. Jesus' message was uncompromising. The Jewish priesthood should be purged of corruption, the temple at Jerusalem "cleansed" of money-making practices. Even more controversially, some of his followers understood him to claim that humans could not gain divine favor by appealing to a kind of bargain with God—the "Covenant" of Jewish tradition. God freely gave or withheld his favor, or grace. According to Jewish doctrine, God responded to obedience to laws and rules. But Jesus' followers preferred to think that, however righteously we behave, we remain dependent on God's grace. No subsequent figure was so influential until Muhammad, the founder of Islam, who died six centuries later, and none thereafter for at least 1,000 years.

The religious teachings of the sages were highlights in a world teeming with other new religions, most of which have not survived. In a period when no one recognized a hard-and-fast distinction between religion and secular life, spiritual ferment stimulated all kinds of intellectual innovation. It is still hard to say, for instance, whether Confucius founded a religion. After all, he ordered rites of veneration of gods and ancestors, but he disclaimed interest in worlds other than our own. The other schools of the axial age in China—so numerous that they were called the Hundred Schools—shared similar priorities but mixed what we would now think of as secular and religious thinking. Confucius' opponent, Mozi, is a case in point. He taught a philosophy of **universal love**, on secular grounds, 400 years before Jesus' religious version.

Some other innovators formulated ideas that belong in what we would now classify as secular thought. Greek sages, for instance, whose work overlapped with that of the founders of new religions in Asia, taught techniques for telling good from evil and truth from falsehood that we still use. The towering figures were two teachers of the fourth century B.C.E.: Aristotle, a physician's son from northern Greece, who was, perhaps, the most purely secular thinker of the age, and his teacher, the Athenian aristocrat, Plato. Aristotle left work on science, logic, politics, and literature unequalled in the West for centuries, while Western philosophy is often jokingly dismissed as "footnotes to Plato." Logicians, scientific observers, and experimenters of the Hundred Schools in China paralleled these achievements, as did thinkers in India of the school known as Nyaya, who shared Greek thinkers' confidence in reason and the urge to analyze it, resolving arguments step by step.

The Thoughts of the Axial Age

There is no easy way to analyze the thinking of the axial age. Textbook writers usually divide the subject by regions because scholars tend to specialize in regions. This method, however, conceals the fact that an almost continuous zone across Eurasia stretching from China, through India, Southwest Asia, and the Mediterranean **Levant**, to Greece linked these regions together.

A thematic approach, of the kind attempted over the next few pages, helps reveal connections and contrasts. We start with religious ideas, bearing in mind the now-familiar warning that religion and secular life were overlapping categories for most thinkers at the time.

Religious Thinking

Of new thoughts of God formulated or developed in the axial age, three proved especially influential in global history: the idea of a divine creator, responsible for everything else in the universe; the idea of a single God, uniquely divine, or divine in a unique way; and the idea of an involved God, actively engaged in the life of the world.

Creation Gods and spirits are hard to imagine. It is even harder to imagine nothing: an idea, beyond experience, at the uttermost limits of thought. The idea of nothing enabled thinkers to understand the order of nature in a new way. For, once you have get your head around the concept of nothing, you can imagine creation from nothing.

Before the axial age, creation narratives, as far as we know, were not really about creation, but were explanations of how the universe came to be the way it is. Ancient Egyptian creation myths, for instance, tell of a creator transforming chaos into a world endowed with time: but the chaos was there for him to mold. The eternal being whom early Indian writings call Brahman created the world out of himself, "as a spider spins its web."

"How could it be so," sneered one of the Upanishads, "that being was produced from non-being?" Most Greek philosophers agreed. Plato's creator-god did not start from nothing, but rearranged what was already there.

Some ancient Greek poetry, however, described a world-beginning without prior matter. Emotion or thought was the prime mover of the universe. As the Gospel according to John put it in the late first century c.e., "In the beginning was the logos"—literally, the thought, which English translations usually render as "the word." Of all the early Christian accounts of Jesus' life, John's was the Gospel Greek thought influenced most heavily. Most other Christian accounts relied heavily on traditions peculiar to Jesus' own people, the Jews, who brought an unusual philosophical twist to divine thinking: the idea of a creator who always existed but who made everything else out of nothing. Conclusions followed. The creator was unique, for nothing else could precede creation; he was purely spiritual, since there was no matter until he made it; he was eternal—he existed, that is, outside time—since he was not himself a product of creation; he was, therefore, unchanging; nothing greater than he could be conceived—his power had no limits.

Monotheism The idea of a unique God, who monopolizes power over nature, is now so familiar, at least in the West, that we can no longer sense how strange it is. Yet, until the first millennium B.C.E., as far as we know, most people who imagined an invisible world—beyond nature and controlling it—supposed that it was diverse: crowded with gods, the way creatures crammed nature. To systematize the world of the gods in the axial age, Greeks arrayed gods in order. Persians reduced them to two—one good, one evil. In Indian *henotheism*, a multiplicity of gods collectively represented divine unity.

For Jews, Yahweh, their tribal deity, was, or became, their only God. The chronology is insecure, and we do not know whether the Jewish creation theory was cause or consequence of this development. Their writings called him "jealous"—unwilling to allow divine status to any rival. Fierce enforcement of his sole right to worship was part of the Covenant in which Yahweh's favor was exchanged for obedience and veneration. "I am Yahweh your God. . . . You shall have no other gods to rival me."

Jews were not obliged to impose the Yahweh cult on others. On the contrary, for most of history, they treated it as a treasure too precious to share with non-Jews. Elsewhere, monotheism seemed unappealing. Buddhism dispensed with the need for a creator by upholding that the universe was itself infinite and everlasting. When asked about the existence of God, Buddha, in the recollection of his disciples, always answered evasively. In India, China, and Greece, the idea of a unique creator left options for polytheism: If one being inhabited eternity, why—in strict logic—might not others? Other forms of uniqueness can be divided: You can shatter a rock, parse a statement, refract light. So maybe the uniqueness of God is of this kind. Alternatively, it could be a kind of comprehensiveness, like that of "Nature," "the Earth," or the sum of everything. God is one—any good Brahmanist would acknowledge—in the sense that everything is one. In any case, if God's power is without limits, surely he can create other gods.

Divine Love. "I am the good shepherd," said Jesus, according to the Gospel of John (10:14), "and I lay down my life for my sheep." During the persecutions that punctuated the first 300 years of the history of the Church, Christian artists interpreted the New Testament's many texts about "straying" and "lost" sheep as metaphors for the souls of martyrs, whom Jesus gathered into his fold. This third-century example shows how Christians continued the heroic and aesthetic conventions of classical sculpture.
Hirmer Fotoarchiv, Munich, Germany

Despite these arguments, three developments have conspired, in the long run, to make the God of the Jews the favorite God of much of the world. First, the Jews' own "sacred" history of sacrifices and sufferings gave a compelling example of faith. Second, a Jewish splinter group, which recognized Jesus as—so to speak—the human face of God, opened its ranks to non-Jews. Christianity built up a vigorous and sometimes aggressive tradition of trying to convert non-Christians everywhere. Thanks in part to a message adaptable to all sorts of cultural environments, it became, over nearly 2,000 years, the world's most widely diffused religion. Finally, early in the seventh century C.E., the Prophet Muhammad studied Judaism and Christianity and incorporated the Jewish understanding of God in Islam. In its turn—in many of the places where it was preached and spread—Islam became at least as appealing as Christianity and today has almost as many followers. Well over a third of the world's population subscribes to this tradition of Jewish, Christian, and Muslim monotheism.

Divine Love Having created, did God remain interested in creation? Most Greek thinkers of the era ignored or repudiated the idea. Aristotle's description of God is of a perfect being, who needs nothing else, who has no uncompleted purposes, and who feels neither sensibility nor suffering. "The benevolence of heaven" was a phrase much used in China around the mid-millennium, but this seems far short of love. Mozi, as even his philosophical adversaries admitted, "would wear out his whole being for the benefit of humankind." But his vision of humankind bound by love was not theologically inspired. Rather, he had a romantic vision of a golden age of "Great Togetherness" in the primitive past.

For humans, the claim that God's interest is specially focused on them seems suspiciously self-centered. Gradually, however, axial age thinking made it believable by insisting that humankind was special—higher than other animals. There were dissenting traditions. Philosophers in southern Italy in the late sixth century B.C.E. taught that "All things that are born with life in them should be treated as kindred." Religious Jains' reverence for animals' souls is so intense that they sweep the ground to avoid walking on insects. But the biblical God makes "man in His own image" as the last word in creation and gives humans dominion over all other animals.

In the second half of the millennium, thinkers in other traditions formulated similar ideas. In the mid-fourth century B.C.E., Aristotle developed a hierarchy of living souls, in which the human soul was superior to those of plants and animals, because it had rational as well as "vegetative" and "sensitive" faculties. The Chinese formula was similar, as, for example, Xunzi put it early in the next century: "Man has spirits, life, and perception, and in addition the sense of justice; therefore he is the noblest of earthly beings." Humans could exploit stronger creatures because they were able to form societies and act collaboratively. Buddhism ranked humans as higher creatures than others for purposes of reincarnation. For Jews, humans were lords or stewards of creation, uniquely empowered to communicate directly with God.

Late in the axial age, some Jews began to use the image of **divine love** to express this relationship—perhaps to cope with the frustrations of their history, in which they had never been able to maintain political independence. Jesus and his followers seized on the identification of God with love. It was emotionally satisfying, because love is a universal emotion. By making God's love embrace all humans—rather than favoring a chosen race or a righteous minority—Christianity acquired universal appeal. Creation became an act of love consistent with God's nature. This solved a lot of problems, though it raised another—why does a loving God permit evil and suffering?

New Political Thinking

The evidence was glaringly ambiguous: Were misdeeds the result of corrupted goodness or inherent evil? Were human beings by their very nature good or bad? "The nature of man is evil—his goodness is only acquired by training," said Xunzi, for instance, in the mid-third century B.C.E. He believed that the original state of humankind was a grim swamp of violence from which progress painfully raised people. Confucius, on the other hand, thought that "Man is born for uprightness. If he lose it and yet live, it is merely luck." Since the axial age, political solutions to the problem of human nature have always been of two contrasting kinds: those that emphasize freedom (to release human goodness) and those that emphasize discipline (to restrain human wickedness).

The biblical account of the creation of humans, in the book of Genesis, contained the most widely favored compromise. God made humans good and free. The abuse of freedom made people bad. Logically, however, this was unpersuasive. If Adam was good, how could he use freedom for evil? To escape this trap, Genesis added a diabolical device. The serpent (or other devilish agents in other traditions) corrupted goodness from outside. This has left politics with a difficult balancing act, which no system has ever adequately accomplished, between freedom and force.

Political Pessimism For pessimists, the way to overcome human deficiencies was to strengthen the state. Plato was a member of an Athenian gang of intellectuals and aristocrats who felt qualified for power and therefore resented democracy. His commendations included censorship, repression, militarism, regimentation, rigid class structure, extreme collectivism, selective breeding of superior human beings, and active deception of the people by the state—all had a distressful influence. The key idea was that political power should be concentrated in a self-electing class of philosopher-rulers called **Guardians**.

Their qualification for office would be intellectual superiority, guaranteed by a mixture of heredity and education, that would make them selfless in their private lives and godlike in their ability to see what was good for the citizens. They would achieve Plato's declared objective: "the greatest happiness of the whole, and not that of any one class." He wrote so persuasively that this reasoning has continued to appeal to state builders ever since. "There will be no end to the troubles of states, or indeed, of humanity," he claimed, "until philosophers become kings in this world, or till those we now call kings and rulers really and truly become philosophers." His Guardians, however, became the inspiration and the intellectual ancestors of elites, aristocracies, party hacks, and self-appointed supermen whose justification for tyrannizing others has always been that they know best.

Chinese counterparts exceeded the severity even of Plato's thinking. For most of the time, they were in the minority: The consensus among the sages was that the ruler should be bound by law (a point in which Aristotle, at the other end of Eurasia, agreed.) Confucius even said that ethics should override obedience to the law. In the fourth century B.C.E., a school of thought in China known as **Legalism** denounced ethics as a "gnawing worm" that would destroy the state. Society required only obedience. Law and order were worth tyranny and injustice.

This was a remarkable new twist in the history of thinking about law. The explanation lies in the terror of the times. Legalist doctrine was born in a time of civil disaster and has tended to resurface in bad times ever since. Legalists laughed off earlier sages' belief in the innate goodness of people. The best penalties were the most severe: cutting off heads, slicing people in half, pulling their bodies apart with chariots, boring a hole in their skulls, roasting them alive, or cutting out their ribs. As well as in the worship of order, ancient Chinese Legalism anticipated modern fascism, for instance, in advocating and glorifying war, recommending economic self-sufficiency for the state, denouncing capitalism, praising agriculture, and insisting on the need to suppress individualism in the interests of state unity.

Political Optimism But most sages of the axial age were optimists. They thought human nature was essentially good. The political doctrines of **Confucianism**, for example, demanded that the state should liberate subjects to fulfill their potential. And some Greek sages advocated democracy, which entrusted citizens (though not, of course, excluded groups, such as women or slaves) with a voice in affairs of state.

Chinese thinkers applied similarly individualistic doctrines, but they did not question monarchy. The state was meant to reflect the universe. Its unity could not be compromised. All that could be expected was that the ruler should consult the people's interests and views and should face, in case of tyranny, the subject's right to rebel. "Heaven sees according as the People see," said Mencius, Confucianism's outstanding spokesman. "Heaven hears according as the people hear." This was a reminder to the ruler, not a recipe for republicanism. Nor does Indian literature of the time mention popular institutions. But some Indian states did have elites numbered in the hundreds—perhaps in the thousands in some cases—which ruled as a group, electing leaders for fixed terms among themselves.

Meanwhile, in Greece, an enormous variety of political experiments unfolded, including republican or aristocratic systems, and even democratic ones. Aristotle made a masterly survey of them in the fourth century B.C.E. He thought monarchy was the best system in theory, but not in practice, because it was impossible to ensure that the best man would always be the ruler. More practical was aristocratic government, in which a manageable number of superior men administered the state. But it tended to degenerate into the self-interested rule of the wealthy or permanent power for an hereditary clique. Democracy could lead to demagogues and mob rule. The best system was a carefully crafted mixture in which aristocracy predominated, under the rule of law. Broadly speaking, this was embodied in the Roman state of the second half of the millennium (see Chapter 7), which became, in turn, the model for most republican survivals and revivals in Western history.

Even when, toward the end of the axial age, Rome abandoned republican government and restored what was in effect a monarchy, Romans still spoke of their state as a republic and the emperor as merely the chief magistrate.

In politics, Jesus preached a subtle subversion. A new commandment to "love one another," he claimed, could replace virtually all laws. The Kingdom of Heaven was more important than the empire of Rome. In one of history's great ironic jokes, Jesus advised fellow Jews, in effect, to despise or even ignore the state: "Render unto Caesar that which is Caesar's and unto God that which is God's." All Jews at the time would have understood what this meant, for everything, to them, was God's.

For society at large, Jesus was equally dangerous, welcoming social outcasts—prostitutes, tax collectors, "sinners," and heretics. He favored the weak against the strong: children, women, the lame, the blind, and beggars—the "meek," who, he promised, "shall inherit the earth." Given the radical nature of this bias, it is unsurprising that Jewish and Roman authorities combined to put him to death. His followers then turned from political activism to spiritual preparation for personal salvation.

Challenging Illusion

New thinking about reason and reality, and the relationship between them, flourished alongside or within the work of the religious leaders. Perhaps the most startling feature that united the thought of the axial age across Eurasia was the sages' struggle against illusion—their effort to see beyond appearances to underlying realities. "People dwelling in a cavern," said Plato, "see only the shadows that fire throws onto the wall of their cave." Senses deceive. We are mental cave dwellers. How can we see out of our cave?

Math

This question inspired innovations in mathematics. Indian sages discovered in numbers a limitless universe. Jain speculators about the age of the cosmos invoked mind-bogglingly big numbers, partly to demonstrate how impossible it was to attain the infinite. Workers in arithmetic discovered unreachable numbers: ratios that could never be exactly determined, yet that seemed to underpin the universe—for instance, those that determined the size of a circle, or the complex ratio that Greek mathematicians called "the Golden Number" (roughly 1.618), and that seemed to represent perfection of proportion. The invention of geometry showed how the mind can reach realities that the senses obscure or warp: a perfect circle, a line without magnitude. Reality can be invisible, untouchable, and yet accessible to reason.

A figure of enormous importance in unfolding these mysteries (for that is what they were to people at the time) was Pythagoras. His life spanned the Greek world. He was born on an island in the Aegean, around the mid-sixth century B.C.E., but spent most of his teaching life in a Greek colony in southern Italy. He attracted stories—he communed with the gods; he had a golden thighbone; he was not a mere man but a unique being, between human and divine.

Pythagoras is most famous today for two relatively trivial insights: that musical harmonies can be expressed as arithmetical ratios and that consistent ratios characterize the lengths of the sides of right-angled triangles. His importance goes much deeper. He was the first thinker, as far as we know, to formulate the idea that numbers are real. They are obviously ways we have of classifying objects—two flowers, five flies. But Pythagoras thought there was more to it than that—that two and five really exist, quite apart from the objects they enumerate. They would still exist, even if there were nothing to count. He went further. Numbers are the basis on which the cosmos is constructed. "All things are numbers" was his way of putting it. Numbers determine shapes and structures—we still speak of "squares" and "cubes"—and numerical proportions underlie all relationships. Geometry, Pythagoras thought, is the architecture of the universe.

Not everyone was equally enthusiastic about the cult of numbers. "I sought the truth in measures and numbers," said Confucius in a text, which, though he probably did not really write it, reflects the prejudices of the third-century B.C.E. Daoist who compiled it, "but after five years I still hadn't found it." Still, the exploration of numbers was a widespread interest among axial-age sages. **Rationalism**—the doctrine that unaided reason can reach the truth and solve the world's problems—was among the results.

Reason

The first pure rationalist we know by name was Parmenides, who was from a Greek colony of southern Italy in the early fifth century B.C.E. He started with geometry. If you believe geometrical figures are real, you believe in the truth of a super-sensible world—for a perfect triangle, for instance, is like God: no one has ever seen one, though crude manmade approximations are commonplace. The only triangles we know about are those in our thoughts. Parmenides therefore suggested that the same might be true of trees—and of everything else.

In some ways, the consequences are impressive. If, say, a pink rose is real by virtue of being a thought rather than a sensible object, then a black rose is equally real. The nonexistence of anything is an incoherent concept. Few of Parmenides' followers were willing to go that far, but reason did seem able to open secret caverns in the mind, where truths lay.

"Fire is not hot. Eyes do not see." These were the numbing, blinding paradoxes of the fourth-century B.C.E. Chinese philosopher Hui Shih, who wrote five cartloads of books. They show that data act directly on the mind, which processes them before they become sensations. Thought does not have to arise from experience. For a true rationalist, the best laboratory is the mind, and the best experiments are thoughts.

In partial consequence, rationalism became an escapist's alternative to reality. Parmenides, for instance, thought he could prove that change was illusory and differences deceptive and that only the unchanging and eternal were real. One of his successors, Zeno of Elea, invented famous paradoxes to demonstrate this: An arrow in flight always occupies a space equal to its size, therefore it is always at rest. You can never complete a journey because you always have to cross half the remaining distance first. Matter is indivisible because "if a rod is shortened every day by half its length, it will still have something left after ten thousand generations."

Early in the second half of the millennium, teachers in India, Greece, and China in proposed rules for the correct use of reason. Practical issues probably underpinned these movements. For pleading in courts, arguing between embassies, persuading enemies and praising rulers, it was important to make arguments watertight. Logic was a fascinating by-product of these practical needs.

The most rigorous and systematic exposition was Aristotle's, strapping common sense into intelligible rules. To this day, even people who have barely heard of him use the techniques he taught, which have seeped into mental habits through the channels of tradition. He was the best-ever analyst of how reason works, in as much as it works at all. According to Aristotle, we can break valid arguments down into phases, called **syllogisms**, in which we can infer a necessary conclusion from two premises that prior demonstration or agreement have established to be true. If the premises are, "All men are mortal" and "Socrates is a man," it follows that "Socrates is mortal."

At roughly the same time in India, the Nyaya school of commentators on ancient texts analyzed logical processes in five-stage breakdowns. Their conception, however, was in one fundamental way different from Aristotle's. They claimed reason was a kind of extraordinary perception that God conferred. Nor were they strictly rationalists, for they believed meaning did not arise in the mind. God, tradition, or consensus conferred it on the object of thought.

Science

Meanwhile, another route through the thought of the axial age led to science. As with the exploration of reason, the starting point was distrust of the senses. As a Daoist text of the third century B.C.E., points out, some metals seem soft but can be combined to form harder ones; lacquer feels liquid but can be made dry by the application of another liquid. First appearances are deceptive. The science of the axial age sought to penetrate the veil and expose underlying truths. "Truth," said Democritus around the turn of the fifth and fourth centuries B.C.E., "lies in the depths." Although no strictly scientific texts from India survive from this period, the Upanishads contain similar warnings about the unreliability of appearances (see Chapter 5).

The idea of a distinction between what is natural and what is supernatural was, as far as we can tell, new. Previously, science seemed sacred, medicine magical. The earliest clear evidence of a shift in thinking is Chinese. In 679 B.C.E., the sage Shen Xu taught that ghosts were the products of the fears and guilt of those who see them. Confucius deterred his followers from thinking "about the dead until you know the living." Confucians professed interest in human affairs—politics and practical morality—and indifference to the rest of nature. But as far as his followers did study nature, it was in an effort to dig out what they regarded as superstition: claims that inanimate substances had feelings and wills, that spirits inhabit all matter, or that the natural world is responsive to human sin or goodness. "The fact," says a Confucian text of 239 B.C.E., "that water leaves the mountains is not due to any dislike on the part of the water but is the effect of height. The wheat has no desire to grow or be gathered into granaries." Thus "natural" causes displaced magic.

In Greece, the origins of science were inseparable from magic, nature worship, and shamanistic attempts to penetrate the mysteries of unseen worlds. For science to thrive in a world that, in most people's minds, gods and sprites and demons still ruled, a method was needed to observe nature systematically, order the information, and test the resulting hypotheses. Aristotle was the best representative of Greek science in its maturity. "We must have facts," he said, and he proceeded to gather them in enormous quantities. Like the perfect example of a "nutty professor," he prowled around his lecture room, dissected flies, and noted every stage in the incubation of birds' eggs. Other highlights of Greek science of the period included Archimedes' discovery of the mechanics of leverage in the mid-third century B.C.E., and, slightly later, the work of Eratosthenes, who produced an almost exactly accurate calculation of the size of the Earth.

Chinese practical science—systematic investigation of nature through observation and experiment—probably arose, around the same time that it did in Greece, from Daoist doctrines of nature. Habits of observation and experiment developed from the magical and omen-seeking practices of early Daoism. The Daoist word for a "temple" means watch tower—a platform from which to observe the natural world and launch naturalistic explanations of its phenomena. Daoism has, in Confucian eyes, a reputation for magical mumbo-jumbo because its priests practice strange ceremonies, many of which seem indebted in their origins to the magical fallacy that nature responds to human ritual. But Daoism also teaches that Nature—to the one who would control it—is like any other beast to be tamed or foe to be dominated—she must be known first.

Daoism encouraged scientific practice: observation, description, classification, and experiment. In second-century B.C.E. China, for instance, the Daoist legend told of Yi the archer, who, on the advice of sages, sought the medicine of immortality away in the West, when the herb that would confer it was growing outside his door. Daoist texts often have amusing dialogues between craftsmen who know their work and rationalists who persuade them to do it in a different way, with ruinous results. Grand theory is discouraged as an intrusion of reason into the workings of wisdom, which can be attained only by gaining knowledge. Chinese science has always been weak on theory, strong on technology.

Medicine

Controversy followed between magic and medicine—or was it just between rival forms of magic? Illness, like any abnormal state, including madness, could be the result of possession or infestation by a spirit, a "demon"—to recycle a commonly used word for it. Or some diseases could have material causes, others spiritual. Or all could be a mixture of the two. Or sickness could be a divine affliction, the result of sin.

In Greece in the late fifth century B.C.E., a secular school known as the Hippocratics tried to monopolize the medical profession, at the expense of rival healers who were attached to temples. The Hippocratics thought that health was essentially a state of balance among four substances in human bodies: blood, phlegm, and black and yellow bile. Adjust the balance, and you alter the patient's state of health. This condemned patients in the West for centuries to treatment mainly by diet, vomiting, laxatives, and bloodletting. The theory was wrong—but it was genuinely scientific, based on observation of the substances the body expels in pain or sickness.

A treatise sometimes attributed to Hippocrates himself—supposed founder of the school—advocates a naturalistic explanation for epilepsy, which many people at the time assumed to be a form of divine possession. The test is: Find a goat exhibiting the same symptoms that a human epileptic does. "If you cut open the head, you will find that the brain is . . . full of fluid and smells foul, convincing proof that the disease and not the deity is harming the body." The method sounds bizarre, but the conclusion is impressive. "Personally," the Hippocratic writer went on, "I believe that human bodies cannot be polluted by a god." A similar shift of business into the hands of secular medical specialists occurred in China. Xunzi, who died in 235 B.C.E., scorned a man who "having got rheumatism from dampness beats a drum and boils a suckling pig as an offering to the spirits." Result: "a worn-out drum and a lost pig, but he will not have the happiness of recovering from sickness." Religious explanations of disease remained. But the Hippocratics and their Chinese counterparts started a presumption that has gained ground ever since: that nothing needs to be explained in divine terms. The physical world is all there is.

These changes had close parallels in India. In the earliest known Indian work of medicine, the *Arthaveda* (ahr-thah-VEH-dah), which dates from the early first millennium B.C.E., diseases and demons are more or less identical and are treated with charms or drugs. From the sixth century B.C.E. onward, however, we see evidence of professional medical training and literature. Work largely complete by the second century C.E. summarizes these medical teachings. Writings attributed to Susutra, who probably lived in the sixth century B.C.E., concern surgery; writings attributed to Charaka (which may be the name of a school rather than a person) concentrate exclusively on diet and drugs. A saying attributed to Charaka is strikingly similar to the morals of the Greek Hippocrates: "If you want your treatment to succeed, to earn wealth, to gain fame, and to win heaven hereafter . . . seek the good of all living creatures, strive with your whole heart to cure the sick." The similarities among Indian, Greek, and Chinese axial age medicine are so remarkable that historians often assume that they influenced each other. There is, however, no direct evidence for this influence.

Skepticism

A consequence of the rise of a scientific point of view was the suspicion that the world is purposeless. In particular, this line of thinking raised an idea that challenged another axial age orthodoxy: If the world had no purpose, it was not made for human beings, who were reduced to insignificance. The idea Aristotle called the "Final Cause"—the purpose of a thing, which explains its nature—becomes incoherent. The world is a random event.

In around 200 B.C.E., this was such a dangerous idea that a skeptical Chinese treatise, the *Liezi* (lee-ay-tzeh), avoided direct advocacy of it by putting it into the mouth of a small boy, who challenged a pious host for praising the divine bounty that provided good things for his table. "Mosquitoes suck human blood, wolves devour human flesh but we do not therefore assert that Heaven created man for their benefit." The greatest-ever exponent of a cosmos without purpose was the Chinese philosopher of the first century C.E., Wangchong (wahng chohng). Humans, he said, live "like lice in the folds of a garment. When fleas buzz in your ear, you do not hear them: How could God even hear men, let alone concede their wishes?" Some materialist thinkers still take pride in asserting that the whole notion of purpose is superstitious and that asking why the world exists or why it is as it is is pointless.

In a world without purpose, there is no need for God. The name of the Greek philosopher Epicurus, who died in 270 B.C.E., has become unfairly associated with the pursuit of physical pleasure—which he certainly recommended, albeit with restraint. A far more important element of his thought was his interpretation of the **atomic theory**. In a world of atoms and voids, there is no room for "spirits." Because atoms are subject to "random swerves," there can be no fate. Because they are perishable, and everything is composed of them, there can be no immortal soul. Gods, if they exist at all, inhabit an imaginary world from which "we have nothing to hope and nothing to fear." Epicurus' arguments were formidable, and materialists and atheists kept returning to them. At about the end of the first century C.E., the Roman writer Sextus Empiricus suggested, like a modern Marxist, that "some shrewd man invented fear of the gods" as a means of social control. The doctrines of an all-powerful and all-knowing god were devised to suppress freedom of conscience. "If they say that God controls everything, they make him the author of evil," he concluded. "We express no belief and avoid the evil of the dogmatizers."

In revulsion from the big, unanswerable questions about the nature of reality, skeptical thinkers and their schools refocused philosophy on practical issues. One of the great anecdote-inspiring characters of ancient Greece was Pyrrho of Elis, who accompanied Alexander the Great's invasion of India in 327–324 B.C.E. (see Chapter 7) and imitated the indifference of the naked sages he met there. On board ship on the way home, he admired and shared the calm response of a pig to a storm. Because, he argued, you can find equally good reasons on both sides of any argument, the only wise course is to stop thinking and judge by appearances. More effective was the argument that all reasoning starts from assumptions; so none of it is secure. Mozi had developed a similar insight in China around the beginning of the fourth century B.C.E. Most problems were matters of doubt. "As for what we now know, is it not mostly derived from past experience?"

Later Greek philosophy focused on the best practical choices for personal happiness or for the good of society. **Stoicism** is the outstanding example of this kind of philosophy, both for the coherence of stoic ideas and because these ideas were so influential. Stoicism appealed to the Roman elite and through them had an enormous effect on Christianity. First taught in the school that Zeno of Citium founded in Athens in the late fourth century B.C.E., stoicism started from the insight that nature is morally neutral—only human acts are good or evil. The wise man therefore achieves happiness by accepting misfortune. Further stoic prescriptions—fatalism and indifference as remedies for pain—were similar to teachings preached at about the same period at the far end of Eurasia, especially by the Buddha and his followers, or Laozi and his. People have sought the "happiness priority" in so many contrasting ways that it is hard to generalize about its overall effect on the history of the world. Stoicism, however, was certainly its most effective manifestation in the West. It has supplied, in effect, the source of the guiding principles of the ethics of most Western elites since it emerged.

The Structures of the Axial Age

Monotheism, republicanism, Legalism, rationalism, logic, science (including scientific medicine), skepticism, the most enduring religions and ethical systems—the tally of new thinking in the axial age looks impressive by any standards, but especially because of its legacy to us. Why was this period so productive and why was it confined, by global standards, to so few societies around the globe?

The structures that underpinned the work of the axial age thinkers were important for making it happen. The schools and sages formed four obvious and sometimes overlapping categories. First, there were professional intellectuals who sold their services as teachers, usually to candidates for professional or public office, but perhaps also to those who sought happiness or immortality or, at least, health. A second class sought the patronage of rulers or positions as political advisers. Many sages belonged to both these groups: Aristotle, for instance, taught in Athens but also served as a tutor to the prince who later became Alexander the Great. Confucius eked out life as a teacher, but not because he did not want to serve states. A third category was made up of prophets or holy men, who emerged from ascetic lives with inspired messages for society; a fourth was composed of charismatic leaders with visions to share with and, if possible, impose on their peoples.

Most sages fitted into networks. Though lonely, hermitlike existence was an ideal that many of them recommended, affected, and even sought, few, if any, of these sages were genuinely isolated thinkers. They usually depended on contacts. Networks stimulated innovation. They nourished competition, fertilized ideas, and gave innovators emotional support. Plato wrote all his works as dialogues and conversations—which make the function of the network visible. The Confucian Mencius, the Daoist Zhuangzi, and Hui Shi, the analyst of language, competed and debated. Plato's teacher Socrates was in contact and conflict with all the Greek schools of his day, attacking those known as Sophists for allegedly valuing the elegance of an argument as more important than its truth. Epicurus and Zeno of Citium established schools in Athens within a few years of each other toward the end of the fourth century B.C.E.

Formal institutions of education played their part in defining networks and stimulating competition. We know little of how they functioned, but the Academy of Athens, founded in 380 B.C.E., had a garden and student lodgings that Plato purchased. Members ate together and contributed to costs according to their means. Master–pupil relationships created traditions or what we might call cross-generational networks. Socrates taught Plato, who taught Aristotle. Traditions of this sort can get rigid, but clever pupils often innovate by reacting against their masters' teaching (something all textbook writers should bear in mind) and set up chains of revisionism from one generation to the next. Confucius was a critic of the establishment of his day. Mohists, similarly, opposed Confucians. A succession of masters as well as a series of conflicts linked Mozi to Confucius. Han Feizi, a Confucian pupil, founded the Legalist school in reaction to his teacher, Xunzi.

The Academic of Athens. Romans continued to admire the philosophy of classical Greece. The Acropolis of Athens is recognizable in the background of this mosaic, preserved in the ruins of Pompeii. The columns and gardens recall what the setting of Plato's Academy at Athens was really like.
Erich Lessing/Art Resource, N.Y.

Disciples confided masters' works to writing. The Upanishads were probably transmitted orally before they were finally written down. Socrates wrote nothing. Jesus wrote nothing that has survived—only, as far as we know, a few words scratched in the dust. The Buddha's teachings were too sacred—his first disciples thought—to confide to writing and had eventually to be retrieved from memories when it was finally decided to write them down. Does this mean that the axial age is a trick of the evidence? That the ideas of its sages became so influential only because they were eventually written down? Not entirely, but it does mean that its thoughts have come down to us in a way that other regions and other periods did not have or did not use.

Some thinkers of the axial age were rich men. Plato could endow his own school with his own money. The Buddha and Mahavira, the founder of Jainism, were princes. Usually, however, intellectuals need patrons or employers to survive. The politically fragmented worlds of axial age Greece, China, and India had plenty of potential patrons. A wandering scholar like Confucius might not retain a patron for long—but he could turn to others. This made for independence of thought and liberated political philosophy to criticize rulers. Every subsequent age has successfully adapted Confucius' message, but he addressed it to his own time—hence his emphasis on the renewal of tradition, the resumption of sacred rites, and the restoration of land and property to their rightful owners. Of course, royal patrons are rarely disinterested. In mid-fourth-century B.C.E. China, Mencius found his patron, the King of Wei, interested only in schemes to improve military efficiency. Also at the court of Wei, Hui Shi turned his talent for argument to negotiations with other states.

To patronize sages became, in itself, a source of princely prestige. In China, the prince of Zhao allegedly had 1,000 scholars at his court toward the mid-third century B.C.E. The Chinese state of Chu supported the followers of Mozi against the Confucians. Qin, supposedly a "barbarian" kingdom on the edge of the Chinese culture area, was home to thousands of scholars. When its ruler burned books in the 220s B.C.E., it was less perhaps an act against learning than a gesture of partisanship on behalf of thinkers he favored.

In India, too, among the states that shared the Ganges valley in the period, similar rivalries and opportunities existed. The *Veda* contains

The Buddha and His Patrons. The Buddha's first sermon, depicted here in a Kushanese relief of the late second or early third century C.E. The Buddha squats under a lotus tree, on a pedestal decorated with a prayer wheel. The attentive figures who stand on small pedestals among the onlookers who surround him are probably the patrons who commissioned this sculpture. Kushanese art—from the mountainous northwest of the Indian subcontinent and Afghanistan—combines influences from India, Persia, Greece, and China, demonstrating the vitality of cultural exchange across Eurasia. *Scenes from the Life of Buddha, late 2nd–early 3rd century, Kushan dynasty, Stone. Courtesy of the Freer Gallery of Art, Smithsonian Institution, Washington, DC*

Making Connections | THINKERS AND THOUGHTS OF THE AXIAL AGE

REGION	SAGE/THINKER	PHILOSOPHY/ RELIGION	DISTINCTIVE IDEAS
Southwest Asia	Jewish sages, ca. 700–500 B.C.E.	Judaism	Monotheism; trials of faith; punishments for sin; covenant with God
	Zoroaster, ca. 600 B.C.E.	Zoroastrianism	Eternal conflict between good and evil (**dualism**)
	Jesus, ca. 30 C.E.	Christianity	Importance of faith, divine love
India	Gautama Siddharta, ca. 560 B.C.E.	Buddhism	Meditation; karma; Four Noble Truths; escaping desire
	Mahavira, ca. 559 B.C.E.	Jainism	Sanctity of life; nonviolence (*ahimsa*)
	Nyaya school, 350 B.C.E.	Rationalism	Logic; reason as an extraordinary perception conferred by God
Greece/Asia Minor	Pythagoras, ca. 550 B.C.E.	Mathematics	Geometrical and mathematical ideas; ratios; ideas that numbers are real
	Parmenides, ca. 425 B.C.E.	Rationalism	Objects of thought are more real than sense perception
	Zeno of Citium, ca. 390 B.C.E.	Stoicism	Nature is morally neutral; happiness achieved by accepting misfortune
	Aristotle and Plato, ca. 380 B.C.E.	Secular philosophy	Logic; science; political thought
	Epicurus, ca. 280 B.C.E.	Skepticism	Centrality of matter; soul is not immortal; if God exists he is indifferent to human affairs

REGION	SAGE/THINKER	PHILOSOPHY/ RELIGION	DISTINCTIVE IDEAS
China	Confucius, ca. 500 B.C.E.	Secular philosophy	Loyalty to God, state, and family; importance of ethics and right conduct
	Mozi, ca. 400 B.C.E.	Secular philosophy	Universal love
	Laozi, ca. 300 B.C.E.	Daoism	Detachment from world; quest for immortality
	Xunzi, ca. 250 B.C.E.	Secular philosophy	Human goodness can be attained through progress and freedom
	Han Feizi, ca. 225 B.C.E.	Legalism	Only good is the good of the state; law and order more important than tyranny and injustice

THE STRUCTURES OF THE AXIAL AGE

155

fragments of sages' dialogues with kings, in which the kings sometimes out argued the sages. Buddhism relied on rulers' patronage in the kingdoms of Kosala and Magadha. Mahavira was related to the rulers of Videha, where his doctrines enjoyed official favor. His followers debated with Buddhists for supremacy in Magadha. As we shall see in the next chapter, political unification and large-scale imperialism did not promote intellectual productivity. One of the reasons Zoroaster had no comparably influential successors in Persia is probably that Persia rapidly became an imperial power. In China, India, and Greece, the axial age waned as empires grew at the expense of small states, even though the empires themselves spread axial age ideas.

In some places, alongside state patronage, popular support nourished the intellectuals. Sages and the holy men are useful to the public in times of political dissolution. Their wisdom and objectivity make them sought after to arbitrate between neighbors or to take the place of absent justice. Public interest is apparent in the multiplicity of schools and the willingness of pupils to seek the benefit of masters' expertise. Learned writings attracted readers. Democritus, an exponent of atomic theory in the early fourth century B.C.E., was credited with sixty books. Heraclitus, one of the first generation of Greek sages around the beginning of the

CHRONOLOGY	
600 B.C.E.–100 C.E.	Teachers and their disciples influence thinking all across Eurasia; spread of Zoroastrianism for next 1,000 years primarily in present-day Iran; teachings about Brahman begin to be written down; Buddhism develops in India; Confucianism, Daoism, and Legalism spread in China; legacy of Plato and Aristotle to Western philosophy; proponents of secular medicine (Susutra in India, Hippocrates in Greece, and Xunzi in China)
580 B.C.E.	Forced migration of Jews from Jerusalem to Babylon creates a "diaspora mentality," influential up to present times
33 C.E.	Jesus and spread of Christianity over the next two millennia
(All dates are approximate)	

sixth century B.C.E., was a notorious loner who refused to take on pupils. But he nonetheless deposited his writings in the famous temple of the goddess Artemis at Ephesus on the western coast of Anatolia—in effect, his local public library.

IN PERSPECTIVE
The Reach of the Sages

Although the new thinking of the axial age was confined to parts of Asia and Europe, it was a worldwide story because of the way axial age thinking later spread and shaped thoughts and feelings in every clime and continent. Empires that are the subject of the next chapter helped to spread it. Trade and colonization, which can be traced at intervals throughout the rest of this book, took axial thought further, until it had spread across the planet. The Roman empire carried Greek science and philosophy into western Europe. Buddhism became a state ideology in the first empire to cover most of India. The Chinese Empire became a growing arena in which Buddhism, as well as native Chinese thought, spread within and across China's widening borders. Japan and Korea fell under Chinese cultural influence, and their intellectual traditions developed from Chinese-inspired starting points. Migration and trade bore Indian thinking into parts of Southeast Asia. Christianity fused Jewish and Greek intellectual traditions and spread them—ultimately—all over the world. Islam shared much of the same heritage and spread it almost as far. Buddhism is the third, in terms of numbers of followers, of the three world religions of today. Alongside Christianity and Islam, both of which developed after the axial age, it has spread over many different countries and cultures, whereas most religions tend to remain specific to their cultures of origin. We do not fully understand why Buddhism succeeded in this way, but we shall trace its history in this book. The scale of demands Buddhism makes on its followers is well suited to a variety of walks of life.

As a result of the spread of the work of the sages and their schools, the thought of the modern world has a familiar ring to a student of the axial age. It seems astonishing that today, after all the technical and material progress of the last 2,000 years, we should remain so dependent on the thought of such a distant era and have added so little to it. We debate the same issues about the nature of reality, using the same tools of logic and science. We struggle with the same problems about the relationship of this world to others, and most of us still follow religious traditions that axial age sages founded. We search for a balance between the same kinds of optimistic and pessimistic assessments of human nature that people of the axial age identified, and we seek to resolve similar conflicts of political ideas that arise as a result. To a remarkable extent, we express ourselves in terms the ancient sages taught.

Although the sages and schools of the axial age were confined to Eurasia, comparisons with other parts of the world help us understand how cultural contacts shape and spread what people think and believe. Over and over again, readers of this book will see and will have seen, for example, how ways of thought and life and worship radiated outward from kernel regions: from Mesoamerica, for example, into North and Central America; or from parts of the Andes along the coasts and mountain chains of South America and across the Amazon valley; or from the Ethiopian highlands into East Africa and South Arabia; or from centers on the Niger River into the Sahel and the forests of West Africa; or, as we shall see in later chapters, from East Asia across Polynesia deep into the Pacific. But the relatively isolating geography of the Americas, sub-Saharan Africa, and the Pacific worked against the kinds of comparatively intense exchange that were possible across Eurasia.

It is impossible to trace to their outer limits the networks that bound the axial age sages. But the similarities among their thoughts across

Eurasia suggest that long-range cultural exchanges must have been going on among them. This was perhaps the critical difference that made Eurasian societies relatively prolific in a period when we know of no comparable achievements in intellectual life anywhere else in the world. Our next task is, therefore, to look not only at the changing political frameworks of the axial age, but also at the evidence of the spread and strength of long-range cultural contacts in the world of the time.

PROBLEMS AND PARALLELS

1. How do the ideas of the great sages of the axial age still influence the way we think today?
2. Why did the idea of divine love change humankind's relationship with God and the world?
3. How did religious ideas affect political thought in the axial age? Why were most axial age sages optimists rather than pessimists?
4. How did axial age science and medicine distinguish themselves from magic?
5. How did networks, schools, and patrons influence and help spread axial age ideas?

The Great Empires

focus questions

1. Why were trade routes so important to axial age empires?
2. How did the Persian Empire benefit its inhabitants?
3. How was Rome able to conquer and rule a vast empire?
4. How did Asoka seek to unify his empire?
5. Why was the Han dynasty so significant for China?
6. Where did the first potentially imperial states arise in the Americas?

In about 33 B.C.E., Maecenas, one of the Roman Empire's leading ministers, gave a small farm to a penniless poet. It was a gift in appreciation of the brilliant satirical verses the poet—whose name was Horace—wrote as evening entertainment for Roman intellectuals and elites. The farm was just what Horace wanted. For the rest of his days, he devoted much of his best poetry—some of the cleverest, loveliest work any wordsmith has ever *forged—to celebrating the simple, rural life and praising his patrons. In one poem, he imagined Maecenas worrying over what the Chinese might be plotting. In others, Horace pictured Augustus, the Roman emperor, intimidating them with his power and fathering a future conqueror of China. This was outrageous flattery, since there was no likelihood of the Roman and Chinese empires having much contact of any kind, let alone going to war. In 97 C.E., China did send an envoy to Rome, but he turned back at the Black Sea.*

That was as close as the Roman and Chinese empires ever came to dealing directly with each other. But that Horace was aware of China— and realized that events at the far end of Eurasia could affect Roman interests—shows how the world was, as we say now, getting smaller as land trade routes opened communications across Eurasia, traffic grew along the existing maritime routes of the Indian Ocean, and sea travel began to connect the Mediterranean with northern Europe's Atlantic shores. The trade routes of the Phoenician and Greek trailblazers described in Chapter 5 led north from the Strait of Gibraltar to the tin-producing British Isles. Their colonies were staging posts in the making of a new economy—helping goods, people, and ideas cross or get around the sharply divisive watershed that separates Mediterranean from Atlantic Europe.

Not only did travelers and trade expand communications, but the need for big armies and the growth of commerce created a demand for stronger, bigger states—empires that included many political communities in common allegiance. The new empires of the period took shape first in Southwest Asia, then around the Mediterranean, and finally in China and India. They established common frontiers or frontier zones of conflict and culture exchange. Around them, chiefs, enriched by trade, turned into kings.

The empires spilled people, technology, and means of life into frontier areas that had been little populated. Cultivated crops and domesticated livestock transformed previously undisturbed ecosystems. At an increasing rate, neighbors who had lived by hunting and foraging for wild plants adopted agriculture, following the empires' example. Those who continued to resist change were cast as enemies and savages. In the great grasslands, the steppes of central Eurasia, where tilling the soil was impossible, empires formed with a different sort of economy, based on herding livestock. A pattern began, lasting some 2,000 years, of violence between these nomad empires that lived by herding and the sedentary farmers who lived near them.

Meanwhile, beyond the routes that connected Eurasian empires, foragers and small-scale farmers survived. They could minimize risk by minimizing change. Most of them took this option. In parts of the New World, however, experiments in embracing change and attempting to control it continued. Large-scale interventions in the environment and imaginative adaptations of human society took forms that were familiar from Eurasia. Agriculture led to urbanization, long-range commerce, and eventually imperialism. Seen from today's perspective, the Americas seemed to be reliving the history of the Old World.

Routes That Drew the Old World Together

As a general rule in history, bigger states mean more exchange over longer distances. In part, this is simply because they facilitate trade and travel within their own expanding borders; in part, because they generate increasing contacts with each other through commerce, diplomacy, and war. To understand the cultural exchanges of the period—how and why they happened and to what extent—we therefore have to understand the political framework: where and how new states formed; how their horizons broadened; what the new institutions were—the mechanisms for conveying commands and exacting obedience—that enabled them to function over unprecedented distances.

State-building and the development of communications are mutually dependent processes. Routes of commerce are the lifelines of empires: pumping them with resources, equipping them with new ideas and technologies, laying down tracks for their armies to follow. We must begin, therefore, by drawing in the long-range causeways of the period: the sea lanes and land routes that crossed Eurasia, making possible the cultural exchanges of the axial age and the new political developments in the empires the routes linked.

The Sea Routes of the Indian Ocean

The world maps Indian geographers of the axial age drew look like the product of stay-at-home minds. Four—then, from the second century B.C.E. onward, seven—continents radiate from a mountainous core. Around concentric rings of rock flow seven seas, made up, respectively, of salt, sugarcane juice, wine, ghee (butter), curds, milk, and water. One should not suppose on the basis of this formal, sacred image of the world that Indians of the time were ignorant of geography. That would be like inferring from the stylized subway map that New Yorkers could not build railways.

We can detect real observations under the metaphors of the maps. The world is grouped around the great Himalaya Mountains and the triangular, petal-like form of India, with the island of Sri Lanka falling from it like a dewdrop. The ocean is divided into separate seas, some imaginary or little known, but others representing real routes to frequented destinations and commercial centers. The Sea of Milk, for instance, corresponds roughly to what we now call the Arabian Sea, and led to Arabia and Persia. The Sea of Butter led to Ethiopia.

Stories of Indian seafaring from late in the first millennium B.C.E. appear in the *Jatakas*, collected tales of Buddhahood—guides to how to become enlightened. Here, piloting a ship "by knowledge of the stars" is a godlike gift. The Buddha saves sailors from cannibalistic goblin-seductresses in Sri Lanka. He puts together an unsinkable vessel for a pious explorer. A merchant, advised by an enlightened sage, buys a ship on credit and sells the cargo at a profit of 200,000 gold pieces. A guardian deity saves shipwreck victims who have combined commerce with pilgrimage "or are endowed with virtue or worship their parents." Similar legends appear in Persian sources, like the story of Jamshid, a hero who is both king and shipbuilder and who crosses oceans "from region to region with great speed."

Accounts of real voyages back these stories. Toward the end of the sixth century B.C.E., Darius I—an emperor enthusiastic for exploration—ruled Persia. He ordered a reconnaissance of the Indian Ocean from the northern tip of the Red Sea, around Arabia, to the mouth of the Indus River in northern India. A canal built from Suez on the Red Sea to the Nile indicates there must have been traffic for it to serve, traffic that the canal increased.

What Indian mapmakers called the Seas of Milk and Butter were, to Greek merchants, "the Erythraean Sea," from which traders brought back aromatics—especially frankincense and myrrh—and an Arabian cinnamon substitute called cassia. Important ports for long-range trade lined Arabia's shores. At Gerrha, for instance, merchants unloaded Indian manufactures. Nearby, Thaj also served as a good place to warehouse imports. Egyptian merchants endowed Egyptian temples with incense in the third century B.C.E. The reason for the long seafaring, sea-daring tradition of the Indian Ocean lies in the regularity of the monsoonal wind system. Above the equator, northeasterlies prevail in winter; but when winter ends, the direction of the winds reverses. For most of the rest of the year, the winds blow steadily from the south and west, sucked toward the Asian landmass as air warms and rises over the continent. By timing voyages to take advantage of the predictable changes in the direction of the wind, navigators could be confident of a fair wind out and a fair wind home.

It is a fact not often appreciated that, overwhelmingly, the history of maritime exploration has been made into the wind, presumably because it was at least as important to get home as to get to anywhere new. This was how the Phoenicians and Greeks opened the Mediterranean to long-range commerce and colonization (see Chapter 5). The same strategy enabled South Sea Island navigators to explore and colonize islands of the Pacific (see Chapter 10). The monsoonal wind system in the Indian Ocean freed navigators from such constraints. One must try to imagine what it would be like, feeling the wind, year after year, alternately in one's face and at one's back. Gradually, would-be seafarers realized how the changes of wind made outward ventures viable. They knew the wind would change and so could risk an outward voyage without fearing that they might be cut off from returning home.

Still, the Indian Ocean is dangerous. Storms wrack it, especially in the Arabian Sea, the Bay of Bengal, and the deadly belt of bad weather that stretches across the ocean below about 10 degrees south of the equator. But the predictability of a homeward wind made this the world's most benign environment for long-range voyaging. The fixed-wind systems of the Atlantic and Pacific were almost impossible to cross with ancient technology. We know of no round trips across them. Even compared with other navigable seas, the reliability of the **monsoon** season offered other advantages. No reliable sources record the length of voyages in this period, but, to judge from later statistics, a trans-Mediterranean journey from east to west, against the wind, would take fifty to seventy days. With the monsoon, a ship could cross the entire Erythraean Sea, between India and a port on the Persian Gulf or near the Red Sea, in three or four weeks in either direction.

Land Routes: The Silk Roads

In the long run, sea routes were more important for global history than land routes. They carried a greater variety of goods faster, more economically, and in greater amounts. Nevertheless, in the early stages, most Eurasian long-range trade was small scale—in goods of high value and limited bulk. Goods moved through a series of markets and middlemen. In the axial age, the land routes that linked Eurasia were as important as the sea routes in establishing cultural contacts: bringing people from different cultures together, facilitating the flow of the ideas of the axial age sages, and transmitting the works of art that changed taste and the goods that influenced lifestyles.

From around the mid-first millennium B.C.E., Chinese silks appeared here and there across Europe—in Athens, and at present-day Budapest in Hungary, and in a series of south German and Rhineland burials. By the end of the millennium, we can trace the flow of Chinese manufactured goods from the southern Caspian to the northern Black Sea, and into what were then gold-rich kingdoms in the southwest stretches of the Eurasian steppe. Meanwhile, roads that kings built and maintained crossed what are now Turkey and Iran, penetrated Egypt and Mesopotamia, reached the Persian Gulf, and, at their easternmost ends, touched the Pamir Mountains in Afghanistan and crossed the Indus River.

Merchants could also use these routes. The first written evidence of presumed commerce across Eurasia appears in a report from Zhang Qian, a Chinese ambassador who set out for Bactria, one of the Greek-ruled kingdoms established in Central Asia in the wake of Alexander the Great—in ca. 139 B.C.E. His objectives were to recruit allies against the aggressive steppeland dwellers on China's northern borders and to obtain horses for the Chinese army from the best breeders, deep in Central Asia.

Captured en route, he remained a hostage with the steppelanders for ten years. He escaped and continued across the Pamir Mountains and the River Oxus. He was captured again, escaped again, and finally reached home, with a steppeland wife in tow, after an absence of twelve years. He never encountered potential allies, but from a commercial point of view, his reports were favorable. The kingdoms beyond the Pamir Mountains had "cities, houses, and mansions as in China." In Ferghana in Central Asia, the horses "sweat blood and come from the stock of the heavenly horses." Zhang Qian saw Chinese cloth in Bactria. "When he asked how they obtained these things, the people told him their merchants bought them in India." From the time of his mission, "specimens of strange things began to arrive" in China "from every direction."

In 111 B.C.E., a Chinese garrison founded the outpost of Dunhuang—the name means "blazing beacon"—beyond China's western borders, amid desert and mountains. Here, according to a poem inscribed in one of the caves where travelers sheltered, was "the throat of Asia," where "the roads to the western ocean" converged like veins in the neck. We now call them the **Silk Roads**. They led to the markets of Central Asia and linked up with routes that branched into Tibet, or doubled back from beyond the Pamir Mountains toward India, or continued westward across the Iranian plateau.

From Dunhuang, the Silk Roads skirted the Taklamakan Desert, clinging to the edges, where water drains from the surrounding mountains, haunted, in Chinese accounts, by screaming demon drummers—personifications of the ferocious winds. The desert was so demanding that it deterred even bandits, while the mountains offered some protection from the predatory nomads who lived beyond them.

A few years after the founding of Dunhuang, a Chinese army, reputedly of 60,000 men, traveled to secure the mountain passes at the western end and to force the horse breeders of Ferghana to trade. A painted cave shows the general, Wudi, kneeling before the "golden

Making Connections | TRADE ROUTES AND THEIR CONNECTIONS

LONG-RANGE ROUTES	ADVANTAGES	GEOGRAPHICAL SCOPE	COMMERCE AND EXCHANGE	POLITICAL SYSTEMS
Sea Route: Indian Ocean	Changeable, predictable monsoon winds lead to reliable schedules; great variety and amount of goods can be carried via ship (emporium trading); seaborne trade usually faster than land routes	East Africa, Arabia, India, Southeast Asia; canal between Red Sea and Nile River eventually connects to Mediterranean	Aromatics (incense), spices, gold, and "thousands of other things" (including wild animals)	African kingdoms, Indian empires and kingdoms, Arabian tribal chiefdoms, Mediterranean empires
Land Route: Silk Roads across Eurasia	Less investment needed to embark on small-scale trading expeditions; more cultural contacts between vastly different peoples; widespread trade of high-value items	China, Bactria, Sogdiana, Persia, Mesopotamia, Anatolia, Caspian/Black Sea, Mediterranean	Spices, silk, gold, silver, cloth, horses, aromatics	Imperial China, Central Asian kingdoms, Egypt, nomadic tribes of Middle East, Persian Empire, Roman Empire, Mediterranean city-states
Sea Route: Mediterranean	Relatively high population densities along the coastal Mediterranean provides more opportunities for trade, numerous ports; shorter distances, calmer waters than vast Indian Ocean routes	Europe, North Africa, Southwest Asia, Black Sea, with Red Sea–Nile canal connections to Arabia, Indian Ocean route	Grain, wine, olive oil, timber, metals	Greek city-states/colonies, Egypt, North African city-states, Roman Empire

men"—idols taken, or perhaps mistaken, for Buddhas—that Chinese forces seized. In ca. 102 B.C.E., the Chinese invaded Ferghana, diverted a river, and obtained 30,000 horses in tribute. Meanwhile, caravans from China reached Persia, and Chinese trade goods became common along the eastern Mediterranean.

Trade across Eurasia exposed great disparities in wealth between East and West. These differences helped to shape the history of that region over the next 2,000 years. Already in the first century C.E., the Roman geographer Pliny worried about it. The Roman world produced little that its trading partners wanted, whereas the silks of China and the spices and incense of Arabia and the Indian Ocean were much in demand in Rome. The only way people in Europe could pay for them was in cash—gold or, more commonly, silver. Nowadays, we would call this an adverse **balance of trade**—the value of Europe's imports from Asia far surpassed the value of its exports. The problems of financing it, by finding enough silver, and ultimately of overcoming and reversing it, by finding and supplying goods Asians wanted to buy, became a major theme of the history of the West and, in the long run, as we shall see, of the world.

The First Eurasian Empire: Persia

Iran commanded a central position in the developing trade across Eurasia, linking Central Asian markets to those of Southwest Asia and the Mediterranean. So—in view of the way trade and empire are mutually nourishing—it is not surprising that the first of the great empires of the axial age originated here.

In earlier periods, Akkadians and Assyrians had carried the traditions of lowland Mesopotamia north into their hills, like booty. Now conquerors from the adjoining and even higher tableland used the same traditions to create a new state. This state became the biggest the world had yet known: the Persian Empire (see Map 7.1).

The Persian Heartland

The heartland consisted of scatterings of good soil and precious water in a vast, arid plateau. Ragae, with its brackish streams and sweet wells, overlooked the Zagros Mountains. Hamadan lay in a valley watered with springs, known for good fruit and inferior wheat. Fars was the richest area in ancient times. Water from the Zayinda Rud—a modest stream much glorified in poetry—enriched the plain of Isfahan, where the inhabitants used pigeon droppings for fertilizer. Rivers—including the Tigris and Euphrates—laced the southwest. Here, at the old trading city of Susa, on the border of the Mesopotamian world, the Persians established the capital of their state. Generally, between mountains and deserts, lay narrow

Persian Empire at its greatest extent   •   place

— Persian royal road   ----   present-day coastline/river

//// irrigation works   —   trade route

Map 7.1 The Persian Empire

strips of good pasture and land, watered by seasonal streams that could be irrigated for farming. Like the old Hittite Empire (see Chapter 4), Persia was another alliance of farmers and flocks. Hymns, which are among the earliest sources for Iranian history, praise herders and husbandmen as followers of truth and pronounce their nomadic enemies "adherents of lies, who uproot crops and waste livestock," which would be better employed fertilizing farmland. Farming communities' depictions of bull sacrifice show spurting blood transformed into sprouting wheat.

The founding of the Persian Empire is traditionally credited to Cyrus the Great, a general from Fars. Toward the mid-sixth century B.C.E., he launched a coup to take over one of the biggest successor-states of Assyria, the kingdom of the Medes. His subsequent campaigns stretched from Palestine to Afghanistan. His power reached almost the farthest limits the Persian Empire would ever attain. His inscriptions call him simply, "I, Cyrus, the Achaemenid"—the name of a proud but previously provincial family to which he belonged. He headed a conquest state, poor in resources, with a need to keep growing. The Persian Empire gradually adopted the Old World–conquering ambitions of Sargon of Akkad (see Chapter 3) and the Assyrians but with a difference: The Persians put these ambitions into practice.

The empire joined two regions—Mesopotamia and Persia—that mountains had formerly divided. At its greatest extent, it reached the Aegean coast, Egypt, and India beyond the Indus River. It relied on long-range trade and needed to invest in communications. By early in the fifth century B.C.E., nearly 1,700 miles of road crossed the empire. Royal armies tramped them at a rate of nineteen miles a day, and "Nothing mortal," it was said, "travels as fast as the royal messengers." The road was also a channel for tribute. Carvings at the imperial city of Persepolis, founded around the end of the sixth century B.C.E., show ivory, gold, and exotic animals arriving at the court of the ruler of Persia.

Persian Government

Persia was more than a robber empire. The empire provided a canal linking the Nile to the Red Sea and irrigation works on the Oxus and the Karun rivers. Forts beyond the Caucasus Mountains kept steppe nomads at bay. At Jerusalem, Cyrus the Great undertook to rebuild the temple that symbolized the city's sanctity for the Jews. The gesture was typical of the way Persian rulers conciliated the subjects they acquired. In gratitude, the biblical prophet Isaiah hailed Cyrus as God's anointed.

Greeks accused Persians of treating their kings like gods, in the Egyptian manner but this charge was unjust. Persian kings were not gods, but their right to rule was god given.

The other Persian practices that Greeks found peculiar were the Persian love of luxury—a criticism excused, perhaps, by envy—and their respect for women. Surviving Achaemenid ration lists—the records of wages and payments in kind that court personnel received—assign professions by sex. These show that royal attendants could be of either sex and that women could supervise mixed groups of men and women and earn higher wages than men. It was not, however, a society of sexual equality. Scribes had to be male, while servers of rations—the lowest category by pay—had to be female. Mothers got extra rations for the birth of boys. Nevertheless, women could hold property in their own right. This gave them a political role as what, in modern American politics, would be called "campaign funders"—backers and patrons of men who sought power. Greek sources, exaggerating the amount of power women enjoyed as a result, blamed every lurch of palace politics on female willfulness. For Greeks, who barred women from political life in their own communities, saw them as dangerous agents of chaos in other cultures' states.

The Persian–Greek Wars

Greeks who lived on and beyond the western edge of the Persian Empire were in a giant's shadow. They needed to cope with insecurity and defeat fear. In about 500 B.C.E., the ruler of Miletus, a Greek colony on the Ionian shore of western Anatolia, had a map of the world that showed two roughly equal areas—an exaggeratedly large Europe at the top, like a protruding lip over Asia, and Africa crammed into the lower half. The agenda was clear. Asia was reduced to a manageable conquest.

The map looked brash, but concealed unease. Rumors claimed that the Persians wanted to conquer Europe because "its trees were too fine for anyone but the Great King to possess." More likely, the empire was committed to expanding because it needed tribute from subject-lands to support it. In any event, the Greeks saw the Persians as a threat, but did not feel threatened enough to stop feuding with each other even when the Persians prepared to invade Greece.

The oracle of Delphi (Chapter 5) even advised submitting to Persian rule, with its reputation for efficiency, generosity, and respect for trade. In the wars that followed, intermittently, throughout the fifth century and into the fourth, Greek unity was sporadic, occurring only in dire moments of Persian invasion. Persia, after testing the difficulties of conquering Greece in unsuccessful invasions in 490 and 480 B.C.E., was generally content to keep these enemies divided, while prioritizing Persian rule over rich, soft Egypt.

The sea became the effective frontier between the Greek and Persian worlds. A Persian decree of 387 B.C.E. sums it up: the king "deems it right that the cities in Asia be his. . . . The other Greek cities, both small and great, shall be independent," while most of the Greek colonies on the islands of the Aegean were divided between Persia and Athens. This was an indication that Athens—best resourced of the Greek cities because it controlled silver mines—had imperial ambitions of its own, which many Greek states found more menacing than those of Persia.

The Empire of Alexander the Great

Not even Athens could assert long-term hegemony in Greece. Macedon, however, could. Macedon is an example of a now familiar fact: On the edges of civilizations, chiefdoms developed into states. This northern kingdom had what to southern Greeks was a barbarian background, but Greece profoundly influenced its culture. Increasingly, in the fourth century B.C.E., Macedonians saw themselves as Greeks: Aristotle (see Chapter 6) served as a tutor to the royal court.

In 338 B.C.E., King Philip of Macedon imposed unity by force on the Greeks and revived the idea of conquering Persia. When he was

Gandharan Sculpture. Soldiers of Alexander the Great (r. 336–323 B.C.E.) founded the kingdom of Gandhara. Greek influence is unmistakable in its art: in the realistic modeling, the sculptural plasticity, the deep reliefs. Buddhist piety dominates the subject matter. Here, the artist illustrates the legend of how King Sibi became a Buddha by sacrificing his eyes and flesh to save the life of a pigeon while gods look on. *Copyright The British Museum*

assassinated two years later—allegedly by a Persian-backed conspiracy— his nineteen-year-old son, Alexander, inherited his father's ambitions. For Philip, attacking Persia was probably intended to focus his uneasily united realm on an external enemy. Alexander's motivation, however, has baffled historians. Was he seeking to vindicate his dead father? Or to reenact legendary romances of Greek campaigns in Asia, which filled his head from his boyhood reading? Or was he full of insatiable ambition to leave "no world unconquered" as some early biographers claimed? Did he have humdrum economic aims? He certainly showed interest in opening up Indian Ocean trade or seizing control of its routes. He ordered reconnaissance by sea of the routes between India, Persia, and Arabia, and began, just before his death, to plan the conquest of Arabia.

Alexander's ambitions probably grew with his success. He destroyed the Persian Empire at lightning speed in three years' campaigns from 334 B.C.E. When the last Persian emperor died at his own officers' hands, perhaps because he had decided to abandon resistance, Alexander proclaimed himself "Great King." His success seems inexplicable except in terms of the interconnected skill and luck of the battlefield. The Persian Empire was essentially strong, well run, and easily governed. Alexander took it over intact, maintained its methods of control, and divided it among his generals.

Success and flattering omens convinced Alexander that he enjoyed divine favor—perhaps, even, that he was divine. His methods became increasingly arbitrary, his character increasingly unpredictable. He dealt with disloyalty first by judicial murder, then assassination, then slaughter by his own hand, then arbitrary executions. In the last years of his life, his control slipped. He failed to impose Persian rituals of homage on his Greek and Macedonian followers who felt that it was demeaning to prostrate themselves before a mere mortal, even if he was a king. He sought conquests beyond Persia's frontiers, but his troops became insubordinate, and he had to halt his invasion of India, shortly after crossing the Indus. Characteristically, Alexander saved face by pretending he had submitted not to the demands of his men, but to warnings from the gods. He had just set the conquest of Arabia as his next objective when he fell dead at age thirty-two, from unknown causes, during a drinking bout—the favorite Macedonian form of excess.

It was what modern publicists might call "a great career move." Alexander became the world's most written-about hero. Epic romancers embroidered his life with wonder stories of his uncontainable prowess. They credited him with exploring the depths of the ocean and ascending to heaven in a chariot drawn by ravens. An epic poem celebrated him in Malay. Kings in India, Ethiopia, and Scotland named themselves after him.

His material legacy was surprisingly meager. His empire did not outlast him. But long-term, long-range cultural exchanges flourished in the states among which it fragmented. On the frontiers of India, the kingdom of Gandhara combined Buddhist religion and Greek-style art. In Alexandria, the city Alexander founded at the Nile delta, Greek and Egyptian traditions fused. Through the kingdoms of Bactria and Sogdiana, the trade of the Silk Roads funneled. The successor-states helped spread Greek as a common language throughout the Middle East and western Asia. A Persian rump state, Parthia, arose in the Iranian heartland. A power vacuum in the eastern Mediterranean that none of Alexander's many imitators and heirs could fill. The eventual beneficiary was Rome.

The Rise of Rome

One of the great unsolved puzzles of history is how a small city-state of obscure origins and limited manpower conquered the Mediterranean, extended its frontiers to the Atlantic and North Sea, and transformed almost every culture it touched. The Romans started as a community of peasants, huddling for defense in an unstrategic spot. Though later Roman writers insisted on Rome's inevitable "destiny" and praised the founders' choice of site, Rome had poor soil, no metals, and no outlet to the sea. Its inhabitants became warlike by necessity. They had no way to gain wealth except at their neighbors' expense.

The Romans organized for war and made victory their supreme value. Roman citizens owed the state at least sixteen years of military service. They learned—to quote Horace again—that "to die for the fatherland is sweet and fitting." Their generals celebrated victories in triumphal public parades, showing off booty and prisoners. Roman education emphasized the virtues of patience and endurance. As a result, Rome was exceptionally well equipped to tough out defeats. Like those other great imperialists, the nineteenth-century British, they could "lose battles but win wars."

This was particularly evident in the Punic Wars the Romans fought against Carthage (see Chapter 5) for domination of the western Mediterranean. The background is clear enough. In the late third century B.C.E., Roman armies reached the limits of landward expansion in Italy. They turned their aggression westward, toward the wealth of Sardinia, Sicily, and Spain. Carthage, the most formidable naval empire of the western Mediterranean, already had colonies, allies, and subject-communities there. Reluctantly, the Romans built a fleet to fight the Carthaginians. This was remarkable, as the Romans hated the sea. "Whoever first dared to float a ship," wrote Horace in about 30 B.C.E., "must have had a heart of oak covered with a triple layer of bronze." Carthage recovered from every defeat, until in 146 B.C.E. Rome finally destroyed it and turned the western Mediterranean into a zone free of rivals. Historians generally regard these wars as the crucial episode in the rise of Rome.

Meanwhile, on its eastern flank, Rome invaded the Balkans and engaged the major powers of the eastern Mediterranean. Macedon was first to fall, annexed to Rome in 148 B.C.E., after fifty years of intermittent wars. The rich kingdom of Pergamum, in Anatolia, once part of the Persian Empire, was next. Its last king willed his kingdom to the Roman people in 133 B.C.E. Then came the rest of Anatolia, Syria, and Palestine. When Rome annexed Egypt in 30 B.C.E., it controlled virtually all the shores of the Mediterranean (see Map 7.2).

The Roman Frontiers

The Roman Empire was an empire of coasts, with the sea as it central axis. It therefore exposed long, vulnerable frontiers to landward. On the African and Levantine shores, Roman territory seemed protected by deserts. The European flank, however, despite one hundred years of further conquests, never seemed secure. There was no reliable barrier against attack. An endless quest for security led beyond the Mediterranean to the Rhine and the

Trade Goods

Food stuffs
- wine
- olive oil
- garum (fish sauce)
- honey

Metals
- gold
- tin
- copper

Cloths
- wool
- flax/linen
- murex (purple dye)

Building material
- timber
- marble

- slaves
- horses

- extent of Roman Empire ca. 120 C.E.
- Parthian Empire ca. 120 C.E.

Celts — peoples

● Fayyum — place

— maritime trade routes

290 B.C.E.: Rome reaches limits of landward expansion in Italy

264 B.C.E.: Outbreak of first war between Rome and Carthage

146 B.C.E.: Rome destroys Carthage in final war

148 B.C.E.: Rome annexes Macedon

51 B.C.E.: Conquest of Gaul completed

30 B.C.E.: Augustus becomes first emperor of Rome

27 B.C.E.: Rome annexes Egypt

43 C.E.: Rome invades Britain

106 C.E.: Conquest of Dacia completed

400 B.C.E. — 300 B.C.E. — 200 B.C.E. — 100 B.C.E. — 1 C.E. — 100 C.E. — 200 C.E.

Map 7.2 The Roman World

173

Danube rivers. In the late first and early second centuries C.E., Rome subdued Dacia (modern Romania), where deadly womenfolk were said to torture prisoners. The result was an even longer and more irrational frontier.

Roman expeditions also tested German defenses as far east as the River Elbe, but the Germans seemed too barbaric to absorb. They were "wild creatures" incapable of laws or civilized arts, according to Velleius, a Roman cavalry officer who fought them around 4 B.C.E. Julius Caesar (d. 44 B.C.E.), whose methodical generalship extended the empire to the Rhine, regarded that river as the limit of civilization. So Rome abandoned the Germans to their own devices. This was probably a mistake. Almost all speakers of Germanic languages beyond Switzerland, Austria, and the Rhineland were left outside the empire, seething with resentment and vengefulness at their exclusion from the wealth they associated with Rome. If Rome had absorbed them and the other sedentary peoples beyond its frontiers, as China did at the other end of Eurasia, the Roman Empire might have proved as durable as China's. The sedentary peoples China absorbed on its frontiers formed a formidable coalition, guarding the Chinese Empire against nomadic outsiders.

Inside the frontiers, oath-taking ceremonies at shrines in Rome, archived at the temple of the ruler of the gods, created real bonds between Romans and regional elites. In 191 B.C.E., when the Greek city of Chalcis stepped up from the status of an occupied conquest to ally, the young girls of the city turned out to dance in celebration, singing, "We revere the good faith of the Romans, which we have solemnly sworn to cherish." Roman rulers knew that they could succeed only by finding collaborators and delivering benefits.

Their methods were predatory as well as placatory. During wars for the conquest of northern Greece, for instance, in 167 B.C.E., Romans sacked seventy enemy towns so thoroughly that the region was still a desert 100 years later. They piled up captured weapons and burned them as an offering to the gods, "to whom it is right," they said, "to dedicate the spoils of the enemy." Loot shipped back to Rome was put on public display before sale to pay the army's wages, and "the gaze of the crowd was no more drawn to a stage show or athletic contests or chariot races than to all the booty of Macedonia." At the same time, 150,000 captives from the war glutted Rome's slave markets. Sometimes Romans overdid the exploitation of their victims and provoked rebellions. On the whole, however, subject-peoples were willing to pay heavily for security or, as they called it, "Roman peace."

Imperial Culture and Commerce

Retired soldiers—Latin-speaking and schooled in allegiance to Rome— helped spread a common culture across the empire, settling in lands where they had been stationed, marrying local women. On his tombstone in Cologne, in the Rhineland, the image of a retired veteran from southern Spain reclines; his wife and slave serve food and wine from an elegant, claw-footed table. A tombstone in northern Britain commemorates a sixteen-year-old boy from Roman Syria. He died, says the inscription, "in the land of the Cimmerians"—the rainy, foggy land that the Greek poet Homer (see Chapter 5) had imagined on the way to the underworld.

Roman culture was so well known in Britain that mints in the third century C.E. could stamp coins with references to the poetry of Virgil—who, in the reign of Augustus (r. 27 B.C.E.–14 C.E.), celebrated Rome's foundation myth. Everywhere, the empire promoted the same classical style for buildings and urban planning: symmetrical, harmonious, regular, and based on Greek architecture. The artistic traditions of subject-peoples became provincial styles. For instance, the last monuments of the funerary art of the pharaohs are the Fayyum portraits, which stare from the surfaces of burial caskets in Roman Egypt. They are recognizably in an ancient Egyptian tradition, yet faces as realistic and sensitive as these might be found in portraits anywhere in the Roman Empire.

Engineering was the Romans' ultimate art. They discovered how to make cement, which made unprecedented feats of building possible. Everywhere the empire reached, Romans invested in infrastructure, building roads, sewers, and aqueducts. Amphitheaters, temples, city walls, public baths, and monumental gates were erected at public expense, alongside the temples that civic-minded patrons usually endowed. The buildings serviced new cities, built in Rome's image, where there were none before, or enlarged and embellished cities that already existed. The biggest courthouse in the empire was in London, the widest street was in Italica, a Roman city in Spain. Colonists in Conimbriga, on the coast of Portugal, where salt spray corroded the mosaic floors, demolished their town center in the first century C.E. and rebuilt it to resemble Rome's. Trade as well as war shipped elements of a common culture around the empire. Rome exported Mediterranean amenities—villas and cities, mosaics—to the provinces, or forced Mediterranean crops like wine grapes, figs, and olive trees to grow in unlikely climates.

As industries became geographically specialized, trade and new commercial relationships crisscrossed the entire empire. In the first century C.E., merchants from the Duero valley in Spain were buried in Hungary. Greek potters made huge jars to transport wine from Spain to southern France. In southwest Spain, huge evaporators survive from the factories where garum—the empire's favorite fish sauce—was made from the blood and entrails of tuna and mackerel. The lives of cloth merchants from northeast France are engraved on a tomb at Igel, on the frontier of Germany. They conveyed bales of cloth by road and river and sold it in elegant shops, lavishing their profits on banquets to lord it over their farming neighbors.

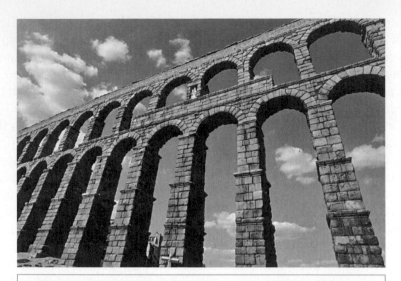

Aqueduct. Nearly 3,000 feet long and rising to 115 feet high, the second-century C.E. aqueduct of Segovia, Spain, is one of the surviving marvels of Roman engineering. In laying the infrastructure of communications and supply, the Romans were not only building up their own power and their ability to shift and sustain armies, they were also spectacularly demonstrating the benefits, self-confidence, and durability of their rule for their subject and "allied" peoples.

Of course, as the empire grew, its political institutions changed. When Rome was a small city-republic, two annually elected chief executives, called consuls, shared power between themselves, subject to checks by the assembly of nobles and notables known as the Senate, and by the tribunes, representatives of the common citizens. Increasingly, however, as the state expanded, in the emergencies of war, power was confided to individuals, called dictators, who were expected to relinquish control when the emergency was over. In the second half of the first century B.C.E., this system finally broke down in a series of struggles between rival contenders for power. In 27 B.C.E., all parties accepted Augustus, who had emerged as victor from the civil wars, as head of state and of government for life, with the right to name his successor.

Effectively, henceforth, Rome was a monarchy, though Romans, schooled in republicanism, hated to use the word. Part of the consequence of Roman distaste for kings was that the rules of succession to supreme power were never perfectly defined. Augustus called himself *princeps*—a word roughly equivalent to "chief" in English. Gradually, however, "emperor" took over as the name people normally used to designate the ruler. The Latin term—***imperator***—originally meant an army commander, and the army, or parts of the army, often in rivalry with each other, increasingly took to itself the role of dethroning and electing emperors.

Unified command and sustained leadership helped to make the growing empire manageable, but the problem remained of melding such diverse and widespread peoples into a single state. A common sense of belonging spread, as Rome granted citizenship to subject-communities. Envoys from allies on the Atlantic and Black Sea came to Rome to hang offerings in the temple of Jupiter, "greatest and best" of Rome's guardian gods. Yet this was by no means a uniform empire. It was so big that it could only work by permitting the provinces to retain their local customs and religious practices. At one level it was a federation of cities, at another a federation of peoples. Spanish notables with barbarous names followed Roman law in legal decisions that they ordered to be carved in bronze. Hebrew princes and Germanic chiefs ruled as imperial delegates. Celts were Rome's partners in the west, Greeks in the east, where Greek rather than Latin was the most widespread common tongue and served at most levels as the official language of government.

The Celts

Celts dominated western Europe by the mid-first millennium B.C.E. They occupied present-day France, Britain, Ireland, and most of Spain. Their settlements were widespread in central Europe and even reached Anatolia. Everywhere they lived in numerous chiefdoms and small states. What united them was language. They all spoke mutually intelligible versions of a single tongue.

Stories about the Celts made Roman gooseflesh ripple. They hunted human heads and hung them on their saddles. They stitched sacrifice victims inside wicker images of gods and burned them alive. They had a reputation for drunkenness. A thirty-five-year-old Celtic hostess at Vix in central France was buried with a Greek wine vessel so large that it had to be imported in sections and assembled on arrival. The Celts' courage was also renowned. Roman sculpture shows them dead or dying but never giving up.

Despite their fierce and undisciplined reputation, the Celts had a way of life that Romans recognized as civilized. They were supposedly suspicious of writing wisdom down, but many inscriptions survive, including laws, administrative records, and a calendar to foretell the future. There were modest Celtic towns in France and Spain. The town of Numancia, which was rich in iron, was a minor metropolis by Celtic standards. Covering almost 1,800 square feet, it was arranged in neat streets up to twenty-one feet wide. Here, on one terrible campaign, the Romans took 3,000 oxhides and 800 horses in booty. The dwellings of Numancia were of mud and thatch on a rubble base, but the inhabitants enjoyed fresh water supplies and sanitary drainage. Some Celtic towns were big. Manching in southern Germany, founded in the third century B.C.E., stretched over 1,000 acres. Nearby Kelheim was half as big again. Most towns minted coins and included workshops for bronze and iron manufacture, glass jewelry, and leather goods.

By the time Rome seriously began to wage war on them—early in the last quarter of the second century B.C.E.—the Celts of what is now France had a society Romans acknowledged as like their own: no longer organized along tribal lines but according to wealth, prowess, and ancestry. Nobility was measured in livestock, not land. Peasant-tenants paid their rents in calves, pigs, and grain. After ferocious initial resistance to Roman conquest, Celts usually accepted Romanization and became enthusiastic subjects of and collaborators in the Roman Empire. Generally, they welcomed the enriching economic consequences of the peace the Romans enforced.

The Beginnings of Imperialism in India

Meanwhile, beyond the eastern frontiers of Persia, in India, Alexander's threat seems to have had an immediately galvanizing effect. When one of his generals recrossed the Indus in 305 B.C.E., he found the states of the Ganges valley confederated under a leader from the delta region, Candragupta. The sources are hazy, however, until the next reign, that of Asoka, which began in the 260s B.C.E. The **Arthasastra**, describes the political world of Asoka. More importantly, his thoughts and deeds come to life in the many decrees and self-reflexive thoughts he had inscribed on pillars and rock faces. Although it is an awful pun, one can say that the rock inscriptions are hard evidence.

The sources show, first, the extraordinarily long reach of Asoka's power. Second, the evidence reveals an expanding realm, constantly reforging environments. "The king shall populate the countryside," says the *Arthasastra*, "by creating villages on virgin land or by reviving abandoned village sites. Like a barren cow, a kingdom without people yields nothing."

The same source describes two main types of environment—one rainy and the other requiring irrigation—and specifies suitable crops for both: rice, millet, wheat, barley, six sorts of beans, four types of oil seeds, vegetables, herbs, and spices. The king is responsible for irrigation and should encourage others to irrigate by exempting them from the water tax. Pasture, mines, and forests (for obtaining war elephants) are all worthy objects of conquest. Roads are emphasized, with signposts and wells at nine-mile intervals. Regulating trade—including coinage, weights, and measures—and processing the raw materials of royal lands are also part of the ruler's job.

Government

Methods and means of government reflected central control. Peasants paid a quarter of their produce in tax, apparently directly to the king, with no mention of any intermediate rulers. Army leaders received pay in cash, rather than being given a share of royal power, as was customary in later Indian states. Asoka's inscriptions portray a hands-on ruler. He "received reports at all times"—in his harem or gardens, his carriage, or his barns, where he inspected his livestock. "And whatever I order by word of mouth, whether it concerns a donation or proclamation or whatever urgent matter is entrusted by my officers, if there is any dispute or deliberation about it at the Council, it is to be reported to me immediately."

The *Arthasastra* expresses an ideology of universal rule and uniform justice. It is hard to know, however, what this meant in practice. India was already becoming a **caste** society, where social rank was inherited, unchangeable, and made sacred by religious sanctions. Brahmanical literature (see Chapter 5) treated women as if they were imperfectly human, though Buddhism admitted them to one form of high status as nuns. Few other occupations were open to them. There were state-run weaving shops for unmarriageable women, including retired prostitutes, the elderly, and the deformed. The king had female bodyguards, but this was because women's social exclusion made them trustworthy: They had nothing to gain by rebelling.

Asoka and His Mental World

The rock inscriptions are, in a sense, Asoka's autobiography, disclosing an extraordinary personal story of spiritual development. The first secure date in his reign is the conquest of Kalinga, a kingdom in eastern India around 260 B.C.E. In his commemorative inscription, he expresses regret for the suffering he caused: 150,000 deportees, 100,000 killed, "and many times that number who perished." He goes on "The Beloved of the gods [meaning Asoka himself] felt remorse, for . . . the slaughter, death and deportation of the people is extremely grievous to the Beloved of the gods, and weighs heavily on his mind." The inscription then gets to what one suspects is the real point: "The Beloved of the gods believes that one who does wrong should be forgiven. . . . And the Beloved of the gods conciliates the forest tribes of his empire, but he warns them that he has power even in his remorse, and he asks them to repent, lest they be killed."

So, in part at least, Asoka's remorse was intended as a warning, and he could hardly have won such a large empire except by war. Still, within a few years, the repudiation of conquest became a major theme of his inscriptions. "Any sons or grandsons I may have should not think of gaining new conquests. . . . The Beloved of the gods considers victory by the teaching of the Buddha to be the foremost victory" Asoka put the policy of conquest-by-conversion into practice, sending missionaries to the kingdoms that replaced the old Persian Empire and to Sri Lanka (see Chapter 5). His descendants, he hoped, would adhere to this policy "until the end of the world."

How are we to explain Asoka's extraordinary behavior? His realm was expanding into areas where city life was only starting or, in northwest India, only reviving after the disappearance of the Harappan civilization. In the absence of existing bureaucracies, Asoka had to resort to the one disciplined, literate group available: the Buddhist clergy. This was the period when Buddhist scriptures were being recorded. Asoka recruited the scribes to his service, decreeing that monks, nuns, and his lay subjects should hear the scriptures frequently and meditate upon them.

These words are the tell-tale trace of Asoka's bargain with the clergy, probably made in the tenth year of his reign, 258 B.C.E. About this time, too, he made a much-publicized pilgrimage to the scene of the Buddha's enlightenment. In a further inscription, he claimed he had made society holy, where "gods mingle with men" for the first time in India.

As the Buddhist clergy became more powerful, however, the monks' rivalry for the gifts of the pious and their disputes over matters of theology threatened the peace of the realm. So Asoka forbade them to speak ill of one another. "Concord is to be recommended, that men may hear one another's principles and obey them." Asoka's alliance with religion was the shape of things to come. As we shall see, it became a practice of kings all over the world, bringing problems and advantages.

The language of Buddhism also infused Asoka's declarations of policy: "All men are my children. . . . There is no better work than promoting the welfare of the whole world." The disadvantaged were specifically included—slaves and servants, women and prisoners. Officials toured the empire to instruct people in Asoka's version of Buddhist ethics: family loyalty, piety for holy men, mercy toward living creatures, and personal austerity. He made such tours himself, taking more pleasure in distributing alms and consulting holy men, he said, than in all other pleasures. These activities replaced hunting, formerly a royal obligation, now banned.

Toward the end of Asoka's reign, it appeared that his enlightenment was beginning to damage the empire. He tightened laws on the treatment of animals, forbidding the slaughter of young livestock and animals that were nursing their young. He forbade the castration of roosters. Fishless days were imposed. "Chaff, which contains living things must not be set on fire. Forests must not be burned to kill living things or without good reason. An animal must not be fed with another animal." Gelding and branding were restricted. These decrees must have caused outrage and threatened livelihoods. The emperor's pride in the twenty-five amnesties he granted to imprisoned criminals can hardly have endeared him to their victims. His condemnation of all rituals as trivial and useless compared with a life in accordance with Buddhist doctrine alienated ordinary people. Perhaps worst of all, his policy against conquests meant the empire could not expand and turned the violence of the military classes inward.

Only twenty-five years after Asoka's death in 232 B.C.E., his empire (which historians call the Mauryan Empire) broke up into separate states. But state-forming, environment-modifying habits had spread throughout India. The economic infrastructure—the routes of commerce, the enhanced range of resources—was not invulnerable. But the Mauryan infrastructure was unforgettable, and it could usually be repaired or reconstructed, if necessary, after future wars and environmental disasters.

Chinese Unity and Imperialism

Even after 500 years of division among warring states, the ideal of imperial unity survived in China. The Hundred Schools (see Chapter 6) kept it alive. Real unity, however, required force. Of all the warring states, Qin was the most marginal, occupying relatively infertile uplands, far from the rice-growing regions. The intelligentsia of most other states considered its people imperfectly civilized.

Toward the mid-third century B.C.E., Qin began what, in retrospect, looks like a systematic strategy of rejecting the very idea of empire. In 256 B.C.E., its ruler discontinued all imperial rites, in effect dissolving the empire. Ten years later, a new king of Qin, Shi Huangdi, declared that having been dismantled, the empire could be replaced. Over the next twenty-five years, he systematically isolated and conquered rival kingdoms and declared himself "First Emperor" of a new monarchy. "If," he declared, "the whole empire has suffered . . . it is because there were nobles and kings." In other words, with himself as sole ruler, a unified China would enjoy peace and prosperity.

Our picture of his reign comes from histories compiled one or two generations later. They are distorted partly by the awe Shi Huangdi inspired and partly by revulsion from his oppressive rule. They were based not on what he actually did, but on the sometimes unrealistic ambitions his decrees reveal. To judge by these sources, he aimed to break the aristocracy,

Terracotta Warriors. Though his life and reign were short, everything else about Shi Huangdi (r. 221–210 B.C.E.), the Qin ruler who conquered China, was on a monumental scale. The size and magnificence of his tomb, guarded by an army of terracotta warriors, echoes the grandeur of his engineering works and the scope of his ambitions and uncompromising reforms.
Nigel Hicks/Nigel Hicks Images

abolish slavery, outlaw inheritance practices that concentrated wealth in noble hands, and replace the power of kings and lords with a uniform system of civil and military districts under his own appointees. He ordered the burning of hundreds of people he considered disloyal and, reputedly, of thousands of books. Only useful technical manuals and the writings of the Legalist school (see Chapter 6) were allowed. Uniformity was the keynote of the new state. Laws, coinage, measures, script, even axle lengths of carts had, by decree, to be the same all over the kingdom. Unauthorized weapons were melted down.

Shi Huangdi's demonic energy is obvious in everything he attempted. He mobilized 700,000 laborers to build a network of roads and canals. He knocked the Great Wall of China together out of older fortifications, as protection against nomad attacks. When he died, he was buried with thousands of life-size clay models of soldiers and servants—each with different facial and body features—to accompany him into the next life. He was a showman of power on a huge scale—which is usually a sign of insecurity. His empire was too fragile to last, but sweeping away the warring states made it easier for his successors to rebuild an enduring Chinese Empire.

Unity Endangered and Saved

The first instinct of the rebels who overthrew Shi Huangdi's feeble son in 207 B.C.E. was to restore the system of the Warring States period. The result was chaotic warfare, with one of the rebel leaders, Liu Bang, emerging victorious over all the others. He put in place a carefully tempered version of Shi Huangdi's system. Restored kings had small territories within military districts. Peasants owed the state two years' military service plus one month's labor a year on state projects, which must have seemed lenient compared to Shi Huangdi's enforced labor and heavy taxation.

Legalism remained the dominant political philosophy. Liu Bang put most of his former allies to death and showed contempt for Confucianism. In the long run, however, only Confucian scholars and officials could supply the literate administrators that a growing state needed. Gradually, especially in the fifty-year reign of Han Wudi, beginning in 141 B.C.E., Confucianism again became the state ideology. Liu Bang called his dynasty "**Han**" after the portion of the country he received in the carving up of Shi Huangdi's realm. In the period of expansion that began in the late second century B.C.E., Han China became the essential China that we see on maps of later eras. Chinese began to call themselves Han.

The return of peaceful conditions under the Han dynasty stimulated a population explosion. The population of 20 million in Shi Huangdi's day probably tripled by the end of the millennium. In part, the huge increase was also a consequence of the increased size and environmental diversity of the state. Rice-growing and millet-growing regions could again exchange supplies in each other's bad times. The government coped with disasters, such as drought, famine, or earthquakes, by massive frontier colonization programs and redistributing population on a large scale. Forced migrations peopled newly conquered provinces in the southeast at the same time that settlers were encouraged to migrate south toward the Huai valley. These movements shifted the distribution of population, making the Yangtze River the main axis of China. Meanwhile, in the north in 120 B.C.E., 700,000 families were moved into a new conquest beyond the province of Shaanxi, which famine had devastated.

The Han dynasty lasted from 206 B.C.E. to 220 C.E., despite a succession system that bred palace conspiracies. Succession was determined by designating a principal wife to be the mother of each emperor's heir. This gave empresses' families a unique opportunity to profit from the emperor's favor. But the advantage rarely lasted more than two generations—less, if the empress failed to produce a future emperor. Consequently, every empress's family was tempted to seize power for itself—and most tried. In these circumstances, a dynasty that survived a long time was a triumph against the odds.

The Menace from the Steppes

The other main problem China faced in this period emerged from the steppelands, north of the Great Wall and the Silk Roads. The region had a bad reputation. Its climate was inhospitable, its soil was unworkable, and its native herdsmen were reputedly savage. In some ways, however, it was a good place in which to start building an empire. It bred plenty of horses and men accustomed to the saddle. Its people were voracious because they were poor. It was a vast, flat tract of land, with few geographical obstacles to the creation of a large state. Because the steppeland fringed the Silk Roads, leaders of steppeland bands could conduct raids, amass treasure, and use their wealth to build up large followings.

Chinese booty, ransom, and protection money enriched war chiefs who became wealthy enough to extend their followings beyond their own kin. According to Chinese evidence, compiled much later—which is all we have—the first great steppelander state emerged late in the third century B.C.E., among people the Chinese called Xiongnu. Their leader styled himself "Son of Heaven," which was a Chinese imperial title and suggests Chinese influence. His warriors hunted heads—exhibiting scalps from their bridles, making enemies' skulls into cups. The basis of their success in war was their skill in mounted archery. Sheep, horses, cattle, and camels were the basis of their economy—guaranteeing the advantages of mixed pastoralism, with milk yields of different species of animals peaking at different times. In about 176 B.C.E., they conquered Gansu, at the western end of the Great Wall, and became a serious, constant nuisance to China.

Confucian doctrine advocated what we would now call appeasement: "Your Majesty has but to manifest your virtue towards them and extend your favors to cover them, and the northern Barbarians will undoubtedly come of their own accord to pay you tribute at the wall." This policy was not as feeble as it sounds. Many neighboring peoples genuinely felt the "peaceful attraction" of Chinese rule, and Chinese culture proved remarkably adept at absorbing huge numbers of subject-peoples. The Xiongnu, however, were unresponsive to such methods.

In the late second century B.C.E., Han efforts to recruit allies against them failed. Zhang Qian's mission, described earlier in this chapter, was part of the effort and part of the failure. But in the 120s B.C.E., the Chinese mounted a series of successful operations. The fortification of the Silk Roads followed. Xiongnu victories became infrequent. Chinese defenses prevailed. For a while around the turn of the millennium, the Xiongnu even abandoned hostilities.

Thereafter, weakened by civil wars, they succumbed to celebrated campaigns by General Ban Zhao in the late first century C.E., while pressure accumulated from neighbors to the north and east, who, in their turn, were beginning to move toward statehood.

Beyond the Empires

The edges of empires bred states. The Xiongnu were not the only example of economic and political development in China's shadow. Large-scale state formation also occurred in the same period in Japan and Korea, under Chinese influence, and at the other end of Eurasia, among the Scythians and Sarmatians, pastoral peoples whose lands bordered the Roman and Persian empires.

Japan and Korea

In the fourth century B.C.E., a rice-growing, bronze-using culture known to archaeologists as Yayoi emerged in Japan. It gradually developed into a state system, under the stimulus of contacts with China. According to Chinese records, in about 200 C.E., one of the Japanese states, Yamatai, conquered the others, under the rule of a female shaman. When she died, 1,000 attendants were burned at her burial. This is the first inkling we have of a unified Japanese state.

Korean states developed faster. The Chinese were in touch with three Korean states—Silla on the Naktong River, Paekche (pek-jay) on the Kum River, and Koguryo on the Taedong River. The Chinese sources are so vague, and the archaeological evidence so scanty, that historians can say nothing reliable about the political history of these realms. But their rulers were buried in impressive tombs—usually with a wooden chamber at their core, piled with stone and earth. Grave goods reveal something of the nature of power and trade: iron weapons, fabulous gold diadems and chains, bronze ornaments that imitate Chinese work.

The Western Eurasian Steppe

Meanwhile, at the other end of the Eurasian steppe, in what is now Ukraine and southern Russia, states formed among the pastoral peoples known as Scythians and Sarmatians. Scythian states formed in and around Crimea, a peninsula that just into the Black Sea, where Greek trader-colonies had been established. Here was the Scythian center of Neapolis, a ruler's court covering forty acres and surrounded by a stone wall. Sarmatian royal courts thrived to the east, beyond the rivers Dneiper and Don.

On one level, Greek writers sensed this pastoral, nomadic world was alien, wild, and menacing. The fifth-century B.C.E. Greek historian, Herodotus, told of a legendary traveler who undertook a mysterious, dreamlike journey to their land, beyond the river Don in modern Ukraine. On another level, the nomads were familiar trading partners. Greek craftsmen depicted them in everyday scenes, milking sheep or stitching their cloaks of unshorn sheepskin. Greek and Celtic trade goods filled princely graves in the last half of the first millennium B.C.E.

Much of this art was produced under the patronage of Scythian and Sarmatian princes and is echoed in their own goldsmiths' work. A gold cup, for instance, from a royal tomb at Kul-Oba, near the Black Sea, shows bearded warriors in tunics and leggings at peace or, at least, between wars. They tend one another's wounds, fix their teeth, mend their bowstrings, and tell campfire tales. A Sarmatian queen of the first century C.E. stares, in Greek clothes and hairstyle, from the center of a gold crown. She looks as if she fancied herself a Greek goddess. Above her head, what look like deer feed on golden fig leaves, or, perhaps, in the steppeland tradition, the artist meant them to be magical horses, crowned with antlers. When we look at their art, we can never be sure whether these people were happy in their own traditions or envious of the sedentary empires—probably a bit of both.

Mesoamerica

Far more remarkable than these cases of state-building by peoples on the edges of existing empires are independent but comparable developments that began in this period in Mesoamerica. Chiefdom-formation and state-building had a long history in this region and in other parts of the Americas, but every innovation had been blocked or frustrated. The geography and vast climate zones of the Americas discouraged communication and cultural change (see Chapter 5).

Now, at least two centers sprang into what might fairly be called a potentially imperial role. Monte Albán in Oaxaca was the first. In a period of social differentiation early in the millennium, the region had deer-fed elite, buried in stone-lined graves with jade-bead lip studs and earrings. Population growth accompanied their supremacy, with increasing exploitation of irrigation and the spread of settlement into areas of sparse rainfall. Around the middle of the millennium, ever-larger settlements appeared, with ritual mounds and the first engraved picture-writing, or **glyphs**. We do not know how to read this writing, and the inscriptions are all short—perhaps no more than names and dates. From about the same time and place, we have the first evidence of what the ritual platforms were for: a carving of a human sacrifice, with blood streaming from a chest sliced open to pluck out the heart.

Not long after this, Monte Albán began to draw in population from surrounding settlements. It was a natural fortress, enhanced by defensive

Monte Albán. The builders of Monte Albán (Oaxaca, Mexico) reshaped the 1,500-foot-high mound on which it stands to fit their idea of how a city should be: fifty acres of terraces supporting temples, palaces, and garrisons. This was truly an imperial metropolis, decorated with gaudy, gory slabs depicting dismembered captives. *Kal Mullar/Woodfin Camp & Associates, Inc.*

walls. From a modest village, Monte Albán became a city of perhaps 20,000 people by about 200 B.C.E., when the population stabilized. Faded carvings proclaim its warlike values in parades of sacrifice victims. A palace and a reservoir that could have held 20,000 gallons of water suggest a familiar story: collective effort under strong rule. The main plaza contains forty huge carved stones—probably of the second century B.C.E. These are "conquest slabs," listing the names of subject-cities from as far as fifty-three miles away, perhaps as many as ninety, if the most daring readings are correct. The slabs record the tribute these cities had to pay.

Monte Albán casts light on the later and, in the long run, more spectacular case of Mesoamerican empire-building. Teotihuacán, in the valley of Mexico, about 450 miles north of Albán, was destined to be a far greater metropolis. At 6,000 feet above sea level, a little higher than Monte Albán, its agriculture was based on what were by then the region's standard products: maize, beans, and squash. Around the end of the millennium, perhaps as the result of a war, a migration as sudden as Albán's shifted almost the entire population of the valley of Mexico to Teotihuacán. The building of the towering Sun Pyramid began. By about 150 C.E., twenty monumental pyramids were in place. The other buildings included some structures apparently for housing people from distant lowland sites: ambassadors, tribute bearers, hostages.

The art of Teotihuacán suggests an ecologically fragile way of life, dependent on rainfall and unreliable gods to deliver fertile soil and crops. The artists imagined the sky as a serpent whose sweat fell as rain and fed the plant life of Earth, where sacrificers in serpent masks scattered blood from hands lacerated with cactus spikes or impaled human hearts on bones. Yet the city and the reach of its trade and power continued to

CHRONOLOGY

Seventh century B.C.E.	First written evidence of the Scythians
Sixth century B.C.E.	Cyrus the Great founds Persian Empire
Fifth century B.C.E.	1,700 miles of road cross Persian Empire; Chinese silks appear in Europe; Silla, Paekche, and Koguryo states dominate Korea
Fourth century B.C.E.	Yayoi culture emerges in Japan
334 B.C.E.	Alexander conquers Persian Empire
Third century B.C.E.	Roman Empire expands beyond Italy; first Xiongnu state emerges north of China
ca. 268–232 B.C.E.	Reign of Asoka (India)
206 B.C.E.	Beginning of Han dynasty in China
200 B.C.E.	Population of Monte Albán reaches 200,000 (Mesoamerica)
127–120 B.C.E.	Chinese mount successful operations against the Xiongnu
27 B.C.E.	Augustus becomes first emperor of Rome
ca. 150 C.E.	Teotihuacán at peak of its influence (Mesoamerica)
220 C.E.	Collapse of the Han dynasty

grow for more than 350 years. At its peak, Teotihuacán was big enough to house well over 100,000 people. Carvings more than 625 miles away depicted its warriors, and its trade goods and tribute came from a similarly wide area. Teotihuacano artifacts of the period have turned up in archaeological digs as far away as Alta Vista in Zacatecas to the north and what is today Honduras in the south.

IN PERSPECTIVE
The Aftermath of the Axial Age

The axial age left three legacies: a remarkably durable heritage of ideas, less secure though lengthening routes for trade and cultural exchange in Eurasia, and a fragile group of empires. In some ways, these legacies seemed interdependent. The empires added little to the intellectual achievements that preceded them, but they did safeguard, enshrine, and nurture them. The Romans, for example, adopted and fostered Greek learning. Persian emperors adopted Zoroastrian rites. Asoka became the patron of Buddhism in India. The Han rehabilitated Confucianism. The empires developed sea and land communications in Eurasia. The road-building programs, the Chinese effort to scout and fortify the Silk Roads, and the interest Alexander and his Persian predecessors took in Indian Ocean navigation all demonstrate that.

The collapse of the Persian Empire and the rapid unraveling of Asoka's empire showed that the world was not yet safe for large-scale imperialism. But the pattern of state-building seems to have been irresistible. New states on the edges of the existing Eurasian empires—and, as we shall see in the next chapter, in parts of Africa where contacts with Eurasia were multiplying—suggest this. The New World resembled a "parallel universe," where, despite the environmental differences, histories similar to those of parts of Eurasia and Africa were beginning to unfold.

PROBLEMS AND PARALLELS

1. How do trade, cross-cultural contacts, and better communications benefit states?
2. What were the advantages and disadvantages of sea routes versus land routes for commerce and communication in the ancient world?
3. What common factors contributed to the fall of the empires discussed in this chapter?
4. How did each empire try to unite diverse peoples in a single state? Did they succeed or fail?

Postimperial Worlds: Problems of Empires in Eurasia and Africa, ca. 200 to ca. 700 C.E.

1. Why did Teotihuacán rise and decline as an imperial power?

2. Why did the Roman Empire collapse in the west but survive in the east?

3. Why was China better adapted for long-term survival than Rome or India?

4. What were the bases for Ethiopian prosperity?

5. Why were the Arabs able to conquer a vast empire so quickly?

6. How did the Muslims treat conquered peoples?

7. How did states arise in Tibet, Korea, and Japan?

They arrived in January 378, soon after the beginning of the rain, in the moist, tropical lowlands of what is now eastern Guatemala. They came from Teotihuacán, 7,500 feet high in the mountain-ringed valley of central Mexico, across hundreds of miles of mountains and forests to the land of the Maya, whose environment, culture, and language were different from their own. The Maya called the leader of the group Siyaj K'ak, meaning "fire born." Previously, historians called him "Smoking Frog"—a literal interpretation of the way his name was carved in stone. Contemporaries in the Maya world added a nickname, "The Great Man from the West." But why had he come?

His destination was Tikal, where limestone temples and gaudily painted rooftop reliefs rose above dense forest. Tikal was one of the oldest and largest of the many city-states among which the Maya world was divided. Its population at the time was perhaps 30,000 or more. But while Tikal was a giant by Maya standards, Teotihuacán was probably more than three times its size: no mere city-state, but the nerve center of an empire that covered the valley of Mexico and spilled into neighboring regions, now called Tlaxcala and Morelos. Teotihuacano influence and tribute-gathering probed further still.

Relations between Tikal and Teotihuacán were important for both cities, because of the complementary ecologies of their regions (see Map 8.1). The Maya supplied Mexico with products unavailable in the highlands, including the plumage of forest birds for ornament, rubber for the ball games the elites of the region favored, cacao, jade, and incense. But visitors like Siyaj K'ak were rare, or even, perhaps, unprecedented. As they approached, day by day, along the river now called San Pedro Mártir, the communities they passed through handed on the news to neighbors down the line. What were the newcomers' intentions? Were they invaders or invitees? Envoys or adventurers? Were they mercenaries, perhaps, or a marriage party? Had they come to arbitrate disputes or to exploit them for their own purposes?

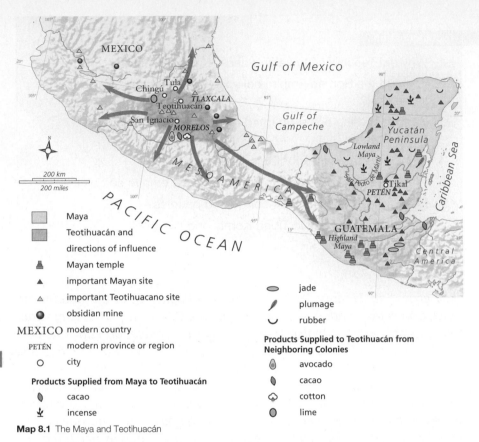

Map 8.1 The Maya and Teotihuacán

The inscriptions that record the events are too fragmentary to answer these questions. But they tell a suggestive story. When Siyaj K'ak reached Tikal on January 31, his arrival precipitated a revolution. On that very day, if the inscriptions can be taken literally, the life of the city's ruler, Chak Tok Ich'aak (or "Great Jaguar Paw," as historians used to call him), came to an end. He "entered the water," as the Maya said, after a reign of eighteen years, ending the supremacy of a royal line that had supplied thirteen kings. The monuments of his dynasty were shattered into fragments or defaced and buried: slabs of stone on which images of kings were carved, with commemorations of the wars they fought, captives they took, astronomical observations they recorded, and sacrifices they offered to the gods—sometimes of their own blood, sometimes of the lives of their captives.

Siyaj K'ak installed new rulers not only in Tikal but also in other, smaller cities in the region over the next few years. The supremacy of Teotihuacán, or at least of Teotihuacanos, was part of the new order. A rash of new cities was founded from Tikal, though they seem quickly, in most cases, to have asserted or exercised independence. It would exceed the evidence to speak of the birth of a new regional state, or the foundation of a new province of the empire of Teotihuacán. But contacts across Mesoamerica

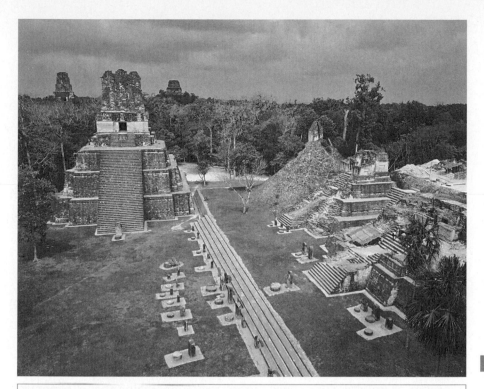

Tikal. The roof-combs of the Maya city of Tikal—hoisted facades set over the temples like mantillas in ladies' hair—rise over the forest of the Petén in Yucatán. Gaudily painted in their day, they warned off enemies, invited trade, celebrated kings. The small stones lining the plaza bear images and records of the deeds of rulers. The great temple in the middle ground was built as a tomb for King Jasaw Chan K'awiil (682–734), who restored the city's fortunes, after a period of impoverishment and defeat, and embarked on the most ambitious building program in Tikal's history.
Dagli Orti/Picture Desk, Inc./Kobal Collection

were growing; state formation was quickening and spreading, and a complex political pattern was emerging: jealous Maya cities, competing and combining, with elites often drawn or sponsored from central Mexico.

The influence and power of Teotihuacán were close to their maximum. Teotihuacanos founded colonies wherever their city needed supplies. Chingú, near the later site of Tula, was one such colony, where lime was exported for Teotihuacán's gigantic building projects. San Ignacio in Morelos was another, supplying avocados, cacao, and cotton, which would not grow in the highlands but was vital for everyday clothing and—increasingly—for the quilted armor warriors favored.

In part, pressure of population drove this expansion. Teotihuacán probably produced or attracted more people than it could contain. In any case, to sustain a growing city, Teotihuacán needed a growing empire. The basic foodstuffs the city consumed—maize and beans—were part of the ecosystem of its own region. But the concentration of population that had to be fed was enormous by the standards of preindustrial cities anywhere in the world and probably required extra supplies from farther away. The cotton and the luxuries and ritual objects on which elite life depended had to come from other climes. Teotihuacán had its own mines of **obsidian**—the glasslike substance of which the cutting blades of tools and weapons were made. But it had no other resources to export. It had to be a military state.

We do not know how the state was organized. Unlike the Maya, the Teotihuacanos produced no art depicting kings and, as far as we know, no chronicles of royal activities. Some curious features, however, show up in the archaeological record. During the fourth century, many families were shifted from small dwellings into large compounds, as if the city were being divided among rival, or potentially rival, focuses of allegiance. From the mid-fifth century, there are signs of internal instability. One of the most lavish temples was demolished. Thick, high internal walls divided different quarters of the city from each other. New building gradually ceased. Meanwhile, Teotihuacano influence over distant areas withered. At an uncertain date, probably around the mid-eighth century, a traumatic event ended Teotihuacán's greatness. Fire wrecked the center of the city, and much of the population fled. Teotihuacán remained a city of perhaps 30,000 people, but it never again displayed imperial trappings or ambition. It is hard to resist the impression that the empire had overreached itself. No single city or empire of comparable dimensions replaced Teotihuacán. But people in Mesoamerica remembered it, conserved its influence, and tried to imitate it, as they entered a period of kaleidoscopic change, in which small, well-matched states fought among themselves without ever settling into an enduring pattern.

Teotihuacán was one of the world's most out-of-the-way empires—isolated from most of the others that arose in or after the axial age. Yet it was typical of its time. Other new imperial initiatives of the era—in the formative Islamic world and in Ethiopia—succumbed to remarkably similar challenges. Even the old empires struggled with similar problems. In Rome, India, China, and Persia, imperial traditions inherited from the axial age were extinguished or suffered periods of fragmentation or submersion by invaders whom the natives regarded as barbaric. And on the edges of empires in transformation, as well as within them, new states felt the effects.

In this chapter and the next two, we have to face the questions of how, if at all, these stories are connected and why their outcomes differed. How, for instance did imperial unity revive in China but not in the other affected areas, or why did Christianity and Islam, but not Buddhism, become almost monopolistic ideologies in the areas they dominated? Less pressing, perhaps, but no less interesting, is the problem of how the history of the rest of the world echoes or connects with the fates of Eurasia's empires.

The Western Roman Empire and Its Invaders

On Rome's Capitoline Hill stands a bronze statue of the Emperor Marcus Aurelius (r. 161–180), triumphantly horsed, holding a globe, wielding Roman power at its height. Yet the empire had abiding problems: sprawling size; long, vulnerable land frontiers; a politicized soldiery, with Roman armies fighting each other to make and unmake emperors; an uneasy, usually hostile relationship with Persia. Two new dangers were increasingly apparent. First, for most of the elite, Christianity seemed subversive. To the pious, Rome's greatness was at the disposal of its gods. To the practical, Roman unity depended on politically charged cults of the divine emperor and patron-gods of Rome. Second, Germanic peoples beyond the empire's borders in Europe coveted Roman wealth. The prosperity gap was like that between "North and South," on a global level, today—inspiring fear in the prosperous and envy in the poor. Marcus Aurelius anticipated ways in which the empire would try to cope with these problems for the next three centuries. He sensed the need to divide government, making his adoptive brother co-emperor and delegating to him responsibility for the eastern frontier. This sort of division was to be a recurrent formula for saving the state from crisis. Marcus Aurelius repudiated fancy theories in favor of practical ethics. His was a dark world, glinting with campfire light, as he fought to keep the Danube frontier secure. He snatched moments on campaign to write his *Meditations* in Greek, which was still the common language of the eastern half of the empire and still the prestige language favored for philosophy. "Renew yourself," he wrote in a memo to himself, "but keep it brief and basic."

In combination with threats from Persia and the convulsions of Roman politics, Germanic invasions in the third century almost dissolved the empire. In the early

The Philosopher at War. *The Meditations* of the Emperor Marcus Aurelius (r. 161–180) were written in military camps while he was campaigning against the barbarians on the empire's northern frontiers. His statue atop the Capitol at Rome has always symbolized dynamism and power, not only because of the commanding gesture of the emperor, but also because of the power his horse displays with its flared nostrils and stamping hoof.
Canali Photobank

fifth century, the struggle to keep the immigrants out became hopeless. They came usually in relatively small, mobile war parties, numbering hundreds or at most a few thousand, composed of men detached from their traditional kinship structures by loyalty to a "ring giver"—a warlord who could buy allegiance with booty, protection money, ransom, extortion, or mercenary service. Trinkets of war-band service survive in burial sites: armbands set with jewels or onyx or inscribed with reminders of loyalty and rings bulging with garnets.

The biggest bands of migrants, numbering tens of thousands at a time, and traveling with women and children, were driven by stresses that arose in the Eurasian steppelands. Here, the mid- to late fourth century was a traumatic time, when war or hunger or plague or exceptional cold or some combination of such events induced unprecedented mobility, conflict, and confusion. The Roman historian and retired soldier, Ammianus Marcellinus, reported a conversation with some Huns, reputedly the most ferocious of the steppeland peoples of the time. "Ask," he said, "who they are and whence they came—and they cannot tell you." Fear of the Huns glistens between the lines of every account: fear of their monstrous appearance, which Roman writers suspected must be produced by self-deformation; fear of their mounted archery; fear of their merciless treatment of enemies. Late in the fourth century, the Huns broke out of their heartlands in the depths of Asia— perhaps on the northeast borders of China, where many scholars identify them with the people the Chinese called Xiongnu (see Chapter 7). A kind of ricochet effect set in, as peoples collided and cannoned off each other, like balls on a pool table. Or perhaps all the turbulence of peoples, Germans and steppelanders alike, was the result of common problems: cold weather; shrinking pastures; or new sources of wealth, such as trade and booty, enriching new classes and disrupting the traditional stability of the societies concerned. Whatever the reasons, in the late fourth and early fifth centuries, displaced communities lined up for admission into the enticing empires of Rome, Persia, China, and India.

The hardest part of the story to appreciate is what it felt like for those who took part. Inklings emerge from the earliest surviving poem in what is recognizably German: the *Hildebrandslied*, the story of a family split in the conflicts of the fifth century. Hildebrand's wife was left "in misery"; his baby grew into his battlefield adversary. The boy, raised in ignorance of his father's identity, unwittingly rejected his present of gold and jewels, "which the King of the Huns had given" to Hildebrand. Only the first few lines survive of the terrible climax, in which father and son fight to the death. The story shows the chaotic, divisive effects of the migrations, the interdependence of the worlds of the Germans and the Huns.

Germans were not nomadic by custom but, according to their own earliest historian, Jordanes, who wrote in the sixth century, were "driven to wander in a prolonged search for lands to cultivate." In 376, for instance, a reputed 200,000 Visigothic refugees were admitted into the Roman Empire. But the Romans then left them to starve, provoking a terrible revenge at the battle of Adrianople in 378, when a Roman emperor died along with most of his army. From 395 to 418, the Visigoths undertook a destructive march across the empire. In 410, they sacked Rome, inspiring speculations about the end of the world among shocked subjects of the empire, before settling as paid "guests" and, in effect, the masters of the local population in southern France and northern Spain. Other Germanic peoples found the Visigoths' example irresistible. Rome's frontier with the Germans was becoming indefensible.

Changes within the Roman Empire

Meanwhile, the center of power in the dwindling empire shifted eastward into the mostly Greek-speaking zone, where barbarian incursions were more limited. In 323, the Emperor Constantine elevated Byzantium, a dauntingly defensible small garrison town, into an imperial capital that he renamed after himself: Constantinople.

From here, in the fourth and fifth centuries, the emperors were able to keep invaders out of most of the eastern provinces or limit immigration to manageable proportions or to numbers needed for imperial defense. In the west, however, the empire could not control the incursions. Supplies and reinforcements from Constantinople could easily reach the provinces from Italy's Adriatic coast eastward, whereas the western Mediterranean lay beyond the terrible navigational bottlenecks between Italy, Sicily, and North Africa. The Rhine was easily crossed—especially in the cold winters of the early fifth century, when the river often froze. From there, invaders usually swung through northern France toward Spain or turned south to reach Italy.

Impeded by war, long-range exchanges of personnel and commerce became increasingly impractical in the west. Communications decayed. Aristocrats withdrew from traditional civic responsibilities—struggling to keep their estates going amid invasions. Bishops replaced bureaucrats. In localities from which imperial authority vanished, holy men took on the jobs of judges. Almost everywhere, barbarian experts in warfare took military commands. Garrisons withdrew from outposts of empire beyond the Rhine, the Danube, and the English Channel. After 476, there was no longer a co-emperor in the west. Regional and local priorities replaced empirewide perspectives. The most extreme form of the dissolution of authority inside the empire was the establishment of kingdoms led by foreigners, as Germans—settled as uneasy allies, entrusted with tasks of imperial defense, and quartered at the expense of their host communities—gradually usurped or accepted authority over non-Germanic populations. Where such kingdoms delivered peace and administered laws, they replaced the empire as the primary focus of people's allegiance.

The "Barbarian" West

At the time, writers of history and prophecy, peering through the twilight of the empire, could not believe Roman history was over. Rome was the last of the world monarchies that the Bible had foretold. Its end would mean the end of time. Everyone, including barbarian kings, connived in pretending that the empire had survived. Germanic settlers were all, in varying degrees, susceptible to Romanization, and their kings usually showed deference to imperial institutions. A Visigothic leader, Athawulf, vowed "to extirpate the Roman name," but ended by marrying into the Roman imperial family and collaborating with Rome. Burgundian kings, in what is now eastern France, continued a flattering correspondence with the emperors in Constantinople for as long as their state survived. The Franks, who occupied most of France in the late fifth and early sixth centuries, adorned their monarchs with emblems of Roman governors and consuls. No barbarians were proof against the appeal of Roman culture. Vandals, whose name has become a byword for destruction, had themselves portrayed in Roman-style mosaics. Even the Germanic settlers of Britain, most of whom had had virtually no contact with the Roman Empire, recalled the rule of Roman "giants" in their poetry.

Yet the limits of barbarian identification with Rome were of enormous importance. The notion of Roman citizenship gradually dissolved. Although the barbarians envied Roman civilization, most of them hankered after their own identities and—not surprisingly amid the dislocation of the times—clung to their roots. Many groups tried to differentiate themselves by upholding, at least for a time, unorthodox versions of Christianity. Some of their scholars and kings took almost as much interest in preserving their own traditional literature as in retaining or rescuing the works of classical and Christian writers. Law codes of barbarian kingdoms prescribed different rules for Germans and Romans.

The realm of the Ostrogothic king, Theodoric, was typically hybrid. He ruled Italy from 493 to 526. A church wall in his courtly center at Ravenna displays his palace, with throne room of gold, curtained like a sanctuary. His tomb is the burial mound of a Germanic king but is also in the style the Roman aristocracy of his era favored. Boethius, his chief minister, who was a Roman senator, not a Goth, worked hard to Romanize him, clinging to the old order, banking on the domestication of barbarian invaders. Imprisoned and then executed by Theodoric for his Roman partialities, he wrote *The Consolation of Philosophy*, fusing the stoical value system of happiness with the Christian tradition of deference to God. Happiness and God, Boethius argued, were identical.

Barbarian invaders had not extinguished the Roman Empire, but they had transformed it, in the areas they occupied, into what were, in effect, independent kingdoms with hybrid cultures. Historians have quarreled over whether to call this transformation a "decline," but in some ways archaeological evidence makes the term seem appropriate: towns shrank; inscriptions were fewer and less literate; the range of circulation of manufactures narrowed; and the quality of the goods people produced—especially pottery—diminished. Imperial institutions survived outside the barbarian kingdoms, and even within them people clung to a sense of continuity with the Roman past. But it is hard to resist the impression that that past was over and that in the Western empire, at least, a poorer, harder way of life had succeeded it.

Steppelanders and Their Victims

Because Germanic peoples lined the zone between Rome's frontier and the Eurasian plains, steppeland peoples like the Huns made relatively few and brief forays into the Roman Empire. Empires centered in China, Persia, and India, by contrast, had to cope with the steppelanders directly. In some ways, invading herdsmen were easier to deal with than the Germans who were used to settled agriculture. The herdsmen's techniques of warfare were less flexible and ill equipped for mountain terrain on the frontiers of Persia or India or amid rice paddies in central and southern China. When successful as conquerors, the steppelanders were usually easier to wean from their cultural traditions than the Germans, assimilating to Chinese or, in some cases, to Indian ways within a few generations.

China

China's empire, moreover, was better adapted for survival than Rome's. Thanks to China's roughly round shape, Chinese armies could get quickly to any point on its frontiers. No invaders threatened the long sea coast. Subject-peoples tended to embrace Chinese identity with a surprising degree of commitment and even enthusiasm. Above all, size, productivity, and technical inventiveness made China self-sufficient, if necessary. There was no adverse balance of trade, such as Rome endured, to drain wealth out of the empire. China's internal market was huge—more internal trade meant more wealth.

But, like Rome, China under the Han dynasty never solved the most basic problem of imperial government: how to secure the succession of emperors. Factionalism and rebelliousness bred in imperial households. To offset the danger, emperors relied ever more heavily on **eunuchs**, whom Roman emperors, too, regarded as perfect servants, and whose inability to father families of their own made them proof against dynastic ambitions. The long-term result was to create another faction and a new focus of resentment, as eunuchs usurped control over the succession. As in Rome, armies in China contended for the power to make and unmake emperors. Rivalry between armies and eunuchs precipitated civil war in 184, when Chang Chueh, a wandering medic, whose plague remedy made him a popular hero, proclaimed rebellion against eunuch rule. The army emerged ascendant from nearly forty years of war that followed.

In 220, the last Han emperor was forced to abdicate in favor of a new, army-backed dynasty, known as Jin. But the former patterns of politics resumed. Civil war became chronic, made worse by emperors' efforts to divide their responsibilities along lines similar to those Rome adopted, giving members of the imperial family regions to run. Steppeland migrants and marauders played increasingly important roles in the wars. Contenders for disputed succession called in rival barbarian armies. In 304, the leader of one of these armies proclaimed himself emperor, and his son drove the Jin south, into the Yangtze valley. The old capital, Chang'an, filled with "weeds and thorns."

Northern China became a kaleidoscope of kingdoms and self-styled empires, continually reshaken by warlords, adventurers, and new migrants, variously Turkic and Mongol. Toward the end of the fifth century, the ruler of the ascendant barbarians, the Xianbei, introduced Chinese rites, including the state cult of Confucius. But the state he founded fragmented in its turn. The old aristocracy resisted Chinese values, while the court practiced Chinese-style cycles of factionalism, family rifts, and civil wars.

India

The invasion routes into India from the steppes were poorly guarded. In the fourth century, a ruler of Maghada who called himself Candragupta, after a hero of the time of Alexander the Great, attempted to restore the unity of the Indian subcontinent. His dynasty, the Guptas, never established as wide a dominion as that of Asoka (see Chapter 7), but it did weaken the states of India's northwest frontier. The Huns who began to infiltrate India around 415—working their way west and south—were, presumably, part of the fallout of the same catastrophes that spilled steppelanders into the Roman and Chinese empires.

The morale of the population favored the invaders. Writers generally agreed that they were living in the *Kaliyuga*, the age of decline. A play written by Kalidasa—who probably lived in the fourth century—depicted alienated classes in a morally corrupt state, where officials practiced torture and the extortion of innocents. It was hard for the empire's poorest subjects to identify with a system that perpetuated their poverty by making social rank inherited. According to Faxian, a Chinese Buddhist pilgrim in India in 405–411, the "untouchables" of the lowest caste had to sound a clapper in the street to warn against their polluting presence.

The loose-knit Gupta political system, which covered most of India as far south as the Deccan showed little resilience. Its decline is conventionally dated from 467—less than a decade before the last emperor in Rome was forced to abdicate and was pensioned off. Subsequent Gupta emperors are shadowy—barely known, except by name, from contemporary sources. Yet within another fifty years or so, the Hunnic realm seems to have become one Indian state among many. Indian unity—such as it was—dissolved among a multitude of principalities in the north and a few relatively large, unstable kingdoms in the south.

New Frontiers in Asia

For the Chinese and Gupta empires, the barbarian invasions inaugurated times of troubles, but it was a time of opportunity for developing states on their frontiers, where imperial power might otherwise have inhibited or repressed development. An early Gupta inscription mentions developing states around the frontiers: the Shaka dynasty in western India and the Vakatakas, whose daughters the Guptas took in marriage in the Deccan. The conditions favored similar effects in other parts of Asia.

Korea

Refugees from China, for instance, fled from the nomad invaders in search of tamer barbarians, to whom they could offer their services as technicians or sages. Dong Shou—to take a case in point—was a scholar who escaped from the Xianbei in 337 and took refuge in neighboring Koguryo, an emerging state that occupied parts of what are now southeastern Manchuria and northern Korea. After a prosperous career, he was buried at Anak, amid wall paintings that document the history of Koguryo at the time. Buddhist and Daoist emblems mingle with scenes of the life of the kingdom: proudly displayed images of prosperity and strength, including irrigation works, rice production, people and horses eating, and a procession of well-armored soldiers. While China dissolved, Koguryo expanded. A memorial of King Kwanggaet'o, erected at the time of his death in 413, credits him with the conquest of sixty-four walled towns and 1,400 villages. Continuing prosperity—the result of the introduction of ox-drawn plows and irrigation for rice fields—can be measured in the results of the census the Chinese took when they eventually conquered Koguryo in 667–668. The country had 176 walled cities and 697,000 families. Unlike other communities whom the Chinese considered barbarians, however, Korean states had, by then, too much self-pride and too long a history of achievement to adopt Chinese identity.

Similar histories unfolded in the southern Korean kingdoms of Silla and Paekche. There, royal tombs were full of gold—spangled crowns in the shape of stylized antlers, golden belts with pendants of gold, jade, and glass. Although the iron trade contributed to the enrichment of the state, Korean states were agrarian kingdoms whose wealth was in manpower. They fought one another to gain population. Paekche paid a ransom of 1,000 households, for instance, when raiders from Koguryo occupied its capital. Silla resolutely followed Chinese models of state-building. In 520, King Pophung began to give positions of power and prestige to Confucian scholars. The kingdom, however, also had a caste system of its own. Many positions were open only to those ranked as possessing "sacred bone"— the rank of the royal family—and "true bone," the birthright of the courtly elite. (This distinction disappeared after 653, when a true bone became king.) Silla unified the Korean peninsula in more than a hundred years of warfare from the mid-sixth century.

Funan

Meanwhile, the turbulence of central Eurasia, which periodically disrupted the Silk Roads, favored states along the maritime route across Eurasia, beside monsoonal seas. Chinese travelers' accounts give us glimpses into their world. Funan occupied a stretch of territory, wrapped around the coast of the Gulf of Thailand. Chinese officials singled it out as a possible tributary or trading partner during a surge of interest in the potential of the region in the third century. Its culture was almost certainly borrowed from India. By Chinese reports, it was a repository of learning, rich enough to levy taxes in "gold, silver, pearls and perfumes." Its success depended on its role as a middleman in Chinese trade with Indonesia and the Bay of Bengal.

The Rise of Ethiopia

The most remarkable state favored by growing commerce across monsoonal seas was Ethiopia, a country at the limit of the Indian Ocean network. The right balance between accessibility and isolation was the key to Ethiopia's success. High altitude made the emergent state defensible and guaranteed it a temperate climate in tropical latitudes. Axum, the capital, was around 7,200 feet up, on a spur of the loftiest highlands.

Outsiders saw Axum as a trading state, where all the exotic goods of black Africa awaited: rhino horn, hippo hides, ivory and obsidian, tortoise shell, monkeys, and slaves. Objects manufactured in China and Greece found their way to Axumite tombs. The frequent use of Greek in inscriptions, alongside the native Ge'ez language, indicates a cosmopolitan community. Ethiopian products could reach the outside world through links with the Mediterranean via Roman and later Byzantine Egypt and with the Indian Ocean via the Red Sea. The highlands could dominate the long Rift valley land route to the south, to lands rich in gold, aromatics, slaves, and ivory.

But the corridor from the Ethiopian highlands to the sea is long and leads to dangerous waters. For the people of Axum, intent on their farming, trade was a sideline. They stamped ears of wheat on their coins. Terraces of grains sprang from valley soils, plowed with oxen and irrigated by stone dams across mountain streams. The highlands were fertile enough to produce two or three crops a year. Food mentioned in inscriptions includes wheat, beer, wine, honey, meat, butter, vegetable oils, and the world's first recorded coffee.

The material remains of the culture include finely worked ivory, metalwork, and huge, cubical tombs lined with brick arches. Three enormous stone pillars, each of a single slab of locally quarried granite, towered over the city. Depictions of many-storied buildings or figures of hawks and crocodiles adorned them. The largest pillar was 160 feet tall and weighed nearly 500 tons—bigger than any other monolith ever made. According to a Greek visitor's description, the central plaza of the city had a four-towered palace and thrones of pure marble, smothered with inscriptions, and statues of gold, silver, and bronze.

Inscriptions from early in the fourth century recorded what people at the time regarded as the key events of politics: numbers of captives; plunder in livestock; oaths of submission; doles of bread, meat, and wine granted to captives; their punitive relocation in distant parts of the empire; and thankful offerings for gods who bestowed victory—native gods at first, then, from the 340s, the Christian God. The ambitions of the kings seemed to tug across the strait to Arabia (see Chapter 5). Early in the sixth century, King Kaleb launched an expedition to conquer southern Arabia, much of which the Ethiopians occupied for most of the rest of the century.

The Crises of the Sixth and Seventh Centuries

Ethiopian control of south Arabia probably faltered because of an environmental crisis in the 530s. Plague played a part in the collapse of the irrigation states of southern Arabia and drove migrants northward, some seeking refuge in Roman-controlled Syria, others swelling the cities of Mecca and Medina. Twice during the Ethiopian occupation, the great dam at Marib broke. The losses of irrigation water were so traumatic that they became a major theme for poets' laments.

These disasters roughly coincided with other, more widespread catastrophes. In 535, the skies of the Northern Hemisphere darkened. A massive volcanic eruption in Indonesia split Java from Sumatra and spewed ash into the atmosphere. Thanks to the diminished sunlight, temperatures fell. The new conditions suited some disease-bearing microorganisms. A plague-bearing bacillus ravaged Constantinople. A disease that resembled smallpox devastated Japan. Even Mesoamerican graves contain evidence of a severe decline in health in what is now central Mexico toward the mid-sixth century. In the same period, the Eurasian steppes overspilled anew, impelling horse-borne war bands into Europe: refugees, perhaps, from plague. Historians still debate how far these events are connected and whether a single volcanic explosion can account for them. Still, the sixth century marked a trough—a low point from which reformers, with varying fortunes, could launch revivals of endangered traditions and rally weakened states.

In India, for instance, early in the seventh century, Harsha, king of Thanesar, tried to fill in the political fissures and reconstruct an empire. He devoted his exceptionally long reign of forty-one years to reunifying most of the Ganges Basin. Rulers in Punjab, Kashmir, and Nepal paid him tribute. He made tireless tours of his realm, collecting tribute, giving alms, and dispensing judgments. But even in the biography Harsha commissioned, practical compromises with kingly ideals are evident. The book describes the poor, gathering fragments of grain left after the king's camp has moved on. The king's elephants trample the hovels of peasants who can defend themselves only by hurling clods of earth. Harsha's dominion was an improvised conquest, and his achievement did not survive him. He had, however, more successful counterparts in China and Rome.

Justinian and the Eastern Roman Empire

Though the eastern Roman Empire remained a single state, it, too, was transformed. In the perceptions of its leaders, it remained "Roman," even after 476, when the emperors no longer had any power in Rome itself. Nowadays, however, historians prefer the term **Byzantine Empire**, from "Byzantium," the former name of Constantinople. From the sixth or seventh century onward, use of Latin—always restricted in the eastern provinces to fairly high levels of administration—dwindled. Most invaders were defeated, turned away, bought off, or deflected by diplomacy, but migrants seeped through the frontiers.

Justinian (r. 527–565) was the last emperor to adopt a grand strategy of imperial reunification, giving equal importance to recovery in the west and defense and expansion in the east. He aimed to be a restorer but was more suited to be a revolutionary—"a born meddler and disturber," as a chronicler who knew him called him. As the heir of a peasant-turned-soldier whom the army had elected to rule, he enjoyed thumbing his nose at established elites. He infuriated bishops with his attempts to reconcile conflicting theological opinions. His tax policies made the rich howl with anguish. He was a great lawgiver who had himself depicted as the biblical Moses and yet broke all the rules. Typically, Justinian outraged straitlaced courtiers by choosing a notoriously dissolute actress named Theodora to be his empress. He relied on her strength and intellect. She was the counselor of every policy and the troubleshooter of every crisis. In the famous mosaic portrait of her in the church of San Vitale at Ravenna in Italy, she wears jewels of triumph and a cloak embroidered with images of kingship and wisdom.

Hagia Sophia. The minarets of the mosque of Hagia Sophia in Istanbul conceal the building's origins as the greatest Christian church of its day, built at the command of the Emperor Justinian to defy time and display the largest dome in the world at the time. The dome collapsed some twenty years after its completion. So the emperor had it rebuilt on an even more ambitious scale. Daring perforations around the base of the dome—more than 100 feet wide and nearly 200 feet high—bathed the sanctuary in light.
Bieber, Tim/Getty Images Inc.–Image Bank

Justinian had the ill-disciplined energy of all insomniacs as he paced the palace corridors at night, "like a ghost," as hostile courtiers said. He thought big. He had himself depicted in a statue, toting a globe in one hand and spreading the other toward the rising sun. His projects included importing the secret of making silk from China and allying with Arabs and Ethiopians against Persia. He built Constantinople's cathedral to be the biggest church in the world and, when its great dome fell down, built it again. He urged his armies against barbarian kingdoms with fanatical perseverance, at crippling cost. The outcome reunited most of the Mediterranean world. Buildings Justinian erected stretched from Morocco to the Persian frontier. He left his partially restored empire impoverished but enlarged.

The robust performance of the eastern empire in the crises that followed was impressive. In the West, however, where Justinian's wars devastated Italy, he probably did more in the long run to dissolve the empire than renew it, for it emerged more vulnerable to subsequent invaders. It was a hag-ridden, doom-fraught world, in which bishops and holy men took over the functions of vanishing public authorities, and relics of saints kept demonic powers at bay.

The New Barbarians

For the barbarian invasions were not yet over. The next invaders of Italy, the Lombards, entered the peninsula in 568 from the north, just in time to gather the spoils of Justinian's wars, in which Romans and Goths had exhausted each other. On a plaque made to adorn the helmet of their King Agilulf, winged figures brandish drinking horns of a traditional Germanic court along with placards marked "Victory" of a kind carried in Roman triumphs. Agilulf's sumptuous cross—all Christian barbarian kings had something similar—is a wand of victory: a sign to conquer by. In the late seventh century, the Bulgars, another invader-people from the steppes, crossed the Danube and set up as the elite of a state that stretched from the northern Balkans almost to the walls of Constantinople. In his shrine at Arkona, on the Baltic, the four-headed deity of the Slavs was perhaps already developing the thirst for wine for which he later became notorious. During the seventh and eighth centuries, in an expansion almost undocumented and never explained, Slavs spread over most of eastern Europe from the Baltic to southern Greece. Meanwhile, in North Africa, the Berbers, upland pastoralists, mobilized camel-borne war bands to terrorize the southern Mediterranean shore. In Scandinavia, in the eighth century, warriors who fought on sleds with prows carved with the heads of monsters took to the sea.

The Arabs

These all proved formidable enemies of what was left of the Roman world. But most formidable of all the loiterers on the threshold were the Arabs, or, more precisely, nomadic, Arabic-speaking peoples of central Arabia. They lived astride the trade routes of the peninsula, between Romanized communities and city-states in the north and the maritime-oriented kingdoms of the seaboard. In the seventh century, they were transformed from a regional nuisance into a dynamic force. The preceding period in Arabia has received bad press—represented as chaotic and morally clueless, until the Prophet Muhammad brought peace and justice in the 620s and early 630s. But the contrast between the periods before and after the Prophet's arrival may be too sharply drawn.

The few glimpses the sources give us suggest that Arab society was already demographically robust, militarily effective, and—at least in its poetry—artistically creative. "Poetry, horses, and numbers of people" were the standards by which different communities measured their rival merits. It is true, however, that Arabia was politically divided and riven by internal wars among tribes. The best-documented war was said to have started when the tribe of Dhubyan cheated in a horse race against the Abs. It lasted for generations and inspired the work of Antarah ibn-Shaddad al-Absi, the most renowned poet and warrior of the age.

It is also true that tribes had come to depend on war: raiding the Byzantine, Persian, and Arab cities that were scattered around the edges of the region and milking their trade. In one respect, the transformation of these Arabs resembled that of other nomadic peoples mobilized for war by social change. As trade and banditry concentrated wealth, new styles of leadership dislocated the traditional, kinship-based structures of society and created an opportunity for a single, charismatic leader to unite an overwhelming force. In the Arabs' case, however, Muhammad's distinctive character marked him out from all other such leaders. His impact changed every aspect of life it touched. The Prophet taught a religion that was as rigorously monotheistic as Judaism, as humane and potentially as universal as Christianity, as traditional as paganism, and—for its time—more practical than any of them. More than a religion, Islam—literally "submission" to God—was also a way of life and a blueprint for society, complete with a demanding but unusually practical moral code, a set of rules of personal discipline, and the outline of a code of civil law.

Islam

A belief central to Islam represents Muhammad as God's mouthpiece and therefore, in human terms, utterly original. His teachings crackle and snap with the noise of a break with the past. He picked up Jewish concepts: monotheism, providence, and history ruled by God. The inspiration of Islam combined elements borrowed from Judaism and Christianity with a measure of respect for some of the traditional rites and teachings of pagan traditions in Arabia.

Muhammad claimed to have received his teaching from God, through the Archangel Gabriel, who revealed divine words into his ear. The resulting **Quran** was so persuasive that hundreds of millions of people believe him to this day. By the time of his death, Muhammad had equipped his followers with a dynamic form of social organization, a sense of their own unique access to the truth of God, and a conviction that war against nonbelievers was not only justified but also sanctified. Warriors were promised an afterlife in a paradise where sensual pleasures were like those of this world—pleasure gardens, young women. Muhammad's legacy gave Muslims (those who "submit" to God's message) administrative and ideological advantages against potential enemies. Yet the opportunity for the Arabs to become an imperial people arose as much, perhaps, from the weakness of the Byzantine and, especially, the Persian empires, as from the dynamics of their own society.

The Arabs against Persia and Rome

Of the old Eurasian empires, Persia's had been the most successful in fending off steppeland turbulence. The Sasanians, however, Persia's ruling dynasty from 226, concentrated their power in the most defensible part of the empire, in the highlands of Fars and in and beyond the Zagros Mountains. A commanding position in the world, along trade routes that linked the Mediterranean to the Indian Ocean and the Silk Roads, gave them the resources to maintain their traditional hostility to Rome— symbolized in a rock carving of 260, where the Roman emperor, Valerian, grovels at the feet of Persian captors. Yet mutual respect tempered Persia's wars against Rome. Each empire recognized the other as civilized, while condemning all other neighbors as barbarians. In the 380s, Rome and Persia responded to the barbarian menace by making peace.

The peace lasted throughout the steppeland turbulence of the fifth century, but at the beginning of the sixth century, as other dangers seemed to recede, war between Romans and Persians resumed with lethal intent—like sparring between boxers that turns deadly. By the time of the Arab conquests, the two giant empires had worn each other out. Mountains had protected Persia from northern steppeland invaders—but the Arab frontier to the southwest was flat. The Muslim Arabs absorbed the Persian Empire in its entirety in a series of campaigns from the late 630s to the early 650s. The Roman provinces of Syria, Palestine, Egypt, and North Africa—Rome's wealthiest and most populous subject-areas— fell to Arab or Arab-led armies by the early eighth century (see Map 8.2).

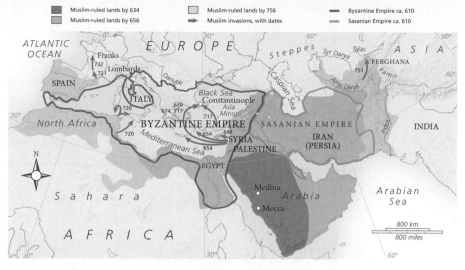

Map 8.2 Islam: Early Conquests

The Muslim World

The Muslims' conquests functioned like a single empire, gradually spreading Islam, the Arabic language, and a common Muslim identity wherever it went, and introducing more or less uniform principles of law and government. Flexibility brought success. Although Arabs and descendants of the Prophet's own tribe enjoyed social privileges, every male Muslim could share a sense of belonging to an imperial elite. Although women were repressed, they at least had important rights: to initiate divorce (albeit under much stricter conditions than those that applied to men); to own property and retain it after divorce; and to conduct business in their own right. Christians and Jews, though vulnerable to periodic persecution and compelled to pay extra taxes, were normally allowed to worship in their own way. So, at first, were the Zoroastrians of Persia, who, though despised as pagans, were too numerous to alienate. Although other forms of paganism were forbidden, many traditional shrines and pilgrimages were resanctified as suitable for Muslim devotion.

The Islamic world was too big to remain a single empire for long. And the precepts Muhammad left his followers at his death were not intended for a large state. For his followers, he was both prophet and ruler. Whereas Jesus invited individuals to respond to God's grace, Muhammad, more straightforwardly, called them to obey God's laws. Whereas Moses legislated for a chosen people, the Jews, and Jesus preached a "kingdom not of this world," Muhammad aimed at a code of behavior covering every department of life. He failed, however, to leave a code that was anything like comprehensive. So schools of jurisprudence

Making Connections | EMPIRES IN TRANSFORMATION

EMPIRE/ REGION	EXTERNAL ENEMIES	INTERNAL WEAKNESSES	STRENGTHS	SURVIVAL STRATEGIES	SUCCESSOR STATE
Teotihuacán/ Mesoamerica	Resentful tributary city-states	Overpopulation; reliance on imports; limited resources to export	Widely emulated culture; extensive trade network	Continual expansion to sustain population growth; installing friendly rulers in neighboring regions	
Roman/ Mediterranean	Germanic border peoples; Huns from Eurasian steppes; Persians	Sprawling, vulnerable land frontiers; politicized military; Christian threat to paganism; internal disorder; mass migrations; uncertain succession of leadership; adverse balance of trade	Occasional strong leaders; strong military tradition; eastern provinces easily defended and supplied	Division of leadership responsibility under Marcus Aurelius (162); division of empire after Constantine (d. 337); transfer of capital to Constantinople	Byzantine Empire in east; Germanic and barbarian kingdoms in west

Hun/China	Steppeland raiders and migrants →	Uncertain succession of leadership; feuding imperial factions; warlords →	Circular shape facilitates movement of troops and information; Chinese culture imitated by barbarians; strong internal economy →	Use of eunuchs for administration; promotion of Chinese customs and language among barbarians → Jin dynasty, followed by civil war and political fragmentation
Gupta/India	Huns →	Cultural pessimism (age of Kaliyuga); poor defenses; inequality fostered by caste system; corrupt bureaucracy →	Several strong leaders (Candra Gupta) →	Differing layers of local authority linked together → Hunnic states and other principalities; kingdom of Harsha
Sasanian/Persia	Romans; nomadic Arabs →	Exhaustion after continuous wars with Rome →	Commanding geographic position; strong defenses; effective diplomacy →	Concentrating power in most defensible areas; diplomacy with Rome → Islamic caliphate

set out to fill in the gaps by inferring Muhammad's principles from laws he made in his lifetime, applying them more generally and, in some cases, adding insights from reason, common sense, or custom. The **Sharia**—literally, "the desert dweller's way to water"—was both a religious discipline and a law code for the state. The principles of law were unchangeable: revealed to the masters of the eighth and ninth centuries, whose interpretations of Muhammad's tradition were regarded as divinely guided. The reconciliation of the various schools' opinions, however, has always allowed some opportunities for development.

One consequence of the way Islam developed was that where Jesus had proclaimed a sharp distinction between the secular and the spiritual, Muslims acknowledged no difference. The supreme Islamic authority, the **caliph**—literally, the "successor" of the Prophet—was, Christians said, both pope and emperor. The problem of identifying who was caliph split Islam between rival claimants and incompatible methods of choosing a caliph within a generation of Muhammad's death. The major division that eventually developed was between **Shia** (meaning "party"), which regarded the caliphate as the prerogative of Muhammad's nephew, Ali, and his heirs, and **Sunni** (meaning "tradition"), which maintained that the Muslim community could designate any member of Muhammad's tribe to hold the office. The rift has never healed, and although Sunnism became the dominant tradition in the Islamic world, the schisms multiplied and, with them, internal conflicts, rival caliphates, and secessionist states.

For as long as unity prevailed, the limits of Arab expansion show both its explosive nature and its reliance on mobilizing the resources and manpower of conquered or converted communities to make further conquests. When Arab expansion began to run out of impetus, in the second decade of the eighth century, armies owing allegiance to the successors of Muhammad, under Arab generalship, were operating in northern Spain. More or less at the same time, they were destroying Zoroastrian temples in Central Asia and a Buddhist shrine in northern India. At its northeast extremity, the Arab effort even touched the outermost frontier of Chinese imperialism, west of the Pamir Mountains, where, in the first half of the eighth century, local rulers played off the Chinese against the Arabs in their efforts to maximize their own power. In 751, Chinese and Arab armies met in direct conflict for the first and last time, on the banks of the Talas River. The result was total victory for the Arabs and their Turkic allies. After this, China withdrew permanently behind the Pamirs, and most of Central Asia became securely part of the world of Islam—but that is part of the stories of chapters still to come.

Recovery and Its Limits in China

At home, China faced relatively familiar problems, with only internal conflicts to weaken it and only the well-known threat from the steppelands to hold at bay. China's recovery from the crisis of the sixth century started later than Rome's under Justinian but lasted longer. In the 570s, a professional soldier, Yang Jian (r. 581–605) became arbiter of power in the Yellow River valley—elevated to civil command because of his outstanding record in wars that had reunited the region. He proclaimed himself emperor, put to death fifty-nine princes of the dynasty he had formerly served, and launched a strategy to re-create the empire by conquering the Yantgze valley. It proved remarkably easy—accomplished in about seven years, perhaps because dynastic instability had undermined the loyalty of southern Chinese to their existing rulers. As a Chinese who had proved that he could master barbarians on the battlefield, Yang Jian was an attractive candidate for the throne.

Conscious of his lack of all traditional credentials except success, the new emperor looked to Buddhism to legitimize his rule and to Legalism (see Chapter 6) for practical guidance in government. Law, Yang Jian said, should "suit the times." In other words, there were no sacred, everlasting, or universal principles. He vowed "to replace mercy with justice"—and demonstrated his commitment by endorsing the condemnation of his own son to death for embezzlement. He affected contempt for Confucian bookworms and controlled the court by violent displays of temper, personally beating underlings who displeased him, sometimes to death. His workaholic and frugal ways—he rationed the palace women's cosmetics—were the characteristics that most impressed observers.

Yang Jian's brutal, strong-arm methods were appropriate to a time of reunification by force. His successor reverted to tradition, announcing the revival of clemency, Confucian learning, and "ancient standards." The great triumph of his reign was the reintegration of the Yellow River and Yantgze valleys by an improved and extensive canal system, the Grand Canal. This was the kind of project that ought to have identified the dynasty with the "ancient virtue" Confucians prized. It was in the tradition of the great engineering emperors of legend. The regime, however, forfeited this potential goodwill by the forced labor and taxes the canal-building effort demanded. An attempt to conquer Korea strained the finances of the empire and the loyalty of the elite. The effort was ruinous and unsuccessful—the usual prelude to a political revolution.

Rise of the Tang

In 617, as the throne toppled, the most respected family in the kingdom, the Li—or those who escaped an imperial attempt to exterminate their clan—led a rebellion. Li Yuan, head of the family after the massacre, was well connected in the army. By promises of future favor, he secured neutrality or support from nomad princes. The reconquest of the country from rival rebels was not complete until about 624, but the exhaustion and disenchantment of the country favored a period of peace. The new dynasty, which called itself **Tang**, relied at first on this comfortable mood. The second emperor of the dynasty, Taizong, took an interventionist, reformist line. He favored the skeptical, scientific tradition; derided omens and magic potions; and held ceremonies when he pleased, not when seers told him to. He rationalized methods of administration, cutting down the number of posts and administrative divisions and subdivisions, creating a new, hand-picked bureaucracy for the provinces that he selected by examination, and simplifying the law codes.

Empress Wu

Taizong's reforms did much to stabilize the empire. Dynastic crises no longer threatened to dissolve the state. A grueling test occurred in 690, when a woman seized the throne. On the face of it, this was unlikely to happen. Two collections of anecdotes—the *Nüjie* and *Nüchunyu*— dominated perceptions of women as idle and promiscuous: a virtuous woman got up early and applied herself to household chores. Women were largely excluded from education—a limitation against which the *Nüjie* protested—and barred from the examinations for the state service. The only route to power was through the dangerous, overpopulated imperial harem. According to later sources, who may have deliberately tried to blacken her reputation because they were appalled at the very idea of a woman ruler, Wu Zhao started as a lowly concubine, but her combination of beauty and brains impressed Taizong. Her recommendation of torture, brutality, and slaughter as methods of government supposedly amused him. It arose during a conversation about horse training, but, Wu Zhao said, "the emperor understood my meaning." She sought power by a characteristically bold stroke: seducing the emperor's heir. As the former emperor's concubine, she was ineligible to be the next empress, but she maneuvered her way around that obstacle with ease. In 655, she married the heir to the throne, replacing his official wife, whom she tortured to death. Similar methods ensured her ascendancy during her husband's lifetime and as effective regent during the next two reigns. To secure her own elevation to the rank of emperor, she mustered every disaffected faction. The Buddhist clergy were her agents, proclaiming her as an incarnation of God, circulating propaganda on her behalf around the empire. Urged by 60,000 petitioners, she became emperor—literally, because she did not rule as an empress but used the masculine title.

Tang Decline

These extraordinary and—to most people at the time—unnatural events hardly disturbed the continuity of the Tang and provoked no serious attempts at provincial secession of the kind that had been routine under previous dynasties. Resentment accumulated, however, under the less resolute rule of Wu's successors. In the mid-eighth century, the defenses of the empire were beginning to look shaky as defeats by nomads became increasingly frequent. A frontier general, An Lushan, was selected as scapegoat. He had little recourse except to rebel. The ensuing civil war confirmed the militarization of society, which, owing to the demands of frontier wars, was already happening anyway. In the 750s, 750,000 men were under arms. Governors became virtually autonomous rulers of their provinces. About a quarter to a third of the empire was effectively outside imperial control. Peasants lived, it was said, "without a penny to their name."

To "bring the provinces under the rule of law" was now the watchword. "Only then can proper order be restored to the realm." Tax reforms in 782 decreed a single, uniform system throughout the empire. In practice, local authorities were left to fulfill quotas. Emperors took the initiative against the autonomous provinces and even began to restore control of provincial armed forces to the central government. But they failed to control the most wayward province, Hebei, which was effectively independent by 822. Meanwhile, the provinces that remained supposedly subject to direct imperial control gained power at the expense of a central

Tang Pottery. The popularity of camels as subjects of fine pottery in Tang China shows the importance of communications with Central Asia along the desert Silk Roads. Here, the potter manages to combine realism and idealism. No camel was ever so lovely, but the tilt of the head, the shape of the braying mouth, the details of the musculature, and the intricacies of the saddle are all lively and typical. *David Gower © Dorling Kindersley*

government that the efforts at recovery had impoverished. Governors enjoyed long tenures, levied unauthorized taxes, appointed local nominees to powerful administrative positions, and acquired ever-larger revenues and retinues. Central government recovered some taxpayers. There were 2.5 million registered households in 807 and 5 million in 839. This was still little more than half the figure attained before An Lushan's revolt. Imperial power became confined to the Yangtze valley.

In the Shadow of Tang: Tibet and Japan

In the shadow of Tang China, promising states emerged. Tibet and Japan provide contrasting examples (see Map 8.3).

Tibet

At the time of the presumed beginnings of the first Tibetan state in the sixth century, the Chinese spoke of Tibetans in the conventional language used for barbarians, as pastoralists who "sleep in unclean places and never wash or comb their hair." In the river valleys of Tibet, however, sedentary agriculture was possible. A little-understood agricultural transformation in the fifth century brought barley to these areas as a staple crop. Once a cereal food was available in large amounts, the advantages of a cold climate for storage helped to create large food surpluses. A land from which small numbers of nomads eked a precarious living now became a breeding ground of armies that could march on far campaigns with "ten thousand" sheep and horses in their supply trains.

Before the seventh century, divine monarchs ruled Tibet, "descended," according to early poems, "from mid-sky, seven stories high," and aspiring to rule "all under heaven." Like other divine kings, they were liable to be sacrificed when their usefulness expired. At an unknown date in the sixth century, kings who ruled until they died a natural death replaced this system. Long reigns, with stability and continuity, were now possible. The first king known from more than fragmentary mentions was Songtsen Gampo. His reign, from about 627 to 650, marked an unprecedented leap in Tibetan power. China bought him off with a Chinese bride in 640. Preserved among a cache of documents in a cave on the Silk Road is the oath of allegiance he exacted: "Never will we disobey any command the king may give." In practice, however, in most of the communities he conquered, he simply levied tribute, rather than practicing direct rule or close supervision.

Tibetan aggression continued for most of the next 250 years. Tibetan armies conquered Nepal and invaded Turkestan in Central Asia. A pillar at Lhasa, the Tibetan capital, erected before 750, records campaigns

Map 8.3 Tang China, Tibet, and Japan, ca. 750 C.E.

Scale varies with perspective

3,333 km
(2,071 miles)

8,392 km
(5,214 miles)

PACIFIC
OCEAN

*Yellow
Sea*

*East China
Sea*

JAPAN

YAMATO

Honshu

KOGURYO

SILLA

PAEKCHE

TAIWAN

*South China
Sea*

Hainan

CHAMPA

Southeast Asia

Turks

Turks

Steppes

Talas

Tien Shan

Samarkand

Bukhara

Kashgar

Yarkand

Pamir

Kabul

Khotan

*Taklamakan
Desert*

*Kunlun
Mountains*

Dunhuang

TIBET

Lhasa

NEPAL

Himalayas

Brahmaputra

Ganges

INDIA

*Bay of
Bengal*

*Arabian
Peninsula*

Persia

Taiyuan

Xiangzhou

Luoyang

Chang'an

Chengdu

Hebei

Yellow River

Yizhou

Weizhou

Bianzhou

Runzhou

Changzhou

Xuanzhou

Yangtze

Yangzhou

Guangzhou

TANG
CHINA

FENAN

Tang Empire at its greatest extent

areas of temporary Tang control

Yamato state

Tibetan invasions

Tibetan Empire ca. 750 C.E.

Silk Roads

Great Wall

Grand Canal

city with over 300,000 inhabitants

other major city

deep inside China. In 821, a Chinese ambassador described the Tibetan war camp, where shamans in tiger skins banged drums before a tent "hung with gold ornaments in the form of dragons, tigers and leopards." Inside, in a turban "the color of morning clouds," the king watched as chiefs signed the treaty with China in blood.

The kings' tastes were increasingly cosmopolitan. Ten of them, including Songtsen Gampo, lie under small mounds at Phyongrgyas, where "dead companions" attended them—now no longer sacrificed but appointed to guard and tend the graves without direct contact with the outside world. Pillars in Indian, central Asian, and Chinese styles, and a guardian lion modeled on a Persian original, attest to the role of Tibet as a cultural crossroads. Their metalsmiths' ingenuity was famous. Mechanical toys of gold dispatched as gifts to the Chinese court included a horse with moving limbs and a tiger with roaring jaws. Tibetan chain mail had an almost magical reputation for deflecting missiles. Yet even this could not protect the Tibetans from the effects of the instability of the era of Tang decline, which must have disrupted trade, while the power of the steppelanders limited Tibetan opportunities to raid or expand. In the early ninth century, Tibet suffered a dreary sequence of defeats on all fronts. Rebellions ensued. Tibet signed its last treaty as an equal with China in 823. Its last known king was assassinated in 842.

Japan

Better prospects of enduring experiments in statecraft existed on the remoter edges of Chinese cultural influence, in Japan, where the steppeland menace could not reach. Chinese culture began to arrive in Japan from Korea when a Buddhist monk became tutor at a Japanese court in about 400. The Korean kingdom of Paekche sent scholars and Buddhist scriptures. The leading state in Japan, Yamato, was a maritime kingdom, attracted by Korean and Chinese civilization, and at least as interested in expanding onto the mainland of Asia as in growing within the Japanese islands. Around 475, the king of Yamato, applied to China for the rank of general and minister. He claimed his ancestors had conquered "55 kingdoms of hairy men to the east and 65 barbarian kingdoms to the west." Crossing the sea to the north, he added, they had subjugated ninety-five kingdoms. "The way to govern is to maintain harmony and peace, thereby establishing order." The ruler, one of the Korean advisers suggested, should "try to make farmers prosperous. . . . After he has followed this policy for three years, food and soldiers will become plentiful." From the mid-sixth century, Japan was following this sort of program, organizing royal estates, taking censuses.

Early in the seventh century, direct contact with China opened. The first Japanese embassy to China presented greetings "from the Son of Heaven in the land where the sun rises to the Son of Heaven in the land where the sun sets." The Chinese dismissed this as impertinence. Their accounts make the queen who ruled Japan at the time say, "As barbarians living in an isolated place beyond the sea, we do not know propriety and justice." It is not clear that the Japanese really saw themselves like that. They staked a claim to equality with China—and imperial rank—that subsequent Japanese regimes never entirely abandoned.

In the 640s, the dynasty narrowly beat off a bid for the throne from a Chinese immigrant family. Reform of the administration then began in earnest. The drive to centralize by breaking up and replacing traditional power structures is reflected in a decree of 645 that blamed clan chieftains for dividing up the land, engaging in conflict, unjustly exploiting labor, and impoverishing peasants "who lack enough land to insert a needle." Landlords were forbidden "to increase, by one iota, the miseries of the weak." Indirectly, China's invasion of Korea in the 660s boosted imperial rule in Japan. One hundred Korean refugees were appointed to court rank. After victory in a civil war of 672, the ruling dynasty of Japan was unchallenged. Japan solved the problem that bedeviled the politics of other empires—devising a secure means to ensure the succession—by two processes. First, women's aptitude to rule was accepted. This increased the dynasty's stock of suitable candidates for the throne. Indeed, until the 770s, when a disastrous empress inspired lasting revulsion against women rulers, most rulers were women. Second, from 749, it became normal for rulers to abdicate and watch over the transmission of power to their heirs. The system worked well until the mid-ninth century, when a single courtly family, the Fujiwara, established an effective monopoly over supply of the chief wives for successive emperors. Thereafter, in the Japanese system of government, the emperor presided over the realm, but a dynasty of court favorites or chief ministers usually did the ruler's job. The last big political development—the search for a means to harness Buddhism for state service while preserving Japan's native religion—belongs in the next chapter.

IN PERSPECTIVE
The Triumph of Barbarism?

Had Siyaj K'ak been able to continue his journey from Teotihuacán and cross the ocean to Eurasia, he might have been gratified by the contrast between the stability and growth of the empire he represented and the

CHRONOLOGY	
220	End of Han dynasty in China
323	Founding of Constantinople
340	Spread of Christianity in Ethiopia
Third and fourth centuries	Germanic invasions of Roman Empire; Huns break out of Central Asia
ca. 375	Teotihuacán (Mesoamerica) at peak of its influence and power
Fifth century	Introduction of barley as a staple crop in Tibet
400	Beginning of Chinese influence in Japan
410	Visigoths sack Rome
415	Huns begin to infiltrate India
467	Death of last-known Gupta emperor (India)
476	End of west Roman Empire
493–526	Reign of Theodoric, Ostrogothic king in Italy
527–565	Reign of Justinian, Byzantine emperor
ca. 535	Massive volcanic eruption in present-day Indonesia
570–632	Life of Muhammed
Seventh century	Beginning of Slav expansion in eastern Europe
609	Grand Canal completed in China
627–650	Reign of Songtsen Gampo in Tibet
630–720	Rapid Arab expansion
667–668	Chinese conquest of Koguryo (Korea)
690	Beginning of reign of Empress Wu (China)
751	Arabs defeat Chinese at battle of Talas

(All dates are C.E.)

perils that beset the empires of the Old World. In the year of his arrival, the Visigoths challenged Roman might at Adrianople. The crises that accompanied the traumas of the Eurasian steppelands and the migrations of Germanic and steppelander peoples into neighboring empires were already beginning. One measure of the instability that ensued is particularly striking. In much of Europe and India, the fifth and sixth centuries were so chaotic that recordkeeping collapsed, and we can no longer reconstruct a complete outline even of the most basic facts of political history—the names and chronology of kings and dynasties. By contrast, in the same period, for the Maya world Siyaj K'ak' visited, we know far more about the rulers of many city-states, whose records are inscribed in stone in meticulous detail.

Yet, despite the waves of migrants and invaders that washed over Old World empires in the half millennium or so from about 200 onward and the crises they provoked, the most remarkable feature of the period is perhaps the durability of old orders. Cultural conflicts usually follow battlefield victories. And even where the so-called barbarians defeated the empires, they tended to get conquered in their turn by the cultures of their victims. The German invaders of the Roman world were partly Romanized, while the eastern Roman Empire survived, centered on Constantinople. Steppeland conquerors played havoc with the political unity of India—but the cultural transformations of India happened from within. "Barbarians" disrupted China politically but did not disturb the continuity of Chinese civilization. On the contrary, when barbarians settled within China, they adjusted to Chinese ways. Indeed, Chinese civilization overspilled China into new areas, such as Korea, Japan, Southeast Asia, and Tibet. The instability of the steppes damaged the land-bound trade of Eurasia, but the commerce of the Indian Ocean continued to grow, and the development of Ethiopia was among the consequences.

Still, despite continuities that survived the barbarians, the world was deeply transformed. Rather than the world of empires that had dominated the densely populated belt of the axial age, it might be proper to speak of a world of civilizations. Western civilization was a hybrid—partly Germanic, partly Christian, partly Roman in heritage. The Islamic world was far more innovative, but it had, in some respects, a similar profile: with a biblical heritage, reinterpreted by Muhammad and the learned legacies of Rome, Greece, and Persia, under an Arab elite from outside the empires, established by conquest but susceptible to the cultural influence of its victims. In both Islam and Christendom, notions of universal empire survived: the caliphate, Byzantium. But neither could maintain unity in practice, and the respective regions became arenas of states contending for the imperial legacy or ignoring it. In India, political fragmentation under the impact of barbarian invasion was more thoroughgoing, in China less so. In both, however, the invaders and immigrants were like chameleons, taking on the cultural hues of their new environments. In both, moreover, the traditional culture spread into new areas and new states, such as those of south India, and China's neighbors. So nowhere, by the eighth century, except in Ethiopia, was there any longer a civilization that was confined to a single state.

Even at the end of a chapter crowded with politics, we still have not reached the deepest transformative influences on the period. One of the traditional limitations of history textbooks is that politics, which generates most of the sources, tends to dominate the foreground. But politics is full of short-term changes, while ideas and environmental influences generate the sea changes. The next two chapters explore the religious transformations that made this world of civilizations distinct, in particular, from the empires that preceded them, and the discovery and development of resources that not only renewed the Old World, but also opened up new frontiers in other parts of the globe.

PROBLEMS AND PARALLELS

1. How does the history of Teotihuacán parallel developments in Eurasia during this period?
2. Why was China more successful than Rome in dealing with steppeland invaders and migrants?
3. How did the Byzantine Empire and the Germanic kingdoms in western Europe both continue and break with the traditions of Rome?
4. How did Ethiopia benefit from its position in the Horn of Africa?
5. Why were the Arabs able to conquer a vast empire so quickly? In what ways was the Muslim world a cultural unity?
6. How did states develop on the edges of empires during this period?

CHAPTER 9

The Rise of World Religions: Christianity, Islam, and Buddhism

focus questions

1. Why did Buddhism, Christianity, and Islam become world religions?
2. How did commerce spread religion in parts of Eurasia and Africa?
3. Why did missionaries seek to convert rulers and elites?
4. How did Christian and Muslim rulers deal with religious minorities?
5. Why was monasticism more important in Buddhism and Christianity than for Islam?
6. What role did women play in the spread of world religions?
7. How did world religions accommodate themselves to local cultures?

In 872, Ibn Wahab, a Muslim traveler from Iraq, arrived in China at the Tang court. The emperor called for illustrated scrolls to be put before him.

Ibn Wahab recognized the portraits of biblical prophets and patriarchs.

"Here is Noah with his ark," he says in his account, "which saved him when the world was drowned. . . ."

At these words, the emperor laughed and said, "You have identified Noah, but, as for the ark, we do not believe it. It did not reach China or India."

"That is Moses with his staff," I said.

"Yes," said the emperor, "but he was unimportant and his people were few."

"There," I said, "is Jesus, surrounded by his apostles."

"Yes," said the emperor. "His mission lasted only thirty months."

"I saw also other pictures, which I did not recognize," Ibn Wahab reports. "The interpreter told me that they were the prophets of China and India."

The anecdote illustrates three themes of the time: the effectiveness of communications across Eurasia; the superiority of Chinese knowledge; and the subject of this chapter—the beginnings of the ascent of Christianity, Islam, and Buddhism as world religions, with followings in all sorts of physical and cultural environments. Most religions do not spread beyond their cultures of origin. Christianity, Islam, and Buddhism were unusual. They aspired to be universal, and became global.

Historians often claim to be interested in the past for its own sake. If we also want to understand our own world, and trace the emergence of its key features, we have to confront the problem of why Christianity, Islam, and Buddhism began to acquire the global acceptance they have today. So, in this chapter, we must stay in Eurasia and Africa—in the parts where these three religions had penetrated by Ibn Wahab's time—and catch up in Chapter 10 with changes that were occurring in other parts of the world.

Spiritual conversions can have enormous impact, not only on the lives of the people who experience them but also on society, inspiring mass movements and initiating social, political, and economic reforms. Most people, however, in most periods, experience religion only superficially. If they do undergo real conversion or spiritual rebirth, it happens sporadically and rarely lasts long. We should not judge the spread of religion by the extent of people's intellectual grasp of it. Instead of understanding religion as belief, or spiritual experience, or doctrine, we can treat it, for our present purposes, as cultural practice, and say that a religion has "spread" where and when people in large numbers take part in its rites and identify with their fellow worshippers as members of a community. Four processes made possible the spread of religions in this sense during the period of takeoff for Islam, Buddhism, and Christianity: war, trade, missionary activity, and elite—especially royal—sponsorship (see Map 9.1).

Map 9.1 The Rise of World Religions to 1000 C.E.

Legend:
- Buddhist heartland
- Muslim world, ca.1000 C.E.
- extent of Christianity, ca.1000 C.E.
- extent of Hinduism, ca.1000 C.E.
- spread of Mahayana Buddhism
- spread of Theravada Buddhism
- Islamic expansion
- spread of Hinduism
- Nestorian missions
- Silk Roads
- maritime routes
- Khazars people

Commerce and Conflict: Carriers of Creeds

Forcible conversion is—strictly speaking—no conversion at all. The Quran says, "there is no compulsion in religion." The Catholic Church forbids using force to spread faith. Buddhism, too, has no place for coercion. But force sometimes works.

In the Islamic World

The Arabic word **jihad** literally means *striving*. The Prophet Muhammad used the word in two contexts: first, to mean the inner struggle against evil that Muslims must wage for themselves; second, to denote real war, fought against the enemies of Islam. These must be genuine enemies, who "fight against you to the death." But in Muhammad's day, the community he led was almost constantly at war, and Chapter Nine of the Quran seems to legitimate war against all "polytheists" and "idolaters."

After the Prophet's death, his successors turned the doctrine of jihad against the "apostates" who abandoned Islam because they considered that their obligations to Muhammad had ended when he died. Jihad was then used to proclaim successful wars of aggression.

Holy war seems an appropriate translation for "jihad": an enterprise sanctified by obedience to what are thought to be the Prophet's commands and rewarded by the promise of martyrdom. According to a saying traditionally ascribed to Muhammad, martyrs go straight to the highest rank of Paradise, for "they fight," as the Quran says, "in the cause of Allah and they slay the enemy or are slain." This is no more bloodthirsty than many passages in the Bible and needs no more to be taken literally than Paul's injunction to Christians to "fight the good fight." But it makes a handy justification for war and implies a link between war and the spread of Islam. The tenth-century Muslim jurist, al-Kayrawani, summed up the tradition as it had evolved by that time. Enemies could either submit to Islam or pay a poll tax for the privilege of persisting in their own religion. "Failing that, we will make war against them."

That was theory. Practice was not always so clear-cut. But in the first couple of centuries of Islamic expansion, victorious Muslim armies normally aimed to wipe out religions they classed as idolatrous and to tax Christians, Jews, and, at times, other privileged groups, such as Zoroastrians in Persia. The result would not necessarily be to convert people to Islam, in the sense of changing their hearts and minds. But the elimination of traditional priesthoods and the destruction of former places of worship opened up spaces in which Islam, the religion of the conquerors, could take root. Moreover, God seemed to endorse Islam. If traditional religion became a badge of resistance to conquest, it withered when that resistance failed. In northwest Africa, for instance, when the last great Berber revolt against the Arabs failed in 703, the woman who had led it sent her sons to receive instruction in Islam.

In Christendom

So, slowly, faith followed the flag. Christian conquerors also abused religion to justify war. In the eighth century, the Frankish king Charlemagne gave the pagan Saxons in eastern Germany a choice of baptism or death. In the ninth, Alfred the Great of England imposed baptism on defeated pagans as a condition of peace. Olaf, king of Norway in the early eleventh century, massacred, mutilated, or blinded pagans who refused Christianity. It seemed consistent with the nature of the Lord of Hosts, as the Bible frequently referred to God, to spread Christianity by war. Yet in all these cases, and others like them, however violent and arbitrary the beginnings of Christianity, the affected communities joined Christian civilization and built springboards for further missions elsewhere.

In the Buddhist World

Less well known is that much of the early spread of Buddhism relied on similar strategies by royal strongmen. As in Christendom, Buddhist rulers practiced remarkable intellectual contortions to justify the imposition by violence of a doctrine of peace and love. Asoka (see Chapter 7) was not alone in priding himself on conquests allegedly achieved "by **dharma**"—the teachings of Buddha. Asoka's near contemporary, Kaniska, King of Peshawar in what is today Pakistan, enforced Buddhism on his own subjects. In the mid-eleventh century C.E., when King Anuruddha introduced Buddhism to Burma, he showed his piety by waging war on the neighboring Mon kingdom to gain possession of holy scriptures.

A Buddhist Pilgrim of the Seventh Century C.E.
Xuanzang was the foremost Chinese Buddhist of the seventh century. He went along the Silk Roads on a pilgrimage to India to visit the sites where the Buddha had lived and taught and to retrieve Buddhist manuscripts. Here, he is depicted, some 250 years after his death, with many of the typical items a Buddhist monk took on pilgrimage.
Reunion des Musees Nationaux/Art Resource, NY

Trade

War can spread religions, but after the time of Asoka, Buddhism never became the ideology of a widely successful conqueror until the sixteenth century—nor did Christianity, until European empires began to spread it around the world. Meanwhile, both religions had to spread with individual journeys beyond political frontiers. Even Islam overspilled the boundaries of Muslim conquests.

Trade was probably as important as war for spreading religion. The temples of Dunhuang are full of images of the role of the Silk Roads in spreading Buddhism. Merchants who rested at the monastery there endowed thousands of paintings that still line chambers carved from the rock. According to tradition, a Chinese monk began to hollow the caves out of the cliff face in 366, when, "traveling the wilds with his pilgrim's staff, he arrived at this mountain and had a vision of a golden radiance in the form of a thousand Buddhas." Many of the paintings portray individual merchants in acts of worship, often with their families, and sometimes in the company of their ancestors. In one image, brigands, converted by a Buddhist merchant they have captured, join him in prayer.

Manichaeanism and the Uighurs

Buddhism met rival religions along the Silk Roads. The Uighurs were a pastoral, Turkic-speaking people who dominated the steppeland north of the roads for a hundred years from the 740s. On service as mercenaries during the Chinese civil wars of the mid-eighth century, they picked up **Manichaeanism**, a religion of obscure origin, probably rooted in a heretical form of Zoroastrianism (see Chapter 6). Mani, its supposed founder in Persia in the third century, divided the universe into realms of spirit—which was good—and matter—which was evil. This kind of dualism, with its stark moral teaching and suspicion of sex, was an ancient and influential idea. But although Mani relentlessly sought to spread his religion, it had never previously captured the allegiance of a state. On the contrary, Zoroastrians, Christians, Muslims, and even—on at least one occasion, in China, in 732—Buddhists persecuted it. Now, however, the Uighur ruler proclaimed himself the "emanation of Mani," and Manichaean zealots became his counselors, rather as Buddhist and Christian rulers chose clergy as advisers and bureaucrats. Indeed, a Uighur bureaucracy developed, using its own language and script. According to a ninth-century inscription, Manichaeanism transformed "a barbarous country, full of the fumes of blood into a land where the people live on vegetables, from a land of killing to a land where good deeds are fostered." Uighur monarchs endowed temples in China and sponsored the collecting of Manichaean scriptures. However, Buddhism and, to a lesser extent, Christianity ultimately replaced Manichaeanism among the Uighurs, and the creed of Mani never caught on to the same extent anywhere else.

Christianity on the Silk Roads

By comparison with Buddhism and even Manichaeanism, Christianity was only moderately successful along the Silk Roads. Relatively few Christians engaged in long-range trade. Among Christian peoples who did have strong vocations for commerce, the Armenians kept to themselves and avoided trying to convert others so as not to invite persecution by non-Christian rulers. **Nestorians**—named after Nestorius, Bishop of Constantinople from 428 to 431, who regarded the human Jesus as merely human, distinct from the divine Jesus—had a network of monasteries and communities that reached China. But the Nestorians remained a thin and patchy presence across a vast area.

Islam on Trade Routes

If Buddhism dominated much of the Silk Roads, Islam spread almost as effectively by trade along the sea routes of maritime Asia and across the

Sahara. As Muslim merchant communities dispersed, they founded mosques, elected or imported preachers, and sometimes attracted local people to join them. Muhammad's commands for peaceful conversion were at least as strong as those for jihad. "Call unto the way of thy Lord with wisdom and fair exhortation," the Quran commands. According to a contemporary estimate, thousands of Muslims constituted the biggest of the foreign merchant communities who perished in Guangzhou in a rebel massacre in 879. In the same period, as East African ports became integrated into the trade routes of the Indian Ocean, so they developed Muslim communities.

In West Africa, way beyond the African frontiers of the caliphates, immigration and acculturation along the Saharan trade routes prepared the way for Islamization. Arab visitors to Soninke chiefdoms and kingdoms from the ninth century noted that some people followed "the king's religion," while others were Muslims. On this frontier, Islam lacked professional missionaries. Occasionally, however, a Muslim merchant might interest a trading partner or even a pagan ruler in Islam. A late-eleventh-century Arab compiler tells such a story, from Malal south of the Senegal. At a time of terrible drought, a Muslim guest advised the king that if he accepted Islam, "You would bring Allah's mercy on the people of your country, and your enemies would envy you." Rain duly fell after prayers and Quranic recitations. "Then the king ordered that the idols be broken and the sorcerers expelled. The king, together with his descendants and the nobility, became sincerely attached to Islam, but the common people remained pagans."

Monarchs and Missionaries

Although not much practiced by Muslims in this period, conversion of kings was one of the main strategies Buddhist and Christian missionaries employed to spread their faiths. They learned to start at the top of society because religion, like other forms of culture, tends to trickle down, encouraged by the example the power of leaders imposes.

For Christians, in particular, the strategy of targeting elites marked a profound innovation in the history of the Church. Christianity in antiquity was branded as a "religion of slaves and women." It appealed to a low level of society and, at first, to those with a low-level education. In its earliest days, it was unwelcoming to persons of high status, like the rich young man in the Gospels whom Jesus sent away grieving, or the well-to-do for whom admission to the Kingdom of God was as if through the eye of a needle. In apostolic times, converts of respectable status were few and modest: a Roman army officer; a tax collector; an Ethiopian envoy mentioned in the Acts of the Apostles; the "most excellent Theophilus," who was probably a Roman official addressed by a Gospel writer. Over the next two to three centuries, the Church grew and embraced people of all classes in the towns of the empire—thanks especially to Christian women, who became the evangelizers of their own husbands and children. But Christianity remained a minority religion, unable to capture the allegiance of rulers or the institutions of states. In the first half of the fourth century, three spectacular conversions inaugurated an era in which efforts at evangelization targeted the top. The rulers of three great states adopted Christianity: the Roman Emperor Constantine, King Ezana of Ethiopia, and King Trdat of Armenia.

Constantine

Like so many future invaders and tourists from the north, Constantine, commander of the Roman army in Britain from 306, was seduced by the feel and flavor of Mediterranean culture. The standard tale of the beginning of his conversion to Christianity is not credible. In 312, he was heading south, intent on capturing the Roman throne in the West for himself. Approaching the decisive battle of his bid for power, at Milvian Bridge, not far from Rome, he saw a vision that he later described as "a cross of light, superimposed on the sun"—perhaps like the crosslike clouds mountaineers have reported in the Alps, or an unusual grouping of planets, or just a dream. As Constantine already worshipped the sun, the image appealed. The priorities reflected in the accompanying message, "In this sign, conquer!" seem to have reflected Constantine's own. He was looking for a Lord of Hosts rather than a God of Love. An alternative account of the conversion may be Constantine's own. It is a stock story of revelation by grace. "I did not think that a power above could see any thoughts which I harbored in the secret places of my heart. . . but Almighty God, sitting on high, has granted what I did not deserve."

Everywhere politics was so deeply implicated in royal religion that it is hard to resist skepticism about royal converts and the sincerity of their conversions, just as today we prudently question politicians who claim to be "born again." Bet hedging was the usual strategy. The emperor was the chief priest of the official pagan cults and was worshipped as divine. His role could not suddenly lose its traditional character. Official religion continued. Court poets and orators classified Constantine's victims in battle as divine sacrifices and his birth as a gift of the gods. One of them constructed a framework of paganism over which the emperor's Christianity could fit: "you have secret communion with the Divine Mind, which, delegating our care to lesser gods, deigns to reveal itself to you alone." The sacredness of the emperor's person could now be redefined in Christian terms by calling him God's deputy on Earth and, in deserving cases, making him a saint after his death. In coins his sons issued, the hand of God guides Constantine into heaven on a chariot, like the prophet Elijah's in the Bible.

Imperial patronage profoundly affected Christianity. Constantine himself became, according to his own propaganda, "like an apostle"—settling disputes between quarreling theologians and influencing the election of bishops. During the fourth century, Christianity gradually began to displace the old cults as the official religion of the empire. Pulpits spread imperial propaganda. Subjects began to go to church—without necessarily embracing, or even understanding, Christian doctrines. More than ever, learned and aristocratic classes, who had previously despised Christianity, blended its teachings with the philosophy of classical antiquity. Christian virtues blended with those of stoicism (see Chapter 6). Traditional Christian pacifism withered as Christians felt obliged to support the empire's wars.

Ezana

The adoption of Christianity at the Ethiopian court at Axum in the 340s illustrates a similar dilemma for a war leader seeking to appropriate a religion of peace. The inscriptions of King Ezana were bloodthirsty documents, full of conquests and captives. As his reign unfolded, they remained bloody but became increasingly high-minded, full of the concept of the good of the people and service to the state. The king still waged wars, but now he was eager to justify them. The king of neighboring Nubia was guilty of boastfulness, raiding, violation of embassies, and refusal to negotiate. "He did not listen to me," Ezana complains, "and uttered curses." The new tone reflects the influence of Christian clergy.

Previously, Ezana had described himself as "son of Mahreb"—a war god. Suddenly, he dropped the claim and waged war in the name of "Lord of Heaven and Earth" or "the Father, Son and Holy Spirit." His last monument proclaims, "I cannot speak fully of his favors, for my mouth and my spirit cannot fully express all the mercies he has done to me. . . . He has made me the guide of my kingdom through my faith in Christ." He toppled the great stone pillars of Axum and began to build churches. Fragments from his sanctuary are still visible in the Old Cathedral of St. Mary of Zion at Axum.

Trdat

To become Christian was to join the growing common culture—at the vertex of a triangle of Christian states, Ethiopia, Rome, Armenia. For Armenia, the evidence is too indistinct to yield a clear picture of what happened. Allegedly contemporary sources exist only in late, contradictory, and probably corrupt versions. A note King Trdat supposedly wrote in the late third century to an anti-Christian Roman emperor declares "loathing for Christians" and a promise to persecute them. His submission to baptism supposedly arose in revulsion from the fate of thirty-three nuns whom he had put to death. Gregory the Illuminator—Trdat's former friend, whom he imprisoned in a pit of snakes—accentuated his remorse. This looks like a theologically crafted tale of a change of heart induced by divine grace. The whole story seems loosely modeled on that of the Apostle Paul in the Bible—the persecutor turned converter. The date of Trdat's conversion cannot be fixed more exactly than between 301 and 314. The latter date seems likely, as by then Constantine had begun to favor Christianity, and Trdat favored alignment with Rome against Persia.

Diplomatic Conversions

Around the same time, in the Caucasus Mountains near Armenia, tradition credits an unnamed slave woman (later called Nino) with converting the people we now know as the Georgians. Her prayers cured a queen's illness. The king proposed to shower the slave with rewards. "She despises gold," said the queen. "The only way we can repay her is to worship divine Christ who cured me thanks to her prayers." The story

The Monastery Church at Jvari ("the Cross") in Georgia occupies a hilltop where St. Nino, a female evangelist traditionally credited with helping to spread Christianity in Georgia in the fourth century, is said to have paused to pray. A church on the site is documented from the seventh century, but the existing building resembles Western churches of the ninth and tenth centuries. Above the entrance, as seen in this photo, angels brandish a cross from which the "living water" of Christian baptism flows.
Natia Chakvetadze

sounds fictional. The verifiable fact, however, is that the priests who launched the Georgian state church came from Constantine's empire. Christianity was a political option for small states in imperial hinterlands, striving to preserve their independence and playing Persia against Rome.

The Georgian kingdoms of Iberia and Lazica pried themselves free of Persian dominance, partly by opting for Roman support. By the early sixth century, a Roman ambassador to Lazica could hardly restrain his enthusiasm for a people who were "in no way barbarians, long association with the Romans having led them to adopt a civilized and law-abiding way of life." From 522, the kings of Lazica ceased to accept election by the emperors of Persia and chose to be invested by those of Rome. King Ztathius had the Roman emperor's portrait embroidered on his robes. His successor held a rank of honor at the court of Constantinople.

Religious allegiances changed with political alliances. Poised between Christian and Muslim powers, the rulers of the Khazars—Turkic pastoralists between the Black Sea and the Caspian, who built up a state that endured for 400 years from the early seventh century—adopted, at different times, Christianity, Islam, and Judaism in their efforts to preserve their independence.

Buddhist Politics

Buddhist missionaries also displayed partiality for royal and imperial disciples. In the late first century, the Chinese emperor Ming was supposed to have introduced Buddhism as the result of a vision. This was untrue, but it is evidence of the importance the Buddhist clergy who invented the tale attached to imperial patronage. As we saw in the last chapter, Buddhism became the favorite spiritual resource of usurpers of the Chinese throne who wanted to legitimize their rule and of monarchs who needed a propaganda machine. But no Buddhist emperor ever suspended the traditional rites and sacrifices that Chinese emperors were required to perform. Only Yang Jian in the sixth century (see Chapter 8)—a skeptic contemptuous of all religion—had the nerve to do that.

Buddhism also had to contend with Chinese belittlement of anything foreign. Indeed, the measure of Buddhism's success is that, until "Westernization" began in the late nineteenth century, it was the only movement of foreign origin ever really to catch on in China. Sporadic bursts of imperial favor enabled Buddhists to establish an enormous network of monasteries that became magnets of piety for millions of people. The scale of Buddhism's ascent appeared during one of the spasms of persecution of Buddhism in which emperors occasionally indulged. In the 820s through the 840s, thousands of monasteries were dissolved, and 250,000 monks and nuns were forced back into lay life.

Korea

In the neighboring Korean kingdom of Koguryo, the rise of Buddhism began in the late fourth century, when barbarian invasions of China enriched Koguryo with refugees. A series of fugitive Chinese monks made themselves indispensable at court and devised ways to reconcile Buddhism with royal responsibilities under the old, indigenous religion. King Kwanggaet'o dedicated a temple with the inscription, "Believing in Buddhism, we seek prosperity." King Changsu, who ruled for most of the fifth century and died in 491, is depicted at the tomb of his predecessor at Pyongyang performing Buddhist as well as native rites. The rest of Korea resisted Buddhist intrusions at first, perhaps because of the importance of local religious rites as part of the ceremonial of kingship. The kings of Silla, for instance, derived prestige from their claim to have arisen from a dynasty of holy men. State formation in Korea was essentially a process of extending uniform religious rites to one community after another.

The launch of Buddhism as a royal religion in southern Korea is traditionally ascribed to the conversions of King Song in Paekche and King Pophung of Silla, despite noble opposition in the 520s or 530s. Monks, like the chief minister Hyeyong in the mid-550s, became useful state servants. Won'gwang, who returned from China in 602 to head the bureaucracy, adapted dharma for political purposes. Serve your lord with loyalty and "face battle without retreating" became precepts of the faith. Having adapted to one political system in the sixth century, Korean Buddhism did so again, under new political conditions, in the tenth century, when the reform of the Korean administration along Chinese lines filled the bureaucracy with men trained in the study of Confucianism. The scholar-administrator Ch'oe Sungno expressed the ensuing compromise well in 982: "Carrying out the teachings of Buddha is the basis for the cultivation of the self. Carrying out the teachings of Confucius is the source for regulating the state."

Japan

Japan was the scene of the most remarkable compromise between a new, universal religion and kingly commitment to traditional paganism. The first image of the Buddha in Japan was said to have arrived as a diplomatic gift from Korea in 538. The pious efforts of the Soga clan—immigrants from China—supposedly spread the new religion around the end of the sixth century. Underlying the tale is a political saga. The traditional "way of the gods"—**Shinto** in Japanese—was the reigning dynasty's special responsibility. The Soga aimed to replace them and saw Buddhism as the path to power

The search was on for a synthesis that would harness Buddhism for the state without disturbing the traditional Shinto ideology and magic of the monarchy. Prince Shotoku (574–622), the first great royal patron of Buddhism in Japan, realized the value of the Buddhist clergy as potential servants of the state. He wrote learned commentaries on Buddhist doctrine and founded monasteries. His injunctions include, "The emperor is heaven and his ministers are Earth. . . . So edicts handed down by the emperor must be scrupulously obeyed." Endorsed from the court, Buddhism flourished. The Japanese census of 624 counted 816 monks. By 690, 3,363 monks received gifts of cloth from the throne.

A reaction set in. The traditional elite feared Buddhism as a foreign intrusion and a menace to the imperial rites. Early eighth-century law codes banned wandering monks from "speaking falsely about misfortunes or blessings based on mysterious natural phenomena," "deluding the people," and begging without permit. Various measures attempted to prevent monasteries from abusing their tax-exempt status.

The advances of Buddhism, however, were irresistible. A Buddhist scripture warned kings that "if they do not walk in the law . . . violent calamities arise." In the 730s, the monk Gembo returned from China with 5,000 volumes of Buddhist scriptures and endeared himself by curing an empress's depression. In 747, 6,563 monks were ordained at a palace ceremony. Buddhist rituals originally intended in India to treat snakebites, poison, and disease were used in Japan to protect the state. The outcome was a characteristically Japanese compromise. No one in Japan, it is often said, was purely Buddhist. The traditional Shinto shrines played a part in the devotions even of monks, as they still do.

Tibet

According to a legend crafted in Tibet about 500 years after the supposed event, a Chinese or Nepalese wife of King Songtsen Gampo brought Buddhism there in the sixth century. The true story was of long, slow monastic colonization. Though Songtsen Gampo probably patronized Buddhist monks and scholars, who frequented his court in the households of the Nepalese and Chinese princesses of his harem, he continued to represent himself as divine.

Even King Trisong Detsen in the second half of the eighth century, whom Buddhists hailed as a model of piety and whom their opponents denounced as a traitor to the traditional royal religion, depicted himself as both the divine defender of the old faith and the enlightened enthusiast of the new. In 792, he presided over a great debate between Indian and Chinese champions on the question of whose traditions better represented the Buddha's doctrine. The issue was decided in favor of the Indian traditional moral disciplines of **Theravada Buddhism**, as it is usually called, by which the soul might advance to Buddhahood by tiny incremental stages of learning and goodness, lifetime after lifetime in the course of reincarnation, rather than the **Mahayana Buddhism**, advocated by Chinese spokesmen, who claimed that the soul could achieve Buddhahood in one lifetime. Mahayana Buddhism, which also took root in Japan, is known as the "greater vehicle" because its proponents believe that it can carry more people to salvation than Theravada Buddhism, the "lesser vehicle," can.

But this debate was premature. Tibet was hardly yet a Buddhist country, nor could one tradition of Buddhism be imposed in the contexts in which Buddhism spread: missionary work and monastery founding; the spread of culture along merchants' routes; and the ebb and flow of armies, who transmitted ideas as the tide shifts pebbles. By the time of Tibet's treaty with China in 821, Buddhism had made real progress. The treaty invoked Buddhist as well as pagan gods, and after traditional sacrifices and blood-smearing rites, the Buddhists among the treaty's negotiators withdrew for a celebration of their own. King Ralpachen was so devout that he let monks sit on his prodigiously long hair. But a reaction set in at his death in 836, and Buddhism survived in Tibet only precariously into the next century, awaiting renewal by a new wave of monastic colonization. Its main rival was not the old religion but **Bon**. Of the origins of this faith, we know nothing reliable, but it was similar and heavily indebted to Buddhism. The sayings of the great Bon-po sage, Gyerspungs, closely resembled those of Buddhist masters: "Existence is like a dream." "Validity is vacuity." Truth must "transcend sounds and terms and words." The main difference lay in the sages' attitude to India. Buddhists acknowledged that their teaching came from there, whereas Bon-pos traced it to a legendary land in the west, and regarded their mythical founder, Shen-rab, as the original Buddha.

India

Ironically, the effort to combine Buddhism with traditional kingship failed most conspicuously in India itself, the Buddha's homeland. In the sixth century, kingdoms multiplied in India, and kings issued many grants of revenue and property to holy men to found religious establishments, in an effort to gain their support. Kings made relatively few grants, however, to Buddhists. The circumstances of the period—the conflicts with the Huns (see Chapter 8) and the crumbling of political unity—seem to have driven popular piety back to its roots in the worship of local gods, as if the troubles of the time were proof that Buddhism had failed.

Rites and practices associated with the traditions we now call **Hinduism** were taking hold. Indeed, some holy men set out to systematize them as an alternative to Buddhism. The development of the caste system—in which an unchangeable ritual rank, defined at birth, determines everyone's place in society—indicates how Hinduism was spreading. The caste system was not yet fully defined, but according to the description of India between 630 and 645 written by Xuanzang, the greatest Chinese Buddhist manuscript collector, butchers, fishermen, actors, executioners, and scavengers were ritually unclean and had to live outside city limits. Almost everyone acknowledged the superiority of the highest caste, the priestly Brahmans. The spread of blood sacrifice also shows that Buddhism was in retreat. Kings sacrificed horses, in defiance of Buddhist teaching, but protected cows, which Hinduism regards as sacred. The first **sati**—the burning to death of a widow on her husband's funeral pyre—was recorded in 510. Most Indian kings preferred to stake their power on devotion to particular traditional gods rather than on Buddhism.

The Margins of Christendom

In **Christendom**, the Constantinian model, according to which conversion begins with the ruler, prevailed for most of what we think of as the Middle Ages. Almost every conversion of a nation or a people, as related in medieval sources, began with the conversion of a king. There were exceptions. Clovis, the Frankish chief who took over most of Gaul (modern France) in the 480s, gave up his claim to descent from a sea god for allegiance to the Church, which promised victories and supplied him with literate administrators. But conversions among the Frankish people preceded or accompanied Clovis's. In Iceland, where "democratic" decision making is generally supposed to have prevailed, the collective adoption of Christianity was resolved in the assembly of the people in 1000, but the lay speaker who presided over the assembly, Thorgeirr Thorkelsson, withdrew to meditate or commune with the gods for a day and a night before lending his decisive influence to the debate. Of course, Christianity was also spread in undocumented or barely documented ways: movements of population and journeys of merchants and envoys. But missionary strategy remained relied on leaders to mobilize peoples.

In northern and eastern Europe, a great sequence of royal conversions in the late tenth and early eleventh centuries more or less established the frontier of Christendom, beginning with Harold Bluetooth in the 960s in Denmark and Mieszko of Poland in 966. In Norway, a year or two after Tryggvason's confirmation as a Christian in 995, a popular assembly endorsed the new religion. In Sweden, King Olof Skötkunung began minting coins with Christian symbols on them before 1000. His reception as king established an uninterrupted sequence of Christian rulers. The coronation of King Stephen of Hungary in 1001 settled the Christian destiny of that country.

Vladimir and the Rus

No conversion was more significant for the future than that of Vladimir, ruler of Kiev in what is today Ukraine, in 987–988, for it ensured that Christianity would be privileged among the eastern Slavs—including the Russians, who became Europe's most numerous people. Vladimir was the descendant of Scandinavians as well as Slavs, pagans on both sides (see Chapter 10). Like many great saints, he sinned with gusto. His harem was said to contain more than 800 girls. Russians trace proverbs in praise of drunkenness to his invention. He left a reputation, in the words of a German chronicler, as "a cruel man and a fornicator on a huge scale."

Among his people, paganism was entrenched by the psychological power of terror. The horror of a human sacrifice among the **Rus** profoundly impressed the caliph's ambassador, Ibn Fadlan, who witnessed it in 922. The slave girl chosen to die with her master sang songs of farewell over her last cups of liquor before ritually copulating with her executioners. An old woman called the Angel of Death then wound a cord around her neck and handed the slack to men standing on either side. While the cord was tightened, the Angel of Death plunged a dagger repeatedly in and out of the girl's breast. The funeral pyre, built on a ship, was then lighted, and the fire fed until it burned to ashes.

To replace this religion, and break the power of its priests, Vladimir needed something equally powerful. In the traditional story, his emissaries' quest led first to the Muslim Bulgars, who "bow down and sit, look hither and thither like men possessed . . . Their religion is not good." Finally, with the Greeks, they are taken to the cathedral of Hagia Sophia at Constantinople: "We knew not whether we were in heaven or on Earth; for on Earth there is no such vision or beauty and we do not know how to describe it. We only know that there God dwells among men."

Vladimir's decision in favor of Orthodox Christianity owed more to politics than aesthetics. Conversion was the price he paid for marriage to a Byzantine princess whom he demanded with threats. Imperial Byzantine princesses were not normally permitted to marry foreign suitors. Marriages between imperial princesses and foreign rulers diminished the sacred, divinely sanctioned dignity of the Byzantine monarchy and opened the way for foreign rulers to claim the Byzantine throne. Vladimir solemnly evicted the occupants of his sacred grove of idols. The golden-haired, silver-moustached thunder god, Perun, was buffeted, insulted, and dragged through the dust before being flung in a muddy river. Vladimir imposed Christianity by violence, while making it more acceptable and perhaps more intelligible by ordering that Christian liturgy be conducted in the Slavonic language the Rus spoke, rather than in Greek.

Islam and the Turks

The magnetism Christianity exerted on the frontiers of Christendom was paralleled in the Islamic world. Around the mid-tenth century, the Karakhanids became the first Turkic people to subscribe to Islam— apparently as a result of the favorable impression they derived from raiding Islamic territory. This was an event pregnant with consequences, because the Turks would bring to the Islamic world a vital infusion of manpower and expertise in war—"the army of God, whom I have installed in the East," according to a legendary saying of the Prophet. Islam's attraction for them is easier to express than explain. Their values were warlike. Boys were not named until they had "lopped off heads in battle." Even women were war-trained and "made the enemy vomit blood." Yet some of their leaders saw attractions in Islam. In 962, Altigin, a Turk who had adopted Islam while serving as a slave in Persia, founded at Ghazni in Afghanistan a Muslim state that was to exert great influence in the future. In about 985, a Turkic chief, **Seljuk**, who dreamed of "ejaculating fire in all directions" and conquering the world, ruled a small state, cobbled together by conquest, in Central Asia. His decision to become a Muslim was of enormous significance, as his descendants supplied some of the Islamic world's most effective frontiersmen.

Trickle Down: Christianization and Islamization

From converted rulers and conquered elites, religions trickled down to the rest of society. For Christians, for example, Constantine's patronage was an extraordinary windfall. At the time, despite the gradual—and, in some eastern provinces, formidable—accumulation of converts among the socially respectable and intellectual, Christianity had remained one among many popular eastern cults. It still bore the marks of its origins as a Jewish heresy, founded by a rabbi whose birth and death were, in the world's eyes, equally disreputable. Its scriptures were, by the sophisticated standards of the Greek schools of rhetoric and philosophy, so badly written as to embarrass all educated Christians.

Now, after the conversion of Constantine, according to the fourth-century Christian historian Eusebius, who had chronicled the persecutions of previous reigns, "It felt as if we were imagining a picture of the kingdom of Christ and that what was happening was no reality but a dream." There were subsidies for the Church, exemptions from fiscal and military obligations for the clergy, jobs in the state service for Christians, and the assurance, from the emperor's own hand, that the worship of Christians benefited the empire.

The rise of the Church from persecution to predominance was completed in 395, when the Emperor Theodosius proclaimed Christianity the official religion of the Roman Empire and reduced pagan cults to the underprivileged status formerly imposed on Christians. From the late fourth century onward, nobility and sanctity converged. So many young aristocrats became monks that monasteries came to resemble "noblemen's clubs." Christianity guaranteed the best opportunities for promotion in the army and bureaucracy and for personal enrichment. Those who accepted it subscribed to a cultural package associated with success. Ethiopian sources are too meager for certainty, but in Armenia, too, the continuing progress of Christianity depended, at least until the Arab conquest in the eighth century, on royal and aristocratic initiatives.

To some extent, parallel considerations applied within the Islamic world. Because the Muslim conquests were vast, and the conquerors relatively few in number, Muslim rulers could not exclude non-Muslims from positions of authority. The Caliph Umar I expelled non-Muslims from Arabia in 635, but without the services of Christians and Jews in the rest of the Middle East, or of Zoroastrians in Persia, the administrations of the eighth- and ninth-century caliphates would have been understaffed. Still, by favoring Muslims, discriminating against non-Muslims, and insisting on the exclusive use of Arabic as the language of administration, rulers created a climate of prejudice in favor of Islam among elites. Even mild persecution could exert considerable pressure. Umar II (r. 717–720) tried to exclude Christians and Jews from public offices and forbade them to lift their voices in prayer, build places of worship, or use saddles for their horses. If a Muslim killed a Christian, his penalty was only a fine. Later caliphs sporadically renewed persecution. In 807, Caliph Harun al-Rashid ordered all churches on the frontiers of his empire demolished. In the 850s, Caliph al-Mutawakkil ordered that Christian and Jewish graves should be level with the ground. Converts to Islam, on the other hand, could rapidly ascend through the ranks of society.

For most Christian and Jewish subjects of Islamic states, the tax system—which exempted Muslims from most charges—was the focus of discrimination. Umar II declared that he would be happy to see Islam spread and revenues diminish, even if it meant he had to till the soil with his own hands. Many people proclaimed themselves Muslims simply to take advantage of reduced tax rates, until Al-Hajjaj, the brutal governor of Iraq in the 690s and early 700s, reimposed the old tax levels on supposedly phoney converts.

Partly because Islam tolerated some other religions, the conquered societies were slow to become Islamized. Indeed, substantial Christian minorities have survived in Egypt, Palestine, Iraq, Syria, and, especially, Lebanon to this day. Some historians have tried to measure the rate of acceptance of

The Dome of the Rock in Jerusalem marks the spot where, according to Muslim tradition, the Prophet Muhammad ascended to paradise. The Caliph Abd al-Malik had it built in the late seventh century, marking as sacred to Islam a city that Christians and Jews already revered. The splendor and scale of the building out-dazzled and dwarfed the nearby Church of the Holy Sepulchre and the remains of the last Jewish temple. *Scala/Art Resource, NY*

Islam by calculating the number of people who gave their children Muslim-sounding names. This method suggested to Richard W. Bulliet, its greatest exponent, that only 2.5 percent of the population of Iran were converted to Islam in the seventh century. Not until the early ninth century was the majority of the population Muslim. In most places, the significance of name-giving is broadly cultural, rather than specifically religious. But the names people were given or adopted do help to demonstrate roughly the rate at which Islam became the dominant influence on the culture of Iran.

Religious Lives: The World of Monks and Nuns

In Buddhism and Christianity, monasticism grew as these religions spread and, in turn, became a major cause of their continuing success.

Christian Monasticism

As a result of the triumph of Christianity as an elite religion, the Church became the great upholder of Roman standards of learning, art, and government. This is not surprising among aristocratic bishops, whose family traditions were of power. In the sixth century, Pope Gregory the Great organized the defenses of Rome (see Chapter 8), launched spiritual missions to pagan parts of western Europe, and reimposed on the western empire a kind of unity by the sheer range of his correspondence. In Visigothic Spain, Isidore of Seville (ca. 560–636) passed the learning of classical Greece and Rome on to future generations in the form of an encyclopedia. Martin of Braga dedicated to a Germanic king a book about virtue, based on a lost Roman work.

It was harder to domesticate the church's own barbarians—the antisocial ascetics and hermits, whose response to the problems of the world was to withdraw from them or rail at them from their caves. The monastic movement made their lives "regular," in houses of work, study, and prayer to benefit society as a whole. There is no scholarly consensus on the origins of monasticism. Christians perhaps got it from Buddhists, or maybe it arose independently in various cultures as hermits and holy men banded together for mutual support. The earliest recorded Christian monastic communities emerged in Egypt in the second century, among ascetics seeking to imitate Jesus' period of self-exile in the desert. Of the many rules of life for monks written in the following centuries, the most influential rule in the western church was that of Benedict of Nursia.

The only certain date in his life is 542, when a king visited him at his monastery of Monte Cassino in southern Italy. Benedict started as a typical, obsessive ascetic, in a cave, where food was lowered to him while he disciplined the lusts of the flesh in a convenient thornbush. When he established his own community, he rededicated the pagan shrine of the Roman god Jupiter on the spot to St. Martin, the patron of poverty, who gave half his cloak to a beggar. The nearby shrine to Apollo became the chapel of John the Baptist, the biblical voice crying in the wilderness. These rededications disclose Benedict's program: the practice of charity in refuge from the world.

His book of rules for monks borrowed freely from others, but its superiority and universality were recognized almost at once. There has hardly been a monastic movement in the West since that it has not deeply influenced. Its animating principles are the quest for salvation in common and the subordination of all individual willfulness. Benedict banned extremes of mortification in favor of steady spiritual progress, manual labor, study, and private and common prayer. He devised a means to make civilization survive, because monastic study also embraced the learning of ancient Greece and Rome. Monasteries became centers for colonizing wasteland and wilderness. Monks sought "desert" frontiers to build new monasteries, and lay people followed them.

The Lotus Sutra. Composed between the first century B.C.E. and the second century C.E., the Lotus Sutra is the most important text of Mahayana Buddhism. The detail from this printed version, from around 1000 C.E., shows the Western Paradise of the Amitabha Buddha and his court of Bodhisattvas. *Courtesy of the Library of Congress*

Buddhist Monks

Monasticism was even more important in Buddhism than in Christianity, because most Buddhist clergy were subject to monastic discipline. In practice Buddhist monasteries performed particular functions, especially in transmitting learning, that made their contributions similar to those of monasteries in Christendom. The 50,000 ancient manuscripts preserved in the library cave of Dunhuang—a precious time capsule, sealed for 800 years in the tenth century—are a measure of the importance of scholarship in Buddhist monasteries. The business of retrieving, translating, editing, and purifying the best written evidence of the Buddha's teachings turned monks into giants and heroes of learning. The first Chinese to be ordained as a Buddhist priest, for instance, in about 250, was Zhu Shixing. He was nearly eighty years old when he made a pilgrimage to India to procure a manuscript of the Buddha. Exhausted by the journey, he handed it to his disciples to carry to China before he died. Kumarajiva, translator into Chinese of the most famous of Buddhist scriptures, the **Lotus Sutra,** in the early fifth century, was said to be able to memorize 30,000 words a day. As in Christendom, Buddhist monastic libraries diversified into secular learning, imaginative literature, and administrative and historical records of life way beyond the monastery walls. They were centers of lay life, too, hosting reading clubs for believers, including groups of women, who would pay fines—such as a jug of wine or bowl of cereal—for failure to attend meetings. And monasteries functioned as objects of pilgrimage, inns for travelers, and granaries to store food against hard times.

Sufism

Strictly speaking, nothing like monasticism should exist in Islam. The Quran condemns it. But Christian influence was not easy to filter out of early Islam. In the early eighth century, Hasan al-Basri quoted Jesus to support his view that asceticism is God's "training ground that his servants might learn to run to him." He advocated fasting and meditation to induce a mystical sense of identity with God. When, toward the end of the same century, the female mystic, Rabia al-Adawiyya, experienced a vision of Muhammad, the Prophet asked her if she loved him. "My love of God has so possessed me," she replied, "that no space is left for loving or hating any but him." Groups of devotees founded houses of common life, or, at least, schools in which they trained in mystical techniques and cultivated the tradition these thinkers established. Though fellow Muslims often suspected these **Sufis** of being heretical, Sufism supplied Islam with some of its supplest thinkers and most dedicated and successful missionaries.

Religious Women

In Christianity, Buddhism, and the Islamic world, women acquired new roles—inside the home as guardians of religious tradition for their children and outside the home as members of religious orders. Nuns played the same role as monks in prayer and scholarship. In some places, both sexes shared the same houses of religion, often under female leadership. At Whitby in seventh-century England, the formidable Abbess Hilda ruled one of the largest and most learned religious establishments of the day. Nunneries played an important part in Buddhist life in China and Japan, as places of education for women. The empresses Shotoku of Japan (see Chapter 10) and Wu of China (see Chapter 8) were nuns before their ascent to power. In the Buddhist world, the nun's vocation was often a stage before returning to secular life, in households where husbands had several wives and concubines. In Islam, which also allowed men to have up to four wives, there was relatively little spare woman power. So female monasticism never developed, and female Sufis—though often individually influential—were rare. Only exceptionally strong-minded women like Rabia al-Adawiyya could pursue their vocations in a life of renunciation of marriage.

CHRONOLOGY	
Second century	Earliest Christian monastic communities (Egypt)
ca. 250	Zhu Shixing becomes first Chinese to be ordained as Buddhist priest
ca. 314	King Trdat of Armenia converts to Christianity
ca. 340	King Ezana of Ethiopia converts to Christianity
366	Founding of Dunhuang monastery, western China
395	Proclamation of Christianity as official religion of Roman Empire
ca. 520	Conversion of kings of Paekche and Silla to Buddhism
538	First image of Buddha arrives in Japan
Sixth century	Life of Benedict of Nursia
Seventh and eighth centuries	Rapid expansion of Islam; spread of Buddhism in Tibet
Ninth century	Seaborne Muslim pilgrims begin to arrive in Mecca
ca. 988	Vladimir of Kiev converts to Orthodox Christianity

IN PERSPECTIVE
The Triumphs of the Potential World Religions

The story of this chapter has been of cultural change rather than religious conversion. Some of the conditions—violence, mass migration, enforced refugeeism, pestilence, famine, natural disaster, "culture shock," and demographic collapse—constitute, on a large scale, influences comparable to the traumas that often precede individual conversion. Yet, when we monitor the public progress of Christianity, Islam, and Buddhism, we glimpse, at best, shadows of individual religious experience. Instead, we see shrines multiplying; congregations growing; influence deepening on laws, rites, customs, and the arts.

By around 1000, all three religions had demonstrated their adaptability to different cultures and climates. Buddhism had big followings in China, Japan, Tibet, and Southeast Asia and had spread into Central Asia along the Silk Roads. Christianity had a near monopoly in western Europe and spilled north and east into Scandinavia and the Slav lands, while

Making Connections | COMPARING THE WORLD RELIGIONS

	CHRISTIANITY	ISLAM	BUDDHISM
Core beliefs	Jesus of Nazareth is the Son of God and the Savior of humankind	There is no God but Allah and Muhammad is His Prophet	The Four Noble Truths: • Suffering is always present in life • Desire is the cause of suffering • Freedom from suffering can be achieved through nirvana (perfect peace and bliss) • The Eightfold Path leads to nirvana
Sacred texts	Bible (Old and New Testaments)	Quran	The *Tripitaka*, various Sutras
Core practices/rites	Baptism, holy Eucharist	The "five pillars" of Islam: • bearing witness • praying five times a day • giving alms • abstinence and fasting during holy month of Ramadan • pilgrimage to Mecca during one's lifetime	The Eightfold Path: • right view • right intention • right speech • right action • right livelihood • right effort • right mindfulness • right concentration
Major traditions	Catholicism, Protestantism, Eastern Orthodox	Sunni, Shia	Mahayana, Theravada

retaining the allegiance of communities scattered through Asia. Islam, dominant in the Middle East and North Africa, spread by conquest, conversion, and migration among Turkic peoples and around the trade routes of the Indian Ocean and the Sahara. Among them, the three religions seemed to have carved up the world known to Ibn Wahab, whom we encountered at the start of this chapter discussing religion with the Chinese emperor. The bases from which all three religions would expand further, especially in the sixteenth and seventeenth centuries (see Chapter 18), had been laid.

Their competitive advantages with religions they displaced were already evident. Pagan groves and temples became churches and Islamic and Buddhist shrines. Local deities reemerged as saints. Excavations at the shrine of the Irish saint, Gobnet, for instance, have yielded 130 anvils dedicated to the blacksmith god, Goibhnin. In Scotland, the goddess Brigid, associated with childbirth, became St. Bride. In the Islamic world, old sacred sites blended into the new religious landscape. The holiest site of Islam, the black stone of the **Kaaba** in Mecca, where Muslims have to perform pilgrimage, was a pagan shrine in the time of Muhammad, housing 360 deities. Muslims still perform the same rites—kissing the sacred stone, running the course of the stream that flows nearby—as their pagan predecessors did. Buddhists had no difficulty incorporating local gods into the vast Buddhist pantheon, or sanctifying local shrines with relics of Buddhas.

This flexibility and adaptability made Christianity, Islam, and Buddhism suitable for projection around the world. But it does not explain, of course, why other religions failed in this respect, or never made the attempt. The blend, which we now call Hinduism, of local Indian religions with the universally applicable philosophy of the Vedas (see Chapter 3) spread throughout India and parts of Southeast Asia, but no farther. Similarly, Daoism never reached beyond China. Nor, until migrants carried it to small colonies abroad, did Zoroastrianism penetrate beyond Southwest Asia, where it struggled to compete with Islam. Traditional paganism, Manichaeanism, and the many cults that came and went, leaving little trace in the record, withered in the face of Christian, Muslim, or Buddhist competition. Some religions, such as Bon in Tibet, Shinto in Japan, and, as far as we know, the religions of sub-Saharan Africa, had no universal aspirations and were designed only for their traditional followers. To judge from later evidence, there was a good deal of exchange between the local and regional religions of Mesoamerica, where, expressed in different languages and called by different names, the divine attributes artists personified were highly similar or, overlapping, from the twelfth century to the sixteenth. We cannot say how much farther they might have spread had Christianity, arriving in the 1500s, not transformed the religious profile of the region. In the Americas, in sub-Saharan Africa, and in regions of which we know even less, such as Australia and the Pacific, the same reasons that inhibited the spread of other forms of culture also tended to limit the communicability of religions. There were no great, long-range avenues of communication, such as the Silk Roads and the monsoonal ocean. The kind of competition that Islam, Christianity, and Buddhism generated never took effect.

Even as they changed the societies in which they triumphed, the new religions changed in their turn, compromising with vested interests; modifying their messages to suit mighty patrons; serving the needs of warriors and kings; even becoming organs of the state, instruments of government, and means of training bureaucrats and communicating with subjects. A further consequence of expansion was that different traditions within each of the religions lost patience or touch with each other. Christians in different parts of the world adopted different theologies. In Ethiopia, for instance, the church believed that Jesus was wholly divine, with no distinctly human person. The Nestorian Christian communities of the Silk Roads preached the opposite doctrine: that the human Jesus was wholly human, leaving his divine nature in heaven. Theological differences gradually drove Christians in Europe apart. After 792, most congregations in western Europe modified the creed, the basic statement of Christian belief, to make the Holy Spirit "proceed" from "the Father and the Son" rather than "the Father" alone. Most churches in eastern Europe denounced—and still denounce—the new wording as heresy. Different Islamic states subscribed variously to Shiism and Sunniism (see Chapter 8) and to different interpretations of Islamic law. In Buddhism divisions between followers of the Theravada and Mahayana traditions were sometimes just as bitter, as rival sects multiplied.

Although all these religions had started by appealing to people of modest or marginal social position, they "took off" by converting rulers and elites, who favored new religions—spiritual merits apart—because they saw advantages in doing so. The support of the church, for instance, was expensive for rulers and aristocrats. But it was worth it because it meant that God and his angels and saints became one's allies and friends. We can measure the value a typical royal convert got from the deal in the weight of gold and jewels in the votive crown that the seventh-century Spanish Visigothic king Reccesvinth hung in the sanctuary of his royal church. In return for such rich gifts, matched by comparable generosity in land, he got the prayers of the priests and monks, the services of a clerical bureaucracy, and the miraculous power of the relics of an army of martyrs. There was also a hidden advantage that no ruler could have banked on and that the next chapter must disclose. In the last three centuries of the first millennium, Islam, Buddhism, and, to a lesser extent, Christianity played vital and spectacular roles in new forms of environmental management.

PROBLEMS AND PARALLELS

1. Why did Buddhism, Christianity, and Islam become world religions? How did they deal with older religious traditions?
2. How did rulers and elites use religion to consolidate and justify their power? Why did Christianity and Islam gain more converts among the masses after rulers and the elites adopted these religions?
3. How did merchants and trade routes spread religious ideas?
4. Why has monasticism been more important in Buddhism and Christianity than it has been in the Islamic world?
5. In what parts of Eurasia had Buddhism, Christianity, and Islam each become dominant by 1000? Why did each of these religions develop differing and rival forms of belief?

10 CHAPTER

Remaking the World: Innovation and Renewal on Environmental Frontiers in the Late First Millennium

focus questions

1. How did geography influence the transmission of culture in sub-Saharan Africa and the Americas?
2. What were the environmental consequences of the Islamic conquests?
3. How did China, Japan, and the states of Southeast Asia seek to stimulate economic growth?
4. How did the Polynesians succeed in colonizing the Pacific?
5. Where did Christendom expand in the eighth and ninth centuries?

One of the oddest monuments of the early Islamic world is the bathhouse of a caliph's hunting lodge at Qusayr Amra in the Jordanian desert. Here, the Prophet Muhammad's successor could relax unseen. He could also relax Islamic condemnations of art that depicted the human form, for Muhammad was supposed specifically to have exempted bathhouses from such bans. Mosaics smother the walls and ceilings. The caliph could lounge in his bath, enjoying scenes of his subject's everyday lives. In one room, he had an image of a naked woman before his eyes. Another wall was decorated with six portraits of failed enemies. Two of the images are too decayed to be recognizable. The others show a Visigothic king from Spain, Roman and Persian monarchs, and an Ethiopian emperor, depicted as the equal of the other great rulers of the world.

In the eighth century, Ethiopia was not yet in the state of collapse that had overcome the Roman and Persian realms, but it was in trouble. Nomadic "barbarians" infiltrated from the north. No coinage was issued. Monumental building stopped. Squatters began to take over abandoned mansions in the Ethiopian capital. At the port of Adulis on the Red Sea, eighth-century ash lies thickly over ruined buildings. Fire had wrecked the city. By the ninth century, central political control was hard or impossible to maintain. Later writers remembered shadowy, allegedly demonic female rulers, who seized power in the tenth century. "God has become angry with us," wrote a fugitive king. "We have become wanderers. . . . The heavens no longer send rain and the earth no longer gives its fruits."

Environmental influences played a big part in Ethiopia's eclipse. Trees vanished from hills overexploited for wood and charcoal. Intensive farming exhausted the soil. Heavy rains aggravated erosion. Mudslides buried buildings. Below volcanic hills, once-rich earth turned to dust. To renew the state and resume expansion, Ethiopians had to find new resources, new frontiers, new techniques.

From around 700 to 1000, states all over the world responded to similar problems. New ways to manage the environment multiplied. They constitute a global story—or at least, a story that spans most of the world. Outcomes, however, continued to vary, and in some regions, such as the Islamic world, China, and Japan, the innovations of the period proved more durable than in others. What we might call the **axial zone** of the world expanded. The densely populated central belt of Eurasia, stretching from China to Europe and North Africa—the region that had seen so many experiments in civilization for so long—got bigger, as it incorporated new frontiers. In the Americas, sub-Saharan Africa, and the Pacific, similar but smaller zones began to take shape but remained fragile.

Isolation and Initiative: Sub-Saharan Africa and the Americas

African Geography

In sub-Saharan Africa, it is tempting to treat Ethiopia as the exception that proves the rule: the one region where developments that historians usually treat as crucial—states and empires, radical modifications of the environment, maintenance of a literate tradition—have been comparable with those in the most favored parts of Eurasia. Geography is often said to imprison sub-Saharan peoples. While great axes of communication cross-fertilize much of the Old World, the Sahara and the Indian Ocean separate most of Africa from those highways of cultural exchange. Except on the Mediterranean and along the coast north of the Mozambique Channel in East Africa, shores exposed to the wind make communication difficult by sea. Rivers fall sharply from the high interior and are hard to navigate. Some of the flows of culture in Africa took centuries longer than comparable transmissions in Eurasia.

The Emergence of Ghana and Gao

Still, it is surprising that there has never been much exchange along the obvious axis of transcontinental communication in Africa: the Sahel, the belt of grassland that links East Africa, where Ethiopian civilization took shape, to another precocious region in the Niger valley in West Africa. Here, urban life, commerce, and industry show up in the archaeological record from the third century B.C.E. onward. By the first century C.E., at Jenne-Jeno, where floods fed the soil, farmers and ironworkers grew millet and rice. The population was reputedly so dense that royal proclamations could be "called out from the top of the city's walls and transmitted by criers from one village to the next."

The region was a natural crossroads, where traders could deal in slaves, salt, copper, and gold from the mines of Senegambia and the middle Volta River. Toward 1000, two states impressed Arab visitors: Ghana and Gao. Ghana was in the territory of the **Soninke**, west of the middle Niger River. Its capital at Kumbi Saleh had houses of stone and acacia wood, and a royal compound—where a sacred snake with a sensitive snout supposedly sniffed out royal quality from contenders for the throne. Enriched by taxes on trade, the monarchs of Ghana and Gao attracted the reverence paid to sacred beings. Subjects prostrated themselves and covered their heads with dust. When the king of Gao ate, all business was suspended, until shouts announced he had finished.

Sacred kingship spread along the Sahel. The Zaghawa of the Chad region in the late ninth century had "no towns," according to an Arab traveler's report, but "they worshipped their king as if he were Allah." In Yoruba territory on the lower Niger River, evidence of divine kingship appears from the tenth century in clay portraits of men and women with elaborate headgear and hairstyles. Had contacts developed across the Sahel between West African realms and Ethiopia, rather in the way that the steppeland linked Europe to China, African history might, in the long run, more closely have resembled that of Eurasia. But the West African kingdoms remained focused on relations north across the Sahara, while Ethiopia's avenues of approach to the rest of the world led in every direction but westward: north to the Nile, east to the Indian Ocean, south along the Rift valley (see Map 10.1).

American Geography

It is tempting to use similar arguments about the geography of the Americas to explain why the New World developed differently from the Old. The shape of the American hemisphere slowed diffusion of new

Map 10.1 African Geography

culture and new crops, which had to travel across climates through the central continental funnel. Most of the great rivers flow east and west from the mountain spines that run up and down the Americas. Only the Mississippi traverses much distance from north to south.

Still, isolation did not prevent civilizations from developing in the Andean region, in parallel with those of Mexico and Central America, taking advantage of the different ecosystems that a world of slopes and valleys, microclimates, and diverse plants and animals provided. The highlands of North America, on the other hand, housed nothing comparable. This may have been, in part, because the Andes and the Sierra Madre in Central America and Mexico are better placed than the mountains of the north: close to rain forests, seas, and swamps for maximum biological diversity.

Moche and Nazca

Similarly, although North and South America both have arid deserts, the effort to civilize them encountered earlier success in the south. One of the strangest deserts in the world is in northern Peru. Except when El Niño drenches the land, almost no rain falls there. Although only five degrees south of the equator, the region is cool and dank with ocean fog. Little grows naturally, but modest rivers streak the flats, creating an opportunity to irrigate. The sea is at hand, with rich fishing grounds. Guano provides rich fertilizer to turn desert dust into cultivable soil. From the third century to the eighth, the civilization known as Moche made this desert rich with corn, squash, peppers, potatoes, and peanuts, which the people admired so much that they modeled them in gold and silver.

Under platforms built as stages for royal rituals, their rulers' graves lie: divine impersonators in golden masks, with earspools decorated with objects of the hunt, scepters and bells with scenes of human sacrifice, necklets with models of shrunken heads in gold or copper, and portraits of a divine sacrificer wielding his bone knife. Farther south, in the same period, in the inhospitable desert of northern Chile, the people known as the Nazca built underground aqueducts to protect irrigation water from the sun. Above ground, they created some of the most ambitious works of art in the world that survive to this day: stunning representations of nature—a hurtling hummingbird, a cormorant spread for flight, sinuous fish—and bold abstract lines, triangles, and spirals, scratched in oxide deposits that film the rock. Some of the images are 1,000 feet wide, too vast to be visible except from a height the artists could not reach, capable of permanently arousing the imagination.

Despite these achievements, the desert remained a fragile environment for ambitious ways of life. The Moche survived repeated droughts.

El Niño events periodically drove away the fish and washed away the irrigation works. These were occurrences frequent enough for the locals to learn to live with. After the mid-eighth century, however, no mounds were built, no great artworks were made, and the irrigated land dwindled. No one knows why, though most scholars speculate that the people overexploited their environment, or an unusually protracted drought may have defeated them.

Andean Developments

The center of gravity of large-scale innovation shifted inland and upslope to the high Andes, though with little long-term gain in security. The city of Huari, 9,000 feet up in the Ayacucho valley in Peru, lasted, as a metropolis, only from the seventh century to the ninth. It had garrison buildings, dormitories for the elite, and communal kitchens, with a population of at least 20,000 clustered around it.

At more than 12,000 feet above sea level, potatoes fed the city of Tiahuanaco in Bolivia because its altitude was hostile to growing grains. The tillers built stone platforms topped with clay and silt. They drew water from Lake Titicaca through channels to irrigate their mounds and protect them from violent changes of air temperature. Beds in this form stretched more than 9 miles from the lakeside and could produce 30,000 tons of potatoes a year. By about 1000, building had ceased, and the site was becoming abandoned—again, for unknown reasons—perhaps because of overexploitation of the soil or a shift in the regional balance of power. Tiahuanaco, as it gradually subsided into ruins, became a source of inspiration for all subsequent efforts to cultivate and build in the Andes.

The Maya

No case has excited more curiosity than that of the Maya. They inhabited (and their descendants still inhabit) three contrasting environments: the volcanic highlands of Guatemala, where microclimates create diverse eco-niches at different altitudes; the limestone plateau of Yucatán, Mexico's Caribbean peninsula, where agriculture depends on irrigation from pools and wells; and tropical lowlands with dense forests of heavy seasonal rain. There is bound to be some cultural diversity across such varied environments, and the chronology of Maya civilization varied considerably among these regions. The lowlands experienced a Classic Age of monumental-scale building and art from about the third to about the tenth centuries, whereas the plateau "peaked" later in these respects. But Maya civilization has some surprisingly uniform features.

The Maya demonstrated, in spectacular ways, common threads of Native American civilizations seen from the Olmecs onward (see Chapter 4).

Maya rulers had three areas of responsibility: war, communication with the gods and the dead, and building monumental ceremonial centers. Royal portraits, often engraved on slabs of stone and displayed in the grand plazas, show rulers in roles similar to those of professional shamans, wearing divine disguises, or engaged in rituals of bloodletting designed to induce visions. Amazingly, we can still confront the images of many kings. At Palenque, in the rain forest of southern Mexico, the seventh-century King Pacal is depicted on his tomb—dead, but refertilizing the world. A ceiba tree, sacred to the Maya, springs from his loins. In Copán in Honduras, the kings of the Macaw dynasty from the fifth century to the ninth, are shown communing together, as if at a celestial conference. At Tikal, when the sun is in the west and gilds the huge temple where he was buried, you can still pick out the vast outline of the fading image of King Jasaw Chan K'awiil, molded onto the temple facade.

Everything the Maya thought important—everything on Earth that they thought worth recording—happened in and around the ceremonial centers. The countryside was there to support and sustain those centers. Monumental buildings housed elites and displayed rites to appease the gods and promote civic solidarity. Elite dwellings were imposing and built of stone, but the facades of some of them are adorned with carvings of humble dwellings, such as the Maya peasantry still inhabit today, built of reeds and thatch with a single stone lintel. The temples, which often doubled as tombs, always evoked the mounds on which, in the lowlands, farming was practiced: structures resembling with vast, terracelike flights of steps, surmounted by platforms on which rituals were enacted. Typically, especially in the highlands and lowlands, false facades topped them, jutting into the sky, decorated with molded reliefs, displaying the symbols of the city, the portraits of the kings, the records of war, and the rewards of wealth. In their time, for travelers, traders, or would-be aggressors, they carried an unmistakable message of propaganda: an invitation to commerce, a deterrent against attack.

Thousands—sometimes many thousands—of peasants' flimsy dwellings surrounded these centers, in a landscape adapted for intensive agriculture. Small fields called *milpas*, were carved into highland terraces or dredged, in the lowlands, between canals that were used for irrigation or fish farming. The fields were sown with the three Native American staples: maize, beans, and squash, supplemented with other foods according to region or locality. Or they were devoted to cash crops, like cacao, which was in high demand as the source of the luxury beverage that accompanied rituals and feasts.

The Maya possessed a singular feature—it is tempting to say, a secret ingredient—because their writing system, the most expressive and complete known in the Native American world before the arrival of

Europeans, did not spread to other culture areas. Much more common in lowland regions than in the plateau and highlands, these writings were carved in stone and therefore able to withstand destruction and decay. Virtually all Maya writing falls into two categories: first, records of astronomical observations and priestly timekeeping—a vital area of interest in Maya efforts to communicate with the gods and appease nature - and, second, dynastic documents, including genealogies of kings and the records of their conquests, sacrifices, and acts of communion with their ancestors.

Of course, all the surviving written evidence is propaganda, produced under the patronage of states. Claims and counterclaims of conquests and captures are evidence not of what the kings actually did but what they thought important. The central drama of kingship—the ritual the inscriptions most often commemorate—was the spilling of royal blood. A king would use a bone needle or spike to draw blood from his penis or scatter it from his hand. A queen might perform the ceremony by dragging a knotted thong, studded with sharp bones or spines, through a perforation in her tongue. Blotted onto bark, the blood would burn with hallucinatory drugs in an open fire. Enraptured by the fumes and blood-loss, the monarch would succumb to a vision, characteristically depicted as a serpent rising from the smoke. The serpent was the mouthpiece of the ancestors. Their message usually justified war.

Maya civilization largely abandoned the lowlands in the ninth and tenth centuries. New building in ceremonial centers ended. Inscriptions ceased. The royal cult disappeared.

Royal Bloodletting. The reign of Itzamnaaj B'alam ("Shield Jaguar") II of Yaxchilán (681–742), in what is today Mexico, produced some of the finest stone reliefs like this one of October 26, 709, in which Maya rulers commemorated important rituals. The most common ritual was royal bloodletting, which was intended to provoke visions. During these bloodlettings, kings communicated with ancestors or gods.
© Erich Lessing/Art Resource

Evidence vanished of rich elites and professions specialized in learning and the arts. Squatters occupied the ruins of decaying ceremonial centers. Traditional scholarship has dramatized and mystified these events as the collapse of classic Maya civilization—an echo of the decline and fall of the Eurasian civilizations of the axial age. It seems more helpful to see what happened as the displacement of the centers of the Maya world from the lowlands to the plateau. Still, it is mysterious. None of the explanations scholars suggest fit the chronology or the evidence. War is unlikely to have put an end to the lowland tradition. The Maya practiced wars so constantly that warfare must have served a useful purpose in their society. Spells of severe and prolonged drought certainly overlapped with the period of decline, but do not seem to have matched it. Political revolutions—rebellions of the masses or struggles within the elite—might have overthrown the regimes. But even if there were direct evidence of such upheavals, we would still need to explain why they occurred at roughly the same time in so many states.

That elite activities ended only in one eco-zone suggests that an environmental explanation should help us understand what happened. The lowlands were always hostile to intensive agriculture and monumental building. In some ways, it is more surprising that such practices should have happened at all, and attained such impressive achievements, than that they should ultimately have failed. To sustain hundreds of cities and what were evidently densely packed populations, the Maya probably had to exploit their environment close to the limit of its possibilities.

Tula

For a while, the influence and, to some degree, the power of the central Mexican empire of Teotihuacán stretched the Maya world. But Teotihuacán itself withered in the eighth and ninth centuries. This vast metropolis was never reoccupied, but became something like what we today would call a heritage site: revered and remembered by peoples who imitated its art and recalled its grandeur in their poetry. A new metropolis arose, well to the northwest, at Tula—the "garden of the gods"—where blood sacrifices irrigated groves of stone pillars and ceremonial enclosures. The region already had a history of unstable settlement, and, by comparison with most earlier Maya cities or with Teotihuacán, Tula did not last long. Its site was abandoned in the twelfth century, but the ruins continued to inspire experiments in urbanization.

The Maize Frontiers

We can sum up all these New World histories of the late first millennium as efforts to open up frontiers of exploitation for intensive agriculture, state formation, and city-building—activities formerly confined to narrowly limited areas, and vulnerable to periodic extinction. Hunter–gatherers, too, could engage with their environment in more productive ways. On the northwest coast of North America, houses got bigger as fishhooks got more plentiful and became more specialized. Along the northern edge of America, whale hunters were working their way along the Arctic coast, spreading new hunting and fishing techniques as they went, reaching Greenland by about 1000.

In other parts of the Americas, new crops and new technologies extended farmers' frontiers, sometimes with transforming effects. Between the Missouri and Ohio River valleys, for instance, a large trading network flourished among peoples of similar material culture from about 200 to about 400. They buried their dead extravagantly and built tombs into mounds of astonishingly elaborate design: one in Ohio is in the shape of a long, coiling serpent—identifiable from a practically unattainable height, like the artworks of the Nazca. Sometime after 500, these practices ended, as leadership of society changed as maize cultivation spread through the region and population grew.

This was the period of the great extension of maize cultivation into regions of North America formerly inhabited almost exclusively by hunter–gatherers, displacing former power groups, coaxing chiefdoms into existence and existing chiefdoms toward statehood. This process looks like another case of a culture not extinguished, but changed and displaced from its former heartland. Maize farming reached the Great Basin of the North American plains, at sites where pottery and rock art were also made for the first time in this period. Beginning after 700, in the North American Southwest, where maize had been long established (see Chapter 5), large dwellings of adobe or stone displaced the semiunderground houses in which people formerly sheltered. Villages got larger, building toward the urban network that emerged around 1000 and that is a subject for the next chapter. Meanwhile, in the Southeast, the arrival of maize and, by around 1000, beans fed the ancestors of the large-scale builders of the early part of the next millennium.

On Marajó Island, in the mouth of the Amazon River in Brazil, people were practicing traditional agriculture with enhanced efficiency in an expanded area. Clusters of villages got denser after the mid-first millennium, with mounds raised for ceremonies as well as for agriculture. Here, the bones of the elite, boiled of their flesh, were buried in pots with clay representations of female genitals and gifts of beads, axes, and other valuables dependent on rank. Richly decorated burial urns provide glimpses of the creatures of their myths: turtles, scorpions, serpents, and almond-eyed humans.

The Islamic World and the Environment

Cultures widely scattered around the New World showed how basic tool kits or new crops could have profound effects. This feature was paralleled in the Old World—especially in the Islamic world. Although Islamic conquests slowed in the eighth century, an even more significant kind of expansion followed them: ecological expansion, as cultivators developed new crops and introduced them to new environments. For the desert pastoralists who bore Islam abroad, every frontier was a revelation. When, for example, the followers of Muhammad captured Basra on the Persian Gulf in what is today Iraq in 637, an eyewitness reported how they found two food baskets that the retreating Persians had abandoned. They ate the basket of dates but assumed the other contained poison, until a horse ate its contents without ill effects. "And their commander said, Pronounce the name of Allah over it and eat. And they ate of it and they found it a most tasty food." It was the Arabs' first taste of rice. When they took the Persian city of Ctesiphon, they mistook medicinal camphor for salt.

Rulers encouraged new introductions, employing agronomists to manage their gardens, enhance their collections of medicinal plants, supply their tables, and improve their estates. For example, between 775 and 785, Yahya ibn Khalid led a mission, on the caliph's behalf, to India to study medicinal drugs. Abd al-Rahman, ruler of Muslim Spain in the mid-eighth century, sent plant collectors to Syria. By the tenth century, Cordova, his capital, had, in effect, a special garden to grow exotic plants with fields for cuttings and seeds from abroad.

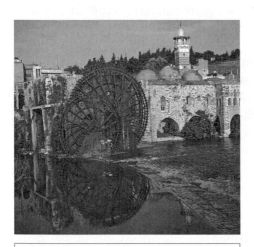

Watermill. Increased agricultural output caused demand for more and bigger mills to grind grain. Most have not survived, but a fine example of medieval watermill technology, pictured here, is on the Orontes River at Hama, Syria. Water wheels on this scale also hoisted water from riverbeds to aqueducts and irrigation channels.
Christopher Rennie/Robert Harding World Imagery

Plants from the tropics made a new summer growing season possible in the Middle East. Sugarcane, for instance, "a reed that produced honey without bees," had reached Persia from India. The Arabs extended its cultivation to the Mediterranean. Eggplant, too, was unknown in the Mediterranean or Middle East before this period. The tenth-century geographer, Ibn Hawqal, tells of a landowner in northern Iraq who doubled his revenues by planting cotton and rice. The most important development to improve mass nutrition was of hard durum wheat in the Middle East. Some crops were transmitted onward, beyond the Muslim world. West Africa got cotton, taro, bananas, plantains, sour oranges, and limes in this period, probably across the Sahara. Christian Europe, by contrast, was slow to receive the benefits of Muslim agronomy. Spinach and hard wheat were not cultivated there until the thirteenth century and rice not until the fifteenth.

The new crops required watering during summer, stimulating irrigation by underground tunnels and wells, which led, in turn, to the adoption for agriculture of more marginalized land. Forest clearance was practiced more widely and intensively than before. Fertile land left uncultivated seems to have been rare in the Muslim world. Islamic law's enforcement of a free market in land meant that farms tended to fall into the hands of owners who used them most productively. Tenants acquired farms, as conquest broke up big holdings that had stagnated under the previous regimes. Tax rates in regions under the rule of the caliphs in Baghdad were low after reforms in the late eighth century—commonly a tenth of output, with summer crops often being exempted. Villages thrived—there were 12,000 along the Guadalquivir River in Muslim Spain by the tenth century. In seventh-century Sawad in Syria, 48,000 square miles were subject to land tax—virtually the entire cultivable area.

Frontier Growth in Japan

The extent of the Islamic world made this rich environmental history possible. But a similar program, on a smaller scale, occurred even in relatively isolated Japan. Here, bureaucrats carefully calculated the hostility of the natural world. Between 806 and 1073, official records list 653 earthquakes, 134 fires, 89 cases of damage to crops, 91 epidemics, 356 supernatural warnings (including volcanic eruptions), and 367 appearances by ghosts. They recorded only 185 favorable events in the same period. In the *Nihongi* of the early eighth century, one of the earliest native Japanese chronicles, the rise of the imperial dynasty is linked with the overthrow of Susa-no-o, a god who "brought many people to an untimely end" by "making green mountains wither" and wrecking rice fields. Japanese rulers took seriously their responsibility to regulate relations with the natural world. Unlike their counterparts in most other cultures, they did not limit themselves to acts and sacrifices intended to appease the forces of nature. From the early eighth century, they had ambitious environmental policies.

Some growth in the yield of agriculture would have happened even without state guidance. Rice yields improved thanks to new, labor-intensive techniques in which whole communities cooperated: growing seedlings in nurseries and transplanting them to the fields. Meanwhile, barley gradually replaced millet as the country's second most important crop after rice, with some benefits for nutrition. Although we lack reliable figures, population was obviously growing. Census returns show—by global standards—exceptionally large households of an average of 10 persons each. Family customs helped. Young mothers commonly spent the first 5 to 15 years of married life in their parents' home, where their husbands visited them. This spread the burden of child care.

The government drive to boost food production was under way by 711, when a decree authorized aristocrats to ask provincial governors for permission to cultivate virgin land at their own expense. The aim, according to a proclamation of 722, was to add 2.5 million acres to the area devoted to rice production. In 723, farmers became eligible to inherit newly cultivated fields for three generations if they irrigated those fields from new ditches or ponds. In 743, farmers acquired absolute ownership of such lands.

As well as a state-sponsored, aristocratic enterprise, the conquest of new environments was a preserve of freelance holy men. In 735, the dismay caused by a devastating smallpox epidemic boosted the appeal and numbers of these zealots. Most of them were Buddhists. The most effective holy man was the monk Gyoki. Traditionalists accused him of embezzling alms, impiously burning the bodies of the dead, and aggressively pursuing converts. But everyone approved of the way he organized his followers to perform public works—building bridges and roads, digging ponds and embankments. The state soon contracted Gyoki's workers to undertake official projects. Frontier expansion at the expense of the "barbarians" of Japan's northeast Honshu Island also increased the amount of available land. The native Emishi were denounced as "hairy people," who dwelt among "evil deities in the mountains and perverse devils on the plains." They were described in terms that seem almost universal among imperial peoples who want to conquer, dispossess, or exterminate others. They were "fierce and wild," dangerous, lacking a recognizable political or legal system. Without chiefs, they "all rob each other. . . . In winter they lodge in holes, in summer they dwell in nests." By 796, the state had settled 9,000 colonists in fortified households on Honshu to cultivate conquered lands.

By the early ninth century, the state was growing more confident about its ability to manage the environment and keep disaster at bay. After performing a successful rainmaking rite, the hermit Kukai began his song of self-praise with a conventional reflection. Nature, he said, responded to human decadence. "And thus," he continued, "even though it is time for rain to fall, the four horizons are blazing with heat." In such circumstances, the emperor intervenes. He fasts and orders appropriate rites in all temples. "As the venerable monks chant the sacred scriptures . . . waterfalls gush forth from high peaks and soak wild animals, while rain fills the fields enough to drown water buffaloes. . . . Peasants! Do not lament any more. . . . See the storehouses, where grain piles up like islands, like mountains."

China and Southeast Asia

In Japan, as in the Islamic world, the human assault on the natural frontier had growing state power to back it. But in the same period, similar developments occurred even in politically unstable and apparently unfavorable conditions in China and India. After the collapse of the Gupta Empire (see Chapter 8), kingdoms in south India and the Deccan boosted their revenues, reach, and power by granting wasteland to priests, monks, and warriors to promote agriculture. In land grants recorded in conquered forest areas in the sixth century, monks and holy men are the biggest beneficiaries. This should not be seen merely—or perhaps at all—as evidence of kings' religious priorities but of monasteries' ability to transform the environment. An inscription on copper, dated 753, shows what happened when a priest received a royal land grant. "We the inhabitants went to the boundaries which the headman of the district pointed out, circumambulated the village . . . and planted milk bushes and placed stones around it. . . . The donee shall enjoy the wet land and the dry land included within these four boundaries, wherever the iguana runs and the tortoise crawls, and shall be permitted to dig river channels and inundation channels." The king would receive taxes on these facilities. The inscription also reveals the collective activities that community contributions supported. The settlers made and operated oil presses and looms. They dug wells. They paid taxes to support the king, the district administration, and the priestly caste out of the yield of crops, including water lilies, "the share of the potter," the price of butter and cloth. To the royal court, they sent huntsmen, messengers, dancing girls, servants, fodder, cotton, molasses, "the best cow and the best bull," and "the fourth part of the trunks of old trees." Irrigation and double cropping appear in many Indian inscriptions of the following two centuries. Marginal land was coming under the plow.

In China, although the emperors of the early seventh century were unable to sustain a lasting dynasty, they did contribute to the enduring infrastructure of the economy, building a canal system that crisscrossed the country, stimulating the grain trade and improving irrigation. In 624, in Shaanxi province, imperial waterworks irrigated more than 80,000 acres. Meanwhile, large-scale land reclamation proceeded by drainage, as population growth and improving food supply stimulated each other. The policy of the Tang dynasty (see Chapter 8) was usually to break up large landholdings and distribute them among taxpayers. A major land reform of 737 divided great estates among their workers. This may have discouraged large landowners from investing in reclamation, but it encouraged cultivation because peasants farmed their holdings more intensively than large landowners did. It was part of an ideology of imperial benevolence that also established price-regulating granaries where food stocks accumulated at government expense when prices were low for redistribution at a discount when prices were high. The resulting stocks helped cushion disaster in the plague-ravaged, famine-fraught 730s through 740s. Improved rice strains, adapted from varieties of rice that Tang armies brought back from campaigns in Vietnam, helped.

Imperial policy also stimulated the southward shift of settlement into regions, far from the threat of steppeland invasion, where rice grew, with beneficial effects on nutrition and therefore on levels of population. In 730, vagrant families were ordered to agricultural colonies under military discipline. Such proclamations often failed to produce results, but some colonies did take shape under this program, cultivating rice on the Huai River in 734. Although governments were prone to periodic bouts of hostility against Buddhism and Daoism, which Confucians tended to despise as superstitious, monasteries were generally encouraged because they could kick-start development in underexploited areas. By the mid-eighth century, a third of China's people lived in the Huai and Yangtze River valleys, and, by the eleventh century, more than half did. As colonization proceeded, Chinese villages replaced aboriginal populations, which were exterminated, assimilated, or driven into marginal areas. Population figures—statistics untrustworthy anywhere at the time except in China—suggest Tang environmental policies paid off. China had about 50 million people after An Lushan's rebellion in the 750s (see Chapter 8). Its population had grown to 60 million by the year 1000.

The extension of the frontier of settlement and of rice cultivation in southern China was part of a bigger phenomenon, extending over the moist, hot, dense forests of mainland Southeast Asia. In the sixth century, Chinese geographers ceased to refer to Funan (see Chapter 8) and located a state they called Chen-la in the interior of what is now Cambodia. This was the first sign of an important change in the region. Alongside the maritime states, founded on trade that lined the routes from China to India, agrarian kingdoms were growing up, based on rice production. For centuries small chiefdoms and aspiring states had dotted the lower Mekong River valley, but in the eighth century, the people of the region, the Khmer, began to coalesce into a single kingdom, centered at the new city of Angkor, on the north shore on the Tonle Sap—a natural reservoir of monsoonal rains. This region had no mines, no great commercial fleets, and no great industries. The wealth of the Khmer derived from a peculiar feature of how the Mekong works. Swollen by the monsoon, the river becomes, in effect, too heavily charged to empty into the sea through its own delta. The water begins to flow backward, flooding the plain of the Tonle Sap. The soil there is so rich that, provided the waters are channeled into reservoirs, it yields three rice crops a year. Angkor was also well placed for contact with other major rice lands in the Maenam and Chao Phraya basins. In 802, it became a capital with explicitly imperial pretensions, when King Jayavarman II proclaimed himself monarch of the universe, and priests in his employ performed a ceremony nullifying all former oaths of loyalty.

Similar experiments occurred across Southeast Asia. The growth of the Viet and Cham kingdoms—the other big states that took shape in Indochina in the period—owed something to the traditional wealth of the region in ivory, rhinoceros horn, and aromatic woods, and much to the bureaucracy that arrived with Buddhism. But it was based mainly on taxes from lumber and food, as forests fell and new fields replaced them. By 1000, a comparable transformation was taking shape in the northwest corner of the region. Here, in the Irawaddy valley on the borders between India and Bangladesh, dry rice cultivation began to transform a near-desert. Meanwhile, offshore, maritime state building shifted toward the Indonesian islands.

Here, in the seventh century, the realm of Srivijaya, on the Sumatran coast, impressed the first Chinese sources to notice it. When the pilgrim I-ching stopped there in 671, the capital had a community of Buddhist monks, said to number 1,000. The court employed Hindu and Buddhist scholars. But the maharajah, as the sources called the king of Srivijaya, was said to use magic to control the sea, with enchanted crocodiles to guard the mouth of his river.

Srivijaya's economy relied on harbor tolls and the profits of piracy. A river-linked domain behind it supplied it with soldiers and rice, because even trading states needed their own food supplies. Srivijaya had big commercial resources in the form of spices and aromatic woods, but the inhabitants still worked to expand rice production. According to a legend of the foundation of Palembang, the fathers of the city chose its site by weighing the waters of Sumatra's various rivers for silt and finding that those of the Musi would be best for irrigating rice lands. Palembang's earliest inscription, dated 685, expresses a king's concern that "all the clearances and gardens his people made should be full, that the cattle of all species raised by them and their bondsmen should prosper."

The capital, where even the parrots spoke four languages, attracted merchants. The maritime strength of Srivijaya was concentrated in the ragged east coast of Sumatra, with its fringe of islands and mangrove swamps, its deep bays and shelters for shipping, its natural coral-reef defenses, its abundant fish and turtles. Its greatness and survival—for it was "invariably described as great," according to a Chinese administrator of its trade in the early eleventh century—depended on Chinese commerce, especially for the sandalwood and frankincense in which it established a dominant trading position.

In eighth-century Java, the Sailendra dynasty rivaled Srivijaya. Their huge temple, Borobodur, seemed to proclaim their patrons' privileged access to heaven. Built of half a million blocks of stone, it arose between about 790 and 830.

The maritime economy of Sailendra has left no archives, but it comes to life in the carvings. One of the most famous depicts a legendary voyage to a promised land that Hiru, the faithful minister of the mythical monk-king Rudrayana, made. Hiru earned the goodwill of heaven by intervening with the king's wicked son and successor, who proposed, among other evil acts, to bury his father's spiritual counselor alive. Miraculously advised to flee in advance of a sandstorm that would smother the court, Hiru fled by sea in a windborne ship to a happy shore. He found granaries, peacocks, varied trees, and hospitable inhabitants. The artist who carved the story had seen such scenes. He knew what a ship looked like and how it worked. The kind of art he produced—evidence, too, of a kind of spirituality—could only come from a world that regarded travel and trade as noble, virtuous activities.

According to later inscriptions—in which we must make allowance for mythical distortions or propagandistic exaggerations—a rival kingdom to the Sailendras arose in regions of Java where forest had been newly converted to rice cultivation on the plains of the Solo and Brantas rivers. Inscriptions credit the expulsion of the Sailendras from these regions in the mid-ninth century to Pikatan, a king who doubled as a holy man, forest clearer, and temple builder.

The Pacific

An even more impressive drive to colonize new lands and exploit new resources occurred deep in the Pacific, where, as far as we know, the commerce of the monsoonal seas barely reached.

To judge from the available archaeological evidence, the Caroline Islands in Micronesia were probably first colonized about 2,000 years ago, not from the relatively nearby Asian mainland but from the southeast, in the Solomon Islands and New Hebrides, by people who made distinctive round pots, intricately patterned by pressing tooth-shaped stamps into the clay, and whose houses were raised on stilts. The way this culture changed—relatively suddenly and at vastly different rates on different islands—awaits explanation. The most precocious island was Pohnpei, at the Carolines' eastern end. It is small—probably incapable of supporting more than 30,000 people—but it was a center of ambitious activity toward 1000. Large-scale labor was mobilized to carve out artificial islets with increasingly monumental ceremonial centers—for tombs and rites including turtle sacrifices and the nurture of sacred eels. On nearby Kosrae Island, a similar history began soon after. Within a couple of centuries, cities were arising around paved streets within high walls of massive construction—observed with "total bewilderment" by the French expedition that came on the city of Lelu by accident in 1824.

Making Connections

ENVIRONMENTAL/GEOGRAPHIC OBSTACLES TO DEVELOPMENT OF STATES

REGION	ENVIRONMENTAL/OBSTACLES	ADAPTIVE STRATEGIES
Sub-Saharan Africa	Isolation—desert in north and lee winds offshore impede communication; widely separated river basins; lack of navigable rivers near coasts; dense forests, malarial jungles	Exploitation of agricultural, mining resources near Sahel grassland; West Africa; trans-Sahara trade routes focusing on copper, salt, gold
North and South America	Bounded by vast oceans—Atlantic and Pacific oceans; most rivers flow east–west preventing north–south contacts; mountainous terrain	Taking advantage of South/Mesoamerican highlands' proximity to rain forests, seas, swamps for resource exploitation; intensive development of fishing/hunting techniques in North America; introduction of new crops and technologies aided by trade networks from Mesoamerica to Mississippi River Basin
Japan	Isolated geography; few navigable rivers; poor soil; earthquake prone	Labor-intensive wetland agricultural techniques; highly regulated society; systematic exploitation of animals as sources of power
Pacific	Vast and isolated region; few food crops, little cultivable soil on many islands	Skillful development of navigational, boat-building techniques; unsurpassed knowledge of ocean and night sky; introduction of basic "tool kit" (fishhooks, taro, coconut, breadfruit, kava, banana plants, chickens, pigs) to uninhabited islands

THE PACIFIC

267

    Beyond the Carolines, in the South Pacific, lay one of the world's most daunting frontiers: an ocean too big to traverse with the technology of the time, where the winds blew almost without stop from the southeast and where vast distances separated islands that could support human life. Speakers of Polynesian languages conquered this environment mainly after 500. They grew taro, yams, coconut, breadfruit, and bananas. They

Polynesian Canoe. Hokule'a is a modern Hawaiian reconstruction of a traditional Polynesian catamaran, in which members of the Polynesian Navigation Society demonstrated the navigability of the island systems of the Pacific in the 1970s, using navigation without instruments, under the guidance of Mau, a pilot from the Caroline Islands.
© Monte Costa

kept chickens and pigs. They named 150 kinds of fish, and exploited them for tools—files made of sea-urchin spines, fish hooks from oyster shells. They drank a brew of fermented roots called kava to induce trances and celebrate rites. Although archaeology cannot retrieve their notions of the sacred, we can infer it from language and later evidence. **Mana**—an ubiquitous life-force—regulated their world, making nets fish or herbs heal.

The Polynesians' was a frontier culture in origin. It grew up in the central Pacific, probably in the islands of Tonga and Samoa, beginning about 2,000 to 3,000 years ago. From their first emergence in the archaeological record, Polynesians ventured ever farther into the paths of the southeast trade winds, which restricted the range of navigation but which at least promised explorers a good chance of getting home. Around 600 there was a period of "takeoff," from which archaeological finds multiplied across the ocean, as far as Easter Island (see Chapter 14). In further phases of expansion, Polynesians colonized northward as far as Hawaii, by about 800, and ultimately settled New Zealand and the Chatham Islands.

To colonize so many islands, many of which seemed dauntingly far apart, was such a surprising achievement that scholars who investigated it long assumed that it must have happened by accident—as a result of seafarers or regional traders drifting off course or being blown to new lands by freak winds. But long-range navigation is part of the logic of life on small islands—a characteristic way to maximize resources, extend economic opportunities, and diversify the ecosystem. The Polynesians, in common with the Caroline Islanders and other sailors of the northern and western Pacific, had impressive maritime technology: double-hulled canoes big enough to carry 200 people, or smaller vessels with outriggers for longer journeys, rigged with claw-shaped sails that kept the mast and rigging light. Their direction-finding techniques were the best in the world. Chants helped navigators remember the complex guidance of the stars in a hemisphere where no single polestar is available to guide voyagers, as it is north of the equator. Navigation was like "breadfruit-picking," star by star. They mapped the ocean's swells—mentally or perhaps with maps made of reeds, of which later examples survive. Eighteenth-century European observers noted that Caroline and Polynesian navigators could literally feel their way around the ocean, identifying their position by the way that waves felt on their own bodies.

By about 1000, the Polynesians may have gotten close to the limits of navigation accessible to them with the technology at their disposal. Oral traditions recall and presumably embellish their history. The most heroic tale is perhaps that of Hui-te-Rangiora, whose journey from Raratonga in the Cook Islands in the remote Pacific in the mid-eighth century took him through bare white rocks that towered over a monstrous sea, to a place of uninterrupted ice. Myths ascribe the discovery of New Zealand to the godlike Maui, who baited giant stingray with his own blood. A less shadowy figure is the indisputably human Kupe, who claimed that a vision of the supreme god Io guided him to New Zealand from Raratonga. Maybe, however, he just followed the migration of the long-tailed cuckoo birds. His sailing directions were: "Let the course be to the right hand of the setting sun, moon, or Venus in the second month of the year."

The Frontiers of Christendom

At the opposite end of Eurasia, in the eighth century, Christendom began to outgrow the frontiers of the Roman Empire (see Map 10.2). Here conquest was the main agent of change. Christendom developed no new crops or technologies. The heavy plow had long been in use. Rye and barley—the grains suitable for the frost-rimmed, dense soils of northern Europe—were ancient crops. Colonization, however, accompanied conquest and transformed environments, as conquerors encouraged settlers in underexploited territories, and armies drove gangways through forests, while monks tamed wilderness and attracted farmers in frontier regions.

Beyond Rome's farthest northern and western frontiers, monastic exiles took memories of antiquity into Scotland and Ireland, like the monk Columba, longing to compose his hymns "on a rocky outcrop, overlooking

Frankish Kingdom, 751
Frankish Kingdom at
ascension of Charlemagne, 771
conquests of Charlemagne
regions recognizing Charlemagne as overlord
Kingdom of Asturias
Byzantine Empire
Kievan Rus
Muslim lands
Slavs   people
Christian missions, 750–1000
Magyar migrations, late 9th century

Map 10.2 The Expansion of Christendom, 751–1000

the coiling surface of the sea." A similar—more dangerous—enterprise flickered in Germany, where Boniface traveled from England in 719 to share the Gospel with his fellow Saxons. Boniface was martyred around 754, but the task of converting the Saxons was taken up 30 years later, from inside the most dynamic spot on the frontier of Christendom: the kingdom of the Franks.

Two events transformed its ruler, Charlemagne, into the self-styled renovator of Rome. His journey to Italy in 774 opened his eyes to ruined

Irish Cross. Outside the Roman Empire, Christianity was slow to take root in Europe—except in Scotland and Ireland. Isolation made Irish Christian art highly distinctive. This eighth-century bronze crucifix was probably made to adorn the cover of a gospel book. The artist was apparently concerned to represent scripture authentically—hence the soldiers who pierce Jesus' side and hoist a sponge to his lips. The angels who perch on the arms of the cross display fragments of what may be intended to represent Christ's shroud, or the cloth used to wipe his face. *National Museum of Ireland*

splendors and enabled him to gather books and scholars. From the 790s, he could afford unprecedented ambitions when he captured the treasure of invading steppelanders, the Avars. Taking advantage of the fact that Irene, an empress of dubious legitimacy, ruled in Constantinople, he proclaimed himself successor of the ancient Roman emperors. While remaining first and foremost a Frankish king, Charlemagne affected what he thought was Roman taste. He appeared on coins in a laurel crown. His seals were stamped with slogans of imperial revival. His court writers, who must have known what he wanted to hear, compared him to Constantine and Justinian (see Chapter 8). The manuscript painters, scribes, and ivory carvers of his palace copied ancient models.

Even before Charlemagne came to the throne, the Frankish realm had incorporated lands beyond the margins of the old Roman Empire, especially along the North Sea and in central Germany. Charlemagne's conquest of Saxony, which took 18 years to complete, was the first annexation of a large new province in Europe by a self-consciously "Roman" emperor since the Emperor Trajan had conquered Dacia in the early second century. More significant yet was the enduring nature of this conquest. Saxony, wrested—said Charlemagne's servant and first biographer—from devil worshippers, became a parade ground of Christendom, converted from an insecure frontier into an imperial heartland.

On Christendom's other exposed flanks, similar expansion made slow progress. In the early ninth century, Mojmir I established a Slav state patterned on Charlemagne's monarchy, beyond the Danube in Bohemia. In 864, the Bulgar Tsar Boris decided to accept Christianity and impose it on his people. The Bulgars rapidly became like the Franks, rival claimants to the mantle of Rome, under a ruler who called himself "emperor of all the Greeks and Bulgars." Yet if the Bulgar Empire was a threat to Constantinople, it was a bulwark for Christendom against pagan steppelanders from farther east.

Despite an isolated position and scant resources, Asturias in ninth-century northern Spain successfully defended Christendom's frontier against the Muslims at the opposite end of the Mediterranean. Part of the sacred armory of its kings lies in Oviedo Cathedral—vessels of gold, ivory, and lapis lazuli, housing even more precious scraps of wood and bone from the saints who could have a magical effect in battle. On a hill above the town, Ramiro I could look out on his kingdom from his summer palace or receive ambassadors in a hall decorated with carvings molded after Persian silverwork from some Roman hoard. By the end of the century, the kingdom began to expand beyond the mountains that screened it to the south.

Exploitation of the shrine attributed to the Apostle James the Great at Compostela gave Asturias advantages over other Christian states in Spain—in pilgrim wealth, monastic colonization, and the chances of recruiting knightly manpower. But a frontier position generally was good for state-building. In the 890s, Wilfrid the Hairy, Count of Barcelona, conquered almost all the counties around his own, south of the Pyrenees. Laborious settlement of underpopulated areas is the subject of all the documents that survive from his time. Wilfrid's story was typical of the edges of Christendom. In lands reclaimed from pagan conquest on the northern frontier, in England, Alfred the Great (r. 871–899) was securing a similar reputation as a state-builder by lavish generosity to monks, the custodians of the historical record. By 924, Alfred's heirs had completed their reconquest of northern and eastern England. The extension or restoration of the frontier of Christendom was pushing Europe outward.

At the same time, a secular political tradition was being spread even farther afield. Christianity, as we saw in the last chapter, was barely beginning to penetrate Scandinavia, which—in terms of the colonists it generated and the new lands it explored—was the most dynamic part of Europe. A letter from the northern Russian city of Novgorod is said to have reached a Viking prince in 862. "Our land," it read, "is great and rich. But there is no order in it. Come and rule us." In response, he founded the state that eventually became Russia. The story shows how territorial statehood was exported, far beyond the limits of the old Roman Empire, to relatively immature political worlds in northern and eastern Europe. Meanwhile, Scandinavian expansion was also going on northward, spreading the frontiers of farming and statehood within its own peninsula, and turning seaward, colonizing Iceland.

CHRONOLOGY	
ca. 200–400	Flourishing of mound-building culture in eastern North America
ca. 600	"Takeoff" of Polynesian expansion
ca. 750	China's population reaches 50 million
754	Martyrdom of Boniface
Third through tenth centuries	Maya Classic Age
Seventh through tenth centuries	Ecological expansion of Islam
Eighth century	Government drive to boost food production in Japan
Eighth through ninth centuries	Decline of Ethiopia
790–830	Construction of Borobodur temple, Java
ca. 800	Settlement of Hawaii
ca. 802	Charlemagne completes conquest of Saxony
ca. 860	Scandinavians begin colonization of Iceland
884	Kiev becomes capital of Russian state
ca. 1000	Andean city of Tiahuanaco abandoned; China's population reaches 60 million
1100s	Tula abandoned

(All dates are C.E.)

IN PERSPECTIVE
The Limits of Divergence

On the face of it, sub-Saharan Africa and the Americas seem to diverge from Eurasia and North Africa from the eighth century to 1000. In Christendom, the Islamic world, China, Southeast Asia, and the western and central Pacific, states came and went, but economies and civilizations were robust—extending frontiers, colonizing new areas, founding new states and empires, or reviving old ones. These regions seem to have bucked the patterns detected by traditional historiography: to have endured beyond periods of decline and fall. At first glance, the contrast with sub-Saharan Africa looks glaring. Ethiopia's dark age really was dark, in the sense that we know virtually nothing about it. Ghana's frustration, and the absence of any evidence of comparable state-building initiatives elsewhere, confirm the traditional picture of a region—like far northern Asia or Australia—about which historians of the period can find almost nothing to say. The myth of Maya collapse has long dominated the way we conventionally think of the Americas in this period as a hemisphere where it was more usual for civilizations to perish than to grow outward or renew themselves. This is an exaggeration—even a caricature. But there is something in it. Teotihuacán, the Moche, the Nazca, the lowland Maya, Huari, Tiahuanaco—these casualties of the era were replaced, if at all, by unstable successors.

Nevertheless, a theme that, if not quite global, genuinely embraces the Old and New Worlds underlies the apparent differences between them. Broadly stated, this was a period of unusual ecological experiment: the exploration or conquest of new environments. In some cases, new frontiers were breached by expansion into neighboring regions and already-familiar environments, like those of the Islamic world or Southeast Asia or most of Christendom. In others, like the Caroline Islands or the Scandinavian expansion, apparently unprecedented adventures were launched from origins that present knowledge cannot adequately explain. In others again, as in China and Japan, internal colonization adapted and transformed previously underexploited wastelands. In others, such as the Andes, central Mexico, and the Maya world, the centers of activity were displaced to new environments—the limestone hills of Tula or Yucatán, the almost incredibly high altitude of Tiahuanaco. In others, which remain necessarily underrepresented in history books because of the absence of evidence, the business of locating resources, developing foodstuffs, and improving production techniques continued without leaving much trace in the record. In the 800s and 900s, for instance, all we have is linguistic evidence for two enormously important developments in the ecology of East Africa. An explosion of new terms shows that banana cultivation and cattle breeding spread inland from the Indian Ocean coast to the Great Lakes of Central Africa. Against this background, the history of the next three centuries, which is the subject of the next part of the book, becomes intelligible. Vibrancy and innovativeness, which became characteristic of most of these regions—and of others where the evidence only begins to mount up from this point onward—grew out of preceding, painstaking efforts to find new, more productive ways to exploit the environment.

The story of the last few centuries of the first millennium c.e. suggests an important point about how history happens. In the past, the search for patterns that help to explain it, and that make it easier to write textbooks about it, has driven historians to grotesque oversimplifications: seeing history as a continuous story of "progress" or decline or representing it as a kind of swing between revolutions and counterrevolutions, or between decadence and dynamism, or between dark ages and rebirths. The reality, it seems, as we get to learn more about the past, is much more subtle and intriguing. At one level, the slow growth of compatible changes—what historians' jargon sometimes calls "structures"—gradually gave the world a new look. Simultaneously, and often with contradictory effect, random or short-term changes stimulate, impede, interrupt, or temporarily reverse those trends, and—sometimes—permanently deflect or end them. Thus, both continuity and discontinuity tend to be visible in the story, pretty much all the time. A picture that omits either is almost certain to be distorted.

In these respects, history is rather like climate, in which many cycles of varying duration all seem to be going on all the time and where random or almost-random changes frequently intervene. With increasing intensity in recent years, historians have struggled to match changes in the human record to knowledge of how these cycles and changes have interacted since the end of the Ice Age. As we are about to see, some of the most remarkable insights to have emerged from this quest illuminate worldwide changes that began—or that we can first begin to detect—around 1,000 years ago.

PROBLEMS AND PARALLELS

1. How did societies take advantage of new ways of managing and exploiting the environment during the late first millennium?
2. How did geography impede the diffusion of culture and crops in sub-Saharan Africa and the Americas?
3. What influences contributed to the flourishing of South American and Mesoamerican cultures and states?
4. What were the effects of environmental expansion in the Islamic world?
5. Why were monks and holy men important for the conquest of new environments and the expansion of states?
6. How were the Polynesians able to colonize the Pacific between 500 and 1000?

Contending with Isolation: ca. 1000–1200

focus questions

1. How did geography influence the spread of culture and state building in the Americas?
2. Why did the Ethiopian Empire begin to expand again in the eleventh and twelfth centuries?
3. Why were the land routes across Eurasia less significant than the sea routes across the Indian Ocean?
4. Which areas of India were most prosperous during these centuries, and what was the basis of their prosperity?
5. How did their relative cultural isolation affect Japan and western Europe during these centuries?

The farewells lasted "all day and into the night." Aboard ship, the travelers prayed for a peaceful crossing. When the clouds cleared, before dawn, "oars pierced the moon's reflection." Winds lashed. Typhoons threatened. Pirates lurked. The voyagers appealed to the gods by flinging tokens, charms, and cupfuls of rice wine into the sea. When perils threatened, they even sacrificed jewels and precious mirrors. It was a routine journey along the coast of Japan in the year 936. The governor of Kochi—at that time, one of the remotest provinces of the Japanese empire—was on his way home to the capital in what is now the city of Kyoto.

A journal that the governor's wife, the "Tosa lady" as she is now called, supposedly wrote recorded the events of the journey. In some ways, the work is obviously a literary creation and a moral tale. The ship navigates between perils. The sea is the arena of the "gods and Buddhas." But despite these dramatizations and fictional conventions, the dangerous sailing conditions the diarist described were true to life. The journey from Tosa to the port of Osaka can hardly have covered more than 400 miles; yet it took well over two months. Hostile seas penned in the Japanese, despite their skill in nautical technology. This helps to explain why, for most of their history, the Japanese have been confined in their own islands and remained in a relatively small country, despite considering themselves to bc an empire.

The experiences of the Tosa Lady, moreover, highlight a startling truth about her times. In other parts of the world, long-range navigations were leaping oceans. For in the amount of time the Tosa Lady took to get to Osaka, an Indian Ocean trader, with the benefit of the reversible wind system, could get all the way from the Persian Gulf to Sumatra: a distance of more than 5,000 miles.

Pilgrim traffic by Muslims to Mecca also stimulated Indian Ocean navigation, as Muslim merchant communities spread across Asia and Muslim holy men traveled and made converts. Meanwhile, beyond the range of the monsoon, migrants from what is now Indonesia crossed the ocean across the path of the southeast trade winds and colonized Madagascar, off the east coast of Africa. Their descendants are still there, speaking the same language the navigators brought—though what inspired such an extraordinary voyage remains unknown. Meanwhile, Polynesian navigators, as we saw in Chapter 10, were penetrating deep into the Pacific Ocean with the aid of some of the world's most regular long-range winds. Even more remarkably, around the year 1000, Thule Inuit from the Pacific and Norse from Scandinavia crossed the Arctic and Atlantic Oceans from opposite directions and met in Greenland.

Pilgrim Ship. The monsoon helped to make the Arabian Sea a Muslim lake. The Indian pilgrim ship depicted in this Iraqi manuscript of the *Maqamaat* of al Hariri of 1238 is equipped with square sails to make the most of the winds on the outward and homebound crossings of the sea.
Bibliotheque Nationale de France

These extraordinarily long-range migrations were part of a double dynamic, as people stretched the resources available to them in one of two ways: exploring for new resources and exploiting existing opportunities in new ways. Region by region, culture by culture, in this chapter and the next, we can see people in widely separated parts of the world using similar strategies: felling forests, extending areas of cultivation and pasture, expanding into new terrain, and enhancing muscle power with new technologies.

In the eleventh and twelfth centuries, these forms of expansion were widespread themes of world history, but they followed divergent courses in different regions. As was so often the case, relative isolation was usually the key to the difference between long-lasting innovation and faltering, short-lived change. Cultures that exchanged information and artifacts were relatively robust. Peoples isolated from fruitful contacts found it much harder to thrive. In the Americas, therefore, as so often before, failures frustrated experiments in new ways of life. But some parts of the Old World, where long-range contacts were easier and more frequent, experienced enduring transformations.

The new opportunities of the period arose partly from the environmental changes of the preceding centuries, described in the last chapter. To see how people responded, we can devote this chapter to a sort of world tour of some of the regions most affected—starting in the Americas, before turning to the world around the shores of the Indian Ocean, including the parts of East Africa that face that ocean, and ending with the extremities of Eurasia in Japan and western Europe. In these parts of the world, we see societies contending with isolation with varying degrees of success.

In other regions of Africa and Eurasia—China, Central Asia, West Africa, the Byzantine Empire, and the Islamic world—the single most important source of new pressures for change arose from the stirrings of nomadic peoples. These are the subject of the next chapter.

American Developments: From the Arctic to Mesoamerica

The history of the Americas in the eleventh and twelfth centuries is scattered with stories of new frontiers, developed by new migrations or new initiatives (see Map 11.1).

Greenland and the North

About 1,000 years ago, a relatively warm spell disturbed the lives of hunters along North America's Arctic edge. Taking advantage of improved conditions for hunting and navigating, migrants worked their way across the southern edge of the Arctic Ocean. The Thule Inuit traveled in vessels made of walrus hides, stretched across wooden ribs. Their vessels were shallow, so that they could hug the shore, and light, so that the voyagers could lift them from between ice floes.

The Thule hunted at sea for whales and polar bears. They mounted their harpoons on floats made from seal bladders, which they blew up like balloons. Game could then be towed home. Alternatively, they attacked their prey on rafts of ice. On land, they hunted with dogs of a breed new to North America. Their spear-armed boatmen trapped reindeer in rivers. For warfare against human enemies, they reintroduced the bow and arrow. By about 1000 they had reached Greenland and the western extremities of North America. The navigation of the Arctic was an astonishing feat, not repeated until the twentieth century.

At the same time, almost equally heroic migrations were under way in the opposite direction, toward the same destinations, across the North Atlantic. Exploitable currents helped navigators from Scandinavia cross the ocean, via Iceland, below the Arctic Circle. It seems extraordinarily daring to risk such a long journey across the open sea without chart or compass, but the Scandinavians knew that the prevailing winds blew from the west in the latitudes they inhabited. So they could always hope to get home. The voyagers probably steered, like the Polynesians (see Chapter 10), by now-unrecoverable techniques, judging their latitude by observing the polestar with the naked eye on cloudless nights.

Whereas the Thule Inuit were blazing a trail of abundance, drawn by the fat-rich foods of the Arctic, the Norse—or Northmen—as the Atlantic voyagers are called, were usually escapees or exiles from poverty or restricted social opportunity. In the early years of their settlement, the environment, harsh as it was, had a lot to offer the newcomers: fish and game, including luxury items valuable as potential exports to Europe, such as hunting falcons and walrus ivory. Greenland was not, however, a land the Norse cared to settle without changing the environment

ATLANTIC OCEAN

Tropic of Cancer

Caribbean Sea

Gulf of Mexico

NORTH AMERICA

UNITED STATES

Prairie

Missouri

Mississippi

ILLINOIS

Cahokia

MISSOURI

Rocky Mountains

COLORADO

San Juan

Chaco Canyon

Pueblo Bonito

NEW MEXICO

Jornada de la Muerte

Rio Grande

Chaco

ARIZONA

Little Colorado

Salt

Colorado

MEXICO

Sierra Madre

MESOAMERICA

Tula

Mixtec

Tutétec

Chichén Itzá

Yucatán Maya

PACIFIC OCEAN

N

500 km

500 miles

40°

80°

80°

100°

100°

110°

20°

20°

canyon cultures
● major city or ceremonial center
Mississippian cultures
↑ roads leading north from Mesoamerica
↑ sea route from Mesoamerica to Mississippi River valley
↑ Mayan trade route

Mixtec peoples
ARIZONA modern state

Economic Basis of Canyon People

● maize
● beans
◈ cotton
▽ irrigation
◯ turquoise

Mississippian Trade Goods

⬒ seashells
✖ deerskins
🦬 bison pelts
✖ horn

Map 11.1 North America and Mesoamerica to ca. 1200

280

profoundly. They introduced grain and European grasses for grazing. They developed a breed of sheep whose wool was prized. The big wooden ships the Norse used, held together with iron nails, in a land with little timber or iron, must have seemed wildly extravagant to the Inuit in their skin canoes. The Norse town of Brattahlid in western Greenland—the remotest outpost of medieval Christendom—was heroically elaborate, with 17 monasteries and churches of stone with bells of bronze. The cathedral at Gardar was built between 1189 and 1200 of red sandstone and molded soapstone, with a bell tower, glass windows, and three fireplaces. The largest farms supported an aristocratic way of life, with big halls in which to feast dependents. But the colony remained precarious and isolated.

The North American Southwest and the Mississippi Region

Beyond the colony in Greenland, the shore station that Greenlanders or Icelanders set up in Newfoundland in about 1000 did not last. There were not enough wealthy or settled communities in the area with whom the Norse could establish contact, trade, and cultural exchange. A glance at the map of North America at the time shows similar cases, deeply inland, of peoples struggling with isolation. The new way of life traveled along two routes: from the heartlands of maize in what is now Mexico, into the arid lands of the North American Southwest, and from the Gulf of Mexico into the wetlands of the Mississippi valley and parts of what is now the United States' Deep South. The results included the rise of cultures with unmistakable similarities to predecessors in Mesoamerica, with urban life, irrigation, elaborate ceramics and shellcraft, gold work and copper work, ball games in some cases, and unmistakable signs of statehood.

In parts, for instance, of what are now the states of Colorado, New Mexico, and Arizona, evidence of some sort of political network spread over 57,000 square miles. An extraordinary system of roadways, up to 12 yards wide, radiated from a cluster of sites around the great canyon near the source of the Chaco River. Either some unknown ritual was being enacted, demanding and reinforcing close ties between the places linked, or the roads were there to move armies.

The environment is surprising: parched and seemingly unsuitable for settled life. Apart from turquoise, which became the basis of trade, natural wealth was scarce. But the region was densely settled, at least in patches. The canyon people built ambitious cities or ceremonial centers around plazas, surrounded by large, round rooms and a honeycomb of small rectangular spaces. Massive outer walls enclosed them. The main buildings were of stone, faced with fine masonry. Roofs were made of great timbers dragged from pine forests in the distant hills—a dazzling show of wealth and power in a treeless desert. To construct the ceremonial center at Chaco Canyon, 200,000 trees were felled. We do not know what the political system was. But we know it was tough. Mass executions have left frightening piles of victims' bones—crushed, split, and picked as if at a cannibal feast.

The economic basis of this civilization was fragile. Sometimes the Chaco River would flood, though not regularly enough to create rich, silty soils. Rainfall levels are likely to have been higher than now, though irrigation was essential to help crops grow in the virtually rainless summer. If water could be delivered to the fields, cotton, maize, and beans would grow predictably, without danger from the sort of fluctuating temperatures that threatened at higher altitudes. Long irrigation canals did the job.

From the twelfth century onward, the climate got drier, putting the irrigation system under a constant strain. The rulers of the canyon people responded by expanding into new zones, building more ambitiously, organizing labor more ferociously. But decline, punctuated by crisis, shows through a series of periodic contractions of the culture area and reorganizations of the settlements. Meanwhile, the harsh peacekeeping methods seem to have stopped working. Settlements withdrew to defensible locations. Revivals of a similar way of life happened frequently, but the problems of isolation defeated or limited all of them until the nineteenth century.

The **canyon cultures** were as remote from Mesoamerican civilizations as the Norse of Greenland were from Europe. Roads north from Mesoamerica led across dangerous territory. Nomadic peoples patrolled the northern edges of the Mesoamerican culture area, practicing raids and conquests, like those launched in Eurasia from the steppes into China or Europe, albeit on a smaller scale. The high road north from what is now Mexico to the nearest patch of easily cultivable soil led through a 61-mile pass known in modern times as the *Jornada del Muerto:*—the "dead man's march"—through rock-strewn defiles and dunes where the glare was so fierce that a traveler's eyes "boiled and bulged" and seemed to burst from their sockets and men "breathed fire and spat pitch."

It was even harder to transmit Mesoamerican crops and traditions beyond the world of Chaco Canyon. The prairie, though a flat expanse, was an ecological barrier, where few patches could sustain sedentary life. It is more likely that Mesoamerica's tool kit, food, and ways of life and thought traveled across the Gulf of Mexico, by seaborne trade, to reach the North American southeast. In parts of this region, the environment was promising. In the Mississippi valley and other riverside floodplains, natural ridges accumulated over centuries, wherever the floods dumped soil. These ridges were the nurseries of the farmers' crops and the inspiration for mounds dredged from the swamps to provide gardens. A hinterland of pools and lakes provided ideal centers for fish farming to supplement the field plants, among which maize was increasingly dominant.

In this region, between the ninth and thirteenth centuries, people laid out ceremonial centers in patterns similar to those of Mesoamerica. Platforms, topped with chambered structures, were loosely grouped around large plazas. **Cahokia**, east of St. Louis, Missouri, is the most spectacular site. Cahokia stands almost at the northwestern limit of the reach of the culture to which it belongs. Its frontier position may have allowed it to act as a commercial gateway between zones of interrelated environments and, therefore, of interrelated products: shells from the Gulf, deerskins from the eastern woodlands, bison pelts and horn from the prairies. Cahokia's central platform is more than 100 feet high. At about 13 acres, the base of the great mound is as big as that of the biggest Egyptian pyramid. Farther away, smaller, similar sites extend from the riverbanks to the uplands of Illinois and Missouri. Cahokia's size gives it the look of a focal point for this scattering of settlements. Its air of importance tempts some scholars to think of it as something like the capital of a state or, at least, a cultural center from which influence radiated.

Graves at Cahokia have given up honored dead. Their treasures included tools and adornments of copper, bones, and tortoiseshell. As time went on, increasing numbers of finely made stone arrowheads were buried in elite graves. This is a precious clue to how Cahokian culture changed but is hard to interpret. Were the arrows trophies of success in war or hunting or simple counters of wealth? In any case, the arrows were aristocratic possessions in a society graded for status and equipped for conflict. When Cahokia lost political power in the thirteenth century, the place retained a sacred aura: its manufactures—pots, shell work, soapstone carvings, and small axe heads that presumably had a place in forgotten rites—circulated over hundreds of miles and for hundreds of years after the mound dwellers died out or dispersed.

When objects of great value are concentrated without evidence of a dwelling, grave, or warehouse, it is tempting to talk of a temple. An impressive cache of this type, found at what is now an automobile showroom, at a site somewhat to the southeast of Cahokia, contains carvings that give us glimpses into a mythic history or symbolic system that attached a high value to two themes: fertility and farming, and especially to maize and squash. One female figure tames a snake whose multiple tails are in the form of squash plants. Another female, kneeling on a mat, holds a stalk of maize.

The people who built Cahokia inaugurated a way of life that was economically successful and artistically productive for not much more than a couple of hundred years—not a bad tally for its place and time, but

AMERICAN DEVELOPMENTS

283

much shorter than the span major cities in Eurasia achieved. After a spell of stagnation or decline, their inhabitants deserted the upper Mississippi valley culture sites over a period of about four generations around the thirteenth and fourteenth centuries.

Though some of its more ambitious features were abandoned, culture of the kind that climaxed at Cahokia was not abandoned. Mound building continued on a smaller scale, at sites scattered over the lower Mississippi valley and across the North American southeast from Florida to Oklahoma. Here, traditions of burying chiefs, with rich grave goods and large-scale sacrifices, were also maintained.

Mesoamerica

In a similar way in Mesoamerica, the collapse of the cities of the classic Maya in the ninth and tenth centuries in Central America and southern Mexico (see Chapter 10) did not put an end to Maya civilization. Although the Maya cities of the lowlands never revived, and their peculiar culture never reappeared in the same form elsewhere, Maya city life and state-building continued in a new environment on the limestone peninsula of Yucatán in eastern Mexico. Here, the environment contrasted with the old lowland heartlands of the Maya. The Yucatan climate was dry, and irrigation relied on pools and wells. But it was possible to reconstruct the old Maya way of life with remarkable fidelity. In Yucatán, lowland tradition met links with central Mexico, which was accessible through a mixture of seaborne and overland routes.

Continuities with the former Maya world are evident in the way the buildings are arrayed in the cities of Yucatán, in layouts that reflect an abiding interest in the observation of the movements of the stars and planets, and in facades decorated with the snouts of curl-nosed gods or the jaws of feathered serpents or scenes of human sacrifice. The greatest Yucatán city, Chichén Itzá, began to arise in the tenth century, at about the time the lowland Maya culture withered. If traditions recorded later are reliable, a dynasty with imperial ambitions, the Cocom, ruled in this city, and their wars with dynasties in rival centers dominated the region for centuries.

Yucatán was a new frontier for the Maya: a region of unprecedentedly intense exploitation in the eleventh and twelfth centuries. It was not the only such area in Mesoamerica. The Pacific-facing regions of Mexico, beyond the Sierra Madre, leap into the historical record in the same period. This is the region where the people known as Mixtec lived, in relatively small communities that one could hardly call cities but that were densely settled and famed for their specialized professions of elite craftsmen, especially in gold work and books made of bark. One of the greatest

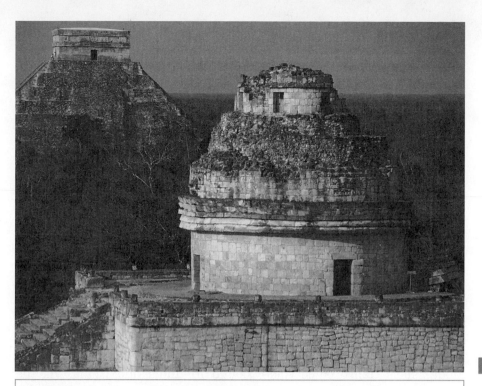

Chichén Itzá. With the end of monumental building, inscription-making, and royal rites among the lowland Maya in the tenth century, Maya civilization did not "die out." Its centers were displaced northward to the limestone peninsula of Yucatán, where Chichén Itzá arose to be the greatest city of the region. Some ways of life continued—lavish building, city-states almost constantly at war with one another, reliance on maize as a staple food, divination, human sacrifice, and elite rituals including chocolate-drinking and ball games. But the cities all have original architectural features. Chichén Itzá, for example, has a ball court of unprecedented size and the unique, round-chambered building known as El Caracol, shown here in the foreground.
Cosmo Condina/Stock Connection

of all Mesoamerican heroes came from here: Eight-Deer Tiger-Claw. From surviving royal genealogies, we can date his life to the years 1063 to 1125. He came from Tututepec in the lowlands of Mexico and spent most of his career among Mixtec communities of the coastal region. His conquests have encouraged scholars to believe in an "empire of Tututepec," but we can best understand them as part of a violent power game to acquire deference, tribute, and victims for sacrifice.

Eight-Deer's wars did not necessarily lead to extensions of power, but they did spawn a great reputation. His activities demonstrate what was expected of a Mesoamerican king. He married frequently and had many children. He visited shrines, mediating between gods and men, offering sacrifices, consulting ancestors. He sent and received ambassadors, played the ball game against rival kings, negotiated peace, and—above all—made war. This model of Mesoamerican kingship was defeated, sacrificed, and dismembered by his enemies—entombed with his royal symbols in an episode vividly recorded in the genealogy of the kings of two small Mixtec towns, who wanted to be remembered as his descendants.

Around the Indian Ocean: Ethiopia, the Khmer, and India

In the Americas, poor communications made it hard for people to exchange wealth and ideas. The Indian Ocean, by contrast, was, as we have seen, the world's great arena of exchange—crossed by trade routes and rimmed with rich societies (see Map 11.2).

East Africa: The Ethiopian Empire

Links across the Indian Ocean lessened East Africa's isolation. By the twelfth century, important changes were occurring there. Arabic-speaking geographers of that period recorded the names of places along the East African coast as far south as the Limpopo River in Mozambique and knew of Muslim communities as far away as the island of Zanzibar. Arab traders already frequented Mogadishu in modern Somalia. By 1200, Muslims from the Persian Gulf ruled it. Muslim geographers mentioned Mogadishu's transoceanic trade, bound for India and China, via the Maldive and Laccadive islands in the Indian Ocean. East Africa was bound to the trade of the ocean by the winds that linked it to Asia and is well marked on thirteenth-century Chinese maps.

The increased trade of coastal kingdoms and cities could affect state-building far inland. This is important, not because state-building is necessarily good or progressive in itself, but because it is a measurable indicator of thoroughgoing, long-term change. In twelfth-century Ethiopia, a new dynasty recovered political unity. In this land, which had now been predominantly Christian for more than 700 years, a time of internal crusade began, recorded in the lives of trailblazing frontier saints. On tireless pilgrimages, for instance, Takla Haymanyot made converts, dethroned idols, and chopped down forests, seizing "devils' trees" to build churches. An ideology of holy war seems to have taken hold.

On the Ethiopian frontier, the monastery churches of Lalibela began to emerge from the rocks: literally so, for they are hewn out of the ground. King Lalibela, after whom their location is named and who is credited with building most of them, is known only from semi-legendary sources. According to legend, a vision of heaven, which he then sought to realize on Earth, inspired Lalibela. After showing him what churches are like in heaven, God said to Lalibela, "It is not for the passing glory of this world that I will make you king, but that you may construct churches, like those you have seen, . . . out of the bowels of the earth."

Stories of angels who worked on the buildings reflect the superiority of the craftsmanship. The monks who wrote Lalibela's life story emphasized that he used wage labor to supplement angelic work. Hatred of slavery was common in the writings of Ethiopian monks.

The Zagwe, as the kings of Lalibela's dynasty were called, were themselves frontiersmen. The metropolitan elites of the central highland region around Axum despised them as provincial intruders. Nor perhaps did the Zagwe carry total conviction when they claimed to be heirs of Solomon. Everyone knew that they were upstarts. Propaganda increasingly identified Ethiopia with the realm of the biblical Queen of Sheba, King Solomon's concubine. Ethiopia was even proclaimed as "the new Israel." These claims to ancient roots favored rivals for the throne, who emerged in the second half of the thirteenth century, representing themselves as the rightful heirs of the Axumite monarchs and calling themselves **Solomids**. In 1270, they seized power. The state was organized for war, its court turned into an army, and its capital into an armed camp. The monasteries of Debra Hayq and Debra Libanos, the little world of religious communities on the islands of Lake Tana, became schools of missionaries whose task was to consolidate Ethiopian power in the conquered pagan lands of Shoa and Gojam.

Ethiopia remained primarily an agrarian state. In some degree, it was always a mountain kingdom, with an ideology of defiance against neighboring states and peoples. But the multiplication of contacts across the Indian Ocean enabled Ethiopia to struggle against the effects of isolation with increasing success.

Southeast Asia: The Khmer Kingdom

At the opposite end of that ocean in Southeast Asia, the same context helps to explain the rise to fabulous wealth and power of another inland, agrarian kingdom: that of the **Khmer** in Cambodia. As we saw in Chapter 10, the Khmer homeland on the Mekong River nourishes three harvests a year. That productivity was the foundation of the kingdom's greatness. The rhythms of its rise, however, matched the growth of Indian Ocean trade, which opened outlets for the Khmer farmers' surplus. The ascent of the kingdom is documented in the growth and embellishment of its great city of Angkor.

The plan of the city reflects influences from India across the Bay of Bengal. Angkor was laid out to evoke the divine design of the world common to both Hindu and Buddhist beliefs: the central mountain or *Meru*, the mountains that ring it, the outer wall of rock, and the seas flowing beyond in circular patterns.

The architecture of the twelfth-century King Suryavarman II proclaims a new era. He had himself carved in the walls of his greatest foundation, the biggest temple in the world, Angkor Wat. Previously, monumental

Map 11.2 The Indian Ocean from Ethiopia to Cambodia, ca. 1000–1200

sculptures had only honored dead monarchs or royal ancestors. Suryavarman appears repeatedly in one of the temple galleries, surrounded by environment-defying goods: umbrellas against the sun and fans against the humidity. Carvings he commissioned reenact the creation of the world, as if his reign were the world's renewal. They show the cosmic tug of war between good and evil gods. Scenes of the churning of the magic potion of life from the ocean suggest that the fortunate age of the world is about to begin. According to Hindu myth, peace and unity will prevail in the new age, and the various ranks of society will willingly perform their roles.

Hindu tradition predicted that this new age would last 1,728,000 years. Suryavarman's reign was over by 1150. But his ambitious building programs continued, especially under King Jayavarman VII later in the century. Jayavarman surrounded Angkor with shrines and palaces, way stations, and—it was said—more than 100 hospitals.

The allocation of resources for the hospitals hints at both the scale and the basis of Khmer wealth. More than 80,000 tributaries provided rice, healing spices, 48,000 varieties of fever medicines, salve for hemorrhoids, and vast amounts of sugars, camphor and other antiseptics, purgatives, and drugs. From no other realm of the time—not even China—do we have figures of this sort or on this scale.

Angkor Wat. By the time of King Suryavarman II (r. 1113–1150), the great central temple of Angkor Wat, rising like the sacred mountain Hindus and Buddhists imagined at the center of the world, already dominated the skyline of Angkor. Thanks to silt deposited by the Mekong River, intensive rice cultivation generated huge food surpluses, making possible the investment of work and wealth required to build the stupendous city.
Andrew Gunners/Getty Images—Digital Vision

Still, the favorite remedy for illness was prayer. In 1186, Jayavarman dedicated a temple to house an image of his mother as "the Perfection of Wisdom." Again, the statistics recorded in surviving documents are dazzling for their precision—which reveals the participation of meticulous bureaucrats—and the sheer volume of wealth they display. The temple received tribute from more than 3,000 villages. Its endowments included vessels made of a mixture of gold and silver, exceeding 1,100 pounds in weight, and a similar set in pure silver. The records itemize thousands of precious stones, together with imported and locally produced luxury textiles. Daily provisions for a permanent establishment of 500 residents included rice, butter, milk, molasses, oil, seeds, and honey. Worshippers at the temple required annual supplies of wax, sandalwood, camphor, and sets of clothing for the temple's 260 cult images of Buddha. This is all evidence of the penetration of Cambodia by Indian Ocean trade.

India: Economy and Culture

The strength of cultural links across the Bay of Bengal, between India and Southeast Asia, is a reminder of another problem. India had long been a fertile source of influences exerted across Eurasia: Buddhism, Hinduism and the science, logic, and technology of the Indian sages. The Indian subcontinent's position athwart Indian Ocean trade routes guaranteed it against isolation and gave it privileged access to far-flung markets. India's long, open coasts could soak up ideas and influences from across the oceans, like the pores of a sponge.

Yet there are signs that from the eleventh century, India's role in originating and recycling cultural influences began to diminish. Whereas earlier generations of Muslim scholars had looked to the sub-continent as a source of useful learning, Al Biruni, who came from Persia and studied India in the 1020s, found Indian science and scholarship disappointing. He was widely regarded as the most learned man of his time; so he should have been in a position to know. Hindu science "presumed on the ignorance of the people." He found the Indian sages of his day complacent and uninterested in learning from abroad. His picture was exaggerated and perhaps distorted by a hidden agenda: the desire to advocate the superiority of Islam over native Indian religion.

There was, however, some truth on Al Biruni's side. At least in the north—the part of India he knew—political dissolution accompanied a decline in the quality and output of works of art and learning. The large states that had filled most of the subcontinent since the early ninth century collapsed under the strain of trying to compete with each other and the impact of invaders and rebellions. Much of central and northern India was not divided among territorial states but among competing royal dynasties that found it hard to sustain the loyalties of their followers. The rich Hindu temples of northern India became the prey of Muslim raiders from Afghanistan.

Nevertheless, though states provide the peace commerce requires—and, if the rulers are wise, the infrastructures that help trade thrive—economies can sometimes function well despite political troubles. In parts of India, the economy was booming. Records of tribute paid to the temples in Rajasthan in northwest India reveal the range of produce sold in local markets and the lively trade in sugar, dyes, textiles, salt, areca nuts, coconuts, butter, salt, and sesame oil. Charcoal makers, distillers, and shopkeepers had to pay taxes in cash. From the eleventh century, we can reconstruct merchant lineages from inscriptions that are astonishing, because they reveal how merchants saw themselves. The Pragvata family, for instance, considered themselves warriors in a trade war against Muslim competitors and advanced loans to rulers to fight real wars. Not only the warrior caste, says one inscription, can fight in "the shop of the battlefield." This is amazingly ambitious, arrogant language. In most societies of the time, merchants would not have dared to liken themselves to the warrior elite. Clearly, however turbulent the politics of the time may have been, the economy was doing well.

India: The Chola Kingdom

Far from the political disorder of the north, states in southern India could enjoy the increase of strength that the wealth of the Indian Ocean made possible. The **Chola** kingdom was the most remarkable. Like that of the Khmer or of Ethiopia, its heartland lay away from the coasts, in rice fields and pastures. The Chola kings almost invariably attached more importance to landward security and expansion than to the sea. A raid that touched the Ganges River did more for the prestige of the monarchy than the remotest seaborne adventure. The Chola labored to extend their landward frontiers and develop their landward resources by ruthless exploitation. Indeed, they felled forests on a gigantic scale. The founding myth of the dynasty concerns King Chola, who was out hunting antelope when, lured deep into the forest by a demon, he came to a place where there were no Brahmans to receive alms. So he cleared the forest and planted temples. His successors followed this pattern.

The power, wealth, and ambitions of the Chola kings fused with those of the merchant communities on the coast. In the kingdom's grand ports, gold was exchanged for pearls, coral, betel nuts, cardamom, dyed cottons, ebony, amber, incense, ivory, and rhinoceros horn. Elephants were luxuriously stabled and were stamped with the royal tiger emblem before being shipped out for export.

The merchants' vocation blended with the pirates'. Chola merchants had private armies and a reputation "like the lion's" for "springing to the kill." The imperial itch seemed strongest in kings whose relations with merchants were closest. King Kulottunga I (r. 1070–1122), who relaxed tolls paid to the crown, imagined himself—there is a pillar inscription to prove it—the hero of songs "sung on the further shore of the ocean by the young women of Persia." Most Chola seaborne "imperialism" was probably just raiding, though there were Chola footholds and garrisons on Sri Lanka and the Maldives and perhaps in Malaya. Its impact, however, crippled Srivijaya in Indonesia (see Chapter 10) and enriched the temples of southern India.

Hindu temples were the allies and support of the Chola kings in managing the state and the biggest beneficiaries of victories in war. While the seaward drive lasted, the registers of gifts inscribed on temple walls show its effects: a shift from livestock and produce of the soil to dazzling bestowals of exotic goods and cash, especially from about 1000 to about 1070. The treasures of the city temple of Tanjore included a crown with enough gold to buy enough oil to keep 40 lamps alight in perpetuity, and hundreds of gemstones and jewels, with plenty of umbrellas and fly whisks for the comfort of the worshippers at ceremonies. When King Rajendra (r. 1012–1042) built a new temple, the site, according to a twelfth-century poet, could overwhelm with joy "all fourteen worlds encircled by the billowing ocean. . . . The very landscape around was made invisible."

The temples are the best evidence of the grandeur of the Chola Empire and the reach of its power and trade. But they also suggest why, ultimately, the Chola withdrew from overseas ventures. The temples invested heavily in land and in the revenues of farmers whom they supplied with capital to make agricultural improvements. In consequence, they may have contributed to a shift of priorities toward agriculture and land-based wealth, and therefore, in the long term, to weakening Chola maritime imperialism—an enfeeblement that became marked in the thirteenth century. So, although India remained as rich as ever, some forms of Indian enterprise turned inward.

Eurasia's Extremities: Japan and Western Europe

The Indian Ocean enclosed the main routes of communication around maritime Asia and between Asia and Africa. Of secondary importance were the land roads across Central Asia and the Sahara, which are subjects for the next chapter. For travelers on both the ocean roads and the land roads, Japan and western Europe—the regions at the easternmost and westernmost extremities of Eurasia—were hard to get to and from. But they were placed close enough to the major communications routes to tap into the great exchanges of culture of the time. During the eleventh and twelfth centuries, both areas emerged from relative isolation.

Japan

While in much of the world people struggled to overcome isolation, in Japan rulers had tried to make a virtue of it. Japanese rulers were fearful of losing migrants to richer regions and apprehensive of Chinese power. They had suspended diplomacy and trade with China in 838 and with Korea nearly a century later. Permission to trade abroad was hard to obtain. Even Buddhist monks had to apply for permission to leave the country on pilgrimage. Of course, illicit trade—or "piracy" as officials called it—went on. But self-sufficiency remained the object of government policy.

The best-known Japanese literature of the tenth and eleventh centuries is focused on a narrow, closed court society in a narrow, closed country. The fiction of Murasaki Shikibu in *The Tale of Genji*, one of the earliest realistic novels ever written, unfolds in palace chambers and corridors dark enough to make her stories of mistaken identity among lovers believable. She depicts a world in which the supreme values seem to be snobbery and sensitivity. Struggles for precedence dominate court life. The emperor grants his favorite cat the privileges "of a lady of middle rank." A nurse can tell from the sound of a visitor's cough to what level of the nobility he belongs. The court is everything. Even an appointment as governor of a province is a disgrace. Court literature scarcely mentions the peasants, beaten down by famine and plague, whose rice taxes sustained the court aristocracy.

Genji. The earliest illustrated manuscripts of *The Tale of Genji* date from the 1120s, more than 100 years after the novel was written. But they demonstrate its enduring popularity and faithfully capture its atmosphere: the leisured opulence of the imperial palace at Heian, the learning and luxury of the court ladies, and the difficulty of leading a private life—let alone conducting the complex love affairs that the story depicts—behind frail partitions that were literally paper-thin. *Japan Society*

Murasaki was an acute observer, and her work portrayed the vices of a faction-ridden system. She was a spokeswoman for courtiers excluded from power by the man she hated, whose amorous advances she claimed to have turned down: the all-powerful courtier, Fujiwara no Michizane, who manipulated the political system by marrying his womenfolk into the imperial family and providing an effective bureaucracy from his own household. After three emperors died in factional struggles, he was left as regent of the empire in 1008. He exploited his opportunities so well that, according to one embittered critic, "not a speck of earth was left for the public domain." Emperors were so preoccupied with ritual duties that the only way they could bid for power was by abdicating and attempting to control their heirs.

Provincial rule was left to administrators supported by retinues of hired tough guys. Despised at court for their "badly powdered faces," these local leaders wielded real power and handled real wealth. Many of them were the descendants of imperial princes who had been sent to the provinces for want of employment at court, or who had opted for provincial careers to pursue autonomy, wealth, and authority of their own. Increasingly, they became warriors whose authority depended on force. As the court began to lose control of the provinces, these provincial warmongers allied in rival bands.

In the 1070s, courtiers, temples, and merchants succeeded in opening Japan to foreign trade in their own economic interests. Trade with Korea resumed for a while as a result of the initiative of Korea's energetic King Munjon (r. 1046–1083). Direct relations between Japan and China followed. The results were dramatic: Newly rich families became players for power. The greatest profiteers were the Taira clan, who relentlessly, during the twelfth century, built up their power by acquiring provincial governorships and penetrating and, by early in the second half of the twelfth century, dominating the imperial court. In a series of civil wars, culminating in 1185, their rivals and relatives, the Minamoto clan, had replaced them as imperial "protectors" or **shoguns**. From then on the emperors never recovered real power. The renowned monk Mongaku was an adviser to successive shoguns. Invited to pray for a new shogun in 1200, he showed just what he thought of the request: "In the dwellings of those who offend, prayer is of no avail."

As the diary of the Tosa Lady shows, it was hard to get around Japan's home islands—even that relatively small part of the islands the Japanese state occupied. Overseas contacts were genuinely difficult, the surrounding seas genuinely daunting. Yet even at its most restrictive, Japan's isolation had never shut out Chinese cultural influence. Some of Murasaki's characters showed impatience with "Chinesified" styles, appealing to the "spirit of Japan." And popular literature did depict China as strange and exotic. But educated Japanese were well aware of their dependence on China for almost all their models of learning, art, and government. Chinese was the language of the upper administration and all serious literature. The elite used handbooks of quotations from Chinese classics to clinch arguments. Confucian ceremonies and Chinese poetry contests (on such subjects as "the thin, solitary voice of the first cicada" and "the freshness of mountains and streams after the sky has cleared") were among the main occupations at court. Murasaki Shikibu, by her own account, repelled Fujiwara's unwanted attentions by capping his Chinese verses.

Western Europe: Economics and Politics

Nowhere else in the world were there long-range trade routes to match those of the Indian Ocean. But—though the subject is poorly documented in this period—the land routes across Eurasia, from Europe to China, and across the Sahara, between the Mediterranean and the Sahel, were probably carrying increasing amounts of traffic through the eleventh and twelfth centuries. Western Europe lay at or just beyond the western and northern extremities of these land routes.

Its relative isolation always threatened the region with backwardness. The Atlantic clouded Europe's outlook to the west. The Sahara cut it off from access to much of Africa. Europe's frontier on the east to the great civilizations of Asia was vital but hard to keep open across plains that hostile steppelanders patrolled or that forests, flanked by vast marshlands, obstructed. There was no direct access to the Indian Ocean. Western European merchants rarely went there—and, when they did, they had to undertake epic overland journeys via the Nile valley or across Arabia or what are now Turkey and Iraq.

A Muslim geographer, al-Istakhri, contemplating the world from Persia in 950, hardly noticed western Europe at all. In his map, the West was squeezed almost out of the picture, dangling feebly off the edge of the known world. Meanwhile, Latin Christians who looked out at the world in their own imaginations probably saw something like the version mapped at about the same time by the monks who drew the illustrations in the *Commentary on the Apocalypse* of Beatus of Liébana in northern Spain: Asia takes up most of the space, Africa most of the rest. Europe consists mainly of three peninsulas—Spain, Italy, and Greece, jutting into the Mediterranean—with a thin strip of hinterland above them. In 1095, urging fellow Christians to new efforts against the Muslims, Pope Urban II expressed the feeling of being under siege:

> *The world is not evenly divided. Of its three parts, our enemies hold Asia. . . . . . . Africa, too, the second part of the world, has been held by our enemies for two hundred years and more. . . . Thirdly there is Europe. . . . Of this region we Christians inhabit only a small part,*

for who will give the name of Christians to those barbarians who live in the remote islands and seek their living on the icy ocean as if they were whales?

Urban wanted Christendom to combine to redress what he saw as an imbalance of power. But disunity fragmented what political scientists call a state system, with lots of interlocking territorial states. From 962, the German ruler Otto I called himself—more in hope than in reality—"Roman emperor" and made a big investment to recover a sense of unity. When his grandson, Otto III, looked back at the reflection of himself that stared, enthroned in power, from an illustration in his Gospel book, he could see lavish images of Germany, Gaul, and the Slav lands humbly bearing their tribute toward him, led by a personification of Rome. These pretensions were hollow. The empire of the Ottos was essentially a German state, covering not much more than modern Germany.

Yet disunity can be stimulating, encouraging rival states to compete with each other. Latin Christendom emerged as a genuinely expanding world, as it stretched between increasingly remote horizons. As we have just seen in Ethiopia, expansion does not only happen outward. There are often inward cracks and gaps to fill, slack to take up. From the eleventh to the early fourteenth centuries, a process of internal expansion, accompanied by new economic activity, was under way in western Europe.

Settlement encroached on marginal soils and headed uphill. Forests fell. Bogs were drained. Farmers moved in. This was more than an economic enterprise: it was a sacred undertaking—reclaiming for God part of the terrain of paganism. The forest was stained with pagan sensuality and alive with sprites, demons, and "wild men of the woods." The pious felled trees sacred to pagans. The most famous example is the best. Unable to sleep "on a certain night" in 1122, Abbot Suger of Saint-Denis, a monastery near Paris, rose to search the forest for 12 trees mighty enough to frame the new sanctuary he was planning for his abbey church, built—he hoped—to be full of light and "to elevate dull minds to the truth." The foresters smiled at him and wondered if the abbot was "quite ignorant of the fact that nothing of the kind could be found in the entire region"; but he found what he needed "with the courage of faith."

It was a representative incident in a vast project to tame underexploited environments. The **Cistercians**, one of the most dynamic new monastic orders of the period, directed their efforts into "deserts" where habitation was sparse and nature hostile. They disputed Suger's views on church architecture—advocating simplicity and austerity in worship—but razed woodlands and drove flocks and ox teams into wildernesses where today, all too often, the vast abbeys lie ruined in their turn. Sometimes, in their craving to escape the greedy secular society that put their souls at risk, Cistercians actually drove existing settlers away from their lands, extending the frontiers of colonization even farther as peasants imitated Cistercian practices on even more marginal lands.

Engineering came to the aid of environmental adaptation. Drainage helped extend the land on which people could dwell. In Holland, rapid population growth seems closely linked with the success of a project Count Floris V (r. 1256–1296) launched to reclaim waterlogged land. New embankments and canals made rivers easier to navigate. Searching out new routes and building roads and bridges were urgent tasks for the common good, for which monarchs accepted some responsibility and for which—for example— Domingo de la Calzada, who built causeways and bridges for pilgrims to the shrine of St. James at Compostela in northern Spain, was made a saint.

Behind the expanding frontiers, modest technical revolutions were boosting production. Among inventions originating in Europe at this time were windmills, ground lenses, and clockwork. Others, brought there thanks to improved communications across Eurasia, were paper mills, the compass, firearms, and—a little later in the fourteenth century—the blast furnace. Large, heavy plows with curved blades bit deeply into the land, which enabled farmers to exploit the dense, wet soil of northern Europe. More effective harnesses enabled horses to pull the plows and take over a lot of hard work in the fields. More efficient windmills and water mills and more exact metallurgy and new products, especially in arms and glassware, extended the range of business and the flow of wealth. The advances in agriculture that began in the Islamic world toward the end of the previous millennium (see Chapter 10) spread hesitantly, across western Europe, improving farming with new strains of wheat and—where it would grow—of rice. More varieties of beans improved nutrition and added nitrates to the soil.

Historians debate who was responsible for extending tillage and coaxing new wealth from the soil. Was it primarily the work of "free peasants"? Or did landowners force peasant dependants into greater productivity? There were many different patterns of landholding, which varied regionally and locally, and the drive to improve efficiency probably happened no matter what form landholding took. In any case, the colonization of new lands created opportunities of enrichment at all social levels. More food meant more people. The population of Europe may well have doubled, from about 35 million around the year 1000, while these changes took place.

As production and population increased, so did opportunities for trade. New trade routes knitted Atlantic and Mediterranean seaboards in a single economy. This was an important development, because western Europe has two natural economic zones—formed, respectively, along the Mediterranean and Atlantic coasts. The Strait of Gibraltar separates them, with widely different sailing conditions along the two seaboards. Inland a chain of breakwaters splits the continent, determining the flow of rivers and, therefore, the directions of exchange. For much of Europe's history, communication between these two zones was not easy. Limited access through routes across France and the Alpine passes kept restricted forms of commerce alive, even when commercial navigation from sea to sea was abandoned.

New kinds of economic activity became possible in growing towns. Lübeck, founded in 1143, was the pioneer city of what became the **Hanseatic League**—a network of allied ports along the North Sea and Baltic coasts that collaborated to promote trade. Soon after, Mediterranean craft, mainly from the Italian city of Genoa, the island of Majorca, and Spain, resumed large-scale ventures along Atlantic coasts, such as had not been recorded since the western Roman Empire collapsed in the fifth century.

Exchange across vast distances made geographical specialization and genuine industrialization possible. For instance, all the industries served by the trade of Genoa depended on geographical specialization. Textiles depended on concentrating wools and dyestuffs from widely separated places of origin. Food processing relied on matching fresh foodstuffs, such as herring, with salt. Shipbuilding demanded a similar marriage of raw materials—wood, iron, sailcloth, and pitch.

The results included urbanization: the revival of old cities and the building of new ones. The best way, indeed, to measure the economic progress of the period in much of Europe is by the growth of towns—ways of organizing life, which, at the time, were prized as uniquely virtuous. "The order of mankind," according to Gerald of Wales in the 1180s, "progresses from the woods to the fields and from the fields to the towns and the gatherings of citizens." In Italy, the **commune**—as the citizen body was collectively called—became an institution of civic government in the late eleventh or early twelfth century. In what seems to have been a conscious reaching back to a Roman model, many Italian cities acquired "consuls" in this period. By the mid-twelfth century, Otto of Freising regarded autonomous city governments as typical of northern Italy. Instead of deferring to some great protector—bishop, nobleman, or abbot—Italian cities became their own "lords" and even extended jurisdiction into the countryside. In effect, some cities were independent republics, forming alliances in defiance of, or in spite of, their supposed lords. Others tried unsuccessfully for the same status.

Self-ruling city-states were most common in Italy, where, perhaps, memories of Rome remained most alive. But similar phenomena occurred over much of Europe, as urban awareness and the numbers and size of towns grew. On the edges of Christendom, planned towns were laid out with the measuring rod and peopled by wagon trains. In Spain, the granting by monarchs of founding documents to tiny new communities marked the progress of settlement on the frontier with the Islamic world. These usually gave the inhabitants some share in judicial or administrative power. All towns of the time were small by modern standards. As few as 2,000 citizens could make a town if it had walls and a charter. "Feelings," it was said, "make the town." If the people felt urban, in other words, they *were* urban. Thirty thousand inhabitants was a metropolis.

For the sake of comparison, it is worth glancing at the farther edge of Christendom, beyond the reach of the **Latin Church**, in western Russia. Here, the cities of Novgorod and Pskov contended against a hostile climate beyond the grain lands on which they relied for sustenance. Famine besieged them more often than human enemies did. Yet control of the trade routes to the river Volga made Novgorod cash rich. It never had more than a few thousand inhabitants, yet its monuments record its progress: its *kremlin* (or palace-fortress) walls and five-domed cathedral in the 1040s; in the early twelfth century, a series of buildings that the ruler paid for; and in 1207, the merchants' church of St. Paraskeva in the marketplace.

Making Connections | CONTENDING WITH ISOLATION, CA. 1000–1200

REGION/PEOPLE OR KINGDOM	OPPORTUNITIES	EXPLOITATION STRATEGIES
Arctic/Inuit	Change in climate: warming weather allows for navigation across Canadian Arctic; introduction of new breed of pack dogs for transportation; introduction of bow and arrow	New techniques for constructing walrus-hide boats; new uses for sealskin, other animal hides for transport, hunting, food
Greenland/ Norse	Warming climate; wealth of fish and game in almost uninhabited region; availability of export items such as hunting falcons, walrus ivory	Improved navigational techniques; new understanding of prevailing winds, ocean currents to improve chances of successful voyages; introduction of European grains and grasses for grazing animals; development of new breed of sheep
North American Southwest and Mississippi Region/ Native Americans	Southwest: introduction of maize from Mexico; defensible canyons with water supply; growing population	Southwest: irrigation canals to expand agriculture; many ceremonial centers; expansion into new zones; intensive organization of labor; development of multistoried residential structures

REGION/PEOPLE OR KINGDOM	OPPORTUNITIES	EXPLOITATION STRATEGIES
	Mississippi: introduction of Mesoamerican "tool kit," food, way of life, thought; expanded trade routes bring deerskin, shells, bison hides, metals, and minerals	Mississippi: expansion of trade routes; new forms of agriculture with maize, beans, squash, and fish farming; larger populations lead to more intensive crafts development/industry
Mesoamerica/ Yucatán: Maya	Abundant forests, wildlife, coastal resources	New forms of irrigation, wells; new communities lead to expanded sea and land trade routes
East Africa/ Ethiopia	Wider access to trade goods	Increased Indian Ocean trade with Arabs, Chinese, Indians helps equip Ethiopian dynasties to expand into new terrain
Southeast Asia/Khmer kingdom (Cambodia)	Growth of Indian Ocean trade opens outlets for Khmer rice surplus; wealth from trade and taxes funds Angkor Wat	Expansion of kingdom coincides with monumental temple complexes at Angkor, complete with expanded amenities for subjects—hospitals, shrines, etc.
India/Chola kingdom	Expansion of frontiers through inland raids brings additional natural resources (forests, agricultural land)	Landward strategy of clearing forests, planting crops and building large temples; coastal merchant communities merge with pirate expeditions sponsored by Chola kings to raid foreign ports
Japan	Provincial warriors break away from imperial court, open Japan to foreign trade; new wealth	Taira and other newly rich families, begin to dominate imperial court, develop shogunate system of govern-ment to rule more efficiently
Western Europe	Expanding settlements into marginal agricultural areas; new engineering techniques to manage rivers, build infrastructure	Intensive land management—felling forests, draining bogs combines with Christianizing efforts to "civilize" barbarian areas; increased commerce leads to economic specialization, growth of towns and communes

From 1136, communal government prevailed in Novgorod. The revolt of that year marks the creation of a city-state on an ancient model—a republican commune like those of Italy. The prince was deposed for reasons the rebels' surviving proclamations specify. "Why did he not care for the common people? Why did he want to wage war? Why did he not fight bravely? And why did he prefer games and entertainments rather than state affairs? Why did he have so many gerfalcons and dogs?" Thereafter, the citizens' principle was, "If the prince is no good, throw him into the mud!"

Western Europe: Religion and Culture

Transformations in art, thought, and worship matched the dynamism of the economy and of political change. New forms of heresy, for instance, were among departures of enormous importance for the future of Western Christendom. If popular heresy existed in western Europe before the eleventh century, no one noticed it. After the year 1000, however, it emerged as a threat. A French peasant named Leutard had a vision in which bees—a traditional symbol of supposedly sexless reproduction—entered his body through his penis. The vision drove him to renounce his wife, shatter the images of Jesus and the saints in the local church, and preach universal celibacy. Among fellow peasants, he attracted a following that survived his death, albeit not for long. In 1015, the first burnings of heretics in the West for more than 600 years were kindled. From then on, popular heretical movements were a continuous and, on the whole, a growing feature of western European history.

Two long, slow changes seem to underlie this phenomenon. By the late eleventh century, a movement of Christian renewal and evangelizing fervor (known to historians as the Gregorian Reform after Pope Gregory VII [r. 1073–1085], its greatest sponsor) was demanding new and exacting standards both of clerical behavior and of lay awareness of the faith and challenging kings and noblemen for control over appointments in the church. More than a power struggle, it was a drive to purge the church of profanity.

At the same time, the evangelical fervor of the clergy was lowering its sights to include the peasantry, to whom clerics had, up to then, paid little attention. This was the result, in part, of a long buildup of dissatisfaction with the shallowness with which Christianity had penetrated popular minds. Among its effects was a new or increased emphasis in saints' lives on how saints could—in today's jargon—"relate" to ordinary people by doing menial jobs. A French count, for instance, who joined a monastery in about 990, was set first to keep the hens, then the sheep, then the pigs, and was astonished at his own delight in each successive task.

On the other hand, the rise of popular dissent bears some signs of a revolution born of prosperity. Lay people were themselves stepping up the demands they made of their clergy. The really popular heresies of the eleventh and twelfth centuries were those ministered to by men of ferocious sanctity, like the preachers who called themselves "the perfect," and whose fanatical renunciation of worldly pleasures made them seem holier than the church. At the same time, the new security of life, the opportunities to gather harvests without being attacked, the leisure that increased yields from the soil gave to people, all bought time for a luxury unavailable in hard times: time to think about the Christian mysteries and to develop a desire to get involved in them. At a relatively high level of education, the church could satisfy these stirrings by providing pilgrimages, private prayers, devotional reading matter, and, ultimately, orders of chivalry for the warrior class. Spiritually minded peasants, like Leutard's enthusiasts, could not be accommodated so easily.

In the struggle to save their souls, European laymen in the Middle Ages were at a disadvantage. The religious life opened heaven's gates; the warrior's life, stained with bloodshed, distracted by the world, closed them. The religious model suggested the idea that obedience to rules—like those of monks and nuns—could sanctify the lay life. The first such rules or "codes of chivalry" in the twelfth century emphasized religious vows of chastity, poverty, and obedience, but lay virtues gathered prominence, redirected against deadly sins: generosity against greed, self-control against anger, loyalty against lies and lust. **Chivalry** became the prevailing disposition among the aristocracy of the age. It did not make warfare any more gentle or moral; nor did it make all aristocrats good. But it did widen the range of the virtues to which aristocrats aspired.

The art of the West in the eleventh and twelfth centuries reveals a sort of cult of the commoner. Images of peasants and artisans appeared alongside saints and angels around church doorways, engaged in the productive economic activities that paid for this art. Here were arrayed the members of a peaceful and orderly society, with everyone in place. The new mood affected the way artists showed heaven. Most people nowadays unfairly associate the art of the era with a cold and distant style of other-worldly portraits: with images of the Virgin staring, passionless, and kingly, judgmental Christs. Yet the humanization of heaven was the essence of the artists' inspiration: the evocation of piercing emotions. Early in the eleventh century, the painter of the Gospel book of Abbess Hilda of Merschede painted a scene of Jesus asleep in a storm on the Sea of Galilee, in which the ship leaps into life and the anxiety of the apostles burdens their brows. The Jesus carved for Archbishop Gero of Cologne in Germany dates from before the end of the tenth century, but no modern master ever chiseled the face of the suffering Jesus with more exquisite agony: drawn lips, taut cheeks, nerveless lids, and a trickle of blood at the brow.

In art, literature, and scholarship, a strong sense of continuity with ancient civilization shines through. Sculptors and builders copied classical works wherever they could find them. The ideas of Abbot Suger on the beauty of light were derived from what he thought was a Greek text from the early first century. The twelfth-century English historian, Geoffrey of Monmouth, claimed to be able to trace the "British" monarchy back to characters from the ancient Greek poet Homer. Poets in England and Germany tried to write like ancient Romans. Lectures in Paris introduced students to the logic of Aristotle. Abelard (1079–1142), the most renowned teacher of the era in Paris, gave audiences the impression that there was nothing logic could not do. In his book on logic, *Sic et Non* of 1122, he exposed the contradictions in many treasured assumptions of the theology and philosophy of his day. The twelfth-century Archbishop of Canterbury, Anselm, too, wrote about God using reason as his only guide—suppressing references to Scripture or the tradition of the church. Indeed, Anselm sought to prove the existence of God—or at least of a real being with the perfection Christianity ascribed to God—by unaided reason. Roughly, his proof says that the most perfect being we can think of must exist, since, if he did not, we should be able to think of another, more perfect being who did.

By the twelfth century, students of nature were beginning to "stand on the shoulders of giants" of antiquity and see farther than they had. In 1092, Walcher of Malvern fixed the difference in time between Italy and England by timing an eclipse. Adelard of Bath noted that light travels faster than sound. He agreed with his younger contemporary, William of Conches, that God likes to work through nature and that miraculous explanations should never be invoked when scientific ones will do. Practical observations piled up: the heights of tides, the habits of volcanoes. Carvers of capitals on pillars in churches imitated natural forms. From this time onward, sculptors chiseled plants and flowers into monastery cloisters.

IN PERSPECTIVE
The Patchwork of Effects

The great leap of Latin Christendom—the renaissance or rebirth in art and thought that began after the year 1000—was possible because people in Western Christendom found ways to cope and contend with their relative isolation. Scholars in the late tenth and eleventh centuries went to Muslim centers of learning in Spain to acquire groundings in science and mathematics and to learn Arabic. Gerbert of Aurillac—the Emperor Otto III's tutor—sweated to learn mathematics in the Spanish Muslim city of Toledo. Adelard of Bath studied Arabic to get access to Arabic

CHRONOLOGY

Tenth century	Flourishing of canyon culture in American Southwest; Chichén Itzá founded
Late tenth century	Norse reach Greenland
ca. 1000	*The Tale of Genji* (Japan); Thule Inuit reach Greenland
1000–1300	Rapid population growth in Europe and development of new technologies; Maya intensively exploit Yucatán peninsula
1000–1100	Flourishing of Chola kingdom (India)
1070s	Opening of Japan to limited foreign trade; restoration of direct relations between China and Japan
Early twelfth century	Building of Angkor Wat (Cambodia) begins
1150	Canyon settlements in American Southwest withdraw to higher ground
1200	Population of Cahokia reaches 10,000
1270	Solomids seize power in Ethiopia
1300	Decline of upper Mississippi valley culture

translations of classical Greek books, lost in the West. In the late eleventh and twelfth centuries, as we shall see in the next chapter, pilgrimages, wars, and trade took western Europeans in unprecedented numbers eastward, to the eastern Mediterranean, and to contact with the Islamic world and Eastern Christendom at Constantinople. At the same time, the westward trickle of communications with south and east Asia probably increased along the Silk Roads.

For Japan, too, isolation might have been frustrating. But there was just enough contact with Korea and China to stoke Japanese art and learning with Chinese influences. The delicately folded poems written by Genji and his friends and real-life counterparts were all in Chinese—part of an ancient renaissance, as influential as anything Europeans wrote or sculpted in imitation of antique models.

In the preindustrial world, the size of states and the scope of economies were functions of time as well as distance. Messages, armies, revenues, and cargoes took a long time to travel across broken country or, by sea, through variable winds. Around the Indian Ocean, increased traffic brought areas in East Africa and Southeast Asia out of isolation and kept India rich, despite its political troubles. Despite the heroic efforts of the Norse in the Atlantic, the Thule Inuit in the Arctic, and the Polynesians in the Pacific, the wealth-creating effects of sustained transoceanic or interoceanic commerce could not yet be reproduced outside the region of the monsoons around the Indian Ocean.

Even so, India was much less influential in world history—far less productive of ideas and movements that affected the rest of the world—after 1000 than it had been before. This is only one of many ways in which India seems to have reached a "peak" of achievement. According to the best available studies, India's population was more than 200 million in 1000, but it fell for the rest of what we think of as the Middle Ages. The Chola kingdom was the last Indian empire to exert major influence in Southeast Asia, where Hinduism began to decline—ultimately, to survive only in patches outside India itself.

In the Americas and parts of sub-Saharan Africa, the arresting effects of isolation could not be overcome. Cultural contacts between Mesoamerica and parts of North America helped, for a while, to produce spectacular experiments in building states and modifying environments. But the networks were still too fragile and temporary for the effects to endure.

In the next century, the thirteenth, changes in the pattern of communications across Eurasia would heighten the differences between the Old and the New Worlds. To understand these events and their effects, we have to turn first to the other great theme of the history of the eleventh and twelfth centuries: the growing contacts and conflicts between sedentary and nomadic peoples in Eurasia and parts of Africa, and their effects on the interactions of surrounding regions.

PROBLEMS AND PARALLELS

1. How did societies around the world contend with their relative isolation between 1000 and 1200?
2. How did isolation affect the Norse colony on Greenland and the cultures of North America? What evidence indicates that the civilizations of Mesoamerica influenced cultural developments in the North American Southwest and Cahokia?
3. How did Buddhism and Hinduism spread in Southeast Asia?
4. How did Japan and Europe overcome their isolation and emerge with powerful political, cultural, and economic systems?
5. How did increased trade across the Indian Ocean affect East Africa during the eleventh century? Why did Ethiopia recover from its "dark age"?
6. What are the benefits and drawbacks of cultural and economic isolation?

CHAPTER 12

The Nomadic Frontiers: The Islamic World, Byzantium, and China, ca. 1000–1200

focus questions

1. How did the Islamic world deal with its steppeland neighbors?
2. What strengths did the Turks bring to the Islamic world?
3. How did Byzantine civilization combine religious and secular values?
4. Why did the Byzantine Empire prove to be so resilient?
5. How did the Crusades affect the Islamic world and Byzantium?
6. Why was Song China such a strong and prosperous state?
7. Why do nomads and settled peoples tend to be enemies?

On a winter's morning in 1021, the Caliph al-Hakim, ruler of a state that stretched from Egypt to what is today Algeria, climbed to his private astronomical observatory in Cairo—then, reputedly, the greatest city in the Islamic world. He intended—so his courtiers supposed—to amuse and instruct himself with the huge copper instrument he used to observe the movements of the stars. It was al-Hakim's habitual way to unwind. But on this occasion, as far as anyone knew, he never came back down. He simply vanished and was never officially heard of again. Some of his followers took it as proof that heaven had absorbed him. He would return at the end of time. A sect in Lebanon, the **Druze***, still regards him as an incarnation of God.*

To most observers, however, he was just mad. His "deeds were without reason," said a typical critic, "and his dreams without interpretation." At different times, he outlawed dogs, churches, evening traffic, canal trade, and women's shoes. He expected the end of the world—which perhaps explains his habits of personal austerity and reckless alms giving. His main defect, in his critics' eyes, was that he was a Shiite (see Chapter 9). He saw himself as the fulfillment of Shiite belief in the divine appointment of an infallible **imam***, or holy ruler, to supplement Muhammad's own teaching.*

The conflict between rival caliphs, the Shiite in Cairo and the Sunni in Baghdad, divided the Islamic world into roughly equal portions. To make matters worse, from the 920s, a third dynasty, with its court in Cordova in Spain, also claimed to be caliph. At intervals in the tenth and eleventh centuries, Shiite rebels or invaders seized Baghdad and humiliated or manipulated the Sunni caliphs. From 1090, the Shiite sect known as the **Assassins** *occupied Alamut—a mountain fortress in Persia—from where they launched raids and unleashed allegedly drug-crazed fanatics to execute political murders. The word assassin comes from "hashish."*

Threads of cultural unity still linked the Islamic world: veneration of the Prophet Muhammad, adherence to the Quran, use of Arabic as the language of religion and learning, and the unifying force of the pilgrimage to Mecca. Mutual obligations among Muslims were still strong, even between Shiites and Sunnis. In 1070, for instance, when famine threatened Cairo, the Shiite caliph sent his womenfolk to Sunni Baghdad to escape starvation. Islamic civilization was still the most widely dispersed civilization the world had ever seen. Muslims ruled a continuous band of territory from Spain to Central Asia and the Arabian Sea.

Nonetheless, political disunity was disturbing for Muslims. Fragmentation weakened Islamic states and wasted their strength in wars against each other. The strain told. In the early eleventh century, the

Spanish caliphate crumbled. In most of Iran and Kurdistan, minor, local dynasties made the rule of the caliph in Baghdad no more than symbolic. The Shiite caliphate had reached the limits of its expansion. In Spain, southern Italy, and Anatolia, aggressive Christian states were active.

The Islamic World and Its Neighbors

Both a challenge to and the salvation of Islam came from unlikely directions: the Sahara and the steppes. The Islamic world was caught up in a sweeping Eurasian confrontation. Settled societies faced warlike, pastoral enemies from Central Asia and North Africa. The relationship was sometimes hostile, always tense. In this chapter, we look at the societies most affected—the Islamic world, with its western neighbors in Spain and West Africa, and then the Byzantine and Chinese empires.

The Coming of the Steppelanders

The steppelands were full of threat, as Turkic peoples overspilled in waves of migrants and invaders. We do not know what set them off. But once the shifts of population began, they rattled a chain reaction, with some groups pushing others ahead of them.

Seljuk Turks seized Baghdad in 1055 and turned the caliph into a client—"a parrot in a cage." Farther east, in Afghanistan, was the self-appointed guardian of Islam, warlord Mahmud of Ghazni, whose 17 raids into India gathered so many captives that prices in Afghanistan's slave markets tumbled. He was the descendant of a Turkish adventurer. Seljuk's sons and grandsons first took service with, then turned on him. Their cavalry overwhelmed Mahmud's war elephants. Muslims called them "the army of God"—not in approval but in fear. God had unleashed these ferocious pagans to punish Muslims' sins.

Just as the Arabs had destroyed the Persian Empire and the western barbarians had broken Rome, the **Turks** might have shattered the Islamic world. After a stunning series of conquests, they stopped, converted by the Islamic culture they had conquered. Seljuk and his sons were among the early converts. The ruins of the capital they built at Konya in Anatolia show how thoroughly they abandoned pastoralism and absorbed urbanism. By the end of the twelfth century, 108 towers enclosed the city. Market gardens stretched far into the surrounding plain, feeding a population of perhaps 30,000. Inns with high-arched aisles accommodated merchants and their camels. But the Seljuks never entirely forgot the steppe. Their coins showed hero-horsemen with stars and haloes round their heads. Their sultans lay in tombs, shaped to recall the tents of their ancestors.

Caravanserai. In 1229, a Seljuk sultan built this imposing structure in Anatolia near Aksaney on the road to Konya as a place where caravans could halt. On either side of the gateway, which had to be big enough to admit laden camels, the slender columns are topped by capitals that still seem to be in the tradition of ancient Rome. There were more than 200 such structures known as *caravanserais,* around the Seljuk realms, facilitating the movement of armies and officials as well as of merchants. *The Art Archive/ Dagli Orti (A)*

Seljuk's experience was typical. No one knows how it happened, but the Islamic world absorbed most of the Turkic invaders and transformed them into its strength and shield. The newly converted conquered Anatolia and Armenia from Christians, Syria and Palestine from Shiites. Success in attracting, converting, and domesticating pastoral peoples—and recycling their violence in Muslim service—is one of the decisive and distinctive features of the history of the Islamic world. Christendom usually dealt with steppelander threats by trying to fight or buy them off. The **Magyars** and Bulgars, who settled in Hungary and Bulgaria, respectively, were Europe's only successfully absorbed steppeland invaders. China seduced steppeland conquerors to Chinese ways of life but was unable or unwilling to turn them permanently into a favorable fighting force. In India, invading pastoralists frequently became ruling elites that sometimes adopted parts of Indian culture, but they usually remained intruders. In none of these regions did native cultures manage to harness nomad energies for wars of their own.

The Crusades

It is worth comparing the Islamic world's response to the steppeland invaders with the fate of the other intruders: the crusaders, who attacked from Christian Europe. Writers of world history usually give the **Crusades** a lot of attention, seeking signs of the vitality of the West—the capacity of western Europeans to reach overseas and make war way beyond their frontiers. For the Islamic world, however, the Crusades were a minor nuisance. Crusaders were few. Their states were small and mostly short lived. They could not be converted, but—thanks to Turkish manpower and leadership—their threat to the Islamic world was neutralized or contained.

The Crusades started as an outgrowth from pilgrimage. Increasingly in the tenth and eleventh centuries, Christians made pilgrimages to places they considered sacred as an act of penance for their sins. Pilgrimages—in theory, peaceful journeys, on which the pilgrims relied on the mercy and charity of people whose lands they crossed—became armed expeditions. Simultaneously, Christians began to adopt a Muslim notion: holy war. Palestine, the land where Jesus had walked, and where so many saints' bones lay buried, was the most sacred land of all. It sanctified those who fought and died to obtain it for Christian rule. Knights need no longer envy monks their easy route to salvation. Warriors could fulfill their vocation for violence and still be saved. "The blood of Muslims," declared a French poet in the early twelfth century, "washes out sins." Even if it were not holy, war for the recovery of Jerusalem would be just, according to Christian theorists: Palestine had once been Christian land, and Muslims had "usurped" it—so it was right to try to win it back.

These trends in thought and devotion came together in the 1090s. Preachers whipped up collective hysteria that sent thousands of poor, ill-armed pilgrims to their deaths in an effort to get to Jerusalem. Pope Urban II (r. 1088–1099) orchestrated a relatively well-planned military expedition. It is often claimed that the crusaders were younger sons, with inadequate inheritances, and adventurers "on the make," escaping from restricted social and economic opportunities. This claim seems false as many crusaders were rich men with a lot to lose. The church is also often thought to have encouraged the Crusades so that it could increase its own wealth. That was one effect—crusaders left property to monasteries and churches to look after in their absence, and, once they got to the East, made grants of conquered land and treasure to religious institutions there.

The early crusaders blundered to surprising success, capturing Jerusalem in 1099 and lining the shores of the Levant with states their own leaders ruled (see Map 12.1). Muslim divisions made these successes possible. Muslim indifference and infighting prolonged them. The crusader kingdoms got support from Italian merchant-communities, which welcomed access to trade, and, occasionally, they received reinforcements from Europe. The newcomers from Europe, however, were often religious zealots who tended to disrupt the delicate tolerance between Christians and Muslims on which the crusader states relied for stability.

In the mid-twelfth century, Zangi—a Turkish chief who dubbed himself "pillar of the faith"—lost patience with the chaos of the Middle East. Or, at least, he saw the opportunities it presented to build an empire. He proclaimed a *jihad* against infidels and Shiites. Zangi and his heirs began to reconquer lands lost to crusaders. Saladin, the Kurdish soldier who seized Zangi's empire in 1170, largely completed the job. He recaptured Jerusalem in 1187, reduced the crusader states to tiny enclaves on the coast, and beat off attempts by new crusaders from Europe to recover Jerusalem. Yet that was not Saladin's greatest achievement. He sought to be remembered above all as the "reviver of the empire of the Commander of the Faithful," a restorer of Islamic unity, a torch of Sunni Islamic orthodoxy.

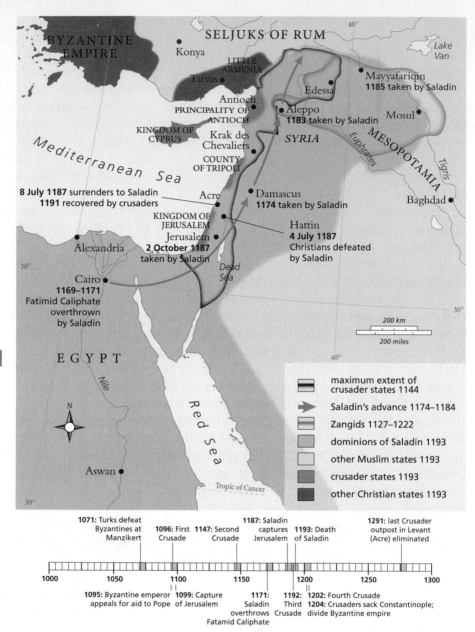

Map 12.1 Crusader Kingdoms and Saladin

The defeat of the crusaders was a sideshow. More important for the future of the Islamic world was the extinction of the Shiite caliphate and the conquest of Egypt for Sunni Islam. Though heresy continued to disrupt Islamic uniformity, no such large or menacing Shiite state outside Iran ever again challenged Islamic solidarity. The other legacy of the Zangids and Saladin was Islamic militancy. Jihad remained a way to legitimize upstart dynasties and regimes.

The Crusades, meanwhile, left an equally sad legacy. For most of the Middle Ages, Christian, Muslim, and Jewish communities in the Middle East, Egypt, and Spain lived alongside one another in relative peace. Christians and Muslims intermarried, exchanged culture, and, in some frontier zones, even worshipped at the same shrines. In war, Christian and Muslim states rarely behaved like natural enemies. They often made alliances against third parties, regardless of religious affiliation. The Crusades, however, fed on religious propaganda and encouraged the traditions to demonize each other. Crusading fervor also contributed to hostility in Europe between Christians and Jews, since Jews were often the victims of rioting aroused by laments over the loss of the Holy Land. In most places, Jews were the only non-Christian communities the mob found to hand.

The common opinion that the Crusades demonstrated the growing power of Latin Christendom seems—at best—exaggerated. There *was* dynamism in the western Europe of the eleventh and twelfth centuries, but most of it was expended on inward development and on expanding the frontiers. If anything, the Crusades contributed indirectly. Their failure helped alert people in Europe to the backwardness and vulnerability of their part of the world compared to the cultures of the Middle East.

The Invaders from the Sahara

It was not only in Asia that Islam successfully mobilized pastoralists. On their westernmost frontier, in Spain and Portugal, Muslims badly needed new strength. Since the eighth century, Muslim rulers had held territory as far north as the Duero and Ebro River valleys. But **al-Andalus**, as Muslims called it, was a sprawling state, hard to hold together and hard to defend. The original Muslim settlers—mostly Berbers from North Africa—were scattered in towns or strung out around the southern and eastern valleys and coasts, uneasily holding down large subject Christian populations. Internal communications relied on roads that the Romans had built centuries earlier to link widely scattered communities. Between the rivers Tagus and Duero was a vast frontier, strewn with fortifications. Wealth made al-Andalus viable: wealth gathered from the huge agricultural surplus of rich soils in the south and east; wealth spent on the fabulous luxuries—ivory, jewels, palaces, gardens—for which Spanish art of the time is renowned.

In the late tenth century, a strong-arm general, Almanzor, kept the potentially mutinous armies and regional aristocracies of the Spanish "caliphate" busy with wars against the Christians. Almanzor died in 1002. In 1009 Berber mutineers sacked his headquarters, "wilder now than the maws of lions, bellowing the end of the world." The Spanish caliphate dissolved into competing kingdoms. The Christian frontier

HISTORICAL BACKGROUND	CAUSE FOR ACTION	EUROPEAN CONSEQUENCES	CONSEQUENCES IN EASTERN MEDITERRANEAN
Tradition of pilgrimage—Christians go to Jerusalem	By 1050, increased danger, disorder, and occasional persecution in Middle East	Transformation of pilgrimage into armed expeditions; adoption of Islamic idea of holy war	Transformation of Holy Land into region of continual battle
Jerusalem formerly a Christian, Muslim, and Jewish city	Muslim kingdoms control the region	Religious leaders whip up mass movement—disorganized expeditions lead to disastrous results; Pope Urban II organizes a military expedition (First Crusade)	Quick capture of Jerusalem; creation of small "crusader kingdoms"
Catholic Church most important institution in western Europe	Church needs land, wealth to fund its clerics, infrastructure, and religious activity; new spirituality favors pilgrimages as a form of penance	Bishops and papacy help coordinate, orchestrate Crusades; crusaders left property to monasteries and churches while abroad	Conquered land and treasure often granted to church institutions
European aristocracy needs means of salvation	Development of chivalric ethos; founding of knightly orders	Aristocratic violence exported on Crusades	Crusades become ruling elite over large Muslim population
Defeat of Muslims by crusaders	Weak, disorganized Muslim kingdoms in eastern Mediterranean	Initial success of crusaders; occupation of Jerusalem and Holy Land	Proclamation of *jihad* by Zangi, Turkic chief; reconquest of Jerusalem by Saladin; overthrow of crusader kingdoms

lurched southward, as the northern Christian kingdoms took advantage. By the 1080s, the Tagus valley was in Christian hands. In alarm, some of the Spanish Muslim kingdoms called on warrior ascetics from North Africa, the **Almoravids**, for help.

In Arabic the Almoravids' name is a pun, suggesting both hermits and soldiers. They emerged as an alliance of pastoral bands from the Sahara, who, through firebrand preaching, were aroused into self-dedication to holy war from the mid-tenth century.

When they received the summons to help Spain's Muslim rulers fend off the Christian states, the Almoravids had already created a state that spanned the Sahara. In the tradition of many Saharan tribes, they had—at least at an early stage of their history—a surprisingly egalitarian attitude to women. A woman, Zaynab al-Nafzawiya, dominated. "Some said the spirits spoke to her . . . others that she was a witch."

In Spain, the Almoravids drove back the Christians, but they also swept away the rulers of the petty Muslim kingdoms, first denouncing their luxury, then seizing it for themselves. The corruption to which the Almoravids submitted in their turn became a provocation and an enticement to other religiously inspired desert pastoralists. In the 1140s, the Almoravids' empire was conquered by a new ascetic alliance, the Almohads—meaning "people of the oneness of God"—who again invaded Spain from North Africa and, for a while, succeeded in propping up the Islamic frontier.

These movements of desert zealots also turned south on Islam's frontier with paganism in Africa. The most celebrated Almoravid general, Abu Bakr al-Lamtumi, apparently abandoned the embraces of Zaynab herself to take up arms against the black pagans. Almoravid efforts focused on the Soninke kingdom of Ghana, which controlled access to the routes of trans-Saharan trade, where gold was exchanged for salt. Muslims—presumably traders—had their own large quarter in or near the Ghanian capital Kumbi Saleh but were kept apart from the royal quarter of the town. The Soninke fought off Almoravid armies until 1076 when Kumbi fell, and its defenders were massacred. The northerners' political hold south of the Sahara did not last, but Islam was firmly implanted in West Africa.

By the mid-twelfth century, Arab writers regarded Ghana as a model Islamic state, whose king revered the true caliph in Baghdad and dispensed justice with exemplary openness. They admired his palace, with its objects of art and windows of glass; the huge gold ingot that was the symbol of his authority; the gold ring by which he tethered his horse; his silk clothes, elephants, and giraffes. This magnificence did not last. After a long period of stagnation or decline, pagan invaders overran the Soninke state and destroyed Kumbi. But Islam had spread so widely by then among the warriors and traders of the Sahel that it retained its foothold south of the Sahara for the rest of the Middle Ages.

The Progress of Sufism

It is doubtful whether war alone could heal the divisions among Muslims and equip the Islamic world to expand. For that, inventive intellectuals were necessary—shapers of a religion that could appeal to a diversity of cultures and engage human sympathies and sensibilities without provoking conflict. Sufism (see Chapter 9) had enormous popular appeal. But most of the Muslim elite rejected it. In the early tenth century, for instance, ordinary people revered the great spokesman of Sufism, al-Hallaj, as a saint, but the Islamic authorities put him to death, because he claimed to have achieved self-extinction and mystical union with God. Gilani, his successor, who became one of the most popular preachers in mid-eleventh-century Baghdad, had a popular reputation as the "perfect man." He offered a simple morality of dependence on God—based on the rule, "Expect nothing from human beings"—as an alternative to the rigid legalism of Islamic scholars.

The divergence between legal-minded and mystic-minded Muslim theologians seemed unbridgeable until al-Ghazali entered the debate. He was blessed, or cursed, with an intellect he described as an "unquenchable thirst for investigation . . . an instinct and a temperament implanted in me by God through no choice of my own." At the height of a career as a conventional theologian in Baghdad, he experienced a sudden awareness of his ignorance of God. He became a Sufi, retired to his native Nishapur in Persia, and, before his death in 1111, wrote a dazzling series of works reconciling Sufism and Sunni orthodoxy. He was a master of reason and science but demonstrated, to the satisfaction of most of his readers, that human minds could not grasp some truths without direct illumination from God. Study could tell you about God, but only a mystical experience can show you who God is. Al Ghazali valued the faith of the poor and uneducated as highly as the learning of the officials of the mosques. His rehabilitation of Sufism was vital for the future of Islam. Because Sufis were indifferent to externals, Sufi mystics could tolerate cultural differences among Muslims and between Muslims and non-Muslims in a way the legal-minded Islamic intellectuals could not. Their habits of holiness satisfied ordinary people's craving for saints. They became Islam's most effective missionaries.

The Byzantine Empire and Its Neighbors

If the pastoralists contributed to the salvation of the Islamic world, their attacks were disastrous for the many non-Muslim states that proved less skillful at absorbing them or deflecting their power. A dramatic case in point is that of the Byzantine Empire.

Byzantium and the Barbarians

The Roman-ness of Byzantium dwindled by degrees. Under Justinian (r. 527–565), the government at Constantinople was actively engaged in trying to reconstruct the Roman world. In the early seventh century, Byzantium still ruled substantial parts of the western Roman Empire, with enclaves as far away as Spain. But events of the seventh and eighth centuries shifted its frontiers and changed its character. Arab expansion after the death of Muhammad (see Chapter 9) stripped away the empire's territory south of the Mediterranean—Syria, Egypt, and North Africa. Meanwhile, from the sixth century to the eighth, speakers of Slav languages slowly colonized much of the Balkans, including Greece. Arabs, Bulgars, and Russians threatened Constantinople itself.

In defense of the empire, missionaries and diplomats were as important as armies. The church virtually monopolized literacy in the areas of the Balkans and Russia, where Byzantine missions were active. Missionaries invented the alphabets in which Slav languages were written. They also helped to spread statehood, legitimating strong rulers, sanctifying weak ones. Many Balkan states slid between allegiance to the Latin- and Greek-speaking churches, but for a while, thanks to missionary efforts launched from Constantinople, Moravians, Croats, and Hungarians hovered in Byzantium's orbit before finally opting for the Latin Church. The greatest success for this religious diplomacy was the conversion of the rulers of much of what is now Russia (see Chapter 9). The policy was most effective when lavish gifts and the hands of Byzantine princesses, who married Bulgar khans and Russian princes, backed it. Instead of an empire like Rome's, a Byzantine "commonwealth" of Christian states was being built up—a diplomatic ring of outer defenses.

Byzantine diplomacy was exceptionally good at economizing on force by intimidating visiting barbarians with elaborate ceremonials. The Emperor Constantine VII (r. 913–959) laid down rules for courtly displays that were designed to embody imperial power and, in effect, to wield it. There was even an official whose job was to bribe paupers to line the streets for imperial processions—or, perhaps, reward those who would turn out anyway. The effect was unashamedly theatrical. When an ambassador arrived at Constantinople in 924, the artificial roar of mechanical lions that guarded the imperial throne surprised him.

The deftness of Byzantine diplomacy, its rulers' ability to impress or intimidate surrounding "barbarians," is part of the repertoire of strategies with which all successful states managed the surge of migrations of the period. The wealth of the empire underpinned those strategies and paid for vital military backup. The Byzantine economy relied on the productivity of the peasantry of Anatolia and on trade that passed through Byzantine territory, for the empire enjoyed a privileged position, close to where great arteries of trade converged: the Silk Roads, the Volga, the Mediterranean.

Yet the system was rickety. Wealth depended on security, which was hard to guarantee. The effectiveness of Byzantine diplomacy had its limits. Most steppeland peoples, and the Muslims who predominated to the east and south, were indifferent to Byzantine religion and unintimidated by Byzantine methods. Caught between the Bulgars and the Turks, Byzantium seemed to lie at the eye of the steppelander storm. Byzantines tended to see their predicament as a test of faith—an episode of sacred history.

Basil II

The longed-for savior appeared from an unlikely quarter. The Emperor Basil II barely survived adolescence. Surprisingly, successive usurpers allowed

Basil II. This is how the Byzantine emperor Basil II (r. 976–1025) liked to see himself. Unlike the German emperor Otto III (see Chapter 11), Basil needs no human helpers. He leans on his own sword while defeated barbarians crawl at his feet and angels crown him and invest him with a scepter. Isolated above the earth, he is perfumed with incense and adorned with a halo. Images of the saints guard him on either hand. Basil may have stressed these divine sanctions for his rule because his family had peasant origins. But the proof that God was on his side was the many victories he won against the empire's foes. *Werner Forman/Art Resource, NY*

him to live on after his father's death until he succeeded to the throne peacefully on coming of age in 976. His image appears on a page from his surviving prayer book—heavily armed, attended by angels, while barbarians cringe at his feet. This is how he wished to be remembered.

Basil ruled intuitively, as if coping with a constant state of emergency, enforcing his own will, administering rough justice, respecting no laws or conventions. In 996, he dealt with a landowner he saw exploiting peasants: "we had his luxurious villa razed to the ground and returned his property to the peasants, leaving him with what he had to begin with and reducing him to the peasants' level." This was an instance of a long conflict between great landowners and the throne. Emperors needed prosperous, independent peasants to provide bedrock taxes and manpower for the armies. Landowners wanted to control the peasants themselves. Aristocratic revolts and resistance to taxation were commonplace.

Basil dealt with the most troublesome of Byzantium's satellite peoples, the Bulgars, by blinding—so it was said—14,000 of their captured warriors and cowing them into submission. He incorporated Bulgaria into the empire in 1018. On the southern front, he made peace with the Arabs. In consequence, he gave the empire virtually ideal borders. In Bulgaria, he followed up his terror stroke by a policy of conciliation, cooperating with the native elite, appointing a Bulgar as the local archbishop. In Greece, he relied on repression, forcing the empire's religion and language on the immigrant Slavs (see Map 12.2).

Force was expensive by comparison with the waiting game, bribes, and tricks characteristic of traditional Byzantine policy. Basil paid for a professional army by heavily taxing the aristocracy. When he died in 1025, his treasury was full, bigger than any emperor's since the sixth century. Prayers cited his name in Russia and Armenia. As late as the 1070s, a Hungarian king accepted a crown from Constantinople. The so-called crown of St. Stephen depicts the king reverencing the rulers of the Byzantine Empire.

The Era of Difficulties

Basil's legacy was unsustainable. His methods of government were personal and arbitrary. The aristocracy could afford his taxes only while his power protected their lands from invaders. As Turkish migrations and invasions began to roll over Byzantine Anatolia, the revenues failed. The succession to the throne was problematic. Basil had no children, and his brother, who succeeded him, had only daughters. These were unusual circumstances: an opportunity for strong women to come to the fore. In the background, deeper, ill-understood social changes were under way. The family—formerly, in theory, a second-best lifestyle to monastic chastity—rose in Byzantine esteem in the tenth century. Women began to be admired for fertility as well as virginity.

In the eyes of influential classes—clergy, landowners, courtiers—eleventh-century experiments did not seem to justify the empowerment of female rulers. Princesses spent their lives confined to the palace, and though they got the same formal education as men in Greek literature, philosophy, and theology, they were denied the opportunity to accumulate useful experience of the world. Basil's niece, Zoe, regarded the throne as a family possession and responsibility. Her "family album" is laid in mosaic in her private enclosure in the gallery of Constantinople's cathedral. Her third husband's portrait smothers that of her second, who murdered his predecessor at Zoe's behest. Zoe outraged Constantinople's snobbish elite by adopting a workman's son as heir—an

ATLANTIC

OCEAN

IRELAND

ENGLAND

London

Normandy
Paris

SCANDINAVIA

SWEDEN

DENMARK

GERMANY

POLAN

Oviedo

40°

FRANCE

Moravians

HUNGARY
(Magyars)

Lisbon

SPAIN
(al-Andalus)

Toledo

Po
Venice

Corsica

Cordova

Granada

A
l
m
o
h
a
d
s

Rome

Sardinia

Zadar
Croats

Ragusa

Serbs

Ca

Balkans

Slavs

Da

BULG

0°

Bari

Thessalonica
T

NORTH

AFRICA

Sicily

1091
Normans
conquer Sicily

Athens

Peloponnese

GREECE

Aegean S

Adriatic Sea

Crete

Mediterranean

250 km

250 miles

20°

	Byzantine empire, ca. 1050
	Byzantine empire, ca. 780
✂	battle of Manzikert, 1071
- - -	frontier with Seljuks of Rum after 1077
■	maximum extent of crusader kingdoms, 1144
Croats	people
→	Fourth crusade route 1202–1204

Map 12.2 Byzantium and Its Neighbors, ca. 1050

CONSTANTINOPLE

1 km

1 mile

Land Walls of Theodosios II

GALATA

Golden Horn

Bosphorus

Cistern

Cistern

Aqueduct

Column
of Marcian

Acropolis

Theatre

Cistern

Cemetery

Philadelpheion

Augustaeum
Senate

Forum of
Arkadios

Forum of
Theodosios

Baths of
Zeuxippos

Signa

(1)

(2)

Golden Gate

Sea of Marmara

✝ Church
(1) Hippodrome
(2) Imperial Palace

RUSSIAN
Principalities

Kiev

Slavs

Dnieper

Bug

Volga

Black Sea

Caucasus

Caspian Sea

60°

Constantinople
(see inset map)

GEORGIA

Nicaea

Trebizond

40°

Anatolia

ARMENIA

Ani

(Seljuks of Rum
after 1077)

Konya

Cilicia

Tigris

Antioch

Aleppo

Cyprus

Euphrates

Damascus

Acre

40°

upstart "pygmy playing Hercules," said the snobs. Zoe's sister Theodora ruled alone in 1055–1056, "shamefully" and "unnaturally"—according to her opponents—refusing to marry. These judgments lack objectivity, but show the outrage the sisters provoked among the elite.

Meanwhile, relations between the Latin- and Greek-speaking churches broke down. Differences had been growing over rites, doctrines, language, and discipline between the sees of Constantinople and Rome for centuries. Underlying the theological bitterness were deep cultural differences. Language was in part to blame. The Greek-speaking Byzantine Empire could not share the common culture of the Latin-speaking elites of western and central Europe, while few in the Latin West could speak or read Greek with fluency. Subtle theological distinctions, inexpressible in Latin, came easily in Greek.

Dogmas that were supposed to be universal turned out differently in the two tongues. For most people, religion is more a matter of conduct than of creed. In this respect, differences between the Roman and Byzantine traditions built up over centuries of relative mutual isolation. The process began as early as the mid-sixth century, when the Eastern churches resisted or rejected the supremacy of the pope. The effects were gradual but great. From the 790s, Greek and Latin congregations recited slightly different versions of the creed, the basic statement of Christian belief. By about 1000, the pope was the supreme authority regarding doctrinal questions and liturgy and the source of patronage in the church throughout western Europe. The Western church still enclosed tremendous local diversity, but it was recognizably a single communion. Eastern Orthodox Christians felt no particular allegiance to the pope. In the West, moreover, the popes generally maintained, with difficulty, their own political independence. In the east, the patriarchs of Constantinople, as that city's bishops were titled, were the emperor's subjects and generally deferred to imperial power.

A moment when it might have been possible to restore Christian unity occurred in the mid-eleventh century. Constantinople and Rome faced common enemies. Norman invaders threatened the pope's political independence and the Byzantine emperor's remaining possessions in southern Italy and Sicily. On June 17, 1053, a Norman army cut the pope's German guard to pieces and, imploring the pope's forgiveness on bended knees, carried him off as a hostage.

Eventually, the papacy would turn the Normans into its sword bearers. At first, however, the pope turned to the Byzantines for help. Meanwhile, in 1054 in Constantinople, the patriarch, who was the head of the Byzantine church, saw an opportunity to exploit the pope's weakness. He closed Latin-speaking congregations' churches. The pope, teaching himself Greek, in the grip of a mortal sickness, sent an uncompromising mission to Constantinople. His representative, Cardinal

Humbert, after weeks of bitter insults, served notice of excommunication on the "false patriarch, now for his abominable crimes notorious." The patriarch responded by excommunicating the pope. At the time, most people assumed this was just a political maneuver, soon to be rescinded or forgotten. But relations between the Eastern and Western churches never fully recovered. A cultural fault line opened across Europe.

The shenanigans of the imperial family and the quarrelsome habits of the church have given Byzantium a bad name as a society doomed by its own decadence. But it was not doomed. There are no irreversible trends in history. Nor, even when beset by difficulties, was the Byzantine Empire decadent. On the contrary, the most unsuccessful emperor of the era was a model of energy and courage. Becoming emperor in 1068, Romanus IV Diogenes had to cope with aristocratic unrest while fighting on two fronts. In the west, the Normans threatened Byzantium's last possessions in Italy. In the east, Turks were penetrating Armenia and Anatolia, stealing the empire's vital food-producing zone. Romanus's military record made him look insuperable, but his generalship proved unequal to the task. In 1071, at the battle of Manzikert, the Seljuk Turks shattered the Byzantine army and forced the emperor to kiss the ground before the feet of their leader, Alp Arslan. Romanus could only raise a fifth of his ransom. He was released but deposed by a coup in Constantinople. Feuding at Constantinople between aristocratic factions paralyzed the government and allowed the Turks to overrun much of Anatolia.

Byzantium and the Crusaders

In 1097, crusaders arrived at Byzantium, ostensibly to help. But by then, the Byzantines had already begun to recover the lost ground on their own. The Byzantine princess Anna Comnena considered the newcomers more of a hindrance. Superbly educated in the classics, she was the official biographer of her father, the Emperor Alexis I (r. 1081–1118). To her, the crusaders seemed "a race under the spell of Dionysos and Eros"—a classical way of saying they were sex-crazed drunkards. Most crusaders, she believed, were enemies whose object was "to dethrone the emperor and capture the capital."

Tense cooperation between Byzantium and the crusaders, which characterized the First Crusade, broke down completely in the twelfth century. The crusaders kept most of the Byzantine territory they recaptured from the Muslims for themselves. Byzantines were convinced of their own moral and cultural superiority over impious, greedy, boorish Westerners, while crusaders blamed "Greek treachery" for their failures. The crusaders might have saved Byzantium, as the Turks saved the Islamic world. Instead, they undermined the empire.

Byzantium's difficulties multiplied. Agriculture was stagnant, despite the boom in other parts of Eurasia. The empire's hinterland beyond Constantinople was too insecure to prosper. In the twelfth century, in a serious reversal of earlier emperors' policy of nurturing the peasants at the landowners' expense, emperors tried to revive their rural revenues by granting control of peasant lands to great lords and encouraging monastic colonization of new lands. To some extent, this was another case of the attempt to exploit new resources, familiar in other societies of the time. The Emperor Isaac II Angelus (r. 1185–1195), for instance, gave a port to a monastery that settled a site at Vera in Thrace, formerly "devoid of men and dwellings, a haunt of snakes and scorpions, just rough ground, overgrown with spreading trees." Measures like these—which so dramatically increased the farmland of Western Christendom, Ethiopia, or, as we shall see, China—were of limited usefulness in a state whose territory was much diminished. Byzantium never recovered most of inland Anatolia from the Turks.

Increasingly, the empire had to look to trade and industry for its wealth. There were, as a Byzantine poet observed, "big merchants" who "for large profits disdain terrors and defy seas." Self-made upstarts coveted money "as a polecat gazes at fat." The huge city of Constantinople, crowded and riotous as it was, benefited from its uniquely favorable position for trade, where Mediterranean and trans-Asian routes met. The Jewish merchant, Benjamin of Tudela, who visited in about 1170, celebrated "a busy city" with inhabitants so rich they "they look like princes" where "merchants come from every country by sea and land." With revenues of 200,000 gold pieces a year from rents, market dues, and the tolls on passing trade, "Wealth like that of Constantinople," Benjamin wrote, "is not to be found in the whole world. Here also are men learned in all the books of the Greeks, and they eat and drink, every man under his vine and his fig tree." For William of Tyre, a Latin bishop who visited at about the same time, the city seemed equally splendid on the surface. But William was a moralist, not a merchant. He was more aware of underlying squalor and inequalities of wealth. "The wealthy overshadow the streets," he wrote—alluding to the teetering mansions of the rich—"and leave dark, dirty spaces to the poor and to travelers." William's prejudices are obvious, but, precisely because he was so keen to criticize the city, we can trust his witness to its wealth.

A special relationship developed between Byzantium and Venice, a maritime republic near the northernmost point of the Adriatic Sea, where trade routes across the Alps converged with the main axis of north Italian commerce, the River Po. Venice's position on marshy, salty islands allowed little scope to accumulate wealth except by piracy, which Venetians practiced, mainly at the expense of Muslim shipping. In the ninth and tenth centuries, however, they began to build up enough capital to become major traders, channeling toward Europe a share of the valuable trade in silks and spices that was concentrated at Byzantium.

Culturally, as well as economically, Venice was close to Byzantium. Though Venetians belonged to the Latin Church and spoke a language derived from Latin, Byzantine models saturated their taste in art and buildings. It could not be otherwise. They knew Byzantium well, and so they had to admire it—and, in some measure, to covet what they saw there.

To would-be attackers, Byzantium's wealth was a magnet and its weakness a motive. Toward the end of the 1190s, in western Europe, popular enthusiasm revived for a new Crusade to recapture Jerusalem. The Venetians agreed to ship the crusading army out at what was to prove an unaffordable price. While the army gathered, an embassy arrived from the pretender to the Byzantine throne, Alexius IV, proposing a detour. If the crusaders put Alexius on the throne, he would reward them with treasure and help them against the Turks. Faced with their inability to pay the Venetians' bill, most of the crusaders agreed to a diversion. The Fourth Crusade, launched in 1202 as a "pilgrimage" under arms to recapture Jerusalem, ended in 1204 by shedding Christian blood, capturing and sacking Constantinople and dividing most of what was left of the Byzantine Empire in Europe and the Aegean among the victors. The big gainer was Venice, which seized—in the words of the treaty that divided the empire—"one quarter and one half of one quarter" of Byzantine territory, achieving virtual monopoly rights in Byzantine trade and becoming an imperial power in the eastern Mediterranean. Meanwhile, in the remnants of the Byzantine Empire in the Balkans and coastal Anatolia, rival dynasties disputed claims to the imperial title.

Byzantine Art and Learning

Throughout the period this chapter covers, even amid the most severe difficulties of the twelfth century, Byzantium remained a beacon of learning and art. The most constant and careful Byzantine work in copying and analyzing the texts of classical authors and of the fathers of the Church was probably over by the tenth century, but mystics, represented by Saint Symeon the New Theologian (as he is called), who died in 1022, proposed an alternative route to learning—through divine illumination. "Orators and philosophers" could not access the wisdom of God. Painters developed a tradition that seemed deliberately unclassical, abandoning realism in favor of stylized, formal figures, usually set against abstract or sketchy backgrounds, more indebted, perhaps, to the mosaic tradition, in which Byzantine artists excelled, than to classical painting or sculpture. Most painters worked only on religious commissions and accepted the artistic vocation as a sacred obligation, aiming at work that captured the spirit of its subject and that would be revered as holy in itself. Innovation happened slowly and subtly, for artists had to treat every subject strictly in accordance with tradition and church dogma.

Nonetheless, in most arts, and in learning, Byzantium preserved and developed the classical legacy, which, in the eleventh and twelfth centuries, revived in an intellectual movement comparable with the renaissance of the same period in the West (see Chapter 11). The historian and biographer Michael Psellus (1018–1078), for instance, wrote in an antique style based on classical Greek models, interpreted the meanings of ancient art, and lectured on Plato and Aristotle (see Chapter 6). Anna Comnena's historical work was saturated in knowledge of Homer, and she commissioned commentaries on neglected works of Aristotle. A renaissance of classical pagan themes in art followed in the twelfth century. The recovery of classical traditions in the West would probably have been impossible without cross-fertilization with the Islamic world and Byzantium.

China and the Northern Barbarians

Beyond the limits of the Turkish steppe, other steppeland peoples were even harder to deal with. Not even the Seljuks seemed able to win battles against them. Fortunately, however, for the Islamic world, none of these remoter nomads yet seemed willing to extend their conquests beyond the steppeland. Their critical relationships lay to the east, with China. We thus need a brief account of what had happened in China in the ninth and tenth centuries.

The End of the Tang Dynasty

Superficially, the history of China in the 800s and 900s looks like a series of disasters. An era of political disintegration began in the ninth century. Eunuchs controlled the succession to the imperial throne. The Xuantong emperor, who died in 859, never named an empress or an heir lest he be "made idle," that is, murdered. Steppelander incursions continued. In 840, in a typical incident, 10,000 Uighurs (see Chapter 9), driven from their Central Asian homeland by rival nomads, arrived on the bend of the Yellow River proposing to garrison the Chinese frontier. A new menace— or, at least, one of unprecedented scale—was the rise of banditry. In a land as densely populated as China, every dislocation, invasion, war, or natural disaster had profound environmental consequences, impoverishing many peasants and driving them to survive by any available means. In the late ninth century, bandit gangs grew into rebellious armies led by renegade members of the elite—students who had failed to pass the examinations for the civil service and Buddhist clergy forced out of monasteries the government had confiscated.

An imperial decree of 877 complained that the bandit forces "come and go just as they please." The emperor's professed wish to "equalize food and clothing so that all might be prosperous" was an admission of weakness. His threat to apply "force without remorse" against those who refused to lay down their arms was empty. In 879, the bandit leader, Huang Chao, unified most of the gangs and crossed the Yangtze River with, reputedly, 600,000 men. He took Chang'an, the seat of the court, with effects described in the verses of one of the most striking poems of the time, the *Lament of Lady Qin*: rape, pillage, and bloodshed. Huang's successor, Zhu Wen, emerged as the most powerful man in China, effectively replacing the Tang dynasty in 907. His state fell in turn in 923 to Turkic nomads whom the Chinese had tried to use against the bandits. The Chinese Empire dissolved into "ten kingdoms."

China's situation recalls that of western Europe, striving to maintain the ancient sense of unity and—for some rulers—even actively seeking to recover it, in times of political dissolution. The Chinese predicament also parallels those of the Islamic world and Byzantium, beset by nomadic migrants and invaders. Chinese responses, as we shall see, were also similar. They tried to fend off the "barbarians" by methods akin to those of the Byzantines: diplomacy, bribery, intimidation, and displays of cultural superiority. As in the Islamic world, Chinese worked to convert invaders to their own culture, usually successfully. As in all the states we have looked at, the reexploitation of internal resources—especially by converting forest to farmland—made an important contribution.

For China, however, the outcome was different from those of other comparable regions. Throughout the period this chapter covers, the reconstruction of unity never seemed perfect or stable, but unity remained an actively pursued and—as we shall see—ultimately recoverable ideal. Divisions over religion, which deepened disunity in Christendom, or in the world of al-Hakim, had no parallel in China. China survived the invaders from the steppes but surrendered much territory to them. And, unlike the Islamic world, China never wholly succeeded in turning invading warriors into a force it could use for its own expansion.

The Rise of the Song and the Barbarian Conquests

The fight for unity after the collapse of the 920s began in 960, when a mutinous army proclaimed its general as emperor. The dynasty he founded, the **Song**, lasted until 1279, but it always had to share China's traditional territory with steppeland invaders who created empires and dynasties of their own in parts of the north. These barbarian states adopted Chinese political ideas and bureaucratic methods and claimed the mandate of heaven—or, at least, a share in it—for themselves. But none of them were able to extend their conquests south of the Huai River, into the intricately patterned lands of rice paddies and dense population the Song retained (see Map 12.3).

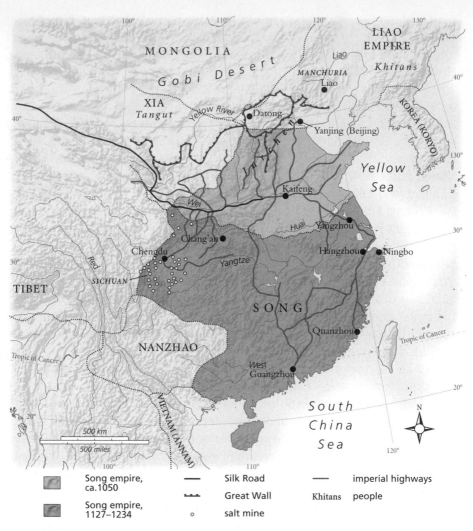

Map 12.3 The Song Empire, ca. 1150

First, from the early tenth to the early twelfth centuries, the Khitan state of Liao loomed over China from heartlands in Mongolia and Manchuria. In the tenth century, under warrior-empresses, the Liao state acquired a southern frontier across the Yellow River valley. The Khitans remained faithful to their pastoral traditions, but they split their empire into two spheres, creating a Chinese-style, Chinese-speaking administration for their southern provinces. They began to build cities, following Chinese urban planning models, apparently to attract migrants. The Khitan Empire had its own civil service, selected on Confucian principles, issuing documents that scholars still do not fully understand. In a treaty of 1004, the Song conceded equality to Liao, which became known as the Northern Kingdom, alongside the Southern Kingdom of the Song. In 1031, they jointly proclaimed "reunification of the universe," but this was a wild exaggeration. The two states lived together in uneasy equilibrium, punctuated by hostilities.

Toward the end of the 1030s, a second steppeland state proclaimed itself an empire—the Xia. The axis of the Xia state was a strip of grazing land, 900 miles long, squeezed between Tibet and the southern Gobi Desert. In 1044 Xia proclaimed itself a kingdom superior to all others except Song and Liao. It had its own system of writing, its own bureaucracy, and an iron coinage much used along the Silk Roads. It also had a scholarly establishment, largely devoted to acquiring and commenting on Buddhist scriptures.

The last state-builders to intrude into the region were the Jurchen, who from 1115 began to build up conquests that eventually included the whole Liao Empire and covered northern China as far as the Huai River. Their homeland was in the forests of northern Manchuria. Their traditional economy relied on hunting rather than herding. They were "sheer barbarians," Chinese envoys reported, "worse than wolves or tigers." On this occasion, for once, we can be reasonably confident about what provoked their migration. It coincided with several years' exceptional cold and rain.

The Jurchen forced the Chinese to acknowledge Jurchen claims to the mandate of heaven. A treaty of 1127 imposed heavy annual tribute on the Song in copper, and silk. Jurchen campaigns penetrated far into the south of China. In 1161, however, the invaders despaired of creating a river navy strong enough to dominate the Yangtze. The Song and Jurchen states learned to live with each other.

Meanwhile, the Jurchen adopted Chinese habits and traditions more fully than even the Khitans had. The Jurchen emperors were uncertain about this trend. On the one hand, they were quick to adopt Chinese bureaucracy and courtly customs themselves. On the other hand, they were afraid that the Jurchen would lose their warlike strength and will to dominate. The Jurchen, after all, were few in number—perhaps a few hundred thousand—compared with their more than 50 million Chinese subjects recorded in a census of 1207. Despite legislation forbidding Jurchen to adopt Chinese language or dress, distinctive Jurchen culture largely vanished.

Chinese thinkers found it hard to adjust to a world in which "barbarians" seemed their equals. On the whole, the Song coped by accepting the reality of the new distribution of power and opting for coexistence and peaceful persuasion, bribing and coaxing the foreigners into remaining quiet. One of the supplest intellects of the Song era was that of the early eleventh-century palace official, Ouyang Xiu. Earlier barbarian attacks, he thought, had been like "the sting of gadflies and mosquitoes." Now they were more serious and could not merely be brushed aside. He advised,

> Put away . . . armor and bows, use humble words and . . . generous
> gifts. . . . Who would exhaust China's resources . . . to quarrel with

serpents and swine? . . . Now is the moment for binding friendship. . . .
If indeed Heaven causes the rogues to accept our humaneness and
they . . . extinguish the beacons on our frontiers, which will be a
great fortune to our ancestral altars.

According to Ouyang Xiu, civilization would always win encounters
with savagery. Barbarians might be invincible in battle, but in the long
run, they could be shamed into submission. There was a lot to be said for
this point of view. China always survived. Barbarian invaders always did
get seduced by Chinese ways and adopt Chinese culture. But the adoption of Chinese ways by barbarians usually followed bloody wars and
costly destruction.

In their way, Ouyang Xiu's arguments simply rewrote the old script—
Chinese superiority would ultimately prevail. This kind of thinking made
defeat by the Jurchen even harder to bear. The traumas the victims of the
wars suffered come to life in pages by the poet Li Qingzhao (lee ching-jhao):
a memoir of her life with her husband, whom she had married for love when
he was a student and she was a teenager. The couple played intellectual
games at teatime, rivaling each other in being able to identify literary quotations. Their books were their most cherished possessions. When the
Jurchen invaded in 1127, the fleeing couple "first gave up the bulky printed
volumes, the albums of paintings, and the bulkiest ornaments." They still
had so many books that it took 15 carts to bear them and a string of boats to
ferry them across the Yangtze. Another Jurchen raid scattered more of the
collection "in clouds of black smoke." When Li Qingzhao finally got beyond
danger, after the couple's parting and her husband's death, only a few baskets of books were left—and most of those were later stolen.

Economy and Society under the Song

Under pressure from the barbarian north, Song rule shrank toward the
south. The Yangtze became the axis of the Song Empire. This potentially
traumatic adjustment—the amputation of the ancient Yellow River
heartlands—was bearable because population, too, had shifted southward. About 60 percent of Chinese lived in the Yangtze valley by 1000.

Away from the steppeland frontier, Chinese expansion went on. Loss
of traditional territory, combined with the growth of population, stimulated
colonization in new directions. The census of 1083 reported 17,211,713
families. By 1124, the number had grown to 20,882,258. Censuses tended
to underestimate numbers, because tax evaders eluded the count. The
Jurchen wars brought the growth of population to an end, but, by then,
Song China must have had well over 100,000,000 inhabitants—perhaps
about half as many again as in the whole of Europe. The state had the
most basic resource: labor. It needed food and space.

The founder of the Song dynasty, Zhao Guangyin, known as the Taizu emperor, realized that China's new opportunities lay in a further shift to the southwest: the vast, underpopulated region of Sichuan. Colonization needed peaceful conditions. So the native tribes had to be suppressed. In a heavily forested, mountainous region, where tribal chiefs had a demonic reputation, this was not an easy task. By repute, the wildest inhabitants were the Black Bone Yi, led by a chief the Chinese called the "Demon Master." In 1001, the Song divided the region into two administrative units called "routes." A campaign in 1014 began the pacification. In 1036, the Demon Master became a salaried state official. The "forbidden hills" of Sichuan were stripped of forests and planted with tea and with mulberries for silk production. The salt mines became resources of the Chinese Empire. A land that poets formerly praised as a romantic wilderness of "streams and grottoes" became China's "heavenly storehouse."

Alongside the colonization of new land, new methods of exploitation enriched China, in a process of internal expansion strikingly reminiscent of what was going on at the same time in many other regions, notably in western Europe and Ethiopia. Environmental change fed the growing population. Wetlands were drained. New varieties of rice arrived from Vietnam, adapted to local conditions by trial and error. Planting and harvesting two crops a year effectively doubled the capacity for food production in the Yangtze valley. From the 1040s, the state promoted agriculture by making loans to peasants for seed grain, at favorable rates. A tax on unharvested timber stimulated deforestation. By 1100, the forests around the city of Kaifeng had disappeared, sacrificed to huge iron-smelting works, employing 3,000 men. In 1132, a new palace at Kaifeng was built with timber from the Qingfeng Mountains, reputedly inaccessible for centuries, like the enchanted forests of fairy tales.

Meanwhile, the money economy boomed. Song mints were always busy, always pumping out new coins—a million strings of coins a year in the early years of the century, six million in 1080—and always devaluing the currency by putting less precious metal—gold and silver—into coins. Paper money became a state monopoly from 1043.

Rice Cultivation. In the second half of the thirteenth century, Zhen Ji illustrated poems on rice cultivation in a long series of paintings, all copied—like the poems—from twelfth-century originals. His art demonstrates the continuity of Chinese agriculture. Even after revolutionary new strains of rice were introduced in China, older varieties of the crop were still cultivated in traditional ways. *The Art Archive/ Freer Gallery of Art*

Towns grew spectacularly. Until the Jurchen captured it, Kaifeng was not just a seat of government but a thriving place of manufacture and trade. A famous twelfth-century painting by Zhang Zeduan depicts the bustling life of the city: craftsmen, merchants, peddlers, entertainers, shoppers, and gawking crowds. Groaning grain ships bring the extra food. Diners enjoyed meals in some of Kaifeng's 72 restaurants, each of up to five pavilions, three stories high, and connected by delicate bridges. In 1147, the poet Master Meng recalled in his *Dream of the Eastern Capital's Splendor* how, in Kaifeng, the entertainers' din "could be heard for miles."

Women rarely appear in Meng's verses or on Zhang's scroll. They never enjoyed the same status in China as among the pastoral cultures of the steppeland, where women were always important partners in managing the herds. Increasingly, in China, women were traded as commodities, and as young girls, their feet were tightly bound with cloth so that they became permanently deformed, in a practice perhaps originally designed to hobble them against escape. Despite the troubled relationship with the nomads and the loss of the northern provinces, the late Song Empire brimmed with wealth. In 1170, an official set off up the Yangtze to his new job in Sichuan. He admired everything he saw: the newness of the bridges, the flourishing commerce, the boats crowded together "like the teeth of a comb." The war readiness of 700 river galleys, with their "speed like flight," excited him. He celebrated ample signs of prosperity. The province to which he was traveling possessed enviable wealth. Two districts in Sichuan had between them 22 centers of population producing annual tax revenue of between 10,000 and 50,000 strings of cash—more than any other district of the Song Empire outside the lower Yangtze. The frontier had been drawn into the empire.

Kaifeng. In this most famous of Song dynasty scroll-paintings, Zhang Zeduan captures the vitality of life on the Yellow River at the city of Kaifeng in the early twelfth century and the wonderful commercial opportunities that the approach of the Spring Festival brought. Hundreds of wares arrive by cart, mule, or camel train or on poles slung across peddlers' backs. *The Art Archive/Picture Desk, Inc./Kobal Collection*

Song Art and Learning

The era left an enduring legacy of intellectual and artistic achievement. To the eleventh-century elite, philosophy was not an occupation of luxury or leisure, but the basis and business of government. On one side of the debate, Ouyang Xiu aimed to restore "the perfection of ancient times"—an ideal age "when rites and music reached everywhere."

Wang Anshi (wahng ahn-sheh), who led the party on the other side of the debate, thought life was like a dream and valued "dreamlike merits" equally with practical results. He carried the notion of socially responsible government to extremes and consulted "peasants and serving girls" rather than relying on Confucian principles and ancient precedents. The policies he pursued, when he was in charge of the government in the 1070s, included progressive taxation, the substitution of taxes for forced labor, cheap loans for farmers, and state-owned pawnshops. Wang mistrusted Confucian confidence in China's ability to tame the steppelanders—he introduced universal conscription. To combat banditry, and prevent the desertion of young peasants to bandit gangs, he organized village society in groups of 10 families, so that each family was held responsible for the good behavior of the others.

Both parties supported reform of the **examination system** that produced the imperial officials with two objectives in mind: to encode in it an ethic of service to society, and to recruit the state's servants from as wide a range of social backgrounds as possible. The old examination tested only skill in composition, especially in verse, and in memorizing texts. The new test asked questions about ethical standards and about how the state could serve the people better. It was a conservative revolution.

While Wang's agenda shaped policy, Ouyang Xiu's dominated the intellectual mainstream. The dominant trend in philosophy for the rest of the Song era was the effort to reinterpret the Confucian classics for the readers' own times. The work of Zhu Xi (1130–1200) summarized and synthesized all previous thinking on this subject. In his own mind, he was an orthodox Confucian, but in some ways, he was what we would now call a secular humanist. He upheld the doctrine of the natural goodness of human beings. He doubted whether "there is a man in heaven judging sin" and dismissed prayer in favor of self-examination and study of the classics. Morality, he thought, was a matter of individual responsibility, not heavenly regulation. But he did accept the tradition on which the Chinese state was based: "heaven" decreed the fortunes of society according to the merits of its rulers. Zhu's synthesis was so influential that it defined what subsequent ages called Confucianism.

The intellectual and economic environment of the Song Empire was favorable to the arts. There was money and enthusiasm for abundant patronage of artists. The painting of the era has always attracted special admiration, not just because it was prolific and technically excellent, but also because it specialized in scenes from the natural world. Admiration for the beauty of nature, untouched by human hands, is, perhaps, a measure of the maturity of a civilization. It is doubtful, however, whether Song artists painted nature, as modern romantics do today, for its own sake. To them, the natural world was a book of lessons about humankind. Su Dongpo (1036–1101) painted virtually nothing but bamboo, because its fragility suggested human weakness. Li Longmian (1049–1106) favored gnarled trees, defying weather, as symbols of the resilience of the sages. Mi Fei (1051–1107) perfected the representation of mist—which is the breath of nature, with power to shape the image, like the spiritual dimension of human beings. With other painters of the same era, they produced some of the world's most influential, most imitated images.

IN PERSPECTIVE
Cains and Abels

The North African Muslim Ibn Khaldun (1332–1406), one of the world's best historians, saw history as a story of struggle between nomads and settled people. To some extent, he based his view on the experience of the

CHRONOLOGY	
907	End of Tang dynasty
960	Beginning of Song dynasty; conversion of Karkhanid Turks to Islam
1040s	Sanhaja conquer Morocco
1054	Schism between Latin and Orthodox Christianity
1071	Battle of Manzikert; end of Byzantine dominance in Anatolia
1076	Kumbi Saleh falls to Almoravid armies
1080s	Muslim kingdoms in al-Andalus call on Almoravids for help
1095	Pope Urban II calls for crusade to capture Jerusalem
1099	Jerusalem falls to crusaders
1111	Death of al-Ghazali, Sufi mystic and theologian
1140s	Almoravid Empire falls to the Almohads
1187	Crusader kingdom of Jerusalem falls to Saladin
1204	Crusaders sack Constantinople

eleventh and twelfth centuries, when, as far as he could make out, pastoralist invaders wrecked the peace and prosperity of his native region and Spain: first, Arab herders whom the Shiite caliphs released or expelled from southern Egypt; then the Almoravids and Almohads from the Sahara. Modern historians have challenged his interpretation. The mutual disdain between tillers and herders was neither as deep nor as destructive as Ibn Khaldun thought. But the tension he perceived was real. The biblical story of Cain and Abel traces the origins of human conflict to the mutual hatred and murderous rivalry of a tiller of the soil and a keeper of flocks.

Nomads threatened their farming neighbors in various ways. The nomadic way of life demanded immeasurably more land per head of population than the intensive agriculture that fed dense farming populations. Nomads were ill equipped for some economic activities, including mining and silk manufacture, and the production of favored commodities, such as tea, fruit, and grain. For these things, therefore, they depended on theft, tribute, or trade from farming communities. The nomads were better equipped for war. Horsemanship made their way of life a preparation for battle. Sedentary peoples had not yet developed firearms or fortifications good enough to tilt the balance in their own favor. The nomads tended to cherish ideologies of superiority—variously of jihad or of divine election for empire—that clashed with the equal and opposite convictions of the settled peoples. Nomads could exploit farmers' lands, but agricultural communities did not yet have the technology—steel plows, mechanical harvesters—needed to turn the unyielding soils of the grasslands into productive farmland.

Yet the hostility of nomads and farmers arose less, perhaps, from conflicts of interest than from mutual misunderstanding: a clash of cultures, incompatible ways of seeing the world and coping with it. There is no moral difference between settled and nomadic lifeways. Each type of community, however, tended to see the other as morally inferior. This was probably because for followers of each way of life, those of the other came to represent all that was alien. Their mutual descriptions were full of incomprehension and even disgust.

Real differences underpinned this mutual revulsion. Pastoralist diets were, for farmers, literally stomach churning. Pastoralists relied on dairy foods, which most farmers' digestive systems rejected, because after early childhood they did not naturally produce lactase—the substance that makes milk digestible. It was also normal for herders to open their animal's veins for fresh blood to drink. This practice enabled nomad armies to take nourishment without halting on the march. Nomad diets tended to be short on plant foods. So to balance their intake, nomads would usually eat the raw organ meats of dead animals. This sort of food contains relatively high levels of vitamin C, which, in other cultures, people get from fruit and vegetables. Indeed, meat processed without cooking was important in the treeless environments of the steppe and the desert, where the only cooking fuel was dried animal dung. One of the great resources of the Eurasian steppe was the fat-tailed sheep, specially bred to drag its tail—as broad as a beaver's—behind it. Its fat is wonderfully soft. Even if nomads have no time to heat this fat, or no available kindling with which to cook it, they can eat it raw and digest it quickly. These were all elements of a rational food strategy for the nomadic life, but they inspired denunciations of the "barbaric" customs of eaters of raw meat and drinkers of blood. The nomads responded with equal contempt. For them, the settled life was soft and corrupted by luxury. Farming involved grubbing and groveling in mud and filth. Cities and rice paddies were cramped and unhealthy.

After successful conquests, the nomads could usually be absorbed and induced to adopt or tolerate settled ways of life; but the conquerors kept coming. The relative success of the Islamic world in absorbing and converting the invaders of the tenth and eleventh centuries was a decisive feature of the history of the period. Byzantium, by contrast, failed to tame the intruders, while Western Christendom could recruit no more pastoralists after the Magyars. China developed no strategy to cope with the nomads, except to retreat and wait for them to adopt Chinese ways. Unprecedented changes in the steppeland, however, were about to upset the balance between nomads and settled peoples and unleash the most formidable steppeland conquerors of all, the Mongols. The outcome would transform the history of Eurasia.

PROBLEMS AND PARALLELS

1. Why was the Islamic world more successful than Christian Europe in absorbing steppeland invaders? How did the Turks strengthen the Islamic world?
2. What were the effects of the Crusades on western Europe, Byzantium, and the Islamic world?
3. Why did the Almoravids and Almohads fail to prevent the expansion of the Christian states in Spain? How did Islam take root in West Africa?
4. Why did the Sufis become the most effective Muslim missionaries?
5. What was the "Byzantine commonwealth"? Why did conflicts arise between Byzantium and the Latin West?
6. How did China deal with steppeland invaders? Why was the Song empire so prosperous in the eleventh and twelfth centuries?
7. Why have relations between pastoralists and farmers been so hostile for much of history?

The World
the Mongols Made

focus questions

1. Why were the Mongols able to conquer such a vast empire?
2. What were the positive and negative effects of the Mongol conquests?
3. Why did the Mongols fail to conquer Egypt, India, and Japan?
4. What key technologies did the West develop in the thirteenth century?
5. Why did nothing comparable to the Mongol Empire develop in Africa or the Americas?

Two coins lie alongside each other in the British Museum in London. One, minted in 1230, is stamped with the name of the queen of Georgia, Rusudan, and the words, "Queen of Queens, Glory of the World and Faith, Champion of the Messiah." Beside it, another Georgian coin, minted 17 years later, shows *"King David, slave of the empire of the Great* **Khan** *Kuyuk." A lot had happened in Georgia in a short time. The changes the coins reflect were important not just for Georgia but for the world, for they were huge in scale, reshaping the politics, communications, and culture of Eurasia.*

In the early thirteenth century, Georgia was a formidable state, capable of imposing rulers on cities as far afield as the Black Sea and the Caspian. In the 1220s, a bishop in Jerusalem admired Georgian pilgrims, who "march into the holy city with banners displayed, without paying tribute to anyone, for the Muslims dare in no way molest them."

The Georgians promised the pope that they would assist in a new crusade. Suddenly, however, in 1224, letters arrived in Rome withdrawing the promise. "A savage people of hellish aspect have invaded my realm," wrote Rusudan. The Mongols were coming. The world would never be the same.

The effects of the events of the rest of the thirteenth century refashioned Eurasia, destroying old states, creating new ones, disrupting existing communications and reforging stronger, wider-ranging links. Though at first the **Mongols** razed cities, destroyed crops, slaughtered elites, and depleted peoples, it looked for a while as if a safer, richer, more interconnected, more dynamic, more expanding, and more enlightened world might emerge. But a century of environmental disasters arrested these changes in most of Eurasia. Catastrophes reversed the growth of populations and prosperity. But previously marginal regions began to be drawn more closely into a widening pattern of contacts and cultural exchange. Some peoples, in Africa and Southeast Asia, for example, looked outward because they escaped disaster. Others, especially in Europe, did so because their reverses were so enormous that there was nothing else they could do.

The Mongols: Reshaping Eurasia

The earliest records of Mongol-speaking peoples occur in Chinese annals of the seventh century, when they emerged onto the steppes of Central Asia, from northern forests, and became horse-borne nomads and sheepherders. In the early twelfth century, the bands or alliances they formed got bigger, and their raids against neighboring sedentary peoples became more menacing. In part, this was the effect of the growing preponderance of some Mongol groups over others. In part, it was the result of slow economic change.

Genghis Khan

Contact with richer neighbors gave Mongol chiefs opportunities for enrichment as mercenaries or raiders. Economic inequalities arose in a society where blood relationships and age had formerly settled every person's position. Prowess in war enabled leaders to build up followers in parallel with—and sometimes in defiance of—the old social order. They called this process "crane catching"—comparing it to caging valuable birds. Successful leaders enticed or forced rival groups into submission. The process spread to involve peoples who were not strictly Mongols, though the same name continued to be used—we use it still—for a confederation of different peoples, including many who spoke Turkic languages. In 1206, Temujin, the most dynamic leader, proclaimed himself ruler "of all those who live in felt tents"—staking a claim to a steppe-wide empire. He was acclaimed by a title of obscure meaning, perhaps signifying "Ocean-King" and therefore, by implication, king of everything the ocean encloses. The title is traditionally rendered in the Roman alphabet as "Genghis Khan."

Today, his memory is twisted between myths. When Mongolia was a communist state between 1921 and 1990, he was an almost unmentionable figure, inconsistent with the peace-loving image the communists tried to project. Now he is Mongolia's national hero. In his own day, he addressed different audiences with conflicting messages. To Muslims, he was an instrument of God, sent to punish them for their sins. To Chinese, he was a candidate for the mandate of heaven. To Mongols, he was a warrior; to monks and hermits, an ascetic. "Heaven is weary of the inordinate luxury of China," he declared. "I have the same rags and the same food as cowherds and grooms, and I treat the soldiers as my brothers."

Genghis Khan. Rashid al-Din (1247–1318) was a former Jewish rabbi, converted to Islam, who became the chief minister of the Mongol rulers of what is now Iran. His Compendium of Chronicles was propaganda that depicted Mongol rulers in Persian style. This is the image of Genghis Khan his successors liked to project—a lone, simple tent-dweller who was the arbitrator and lawgiver to petitioners from many nations. *Bibliotheque Nationale, Paris, France/The Bridgeman Art Library*

The violence endemic in the steppes now turned outward to challenge neighboring civilizations. Historians have been tempted to speculate about the reasons. One explanation is environmental. Temperatures in the steppe fell. People farther west on the Russian plains complained that a cold spell in the early thirteenth century caused crops to fail. So declining pastures might have driven the Mongols to expand from the steppes. Population in the region seems to have been relatively high, and the pastoral way of life demands large amounts of grazing land to feed relatively few people. So perhaps the Mongol outthrust was a consequence of having more mouths to feed. Yet the Mongols were doing what steppelanders had always sought to do: dominate and exploit sedentary peoples. The difference was that they did it with greater ambition and efficiency than their predecessors.

Genghis Khan enforced or induced unity over almost the entire steppeland. A single ideology came to animate, or perhaps reflect, his program: the God-given right of the Mongols to conquer the world. Mongol-inspired sources constantly insist on an analogy between the overarching unity of the sky and God's evident desire for the Earth to echo that unity through submission to one ruler.

This imperial vision probably grew gradually, from raiding, ransoming, and tribute gathering, to constructing an empire. Tradition alleges a turning point. When one of his generals proposed to exterminate 10 million Chinese subjects and convert their fields into pasture for Mongol herds, Genghis Khan realized that he could profit more by sparing the peasants and taxing them to the tune of 500,000 ounces of silver, 400,000 sacks of grain, and 80,000 bolts of silk a year. Genghis Khan's initially limited ambitions are clear from the oath Mongol chiefs took at his election: "If you will be our khan, we will go as your vanguard against the multitude of your enemies. All the beautiful girls and married women that we capture and all the fine horses we will bring to you." The khan acquired an unequaled reputation for lust and bloodlust. "My greatest joy," he was remembered for saying, "is to shed my enemies' blood, wring tears from their womenfolk and take their daughters for bedding." Even after he had introduced more constructive policies, terror remained an instrument of empire. Mongol sieges routinely culminated in massacre.

Wherever Mongol armies went, their reputation preceded them. Armenian sources warned Westerners of the approach of the "precursors of Antichrist who rush with joy to carnage as if to a wedding feast or orgy." Matthew Paris, the thirteenth-century English monk who, in his day, probably knew as much about the rest of the world as any of his countrymen, summed up the Mongols' image: "They are inhuman and beastly, rather monsters than men . . . ravaging and slaughtering, striking everyone with terror and with incomparable horror."

The Mongol conquests reached farther and lasted longer than those of any previous nomad empire. At its fullest extent the empire stretched from the Volga River to the Pacific, encompassing the whole of Russia, Persia, China, the Silk Roads, and the steppes. It was the largest empire the world had seen.

Efforts to explain this success appeal to Genghis Khan's military genius, the effectiveness of the Mongols' curved bows and inventive tactics, the demoralizing impact of their ruthless practices. Of course, they had the usual steppelander advantages of superior horsemanship and unrivaled mobility. It is likely that they succeeded, in part, through sheer numbers. Though we call it a Mongol army, Genghis Khan's was the widest alliance of steppelander peoples ever. And it is probable—though the sources are not good enough for certainty—that, relatively speaking, the steppeland was more populous in his day than ever before.

Above all, the Mongols were exceptionally adaptable warmongers. They triumphed not only in cavalry country, but also in environments where previous steppelander armies had failed, pressing into service huge forces of foot soldiers, mobilizing complex logistical support, organizing siege trains and fleets, and appropriating the full potential of sedentary economies to finance further wars. The mountains of Georgia could not stop them. Nor could the rice paddies and rivers of southern China, where the Mongols destroyed the Song dynasty in the 1270s. Toward the end of the century, when another supreme khan wanted to conquer Java and Japan, they were even willing to take to the sea.

The Mongol Empire was also remarkable, by steppelander standards, for longevity. As his career progressed, Genghis Khan became a visionary lawgiver, a patron of letters, an architect of enduring empire. Gradually, a code took shape, regulating hunting, army discipline, behavior at feasts, and social relationships, with death the penalty for murder, serious theft, conspiracy, adultery, sodomy, and witchcraft. Initially, the khan relied on Uighurs (see Chapter 9) for his administrators and ordered the adoption of the Uighur script for the Mongols' language. But he recruited as and where he conquered, without favoritism for any community or creed. His closest ministers included Muslims, Christians, and Buddhists.

In 1219, a Chinese Daoist sage, Changchun, answered the khan's call for wise experts. At the age of 71, he undertook an arduous three-year journey from China to meet the khan at the foot of the Hindu Kush mountains. There were sacrifices of principle Changchun would not make. He would not travel with recruits for the imperial harem, or venture into the steppe, "a land where vegetables were unavailable." Yet he crossed the Gobi Desert, climbed mountains, and braved wildernesses where his escort smeared their horses with blood to ward off demons. Changchun's meeting with the khan was disappointing. The question the conqueror was most eager to put was not about the art of government, but about a potion to confer longevity on himself.

The Mongol Steppe

Still, many lettered and experienced officials from conquered states took service at the khan's court. The result was an exceptional, though short-lived, era in steppeland history: the **Mongol peace**. A European, who witnessed it in the 1240s, described it to reproach his fellow Christians: "The Mongols are the most obedient people in the world with regard to their leaders, more so even than our own clergy to their superiors. . . . There are no wranglings among them, no disputes or murders." This was obviously exaggerated, but Mongol rule did make the steppeland safe for outsiders. This was new. A previously inaccessible road through the steppes opened across Eurasia north of the Silk Road. The Mongols became its highway police. Teams of Mongol horses, for instance, took the pope's ambassador, John of Piano Carpini, 3,000 miles in 106 days in 1246, an exceptionally fast pace for the time (see Map 13.1).

William of Rubruck, a Franciscan envoy, recorded vividly his mission to Mongke Khan, Genghis Khan's grandson, in 1253. After taking leave of the king of France, who hoped for an alliance with the Mongols against the Muslims, William crossed the Black Sea in May and set out across the steppe by wagon, bound for Karakorum, the new city in Mongolia where the khan held court. By November, he was in Transoxiana, "famished, thirsty, frozen, and exhausted." In December, he was in the dreaded Altai Shan, the mountain barrier that guarded the road to Karakorum. Here he "chanted the creed, among dreadful crags, to put the demons to flight." At last, on Palm Sunday, 1254, he entered the Mongol capital.

William always insisted that he was a simple missionary, but he was treated as an ambassador and behaved like a spy. Little useful intelligence escaped him. But he also showed interest in the culture he tried unsuccessfully to convert to Christianity. His description of a Mongol tent dwelling still holds good. The layout, social space, and way of life that took place in the tents William saw have not changed much since his day. A frame of interlaced branches stretched between supports made of branches, converging at the top. The covering was of white felt, "and they decorate the felt with various fine designs." Up to 22 oxen hauled these tent houses on wagons 20 feet broad.

Each wife of the master of the household had her own tent, where the master had a bench facing the entrance. In an inversion of Chinese rules of precedence, the women sat on the east side, the men to the right of the master, who sat at the north end. Ancestral spirits resided in felt bags arrayed around the walls. One each hung over the

Map 13.1 European Travelers of the Mongol Roads, 1245–1295

John of Piano Carpini 1245–1247 and
William of Rubruck 1253–1254

Marco Polo 1271–1275

Marco Polo 1275–1295

Khanate of the Golden Horde

Il-Khanate

Chagatai Khanate

Empire of the Great Khan

Silk Road

heads of master and mistress, with a guardian image between them. Others hung on the women's and men's sides of the tent, adorned with the udders of a cow and a mare, symbols of the sources of life for people who relied on dairy products for their diet. The household would gather to drink in the tent of the chosen wife of the night. "I should have drawn everything for you," William assured his readers, "had I known how to draw."

Shamans' trances released the spirits from the bags that held them. Frenzied drumming, dancing, and drinking induced the shamans' ecstasies. The power of speaking with the ancestors' voices gave **shamans** enormous authority in Mongol decision making, including the opportunity to interfere in making and unmaking khans. This was a point William missed. The Mongols leaders' interest in foreign religions, and their investment in the cult of heaven, were, in part at least, strategies to offset the power of the native priests.

Outside the tent, William vividly captured the nature of the terrain—so smooth and flat that one woman could pilot 30 wagons, linked by trailing ropes. He described a way of life that reflected steppeland ecology. The Mongols had mixed flocks of various kinds of sheep and cattle. Mixed pastoralism is essential in an environment in which no other source of food is available. Different species have different cycles of lactation and fertility. Variety, therefore, ensures a reliable food supply.

The horse was the dominant partner of life on the steppe. Mare's milk was the Mongols' summer food. By drawing blood from living horses, Mongols on campaign could refresh themselves without significantly slowing the herds. This was the basis of their reputation for blood-sucking savagery among their sedentary neighbors. They made, said William, "very fine shoes from the hind part of a horse's hide." Fermented mare's milk was the favorite intoxicating drink. The Mongols revered drunkenness and hallowed it by rites: offerings sprinkled over the bags of ancestral spirits, or poured out toward the quarters of the globe. Challenges to drinking bouts were a nightly entertainment. To the accompaniment of singing and clapping, the victim would be seized by the ears, with a vigorous tug "to make him open his gullet."

William related in detail his conversations with the habitually drunken Möngke Khan. Despite the khan's bluster and self-righteousness, the conversations revealed some of the qualities that made the Mongols of his era great: tolerance, adaptability, and respect for tradition. "We Mongols believe," Möngke said, "that there is but one God, in Whom we live and in Whom we die, and towards him we have an upright heart." Spreading his hand, he added, "But just as God has given different fingers to the hand, so He has given different religions to people." Later in the thirteenth century, Kubilai Khan, another of Genghis Khan's grandsons, expressed himself to the Venetian traveler, Marco Polo, in similar terms. So this was genuinely a Mongol saying.

The Mongol World beyond the Steppes: The Silk Roads, China, Persia, and Russia

The steppeland route was ideal for horseborne travelers. Trading caravans, however, favored the traditional **Silk Roads**, which crossed Eurasia to the south of the steppe through the Taklamakan Desert. These routes had developed over centuries because high mountains protected them from steppeland raiders. But they had never been secure before the Mongol peace. The new security boosted the amount of traffic the roads carried. Mongol partiality for merchants also helped. Mongols encouraged Chinese trade, uninhibited by any of the traditional Confucian prejudices against commerce as an ignoble occupation held by the Chinese elite. In 1299, after the Mongol Empire had been divided among several rulers, a Persian merchant was made the ambassador of the Supreme Khan to the court of the subordinate Mongol **Il-khan** in Persia—an elevation unthinkable under a native Chinese dynasty, which would have reserved such a post for an official educated in the Confucian classics. The khans gave low-cost loans to Chinese trading companies. Chinese goods—and with them, patterns and styles—flowed to Persian markets as never before. Chinese arts, under Mongol patronage, became more open to foreign influences.

Yet geography still made the Silk Roads hard to travel. Marco Polo, as a young Venetian who accompanied his father and uncle on a trading mission to Mongol-ruled China in the early 1270s, reported that "they were hard put to it to complete the journey in three and a half years." The Taklamakan Desert, whose modest water sources could not sustain many more than 50 men at a time with their beasts, was the great obstacle. Though there might be an occasional salt-marsh oasis or unreliable river, it was normal to go for 30 days without finding water. But, the worst danger was getting lost—"lured from the path by demon-spirits." As a fourteenth-century painter at Persia's Mongol court imagined them, the demons were black, athletic, and ruthless, waving dismembered limbs of horses as they danced.

A fourteenth-century guide included tips for Italian merchants who headed for East Asia to extend the reach of the commerce of their cities. At the port of Tana, on the Black Sea, you should furnish yourself with a good guide, regardless of expense. "And if the merchant likes to take a woman with him from Tana, he can do so." On departure from Tana, 25 days' supply of flour and salt fish were needed—"other things you will find in

The Silk Roads. Cresques Abraham was the finest mapmaker of his day. He painted this image of a caravan on the Silk Roads in the late 1370s or early 1380s in an atlas probably commissioned for the king of France. By that date, the Mongols no longer controlled the whole of the route, though the lances of an armed escort, presumably of Mongols, are visible behind the merchants. The caption says the caravan is bound for China, but it is heading in the opposite direction.
The Art Archive/Bibliotheque Nationale, Paris

sufficiency and especially meat." The road was "safe by day and night," protected by Mongol police. But it was important to take a close relative for company. Otherwise, should a merchant die, his property would be forfeit. The text specified rates of exchange at each stop and recommended suitable conveyances for each stage of the journey: oxcart or horse-drawn wagon to the city of Astrakhan where the Don River runs into the Caspian Sea, depending on how fast the traveler wanted to go and how much he wanted to pay. Thereafter, camel train or pack mule was best, until you arrived at the river system of China. Silver was the currency of the road, but the Chinese authorities would exchange it for paper money, which—Westerners were assured—they could use throughout China.

After the deserts, the next obstacles were the mountains on their rims. The Tian Shan, which screens the Taklamakan Desert, is 1,800 miles long, up to 300 miles wide, up to 24,000 feet high, and punctuated by deep chasms. Farther north, the Altai Mountains guard the Mongolian heartlands. "Before the days of the Mongols," wrote the bishop of the missionary diocese the Franciscans had established in China, "nobody believed that the Earth was habitable beyond these mountains . . . but by God's leave and wonderful exertion the Mongols crossed them, and . . . so did I."

Europeans frequently made the journey to China. That reflects the balance of wealth and power at the time. China was rich and productive, Europe a needy backwater. We know of only one subject of the Chinese emperor who found it worthwhile to make the journey in the opposite direction. Rabban Bar Sauma was a Christian who set out from China on a pilgrimage to Jerusalem. He got as far as Maragha in what is now Azerbaijan, the intellectual capital of the western Mongol world, reputedly with a library of 400,000 books and a new astronomical observatory. Then in 1286, he was appointed the Mongols' ambassador to the kingdoms of the Christian West, to negotiate an alliance against Muslim Egypt.

When he got to Rome, Bar Sauma was accorded a signal honor: reception by the cardinals who had assembled to elect a pope. In Paris, he recognized the university there as an intellectual powerhouse reminiscent of Maragha, with schools of mathematics, astronomy, medicine, and philosophy. Persian was the only language in which Bar Sauma could communicate with Western interpreters. He mistook diplomatic evasions for assent and vague expressions of Christian fellowship for doctrinal agreement. But that he completed the journey at all shows how the Mongols made it possible to cross Eurasia.

China

The Mongols never ran their dominions as a centralized state. Three main areas of conquest beyond the steppeland—in China, Persia, and Russia— were added after Genghis Khan's death. All were exploited in different ways, specific to the Mongols' needs and the peculiarities of each region.

The conquest of Song China was long and difficult for two reasons. It was a more powerful state than any the Mongols faced elsewhere, and it was highly defensible: its armies could maneuver on interior lines of communication, and its rice paddies made it difficult for Mongol horsemen to maneuver. But, fueled by resources from the Mongols' other conquests, and pursued with tenacity, the conquest unfolded relentlessly bit by bit. Letters from the Chinese court seeped desperation as the Mongols closed in for the kill. In 1274, the Chinese empress mother, Xie Qiao, reflected on where the blame lay:

> The empire's descent into peril is due, I regret, to the instability of our moral virtue. . . . The sound of woeful lament reverberated through the countryside, yet we failed to investigate. The pall of hunger and cold enveloped the armed forces, yet we failed to console.

Unlike previous steppelander invaders of China, the Mongols spared no resources to pursue all-out victory and hired the troops and equipment needed to subdue a country of cities, rice paddies, and rivers. Clearly, the size of the Mongols' existing empire helped. Persian

Kubilai Khan. Liu Guandao was Kubilai Khan's favorite painter. So we can be fairly sure that this is how the khan would like to be remembered: not just in the traditional inert Chinese pose (which Liu also painted), but also active, dressed and horsed like a Mongol ruler, engaged in the hunt. A woman, presumably his influential consort, Chabi, is at his side. The blank silk background evokes the featurelessness of the steppe, while also highlighting the human figures. *National Palace Museum, Taipei, Taiwan/The Bridgeman Art Library*

engineers built the siege engines that helped overcome southern Chinese cities. The last battle was at Changzhao in 1275. The Chinese poet Yi Tinggao was there, "smelling the acrid dust of the field," spying "the green irridescence of the dead." The human misery could be measured in the grief-stricken literature that survives: the suicide notes, the cries of longing for loved ones who disappeared in the chaos, massacred or enslaved. Years later, Ni Bozhuang, bailiff of a Daoist monastery, recalled the loss of his wife: "I still do not know if you were taken because of your beauty, or if, surrounded by horses, you can still buy cosmetics." In 1276, with his advisers fleeing and his mother packed for flight, the young Song emperor wrote his abdication letter to the Mongol khan: "The **Mandate of Heaven** having shifted, your Servant chooses to change with it,. . . yet my heart is full of emotions and these cannot countenance the prospect of the abrupt annihilation of the . . . altars of my ancestors. Whether they be misguidedly abandoned or specially preserved intact rests solely with the revitalized moral virtue you bring to the throne."

For the Mongols, the conquest of China was a logical continuation of the policies of Genghis Khan and a stage in fulfilling the destiny of world conquest heaven supposedly envisaged. But it was also the personal project and passion of Kubilai Khan (1214–1294), Genghis's grandson, who became so immersed in China that he never asserted his supremacy against those Mongol leaders in the extreme west of the Mongol world who resisted his claims. Some of his Chinese subjects resented Kubilai's foreign ways: the libations of fermented mare's milk with which he honored his gods, his barbarous banquets of meat, the officials he chose with great freedom from outside the Confucian elite and even from outside China. Marco Polo reported that all the Chinese "hated the government of the Great Khan, because he set over them steppelanders, most of whom were Muslims, and . . . it made them feel no more than slaves." In this respect, the khan broke with Chinese tradition, which was to confine administrative positions to a meritocracy, whose members were selected by examination in the Confucian classics. Kubilai showed his reverence for Confucius by building a shrine in his honor, but he needed to recruit, as Genghis Khan had, from the full range of talent the Mongol Empire supplied.

Kubilai remained a Mongol khan. In some respects, he flouted Chinese conventions. He showed traditional steppelander respect for the abilities of women, giving them court posts and, in one case, a provincial governorship. His wife, Chabi, was one of his closest political advisers. He introduced a separate tier of administration for Mongols, who became a privileged minority in China, ruled by their own laws, and resented for it by most Chinese. In defiance of Confucian teachings, Kubilai felt obliged to fulfill the vision of world conquest he inherited from Genghis Khan. But beyond China, he registered only fleeting success. In Java, the Mongols replaced one native prince with another, without making permanent gains. In Vietnam, the Mongols were only able to levy tribute at a rate too low to meet the cost of their campaigns there. So-called *kamikaze* winds—divine typhoons that wrecked the Mongol fleets—drove Kubilai's armies back from Japan.

While upholding Mongol traditions, Kubilai also sought, emphatically, to be a Chinese emperor who performed the due rites, dressed in the Chinese manner, learned the language, patronized the arts, protected the traditions, and promoted the interests of his Chinese subjects. Marco Polo, who seems to have served him as a sort of professional storyteller, called him "the most powerful master of men, lands, and treasures there has been in the world from the time of Adam until today."

Persia

In Persia, meanwhile, the Mongol rulers were like chameleons, adopting the tenets of the culture they conquered. But, as in China, they were anxious to maintain a distinct identity and preserve their own traditions. The court tended to stay in the north, where there was grazing for the kinds of herds their followers brought with them from the steppe. The Il-khans—"subordinate rulers," so called in deference to Kubilai Khan's nominal superiority—retained nomadic habits, migrating every summer and winter to new camps with palatial tents. In southern Iran and Iraq, the Il-khans tended to entrust power to local dynasties, securing their loyalty by marriages with the ruling family or court nobility. In effect, this gave them hostages for the good conduct of provincial rulers.

Eventually in 1295, the Il-khans adopted Islam, after flirtations with Christianity and Buddhism. This marked an important departure from the tradition of religious pluralism Genghis Khan had begun and Kubilai upheld. From the moment the Il-khan Ghazan (r. 1295–1304) declared his conversion to Islam, the state began to take on a militantly religious character, excluding the Christians, Zoroastrians, Buddhists, and Jews formerly admitted to the khan's service. Moreover, for a time, one Il-khan embraced Shiite doctrines (see Chapter 9) most Muslims rejected: that Muhammad's authority descended via his nephew Ali; that a divinely selected leader or imam would perfect the Prophet's message; and that, in the meantime, the clergy had the right to interpret Islam. The Il-khan's option helped ensure that Persia would be an exceptional region in the Muslim world, with a large Shiite constituency.

The religious art of the Il-khanate was unorthodox according to Muslim standards, full of human figures, especially those of Muhammad and Ali, whose images were never portrayed in the rest of the Muslim world. Persian painters even copied Christian nativity scenes to produce versions of the Prophet's birth. The Il-khans' Persia, however, was not isolated from neighboring states. On the contrary, as was usual in the Mongol world, the presence of rulers descended from Genghis Khan promoted trans-Eurasian contacts and exchanges of goods, personnel, and ideas. Persia supplied China, for instance, with engineers, astronomers, and mathematicians, while Persia received Chinese porcelain and paper money, which, however, did not take root in Persia before the twentieth century. Chinese designs influenced Persian weavers, and Chinese dragons appeared on the tiles with which Persian buildings of the time were decorated. Mongol rule ended in Persia in 1343 when the last Il-khan died without an heir.

Russia

Meanwhile, the Mongols who remained in their Central Asian heartlands continued their traditional way of life. So did those who formed the elite in the remaining areas the heirs of Genghis Khan inherited: in

Turkestan and Kashgaria in Central Asia, and the steppes of the lower Volga River. From the last of these areas, where the Mongols were known as the Golden Horde, they exercised overlordship over Russia, where they practiced a kind of imperialism different from those in China and Persia. The Mongols left the Christian Russian principalities and city-states to run their own affairs. But their rulers had to receive charters from the khan's court at Saray on the lower Volga, where they had to make regular appearances, loaded with tribute and subject to ritual humiliations. The population had to pay taxes directly to Mongol-appointed tax gatherers—though as time went on, the Mongols assigned the tax gathering to native Russian princes and civic authorities.

The Russians tolerated this situation—albeit unhappily, and with many revolts—partly because the Mongols intimidated them by terror. When the Mongols took the great city of Kiev in 1240, it was said, they left only 200 houses standing and strewed the fields "with countless heads and bones of the dead." Partly, however, the Russians were responding to a milder Mongol policy. In most of Russia, the invaders came to exploit rather than to destroy. According to one chronicler, the Mongols spared Russia's peasants to ensure that farming would continue. Ryazan, a Russian principality on the Volga, southeast of Moscow, seems to have borne the brunt of the Mongol invasion. Yet there, if the local chronicle can be believed, "the pious Grand Prince Ingvary Ingvarevitch sat on his father's throne and renewed the land and built churches and monasteries and consoled newcomers and gathered together the people. And there was joy among the Christians whom God had saved from the godless and impious khan." Many cities escaped lightly by capitulating at once. Novgorod, that hugely rich city (see Chapter 11), which the Mongols might have coveted, they bypassed altogether.

Moreover, the Russian princes were even more fearful of enemies to the west, where the Swedes, Poles, and Lithuanians had constructed strong, unitary monarchies, capable of sweeping the princes away if they ever succeed in expanding into Russian territory. Equally menacing were groups of mainly German adventurers, organized into crusading "orders" of warriors, such as the Teutonic Knights and the Brothers of the Sword, who took monastic-style vows but dedicated themselves to waging holy war against pagans and heretics. In practice, these orders were self-enriching companies of professional fighters, who built up territorial domains along the Baltic coast by conquest. In campaigns between 1242 and 1245, Russian coalitions fought off invaders from the west, but they could not sustain war on two fronts. The experience made them submissive to the Mongols.

The Limits of Conquest:
Mamluk Egypt and Muslim India

Mamluk Egypt

In the 1200s, Egypt was in chaos because of rebellions by pastoralists from the southern desert and revolt by the **Mamluks,** the slaves who formed the elite fighting force. It seems counterintuitive to arm slaves. But for most of the thirteenth century, the policy worked well for Saladin's heirs, who had ruled Egypt since 1192. The rulers handpicked their slave army. The slaves came overwhelmingly from Turkic peoples that Mongol rebels displaced or captured and sold. These slaves had nowhere else to go and no future except in the Egyptian sultan's service. They were acquired young. They trained in barracks, which became their substitutes for families and the source of their pride and strong sense of comradeship. They seemed, from the ruler's point of view, ideally reliable: a dependent class. Increasingly, however, the Mamluks came to know their own strength. In the 1250s, they rebelled "like an unleashed torrent." Their own propaganda cites the sultan's failure to reward them fairly for their services and their outrage at the promotion of a black slave to one of the highest offices in the court.

While contending with internal enemies, the rebels perceived the Mongols as a greater threat and turned to face them. In September 1260, they turned back the Mongol armies at one of the decisive battles of the world at Ain Jalut in Syria. It was the first serious reversal the Mongols had experienced since Genghis Khan united them. And it gave the Mamluk commander, Baybars, the chance to take over Egypt and Syria. He boasted that he could play polo in Cairo and Damascus within the space of a single week. The Mamluks mopped up the last small crusader states on the coast of Syria and Palestine between 1268 and 1291. In combination with the effects of the internal politics of the Mongol world, which inhibited armies from getting too far from the centers of power, the Mamluk victory kept the Mongols out of Africa.

Mamluk victory also marked a further stage in the Islamization of Africa. The Mamluks levied tribute on the Christian kingdoms of Nubia. Then, in the next century, they imposed Islam there. Cairo became a stopping place on the pilgrimage route to Mecca for Muslim kings and dignitaries from West Africa. Islam percolated through the region of Lake Chad and into Hausaland in what is today Nigeria.

Muslim India: The Delhi Sultanate

After the disruptions caused by the violent Turkic migrations of the twelfth century, it took a long time for a state in the mold of Mahmud's to reemerge in Ghazna (see Chapter 12). By the 1190s, however, a Muslim

Turkic dynasty and people, the Ghurids, had resumed the habit of raiding into Hindu India, where they levied tribute and scattered garrisons. One of their most far-flung outposts—and therefore one of the strongest—was at the city of Delhi in northern India. The adventurer Iltutmish took command there in 1211. He was a former slave who had risen to general and received his freedom from his Ghurid masters. He avoided war with Hindus—which was, in essence, his job—in favor of building up his own resources. In 1216, he effectively declared himself independent. Over the next 12 years, he played the power game with skill, exploiting the rivalries of Muslim commanders to construct a state from the Indus River to the Bay of Bengal. Meanwhile, the effects of the Mongol conquests on Central Asia protected this new realm, which became known as the Sultanate of Delhi, against outside attack (see Map 13.2). As one of the early chroniclers of the sultanate said, "Rulers and governors, . . . and many administrators and notables came to Iltutmish's court from fear of the slaughter and terror of the accursed Mongol, Genghis Khan."

The sultanate had no consistent form of administration. In most of the more remote territories, the Delhi sultan was an overlord, mediating between small, autonomous states, many of which Hindus ruled. Bengal was exceptional—a forest frontier, in which governors tried to promote Muslim settlement by making land grants to pioneering holy men and religious communities. But a core of lands was the sultan's personal property, exploited to benefit his treasury and run by administrators he appointed. Lands the sultan granted in exchange for military service ringed this core. At great oath-taking ceremonies, the aristocracy—effectively freelance warriors and local rulers whom it was difficult or impossible for the sultan to dismiss—would make emotional but often short-lived declarations of loyalty.

As an ex-slave, Iltutmish was no respecter of conventional ideas of hierarchy. Denouncing his sons for incompetence, he chose his daughter, Radiyya, as his successor in 1236. In the steppes, women often handled important jobs. In the Islamic world, a woman ruler was a challenge to what was thought to be the natural order of the world. When, in 1250, a little before the Mamluks took over in Egypt, a woman had seized the throne there and applied to Baghdad for legitimation by the caliph, he is supposed to have replied that he could supply capable men, if no more existed in Egypt. Radiyya had to contend both with a brother who briefly ousted her—she had him put to death—and, what was harder, with male mistrust. Some of her coins emphasize claims to unique feminine virtues as "pillar of women." Others have modest inscriptions, in which all the glorious epithets are reserved for her father and the caliph in Baghdad. Her best strategy was to behave like a man. She dressed in male clothing, refused to cover her face, and according to a slightly late source, "mounted horse like

Delhi Sultanate 1236

area subject to sporadic influence
by Delhi Sultanate

border of Ghaznavid Empire 1186

Map 13.2 The Delhi Sultanate

men, armed with bow and quiver." To conventional minds, these were provocations. She was ousted on grounds that—true or false—reflect male prejudices about female behavior. Accused of taking a black slave as a lover, she was deposed in 1240 in favor of a brother. Her real offense was self-assertion. Those modest coin inscriptions suggest that power brokers in the army and the court were willing to accept her, but only as a figure-head representative of her father, not as an active leader of men.

The sultanate had to cope not only with its turbulent elite, but with Hindu subjects and neighbors. Dominion by any state over the entire

Indian subcontinent remained, at best, a dream. Frontier expansion was slow. **Deforestation** was an act of state, because, as a Muslim writer of the fourteenth century complained, "the infidels live in these forests, which for them are as good as city walls . . . so that they cannot be overcome except by strong armies of men who go into these forests and cut down those reeds." In Bengal, the eastward shift of the Ganges River made Islamization easier. Charismatic **Sufis,** with tax-free grants of forest land for mosques and shrines, led the way.

For most of the thirteenth century, the Mongol menace overshadowed the sultanate. The internal politics of the dynasty of Genghis Khan caused dissensions and hesitancies that protected Delhi. Mongol dynastic disputes cut short periodic invasions. Moreover, a buffer state that dissident Mongols created in Delhi's western territories diminished the sultanate but also absorbed most of the khans' attacks. In the 1290s, however, the buffer collapsed. By what writers in Delhi considered a miracle, the subsequent Mongol attacks failed, faltered, or were driven off.

Europe

With the scare the Mongol invasions caused and the loss of the last crusader states in Syria to the Mamluks, Latin Christendom looked vulnerable. Attempts were made to revitalize the crusading movement—especially by King Louis IX of France (r. 1226–1270), who became a model monarch for the Western world. But they all failed. A further reversal was the loss of Constantinople by its Latin rulers to a Byzantine revival. The Mongols destroyed or dominated most of the successor states that claimed Byzantium's legacy, but at the city of Nicaea in western Anatolia, rulers who continued to call themselves "Roman emperors" maintained the court rituals and art of Byzantine greatness. In 1261, they recaptured the old capital from the crusaders "after many failures," as Emperor Michael VIII, admitted, "because God wished us to know that the possession of the city was a grace dependent on his bounty."

Nevertheless, Latin Christendom grew on other fronts, extending the frontier deep into formerly pagan worlds along the Baltic in Livonia, Estonia, Prussia, and Finland. Between the 1220s and the 1260s, Christian kingdoms seized most of the Mediterranean seaboard of Spain and the Balearic Islands from the hands of Muslim rulers. Here, the existing economy and population were not much disturbed, but in Atlantic-side Spain conquerors expelled Muslims, creating a sort of Iberian Wild West of sparse settlements, tough frontiersmen, and vast cattle and sheep ranches. Meanwhile, traders of the western Mediterranean increased their commerce with northern Europe along the coasts the Spaniards conquered, through the Strait of Gibraltar.

Toward the end of the thirteenth century, as they became accustomed to Atlantic sailing conditions, some of them began to think of exploring the ocean for new routes and resources. In 1291, an expedition set off from the Italian city of Genoa to find "the regions of India by way of the ocean." The voyagers were never heard of again, but their voyage marked the beginning of a long, faltering effort by maritime communities of western Europe to exploit the ocean at their feet.

The big new opportunities, however, lay to the east, from which transforming technologies reached Europe. Paper was a Chinese invention that had already reached the West through Arab intermediaries, but only in the thirteenth century was it manufactured in Europe on a large scale. European maritime technology—a prerequisite of the prosperity borne by long-range trade and of the reach of most long-range imperialism—was especially primitive by non-European standards up to this time. Though the compass was first recorded in Europe in about 1190, the West had as yet no maritime charts. The earliest reference to such a device dates only from 1270. Gunpowder and the blast furnace were among the magical-seeming technologies that first reached Europe from China in the thirteenth and fourteenth centuries.

Meanwhile, with consequences for the future that can hardly be overestimated, Western science grew more **empirical**, more committed to observation and experiment. The cosmos became measurable, portrayed between the dividers of Christ the geometer, like a ball of fluff trapped between tweezers. At the University of Paris, which the Rabban Bar Sauma so admired, scholars cultivated a genuinely scientific way of understanding the world. The work of encyclopedists arrayed in precise categories, everything known by experience or report. The greatest intellect of the age, Thomas Aquinas (1225–1274), compiled marvelously comprehensive schemes of faith and secular knowledge. In the third quarter of the thirteenth century, Parisian teachers, of whom the most insistent was Siger of Brabant, pointed out that the doctrines of the church on the creation and the nature of the soul conflicted with classical philosophy and empirical evidence. "Every disputable question," they argued, "must be determined by rational arguments." Another professor, Roger Bacon, stated that excessive deference to authority—including ancestral wisdom, custom, and consensus—was a cause of ignorance. He insisted that scientific observations could help to validate holy writ and that medical experiments could increase knowledge and save life. He also claimed—citing the lenses with which Archimedes reputedly set fire to a Roman fleet during the siege of the Greek city of Syracuse in Sicily in 212 B.C.E.—that science could cow and convert infidels.

Bacon was a Franciscan friar, a follower of Francis of Assisi (1181–1226), and his enthusiasm for science seems to have owed something to Francis's doctrine that because the world made God manifest, it was worth observing. Francis was a witness and maker of the new European imagination. He was a rich man's son inspired by Jesus's advice. He renounced riches for a life of total dependence on God. In anyone less committed and charismatic, his behavior might have been considered insane or heretical. He launched his mission by stripping naked in the public square of his native city as a sign that he was throwing himself, unprotected, on God's mercy. He relied for sustenance on what people gave him. He attracted a following and modeled his followers' way of life on the way he thought Christ and the apostles lived, refusing to accept property, sharing the alms the brethren received.

The **Franciscans** became the spearhead of the church's mission to the poor and inspired other orders of friars—clergy who combined religious vows of poverty, chastity, and obedience with work in the world. In an age of urbanization, friars could establish bonds of sympathy with the rootless masses, who had lost the familiar companionship of rural parishes. Friars were also a valuable counterforce to heretics who denounced the church for worldliness. In his attitude toward nature, Francis was representative of his time. Against heretics who condemned the world as evil, he insisted on the goodness of God's creation, which was all "bright and beautiful." Even its conflicts and cruelties were there to elicit human love. He tried to enfold the whole of nature in love. He preached to ravens and called creatures, landscapes, sun, and moon his brothers and sisters, eventually welcoming "Sister Death." He communicated his sensibilities to his followers. As a result, Franciscans were prominent in scientific thinking in the West. Love of nature made them observe it more closely and keenly and scrutinize it for good uses.

Franciscans also became patrons of increasingly naturalistic art. The art they commissioned for their churches drew the onlooker into sacred spaces, as if in eyewitness of the lives of Jesus and the saints. The devotion of the rosary, introduced early in the thirteenth century, encouraged the faithful to imagine sacred mysteries, while praying, with the vividness of scenes of everyday life in mind, as if witnessed in person, looking at the world with eyes as unblinking as those of the new scientific thinkers. Considered from one point of view, the realism Western painting increasingly favored was a tribute to the enhanced prestige of the senses. To paint what one's eyes could see was to confer dignity on a subject not previously thought worthy of art. So art linked the science and piety of the age.

The revolutionary experiences of the West at the time—the technical progress, the innovations in art, the readjustment of notions of reality through the eyes of a new kind of science—were owed, in part, to influences transmitted along routes the Mongols maintained. None of this experimentation and imagination put Western science abreast of that of China, where observation and experiment had been continuous in scientific tradition since the first millennium B.C.E. In two technologies, however—key technologies, as they later proved to be, for their influence on world history—western Europe came to house the world's leading centers of development and production.

Francis of Assisi. Franciscan art patronage rewarded painters like Giotto, who were interested in creating vivid versions of sacred scenes in which the actors seemed real rather than abstract. Francis preached to the birds because humans failed to heed his message—but the image suggests, too, how the Franciscans promoted awareness of the natural world. Piety and science coincided in the observation of nature. *Canali Photobank*

The first was glassmaking. In the thirteenth century, demand for fine glassware leapt in the West because of the growing taste for using church windows made of stained glass to illuminate sacred stories and to exhibit glowingly the wonders of creation. Glassmakers adapted their skills to meet domestic demand for glass mirrors and optical lenses. These objects were not manufactured on a significant scale anywhere else in the world, though for centuries scholars writing in Arabic had known how to make them and use them as aids to scientific observation. Now Western savants could repeat the same experiments themselves and even improve on them.

Second, the West drew ahead in the technology of clockwork. Mechanical clocks had a long history in China and the Islamic world. But clockwork never caught on except in Europe, perhaps because it is too regular to match the movements of the heavens. It divides the day into arbitrary hours of equal length that do not match those of the sun. But this way of organizing life suited Western monasteries, where, apart from the prayers prescribed for the dawn and nightfall, the services of prayer were best arranged at regular intervals, independently of the sun.

For city churches in an age of urban growth, regular timekeeping was also convenient. Clockwork suited the rhythms of urban life. Civic authorities began to invest heavily in town clocks in the thirteenth and fourteenth centuries. This was the beginning of the still-familiar Western convention of an urban skyline dominated by the town hall clock tower.

The combination of lenses and clockwork mattered in the long run because eventually—not until the seventeenth century, when telescopes were combined with accurate chronometry—they gave Western astronomers an advantage over Muslim and Chinese competitors. This in turn gave Western scientists the respect of their counterparts and secured the patronage of rulers all over the world in societies interested in astronomy either for its own sake or—more often—because of astrology.

CHRONOLOGY	
1181–1226	Life of Francis of Assisi
1190	First European recorded reference to a compass
1206	Temujin proclaims himself khan
1211–1236	Reign of Iltutmish, sultan of Delhi
1225–1274	Life of Thomas Aquinas
1234	Mongols conquer Georgia
1241–1242	Mongol armies reach Elbe River, Germany
1253–1254	Mission of William of Rubruck to Mongolian court
1258	Mongols capture Baghdad, last caliph put to death
1260	Mamluks defeat Mongols at battle of Ain Jalut
1261	Byzantine Empire regains Constantinople
1268–1291	Mamluks overthrow last crusader states on coast of Palestine
1270	Earliest European reference to maritime charts
1271–1275	Marco Polo's first journey to China
1274, 1281	Failed Mongol attempts to invade Japan
1279	Mongol conquest of China completed
1286	Rabban Bar Sauma appointed Mongol ambassador to Christian West

Making Connections

TRADE AND TRANSPORTATION	TECHNOLOGY AND SCIENCE	POLITICS	RELIGION
Increased communication across Eurasia leads to introduction of Chinese and Arabic technology, medicine, and inventions	Imported inventions such as paper, magnetic compasses, gunpowder, and blast furnace combine with focus on empiricism	Christian kingdoms seize Muslim lands in Spain, Mediterranean islands; revival of Crusades, extension of frontier north to the Baltics, Finland, and Scandinavia	Francis and his religious order place new emphasis on observing nature, serving the poor, and renouncing wealth; increased emphasis on sacred mysteries
Increased transportation and trade links within Europe aided by new infrastructure (roads, canals); growth of towns; economic and political stability leads to larger towns and cities; more productive industry	Better maritime technology expands range of sea voyages; demand for elaborate church windows spurs glassmaking and innovation in glass lenses; clocks provide regularized timekeeping for monasteries and cities; availability of paper multiplies books and empowers states with a medium for their messages	Bigger, richer states with more scope to communicate and enforce commands; more church-state competition and conflict	Mendicants prominent in scientific thinking in West; spearhead Church's mission to poor in growing towns

IN PERSPECTIVE
The Uniqueness of the Mongols

Like many great revolutionaries, the Mongols started bloodily and became constructive. For 100 years after the initial horror of the Mongol
conquests, the steppe became a highway of fast communication, linking
the extremities of the landmass and helping transfer culture across two
continents. Without the Mongol peace, it is hard to imagine any of the

rest of world history working out as it did, for these were the roads that carried Chinese ideas and technology westward and opened up European minds to the vastness of the world. The importance of the Mongols' passage through world history does not stop at the frontiers of their empire. It resonated across Eurasia.

The Eurasian experience was unique. Why did nothing like it happen in Africa or the Americas? Cultural exchanges across the grasslands of prairie, pampa, and Sahel never spread far until the nineteenth century. None of those regions saw conquerors like the Mongols, able to unify the entire region and turn it into a causeway of civilizations, shuttling ideas and techniques across a continent.

In the Americas, geography was an inhibiting influence. The North American prairie is aligned on a north–south axis, across climatic zones, whereas the steppe stretches from east to west. Plants and animals can cross the steppe without encountering impenetrable environments. Seeds can survive the journey without perishing and without finding, at the end of the road, an environment too sunless or cold to thrive in. In North America, it took centuries longer to achieve comparable exchanges. As we have seen repeatedly—almost whenever the Americas have entered our story—transmissions of culture across latitudes are much harder to effect than those that occur within latitudes, which have relatively narrow boundaries, where climate and conditions are familiar.

Moreover, to function, an avenue of communications needs people at either end of it who want to be in touch. The Eurasian steppe was like a dumbbell, with densely populated zones and productive economies at either end of it. For people in Europe, Southwest Asia, and North Africa, access to the products of South, Southeast, and East Asia was highly desirable. For the suppliers of spices, drugs, fine textiles, and luxury products in the east, it was good to have customers who paid in silver. In the Americas, there was no chance to reproduce such relationships. The concentrations of wealth and population were in two regions—Mesoamerica and the Andes— that neither grasslands nor any other easily traveled routes linked. Though societies in other parts of the hemisphere drew lessons, models of life, technologies, and types of food from those areas, the results, as we have seen, were hard to sustain because communications between these areas and outlying regions were difficult to keep up. Without the horse—extinct in the Americas for 10,000 years—the chances of an imperial people arising in the prairie or the pampa to do the sort of job the Mongols did in Europe were virtually zero. (Much later, as we shall see in Chapter 21, when European invaders reintroduced the horse in the Americas in the 1500s, experiments in grassland imperialism by peoples such as the Sioux followed.)

In Africa, the constraints were different. The **Sahel** might have played a role similar to that of the steppes in Eurasian history. There was a viable corridor of communication between the Nile and Niger valleys. In theory, an imperial people might have been able to open communications across the continent between the civilizations of East Africa, which were in touch with the world of the Indian Ocean, and those of West Africa, which the trade routes of the Sahara linked to the Mediterranean. But it never happened. For long-range empire building, the Sahel was, paradoxically, too rich compared with the Eurasian steppe. The environment of the Sahel was more diverse. Agrarian or partly agrarian states had more opportunity to develop, obstructing the formation of a Sahel-wide empire. Although pastoral peoples of the western Sahel often built up powerful empires, they always tended to run into either or both of two problems. First, as we have seen, and shall see again, invaders from the desert always challenged and sometimes crushed them.

Second, while they lasted, the empires of the Sahel never reached east of the region of Lake Chad. Here states grew up, strong enough to resist conquest from outside, but not strong enough to expand to imperial dimensions themselves. The accounts of early Muslim visitors reviled the region for its "reed huts . . . not towns" and people clad only in loin cloths. But by the twelfth and thirteenth centuries, states like Kanem and Bornu commanded respect in Arab geography. Lakeshore floodplains for agriculture enriched them, together with the gold they obtained from selling their surplus millet. Around 1300, according to Arab sources, the region enclosed 12 "kingdoms."

The Mongols, after their initial bout of extreme destructiveness, brought peace and, in the wake of that peace, wealth and learning. But with increased travel, it was not only goods and ideas that circulated with increased freedom. The steppeland also became a highway to communicate disease. The Mongol peace lasted less than 150 years. The age of plague that was now about to begin would influence the history of Eurasia, and therefore of the world, for centuries.

PROBLEMS AND PARALLELS

1. How did the Mongols transform Eurasia? How did Mongol rule affect travel and trade along the Silk Roads? What was the Mongol peace?
2. How did Kubilai Khan blend Mongol and Chinese traditions? Why did the Russian princes grudgingly submit to Mongol rule? Why was the Il-khans' conversion to Shiite Islam in Persia so important?
3. Why did Egypt and India show such vitality in the thirteenth century?
4. How did the Franciscans influence medieval European art and science?
5. Why did geography hinder the rise of continent-wide empires in Africa and the Americas?

CHAPTER 14

The Revenge of Nature: Plague, Cold, and the Limits of Disaster in the Fourteenth Century

focus questions

1. How did the global climate change in the fourteenth century?
2. Which parts of the world suffered most and least from the onset of the age of plague?
3. What were the social and political effects of the plague in China, the Islamic world, and western Europe?
4. How did the absence of plague affect India, Southeast Asia, Japan, Mali, and the cultures of the Pacific?

"The people of Cairo are fond of pleasure and amusement," wrote Ibn Battuta, when he first visited the Egyptian city in 1325. Wanderlust had made this Muslim pilgrim from Morocco the world's most traveled man. Yet he had never seen a city so big. Cairo had—he was told—12,000 water carriers, 30,000 donkey-rental businesses, and 36,000 river craft transporting food and goods. Among sources of pleasure he noted were "boys and maids with lustrous eyes" and the gardens and buildings, "peerless in splendor." On his next visit, in 1348, plague devastated the city; corpses filled its streets. "I was told that . . . deaths there had risen to 21,000 a day. . . . All the sheikhs I had known were dead. May God Most High have mercy upon them!"

Ibn Battuta was witnessing the most devastating natural catastrophe ever to have hit Eurasia. The **Black Death** killed millions of people, disrupted states, and checked expansion. In a climate that was growing colder, Eurasia's densely populated zone contracted. The growth of trades and states slowed or stopped. Cultural transmissions across the landmass diminished. Isolation from the main routes of trade and travel suddenly became, in some respects, an advantage.

Among the hardest-hit societies were the most ambitious—those with the longest and most active records in challenging their environments. It was as if nature had struck back. Indeed, Muslim theologians argued that plague was a warning from God: "a martyrdom and a mercy," for Muslims, but "a punishment for an infidel." In China conventional wisdom understood natural disasters as examples of what historian Mark Elvin calls "moral meteorology"—the corrections of heaven, unleashed to restore the balance of nature disturbed by human wickedness.

Climate and microbes resist human power. The fourteenth century was exceptional because, in some parts of the world, climate change and disease coincided to menace or undermine human activities.

The best—or even, because of the evidence available, the only—way to approach the changes of the fourteenth century is to start in those parts of the northern hemisphere, especially in Eurasia and North Africa, where the effects of cold and plague combined. We can then turn to areas that escaped plagues, or escaped their worst consequences, in India, sub-Saharan Africa, Japan, and Southeast Asia. Finally, we shall turn to faraway and out-of-touch societies in and around the Pacific to appreciate how isolation—which usually retards change—acted as a form of quarantine against disease. As plagues affected some of the planet's previously most dynamic regions, other parts of the world leaped into the sight lines of global history.

Climate Change

Climate change is full of conflicting shifts. Three levels are detectable. At one level, ice ages, which periodically smother great parts of the globe, alternate with global warming, when some glacier-covered areas reemerge. We are between ice ages now. The fluctuations of the period this book covers have happened in a relatively warm era of the planet's history. Meanwhile, periods of a few hundred years of relative cold and warmth alternate within eras of global warming. But even within these periods, changes in winds and currents can reverse the overall trend, producing spells, lasting from 10 to 50 years or so, of warmer or cooler temperatures. Finally, there are sudden interruptions of normal conditions—occurring irregularly and unpredictably—when the distribution of atmospheric pressure is disturbed for unknown reasons. This produces the notorious **El Niño** effect in the tropics and the southern hemisphere (see Chapter 4). In Europe, reversals of normal patterns produce longer spells, often of a decade or so, of extremely cold weather.

Short-term fluctuations are sometimes traceable to particular causes. The middle of the second decade of the fourteenth century, for instance, was a cold period all over the Northern Hemisphere, probably because of a sudden, localized occurrence: the explosion of Indonesian volcanoes, pumping ash into the atmosphere and clouding the sun. But the fall in temperatures was not confined to a few exceptional years. It was part of a general, long-term trend.

Broadly speaking, global temperatures had been relatively warm since the tenth century, with much erosion of natural environments as people converted previously underexploited land for farming or grazing. Now a cool period—of fluctuating but relatively low temperatures—would last for about 500 years.

The cooling trend began in the Arctic in the thirteenth century. The ice cap crept south. Glaciers disrupted shipping. Mean annual temperatures in China, which had stayed above freezing from the seventh century to the eleventh, dipped below freezing from the thirteenth century until the late 1700s. Evidence of glacier growth suggests that North America, too, felt the cold in the fourteenth century. Other indicators for the same century include the persistence of pack ice in summer in the seas around Greenland and the disappearance of water-demanding plants from the hinterland of Lake Chad in Central Africa from about 1300 onward. This is important because glacier growth affects precipitation. When water ices over, less of it evaporates and falls as rain.

While temperatures were lower than previously in the early fourteenth century, it was not cold in any absolute sense. Nonetheless, the weather seemed hostile to people who had to endure it. The cold was, an English poet wrote, "a new kind of affliction, . . . not known for a thousand years. . . . No horror left us e'er so like a ghost." In England uplands were abandoned. Glaciers forced Norwegian farmers to retreat to lower altitudes.

In 1309–1310, wrote an English chronicler, "bread wrapped in straw or other covering froze and could not be eaten unless it was warmed." During the prolonged cold of 1315–1316, before the ice grew sufficiently to disrupt rainfall, heavy rains all over northern Europe destroyed the crops, inflicting famine. Grain "could not ripen," complained an English chronicler. A chronicler in Austria likened the rains to Noah's flood. During 1316, from May to October, cities in Belgium lost 5 or 10 percent of their population. Calamitous flooding and coastal erosion became common around the North Sea, culminating in the "Great Drowning" of 1362, when the sea swallowed vast areas of Holland, Denmark, and England. Far from the sea, cooling in the Northern Hemisphere brought droughts and famines. In Central Asia, the accumulated abundance that fueled Mongol conquests in the previous century seems to have run out. The Mongol world began to contract. According to official chronicles, China experienced exceptionally severe winters for 36 of the fourteenth century's 100 years. In partial consequence, famines struck some part of China in every year of the reign of the Shundi emperor (r. 1333–1368).

At about the same time, climate change seems to have helped to destroy an impressive regional system of agriculture and urban life deep in the North American interior, between the Gila and San Juan rivers and in the neighborhood of present-day Phoenix, Arizona. First the **Hohokam people**—as archaeologists called them—relocated from their scattered villages and sought closer collaboration in relatively few, dense settlements. At Paquimé, they regrouped in a city with all the traditional amenities of earlier indigenous civilizations: ball courts, carved facades for temples and palaces, wells and irrigation works, workshops for copper workers and jewelsmiths. There was even a macaw hatchery to produce the ornamental feathers the elite coveted. It was a splendid effort, but it was a response to stress. Every indicator shows severe population loss throughout the Southwest in the thirteenth and fourteenth centuries. By around 1400, even the new settlements were abandoned. Ruins remain. Casa Grande, in Pinal County, Arizona, leaves onlookers amazed at the ambition of the builders and clueless about what befell them. Some scholars have speculated that the conditions that crushed the Hohokam may also have driven migrants south to colonize central Mexico and found the state that later became the kernel of the Aztec world (see Chapter 15). But the only evidence for this is in later, untrustworthy legends.

The Coming of the Age of Plague

In Eurasia the cold spell coincided with the beginning of an age of plague. Starting in the 1320s, unprecedented bouts of pestilence culminated in the Black Death. Recurrences—less widespread and less intense—of similar or identical diseases remained frequent in Eurasia until the eighteenth century. The age of plague was so unusual and significant that we want to know what the disease was, where it came from, what caused it, and how much damage it did. All these questions are hard to answer.

Most attempts to write the history of disease have foundered on a false assumption: that we can recognize past visitations of identifiable diseases, known to modern medical science, from symptoms historical sources describe. For two reasons, this is an unrealistic expectation.

First, people in the past looked at disease with perceptions different from ours. The symptoms they spotted would not necessarily be those an observer today would note, nor would they use the same sort of language to describe them. Second, diseases themselves change. Many of the microorganisms that cause disease evolve fast because they reproduce rapidly and respond quickly to changing environments.

The plagues of the age of plague need not all have been visitations of a single disease. They may have included some diseases that today's medical handbooks identify. But the likelihood—stronger than a possibility—is that some diseases that devastated Eurasia in the age of plague were peculiar to that period. New pathogens are deadly because they are unfamiliar. When they strike, no one has built up immunity to them.

Of diseases now known to medical science, bubonic plague—not, perhaps, of the same variety we know today—most likely played a part in the age of plague. Bubonic plague is a rat-borne disease. When they bite, rats' fleas regurgitate the bacillus, ingested from rats' blood, into human victims. In cases of septicemic plague (a systemic, blood-poisoning disease), one of the first symptoms is generally death. Otherwise, swellings appear—small like Brazil nuts or big and ridged like grapefruit—over the neck and groin or behind the ears. Jitters, vomiting, dizziness, and pain might follow, often accompanied by an inability to tolerate light.

Fourteenth-century sources describe these symptoms, together with sudden fainting, before victims, as one observer explained, "almost sleeping and with a great stench eased into death." The trouble is that during the first hundred years of the age of plague, of all the sources that describe the symptoms, fewer than one in six lists symptoms of this kind. Moreover, almost everyone at the time was convinced that plague spread by infection or contagion. Rats—the normal agent for the spread of bubonic plague—play little part in the accounts in the sources. The black rat, culprit species in the transmission of bubonic plague, seems not to have existed at the time in plague-stricken Iceland and was rare or absent in other afflicted places. Finally, it seems most unlikely that frequent epidemics reported in China from the 1320s to the 1360s can have been bubonic plague in the form now familiar to us, which hit an unimmunized China in the late eighteenth century. The suddenness and virulence of these visitations suggest the arrival of a new and previously unexperienced pathogen. The Chinese, with their long experience in farming and animal domestication, enjoyed highly developed natural immunities to the familiar diseases that breed in farming environments.

Many accounts of the Black Death include a bewildering variety of symptoms that are not associated with bubonic plague: complications in the lungs, spitting blood, headaches, rapid breathing, discolored urine. The emphasis of some sources on lung disorders suggests a mixture of bubonic and pneumonic plague, which primarily attacks the lungs. To judge from other surviving descriptions, outbreaks of typhus, smallpox, various kinds of influenza, and hemorrhagic fevers coincided with some visitations of plague. In the Mediterranean, the plague usually struck in summer, while in northern Europe, autumn seems to have been the deadliest season. But, looked at as a whole, the plagues of the period had no seasonal pattern and no obvious connection with any particular weather systems or atmospheric conditions. This again points to the involvement of more than one pathogen.

Domestic animals were probably an essential part of the background—as carriers of disease, as a reservoir of infection, and even as sufferers. One of the curious features about the way some early plague victims described the disease is that they were sure that their domestic animals suffered from it, just as they did themselves. A chronicler in Italy listed "dogs, cats, chickens, oxen, donkeys, and sheep" among the sufferers, with the same symptoms as human victims, including swellings in the groin and armpits. At Salona on the Adriatic coast, the Black Death's first victims were "horses, oxen, sheep, and goats." The Egyptian chronicler, al-Maqrizi, who was among the most observant and thoughtful witnesses, believed that the disease started, like so many others, among animals

Plague Victims. The illustrator of an early fifteenth-century German chronicle imagined the biblical plague of Egypt with the same symptoms as the Black Death. In the background, Moses brings the plague down on Egypt by prayer. By implication, prayer and obedience to the will of God could also be remedies for plague.
© Bildarchiv Preussischer Kulturbesitz/Art Resource, NY

before transferring to human hosts. It had spread from grazing flocks on the steppe in 1341, after which "the wind transmitted their stench around the world." Al-Maqrizi and other Muslim commentators thought wild animals caught it, too. If any of these sources are correct, the Black Death must have been—or included—a disease unknown today.

An unanswered question is, *How, if at all, were changes in climate and disease patterns linked?* The plague pathogens, as we have seen, were remarkably indifferent to weather, striking at different seasons and in climatically different regions of Eurasia, from cold Scandinavia and rain-drenched western Europe to the hot, dry Middle East. The plagues were less penetrative, however, in hot, moist regions and do not seem to have reached across the Sahara to tropical Africa, even though many potential disease carriers crossed that desert to trade. It is worth bearing in mind that the plague pathogens seem to have included new arrivals in the microbial world that remained active for as long as global cooling lasted.

The Course and Impact of Plague

It is easier to describe the routes by which the plague traveled (see Map 14.1) than to say what it was. The Italian chronicler Matteo Villani said the plague came from China and Central Asia, "then through their surrounding lands and then to coastal places across the ocean." Arabic sources cite a similar path.

The age of plague does seem to have started in China. But that is not the same as saying that subsequent outbreaks elsewhere were the result of communication from China, or even that they were necessarily outbreaks of the same disease or diseases. Repeated occurrences—or, perhaps, a continuous visitation—of massively lethal maladies were recorded in southwest China, and over much of central China, north of the Yangtze River, in the early 1320s. In 1331, mortality rates in parts of northeast China that had endured five reported outbreaks of plague in the previous two decades reputedly reached 90 percent. Two years later, a plague claimed 400,000 lives in the Yangtze and Huai valleys. In 1353–1354, chroniclers reported that around two-thirds of the population perished from pestilence in eight distinct Chinese districts. Most of those areas experienced repeated bouts of disease of the same sort in the late 1350s or early 1360s.

Doubt persists, however, over whether the diseases rampant in China were the cause of—or even the same as—those found farther west. From the perspective of most commentators at the time in Europe and the Middle East, plague, like the Mongols, seemed to be an invader from the steppeland. Many observers at the time noted that the Mongols transmitted plague.

Trade Routes

— land route

▬ Silk Roads

- ▨ area of outbreak of plague
- ☻ recorded outbreak of plague
- UZBEKISTAN modern country

Stockholm 1349
Edinburgh 1350
Dublin 1349 York
London 1348
Bruges
Paris
Cologne 1349
Lübeck
Danzig
Kiev
Riga
Novgorod
Nizhniy Novgorod
Moscow
MUSCOVY 1351
New Saray
Rostov Dana
Kaffa 1346
Trebizond
Buda 1349
Salona
Florence 1348
Venice
Milan
Augsburg
Bordeaux 1348
Genoa
Marseille 1347
Rome
Naples
Barcelona
Lisbon 1349
Constantinople 1347
Athens 1348
Palermo
Tunis 1347
Tripoli 1348
Algiers
Ceuta
Fez Melilla
Marrakesh 1349
Wadan
Timbuktu
Alexandria 1347
Cairo 1348
Aydhab
Jedda Mecca 1348
Zeila
Aden 1351
Mogadishu
Tbilisi
Tabriz
Rayy
Aleppo
Damascus 1347
Baghdad 1347
Basra
Isfahan
Shiraz
Hormuz
Muscat
Balasaghun
Tashkent
Bukhara
Merv
Balkh
Herat
Samarka
Fergha Val
Socotra

SCANDINAVIA
North Sea
Baltic Sea
BRITAIN
GERMANY
POLAND
EUROPE
FRANCE
SPAIN
ITALY
Sicily
GREECE
Anatolia
Mediterranean Sea
Atlas Mountains
Sahara
AFRICA
EGYPT
SUDAN
Nile
Red Sea
Gulf of Aden
Arabian Peninsula
Persian Gulf
Arabian
Tigris
Euphrates
SYRIA
ARMENIA
GEORGIA
PERSIA
TURKMENISTAN
UZBEKISTAN
Black Sea
Caspian Sea
Aral Sea
Syr Darya
Hindu K
RUSSIA
MUSCOVY
LITHUANIA
Steppes
Ural Mountains
Irtysh
Ural
Volga
Don
Dnieper
Danube
ATLANTIC OCEAN
Tropic of Cancer
Equator

Map 14.1 The Black Death, 1320–1355

60°
160°

40°
40°

Sea of Okhotsk

160°

Siberia

Amur

Sea of Japan
(East Sea)

JAPAN

20°

Lake Baikal

Kyoto

MANCHURIA

Karakorum

Shangdu

Beijing

Nagasaki

East China Sea

A

MONGOLIA

Taiyuan

Beijing

1345 ☠

Tropic of Cancer

Altai Mountains

Gobi

1351 ☠

1354 ☠

PACIFIC OCEAN

lmalyk

Beshbalik

Yellow R.

Ningxia

Kaifeng

Luoyang

1335

1351 ☠

1323 ☠

Hangzhou

Anxi

Lanzhou

Xian

1320 ☠

Nanchang

Shan

Takla Makan

Cherchen

Chengdu

1332 ☠

Wuchang

Chongqing

Changsha

1345 ☠

Zaitun

Formosa

gar

Khotan

CHINA

1356 ☠

Yangtze

South China Sea

Leh

Plateau of Tibet

Lhasa

Guangzhou

1354 ☠

Brahmaputra

Nanning

Yunnan

Himalayas

Irrawaddy

Equator

ultan

Delhi

Ganges

Patna

Chittagong

Pagan

ANNAM CHAMPA

40°

Thar
esert

INDIA

BURMA

Pegu

Mekong

Angkor

SIAM

Puri

Bay of
Bengal

Thon
Buri

Brunei

Moluccas

ian
ea

Cambay

Andaman
Islands

Borneo

120°

Nicobar
Islands

Malacca

Calicut

Ceylon

Sumatra

Palembang

Java

Quilon

Equator

80°

INDIAN OCEAN

100°

1,000 km

1,000 miles

ca. 1320: Outbreak of
plague in southern
and central China

ca. 1346: Outbreak of
plague in Kaffa
on Black Sea

1351: Plague
strikes Russia

1320   1330   1340   1350

ca. 1331: Mortality rates
in northern China
reach 90 percent

ca. 1347–1349: Plague
rages throughout Middle East,
North Africa, and
much of Europe

ca. 1360: Outbreak
of plague
reported in China

Chroniclers' estimates of mortality are notoriously unreliable, but verifiable evidence bears out some of the most shocking assessments of the damage. In Barcelona on the Mediterranean coast of Spain, 60 percent of jobs in the church fell vacant. Records in northern England suggest the first visitation of the plague killed 40 percent of clergy there. Clergy were, perhaps, members of a high-risk profession, but the laity suffered just as much. In some manors in England, up to 70 percent of tenants died. Villages in southern France lost 80 percent of their population. Towns ran out of cemetery space. The living had to pile the dead in quicklime pits to speed decomposition and minimize rot. Half the villages of Sicily and a third of those around Rome were abandoned.

When the plague reached the Middle East, Ibn Battuta was there to observe it. Arriving in Syria in May 1348, he found that deaths in Damascus reached 2,400 a day. The plague spread along the coast of North Africa, causing—so people claimed—1,000 deaths a day at its height in Tunis. In Morocco, Ibn Battuta's mother was among the victims.

In Central Asia, Arab sources reported that many steppeland dynasties and Mongol warriors succumbed to plague. Headstones at a cemetery in Chwolson in what is now Turkmenistan refer to plague as cause of death in 1338 and 1339. In 1345 and 1346, according to Russian chronicles, pestilence devastated cities in the Mongol-ruled parts of southern Russia. Uzbek villages emptied. In 1346–1347, an official in Crimea reputedly counted 85,000 corpses.

In China, there seems little doubt that the population fell overall. The census of 1393, with adjustments demographers made to compensate for the official habit of underestimating the numbers, suggests a total population of perhaps a little more than 80 million—compared with about 120 million in the mid-fourteenth century.

Moral and Social Effects

Natural disasters always inspire moralizing. Although the Black Death killed people indiscriminately—the vicious and the virtuous alike—it was tempting, especially for Christians, to see it as a moral agent, even a divine instrument to call the world to repentance and make people good. For many who experienced it, the plague was a test of faith, first eliciting selfish reactions of terror and flight, profiteering and despair; then as a Florentine chronicler observed, "people . . . began to help one another, so that many were cured." Dice makers, claimed an abbot in northern France, began making rosary beads. In China, plague, combined with other natural disasters, helped to stir up religious movements that sparked political revolution. In the Islamic world, fear of plague stimulated a revival of popular religion: summoning spirits, casting magical spells, and wearing charms.

Medicine and Morals

Plague also stimulated science as people searched for a cure. It was normal to speak of sin as if it were the cause of the plague. But most people did not take such talk literally. Moralistic explanations of disease were hardly more convincing in the fourteenth century than they are today. Scientific inquiry soon replaced lamentations. The University of Paris medical faculty blamed "a year of many fogs and damps. . . . We must not overlook the fact that pestilence proceeds from divine will, . . . but this does not mean forsaking doctors." Astrologers produced fatalistic explanations based on the alignments of the planets. "Corrupt air" was widely blamed, perhaps caused by polluted wells, perhaps by earthquakes. Muslim physicians also blamed corrupt air, caused in its turn by irregular weather, decaying matter, and astrological influences.

As for how to treat plague, practices were wildly different. In Cairo, healers smeared the swellings with clay. In Spain, the Muslim physician Ibn Khatib advised abstention from grains, cheese, mushrooms, and garlic. Barley water and syrup of basil were widely prescribed. In Italy, Gentile of Foligno, who died of plague in 1348, recommended dried snake's flesh, at least a year old. Another Italian, Gabriele de' Mussis, favored bloodlettings and plasters of mallow leaves. Turks sliced off the heads of the boils on the bodies of the sick and supposedly extracted "green glands." The medical consensus saw infection and contagion as the main threats, and where authorities imposed quarantine, lives were indeed spared.

But where it could not be averted, plague shattered morale. A poet in Cairo, described the psychological effect of the disease: "God has not just subdued Egypt, he has made her crawl on her knees." The Florentine poet, Petrarch, raged at his fellow survivors: "Go, mortals, sweat, pant, toil, range the lands and seas to pile up riches you cannot keep. . . . The life we lead is a sleep; whatever we do are dreams. Only death . . . wakes us . . . I wish I could have woken before this."

Plague had winners and losers. In Europe, **anti-Semitism** ensured that Jews were among the losers because popular prejudice made them scapegoats for causing the plague. A skeptical German Franciscan friar reported the common opinion that Jews started the plague by poisoning wells: "many Jews confessed as much under torture: that they had bred spiders and toads in pots and pans, and had obtained poison from overseas. . . . Throughout Germany, and in all places, they were burnt. For fear of that punishment many accepted baptism and their lives were spared." The massacres of Jews that ensued, especially in Germany, were nearly always the result of outbreaks of mob violence despite the efforts of authorities to absolve the Jews of blame and prevent violence. In July 1348, Pope Clement VI declared the Jews innocent of the charge of well poisoning and excommunicated anyone who harmed them. In January 1349, Cologne's city council warned authorities in other German cities that anti-Jewish riots could ignite popular revolt. But massacres continued.

Why did some people in Europe victimize Jews? Jewish communities had existed all over the Mediterranean since Roman times. Like other eastern migrants—Greeks, Syrians, and Arabs—Jews were an urban and often a commercial people. The itinerary of the twelfth-century Jewish merchant, Benjamin of Tudela, describes their close-knit world, in which a structure of family firms and the fellow feeling of co-religionists gave Jews a commercial advantage and helped them to trade between the Christian and Muslim worlds. An isolated reference to Jews in Cologne occurs as early as 321 C.E., when the Rhineland was part of the Roman Empire, but Mediterranean communities were probably the springboard for Jewish colonization of northern European cities between the sixth and eleventh centuries.

Wherever they went, Jews were alternately privileged and persecuted: privileged, because rulers who needed productive settlers were prepared to reward them with legal immunities; persecuted, because host communities resented intruders who were given special advantages. Some scholars trace anti-Semitism to the influence of Christianity. Indeed, medieval anti-Semitism did exploit Christian prejudices. Gospel texts could be read—as they were, for example, at the time of the First Crusade—to saddle Jews with collective responsibility for the death of Jesus. In the Greek world, however, anti-Semitism was older than Christianity. Medieval anti-Semitism, moreover, was just one aspect of a wider phenomenon: society's antipathy for groups it could not assimilate—comparable, for instance, to the treatment of lepers, Muslims, and, later, Gypsies. Outbreaks of anti-Jewish hatred are intelligible, in part, as examples of the prejudice outsiders commonly attract. At the time of the Black Death, lepers were also accused of well poisoning. So were random strangers and individuals unpopular in their communities. Similar phenomena occur in almost every culture.

The increased intensity of persecution in the fourteenth century drove Jews to new centers. England had already expelled those Jews who did not convert to Christianity in 1290. The Jews were forced out of most of France in the early fourteenth century, and from many areas of western Germany in the early fifteenth century. (Spain and Portugal followed suit in the 1490s.) The effect was to shift Jewish settlement toward the central and eastern Mediterranean, Poland, and Lithuania.

Though the evidence relates almost entirely to Europe, there were also groups of people who benefited from the effects of plague. In western Europe, propertied women were among them. The aristocratic marriage market could be fatal to women who married young and faced repeated pregnancies, but it also left many young widows—the last wives of aging, dying husbands. Property law had to provide for widows by ensuring them an adequate share in their dead husbands' estates and reversion of the property the women had brought to their marriages as dowries. More widows burying more husbands could shift the balance of property ownership between the sexes.

The plagues of the fourteenth century, taken as a whole, seem to have hit men harder than women, presumably because women led relatively more secluded, and therefore protected, lives than men. Rich widows, often accumulating property from successive marriages, wielded power in their own right. The same considerations applied lower down the ranks of society. For instance, during the period of high mortality associated with cold and famine in the second decade of the fourteenth century, more than half the weddings among the peasants of the manor of Taunton in southwest England involved rich widows. After the Black Death, the lords of the manor introduced massive license fees for anyone who wanted to make such marriages, ostensibly to protect widows from predatory Romeos. In unprecedented numbers, widows became the administrators of estates. Women of leisure, education, and power played a bigger part in Western society after this. The increased prominence of women in political, literary, and religious life from the fifteenth century onward might not have been possible without the damage plague did to men.

In western Europe, peasants—if they survived the plague—also benefited from it. In the long run, owners could only keep great properties viable after plague had scythed the labor force by splitting the proceeds with their workers or by breaking the estates up and letting peasants farm the parcels as tenants. Instead of taking orders from the lord's agent or bailiff, tenants paid rent and could manage their landholdings to their own best advantage. The trend toward "free" peasantries started long before the Black Death struck because in many cases it suited landowners, too. Peasants often made the land more productive. It made economic sense to allow them the initiative to improve their holdings. In England, where the royal courts encouraged peasant freedom to expand their own jurisdiction at aristocrats' expense, about half the peasants in the south of the country were already free when the plague arrived.

Lords wrote off their rights to labor services because, as a steward on an English estate admitted in 1351, "the lord's interest made it necessary." The contract peasant dependants of an English abbey renegotiated is revealing: "At the time of the mortality or pestilence which occurred in 1349, scarcely two peasants remained on the manor." They threatened to leave unless the abbey made a new contract. Most of their former services—including plowing, weeding, carting, and preparing soil for planting—were commuted for rent "as long as it pleases the lord—and would that it might please the lord for ever," added the scribe, "since the aforesaid services were not worth very much." It is remarkable, however, that the growth of leaseholding and the relaxation of lordly controls over peasant farmers happened on a large scale in the late fourteenth and fifteenth centuries in the parts of western Europe plague affected. In areas the Black Death bypassed—such as Poland, much of Russia, and what is now the Czech Republic and Slovakia—the opposite happened. Peasants became tied to their lords' land and subject to the landholders' jurisdiction.

Were the effects on the European peasantry duplicated in other plague-ridden lands? Certainly, the rural population became more restive and mobile in Egypt and Syria, where, in 1370, one jurist railed against the laws that obliged justices to return peasant refugees to the places from where they had fled. Villages in Egypt often had their tax burdens reduced in acknowledgment of the loss of population. The cost of labor services rose as population fell, creating opportunities for economic mobility among peasants and urban workers, and stimulating a further decline in rural population levels as peasants migrated to towns. But these changes did not disturb landowners' grip on their holdings. Peasants and landowners seem to have suffered together the effects of declining rural productivity.

Moreover, most governments responded to the demographic disaster, loss of revenue, and loss of labor by raising taxes and trying to limit labor mobility. In previous centuries, ecological disasters and political oppression had often driven peasants into religious extremism or rebellion. Now, popular revolt took on a new agenda: **revolutionary millenarianism**—the doctrine that in an imminent, divinely contrived relaunch of history, God would empower the poor. This happened independently but in strikingly similar ways, in both Europe and China. A popular preacher who incited peasant rebels in England in 1381, expressed the doctrine of egalitarianism:

> How can the lords say or prove that they are more lords than we—
> save that they make us dig and till the ground so that they can
> squander what we produce? . . . But it is from us and our labor that
> everything comes with which they maintain their pomp.

Prophecies helped nourish revolt. Some Franciscans, with their special vocation to serve the poor, excited expectations that the end of the world could not be far off and that a new age was at hand when God would release riches from the bowels of the Earth and eliminate inequality. In China, a similar doctrine inspired peasant rebels in the 1350s. A new Buddha would inaugurate a golden age and give his followers power over their oppressors. According to both movements, a divinely appointed hero would put a bloody end to the struggle of good and evil.

The next chapter describes the politics of the ensuing revolt in China. According to popular traditions dating from soon after the time, the leader of the rebellion, the founder of the Ming dynasty, who claimed to be the prophesied hero, experienced the effects of ecological crisis himself. In one story, he rose to prominence by inventing a medicine that could cure a devastating new plague "which killed half the people and which no known medicine could combat."

The plagues also helped transform the Mongol world. The region the Mongols dominated spanned the plague's trans-Eurasian corridors of transmission. Though the evidence comes from European observers, it is a safe assumption that Mongol manpower suffered and that population levels in some regions from which the Mongols levied recruits and collected taxes also fell. The loss of China in 1368 was the Mongols' most spectacular forfeiture of power. But Mongol control slackened in other dominions, and, on the Chinese front, it never recovered.

In general, plague-stricken societies showed more of what we now call social mobility. The ranks of aristocracies, which were always subject to rapid turnover as families died out, thinned and refilled faster than ever. This seems to have applied as much to China's scholar elite, whose hold on power lapsed and was not fully reasserted until well into the fifteenth century, as to western European nobilities, whose composition changed. In western Europe, the increase in the number of free peasants and tenants created a form of rural capitalism. Families formerly restricted to modest social ambitions could accumulate wealth and bid for higher status, buying education, business opportunities, or more land.

The Limits of Disaster: Beyond the Plague Zone

How far did the plagues of the fourteenth century reach? In terms of effects, the plague was a regional phenomenon, changing the history of China, western Europe, the Middle East, and the steppeland empires. But parts of central and eastern Europe escaped. So did areas that ought to have been vulnerable, such as Southeast Asia, and the parts of Africa that were in touch, by way of the Indian Ocean or the Saharan caravan routes, with affected regions. Relative isolation protected Japan. Apart from a pestilence in the capital Kyoto in 1342, which chroniclers were inclined to attribute to the vengeful spirit of a former emperor, Japan suffered no visitations of any disease on a scale resembling that of the Black Death. The principalities and city-states of central and northern Russia suffered relatively little and late—not before 1350, which is surprising in view of Russia's openness to the steppeland and close contact with the Mongols. India was relatively little affected.

Beyond the reach of the plagues—or, at least, beyond the zone of their most severe effects—the fourteenth century was an era of opportunity in Eurasia. The Mongols were now troubled giants, from whom states in India, Japan, and Southeast Asia were at last safe. We can look at those regions first (see Map 14.2) before turning to sub-Saharan Africa and the Pacific where as far as we know the plague never penetrated.

India

The sultanate of Delhi profited from the Mongols' decline. Sultan Muhammad Ibn Tughluq (r. 1325–1351) was the driving force of a policy of conquest that almost covered the subcontinent with campaigns. Ibn Battuta, who knew the sultan well, called him "of all men the most addicted to the making of gifts and the shedding of blood. His gate is never without some poor man enriched or some living man executed." Emphasis on the sultan's generosity reflects Ibn Battuta's own priorities. He was always on the lookout for rich patrons. But the key facts about Ibn Tughluq's methods are clear. He ran his court and army by balancing lavish gifts with intimidating displays of wrath.

His administration was a machine for recycling wealth. Ibn Battuta describes the regular arrival of revenue collectors from villages, casting gold coins into a golden basin: "These contributions amount in all to a vast sum which the sultan gives to anyone he pleases." Annually, "the daughters of the infidel kings and who have been taken as captives in war during that year" were distributed among the sultan's chief supporters, after performing a sort of audition—singing and dancing, presumably to establish which girls were the most valuable.

While praising Ibn Tughluq's sense of justice, Ibn Battuta indicts him for the use of terror, abuses of power, and judicial murder: "The Sultan was far too free in shedding blood. . . . Every day there are brought to the audience hall hundreds of people, chained, beaten and fettered, and those who are for execution are executed, those for torture tortured, and those for beating beaten." He put one of his brothers to death on a charge of rebellion, which Ibn Battuta clearly felt was trumped up—the first of many judicial murders. On one occasion, the sultan executed 350 alleged deserters at once. A sheikh who accused him of tyranny was fed with excrement and beheaded.

Ibn Tughluq's was a personal empire. His own dynamism and reputation and a policy of religious toleration held it together—the only policy workable for a Muslim elite in a largely Hindu country. But Ibn Tughluq's state was not built to last. It relied on conquest to fuel the system. The Turkic elite, who provided the muscle for revenue collection at home and

Map 14.2 South and Southeast Asia, ca. 1350

Traded Goods

- 🫒 pepper
- ⬭ cinnamon
- 🌿 sandalwood
- 🥥 nutmeg
- ✳ cloves
- 🌱 mace

region where Majapahit claimed tribute

Delhi sultanate at its greatest extent, ca. 1335

area subject to sporadic influence by Delhi Sultanate

— main trade route

• important trade centers

for war on the frontiers, demanded constant rewards. When they did not get them, they seceded from the state. This began to happen on a large scale toward the end of Ibn Tughluq's life. Conquest is, in any case, a gambler's game. Military fortunes change, and military systems, even of the most crushing superiority, can fail unpredictably. Disaster struck Ibn Tughluq, for instance, when a plague devastated his army. "The provinces withdrew their allegiance," Ibn Battuta reported, "and the outer regions broke away."

Moreover, the Delhi sultans were under constant pressure from the Muslim establishment to impose Islam by force, launch holy war, and ease the tax burden on Muslims at the expense of "infidels." The discontent evident among sheikhs and some Muslim notables during Ibn Tughluq's reign owed something, no doubt, to fear of the sultan's arbitrary measures. But frustration with his policies of toleration also inspired much of it. Ibn Tughluq's successor succumbed to these pressures and forfeited Hindu allegiance. Beyond the frontier, Hindu states adopted a counter ideology of resistance to Islam—at least at the level of rhetoric, since religion rarely took priority over politics. In southern India, a Hindu state with imperial ambitions arose at Vijayanagar. The conquest juggernaut of the sultanate of Delhi stopped rolling, and provincial elites in outlying regions dropped out of the empire. Again, as so often happened in Indian history, both the difficulties of and the capacity for an India-wide empire had been demonstrated. But again, the problems of maintaining such a large and diverse state were obvious. Future attempts would run into the same kinds of difficulties as those that caused the sultanate's control of the outer edges of the state to unravel and its expansion to come to a halt.

Southeast Asia

Rather as Delhi did in India, a kingdom in Java exploited the opportunity that emerged as the Mongol threat waned. The offshore world of Southeast Asia produced goods the Chinese market wanted. Some states in the region were in a position to threaten or control the passage of those goods by sea: pepper and cinnamon from southern India and Sri Lanka; sandalwood from Timor; timber and aromatic spices—nutmeg, cloves, and mace—from Borneo and the Moluccas. Control of the strait between Malaya, Java, and Sumatra was strategically vital for China-bound trade, and the shipping of Java made an important contribution to the commerce of the region. That is why Kubilai Khan focused on Java when he tried to extend his empire into Southeast Asia (see Chapter 13).

The establishment of a powerful state on Java, centered on the secure, inland city of Majapahit (Mah-jah-PAH-heet), was the achievement of Kertanagara, who died in 1292. Chroniclers credited him with magic powers or saintly virtues, according to their own prejudices. He seems to have balanced the rituals of Buddhist, Hindu, and indigenous religions to keep a diverse array of followers together. Kertanagara repulsed Kubilai Khan's Mongol invasion.

The king who launched Majapahit on its own imperial career in the mid–fourteenth century was Hayan Wuruk (died 1389). He had dazzling ambitions. We know this because his childhood playmate, who became one of his chief ministers, wrote a poem in his praise. The verses reveal what the king wanted people to think of him. The poem lovingly describes the royal palace at Majapahit, which had gates of iron and a "diamond-plastered" watchtower. Majapahit was like the sun and moon, while the villages of the rest of the kingdom are "of the aspect of stars." When Hayan Wuruk traveled the country, his court filled numberless carts. Through the streets of his capital, he paraded, clad in gold, borne on a throne carved with supporting lions, to the music of lutes and drums, conches and trumpets, and singers. Ambassadors from foreign courts brought him praises in Sanskrit verse.

Hayan Wuruk was both "Buddha in the body" and "Shiva incarnate"—worshipful to Buddhist and Hindu subjects alike. He was also a master of native rituals, skilled in the theater, dance, and song. "The king's song put them under a spell," the poet assures us, "like the cries of a peacock." Hayan Wuruk's realm, according to the poet, was more famous than any country in the world except India. In reality, the kingdom occupied little more than half the island of Java. The king, however, aimed to make it bigger. The poet listed tributaries in many islands in what is today Indonesia and "protectorates" in northern Malaya, Thailand, and Indochina. Even China and India, he claimed, defer to Hayan Wuruk. "Already the other continents," he boasts, "are getting ready to show obedience to the illustrious prince" and a state "renowned for its purifying power in the world."

That was all the exaggeration of propaganda. But a disinterested foreign chronicler confirmed much of the picture:

> The empire grew prosperous. . . . There was a ceaseless coming and going of people from the territories overseas which had submitted to the king. . . . Everywhere one went there were gongs and drums being beaten, people dancing to the strains of all kinds of loud music, entertainments of all kinds like the living theater.

Surviving temple reliefs show what the Java of Hayan Wuruk was like. Wooden houses, perched on pillars over stone terraces, formed neat villages. Peasants grew paddy rice, or coaxed water buffalo over dry fields to break up the soil. Women did the harvesting and cooking. Orchestras, beating gongs with sticks, accompanied masked dancers. Royal charters fill out the picture of economic activities. Industrial processes included salt making by evaporation, sugar refining, process-ing cured water-buffalo meat, oil pressing from seeds, making rice noo-dles, ironmaking, rattan weaving, and dyeing cloth. More sophisticated ceramics and textiles were imported from China. The same charters re-veal the extension of royal power and impact into the hinterland. They establish direct relationships between the royal court and members of lo-cal elites. They favor the foundations of new temples and encourage the spread of communications, the building of bridges, the commissioning of ferries, and the erection of "rest houses, pious foundations, and hospi-tals" mentioned in the king's praise poem.

Majapahit was an expanding realm. As Mongol vigilance in the region relaxed, Majapahit's power increased. In the 1340s, a network of ports in the hands of Majapahit garrisons spread over Bali and Sumatra. Majapahit indeed seems to have annihilated commercial rivals in Sumatra and to have maintained fortified outposts on the coast of that is-land. In 1377, Hayan Wuruk launched an apparently successful expedi-tion against Palembang, the major way station on the route from India to China. A struggle was on to profit from Southeast Asia's trade.

Japan

Japan, like Java, was a region the plagues spared and the Mongols failed to conquer. Here, however, security from the Mongol menace had a con-trasting effect. As the threat receded, so did pressure to stay united and serve the state. Potential rebels could now raise armies with increasing ease. Japan had enjoyed more than a century of stability. The warrior class had been pacified—maintained by grants of estates and revenues. Now people at all social levels were accumulating wealth. Social status, which was supposedly protected by complicated standards of eligibility for different ranks, was up for grabs. Warriors began to diversify into new occupations, to sell or break up their estate rights, and, in increasing numbers, to resort to violence as a way of life.

At the top of this volatile society, rival branches of the imperial family contested the throne. The Emperor Godaigo (r. 1318–1339) fought to exclude family competitors and to take back the power the shoguns exer-cised in the emperor's name. He accused them of "drawing water from a stream and forgetting its source." Godaigo had his portrait painted show-ing himself with a sword—an accessory normally considered too active for an emperor, but one that signified his intentions to recover real power.

Godaigo found, however, that he could not simply take up the reins of power himself. Traditional methods could no longer govern the coun-try. Loyalty, though much talked of by writers at the time, became an unpredictable commodity, liable to change hands as circumstances changed. "Then was then," proclaimed a saying of the time. "Now is now: rewards are lord!"

Godaigo's army deserted in dissatisfaction over the rewards he could provide. "How," complained one of his officials, "can those who tend to have the outlook of a merchant be of use to the court?" Clearly, the new disorder was, for some, a kind of social revolution: the result of violations of the proper boundaries of class and rank.

In 1335, the most powerful of the warlords, Ashikaga Takauji, seized the position of supreme power as **shogun** in defiance of Godaigo's wishes. In 1336, he overwhelmed Godaigo's remaining supporters at the Battle of Minato River. The Ashikaga dynasty survived as shoguns almost until 1573 by accepting the realities of the changed world, withdrawing into a role as the greatest of a number of regional powers, and attempting only modest interventions in the spheres of other major warlords. The Ashikaga also restored the old relationship between shogun and emperor, in which pieties smothered the real displacement of authority into the shogun's hands.

The chaos of the fourteenth century favored the rise of **Zen**, a tradition of Buddhism that valued personal extinction as a part of mystical experience. A twelfth-century Japanese text defined it: "a special transmission outside the scriptures, not founded on words or letters, which allows one to penetrate the nature of things by pointing directly to the mind." Zen made progress partly because of the influx of monks from China who were escaping from the Mongols, and partly because Zen ideas suited the warriors and warlords who now effectively ruled Japan. Discipline, self-denial, and willingness to die are martial virtues. The warriors recognized Zen monks as kindred spirits.

A Shogun's Armor. This armor is believed to have belonged to Ashikaga Takauji, who was shogun from 1338 to 1358. The quality and costliness of the gilt copper breastplate and helmet mountings show that the armor belonged to a person of high status. Stenciled in lacquered doeskin, an image of Fudo Myo-o—the god who personified the samurai virtues of outward ferocity and inner calm—adorns the breastplate.
The Metropolitan Museum of Art, Gift of Bashford Dean, 1914 (ART322237) Photograph © 1991 The Metropolitan Museum of Art. Art Resource, NY

Zen Garden. Zuiho-in is one of 24 temples within the temple complex of Daitokuji in Kyoto, one of Japan's biggest Zen communities. Most temples have a garden of meditation designed to be observed from a single viewpoint to encourage solitude. The hallmarks of these gardens are the expanses of gravel raked to resemble waves and rocks arranged like islands within it. Greenery is not a normal part of most Zen garden designs, perhaps because living plants are mutable—they change too easily with the passing seasons, whereas rocks are deceptively unchanging. But to ask what a Zen garden "means" is to invite an evasive answer.
© Catherine Karnos/CORBIS All Rights Reserved

Warrior families made Zen practitioners the custodians of their ancestral temples and tombs.

For the women of families of warrior and aristocratic rank, the changes of the period were oppressive. Women could attain responsible positions in the emperor's court. Hino Meishi, for instance, was in charge of the sacred imperial symbols in 1331, when the shogun tried to depose Godaigo. But changing marriage customs were unfavorable to women's personal independence. Until the fourteenth century, marriage in Japan was predominantly a private, essentially sexual relationship. Now it became increasingly formalized, as a union of two families. Wives moved into the homes of their husbands' families, instead of remaining in their own homes. Hino Meishi, for instance, started her experience of married life in 1333 in traditional manner, when her lover started visiting her openly. This publicly acknowledged the relationship as a permanent one. She worried, not because the arrangement was informal, but because her husband's family was of higher rank than her own. In the confused conditions of the civil war then raging, Meishi was forced to move house, but she ended up in her husband's home.

A sign of women's changed circumstances is that they stopped writing fiction and the kind of personal diaries familiar from earlier periods. Hino Meishi herself was the author of the last autobiographical memoir by a woman—which is why we know so much about her life. Self-expression was now considered inappropriate for the female sex. Wives came to be thought of as their husbands' property. In the same period, following changes in the practices of the imperial family, it became common for women aristocrats to receive a life interest in a share of family property, rather than inheriting property outright. Property rights were steered toward a single male heir. Among commoners, however, this practice failed to take hold, and women held growing amounts of property and engaged in more business in their own right.

The peasants profited from the changes that were transforming the warrior class. Relaxation of central authority freed villagers from intrusive legislation. They could get on with improving crop yields as they saw fit. The new regime of rewards for military service meant that the landlords were always changing—dispossessed and replaced as the fortunes of war shifted. The rapid turnover of lords, who were usually absentees, also allowed the peasants to get on with their business. There were no epidemics in the fourteenth-century countryside in Japan, and serious crop failures were rare. Nor were population growth and the extension of cultivated land interrupted. As a result of the successful exploitation of formerly marginal lands outside the great estates, the numbers of small independent farmers multiplied, though not on anything like the scale that occurred at the same time in western Europe.

Mali

Just as Java and Japan seemed to grow in stature by comparison with the afflictions of China and the Mongols, so parts of West Africa projected an image of abundance toward the devastated Mediterranean world. Conspicuous evidence for West African prosperity is the Catalan Atlas, made in the studio of the finest mapmaker in Europe, Cresques Abraham, on the island of Majorca, in the 1370s or 1380s. Among bright images in costly pigments, like the contents of a spilled jewel box, the map depicts a black king in West Africa—bearded, crowned, enthroned, surrounded by depictions of rich cities of many turrets—holding a huge nugget of pure gold. "This is the richest king in all the land," says a caption.

His kingdom, **Mali**, occupied grassland and mixed savanna between the Sahara Desert and the tropical forest. The desert sealed it from plague (see Map 14.3). According to tradition, a hero known as **Sundiata** founded the kingdom in the early thirteenth century. His story has obviously

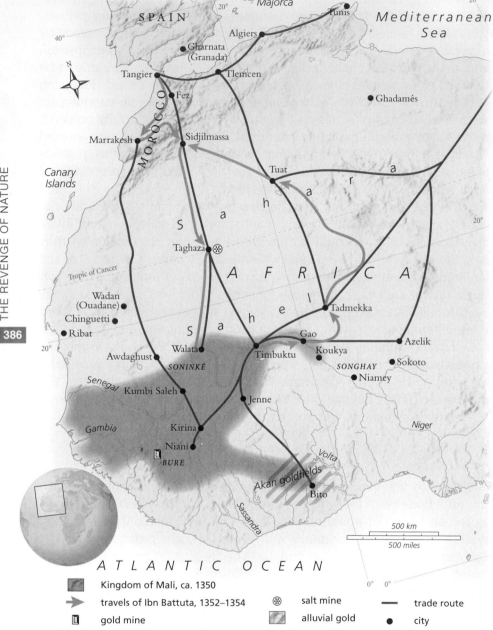

Map 14.3 The Kingdom of Mali, ca. 1350

mythical features. He was a cripple, mocked and exiled, who returned home as a conqueror and avenger. The strength of his army, and those of his successors, was horsemen. Terracotta sculptures show us what they were like. Helmed and armed, with round shields and breastplates over slashed leather jackets, they kept their heads haughtily tilted and their horses on short rein, with elaborately braided bridles. Their great age of conquest came in the 1260s and 1270s when, according to the Muslim historian Ibn Khaldun, "they overcame the neighboring peoples . . . and all nations of the land of the blacks stood in awe of them."

The "mansas," kings of Mali, made pilgrimages to the Muslim holy city of Mecca at intervals from the late thirteenth century. The mere fact that they dared leave for the year-long journey shows how stable the state must have been. In about 1324, Mansa Musa stayed in Egypt for three months on his way to Mecca. He gave 50,000 gold coins to the Mamluk sultan and distributed ingots of gold to officials. He endowed so many mosques and shrines that he caused inflation. The value of gold in Egypt fell as a result of his stay. On his homeward journey, he raised loans that, it was said, he repaid at the rate of 700 coins for every 300 of the same value he borrowed.

The location of West Africa's gold mines was a closely guarded commercial secret, but it was probably in Bure, around the upper reaches of the Niger River and the headwaters of the Gambia and Senegal rivers. The merchants of Mali handled the gold trade but never controlled its production. The mansa took nuggets for tribute—hence the image on Cresques Abraham's map.

The gold bought salt. Mali was so rich in gold and so short of salt that the price of salt reputedly tripled or quadrupled in the kingdom's markets.

In 1352, Ibn Battuta joined a salt caravan across the Sahara. He detested the manners, food, and what he considered to be the sexual promiscuity he found in Mali, "and their contempt for white men," but he praised the Malians "abhorrence of injustice." The mansa's court impressed him, as it impressed other visitors in the same period. This consensus is striking, because North African Muslims rarely praised black achievements. The mansa, according to Ibn Battuta, commanded more devotion from his subjects than any other ruler in the world, though most of the court ceremonial was traditional among black kingdoms in West Africa. The ruler, for instance, spoke only through an intermediary, for to raise his voice was beneath his dignity. Supplicants had to prostrate themselves and sprinkle dust on their heads as they addressed him. When his words were relayed to the people, guards strummed their bowstrings, and everyone else hummed appreciatively. Sneezing in the mansa's presence was punishable by death. Hundreds of servants attended him with gilded rods. Court poets and scholars came to serve the mansa from Muslim Spain and North Africa.

Meanwhile, West African gold inspired heroic European efforts to get some of it. Western Europe produced only small amounts of silver, and its economies were permanently short of precious metals with which to trade. There was a longstanding adverse trade balance with more productive Silk Road economies. To keep it going, this trade always needed infusions of cash. So, as Mali's reputation grew, the search for African gold obsessed European adventurers. Cresques Abraham depicted the fate of one of them, the Spaniard Jaume Ferrer, lost to shipwreck off the West African coast in 1346 in an attempt to find a sea route to Mali. The endeavor was hopeless. Mali was land-locked, and the African coasts had little gold until well into the fifteenth century.

The Pacific: Societies of Isolation

Beyond the world that escaped the worst of the Black Death lay regions contagion did not threaten. Isolation, which had arresting effects in so many cases, was a privilege in the fourteenth century. To understand this unaccustomed reversal of what can only be called the normal pattern of global history, we need to look at some relatively isolated societies. The vastness of the Pacific—which the technology of the time could not cross—ensured that exceptionally isolated cultures lay scattered around and about that ocean.

Easter Island

No part of the inhabited globe was more isolated than Easter Island, which lay, at the time, more than 2,000 miles away from any other human habitation. The island covers only 64 square miles of the Pacific Ocean. It is hard to believe that the Polynesian navigators who first colonized the island, possibly more than 1,500 years ago, would have stayed if they had been able to continue their journey or turn around and go home. Most of the soil is poor. Nowadays, there are no nearby fisheries, though native traditions recall a time when the island's elite feasted on porpoise and dolphin. The first settlers brought chickens and the starchy plant called taro. But not much that was edible was available to them when they arrived. Migrant birds were their renewable source of food. The old-est art on the island shows a birdman. Feasts of fowl and egg-stealing competitions greeted the annual arrival of flocks of sooty terns.

Despite the natural poverty of the island and its isolation from other societies, in the fourteenth century it housed a people at the height of their ambition. Probably late in the first millennium, they had begun to erect monumental statues for reasons we can no longer determine. The statues, called *Moais*, resemble those other Polynesian peoples erected: tall, elongated, stylized faces hewn of stone. They were originally adorned with red topknots—sitting hatlike on their heads—and white coral eyes, looking out with a fixed stare. The Easter Island statues are

Moais. Monumental statue making on Easter Island was probably at its most intense in the fourteenth century. For a small population on a poorly provided and remote island, the investment of energy the practice required seems astounding. The images are similar to those of ancestor cults elsewhere in Polynesia, but they are exceptional in being huge, numerous, and carved from stone rather than wood. Isolation apparently made Easter Island culture distinctive, but still recognizably like that of other Polynesian colonies.
Dallas and John Heaton/Stock Connection

unique compared with other Polynesian works of the same sort only because they are so big and there are so many of them—878 in all, including those abandoned, incomplete, in the quarries. Some 600 finished examples survive, most of them more than 20 feet tall.

It took real communal effort to make and erect the statues, each carved from a pillar of rock weighing between 30 and 40 tons. A single extended family—say, about 400 people—joining together to provide the labor and feed the workers, would have taken more than a year to complete the task. As time went on, the statues got bigger—a clear case of competition, driving up the costs of the culture and, perhaps, condemning it to collapse, a century or two later. An enterprising community could buck the effects of isolation, and even turn isolation to advantage—but, in an extreme case like that of Easter Island, the effort was evidently hard to sustain. Statue building slowed and, in the sixteenth or seventeenth century, stopped.

New Zealand

New Zealand was another, almost equally remote outpost of the Polynesian world, but with infinitely more resources than Easter Island and, therefore, with better prospects of sustainable development. Although the date of the first settlement of New Zealand is disputed, fairly secure dates are possible for changes that were under way by the fourteenth century. Population increased. Hunting resources diminished in populated areas as the fur seal and moa began to get scarce; the moa, a huge, flightless bird, with eggs as big as a hundred hen's eggs, was among the early settlers' main sources of food. Human overexploitation was almost certainly responsible for the moa's extinction. Its meat was processed in immense butcheries. At the biggest butchery, at the mouth of the Waitako River in South Island, up to 90,000 birds were dismembered with blades made of obsidian, a volcanic stone that can be honed to a razor-sharp edge. The same region had more than 300 smaller sites, each handling at least 5,000 moa.

As the balance of the way of life shifted from hunting toward farming, mobile colonies settled down. The kind of wear the teeth of people buried in this period shows is different from that of their predecessors: fibrous foods and gritty mollusks ground their dental bites, which show fewer traces of the effects of a meat-rich diet. The results included stronger community identification with land and, therefore, more competition for cultivable resources. Part of the farming surplus was invested in war. From the fifteenth century, the number of places where weapons were made grew enormously. So did the number of fortified villages, especially in the North Island. War was only one of many forms of new or newly intensive activity that favored the power of chiefs. Farming required strong centers of power to organize collective activity and regulate the distribution of food. So did new fishing technologies with gigantic nets that needed many hands to operate them.

Ozette

Meanwhile, on the Pacific rim of the New World, people experimented with contrasting responses to isolation. Good evidence has survived for two different communities. One body of evidence comes from a community of hunters in the north of the hemisphere. Exact dates are hard to assign, but probably toward the end of the fifteenth century, a mudslide at Ozette, in Washington State, buried the homes of a community of whalers and seal fishers. The mud perfectly preserved the site. Archaeologists have revealed layers of sediment that show that ways of life had not changed here significantly for centuries before the disaster. The mud of Ozette gives us a unique glimpse into the lives of a hunting culture in what we think of in European terms as the late Middle Ages.

The victims of the mudslide lived in big cedarwood buildings, each more than 50 feet long and 30 feet wide. Each building housed about 40 people, divided typically by partitions into half a dozen smaller family units with their own hearths. Hanging mats helped insulate the walls. The

Ozette people ate almost no vegetable matter except wild berries. Though they hunted land animals and birds, the sea was their main hunting ground. Fur seals provided nearly 90 percent of their meat. For cooking, they filled watertight cedarwood boxes with hot water and boiled or steamed their food. They hunted and fished in dugouts. Whale images dominated their art, probably because the art had a ritual or magical function in bringing good fortune to the whale hunt. Carvers also made bowls in the shape of men, depicted realistically except for big cavities, where the belly should be, to hold food or offerings. Their way of life was, broadly speaking, similar to that of the Thule Inuit centuries earlier (see Chapter 11).

Chan Chan

On the Pacific's South American edge, we can trace new activity to roughly the same period. Of course, this was not a region as isolated as New Zealand, Easter Island, or even Ozette. As we have seen many times in this book, the coasts of what are now Peru, Ecuador, and Pacific-side Colombia were always in touch with the cultures of the high Andes and, through them, with the lowlands beyond. In South America, in and around the fourteenth century, the latest experiment in state-building, intensive agriculture, and city life was under way at Chan Chan. This city was in the coastal desert region of Peru, where the Moche had formerly built complex irrigation works and prosperous cities in defiance of a hostile environment (see Chapter 10). The methods of the **Chimú** people of Chan Chan were different. They concentrated agriculture around the city, where 30,000 people lived. The population of Chan Chan's hinterland was thinly distributed and not much greater than that of the city itself.

Cotton production was a major economic activity. Fishing seems to have mattered little. For protein, the people of Chan Chan—or, perhaps, just the elite—relied on llamas. Pasture was limited, so the llamas were farmed in corrals in and around the city. Fodder supplemented grazing.

The city of Chan Chan covered almost 7 square miles. Spaces in Chan Chan served as the tombs of kings, dwellings for elites, and warehouses to store and distribute food. The layout shows that the Chimú state was oppressive, with a security-obsessed elite. High walls, fortified gateways and dog-leg corridors, designed with sharp turns to delay attackers and favor defenders, protected the rulers' quarters from their own people.

The warehouses were the most important buildings. Access to them was through chambers where costly ceremonies unfolded: sacrifices of llamas and men, deposits of precious objects. The storerooms were vital—the most vital part of the state—because El Niño periodically and unpredictably washed away the irrigation works. Stockpiling enabled the Chimú to recover when disaster struck.

The rulers' tombs were so rich that colonial-era Spaniards spoke of "mining" them. The Chimú elite favored gold for their precious ornaments and ritual objects. But gold did not occur naturally in this part of Peru. Trade or tribute must have brought it to Chimú, which was evidently an expansionist state. Perhaps it had to be to boost its resources in a difficult and depleted environment. Sites of towns built in the style of Chan Chan stretch between the Sana and Supe rivers.

CHRONOLOGY	
1290	England expels Jews
Thirteenth and fourteenth centuries	Climate change in Northern Hemisphere; population rises in New Zealand and agriculture replaces hunting as way of life; rise of Chimú state (Chan Chan) in Peru
1309–1310	Thames River freezes (London)
1315–1316	Heavy rains in northern Europe
1320s	Plague epidemics in southwest and central China
1324	Mansa Musa makes *hajj* to Mecca
1325–1351	Reign of Ibn Tughluq (Delhi Sultanate, India)
1330s	Mortality rates in northeast China reach 90 percent
1335	Ashikaga Tokauji seizes shogunate (Japan)
1343	Last Il-khan dies in Persia
1346	Plague reported in Crimea (Black Sea)
1347	Last Icelandic voyage to America
1347–1349	Plague rages in western Europe, Middle East, and North Africa
1350s	Peasant rebellions spread in China
1351	Plague strikes southern Russia
1352	Ibn Battuta sets off for Mali
1354	Ottoman Turks cross Dardanelles to occupy Byzantine city of Gallipoli
1360	Plague in China
1389	Death of Hayan Wuruk (Majapahit in Java)
ca. 1400	Settlements in American Southwest abandoned

IN PERSPECTIVE
The Aftershock

Ibn Khaldun left an often-quoted but unforgettable description of the effects of the Black Death on the Muslim world:

> *Civilization shrank with the decrease of mankind. Cities and buildings were bared, roads and signposts were abandoned, villages and palaces were deserted. Tribes and dynasties were expunged. It was as if the voice of existence in the world had called out for oblivion, and the world had responded to the call.*

But how serious and enduring were the consequences? For western Europe, many promising initiatives of the preceding period ended. North Atlantic navigation, which Norse seafarers had developed so heroically in previous centuries, dwindled. The last Icelandic voyage to mainland America was in 1347. The Norse Greenland colonies became increasingly isolated. When a bishop's representative sailed to the more northerly of them in the 1340s, he "found nobody, either Christians or heathens, only some wild cattle and sheep, and they slaughtered the wild cattle for food, as much as the ships would carry, and then sailed home therewith themselves." When the Greenland colony was finally extinguished in the fifteenth century, it was by mysterious raiders of savage ferocity known to the Norse as Skraelingar—presumably, the Thule Inuit with whom the Norse had long shared the island. Exploration of other parts of the Atlantic virtually stopped at the time of the Black Death. In the half century preceding the onset of the plague, explorers from maritime communities in western Europe had made considerable progress. Mapping of the African Atlantic had begun, with the Canary and Madeira Islands, and navigators had begun to investigate the pattern of the northeast trade winds. Jaume Ferrer's shipwreck was symbolic. Few similar voyages were recorded in the second half of the fourteenth century.

Human foes supplemented the plague, famine, and cold. In 1354, an earthquake demolished the walls of the Byzantine city of Gallipoli on the European side of the entrance to the Dardanelles, the narrow strait that divides Europe from Anatolia. Ottoman Turks were waiting to cross the strait and take over the ruins, inaugurating a history of European anxiety about the defensibility of Christendom's eastern Mediterranean frontier—anxiety that would last, with fluctuations, for more than 300 years. In the northeast, pagan Lithuanians eroded the conquests of the Teutonic Knights along the Baltic (see Chapter 13). To some extent, the gradual diffusion of Catholic faith, under Polish influence, into Lithuania made good these losses—for Christendom, if not for the Germans. Meanwhile,

THE REVENGE OF NATURE

REGION	➤ TENTATIVE REASON FOR ABSENCE OF PLAGUE	➤ CONSEQUENCES
Japan	Protected by relative isolation	Protected from Mongols; new threats emerge from prosperous provincial warlords; the imperial family divides into rival factions; new dynasty of shoguns emerges; Zen Buddhism becomes influential
Northern Russia	Unknown—interaction with Mongols should have made Russians vulnerable	Grand Duchy of Moscow begins to throw off Mongol rule in late 1300s
India	Unknown—although Silk Roads and sea trade connected it to other parts of Eurasia and Africa	Sultanate of Delhi profits from Mongols' decline, initiating policy of conquest; Turkic elite responsible for war and revenue collecting eventually secedes; Hindu/Muslim relations are always problematic
Southeast Asia	Unknown—trade routes from China, Europe, Africa should have made the region vulnerable	Establishment of powerful state on Java (Majapahit), to control trade with China and India, creating stable and prosperous society
Pacific	Isolation	Existing societies expand; shift from hunting to agriculture in New Zealand; Chimú state (Chan Chan) flourishes in Peru
Sub-Saharan West Africa	Unclear—trans-Saharan trade routes should have carried plague	Mali becomes rich and powerful from control over gold trade; European need for gold creates obsession with reaching Mali

in parts of eastern Europe, state-building continued, under rulers whose longevity helped bring stability. The period of the Black Death was spanned by the reigns of Charles the Great in Bohemia (r. 1346–1378), Casimir the Great in Poland (r. 1333–1370), and Louis the Great of Hungary (r. 1342–1382). On the whole, even in western Europe, the effects of plague favored the state, because afflicted populations turned to monarchs as potential saviors and were willing to trust them with enhanced powers. Even peasant rebels tended to focus their resentments on the rest of the elite and appealed for aid directly—albeit, usually, unsuccessfully—to monarchs.

In the Mongol dominions, the case was different. Mongol expansion ceased. Russian principalities began to pry themselves free of Mongol control. The Mongol state in Persia fragmented. From the ruins of Mongol domination, a new state arose in Anatolia, under a Turkish dynasty, known as the Ottomans, whose center of operations from 1326 was at the formerly Byzantine city of Bursa, in what is now western Turkey, from where they were able to profit from the dislocation the Black Death caused (see Map 14.4). They gradually came to dominate Byzantium, invaded the Balkans, and established a close trading relationship with the Italian city of Genoa. Toward the end of the fourteenth century, they began to construct a navy, to extend their power into the Mediterranean. In China, as we shall see in the next chapter, the strain of the ecological crisis of the mid-fourteenth century contributed to the dissolution of the Mongol state and its replacement by a new regime of native Chinese rulers, under the Ming dynasty.

At a deeper level than that of the rise and fall of states and political elites, the coming of the age of plagues, made worse by unpredictable changes in climate, affected the balance of population—and therefore of power—among Eurasian civilizations. Natural disasters do not usually

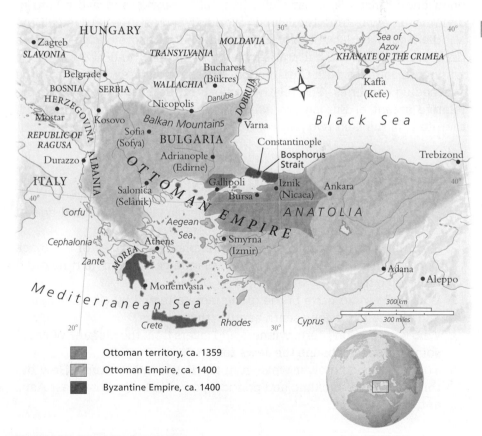

Ottoman territory, ca. 1359
Ottoman Empire, ca. 1400
Byzantine Empire, ca. 1400

Map 14.4 The Ottoman Empire, ca. 1400

affect population trends for long. Population can recover with surprising speed. Recovery was harder in the wake of the Black Death because, although plagues became less ferocious, and populations built up immunity, pestilence affected the same regions for centuries to come, at a rate too rapid to enumerate. In Egypt, for instance, visitations of plague struck more than once, on average, every four years in the two centuries following the Black Death. The population of Eurasia probably remained static during the late fourteenth century and for most of the fifteenth. In the long run, of the three culture areas that suffered most, it appears that the Islamic world may have been more affected than Christendom or China, both of which seem to have recovered faster and resisted better. This can only be a tentative conclusion, because the evidence is unreliable. It does seem, however, that the populations of Christendom and China recovered to pre-plague levels by the end of the fifteenth century, whereas in Egypt, Syria, and, perhaps, other parts of the Islamic world, the recovery did not even begin until then. The increase of population thereafter was generally slower in the Islamic world than in Christendom and China until the twentieth century. If correct, this conclusion may help to explain one of history's great shifts in wealth, power, and every kind of dynamism—away from the Islamic world. Whereas in what we call the Middle Ages, the Islamic world had contributed enormously—far more than Christendom—to cultural exchange in Eurasia, and had tended to win out in conflicts with Christendom, Muslim power dwindled over the succeeding centuries. The relative eclipse of the Islamic world and the relative ascent of Europe are major themes of the age of plague and, therefore, of the next two parts of this book.

PROBLEMS AND PARALLELS

1. What were the long-term effects of the climate change and age of plagues that began in the fourteenth century?
2. How did contemporaries attempt to explain the causes of the Black Death? Where did they believe the plague came from, and how did they try to treat it?
3. Why were some parts of the globe more affected by climate change and plague in the fourteenth century than others?
4. Who were the long-term winners and losers from the plague? Why did some Europeans blame the Jews for the Black Death?
5. Why did Mongol power weaken in the fourteenth century? How did this affect state-building and political power in India, Southeast Asia, and Japan?

CHAPTER 15

Expanding Worlds: Recovery in the Late Fourteenth and Fifteenth Centuries

focus questions

1. Why were African empires able to expand on such an impressive scale during this period?
2. What role did geographical diversity play in the Inca and Aztec empires?
3. What strong new states arose on the European borderlands?

4. Why did Ming China turn away from overseas imperialism?

5. Why did western Europe begin to reach out and cross the oceans in the late 1400s?

Abd-ar-Razzak was a landlubber. The stories he knew about navigation on the Indian Ocean presented the sea as God's arena, where luck changed with the wind and storms fell like divine arrows. Every story ended with a shipwreck. But he had a journey to face that he could only make by sea. In 1417, he was appointed Persian ambassador to Vijayanagar, a powerful state in southern India, and there were too many hostile kingdoms between it and Persia for him to cross by land. But his ship sailed late,

> *so that the favorable time for departing by sea, that is to say the beginning or middle of the monsoon, was allowed to pass, and we came to the end of the monsoon, which is the season when tempests and attacks from pirates are to be dreaded. . . . The merchants, who were my intimate friends, cried with one voice that the time for navigation was past, and that everyone who put to sea at this season was alone responsible for his death.*

Abd-ar-Razzak's predicament, however, had a positive side. The late monsoon is so fierce that ships speed before it. He made the journey in only 19 days, about two-thirds of the time one might normally expect.

Abd-ar-Razzak's voyage demonstrates the crucial importance of winds in world history. Most of the Earth's surface area is sea. Long-range communications have to traverse wide waters. Throughout the age of sail—that is, for almost the entire history of travel—winds and currents set the limits of what was possible: the routes, the rates, the mutually accessible cultures. More particularly, Abd-ar-Razzak's experience illustrates the paradox of Indian Ocean navigation in his day. The monsoon winds made travel speedy, but the ocean was stormy, unsafe, and hard to get into and out of. Access from the east was barely possible in summer, when typhoons tore into the shores. Fierce storms guarded the southern approaches. No one who knew the reputation of these waters cared to venture between about 10 and 30 degrees south and 60 or 90 degrees east during the hurricane season. Many European maps of the fifteenth century depicted the Indian Ocean as landlocked—literally inaccessible by sea. Yet it was the biggest and richest zone of long-range commerce in the world.

By the end of the fifteenth century, European navigators had found a way to penetrate it. Meanwhile, the Atlantic was developing into a rival zone, with transoceanic routes ready to be exploited. Indeed, seafaring on the Atlantic would transform the world by bringing cultures that had been torn apart into contact, conflict, commerce, and cultural and ecological exchange. The divergent, isolated worlds of ancient and medieval times were coming together to form the interconnected world we inhabit today.

How did it happen? How did the world rebound from the plagues and climate changes of the fourteenth century? For one thing, populations gradually acquired immunity against plague, as susceptible people died and those who were naturally most resistant passed on their genes. As for worsening climates, survivors relocated or just got used to colder, wetter conditions. To some extent, technological advance made up for—indeed, was a response to—decreased population. Across Eurasia, and in parts of Africa that were in contact with Eurasia, the long period of accelerated exchange in the Song and Mongol eras had equipped expanding economies with improved technology. In regions that escaped the catastrophes of the fourteenth century, long-term population growth continued to strengthen states and economies. So it is not surprising that the world of the late fourteenth and fifteenth centuries was a world in recovery and even a world of resumed expansion.

Toward the end of the period, from about 1460 on, in states in widely separated parts of the world, expansion speeded up like springs uncoiling. An age of expansion really did begin, but the phenomenon was of an expanding world, not, as some historians say, of European expansion. The world did not wait passively for European outreach to transform it, as if touched by a magic wand. Other societies were already working magic of their own, turning states into empires and cultures into civilizations. Beyond the reach of the recurring plagues that stopped demographic growth in much of Eurasia, some of the most dynamic and rapidly expanding societies of the fifteenth century were in the Americas and sub-Saharan Africa. Indeed, in terms of territorial expansion and military effectiveness against opponents, African and American empires outclassed any state in western Europe until the sixteenth century.

As we shall see, some European communities played big and growing roles. And their expansion did have unique features—exceptional range, above all, which enabled people from western Europe to cross unprecedented distances on previously unexplored routes. But to appreciate what was special about Europe, we have to see it in global context and acknowledge that expansion was a worldwide phenomenon. If we start in Africa and approach Europe only after looking at the Americas and following Abd-ar-Razzak's route in Asia, we can begin to make sense of the peculiar features of the history of Atlantic-side European peoples, as they launched empires that will take up more and more space in the rest of the book.

Fragile Empires in Africa

East Africa

Ethiopia emerged relatively early from its period of quiescence. In the late fourteenth century, the highland realm again began to reach beyond its mountains. Monasteries became schools of missionaries whose task was to consolidate Ethiopian power in the conquered pagan lands of Shoa and Gojam. Rulers concentrated on reopening outlets to the Red Sea and thereby the Indian Ocean. By the time they recaptured the port of Massawa in 1403, Ethiopian rule stretched into the Great Rift valley. The resulting wealth funded defense of the empire and fueled expansionist ambitions.

Saints' lives tell of internal expansion. Wasteland was converted to farmland and settled by monks. When Portuguese diplomatic missions began to arrive in Ethiopia—the first in the 1490s, a second in 1520— "men and gold and provisions like the sands of the sea and the stars in the sky" impressed them. As we shall see in the next chapter, however, they overestimated the empire's stability. Ethiopia had probably already overreached its resources.

Southward from Ethiopia, at the far end of the Rift valley, lay the gold-rich Zambezi valley and the productive plateau beyond, which stretched to the south as far as the Limpopo River and was rich in salt, gold, and elephants. Like Ethiopia, these areas looked toward the Indian Ocean for long-range trade with the economies of maritime Asia, but their outlets to the sea lay below the reach of the monsoon system and, therefore, beyond the normal routes of trade. Still, adventurous merchants—most of them, probably, from southern Arabia—risked the voyage to bring manufactured goods from Asia in trade for gold and ivory. Some of the most vivid evidence comes from the mosque in Kilwa, in modern Tanzania, where fifteenth-century Chinese porcelain bowls line the inside of the dome.

Further evidence of the effects of trade lie inland between the Zambezi and the Limpopo Rivers, where fortified, stone-built administrative centers—called **zimbabwes**—had been common for centuries. Now, in the late fourteenth and fifteenth centuries, the zimbabwes entered their greatest age. The most famous, Great Zimbabwe, included a formidable citadel on a hill 350 feet high, but remains of other citadels are scattered over the land. Near stone buildings, the beef-fed elite were buried with gifts: gold, jeweled ironwork, large copper ingots, and Chinese porcelain.

In the second quarter of the fifteenth century, the center of power shifted northward to the Zambezi valley, with the expansion of a new regional power. Mwene Mutapa, as it was called, arose during the northward migration of bands of warriors from what are now parts of Mozambique and KwaZulu-Natal. When one of their leaders conquered the middle Zambezi valley, he took the title Mwene Mutapa, or "lord of the

The Turreted Walls of Great Zimbabwe. These walls surround a 350-foot-high hill, crowned by a formidable citadel, which housed the elite, who ate beef and were buried with gifts of gold, copper, jewels, and Chinese porcelain. Though it was the biggest of the stone-built settlements of the period, Great Zimbabwe was typical, in style and substance, of other buildings in the region south of the Zambezi River during what we think of as the late Middle Ages. *Casement Creative Services Inc.*

tribute payers," a name that became extended to the state. From about the mid-fifteenth century, the pattern of trade routes altered as conquests spread toward the coast. But Mwene Mutapa never reached the ocean. Native merchants, who traded at inland fairs, had no interest in a direct outlet to the sea. They did well enough using middlemen on the coast and had no incentive for or experience of ocean trade. Like Mali in West Africa, Mwene Mutapa was a landlocked empire, sustained by trade in gold and salt. The colonists were drawn, not driven, northward, though a decline in the navigability of the Sabi River may have stimulated the move.

West Africa

New states emerged in West Africa, following the decline of the old regional power, Mali (see Map 15.1). Like many empires of promise in out-of-the-way places, Mali became a victim of its relative isolation. From

EUROPE

Azores

Lisbon

Granada

Tangier
Strait of Gibraltar
Fez

Rome

Tunis

Mediterranean Sea

Madeira

Marrakesh

Tripoli

Alexandria

Cairo

Nile

Canary Islands

Tropic of Cancer

Cape Bojador

S a h a r a

Cape Blanc

Taghaza

S a h e l

20°

Walata

Senegal

Cape Verde

Cape Verde Islands

Gambia

Timbuktu

Gao

Niger

Kano

La

Bissagos Island

Niani

Ife

Benin

A F R I C A

Elmina

São Jorge de Mina

Equator

Cape Palmas

Gulf of Guinea

Príncipe
São Tomé
Cape St. Catherine

Lake Victoria

Lake Tanganyika

ATLANTIC OCEAN

Ascension Island

Congo

La
Nya

St. Helena

Cape St. Mary (Cape Lobo)

Zambezi

20°

Tropic of Capricorn

Cape Cross
Walvis Bay

Great Zimbabwe

Limpopo

S

KwaZulu Natal

Cape da Volta (Dias Point)

Orange

N

1,000 km

1,000 miles

St. Helena Bay

Cape of Good Hope

Mossel Bay

Algoa

Map 15.1 Major African States, 1400–1500

402

ASIA

Hornuz

Bahrain

Persian Gulf

Tropic of Cancer

mascus

alem

Jedda

Mecca

Arabia

Arabian
Sea

20°

India

Dhofar

Calicut

Massaweh

Sana

Aden

Mogadishu

INDIAN

Equator

OCEAN

alindi

ombasa

Dar es Salaam

Kilwa

Cape
Delgado

60°

Mozambique

20°

Madagascar

Tropic of Capricorn

ala

Cape
Correntes

40°

60°

40°

80°

	Ethiopia
	Mwene Mutapa
	Zimbabwes
	Mali
	Songhay
	Benin / Ife
	Kongo
- -	other African states
→	Indian Ocean trade route
→	Trans-Saharan trade route
	extent of Portuguese exploration of West African coast up to 1487
✚	Portuguese markers erected in token of their claim to sovereignty
MOZAMBIQUE	modern country or state

about 1360, a power struggle pitted the descendants of Mansa Musa against those of his brother, Mansa Sulayman. Around 1400, the Songhay, a people from lower down the Niger River, broke away and seized Gao. This was disastrous for Mali, because Gao was one of the great trading cities between the rain forest and the desert. Traders could now outflank Mali's trading monopoly. Mali was further weakened in the 1430s when invaders from the Sahara seized its northernmost towns.

Two decades later, in the 1450s, when Portuguese expeditions, pushing up the river Gambia, made the first recorded European contact with Mali, the mansa's power was virtually confined to the original heartland. The result was a tragedy for the history of the world, for the absence of a strong West African empire undermined Europeans' view of black Africans as equals. The Portuguese expected to find a great, rich state. Instead, they found Mali a ramshackle wreck. Their disappointment prejudiced them, and they wondered if black Africans had any capacity for political greatness. In European maps, instead of the magnificent depictions of the Mansa of Mali typical of the fourteenth century—bearded and costumed in Western fashion—the ruler of Mali became a figure of fun. Though some Europeans continued to treat black Africans as equals—and the Portuguese crown, in particular, maintained the affectation that black kings were fellow monarchs on a par with those of Europe—from now on, white people in Africa could nourish convictions of superiority.

Songhay gradually succeeded Mali as the most powerful state in the region, but it never controlled as much of the Saharan trade as Mali had. Muhammad Touray Askia, an upstart general who used Islam to justify seizing the throne, wrenched Songhay into the Islamic mainstream in the late fifteenth century. In 1497, he undertook a pilgrimage to Mecca on a scale of magnificence calculated to echo that of Mansa Musa in 1324–1325 (see Chapter 14). Askia's ascent to power ensured that Sahelian Africa—the band of dry grasslands south of the Sahara—would be predominantly Muslim. His alliance with the Muslim intelligentsia made Songhay a state "favored by God" in the eyes of religious Muslims—the class on which the state depended for administrators. He stimulated trade by imposing peace and so increasing Saharan merchants' sense of security. He promoted a modest sort of capitalism by concentrating resources in the hands of religious foundations, which had the personnel and range of contacts to maximize their holdings' potential. New canals, wells, dikes, and reservoirs scored the land. Cultivated terrain was extended, especially for rice, which had long been known in the region but never previously farmed on a large scale.

Songhay, like Mali before it, benefited from the trade routes of the Sahara, which linked the Mediterranean coast to the Niger valley. The Niger River is navigable for almost its entire length, but the Atlantic's adverse winds and currents limited opportunities for long-range communications by sea. The states and cultures of the tropical forest and coast in the African "bulge" were confined to regional power and wealth. Nevertheless, they have left plenty of evidence of economic expansion and of the growing wealth and power of their kings in the fifteenth century: the fortifications, for instance, of the city-state of Benin and the splendid metal weapons, adornments and courtly furnishings of Benin and the Ife.

The whole African coast from Senegambia to the mouth of the Niger impressed Europeans at the time. In 1486, the Portuguese crown celebrated the baptism of a Senegambian chief in Lisbon with a lavish display. The trading post that Portugal opened at São Jorge da Mina, on the underside of the African bulge, in 1482, appeared on maps as a gilded, turreted fantasy city. It suited the Portuguese monarchs to exaggerate the grandeur, but their propaganda reflected the reality of a region of rich kingdoms, busy commerce, and patches of urban life.

Farther south, too, in the Congo Basin, the opportunities for states to reach out by sea were limited. The Kingdom of Kongo dominated the Congo River's navigable lower reaches, probably from the mid-fourteenth century. The ambitions of its rulers became evident when Portuguese explorers established contact in the 1480s. Kongo enthusiastically adopted the religion and technology of the visitors. The kingdom became host to Portuguese missionaries, craftsmen, and mercenaries. The royal residence was rebuilt in Portuguese style. The kings issued documents in Portuguese, and members of the royal family went to Portugal for their education. One prince became an archbishop, and the kings continued to have Portuguese baptismal names for centuries thereafter. Portuguese firepower gave the kings a military advantage over their neighbors. They gained territory and, more importantly, slaves, many of whom they sold to the Portuguese for export.

The Portuguese connection made Kongo the best-documented kingdom in West Africa in the sixteenth century. Missionary reports extolled the zeal of the "angelic" King Affonso I (r. 1506–1545) and commended him for "burning idolaters along with their idols," but Affonso's own letters to the king of Portugal reveal tensions with white slavers, who infringed the royal monopoly of European trade goods and seized slaves indiscriminately.

Although Ethiopia, Mwene Mutapa, Songhay, and Kongo were all formidable regional powers, and although many small states of the West African coast expanded commercially and territorially, little of this activity was on an unprecedented scale. Ethiopia's resumed rise was part of a sequence of expansion and decline that had been going on for centuries. Songhay was the latest in a series of empires in the Sahel. Trading states had long studded West Africa. Mwene Mutapa was the successor state of the builders of the zimbabwes. What was happening in Africa at this time was part of a wider phenomenon. Like some states in Eurasia, African empires grew at impressive rates and to impressive extents in part because they were in touch with other phenomena of commercial and political expansion: Songhay across the Sahara, Ethiopia and Mwene Mutapa across the Indian Ocean, the coastal trading cities and Kongo with the Portuguese. In the Americas, however, in the late fifteenth century, even states that had to contend with isolation could expand on a new scale.

Ecological Imperialism in the Americas

Since the inventive historian Alfred Crosby coined the term **ecological imperialism** in 1972, historians have used it to refer to the sweeping environmental changes European imperialists introduced in regions they colonized. But the term also suits Native American empires, especially in mountainous regions of Mesoamerica and the Andes, where the key to success in large-scale state-building lay in combining diverse regions and exploiting the complementary products of contrasting ecosystems.

The Inca Empire

In the late fifteenth century, the world's fastest-growing empire was the Inca Empire of the Andes (see Map 15.2). Inca chronology is always uncertain because until the 1530s, the **Incas** made records in forms that are now indecipherable. But they seem to have built their empire during the reigns of three rulers in the late fifteenth and early sixteenth centuries.

Probably early in the second half of the fifteenth century, the founders of the Inca state descended from the highlands to find fertile land. They occupied Cuzco in what is today Peru, which became their biggest city, and began subjugating their neighbors. Their story was typically Andean. They gathered many diverse environments into one state to facilitate exchanging and stockpiling a wide range of products. The Incas, however, took this well-established practice to new lengths. Theirs was one of the most environmentally diverse empires of the time. It was long and thin, with the Andes forming its spine and creating valleys. Abrupt mountains multiplied microclimates, where sun, wind, and rain hit different slopes in different ways. The Inca realm encompassed coastal lowlands and the fringes of the rain forest. The tribute system was based on the exchange of products between contrasting zones, as a form of insurance against disaster. When the maize of the lowlands failed, for instance, potatoes from the highlands might still be abundant. The Inca uprooted populations and transferred

Map 15.2 The Aztec and Inca Empires, ca. 1500

- important center
- MAYA native state or people
- ⎯⎯⎯ Aztec trade route
- ⎯ Inca road

The Inca City of Machu Picchu. Machu Picchu in Peru is a miracle of urban engineering. It was built on a sharp 2,000-foot rise in the high Andes. Unrecorded in colonial times, it was discovered early in the twentieth century when the eccentric and adventurous American archaeologist, Hiram Bingham, was searching for another lost Inca city, Vilcamba. Unknown to Bingham, however, Vilcamba was in the tropical lowlands of Peru. The vast difference in climate between the two cities is stunning evidence of the environmental diversity of the Inca world.
© Danny Lehman/CORBIS All Rights Reserved

them to new locations according to the needs of the system.

Economic security, however, came at a political price. To maintain the state, the Incas had to acquire new territories, leading to hectic and, in the long run, perhaps, unsustainable expansion. Moreover, their methods of subjugation were extreme. For example, they extinguished the coastal civilization of Chimú (see Chapter 14), razing its capital at Chan Chan almost to the ground and deporting its population. An Inca ruler was said to have drowned 20,000 enemy warriors when he conquered the Cañaris. The survivors became irreconcilable opponents. Many subject-peoples harbored grievances arising from memories of massacred warriors and forced migrations. Even the Incas' allies and elites were dissatisfied. The Checa, for instance, a people important to the Inca system of control because their homeland straddled the route from Cuzco to the coast, never forgave the Inca emperor for breaking his promise to perform ritual dances at their principal shrine in acknowledgment of their alliance. The Inca never seemed to have enough rewards to go around. The cults of dead leaders—who lay, mummified, in expensive shrines maintained by huge payrolls—existed to appease key Inca clans and factions, whose resources they boosted at the state's expense because tribute had to be diverted to meet the costs. Toward the end of the fifteenth century, the Inca Empire approached its greatest extent, from Quito in what is today Ecuador in the north, to the Valle Central in what is today Chile in the south. But at its core, the empire was shaky.

The Aztec Empire

In the same period, rapid expansion and environmental diversity characterized Mesoamerica. Here, an exceptionally dynamic state grew from the city of Tenochtitlán in the valley of Mexico (and some neighboring, allied cities). Tenochtitlán stood in the middle of a lake, some 5,000 feet above sea level. The ground was swampy, and there was too little cultivable soil to grow enough maize and beans to feed the city. Tenochtitlán was too high and the climate too severe for cacao and cotton. Its people, whom we have traditionally called **Aztecs**, had only two options: poverty or warfare. They chose the latter.

Aztec expansion, like Inca expansion, was largely a late fifteenth- and early sixteenth-century phenomenon (see Map 15.2). At its peak, the Aztec Empire stretched from the Pánuco River in the north to what is now the Mexican–Guatemalan border on the Pacific coast and encompassed hundreds of tributary communities.

The tribute demonstrated the ecological diversity of the regions. The Aztec bureaucracy meticulously listed and depicted it. From the "hot countries" in the south came ornamental feathers and jaguar pelts, jade, amber, gold, rubber, and resin for incense. Overlapping regions supplied cacao, the essential ingredient of the addictive, high-status drink essential at Aztec ceremonies and parties. Ornamental shells arrived from the Gulf of Mexico and live eagles, deerskins, and tobacco from the mountain lands that fringed the valley of Mexico. For war and for the ball game, which was a form of mock warfare and an aristocratic exercise, Aztec nobles and priests dressed as gods. On almost every folio of the tribute roll appear magnificent ritual garments and divine disguises. The tribute system brought necessities as well as luxuries: hundreds of thousands of bushels of maize and beans every year, with hundreds of thousands of cotton garments and quilted cotton suits of armor. Finally, there was the product that best expressed Aztec power and—perhaps in Aztec minds—supplied the blood that fueled the universe: human-sacrifice victims, captured in war or tendered in tribute. In 1487, for instance, at the dedication of a temple in Tenochtitlán, thousands of captives were said to have been slaughtered at once.

Tributary networks were complex. Some communities exchanged tribute, often collecting it from some tributaries to pass part of it on to others. Tenochtitlán was at the summit of the system, but it left most communities to govern themselves as long as they paid tribute. This was contrary to the highly interventionist politics of the Incas. According to records copied in the sixteenth century, Tenochtitlán only garrisoned or directly ruled 22 communities. The Aztecs did, however, share some of the same problems that afflicted the Incas. They relied on fragile alliances, bore the resentment of tributary peoples, and expanded so rapidly that their reach always threatened to out-run their available manpower and technology.

The Aztecs and Incas saw themselves as continuing the traditions of earlier empires. They recalled ruined supremacies of the past: Tula and Teotihuacán in the Aztec case, Tiahuanaco for the Incas. The reach of their power seems, however, to have exceeded anything either Mesoamerica or the Andes had witnessed before. So how did they do it? Long-range ex-changes with other cultures helped to propel empires in Eurasia and Africa into expansion, but these advantages scarcely applied in the Americas. The Incas and the Aztecs did not benefit from new technology. Nor, as far as we know, were people in the Andes or Mesoamerica bouncing back from any-thing resembling the demographic catastrophe that had struck parts of the Old World in the previous century. There was no momentum of recovery be-hind the enormous extensions of Aztec and Inca power. The most likely explanation is that demographic growth crossed a critical threshold in both areas. Probably, only imperial solutions could command the resources and compel the exchanges of goods needed to sustain the growing cities in which the Aztecs and Incas lived. In any case, both empires, as we shall see in the next chapter, were short lived. Essentially, they were empires of types traditional in the region and overreached the realistic limits of their potential.

New Eurasian Empires

The expanding states of fifteenth-century Africa and the Americas proved relatively fragile. Sixteenth-century European conquerors swal-lowed the Aztec and Inca states almost at a gulp. The Christian Ethiopian Empire barely survived in the sixteenth century, eroded by conflicts with Muslims and waves of pagan, pastoralist immigrants. Songhay fell to invaders from Morocco in the late sixteenth century. Finally, though Mwene Mutapa survived into the seventeenth century, having fought off would-be conquerors from Europe, it then dissolved into numerous petty states. It was the borderlands that straddle Europe and Asia that nurtured the really big, really enduring new or resumed empires of the age, those of the Turks and Russians.

The Russian Empire

The rise of a powerful Russian state was without precedent. Previously, the geography of the region produced unstable empires. Open, flatlands and scattered populations contributed to an environment in which states formed with ease but survived with difficulty. Most came and went quickly, vulnerable to external attack and internal rebellion.

In the fifteenth century, however, the rulers of Moscow established a state of imperial dimensions. Muscovy—as the early Russian Empire was called—has always been volatile at the edges, but it has been exceptionally enduring. One of the features that made Muscovy different was the shape of its heartland, based on control of the Volga River, a north–south axis of

Making Connections | EXPANSION AND ITS LIMITS: AFRICA AND THE AMERICAS IN THE FIFTEENTH CENTURY

REGION/ STATE OR EMPIRE	CAUSES FOR EXPANSION	EVIDENCE/ EFFECTS OF EXPANSION	LIMITATIONS
East Africa/ Ethiopia	Access to long-range trading routes to Indian Ocean via Red Sea ports	Recapture of coastal cities in 1400s, increased trade in slaves, ivory, gold, incense; creation of main access road to Indian Ocean	Limited agricultural land; need to control mountainous and lowland areas to access trade routes; major river systems to south and east with large populations; gradually encroaching Portuguese and Muslim influence by sixteenth century
East/ Central Africa/ Zambezi River Valley, Great Zimbabwe	Difficult access to Indian Ocean seaports; large populations with ivory, gold, metal resources	Manufactured goods from Asia (porcelain, silk, etc.) traded for gold, ivory; increasingly large administrative centers in stone, large amounts of coins, jewelry, gold, etc.	Landlocked; altered trade routes; decline in navigability of rivers
West Africa/ Songhay Empire	Trade routes of the Sahara, linking Mediterranean and Niger valley; astute leadership (Muhammad Askia) and alliance with Muslim clerics, scholars	Canals, dikes, reservoirs; extension of cultivable land; rich trade with Niger valley goldfields	Limited long-range communication; adverse Atlantic winds/currents

Continued

REGION/ STATE OR EMPIRE	CAUSES FOR EXPANSION	EVIDENCE/ EFFECTS OF EXPANSION	LIMITATIONS
Central Africa/ Kongo	Domination of Congo River; alliance with Portuguese; abundant natural resources	Use of Western firearms, Christian religion and symbols to legitimate and maintain control; trading of slaves from conquered territories to Portuguese	Ultimate loss of control over slave trade to Portuguese leads to decline and fall
South America/ Inca	Diversity of environments, resources; tribute system allows exchange of products between zones	Quick expansion and use of extreme methods of control; extensive road system; large shrines for dead leaders	Mass executions and other methods of subjugation alienate subject peoples and allies
Mesoamerica/ Aztecs	Environmental diversity; hundreds of tributary communities; efficient recordkeeping; large array of natural resources	Intensive transformation of environment in/around capital (Tenochtitlán); abundance of commodities, both neces- sities (food, tools) and luxuries; wide- spread human sacrifice; monumental architecture	Loose administrative control; fragile alliances; alienation of tributary peoples; excessively rapid expansion

trade. Earlier empires, including the Mongols', were based on the east–west axis of the steppes, which served as highways for horse-borne armies.

The new empire's beginnings were almost imperceptible to those who experienced them or witnessed their effects. The Russian world expanded northward in the late fourteenth and early fifteenth centuries, as missionaries opened roads to convert people in the forests and tundra. An astonishing example of expansion by sea occurred in the 1430s. The evidence comes from a monastery on an island—bare, poor, and ice bound for much of the year—in the White Sea, on the edge of the Arctic. The monks painted their home not as it was but as they envisioned it, with a golden sanctuary and domes like candle flames. They showed the founders of their monastery rowing to the island, while whip-wielding angels expelled the original inhabitants. Monks appeared, rescuing shipwrecked merchants, while angels supplied bread, cooking oil, and salt. All the ingredients of a typical story of European colonialism appeared: the religious inspiration, the heroic voyage into a perilous environment, the ruthless treatment of the natives, the struggle to adapt and establish a viable economy, the quick arrival of commercial interests, and, finally, success through perseverance.

Muscovy's sudden take-off in the second half of the century, when conquests of neighboring peoples turned it into an imperial state, overshadowed early efforts at expansion. Indeed, when Constantinople fell to the Turks in 1453, Muscovites could see their city as, potentially, the **Third Rome**, replacing Constantinople as Constantinople had replaced Rome, the former imperial capital. By the 1470s, Ivan the Great (r. 1462–1505) had absorbed most of Russia's other principalities. He married a Byzantine princess, incorporated an imperial eagle into his coat of arms, forged a genealogy that traced his family back to the Roman Caesars, imported Italian technicians to fortify his palace, and contemptuously dismissed an offer from the German emperor to invest him as king. "We have been sovereign in our land from our earliest forefathers," he replied, "and we hold our sovereignty from God."

During his reign, Ivan the Great more than trebled the territory he ruled—to more than 240,000 square miles. His realm also took a new shape around most of the vast length of the Volga across the breadth of Eurasia, uniting the fur-rich north and the cash-rich fringes of Asia. Fur was the "black gold" of the north, inducing Russians to conquest and colonization, just as gold and spices lured other European peoples to Africa and the East.

War parties gathered pelts as tribute along a northern route that missionaries pioneered in the late fourteenth century, by way of the Vym and Pechora rivers. Repeatedly from 1465, Ivan sent expeditions to the Perm and Ob rivers to levy tribute. The expedition of 1499 numbered 4,000 men, equipped with sleds drawn by reindeer and dogs. They crossed the Ob in winter, returning with 1,000 captives from the forest-dwelling peoples who hunted for the furs. Ivan's ambassador to the rich Italian duchy of Milan boasted that his master received 1,000 gold ducats' worth of tribute annually in furs—five or six times an Italian nobleman's income.

Timurids and the Ottoman Empire

In the early fifteenth century, Turkish—and therefore Muslim—expansion resumed in southern Europe and Asia, still under the leadership of the Ottoman dynasty. The Mongol supremacy had been a traumatic challenge to the Islamic world, shattering the reputation of Muslim armies, breaking the monopoly of Sharia or Islamic law, exposing the limitations of the clergy, and inspiring the religious minded to withdraw from the world in a spirit of resignation. The Black Death had also battered the Islamic world. Muslims' numerical preponderance over Christians never got back to earlier levels. But, for global history, the Islamic recovery is a much bigger story than the temporary setback.

To understand recovery, we turn to one of its most brilliant Muslim observers after the Black Death, the historian Ibn Khaldun, whose theory about the conflict between nomads and settled peoples we discussed at the end of Chapter 12. In 1377, he sat down in a village in what is now Algeria "with ideas pouring into my head like cream into a churn." His efforts produced one of the most admired works of all time on history and political philosophy, the *Muqaddimah*. Its theme, as we have seen, was the counterpoint of herder and tiller, which Ibn Khaldun saw as the motivating force of historical change. Everywhere in his day, the Islamic world's survival and success depended on Muslims' ability to tame the invaders from the deserts and the steppes and turn their power to the service of Islam. Most Turkic peoples and many Mongols were converted into warriors for Islam. Consequently, Central Asia stayed Muslim, and the Indian Ocean linked mainly Muslim shores. In other words, the Silk Roads and maritime routes of Eurasia had to pass through Muslim-ruled territory. Equally important, human fuel renewed the Islamic world's capacity to wage war and expand its frontiers.

The most conspicuous mobilizer of steppeland manpower in Muslim service in the late fourteenth and early fifteenth centuries, was the self-proclaimed "world conqueror," Timur the Lame. His court historian represented him as "the being nearest to perfection" and a pious devotee of holy war, but his role models were the pagans, Alexander the Great (see Chapter 5) and Genghis Khan.

When Turkic nobles rebelled against their Mongol masters in his homeland in Central Asia, Timur emerged as their leader. Deftly eliminating rivals, he ruled the region by 1370. By the time he died in 1405, he had conquered Iran, defeated the Ottoman Turks and put their sultan in a cage, invaded Syria and India, and planned the conquest of China. Wherever he went, he heaped up the skulls of citizens unwise enough to resist his sieges. But this destruction was for efficiency, not for its own sake. It made most conquests submit cheaply. His success was by no means uniform, but it was impressive enough, and consistent enough, to seem decreed by God. He addressed enemies in terms reminiscent of Mongol tradition: "Almighty God has subjugated the world to my domination, and the will of the Creator has entrusted the countries of the Earth to my power."

The day after his death, as his heirs turned on one another, his achievements seemed transitory. Even today, Timur's impact on the

Islamic world is usually seen as negative. His success against the Ottomans gave Christendom a reprieve. By humbling the Mongols, he encouraged Christians in Russia. By weakening the Muslim sultans of Delhi, he liberated millions of Hindus. These reflections, however, overlook his psychological legacy. He was a champion of Islamic orthodoxy and a patron of Muslim education and arts. He is also important as an example of the process that converted pastoralists. Having been the scourge of the Islamic world, they became its sword.

Timur was like a hurricane—his force was terrific but soon spent. The Ottomans were more like a monsoon: Their armies returned and receded as each season came and went, but they constantly made new conquests. The fate of the Mongols—expelled from China, retreating from Russia—shows how hard it was for a great Eurasian empire to survive in the aftermath of the Black Death, which jarred economies and felled manpower. Yet, falteringly in the early fifteenth century but with renewed strength thereafter, the **Ottoman Empire** managed to do so.

The Ottomans' great advantage was location. The heartlands of the empire were at the crossroads of some of the world's great trade routes, where the Silk Roads, the Indian Ocean routes, the Volga, the Danube, and the Mediterranean almost converged. The history of the Byzantine Empire showed the importance of holding on to this location. Byzantium flourished while it occupied these lands and faltered when its control there slackened and ceased (see Chapter 12). From their own past, the Ottomans inherited the traditions of steppeland imperialism. They were content, at first, to levy tribute and allow their tributaries to govern themselves or to exist as puppet states, manipulated according to Ottoman needs.

Gradually, the Ottomans adapted to the environments they conquered: agrarian, urban, and maritime. Other empires of nomadic origins failed when required to adapt to new military technologies, but the Ottomans readily became a gunpowder empire. Their forces could blow away cavalry or batter down city walls. They even took to the sea. In the 1390s, the sultans began to build permanent fleets. It was a long process and hard to catch up with long-established naval powers. As late as 1466, a Venetian merchant in Constantinople claimed that to win a battle, Turkish warships needed to outnumber those of Venice by four or five to one. By the end of the century, however, the Ottomans had overturned the 400-year-old Christian maritime supremacy in the Mediterranean. Never since Rome defeated Carthage (see Chapter 7) had such an unlikely candidate become a naval power.

Like other imperialists of steppeland origin, the Ottomans mastered the art of keeping subjects of diverse religions loyal to them. They tolerated Jews, Christians, and Shiites, but had no qualms about levying punitive taxes on these minorities. From the 1420s, the sultan functioned

Sultan Mehmet II. Mehmet (r. 1451–1481) extended the Ottoman Empire westward into Europe, taking great interest in the culture of lands that had once belonged to the Roman Empire—especially after he captured the old Roman capital of Constantinople in 1453. Gentile Bellini, who worked at Mehmet's court and was one of the best Venetian painters of the day, painted this portrait of the sultan in the realistic style that was popular in Italy at the time. Bellini framed the sultan's image with columns decorated in the European style.
© National Gallery, London/Art Resource, NY

as head of two linked systems of law and justice. The first consisted of secular laws and customs that the sultan's appointees administered. The second was enshrined in the Quran and the traditions of Islamic law, with a body of experts to run it, who met in the sultan's palace.

In 1451, Mehmet II became sultan at the age of 19, uninhibited by caution, committed to reform. Mehmet's predecessors had prudently allowed self-rule to continue in the city of Constantinople and its few surviving dependencies—the last fragments of the Byzantine Empire that still proclaimed itself the heir of Rome. The Ottomans controlled what happened in Constantinople by threatening and bribing political factions there. But some factions in the city were determined to challenge the Turks and formed an alliance with Western Christendom. In 1453, Mehmet laid siege to Constantinople. He built huge forts to command the sea approaches to the city and fired the heaviest artillery yet made at its walls. He transported ships overland to elude Byzantine naval defenses. In the end, weight of numbers was decisive. The attackers climbed the walls over the bodies of dead comrades. The last Byzantine emperor fell fighting—only the eagles on his purple boots identified his corpse.

With the fall of Constantinople, Mehmet II could see his empire as a continuation of Rome's. He looked westward for fashions to incorporate into his court culture and chose Italians to paint his portrait, sculpt his medals, and write some of his propaganda. The direction of Ottoman conquests tilted toward Europe, extending over most of what are now Greece, Romania, and Bosnia, seeking to control the shores of the Adriatic and Black seas.

The Limitations of Chinese Imperialism

Ottoman imperialism in the fifteenth century resumed its former course after setbacks caused by the Black Death and the rise of Timur. An observer at the time might have predicted that China, too, would resume expansion and even anticipate the Ottomans in bidding for a maritime empire. The best way to understand why such developments seemed likely—and why they were frustrated—is to look back at China's recovery from the mid-fourteenth-century plagues. Like so many decisive episodes of Chinese history, the story begins among the people on whose labor the empire depended: peasants.

Peasants sometimes defer hope and wait for the millennium—a fabled future, when divine intervention will either perfect the world or end it. Often, however, in times of extreme disaster, peasant movements arise to try to trigger the millennium. One of the most explosive of all such movements began among Chinese canal workers in 1350.

In mid-fourteenth-century China, peasants were the victims of the slow-grinding effects of economic misery and the survivors of terrible environmental disasters. The plagues that began in the 1320s kept returning. Not until well into the 1350s did the plagues in China begin to lose their virulence or to encounter naturally immunized populations. In 1344, the Yellow River flooded. Persistent droughts followed. In this setting, peasants were forced to repair the Grand Canal, which carried essential food supplies from southern and central China to Beijing.

The peasants' millenarianism—their hope of deliverance in a transfigured world—was based on a Buddhist myth. The lord Maitreya, the last of the earthly Buddhas, would come to prepare the world for extinction. Now, however, given the peasants' miserable lives, the myth acquired a political edge. Maitreya would put a triumphant end to the struggle of good against evildoers and give his followers power over their oppressors. A similar movement was current at the same time in western Europe, where the Fraticelli, a group of Franciscan friars, identified with the needs and interests of the wretched of the Earth. The Franciscans predicted that a cosmic hero would come to wrest treasures from the soil and enrich the poor. Fulfilling a prophecy uttered by the mother of Jesus, which the prayer of the church repeated every day, he would put down the mighty from their seat and exalt the humble and meek.

In China, along with their desire for deliverance, peasants harbored a folk memory of the Song dynasty (see Chapter 12) and a hankering for the good times supposed to have preceded the Mongol invasions of a century before. Peasant revolts are often revolutionary in the most literal sense of the word, wanting to turn the world back, "revolve" it full circle, to an imagined or misremembered golden age. Therefore, in 1351 when

China's Mongol rulers executed a pretender to the throne who claimed to be the heir of the Song, a revolt broke out among his followers. They easily recruited thousands to their cause. Some members of the elite joined in, out of resentment at the ruling dynasty's partiality for foreign advisers.

The leader who emerged from the chaos of rebellion was Zhu Yuanzhang, the recruiting officer of a rebel band. By the end of the 1350s, the Yangtze region had dissolved into a chaos of small states run by similar upstarts. In river warfare of reckless daring, Zhu conquered his rivals. In 1368 he proclaimed a new dynasty.

Zhu cleverly managed the coalition that had brought him to power. He juggled the rebels' conflicting ideologies while reconciling former enemies. To please the Confucian establishment, he restored ancient court ceremonies and the examinations for public service that the Mongols had neglected or ignored. He kept the military command structure and even dressed in some of the same ways as the previous Mongol dynasty had. He renounced the cult of Maitreya, but only after making it clear that he had fulfilled it in his own person by adopting the buddha's traditional epithet, "Ming" or "bright", as the name of his dynasty.

Zhu had the auto-didact's contempt for the academic establishment. "Chewing on phrases and biting on words," he said, "they have never had any practical experience." But he recognized that the Confucian bureaucrats had expertise he could use. He therefore kept the traditional power centers of his court in balance: the military top brass, the eunuchs who ran the imperial household, the foreign and Muslim advisers and technicians, the Buddhist and Daoist clergies, and the merchant lobby. Together, they limited the power of the Confucian elite.

The result was a brief period when expansionist policies prevailed over Confucian caution. Zhu's son, the Yongle emperor (r. 1402–1424) aggressively sought contact with the world beyond the empire. He meddled in the politics of Vietnam, fought Mongols, and enticed the Japanese to trade.

The most spectacular manifestation of the new outward-looking policy was the career of the Muslim eunuch-admiral, Zheng He. In 1405, he led the first of a series of naval expeditions. Their purpose has been the subject of long and unresolved scholarly debate, but in part, at least, it was to show China's flag all over the Indian Ocean. Zeng He replaced unacceptable rulers in Java, Sumatra, and Sri Lanka, founded a puppet state on the commercially important Strait of Malacca and gathered tribute from Bengal in India. He displayed Chinese power as far away as Jiddah, on the Red Sea coast of Arabia, and in major ports in East Africa as far south as the island of Zanzibar. "The countries beyond the horizon," he announced with some exaggeration, "and from the ends of the Earth, have become subjects." He restocked the imperial zoo with giraffes, ostriches, zebra, and rhinoceroses—all hailed as beasts bringing good luck—and brought Chinese geographical knowledge up to date.

Can Zheng He's voyages be called an imperial venture? Their official purpose was to pursue a fugitive pretender to the Chinese throne—but that would not have required such vast expeditions to such distant places. The Chinese called the vessels treasure ships and emphasized what they called tribute gathering (in the more distant spots Zheng He's ships visited, what happened was more like a commercial exchange). Commercial objectives may have been involved. Almost all the places Zheng He visited had long been important in Chinese trade. In part, the voyages were scientific missions: Ma Huan, Zheng He's interpreter, called his own book on the subject *The Overall Survey of the Ocean's Shores,* and improved maps and data on the plants, animals, and peoples of the regions visited were among the expeditions' fruits. But flag showing is always, to some extent, about power or, at least, prestige. And the aggressive intervention Zheng He made in some places, together with the tone of his commemorative inscriptions, demonstrates that the extension or reinforcement of China's image and influence was part of the project.

Indeed, it is hard to see how else the huge investment the state made in his enterprise could have been justified. Zheng He's expeditions were on a crushing scale. His ships were much bigger than anything European navies could float at the time. His first fleet was said to comprise 66 of the largest junks ever built, 225 support vessels, and 27,870 men. The seventh voyage—probably the longest in reach—sailed 12,618 miles. The voyages lasted, on average, more than two years each. Some silly claims have been made for Zheng He's voyages. Ships of his fleet did not sail beyond the limits of the Indian Ocean— much less discover America or Antarctica. His achievements, however, clearly demonstrated China's potential to become the center of a maritime empire of enormous reach.

But the Chinese naval effort could not last. Historians have debated why it was abandoned. In many ways, it was to the credit of Chinese decision makers that they pulled back from involvement in costly adventures far from home. Most powers that have undertaken such expeditions and attempted to impose their rule on distant countries have had cause to regret it. Confucian values, as we have seen, included giving priority to good government at home. "Barbarians" would submit to Chinese rule if and when they saw the benefits. Attempting to beat or coax them into submission was a waste of resources. By consolidating their landward empire, and refraining from seaborne imperialism, China's rulers ensured the longevity of their state. All the maritime colonial empires founded in the world in the last 500 years have crumbled. China is still there.

Part, at least, of the context of the decision to abort Zheng He's missions is clear. The examination system and the gradual discontinuation of other forms of recruitment for public service had serious implications. Increasingly, Confucian scholars, with their indifference to expansion, and gentlemen, with their contempt for trade, governed China. In the 1420s and 1430s, the balance of power at court shifted in the bureaucrats' favor, away from the Buddhists, eunuchs, Muslims, and merchants who had supported Zheng He. When the Hongxi emperor succeeded to the throne in 1425, one of his first acts was to cancel Zheng He's next voyage. He restored Confucian office holders, whom the Yongle emperor had dismissed, and curtailed the power of other factions. In 1429, the shipbuilding budget was cut almost to extinction. The scholar-elite hated overseas adventures—and the factions that favored them—so much that they destroyed all Zheng He's records in an attempt to obliterate his memory. Moreover, China's land frontiers became insecure as Mongol power revived. China needed to turn away from the sea and toward the new threat. The Chinese state never resumed overseas expansion. The growth of trade and Chinese colonization in Southeast Asia was left to merchants and migrants. China, the empire best equipped for maritime imperialism, opted out. Consequently, lesser powers, including those of Europe, were able to exploit opportunities at sea.

By the late fifteenth century, the scholars' position seemed unshakable, and the supremacy of Confucian values could not be challenged. The Hongxi emperor aspired to Confucian perfection. He ordered the slaughter or expulsion of court magicians and exiled 1,000 Buddhist and Daoist monks. He resumed a Confucian priority: study of the penal code, which previous Ming emperors had neglected. He reintroduced the palace lectures, during which Confucian professors instructed the emperor. He endowed a library alongside the Confucian temple at the sage's birthplace in Qufu. He patronized artists whose work radiated Confucian serenity. Wu Wei, the emperor's favorite painter, had Daoist patrons, too, but his representations of ascetics meditating in sketchy landscapes demonstrate the triumph of thought over nature and, therefore, by implication, of Confucianism over Daoism.

The Beginnings of Oceanic Imperialism

Even under the Yongle emperor, China confined its seaward reach to the monsoonal seas of maritime Asia and the Indian Ocean—seas of terrible hazards and fabulous rewards. As we have seen, the Indian Ocean was relatively easy to cross but relatively hard to enter or exit. For most of history, therefore, it was the preserve of peoples whose homes bordered it or who traveled overland—like some European and Armenian traders—to become part of its world. Moreover, all the trade was internal. Merchants took no interest in venturing far beyond the monsoon system to reach other markets or supplies.

From Europe, however, access to the Indian Ocean was well worth seeking. Merchants craved a share of the richest trades and most prosperous markets in the world, especially the spices, drugs, and aromatics that were the specialities of producers in Sri Lanka, India, and Indonesia. These products—sold to rich buyers in China and Southwest Asia, and, to a lesser extent, in Europe—were the most profitable in the world, in terms of price per unit of weight. Many Europeans sought to find out where they came from and to take part in the trades. But the journey was too long, laborious, and hazardous to generate much profit. From the Mediterranean, merchants had either to travel up the Nile and proceed by camel caravan to a Red Sea port or to negotiate a dangerous passage through the Ottoman Empire to the Persian Gulf. In either case, they obviously could not take ships with them. This was a potentially fatal limitation because Europeans had little to offer to people in the Indian Ocean basin except shipping services. For most of the fifteenth century, until the 1490s, Europeans were not sure if it was possible to approach the Indian Ocean by sea at all.

Europe's only effective access by sea to the rest of the world is along its western seaboard, into the Atlantic. For the Atlantic to become Europe's highway to the rest of the world, explorers had to discover the winds that led to commercially important destinations. There were, first, the northeast trade winds, which led to the resource-rich, densely populated regions of the New World, far south of the lands the Norse reached. There was also the South Atlantic wind system, which led, by way of the southeast trade winds and the westerlies of the far south, to the Indian Ocean.

The technology to exploit the Atlantic's wind systems only gradually became available during a period of long, slow improvements to ships' hulls, rigging, and water casks in the thirteenth, fourteenth, and fifteenth centuries. Historians have traditionally emphasized the contribution of formal science in developing maritime charts and instruments for navigating by the stars. Now it seems that these innovations were irrelevant. No practical navigator of this period in Europe seems to have used them.

Only the long accumulation of information and experience could make a breakthrough possible. Several attempts were made during the fifteenth century to explore Atlantic space, but most doomed themselves to failure by setting out in the belt of westerly winds. Presumably explorers chose this route because they wanted to be sure that they would be able to get home. Shortly after 1450, the westernmost islands of the Azores were reached. Over the next three decades, the Portuguese crown often commissioned voyages of exploration farther into the Atlantic, but none is known to have made any further progress. Not only was exploitation of the Atlantic slow, but at first it yielded few returns. In the 1480s, however, the situation changed, and Atlantic exploration began to pay off. In the North Atlantic, customs records of the English port of Bristol indicate that quantities of whaling products, salt fish, and walrus ivory from the ocean increased dramatically. In West Africa, the Portuguese post at São Jorge da Mina, near the mouth of the Benya River, was close to gold fields in the Volta River valley, and large amounts of gold now began to reach European hands. In 1484, sugar production at last began in the Canary Islands. In the same decade, Portuguese made contact with the kingdom of Kongo. Although voyages toward and around the southernmost tip of Africa encountered unremittingly adverse currents, they also showed that the far south of the Atlantic had westerly winds that might at last lead to the Indian Ocean. By the end of the 1480s, it was apparent that Atlantic investment could yield dividends.

The 1490s were a breakthrough decade in Europe's efforts to reach out across the ocean to the rest of the world (see Map 15.3). In 1492–1493, Christopher Columbus, financed by Italian bankers and endorsed by Spanish monarchs, discovered fast, reliable routes across the Atlantic that linked the Mediterranean and the Caribbean. In 1496, John Cabot, another Italian adventurer, backed by merchants in Bristol and the English crown, discovered a direct route across the North Atlantic, using variable spring-time winds to get across and the westerlies to get back. His route, however, was not reliable and, for more than 100 years, was mainly used to reach the lucrative cod fisheries of Newfoundland.

Meanwhile, the Portuguese sought to determine whether the Indian Ocean was genuinely landlocked. In 1497–1498, a Portuguese trading venture, commissioned by the crown and probably financed by Italian bankers, attempted to use the westerlies of the South Atlantic to reach the Indian Ocean. Its leader, Vasco da Gama, turned east too early and had to struggle around the Cape of Good Hope at the tip of Africa. But he managed to get across the Indian Ocean anyway and reach the pepper-rich port of Calicut at the tip of India. The next voyage, in 1500, reached India without a serious hitch.

The breakthroughs of the 1490s opened direct, long-range routes of maritime trade across the world among Europe, Asia, and Africa. Success may seem sudden, but not if we view it against the background of slow developments in European chronology and knowledge and the accelerating benefits of Atlantic exploration in the previous decade. Was there more to it than that? Was there something special about European culture that would explain why Europeans, rather than explorers from other cultures, discovered the world-girdling routes, linking the Old World to the New and the Indian Ocean to the Atlantic? Some European historians have argued just that—that Europeans had something others lacked.

Such a suggestion, however, seems ill conceived. Compared to the peoples of maritime Asia, Europeans were special mainly in being slow to launch long-range voyages. Moreover, the breakthrough explorations were not the work of "Europe" but of people from a few communities on the Atlantic seaboard and in the Mediterranean. What distinguishes them is not so much that they set off with the right kind of culture–though, as we shall see, culture was relevant in surprising ways–as that they set off from the right place, near to where ocean-spanning winds and currents arose and returned.

The European Outlook: Problems and Promise

In some ways, indeed, western Europe in the fifteenth century was beset with problems. Recovery from the disasters of the fourteenth century was slow. Though plagues were less severe, they remained frequent. And though used to the severe climate that began in the early fourteenth century, western Europeans did not reoccupy the high ground and distant colonies that they had abandoned. In most places, population increase was modest and probably did not reach levels attained before the Black Death. Food supplies were unreliable, and harvests frequently failed.

Human foes joined impersonal enemies—plague, war, and famine. In 1396, a crusade to drive the Turks from the Balkans failed. It marked the beginning of a long period of Turkish advance on the Balkan and eastern Mediterranean frontiers of Christendom. Meanwhile, in the northeast, Lithuanians, most of whom remained pagan until the late fourteenth or early fifteenth century, eroded the conquests of German knightly orders along the Baltic Sea (see Chapter 12). In the early fifteenth century, Thule Inuit raiders finally obliterated the Norse colony on Greenland (see Chapter 14).

Meanwhile, hard times created opportunities for those with the skill or luck to exploit them. High mortality opened gaps in elites, which bureaucrats could fill, thanks, in part, to a revolution in government. To help legitimize the newcomers' power, Western moralists redefined nobility as the product of virtue or education rather than ancestry. "Virtue is the sole and unique nobility," declared a Venetian coat of arms. A doctrine of late fifteenth-century Italian social thought invoked Greek mythology to make its point: "Neither the wealth of Croesus nor the antiquity of the blood of Priam could rival reason as an ingredient of nobility."

New economic divisions appeared. The line of the Elbe and northern Danube rivers and the lands between became a cultural fault line. To the west of this line, underpopulation boosted the value of labor. The effects were to liberate peasants and urban communities from landowners' control, split up landholdings, encourage tenancies, and convert cropland to pasture. In the east, the opposite occurred. Landholders responded to the loss of manpower and revenue by clamping down on peasants' rights and forcing formerly free towns into submission. New definitions of

Map 15.3 European Oceanic Exploration to 1500

→	European explorers with names and dates
→	Norse voyages of the 10th and 11th centuries
▬	extent of Portuguese exploration of West African coast up to 1487
✚	Portuguese markers erected in token of their claim to sovereignty
Thule Inuit	people

nobility were rejected. East of the Bohemian forest, nobility was ancient blood or acquired "by martial discipline," and that was that.

Scored by heresies, trenched by conflicting social values, and riven by economic cracks, western Europe nevertheless showed signs of self-confidence and optimism. Scholars and artists pursued, with renewed vigor, the project of recovering the legacy of classical antiquity—the cultural achievements of ancient Greece and Rome. The movement is commonly called the **Renaissance** on the grounds that the civilization of classical antiquity was reborn—but scholarship has now identified renaissances in almost every century for the previous 1,000 years. No radically new departure occurred in the fifteenth century from what had gone before, but long-accumulating tendencies were accentuated (see Chapter 18).

Humanist students adopted a predominantly secular curriculum: grammar, rhetoric, poetry, history, and moral philosophy, imbibed mainly from classical texts. The classics as well as—even, instead of—Christianity came to inform common ideas of morality, politics, and taste. Spreading, at first, from a few French and north Italian schools, **humanism** gradually became Europe's most prestigious form of learning. Political thinkers turned back to Greek and Roman history for instruction. Religious innovators modeled their ideas on evidence from early Christianity. Artists adopted realism and perspective from what they thought were Greek and Roman models.

Florence demonstrates humanism's power and limitations. In the fifteenth century, classical taste transformed its art and architecture. Comparisons with the Roman republic inspired its citizens to think of themselves as free and self-governing. Yet power gradually fell into the hands of a single family, the Medici, who patronized art in the classical tradition but who actually spent more on jewels and on gaudy, gemlike artworks that could display their wealth. When they were temporarily overthrown in 1494, after their banking business collapsed, the state that replaced them was no Roman-style republic. Rather, it was the rule of a "godly" clique, inspired by a hell-fire preacher, who preferred piety to humanism. Botticelli (1444–1510), the great artist who had painted pagan erotica for a Medici villa, turned to biblical subjects.

Still, across Europe, the rise of humanism had lasting consequences. Humanists painstakingly scrutinized the language of the Bible and the historical traditions of the church, exposing incorrect translations and departures from the practices of early Christianity. New styles in church architecture reflected classical taste and, more deeply, arose from the desire to create a setting for the kind of devotion that humanism inspired. Open sanctuaries, brilliantly lit and approached through wide naves and aisles, allowed worshippers to see and take part in events at the altar.

Humanism also helped arouse European interest in the wider world. In the early fifteenth century, the work of the ancient Greek scholar

The Church of San Lorenzo. Filippo Brunelleschi, the trend-setting architect of Florence, got the commission to design the parish church of the ruling Medici family in 1418. He based his concept on laws of mathematical proportion that, he believed, ancient Greek and Roman architects had followed. He copied the ground plans of the most ancient churches he knew, and, to support the clergy's growing desire to make congregations participate actively in worship, he opened domes above the sacred spaces to fill them with light.
The Art Archive/Dagli Orti (A)

Ptolemy, originally written in Alexandria in the second century, invited intense speculation about geography, mapping the world, and the limits of exploration. The first-century B.C.E. work of Strabo, a Greek geographer who sought to reconstruct Homer's mental map of the world, prompted questions about finding previously unknown continents in the ocean. Humanists' fascination with the history of language reinforced the search for "primitive" peoples, who might cast light on the question of how language originated.

Chivalry, however, was more characteristic than humanism in stimulating overseas exploration. **Chivalry** could not, perhaps, make men good, as it was supposed to do. It could, however, win wars. In 1492, for instance, the monarchs of the Spanish kingdom of Castile extended the frontier of Christendom by conquering Granada, the last Muslim kingdom in Spain, in "a beautiful war," said the Venetian ambassador. "There was not a lord present who was not enamored of some lady," who "often handed warriors their weapons . . . with a request that they show their love by their deeds." The queen of Castile died uttering prayers to the Archangel Michael as "prince of the chivalry of angels."

The typical chivalrous hero of the time took to the sea, conquered an island, married a princess, and became a ruler. Explorers—often men of humble social origins—tried to embody these fictions in real life. Adventurers in the service of the Portuguese Prince Henry (1394–1460) included former pirates and violent criminals. They indulged in chivalric rituals and gave themselves storybook names, like Lancelot and Tristram of the Island. They also colonized the Madeira Islands and parts of the Azores and explored the coast of West Africa as far as Sierra Leone. The commercial sector that helped to back overseas adventures was looking for new opportunities—especially the Genoese, whose role in the eastern Mediterranean at this period was largely confined to high-bulk, low-profit shipping and trading. Marginal noblemen, shut out from advancement at home and imbued with chivalric ideas, were willing to take amazing risks. That, together with the availability of high-risk investment, helps to explain many early forays in Atlantic exploration.

Prince Henry himself—traditionally misrepresented as a navigator motivated by scientific curiosity—imagined himself a romantic hero, destined to perform great deeds and win a kingdom of his own. The truth is that he never went exploring, and his desperate efforts to make enough money to pay his retainers included slave raiding and a soap monopoly. His followers included the father-in-law of Christopher Columbus, a weaver by training who reinvented himself as a "captain of cavaliers and conquests" and who took to exploration to escape the restricted social opportunities of home.

Alongside chivalry, millenarian fantasies may have influenced overseas expansion. The first king of Portugal's ruling dynasty was called "Messiah of Portugal." Columbus claimed that the profits of his discoveries could be used to conquer Jerusalem and help complete God's plans for a new age. Franciscan friars who supported Columbus believed that an "Age of the Holy Spirit," which would precede the end of the world, was coming soon, and some of them came to see the New World as the place where such an age might begin.

Europe's outreach into the Atlantic was probably not the result of science or strength so much as of delusion and desperation. This was a space race, where it helped to come from behind. The prosperous cultures with access to the Indian Ocean felt no need to explore remote lands and seas for new resources. For cash-strapped Europe, however, the attempt to exploit the Atlantic for new products was like the efforts of underdeveloped countries today, anxiously drilling for offshore wealth from oil or natural gas. In some ways, it paid off.

CHRONOLOGY

ca. 1325	Aztecs found city of Tenochtitlán
1368	Beginning of Ming dynasty
1370–1405	Reign of Timur
Late fourteenth century	Ethiopia expands into surrounding regions
1401	Lorenzo Ghiberti wins competition for the bronze doors of the Baptistery in Florence
1405	First voyage of Zheng He
1417	Voyage of Abd-ar-Razzak to Vijayanagar (India)
1430s	Portuguese establish way stations in Azores
1440s	Portuguese begin to obtain slaves from West Africa
ca. 1450	Inca begin period of expansion and conquest
1453	Ottomans capture Constantinople
1462–1505	Reign of Ivan the Great
ca. 1475	Center of power in southern Africa shifts from Zimbabwe to Mwene Mutapa
1480s	Portuguese make contact with kingdom of Kongo
1482	Portuguese establish trading post of São Jorge da Mina on West African coast
1484	Sugar production begins in Canary Islands
1490s	First Portuguese diplomatic missions arrive in Ethiopia
1492–1493	First voyage of Christopher Columbus; Spanish kingdom of Castile captures Granada, last Muslim kingdom in Spain
1496	John Cabot discovers direct route across North Atlantic
1497	Pilgrimage of Muhammed Touray Askia, ruler of Songhay, to Mecca; first voyage of Vasco da Gama
1500	Vasco da Gama reaches India

IN PERSPECTIVE
Beyond Empires

The imperial habit was spreading, and new empires were forming in environments that had never experienced imperialism before. Russia, for example, extended empire to the Eurasian far north. Mwene Mutapa introduced it in sub-Saharan East Africa. The Aztecs and Incas practiced it in the Americas on an unprecedented scale. Nonetheless, most of Africa and the Americas, as well as the whole of Australia and most of the Pacific island world, as far as we know, had still not experienced anything like empire. While some empires revived, most of the world remained in the hands of communities with modest political ambitions. These were still organized as kinship networks, chiefdoms, or small states. More remarkably, perhaps, some regions with an imperial past, or under imperialist threat, shied away. Instead, they developed systems in which independent states coexisted with varying degrees of mutual hostility.

In North Africa, for instance, Mamluk Egypt was an immensely rich and productive state but remained confined to the Nile valley, unable to expand beyond the deserts that fringed it. Westward, along North Africa's Mediterranean coast lay numerous small states, founded on the profits of trade or piracy, where Mediterranean and Saharan trade routes met. At the western end of North Africa, Morocco emerged as a kingdom on the edge of the Islamic world, holding Christendom at bay.

South and Southeast Asia also housed state systems. In India, the sultanate of Delhi never fully recovered from the setbacks of the mid-fourteenth century. Hindu states proliferated, some warlike, specifically, toward Islam. The most militaristic, perhaps, was Vijayanagar (the "City of Victories")—Abd-ar-Razzak's destination as he crossed the ocean from Iran in 1417. It impressed another Muslim visitor in 1443 as "such that the eye has seen nothing like it." Chinese expansion nibbled at the edges of Southeast Asia, but China's renunciation of imperialism left the native states of the region free to try one another's strength. The Thai—founders of what is now called Thailand—certainly had expansionist ambitions. In the early fifteenth century, they created the region's largest state at the expense of their neighbors, the Burmese, Khmer, Mons, and Malays. Nonetheless, the region lacked a dominant empire and remained home to a state system in which a number of regional states contended with each other.

Most of Europe, too, continued to enclose a state system. East of the Vistula River, where geography favored the formation of large states, Russia, as we have seen, undertook a massive imperial enterprise. A union of the Polish and Lithuanian states in 1386 created what, on the map, at least, also looked like an empire from the Baltic to the Black Sea. Farther west, however, small or middling states got stronger, and the dream of reuniting them and recreating the old Roman Empire faded—or began to look unrealistic.

Something like national feeling emerged from mutually intelligible speech and a common sense of identity defined by birth. National communities adopted patron saints. At European gatherings such as universities and church councils, people defined themselves according the nation to which they belonged and engaged in ferocious disputes over precedence.

States increasingly asserted absolute sovereignty, rejecting any obligation to defer to such traditionally supranational authorities as the church or the Holy Roman Emperor. When, for instance, the Emperor Sigismund visited England in 1415, a knight rode into the sea to challenge him to renounce all claim to authority in England before he was allowed to disembark. Kings of France called themselves "emperors in their own realm," and those of Castile in Spain asserted "my sovereign absolute power."

Some rulers developed ideological grounds for their claims to absolute sovereignty. French kings were supposedly endowed with divine powers to heal and to perform "miracles in your own lifetime." Richard II of England (r. 1377–1399) had himself painted attended by angels, opening his hands to receive the body of Christ from the Virgin Mary herself.

At the same time, the power of the state really did increase. One reason was improved communications. As paper replaced parchment, increasing the output of documents, royal bureaucracies reached more people in more parts of the realm. Changes in the concept of law also strengthened the state. Traditionally, the law was a body of wisdom handed down from the past. Now it came to be seen as a code that kings and parliaments could endlessly change and recreate. The state's power also expanded over vast new areas of public life and common welfare: labor relations, wages, prices, forms of land tenure, markets, the food supply, livestock breeding, and even, in some cases, what personal adornments people could wear.

Finally, while the state was growing more powerful, the power of the church declined. Between 1378 and 1415, rulers in Latin Christendom could not agree on whom to recognize as pope. The power vacuum eroded what little unity Christendom still had. Secular states became stronger as heresies arose. Under the influence of reformers who demanded—among other changes—lay control of appointments in the church and worship in everyday language instead of Latin, Bohemia for a time refused to recognize papal authority. Reformers known as conciliarists argued that the church should become a kind of republic, with power transferred from Rome to a council of bishops who would meet periodically in a kind of parliament.

How much difference did the state system make to Europe's prospects? Historians have engaged in a pointless debate over this question. On the one hand, the state system deprived Europeans of unified command, of the sort found, for instance, in the Chinese or Ottoman empires. On the other hand, it stimulated competition among rulers, multiplying the possible sources of patronage available to innovators. For European maritime expansion, the state system was not decisive in launching most initiatives. Explorers and would-be empire builders relied on private enterprise, with little or no state backing. Columbus, for instance, got no direct financial support from the Spanish crown—the myth that Queen Isabella of Castile pawned her jewels for him is nonsense. His funding came from bankers and private investors. Prince Henry's Atlantic enterprise was also a private venture. Furthermore, as the example of Southeast Asia shows, a state system was not in itself sufficient to produce overseas imperialism; for that, the stimulus of coming from behind was necessary. Asian states were at the nodes of the world's richest trades. They had no need to explore new markets or conquer new centers of production, because everything came to them anyway. Europeans, on the other hand, had to expand if they were to gain access to anything worth exploiting.

For all its hesitations and limitations, fifteenth-century expansion was new and potentially world changing. The new routes pioneered in the 1490s linked the populous central belt of Eurasia to the Americas and Africa, and Europe to Asia by sea. We can see the beginnings of an interconnected globe—a **world system** able to encompass the planet. The expanding empires of the age were reaching toward each other. Where they made contact, they became arenas of unprecedented scale for trade and for transmitting technology, ideas, sentiments, and ways of life. The consequences would transform the world of the next three centuries: Worldwide encounters, commerce, conflict, contagion, and cultural and ecological exchange would follow.

PROBLEMS AND PARALLELS

1. Why did powerful new states emerge in Africa and the Americas during this period? Why were these states relatively short lived?
2. What does the term "ecological imperialism" mean? How did the Inca and Aztec empires exploit the ecological diversity of the Andes and Mesoamerica?
3. How did the Russian and Ottoman empires expand during the fourteenth and fifteenth centuries?
4. Why did China turn away from maritime expansion in the fourteenth century?
5. Why was western Europe motivated to try to expand overseas? What roles did geography and culture play in European overseas expansion?

Abolitionism   Belief that slavery and the slave trade are immoral and should be abolished.

Aborigines   Indigenous people of Australia.

Afrikaans   An official language of South Africa, spoken mostly by the Boers. It is derived from seventeenth-century Dutch.

Ahriman   The chief spirit of darkness and evil in Zoroastrianism, the enemy of Ahura Mazda.

Ahura Mazda   The chief deity of Zoroastrianism, the creator of the world, the source of light, and the embodiment of good.

Al-Andalus   Arabic name for the Iberian Peninsula (Spain and Portugal).

Alluvial plains   Flat lands where mud from rivers or lakes renews the topsoil. If people can control the flooding that is common in such conditions, alluvial plains are excellent for settled agriculture.

Almoravids   Muslim dynasty of Berber warriors that flourished from 1049 to 1145 and that established political dominance over northwest Africa and Spain.

Alternative energy   Energy sources that usually produce less pollution than does the burning of fossil fuels; these sources are renewable in some cases.

Alternative medicine   Medicines, treatments, and techniques not advocated by the mainstream medical establishment in the West.

Americanization   The process by which other cultures, to a greater or lesser degree, adopt American fashions, culture, and ways of life.

Anarchists   Believers in the theory that all forms of government are oppressive and undesirable and should be opposed and abolished.

Animal rights   Movement that asserts that animals have fundamental rights that human beings have a moral obligation to respect.

Anti-Semitism   Hostility or prejudice against Jews or Judaism.

Arthasastra   Ancient Indian study of economics and politics that influenced the Emperor Asoka. The Arthasastra expresses an ideology of universal rule and emphasizes the supremacy of "the king's law" and the importance of uniform justice.

Artificial intelligence   The creation of a machine or computer program that exhibits the characteristics of human intelligence.

Arts and Crafts Movement   Nineteenth-century artists and intellectuals who argued that the products produced by individual craftsmen were more attractive than and morally superior to the mass, uniform goods produced by industry.

Assassins   A secret order of Muslims in what is today Syria and Lebanon who terrorized and killed its opponents, both Christian and Muslim. The Assassins were active from the eleventh to the thirteenth centuries.

Atlantic Slave Trade   Trade in African slaves who were bought, primarily in West Africa, by Europeans and white Americans and transported across the Atlantic, usually in horrific conditions, to satisfy the demand for labor in the plantations and mines of the Americas.

Atomic theory The theory that matter is not a continuous whole, but is composed of tiny, discrete particles.

Australopithecine (Trans.) "Southern apelike creatures." Term used to describe prehuman species that existed before those classed under the genus *Homo*.

Axial age A pivotal age in the history of world civilization, lasting for roughly 500 years up to the beginning of the Christian era, in which critical intellectual and cultural ideas arose in and were transmitted across the Mediterranean world, India, Iran, and East Asia.

Axial zone The densely populated central belt of world population, communication, and cultural exchange in Eurasia that stretches from Japan and China to western Europe and North Africa.

Aztecs People of central Mexico whose civilization and empire were at their height at the time of the Spanish conquest in the early sixteenth century.

Balance of trade The relative value of goods traded between two or more nations or states. Each trading partner strives to have a favorable balance of trade, that is, to sell more to its trading partners than it buys from them.

Bantu African people sharing a common linguistic ancestry who originated in West Africa and whose early agriculture centered on the cultivation of yams and oil palms in swamplands.

Big bang theory Theory that the universe began with an explosion of almost infinitesimally compressed matter, the effects of which are still going on.

Black Death Term for a lethal disease or diseases that struck large parts of Eurasia and North Africa in the 1300s and killed millions of people.

Boers Dutch settlers and their descendents in southern Africa. The first Boers arrived in South Africa in the seventeenth century.

Bon Religion that was Buddhism's main rival in Tibet for several centuries in the late first millennium C.E.

Brahman A member of the highest, priestly caste of traditional Indian society.

Bureaucratization The process by which government increasingly operates through a body of trained officials who follow a set of regular rules and procedures.

Business imperialism Economic domination and exploitation of poorer and weaker countries by richer and stronger states.

Byzantine Empire Term for the Greek-speaking, eastern portion of the former Roman Empire, centered on Constantinople. It lasted until 1453, when it was conquered by the Ottoman Turks.

Cahokia Most spectacular existent site of Mississippi Valley Native American civilization, located near modern St. Louis.

Caliph The supreme Islamic political and religious authority, literally, the "successor" of the Prophet Muhammad.

Canyon cultures Indigenous peoples of the North American Southwest. The canyon cultures flourished beween about 850 and 1250 C.E.

Capitalism An economic system in which the means of production and distribution are privately or corporately owned.

Caste system A social system in which people's places in society, how they live and work, and with whom they can marry are determined by heredity. The Indian caste system has been intertwined with India's religious and economic systems.

Centralization The concentration of power in the hands of a central government.

Chaos theory Theory that some systems are so complex that their causes and effects are untraceable.

Chicago-style economics   The economic theory associated with economists who taught at the University of Chicago that holds that low taxes and light government regulation will lead to economic prosperity.

Chimú   Civilization centered on the Pacific coast of Peru that was conquered by the Inca in the fifteenth century.

Chinese Board of Astronomy   Official department of the Chinese imperial court created in the early seventeenth century that was responsible for devising the ritual calendar.

Chinese diaspora   The migration of Chinese immigrants around the world between the seventeenth and nineteenth centuries.

Chivalry   The qualities idealized by the medieval European aristocracy and associated with knighthood, such as bravery, courtesy, honor, and gallantry.

Chola   Expansive kingdom in southern India that had important connections with merchant communities on the coast. Chola reached its height around 1050 C.E.

Christendom   Term referring to the European states in which Christianity was the dominant or only religion.

Cistercians   Christian monastic order that built monasteries in places where habitation was sparse and nature hostile. Cistercians practiced a more ascetic and rigorous form of the Benedictine rule.

Civilizing mission   The belief that imperialism and colonialism are justified because imperial powers have a duty to bring the benefits of "civilization" to, or impose them on, the "backward" people they ruled or conquered.

Clan   A social group made up of a number of families that claim descent from a common ancestor and follow a hereditary chieftain.

Class struggle   Conflict between competing social classes that, in Karl Marx's view, was responsible for all important historical change.

Climacteric   A period of critical change in a society that is poised between different possible outcomes.

Code Napoléon   Civil code promulgated by Napoleon in 1804 and spread by his armies across Europe. It still forms the basis for the legal code for many European, Latin American, and African countries.

Cold War   Post–World War II rivalry between the United States and its allies and the Soviet Union and its allies. The cold war ended in 1990–1991 with the end of the Soviet Empire in eastern Europe and the collapse of the Soviet Union itself.

Commune   Collective name for the citizen body of a medieval and Renaissance Italian town.

Communism   A system of government in which the state plans and controls the economy, and private property and class distinctions are abolished.

Confraternities   Lay Catholic charitable brotherhoods.

Confucianism   Chinese doctrine founded by Confucius emphasizing learning and the fulfillment of obligations among family members, citizens, and the state.

Constitutionalism   The doctrine that the state is founded on a set of fundamental laws that rulers and citizens make together and are bound to respect.

Consumerism   A system of values that exalts the consumption and possession of consumer goods as both a social good and as an end in themselves.

Coolies   Poor laborers from China and India who left their homelands to do hard manual and agricultural work in other parts of the world in the nineteenth and early twentieth centuries.

Copernican revolution   Development of a heliocentric model of the solar system begun in 1543 by Nicholas Copernicus, a Polish churchman and astronomer.

Council of Trent   A series of meetings from 1545 to 1563 to direct the response of the Roman Catholic Church to Protestantism. The council defined Catholic dogma and reformed church discipline.

Counter Reformation   The Catholic effort to combat the spread of Protestantism in the sixteenth and seventeenth centuries.

Countercolonization   The flow of immigrants out of former colonies to the "home countries" that used to rule them.

Country trades   Commerce involving local or regional exchanges of goods from one Asian destination to another that, while often handled by European merchants, never touched Europe.

Creoles   People of at least part-European descent born in the West Indies, French Louisiana, or Spanish America.

Crusades   Any of the military expeditions undertaken by European Christians from the late eleventh to the thirteenth centuries to recover the Holy Land from the Muslims.

Cubism   Artistic style developed by Pablo Picasso and Georges Braque in the early twentieth century, characterized by the reduction and fragmentation of natural forms into abstract, often geometric structures.

Cultural relativism   The doctrine that cultures cannot be ranked in any order of merit. No culture is superior to another, and each culture must be judged on its own terms.

Cultural Revolution   Campaign launched by Mao Zedong in 1965–1966 against the bureaucrats of the Chinese Communist Party. It lasted until 1976 and involved widespread disorder, violence, killings, and the persecution of intellectuals and the educated elite.

Culture   Socially transmitted behavior, beliefs, institutions, and technologies that a given group of people, peoples, or animals share.

Cuneiform   Mesopotamian writing system that was inscribed on clay tablets with wedge-shaped markers.

Czars   (Trans.) "Caesar." Title of the emperors who ruled Russia until the revolution of 1917.

Dada   An early twentieth-century European artistic and literary movement that flouted conventional and traditional aesthetic and cultural values by producing works marked by nonsense, travesty, and incongruity.

Dahomey   West African slave-trading state that began to be prominent in the sixteenth century.

Daimyo   Japanese feudal lord who ruled a province and was subject to the shoguns.

Dalai Lama   The ruler of Tibet.

Daoism   Chinese doctrine founded by Laozi that identified detachment from the world with the pursuit of immortality.

Declaration of the Rights of Man and Citizen   Declaration of basic principles adopted by the French National Assembly in August 1789, at the start of the French Revolution.

Decolonization   The process by which the nineteenth-century colonial empires in Asia, Africa, the Caribbean, and the Pacific were dismantled after World War II.

Deforestation   The process by which trees are eliminated from an ecosystem.

Democracy   Government by the people, exercised either directly or through elected representatives.

Dharma   In the teachings of Buddha, moral law or duty.

Diffusion   The spread of a practice, belief, culture, or technology within a community or between communities.

Dirlik   (Trans.) "Wealth." The term applied to provincial government in the Ottoman Empire.

Divine love   God's ongoing love for and interest in human beings.

Dominicans   Order of preaching friars established in 1216 by Saint Dominic.

Dutch East India Company   Dutch company founded in 1602 that enjoyed a government-granted monopoly on trade between Holland and Asia. The company eventually established a territorial empire in what is today Indonesia.

Dutch East Indies   Dutch colonies in Asia centered on present-day Indonesia.

East India trade   Maritime trade between western Europe and New England and Asia (predominantly India and China) between 1600 and 1800. Westerners paid cash for items from Asia, such as porcelain, tea, silk, cotton textiles, and spices.

Ecological exchange   The exchange of plants and animals between ecosystems.

Ecological imperialism   Term historians use for the sweeping environmental changes European and other imperialists introduced in regions they colonized.

Ecology   The interaction of people with their environment.

Economic liberalism   Belief that government interference in and regulation of the economy should be kept to a minimum.

Economies of scale   A concept in economics whereby a business saves on costs by making big investments and consequently gets disproportionately large returns.

Edo   Former name of Tokyo when it was the center of government for the Tokugawa shoguns.

El Niño   A periodic reversal of the normal flow of Pacific currents that alters weather patterns and affects the number and location of fish in the ocean.

Elan vital   The "vital force" hypothesized by the French philosopher Henri Bergson as a source of efficient causation and evolution in nature.

Emancipation   The act of freeing; liberation.

Empiricism   The view that experience, especially of the senses, is the only source of knowledge.

Encyclopedia, The   Twenty-eight volume compendium of Enlightenment thought published in French and edited by Denis Diderot. The first volume appeared in 1751.

English East India Company   British trading company founded in 1600 that played a key role in the colonization of India. It ruled much of the subcontinent until 1857.

Enlightened despotism   Reforms instituted by powerful monarchs in eighteenth-century Europe who were inspired by the principles of the Enlightenment.

Enlightenment   Movement of eighteenth-century European thought championed by the *philosophes*, thinkers who held that change and reform were desirable and could be achieved by the application of reason and science. Most Enlightenment thinkers were hostile to conventional religion.

Environmentalism   A deepening and spreading conviction that humans are part of the web of the natural world; that our relationship with our environment is the inescapable framework for everything we do; and that, in consequence, care of the environment is our essential priority, whether as a self-interested strategy or as a moral or religious duty that we owe to other forms of life.

Epistemology The branch of philosophy that studies the nature of knowledge.

Eugenics The theory that the human race can be improved mentally and physically by controlled selective breeding and that the state and society have a duty to encourage "superior" persons to have offspring and prevent "inferior" persons from reproducing.

Eunuchs Castrated male servants valued because they could not produce heirs or have sexual relations with women. In Byzantium, China, and the Islamic world, eunuchs could rise to high office in the state and the military.

European Union (EU) Loose economic and political federation that succeeded the European Economic Community (EEC) in 1993. It has expanded to include most of the states in western and eastern Europe.

Evolution Change in the genetic composition of a population over successive generations, as a result of natural selection acting on the genetic variation among individuals.

Examination system System for selecting Chinese officials and bureaucrats according to merit through a series of competitive, written examinations that, in theory, any Chinese young man could take. Success in the exams required years of intense study in classical Chinese literature. The examination system was not abolished until the early twentieth century.

Existentialism Philosophy that regards human existence as unexplainable, and stresses freedom of choice and accepting responsibility for the consequences of one's acts.

Expressionism Term describing a work of art in which forms are created primarily to evoke subjective emotions rather than to portray objective reality.

Factories Foreign trading posts in China and other parts of Asia. The chief representative of a factory was known as a "factor." Though the earliest trading posts were established by the Portuguese in the sixteenth century, the number of factories grew rapidly in the eighteenth and nineteenth centuries, with European and American merchants trading for silk, rhubarb, tea, and porcelain.

Fascism A system of government marked by centralization of authority under a dictator, stringent socioeconomic controls, and suppression of the opposition through terror and censorship.

Feminism The belief that women collectively constitute a class of society that has been historically oppressed and deserves to be set free.

Fossil fuels Fuels including peat, coal, natural gas, and oil.

Franciscans Religious order founded by Francis of Assisi in 1209 and dedicated to the virtues of humility, poverty, and charitable work among the poor.

Free trade The notion that maximum economic efficiency is achieved when barriers to trade, especially taxes on imports and exports, are eliminated.

French Revolution Political, intellectual, and social upheaval that began in France in 1789. It resulted in the overthrow of the monarchy and the establishment of a republic.

Fulani Traditional herdsmen of the Sahel in West Africa.

Functionalism An architectural style that favored machine-like buildings, fashioned by necessity and stripped to their most elementary forms.

Fundamentalism The idea that a sacred text or texts contains fundamental truths that cannot be questioned, either by critical inquiry or by scientific evidence.

Futurism   Artistic vision articulated by Emilio Filippo Marinetti in 1909. He believed that all traditional art and ideas should be repudiated, destroyed, and replaced by the new. Futurists glorified speed, technology, progress, and violence.

Gauchos   Argentine cowboys.

General will   Jean-Jacques Rousseau's concept of the collective will of the population. He believed that the purpose of government was to express the general will.

Genetically modified (GM)   Crops that have been *genetically modified* to produce certain desired characteristics.

Genocide   The systematic and planned extermination of an entire national, racial, political, or ethnic group.

Ghana   A medieval West African kingdom in what are now eastern Senegal, southwest Mali, and southern Mauritania.

Global gardening   The collecting in botanical gardens of plants from around the world for cultivation and study.

Globalization   The process through which uniform or similar ways of life are spread across the planet.

Glyph   A form of writing that uses symbolic figures that are usually engraved or incised, such as Egyptian hieroglyphics.

Golden Horde   Term for Mongols who ruled much of Russia from the steppes of the lower Volga River from the thirteenth to the fifteenth centuries.

Grand Vizier   The chief minister of state in the Ottoman Empire.

Green revolution   Improvements in twentieth-century agriculture that substantially increased food production by developing new strains of crops and agricultural techniques.

Greenhouse effect   The increase in temperature caused by the trapping of carbon in the Earth's atmosphere.

Guardians   Self-elected class of philosopher-rulers found in Plato's *Republic*.

Habsburgs   An Austro-German imperial family that reached the height of their power in the sixteenth century under Charles V of Spain when the Habsburgs ruled much of Europe and the Americas. The Habsburgs continued to rule a multinational empire based in Vienna until 1918.

Hajj   The pilgrimage to Mecca that all faithful Muslims are required to complete at least once in their lifetime if they are able.

Han   Dynasty that ruled China from ca. 206 B.C.E. to ca. 220 C.E. This was the period when the fundamental identity and culture of China were formed. Chinese people still refer to themselves as "Han."

Hanseatic League   Founded in 1356, the Hanseatic League was a powerful network of allied ports along the North Sea and Baltic coasts that collaborated to promote trade.

Herders   Agriculturalists who emphasize the raising of animals, rather than plants, for food and products, such as wool and hides.

High-level equilibrium trap   A situation in which an economy that is meeting high levels of demand with traditional technology finds that it has little scope to increase its output.

Hinduism   Indian polytheistic religion that developed out of Brahmanism and in response to Buddhism. It remains the majority religion in India today.

Hispaniola   Modern Haiti and the Dominican Republic.

Hohokam people   Native American culture that flourished from about the third century B.C.E. to the mid–fifteenth century C.E. in south-central Arizona.

Holocaust   Term for the murder of millions of Jews by the Nazi regime during World War II.

Holy Roman Empire   A loose federation of states under an elected emperor that consisted primarily of Germany and northern Italy. It endured in various forms from 800 to 1806.

Homo erectus   (Trans.) "Standing upright." Humanlike tool-using species that lived about 1.5 million years ago. At one time, Homo erectus was thought to be the first "human."

Homo ergaster   (Trans.) "Workman." Humanlike species that lived 800,000 years ago and stacked the bones of its dead.

Homo habilis   (Trans.) "Handy." Humanlike species that lived about 2.5 million years ago and made stone hand axes.

Homo sapiens   (Trans.) "Wise." The species to which contemporary humans belong.

Human rights   Notion of inherent rights that all human beings share. Based in part on the assumption that being human constitutes in itself a meaningful moral category that excludes nonhuman creatures.

Humanism   Cultural and intellectual movement of the Renaissance centered on the study of the literature, art, and civilization of ancient Greece and Rome.

Huron   A Native American confederacy of eastern Canada. The Huron flourished immediately prior to contact with Europeans, but declined rapidly as a result of European diseases such as smallpox. They were allied with the French in wars against the British, the Dutch, and other Native Americans.

Husbandry   The practice of cultivating crops and breeding and raising livestock; agriculture.

Ice Age affluence   Relative prosperity of Ice Age society as the result of abundant game and wild, edible plants.

Il-Khanate   A branch of the Mongol Empire, centered in present-day Iran. Its rulers, the Il-Khans, converted to Islam and adopted Persian culture.

Imam   A Muslim religious teacher. Also the title of Muslim political and religious rulers in Yemen and Oman.

Imperator   A Latin term that originally meant an army commander under the Roman Republic and evolved into the term *emperor.*

Imperialism   The policy of extending a nation's authority and influence by conquest or by establishing economic and political hegemony over other nations.

Incas   Peoples of highland Peru who established an empire from northern Ecuador to central Chile before the Spanish conquest in the 1530s.

Indirect rule   Rule by a colonial power through local elites.

Individualism   Belief in the primary importance of the individual and in the virtues of self-reliance and personal independence.

Indo-European languages   Language family that originated in Asia and from which most of Europe's present languages evolved.

Inductive method   Method by which scientists turn individual observations and experiments into general laws.

Industrial revolution   The complex set of economic, demographic, and technological events that began in western Europe and resulted in the advent of an industrial economy.

Industrialization The process by which an industrial economy is developed.

Inquisition A tribunal of the Roman Catholic Church that was charged with suppressing heresy and immorality.

Isolationism Belief that, unless directly challenged, a country should concentrate on domestic issues and avoid foreign conflicts or active participation in foreign affairs.

Jainism A way of life that arose in India designed to free the soul from evil by ascetic practices: chastity, detachment, truth, selflessness, and strict vegetarianism.

Jesuits Order of regular clergy strongly committed to education, scholarship, and missionary work. Founded by Ignatius of Loyola in 1534.

Jihad Arabic word meaning "striving." Muhammad used the word to refer to the inner struggle all Muslims must wage against evil, and the real wars fought against the enemies of Islam.

Joint-stock company A business whose capital is held in transferable shares of stock by its joint owners. The Dutch East India Company, founded in 1602, was the first joint-stock company.

Kaaba The holiest place in Islam. Formerly a pagan shrine, the Kaaba is a massive cube-shaped structure in Mecca toward which Muslims turn to pray.

Keynesianism John Maynard Keynes, based on the premise that governments could adjust the distribution of wealth and regulate the functioning of the economy through taxation and public spending, without seriously weakening free enterprise or infringing freedom.

Khan A ruler of a Mongol, Tartar, or Turkish tribe.

Khedive Title held by the hereditary viceroys of Egypt in the nineteenth century. Although nominally subject to the Ottoman sultans, the khedives were, in effect, sovereign princes.

Khmer Agrarian kingdom of Cambodia, built on the wealth produced by enormous rice surpluses.

Kongo Kingdom located in west central Africa along the Congo River, founded in the fourteenth century. The Portuguese converted its rulers and elite to Catholicism in the fifteenth century.

Kulturkampf (Trans.) "The struggle for culture." Name given to the conflict between the Roman Catholic Church and the imperial German government under Chancellor Otto von Bismarck in the 1870s.

Laissez-faire An economic policy that emphasizes the minimization of government regulation and involvement in the economy.

Latin Church Dominant Christian church in western Europe.

Latitude The angular distance north or south of the Earth's equator, measured in degrees along a meridian.

Law of nations Law that, according to Thomas Aquinas, all states must obey and that governs the relationships between them. This law, which Aquinas never defined, is to be distinguished from the laws of individual states. Francisco Suárez later clarified this as "simply a kind of positive human law" that is distinct from "natural law."

League of Nations International political organization created after World War I to resolve disputes between states peacefully and create a more just international order.

Legalism Chinese school of thought that emerged in the fourth century B.C.E. Legalists believed that morality was meaningless and that obedience to the state was the supreme good. The state thus had the right to enforce its laws under threat of the harshest penalties.

Levant   The countries bordering on the eastern Mediterranean from Turkey to Egypt.

Liberation Theology   Religious movement in Latin America, primarily among Roman Catholics, concerned with justice for the poor and oppressed. Its adherents argue that sin is the result not just of individual moral failure but of the oppressive and exploitative way in which capitalist society is organized and functions.

Logograms   A system of writing in which stylized pictures represent a word or phrase.

Longitude   An imaginary great circle on the surface of the Earth passing through the north and south poles at right angles to the equator.

Lotus Sutra   The most famous of Buddhist scriptures.

Low Countries   A region of northwest Europe comprising what is today Belgium, the Netherlands, and Luxembourg.

Magyars   Steppeland people who invaded eastern Europe in the tenth century and were eventually converted to Catholic Christianity. The Magyars are the majority ethnic group in present-day Hungary.

Mahayana Buddhism   One of the major schools of Buddhism. It emphasizes the Buddha's infinite compassion for all human beings, social concern, and universal salvation. It is the dominant branch of Buddhism in East Asia.

Mahdi   A Muslim messiah, whose coming would inaugurate a cosmic struggle, preceding the end of the world.

Maize   The grain that modern Americans call "corn." It was first cultivated in ancient Mesoamerica.

Mali   Powerful West African state that flourished in the fourteenth century.

Malthusian   Ideas inspired by Thomas Malthus's theory that population growth would always outpace growth in food supply.

Mamluks   Egyptian Muslim slave army. The mamluks provided Egypt's rulers from 1390 to 1517.

Mana   According to the Polynesians, a supernatural force that regulates everything in the world. For example, the mana of a net makes it catch a fish, and the mana of an herb gives it its healing powers.

Manchurian Incident   Japanese invasion of Manchuria in 1931, justified by the alleged effort of the Chinese to blow up a Japanese train. In fact, Japanese agents deliberately triggered the explosion to provide a pretext for war.

Manchus   A people native to Manchuria who ruled China during the Qing dynasty.

Mandate of heaven   The source of divine legitimacy for Chinese emperors. According to the mandate of heaven, emperors were chosen by the gods and retained their favor as long as the emperors acted in righteous ways. Emperors and dynasties that lost the mandate of heaven could be deposed or overthrown.

Manichaeanism   A dualistic philosophy dividing the world between the two opposed principles of good and evil.

Manifest destiny   Nineteenth-century belief that the United States was destined to expand across all of North America from the Atlantic to the Pacific, including Canada and Mexico.

Manila galleons   Spanish galleons that sailed each year between the Philippines and Mexico with a cargo of silk, porcelain, and other Asian luxury goods that were paid for with Mexican silver.

Maori   Indigenous Polynesian people of New Zealand.

Marathas   Petty Hindu princes who ruled in Maharashtra in southern India in the eighteenth century.

Maritime empires   Empires based on trade and naval power that flourished in the sixteenth and seventeenth centuries.

Maroons   Runaway slaves in the Americas who formed autonomous communities, and even states, between 1500 and 1800.

Marshall Plan   Foreign-aid program for Western Europe after World War II, named after U.S. Secretary of State George C. Marshall.

Material culture   Concrete objects that people create.

Maya   Major civilization of Mesoamerica. The earliest evidence connected to Maya civilization dates from about 1000 B.C.E. Maya civilization reached its peak between 250 and 900 C.E. Maya cultural and political practices were a major influence on other Mesoamericans.

Meiji Restoration   The overthrow of the Tokugawa *bakufu* in Japan in 1868 and the "restoration" of power to the imperial government under the Emperor Meiji.

Mesoamerica   A region stretching from central Mexico to Central America. Mesoamerica was home to the Olmec, the Maya, the Aztecs, and other Native American peoples.

Messiah   The anticipated savior of the Jews. Christians identify Jesus as the Messiah.

Mestizos   The descendents of Europeans and Native Americans.

Microbial exchange   The exchange of microbes between ecosystems.

Military revolution   Change in warfare in the sixteenth and seventeenth centuries that accompanied the rise of firepower technology.

Millenarianism   Belief that the end of the world is about to occur, as foretold in the biblical Book of Revelation.

Minas Gerais   (Trans.) "General Mines." Region of Brazil rich in mineral resources that experienced a gold rush in the early eighteenth century.

Ming dynasty   Chinese dynasty (1368–1644) noted for its flourishing foreign trade and achievements in scholarship and the arts.

Mongol peace   Era in the thirteenth and fourteenth centuries when Mongol rule created order and stability in Central Asia and enabled goods and ideas to flow along the Silk Roads.

Mongols   Nomadic people whose homeland was in Mongolia. In the twelfth and thirteenth centuries, they conquered most of Eurasia from China to eastern Europe.

Monocultures   The cultivation of a single dominant food crop, such as potatoes or rice. Societies that practiced monoculture were vulnerable to famine if bad weather or disease caused their single food crop to fail.

Monroe Doctrine   The policy enunciated by President James Monroe in 1823 that the United States would oppose further European colonization in the Americas.

Monsoon   A wind from the southwest or south that brings heavy rainfall each summer to southern Asia.

Mughals   Muslim dynasty founded by Babur that ruled India, at least nominally, from the mid-1500s until 1857.

Multiculturalism   The belief that different cultures can coexist peacefully and equitably in a single country.

Napoleonic Wars   Wars waged between France under Napoleon and its European enemies from 1799 to 1815. The fighting spilled over into the Middle East and sparked conflicts in North America and India and independence movements in the Spanish and Portuguese colonies in the Americas.

Nationalism   Belief that a people who share the same language, historic experience, and sense of identity make up a nation and that every nation has the right to assert its identity, pursue its destiny, defend its rights, and be the primary focus of its people's loyalty.

Natural selection   The process by which only the organisms best adapted to their environment pass on their genetic material to subsequent generations.

Nature versus nurture   Debate over the relative importance of inherited characterizes and environmental factors in determining human development.

Nazis   Members of the National Socialist German Workers' Party, founded in Germany in 1919 and brought to power in 1933 under Adolf Hitler.

Neanderthal   (Trans.) "Neander Valley." Humanlike species, evidence for whose existence was found in the Neander River valley in northern Germany in the mid-nineteenth century. Neanderthals disappeared from the evolutionary record about 30,000 years ago.

Négritude   The affirmation of the distinctive nature, quality, and validity of black culture.

Neo Europes (or New Europes)   Lands in other hemispheres where the environment resembled that of Europe and where immigrants could successfully transplant a European way of life and European culture.

Nestorianism   The Christian theological doctrine that within Jesus are two distinct and separate persons, divine and human, rather than a single divine person. Orthodox Christians classed Nestorianism as a heresy, but it spread across Central Asia along the Silk Roads.

New rich   Rich people whose wealth was acquired in the recent past, often in industry or commerce.

Nirvana   The spiritual goal of Buddhism, when a person ends the cycle of birth and rebirth and achieves enlightenment and freedom from any attachment to material things.

Noble savage   Idealized vision that some people in the West held about certain non-Europeans, especially some Native Americans and Polynesians. It was based on the notions that civilization was a corrupting force and that these peoples lived lives more in tune with nature.

Nomadism   Communities of people who move from one place to another instead of settling into one permanent location.

Obsidian   Volcanic glass used to make tools, weapons, and mirrors.

Ongons   Tibetan images in which spirits are thought to reside. Shamans claimed to communicate with the ongons.

OPEC   The Organization of Petroleum Exporting Countries, an alliance of the world's major oil producers.

Opium Wars   Two wars resulting from a trade dispute between China and Great Britain over China's efforts to curtail the sale of opium by Great Britain. The first Opium War took place from 1839–1842 and the second from 1856 to 1860.

Oracle   A person or group that claims to be able to have access to knowledge of the future by consulting a god. Ancient rulers often consulted oracles.

Oriental despotism   Arbitrary and corrupt rule. Eighteenth-century Europeans saw it as characteristic of Asian or Islamic rulers.

Orthodox Church   Dominant Christian church in the Byzantine Empire, the Balkans, and Russia.

Ottoman Empire Islamic empire based in present-day Turkey, with its capital at Istanbul. At its height in the sixteenth century, the Ottoman Empire stretched from Iraq across North Africa to the borders of Morocco and included almost all the Balkans and most of Hungary. The empire gradually declined, but endured until it was dismembered after World War I.

Pampa A vast plain of south-central South America that supports huge herds of cattle and other livestock.

Pan-African Congress A series of five meetings held between 1919 and 1945 that claimed to represent all black Africans and demanded an end to colonial rule.

Partition of India The division in 1947 along ethnic and religious lines of the British Indian Empire into two independent states: India, which was largely Hindu, and Pakistan, which was largely Muslim. The division involved widespread violence in which at least 500,000 people were killed.

Paternalism A social or economic relationship that resembles the dependency that exists between a father and his child.

Philosopher's Stone A substance that was believed to have the power to change base metals into gold.

Physiocrats Eighteenth-century French political economists who argued that agriculture was the foundation of any country's wealth and recommended agricultural improvements.

Positivism Doctrine that asserts the undeniability of human sense perception and the power of reason to prove that what our senses perceive is true.

Pragmatism Philosophy advocated by William James that holds that the standard for evaluating the truth or validity of a theory or concept depends on how well it works and on the results that arise from holding it.

Proletarian Members of the working class, which according to Karl Marx, would overthrow the bourgeoisie.

Protectorate A country or region that, although nominally independent and not a colony, is in fact controlled militarily, politically, and economically by a more powerful foreign state.

Protestantism The theological system of any of the churches of Western Christendom that separated from the Roman Catholic Church during the Reformation. The advent of Protestantism is usually associated with Martin Luther's break from the Catholic Church in the 1520s.

Psychoanalysis Technique developed by Sigmund Freud to treat patients suffering from emotional or psychological disorders by making them aware of their subconscious conflicts, motivations, and desires.

Public sphere Sites for the public discussion of political, social, economic, and cultural issues.

Qing dynasty Last imperial Chinese dynasty (1644–1912), founded when the Manchus, a steppeland people from Manchuria, conquered China. It was succeeded by a republic.

Quantum mechanics Mechanics based on the principle that matter and energy have the properties of both particles and waves.

Quran The sacred text of Islam dictated from God to the Prophet Muhammad by the Archangel Gabriel. Considered by Muslims to contain the final revelations of God to humanity.

Rape of Nanjing Atrocities committed by the Japanese during their occupation of the city of Nanjing, China, in 1937.

Rastafarianism   A religious and political movement that began among black people in Jamaica in the 1930s. Its adherents believe that former Emperor Haile Selassie of Ethiopia (r. 1930–1974) was divine and the Messiah whose coming was foretold in the Bible.

Rationalism   The doctrine that reason by itself can determine truth and solve the world's problems.

Realpolitik   Political doctrine that says that the state is not subject to moral laws and has the right to do whatever safeguards it and advances its interests.

Reformation   The Protestant break from the Roman Catholic Church in the sixteenth century.

Renaissance   Humanistic revival of classical art, architecture, literature, and learning that originated in Italy in the fourteenth century and spread throughout Europe.

Renewable energy   Energy that is not derived from a finite resource such as oil or coal.

Revolutionary militarization   The trend toward larger and more powerful armed forces and the organization of society and the economy to achieve that goal.

Rig Veda   A collection of hymns and poems created by a sedentary people living in the area north of the Indus valley where northern India and Pakistan meet. The Rig Veda provides evidence for the theory that invaders destroyed Harappan civilization.

Romanticism   Intellectual and artistic movement that arose in reaction to the Enlightenment's emphasis on reason. Romantics had a heightened interest in nature and religion, and emphasized emotion and imagination.

Rus   A Slavic-Scandinavian people who created the first Russian state and converted to Orthodox Christianity.

Safavids   Shiite dynasty that ruled Persia between 1501 and 1722.

Sahel   A semiarid region of north Central Africa south of the Sahara Desert.

Saint-Domingue   A French colony on Hispaniola that flourished in the eighteenth century by cultivating sugar and coffee with slave labor. It became the modern republic of Haiti after a protracted struggle that began in the 1790s.

Samurai   The hereditary Japanese feudal-military aristocracy.

Sati   In Hinduism, the burning of a widow on her husband's funeral pyre.

Satyagraha   (Trans.) "The force of truth." Nonviolent movement launched by Mohandas K. Gandhi, with the goal of achieving Indian independence.

Scientific revolution   The sweeping change in the investigation of nature and the view of the universe that took place in Europe in the sixteenth and seventeenth centuries.

Scientism   The belief that natural science is the only viable method to be used for understanding the world. All other belief systems—metaphysics, religion, philosophy—are to be rejected in favor of natural science.

Scramble for Africa   Efforts in the late nineteenth century by European nations to carve up the African continent and take control of various regions to establish vast empires.

Sea Peoples   The term used for a confederation of seafaring raiders of the second millennium B.C.E. who sailed into the eastern Mediterranean, causing political unrest, and attempted to enter or control Egyptian territory during the late nineteenth and twentieth dynasties.

Self-strengthening   Mid-nineteenth-century Chinese reform movement initiated in response to Western incursions.

Seljuks   A Turkish dynasty ruling in Central and western Asia from the eleventh to the thirteenth centuries.

Serf   Agricultural laborer attached to the land owned by a lord and required to perform labor in return for certain legal or customary rights. Unlike slaves, serfs could not usually be sold away from the land.

Shaman   A person who acts as an intermediary between humans and spirits or gods. Such a person functions as the medium though which spirits talk to humans.

Sharia Islamic law   The word *sharia* derives from the verb *shara'a*, which is connected to the concepts of "spiritual law" and "system of divine law."

Shiites   Members of the most important minority tradition in the Islamic world. Shiites believe that the caliphate is the prerogative of Muhammad's nephew, Ali, and his heirs. Shiism has been the state religion in Iran since the sixteenth century.

Shinto   A religion native to Japan, characterized by veneration of nature spirits and ancestors and by a lack of formal dogma.

Shogun   A hereditary military ruler of Japan who exercised real power in the name of the emperor, who was usually powerless and relegated to purely ceremonial roles. The last shogun was removed from office in 1868.

Sikhism   Indian religion founded by Nanak Guru in the early sixteenth century that blends elements of the Hindu and Muslim traditions.

Silk Roads   Key overland trade routes that connected eastern and western Eurasia. The route first began to function in the aftermath of Alexander the Great's expansion into Central Asia at the end of the fourth century B.C.E.

Sioux   A nomadic Native American people of central North America who, with the benefit of horses introduced to the Americas by the Spanish, formed a pastoralist empire in the late eighteenth and mid–nineteenth centuries.

Social Darwinism   The misapplication of Darwin's biological theories to human societies, often to justify claims of racial superiority and rule by the strong over the weak.

Socialism   Any of various theories or systems in which the means of producing and distributing goods is owned collectively or by a centralized government.

Socialist realism   An artistic doctrine embraced by many communist and leftist regimes that the sole legitimate purpose of the arts was to glorify the ideals of the state by portraying workers, peasants, and the masses in a strictly representational, nonabstract style.

Sociobiology   The study of the biological determinants of social behavior.

Soft power   The cultural influence and the appeal of American institutions and ways of life on a world scale during the twentieth century.

Solidarity   Polish trade union founded in 1980 that played a key role in bringing down Poland's communist regime.

Solomids   Dynasty that seized power in Ethiopia in 1270 C.E. and claimed descent from the Biblical King Solomon.

Song Dynasty   Dynasty (960–1279) under which China achieved one of its highest levels of culture and prosperity.

Songhay   An ancient empire of West Africa in the present-day country of Mali. It reached the height of its power around 1500 C.E.

Soninke   West African kingdom on the upper Niger River.

Soviet   Russian term for a workers' collective.

State system   Organization of early modern Europe into competing nation-states.

Steppe   A vast semiarid, grass-covered plain, extending across northern Eurasia and central North America.

Stoicism   Philosophy founded on the belief that nature is morally neutral and that the wise person, therefore, achieves happiness by accepting misfortune and practicing self-control.

Stranger effect   The tendency some peoples have to esteem and defer to strangers.

Subsidiarity   Doctrine that decisions should always be made at the level closest to the people whom the decisions most affect.

Suez Canal   Canal linking the Mediterranean and the Red Sea. It was built by French engineers with European capital and opened in 1869.

Sufis   Members of Islamic groups that cultivate mystical beliefs and practices. Sufis have often been instrumental in spreading Islam, but Muslim authorities have often distrusted them.

Sundiata   Legendary hero said to have founded the kingdom of Mali in West Africa.

Sunnis   Members of the dominant tradition in the Islamic world. Sunnis believe that any member of Muhammad's tribe could be designated caliph.

Surrealism   Literary and artistic movement that attempts to express the workings of the subconscious.

Syllogisms   A form of argument in which we can infer a necessary conclusion from two premises that prior demonstration or agreement has established to be true.

Syncretic   Characterized by the reconciliation or fusion of differing systems of belief.

Taiping Rebellion   Rebellion (1852–1864) against the Qing Empire that resulted in tens of millions of deaths and widespread destruction in southern China.

Tang Dynasty   Chinese dynasty (618–907) famous for its wealth and encouragement of the arts and literature.

Theravada Buddhism   A conservative branch of Buddhism that adheres to the nontheistic ideal of self-purification to nirvana. Theravada Buddhism emphasizes the monastic ideal and is dominant in present-day Sri Lanka and southeast Asia.

Third Rome   Term Russians used for Moscow and Russian Orthodox Christianity. It expressed the belief that the Russian czars were the divinely chosen heirs of the Roman and Byzantine emperors.

Thule Inuit   Indigenous Native American people who crossed the Arctic and arrived in Greenland around 1000 C.E.

Tillers   Agriculturalists who emphasize the cultivation of plants for food and products, such as timber and cotton.

Tokugawa   A family of shoguns that ruled Japan in the name of the emperors from 1603 to 1868.

Trading-post empires   Term for the networks of imperial forts and trading posts that Europeans established in Asia in the seventeenth century.

Treasure fleets   Spanish fleets that sailed from the Caribbean each year to bring gold and silver from mines in the Americas back to Europe.

Tundra   A treeless area between the ice cap and the tree line of Arctic regions.

Turks   A member of any of the Turkic-speaking, nomadic peoples who originated in Central Asia. The Turks eventually converted to Islam and dominated the Middle East.

Uncertainty principle   Niels Bohr and Werner Heisenberg's theory that because observers are part of every observation their findings can never be objective.

United Nations   International political organization created after World War II to prevent armed conflict, settle international disputes peacefully, and provide cultural, economic, and technological aid. It was the successor to the League of Nations, which had proved to be ineffectual.

Universal love   Love between all people, regardless of status, nationality, or family ties.

Upanishads   The theoretical sections of the Veda (the literature of the sages of the Ganges civilization). The Upanishads were written down as early as 800 B.C.E.

Urbanization   The process by which urban areas develop and expand.

Utilitarianism   System of thought devised by Jeremy Bentham, based on the notion that the goal of the state was to create the greatest happiness for the greatest number of people.

Utopianism   Belief in a system or ideology aimed at producing a perfect or ideal society.

Virtual reality   A computer simulation of a real or imaginary system.

Wahhabism   Muslim sect founded by Abdul Wahhab (1703–1792), known for its strict observance of the Quran. It is the dominant form of Islam in Saudi Arabia.

Westernization   The process by which other cultures adopt Western styles or ways of life.

World system   The system of interconnections among the world's population.

World War I   Global war (1914–1918) sparked by the assassination of Archduke Francis Ferdinand of Austria by a Serb terrorist in June 1914.

World War II   Global conflict that lasted from 1939 to 1945 and ended with the defeat and occupation of Fascist Italy, Nazi Germany, and Japan.

Zen   A school of Mahayana Buddhism that asserts that a person can attain enlightenment through meditation, self-contemplation, and intuition.

Ziggurats   A tall, tapering Mesopotamian temple. Ziggurats were the physical and cultural centers of Mesopotamian cities.

Zimbabwes   Stone-built administrative centers for rulers and the elite in southern Africa. The zimbabwes flourished in the fifteenth century.

Zoroastrianism   Iranian religious system founded by Zoroaster that posited a universal struggle between the forces of light (the good) and of darkness (evil).

index

*Page numbers in italic refer to maps and photos

additional titles of interest

Note to Instructors: These and other Penguin titles can be packaged with this book at a significant discount. Contact your local Pearson sales representative for details on how to create a Penguin Value Package.

Anonymous, *Bhagavad-Gita*
Anonymous, *Epic of Gilgamesh*
Anonymous, *The Upanishads*
Anonymous, *The Koran*
Belcher, *African Myths of Origin*
Confucius, *The Analects*
Dante, *The Inferno*
de las Casas, *A Short Account of the Destruction of the Indies*
Equiano, *The Interesting Narrative*
Descartes, *Discourse on Method and Related Writings*
Einhard, *Two Lives of Charlemagne*
Gonzalez, *Harvest of Empire*
Ibsen, *Four Major Plays: A Doll's House, Wild Duck, Hedda Gabler,
    Master Builder*
Marx/Engels, *The Communist Manifesto*
Moliere, *Tartuffe and Other Plays*
More, *Utopia*
Murasaki, *Diary of Lady Murasaki*
Narayan, *The Ramayana: A Shortened Modern Prose Version of the
    Indian Epic*
Seager, *Penguin Atlas of Women in the World*
Spence, *The Death of Woman Wang*
Spence, *Mao Zedong*
Voltaire, *Candide Zadig and Selected Stories*
Woolf, *Jacob's Room*

For a complete list of titles, go to: http://www.pearsonhighered.com/history and select "Penguin Packs."